The Way Class Works

Since the 1980s, the relationship between social class and education has been overshadowed by scholarship more generally targeting issues of race, gender, and representation. Today, with the global economy deeply immersed in social inequalities, there is pressing need for serious class-based analyses of schooling, family life, and social structure. *The Way Class Works* is a collection of twenty-four groundbreaking essays on the material conditions of social class and the ways in which class is produced "on the ground" in educational institutions and families. Written by the most visible and important scholars in education and the social sciences, these timely essays explore the production of class in and through the economy, family, and school, while simultaneously interrogating and challenging our understandings of social class as linked to race, gender, and nation. With essays by distinguished scholars and questions for further reflection and discussion, *The Way Class Works* will be an invaluable resource for students and scholars in education, sociology, and beyond.

Lois Weis is State University of New York Distinguished Professor of Sociology of Education at the University at Buffalo, State University of New York.

The Way Class Works

Readings on school, family, and the economy

Edited by
Lois Weis

Routledge
Taylor & Francis Group

NEW YORK AND LONDON

First published 2008
by Routledge
270 Madison Ave, New York, NY 10016

Simultaneously published in the UK
by Routledge
2 Park Square, Milton Park, Abingdon, Oxon OX14 4RN

Routledge is an imprint of the Taylor & Francis Group, an informa business

© 2008 by the Taylor & Francis Group

Typeset in Sabon by
Book Now Ltd, London
Printed and bound in the United States of America on acid-free paper by
Edwards Brothers, Inc.

Library of Congress Cataloging in Publication Data
The way class works: readings on school, family, and the economy/Lois
Weis, editor.
    p. cm.
Includes bibliographical references and index.
1. Social classes—United States. 2. Social stratification—United States. 3.
Equality—United States. 4. United States—Social conditions. I. Weis, Lois.
HN59.2.W39 2008
305.5′120973—dc22   2007019111

British Library Cataloguing in Publication Data
A catalogue record for this book is available from the British Library

ISBN10: 0–415–95707–9 (hbk)
ISBN10: 0–415–95708–7 (pbk)
ISBN10: 0–203–93500–4 (ebk)

ISBN13: 978–0–415–95707–6 (hbk)
ISBN13: 978–0–415–95708–3 (pbk)
ISBN13: 978–0–203–93500–2 (ebk)

Contents

T2U
T2U

SECTION 4
Complicating class, race, and gender intersectionality   289

Figures

Tables

Contributors

Jean Anyon is author of *Radical Possibilities: Public Policy, Urban Education, and A New Social Movement* and *Ghetto Schooling: A Political Economy of Urban Education*. Her articles on cities, race, social class, and schools have been reprinted in over 40 edited collections, and translated into several languages. She teaches Education and Social Policy in the Doctoral Program in Urban Education at the City University of New York.

Stanley Aronowitz is Distinguished Professor of Sociology at CUNY Graduate Center and Director of Center for the Study of Culture, Technology, and Work. He is founding editor of *Social Text* and *Situations*; book review editor of *Social Policy*; and on the editorial boards of *Ethnography* and *Cultural Critique*. He is also the author/ editor of 23 books, including *How Class Works* and *Just Around the Corner: The Paradox of the Jobless Recovery*. He is currently working on a biography of Mills for Columbia University Press.

Angela Bell is a doctoral candidate at the Institute of Higher Education at the University of Georgia. Her primary research interest is the impact of state higher education policy. She received her BA in Classics with a minor in Women's Studies from Princeton University in 1993 and her MEd in Language Education from the University of Georgia in 1996. She taught high school Latin for nine years before returning to the University of Georgia to begin her doctorate in Higher Education.

Ellen Brantlinger retired from the Department of Curriculum and Instruction at Indiana University in 2004. During her time at Indiana University she directed the Undergraduate Special Education Teacher Education Programs and the Graduate Program in Curriculum Studies. She has published *Politics of Social Class in Secondary Schools, Fighting for Darla, Sterilization of People with Mental Disabilities*, and *Dividing Classes: How the Middle Class Negotiates and Rationalizes School Advantage* and edited a multi-author volume entitled *Who Benefits from Special Education?: Remediating (Fixing) Other People's Children*. Her well-known article "Using Ideology: Cases of Nonrecognition of the Politics of Research and Practice in Special Education" was published in the *Review of Educational Research* in 1997.

April Burns is a doctoral student in Social-Personality Psychology at the City University of New York, Graduate Center. Her research focuses broadly on the psychology of social class and education, and issues of classed subjectivity. She is currently investigating family and individual narratives surrounding the educational experiences of first-generation college graduates. She has been published in *JSI* and *Feminism & Psychology*, and is author of "The Racing of Capability and Culpability in Desegregated Schools: Discourses of Merit and Responsibility."

Fiona Devine is Professor of Sociology at the University of Manchester, UK. She is the author of *Affluent Workers Revisited*, *Social Class in America and Britain*, and *Class Practices*. She has edited a number of collections including *Social Inequalities in Comparative Perspective* with Mary C. Waters.

Jo-Anne Dillabough is an Associate Professor in the Department of Educational Studies at the Peter Wall Institute for Advanced Studies, University of British Columbia. She is co-editor of *Challenging Democracy: International Perspectives on Gender, Education and Citizenship* (with Madeleine Arnot) and of *Globalisation, Education and Social Change* (with A. Halsey, H. Lauder, and P. Brown). She is currently the holder of two large-scale SSHRC grants (Social Sciences and Humanities Research Council Grants) and a Spencer Foundation grant.

Greg Dimitriadis is Associate Professor of Sociology of Education at the University at Buffalo, SUNY. He is interested in new ways of thinking about urban education and the policies which serve urban youth. Dimitriadis is author or editor (alone and with others) of nine books and over fifty articles. His most recent books (co-authored with George Kamberelis) are *On Qualitative Inquiry* and *Theory for Education*.

Michelle Fine is Distinguished Professor of Social Psychology, Women's Studies, and Urban Education at the Graduate Center, CUNY. Her recent publications include: "Sexuality Education and Desire: Still Missing After All These Years" (with Sara McClelland), *Harvard Educational Review*, 2006; *Working Method: Research and Social Injustice* (with Lois Weis); *Off White: Essays on Race, Privilege and Contestation* (with Lois Weis, Linda Powell Pruitt, and April Burns); *Echoes of Brown: Youth Documenting and Performing the Legacy of Brown v. Board of Education*; and *Changing Minds: The Impact of College in Prison*.

Timothy G. Ford is a doctoral student in the Curriculum, Teaching, and Educational Policy program at Michigan State University and a Research Associate at the Data Research and Development Center. His primary research interests center on the sociology of education, with an emphasis on how education relates to issues of mobility, social inequality and/or stratification, and parenting and family life. Tim holds a bachelor's degree in linguistics from Truman State University and an MA in Teaching English as a Second Language from the University of Kansas.

Adam Gamoran is Professor of Sociology and Educational Policy Studies at the University of Wisconsin-Madison and is Director of the Wisconsin Center for Educational Research. He earned his PhD in education from the University of Chicago. Gamoran was a visiting professor at Tel Aviv University, Israel and was a Fulbright Scholar at the University of Edinburgh, Scotland. In 2001, he was elected to the National Academy of Education and in 2002 was elected to the Sociological Research Association for his significant academic contributions to the field of sociology. His research interests include organizational and occupational analysis, social stratification, and sociology of education. Among Gamoran's numerous published books and articles, his most recent work, *Stratification in Higher Education: A*

Comparative Study (2007), co-edited with Yossi Shavit and Richard Arum, includes authors from 15 countries addressing the expansion of higher education and inequality. He is co-author of *Transforming Teaching in Mathematics and Science: How Schools and Districts Can Support Change* (2003) and co-editor of *Stability and Change in American Education: Structure, Process, and Outcomes* (2003). Gamoran's current research focuses on the resegregation of public schools in Nashville, Tennessee.

Sean Patrick Kelly is Assistant Professor of Sociology at the University of Notre Dame, and a researcher at the Center for Research on Educational Opportunity. His research has focused on several educational issues facing US schools, including problems of student engagement, the process of matching teachers to classrooms, the assignment of diverse students to course sequences in high school, and the causes of teacher attrition.

Jacqueline Kennelly is a Killam doctoral fellow currently completing her SSHRC-funded doctoral studies in the Department of Educational Studies at the University of British Columbia. Her research focuses on youth subcultures, citizenship, exclusion, and belonging within the Canadian nation-state. She has received numerous awards and scholarships in recognition of her work, and is the author or co-author of several journal articles and book chapters, including publications in the *Canadian Journal of Education, Canadian Woman Studies, Journal of Curriculum Theorizing*, and the *Canadian Journal of Environmental Education*.

Annette Lareau teaches in the Department of Sociology at the University of Maryland, College Park. Her books *Unequal Childhoods: Class, Race, and Family Life* and *Home Advantage: Social Class and Parental Involvement in Elementary Education* won ASA awards. With Jeff Schultz, she is the co-editor of *Journeys Through Ethnography: Realistic Accounts of Fieldwork*. With Elliot Weininger she is beginning a new study of the role of school in the first-home purchase of families with young children. This mixed-method research project is funded by the Spencer Foundation.

Stacey J. Lee is Professor of Educational Policy Studies at the University of Wisconsin-Madison and Professor in the Program in Urban Education, CUNY Graduate Center. She is the author of *Unraveling the "Model Minority" Stereotype: Listening to Asian American Youth* and *Up Against Whiteness: Race, School, and Immigrant Youth*.

Henry M. Levin is the William Heard Kilpatrick Professor of Economics and Education at Teachers College, Columbia University and Director of the National Center for the Study of Privatization in Education. He is also the David Jacks Professor of Higher Education and Economics, Emeritus, at Stanford University where he served after working as an economist at the Brookings Institution in Washington. He has been the Director of the Institute for Research on Educational Finance at Stanford, the Director of the Accelerated Schools Project, and Editor of the *Review of Educational Research*. He is also a recipient of the 2004 Outstanding Service Award of the American Educational Finance Association. Levin is a specialist in the economics of education and human resources and has published 20 books and about 300 articles on these and related subjects. His most recent books are: *Cost-Effectiveness Analysis: Methods and Applications; Privatizing Education; Cost-Effectiveness and Educational Policy; Readings in the Economics of Higher Education;* and *Privatizing Educational Choice*.

Guofang Li is Associate Professor of Second Language and Literacy Education in the Department of Teacher Education, Michigan State University. Li's major publications include three books, *East is East, West is West? Home Literacy, Culture, and Schooling*; *Culturally Contested Pedagogy: Battles of Literacy and Schooling Between Mainstream Teachers and Asian Immigrant Parents* (winner of 2006 Ed Fry Book Award, National Reading Conference); *Strangers of the Academy: Asian Women Scholars in Higher Education*; and a monograph entitled *Asian-American Education Across the Class Line: A Multisite Report*.

Jennifer Logue is a doctoral student in Educational Policy Studies, specializing in Philosophy of Education and Gender and Women's Studies. She has published in the areas of sexuality studies, critical pedagogy, and social justice education in the *Journal for Philosophical Studies in Education* and the *Philosophy of Education Society Yearbook*.

Setha Low is Professor of Environmental Psychology, Anthropology, and Women's Studies, and Director of the Public Space Research Group at the Graduate Center, City University of New York. She has been awarded a Getty Fellowship, an NEH fellowship, and a Guggenheim for her ethnographic research on public space in Latin America and the USA. She is widely published and lectures internationally on these issues. Her most recent books include: *Politics of Public Space* (with Neil Smith); *Rethinking Urban Parks: Public Space and Cultural Diversity* (with S. Scheld and D. Taplin); *Behind the Gates: Life, Security and the Pursuit of Happiness in Fortress America*; and *The Anthropology of Space and Place: Locating Culture* (with D. Lawrence-Zuniga). Dr. Low is currently President-elect of the American Anthropological Association. Her current research is on the impact of private governance on New York City co-op residents, and she is writing a book on *An Anthropological Theory of Space and Place*.

Wendy Luttrell, Aronson Associate Professor of Human Development and Education at Harvard Graduate School of Education, studies the relationship between culture, identity, and schooling. Her research focuses on US schools as sites where beliefs about worth, value, knowledge, and power are acquired and contested, and as contexts for the formation of self-understandings and social identities (especially regarding gender, race, ethnicity, class, and sexuality). These issues are explored in her two books, *School-smart and Mother-wise: Working-Class Women's Identity and Schooling* and *Pregnant Bodies, Fertile Minds: Gender, Race, and the Schooling of Pregnant Teens*.

Kimberly S. Maier is Assistant Professor of Measurement and Quantitative Methods and affiliate of Educational Policy in the College of Education at Michigan State University. Dr. Maier's current research focuses on the application of multilevel item response theory to educational achievement measures and attitudinal surveys. Other areas of interest include Bayesian data analysis methods for educational research, the study of familial impacts on adolescent achievement and aspirations, adolescent motivation in science and mathematics education, and the application of multilevel models to policy research.

Cameron McCarthy teaches Mass Communications Theory, Cultural Studies, and the Sociology of Knowledge in the Department of Educational Policy Studies and the

Institute of Communications Research at the University of Illinois's Urbana campus. With Lois Weis and Greg Dimitriadis he recently published *Ideology, Curriculum, and the New Sociology of Education: Revisiting the Work of Michael Apple*.

Julie McLeod is an Associate Professor in the Faculty of Education, University of Melbourne. Her areas of research include gender and youth studies, sociological and historical studies of subjectivity, curriculum and schooling, and social and feminist theory in education. She is co-author (with Cherry Collins and Jane Kenway) of *Factors Influencing the Educational Performance of Males and Females at School and their Initial Destinations after Leaving School* (DETYA 2000); co-editor (with Andrea Allard) of *Learning from the Margins: Young Women, Social Exclusion and Education*; and co-author (with Lyn Yates) of *Making Modern Lives: Subjectivity, Schooling, and Social Change*.

Yasser A. Payne is Assistant Professor in the Black American Studies Program at the University of Delaware. Dr. Payne completed his doctoral work at the Graduate Center, City University of New York, where he was trained as a social-personality psychologist and has recently completed a postdoctoral fellowship funded by the National Institute of Drug Abuse whereby he worked on a re-entry and intervention-based research project in New York City's largest jail, Rikers Island. Further, he has published numerous articles in: *Teachers College Record, Culture Diversity and Ethnic Minority Psychology, Men and Masculinities, Journal of Social Issues*, and the *International Journal of Critical Psychology*. Also, Dr. Payne co-authored *Echoes of Brown: Youth Documenting and Performing the Legacy of Brown v. Board of Education*.

Diane Reay is a Professor in the Faculty of Education, University of Cambridge, UK. Her interests are in social justice issues in education, Pierre Bourdieu's social theory, and cultural analyses of social class. Her most recent book *Degrees of Choice: Social Class, Race and Gender in Higher Education* (with Stephen Ball and Miriam David) utilizes Bourdieu's conceptual framework to examine inequalities in access to higher education.

Robert B. Reich has served in three national administrations, most recently as Secretary of Labor under President Bill Clinton. He is co-founder and national editor of *The American Prospect*, and his writings have appeared in *The New Yorker, The Atlantic Monthly, New York Times, Washington Post*, and the *Wall Street Journal*. He has written eight books, including the highly influential volumes *The Future of Success* and *The Work of Nations*.

Alan R. Sadovnik is Professor of Education and Sociology at Rutgers University, Newark, New Jersey. He is the author of many books on education, including: *Equity and Excellence in Higher Education* (1995); *Sociology of Education: A Critical Reader* (2007); *Founding Mothers and Others: Women Educational Leaders During the Progressive Era* (2002); and *No Child Left Behind and the Reduction of the Achievement Gap: Sociological Perspectives on Federal Educational Policy* (2007). He received the Willard Waller Award in 1993 from the ASAS for the outstanding article published in the field, as well as several AESA Critics Choice Awards. He is co-editor, with Susan F. Semel, of the "History of Schools and Schooling Series" at

Peter Lang Publishing, the "Palgrave Series in Urban Education" at Palgrave-Macmillan, and the "Schooling Around the World Series" at Greenwood Press. He has served as the Program Chair for the Sociology of Education SIG and the Sociology of Education Section of ASA and is on the editorial boards of *Teachers College Record*, *History of Educational Quarterly*, *Sociology of Education*, *Educational Foundations*, and *The Urban Review*.

Barbara Schneider is the John A. Hannah Distinguished Professor in the College of Education and the Department of Sociology at Michigan State University. She holds many positions at NORC and the University of Chicago, including Principal Investigator for the Data Research and Development Center, and Co-Director of the Alfred P. Sloan Center on Parents, Children, and Work. Schneider has numerous publications, including: *Trust in Schools: A Core Resource for Improvement* (co-authored with Anthony Bryk); *The Ambitious Generation: America's Teenagers, Motivated but Directionless* (co-authored with David Stevenson); and *Becoming Adult: How Teenagers Prepare for the World of Work* (co-authored with Mihaly Csikszentmihalyi). Schneider serves on a number of advisory boards including the American Educational Research Association Grants Board. She has also served on the Social Science Research Council's Committee on Transitions into Postsecondary Education, the National Academies Committee on Populations, Panel on Hispanics in the US, and the National Academy of Sciences Committee on Research in Education. In 2005, the ASA selected her as the new editor of *Sociology of Education*.

Scott L. Thomas is Associate Professor at the Institute of Higher Education at the University of Georgia. Thomas' current work focuses on college access issues with special attention to the K-12 achievement gap and college affordability. His interests in these areas revolve around within-school processes that sort students into widely varying college opportunity sets. Relevant published work in this area can be found in *Sociology of Education*, *Research in Higher Education*, and various chapters in the highly regarded *Higher Education: Handbook of Theory and Research*.

María Elena Torre is Chair of Education Studies at Eugene Lang College of The New School. Her current research focuses on urban education, youth definitions of rights and "citizenship," and youth and community engagement in participatory action research. She is a co-author of *Echoes of Brown: Youth Documenting and Performing the Legacy of Brown v. Board of Education* and *Changing Minds: The Impact of College on a Maximum Security Prison*.

Eugenia Wang is a PhD candidate in Human Geography at the University of British Columbia. Her research interests include youth geographies, critical legal studies, ethnographies of the state, and refugee studies. Eugenia's dissertation examines the legal, cultural, and spatial dynamics of power as they are manifest in Canadian state responses to unaccompanied minor asylum seekers. She is a founding member of the Canadian Association for Refugee and Forced Migration Studies. She is also an active caseworker with Amnesty International's Refugee Network in Vancouver and a Canadian representative with the Canadian Council of Refugee's International Refugee Rights Network.

Lois Weis is State University of New York Distinguished Professor of Sociology of Education at the University at Buffalo, State University of New York. She is the author and/or editor of numerous books and articles relating to race, class, gender, education, and the economy. Her most recent volumes include *Class Reunion: The Remaking of the American White Working Class* and *Beyond Silenced Voices: Class, Race and Gender in United States Schools* (edited with Michelle Fine). She is a winner of the outstanding book award from the prestigious Gustavus Meyers Center for the Study of Bigotry and Human Rights in North America, as well as a seven-time winner of the American Educational Studies Association's Critic's Choice Award, given for an outstanding book. She is past-president of the American Educational Studies Association, and is the editor of the "Power, Social Identity and Education" series for SUNY Press.

Erik Olin Wright is Vilas Distinguished Professor of Sociology at the University of Wisconsin. Since 1992 he has directed *The Real Utopias Project* which explores a range of proposals for new institutional designs that embody emancipatory ideals and are attentive to issues of pragmatic feasibility. His principal publications include: *Classes*; *The Debate on Classes*; *Reconstructing Marxism: Essays on Explanation and the Theory of History* (with Elliott Sober and Andrew Levine); *Interrogating Inequality*; *Class Counts: Comparative Studies in Class Analysis*; and *Deepening Democracy: Institutional Innovations in Empowered Participatory Governance* (with Archon Fung).

Lyn Yates is Foundation Professor of Curriculum at the University of Melbourne, Australia and is a past president of the Australian Association for Research in Education. Her recent books include *Making Modern Lives: Subjectivity, Schooling and Social Change* (with Julie McLeod), *What DOES Good Education Research Look Like? Situating a Field and its Practices*, and *Reconstructing the Lifelong Learner: Pedagogy and Identity in Individual, Organisational and Social Change* (with Chappell, et al.).

Acknowledgments

This volume owes its existence to numerous individuals. Catherine Bernard of Routledge supported the project from the very beginning and it has been my privilege, once again, to work with both Catherine and Routledge. Authors worked tirelessly to produce chapters aimed at re-centering social class as a key analytic lens through which social life must be interrogated, and all contributed immensely to the final product. A team of incredibly talented Sociology of Education and Comparative Education PhD students at the University at Buffalo, State University of New York, led by Rima Aranha, authored discussion questions for each chapter. This team engaged its task with great intensity, collectively reading and thinking about each chapter, ultimately coming up with a set of key questions for class discussion. Students include Rima Aranha, Heather Jenkins, Chien-Chen Kung, Mustafa Sever, Amy Stich, and Carolyn Stirling. Both Rima Aranha and Amy Stich played a major role in the overall volume, being in constant contact with authors, attending to revisions, and wrapping up a myriad of details related to volume assembly and production. Kristin Cipollone, along with Amy Stich and Carolyn Stirling, played an invaluable role as the volume moved toward final publication. Heather Jarrow of Routledge was similarly helpful as we posed seemingly unending questions with regard to technical details. Amy Ferry, once again, produced the final product with great dedication and skill. The Baldy Center for Law and Social Policy at the University at Buffalo, State University of New York made my work far easier by providing me with a small grant to offset necessary costs.

My husband, Tereffe Asrat, and daughters, Sara Asrat and Jessica Asrat, continue to inspire me. It is their collective social vision, strength, and love that make such work worth doing.

With thanks,
Lois Weis
April 2007

Introduction

Lois Weis*

Increasing attention is being paid in the US mass media to issues of social class. In 2005, *The New York Times* ran a series of well-received pieces devoted to class inequality, and even David Brooks, conservative columnist, is a frequent commentator on the subject. As Brooks notes:

> Economic stratification is translating into social stratification. Only 28 percent of American adults have a college degree, but most of us in this group find ourselves in workplaces in social milieus where almost everybody has been to college. A social chasm is opening up between those in educated society and those in non-educated society, and you are beginning to see vast behavioral differences between the two groups.
>
> (September 25, 2005, *The Times Union*)

More recently, *The New York Times* reports that "income inequality grew significantly in 2005, with the top 1 percent of Americans—those with incomes that year of more than $348,000—receiving their largest share of national income since 1928" (March 29, 2007, *The New York Times*). Given recognition of deepening class inequality by both journalists and scholars (Aron-Dine & Shapiro, 2006; Piketty & Saez, 2003; Reich, 2001), *The Way Class Works*—a volume devoted to key readings on the economy, social class, family, and schooling—could not be timelier.[1]

Noteworthy ethnographic work has been conducted which both elicits class culture and identity (Bensman & Lynch, 1987; Halle, 1984; Kefalas, 2003; Lamont, 2000; Rubin, 1976) and describes and theorizes this identity in relation to schools (Everhart, 1983; Gaskell, 1992; London, 1978; Valli, 1986; Willis, 1977). Such discussion has been tempered, if not altogether ignored, over the past twenty-five years by those of us who do research on schools and schooling, as scholarship, particularly in the United States, targeted more specifically to issues of race and/or gender as well as broader issues of representation, has taken hold. Such scholarship, while critically important, has often delved into issues of race, gender, and/or representations irrespective of a distinct social class referent, much as earlier scholarship on social class ignored gender and race—a point which critical race theorists (Kelley, 1994; Marable, 1997; McCarthy, 1990, 1993), theorists of "whiteness" production (Fine, Weis, Powell & Wong, 1997; Fine,

* State University of New York Distinguished Professor of Sociology of Education at the University at Buffalo, State University of New York.

Weis, Pruitt & Burns, 2004; Giroux, 1997; Kinchloe, Steinberg, Rodriguez & Chenault, 1998), and feminist theorists across race and ethnicity have commented upon at length (Crenshaw, 1989; Lather, 1991; Mullings, 1997; Roman & Christian-Smith, 1988; Spelman, 1988). With the clear turn in the global economy, one accompanied by deep intensification of social inequalities (Katz, 2001; Levin & Rumberger, 1987; Piketty & Saez, 2003, 2006; Reich, 1991, 2001), the need for serious class-based analyses of schooling, family life, and social structure could not be more pressing. Although Anyon (1981a, 1981b), Arnot (2002), Bernstein (1990), Bourdieu (1979), Bourdieu and Passeron (1970), Davis (1986), Gaskell (1992), Hogan (1982, 1985), McRobbie (1978), Sennett and Cobb (1972), Weiler (2000), Willis (1977), and others have done truly outstanding work that informs us about social class and schooling, both in the United States and in Britain, France, Canada, and Australia, much of this scholarship was produced in the 1970s and 1980s (or, in the case of Hogan and Davis, is historical in nature), including that contained in more recently released volumes (for example, Arnot, 2002; Bernstein, 1990; Gaskell, 1992). Although powerful then, given the "moment" of scholarly production, such work cannot take the restructured world economy fully into account.

Pulling together new research on school, family, culture, economy, and social class, coupled with several classic pieces, *The Way Class Works* seeks to re-invigorate discussion and research in this area by re-introducing class as a key and simultaneously indispensable analytic strategy in our work on schools, schooling, and family life. In addition, the volume seeks to introduce the next generation of scholars and students to a range of important class-related research formulations and findings.

In so doing, I assume that social class, while perhaps a "phantasmatic" category, organizes the social, cultural, and material world in exceptionally powerful ways.[2] While class is clearly connected to income and occupation, and there is ample evidence that income inequalities are widening in the United States as well as in nations across the globe (Piketty & Saez, 2003, 2006), class must also be understood as practices of living— "the social and psychic practices through which ordinary people live, survive and cope" (Walkerdine, Lucey & Melody, 2001, p. 27). The following are examples of *profoundly* classed experiences, rooted not only in material realities but also in shared culturally based expectations, whether recognized or not: the books we read (or if we read at all); our travel destinations (if we have them) and modes of travel (bus, car, private jet); the films we see; clothes we wear; foods we eat; whether we have orthodontically straightened teeth; where our children go to school, with whom, and under what staff expectations and treatment; the "look" and "feel" of home and school-based interventions if our children "fail"; where we feel most comfortable and with whom; sports our children play and where they play them; the extent and type of extracurricular activities our children engage in; where we live and the nature of our housing; where and if we apply to college/university, under what expectations for success and imagined and/or taken for granted financing (parents, federal money, work/study); the extent to which we are "prepped" for college admission procedures and competition (nature of school-based and/or private college counseling, SAT prep tests, and so forth); and, in the United States at least, whether we have health insurance and, if so, what kind, with what coverage, and for how long. While class certainly has its roots in economic realities, individuals and collectivities create and live class in response to such realities, and families and schools are important mediators in this regard. Such recognition of both the structuring effects of class and the ways in which class is lived out has never been more pressing, given key shifts in the global economy and accompanying deepening social inequalities.

This is not to deny the ongoing and independent effects of race in relation to the production of inequality, a point that is particularly salient in the United States, yet perhaps increasingly important in the UK, France, Germany, and Canada, where large immigrant populations of color have significantly altered the social and economic landscape. Rather it is to suggest that class is a *fundamental organizer* of social experience, both "objective" and "subjective," an organizer that has been largely eclipsed in scholarly literature over the past twenty-five years, particularly in the United States, by other forms of interrogation and analyses, no matter how important. As Cameron McCarthy (1988) reminds us, however, the experiences and subjectivities of racially subordinated groups cannot be read entirely off class, as race has its own independent trajectory with regard to the production of subjectivities and lived-out inequalities (Massey & Denton, 1993; Oliver & Shapiro, 1995).

Although chapters in this volume are based primarily on quantitative and qualitative research rooted in the United States, it is arguably the case that what goes on inside the United States is both similar to and simultaneously increasingly linked to what goes on in the rest of the world. Issues raised in this volume inevitably play out in a wide variety of countries, although in specific national and local parlance. A variety of jobs, for example—whether those for working-class or middle-class individuals—are increasingly exported from highly industrialized countries such as the United States, the UK, and Japan to places where multinational companies can hire both unskilled and highly skilled/well-educated laborers at lower pay and without benefits. In the United States, for example, we are witnessing decreasing opportunities for the working class and poor (outside the military and prisons) who live in particular gender and racial/ethnic relational forms, as well as intensified and pressure-packed expectations directed toward the privileged. This can only be comprehended if we set in motion understanding of a global economy under which a variety of jobs—whether for working-class, poor, and/or middle-class/upper middle-class individuals—are increasingly exported from highly industrialized countries to places where multinational companies can hire highly skilled, well-educated laborers for lower pay and without benefits. This evolving set of international economic and human resource relations affects the educational aspirations and apathies of younger generations in a variety of exporting and importing countries. Those who are educated, as well as those who are not, now live and work inside a global community. At the same time, the push and pull dynamics of globalization (in the sense of pushing certain kinds of jobs outside the borders of first-wave industrialized nations while simultaneously pulling such jobs to nations such as China and India) exert particular class-linked forms of pressure on schools, families, and youth—forms of pressure that are shared in a wide variety of nations, although locally specific iterations are obviously important in this regard.

In addition, the movement of peoples across national borders, including those who possess "flexible citizenship" by virtue of possession of high status knowledge—those who can transcend nation-state boundaries with their inherited and/or earned cultural and intellectual capital (for example, high powered intellectuals, engineers, and medical professionals who are seduced to work in economically powerful nations)—bring new demands to, among others, US and Canadian school systems. By way of example, upper middle-class Hong Kong Chinese parents in Vancouver have little use for what they see as the "soft" curriculum associated with North American schooling (Li, 2005). Given class linked cultural and economic capital, such privileged world citizens are demanding more strongly framed knowledge and less of the "fluff" that they associate with western, particularly North American, schooling, even though they currently reside in Canada. This scene is being played out in schools up and down the Pacific North American coast, where a new form of "white flight" is taking place as white parents are removing their children from schools heavily populated by Asians, a phenomenon linked both to what white parents often see as the inappropriate demand for more strongly framed and inten- sified knowledge on the part of Asian parents as well as the indisputable fact that their children are not, overall, performing as well. This has implications for class formation in the US and elsewhere, as class is now being produced and re-aligned in relation to large numbers of recent immigrants, whether those who possess "flexible citizenship" such as in the case noted above, or those who enter economically powerful nations as immigrants with little more than the clothes on their back, yet subsequently do relatively well in school (Centrie, 2004).

This increasingly interconnected world—of commerce and capital coupled with new patterns of emigration—means that social class is being produced and realigned every- where and that the production of classed communities must take into account the experi- ences and practices of migrants/immigrants in economically powerful nations (see chapters by Li and Weis in this volume). Given shared international press in relation to the flight of jobs from first-wave industrialized nations, as well as the movement of both unskilled and professional workers *to* such job-exporting nations (at one and the same moment as a greater number and variety of jobs are being *exported* to nations such as India), select chapters in this volume probe class structure and re-alignment in Britain (Reay), Canada (Dillabough, Kennelly, and Wang), and Australia (McLeod and Yates), as well as the ways in which class structuration is constitutive of race/ethnic and gender dynamics in national and international contexts.

Adam Gamoran (2001, and in this volume) argues that inequality in educational outcomes as related to social class background "will persist largely unabated throughout the twenty-first century despite much rhetoric and a few policies directed against it" (2001, p. 135). Deepened segregation (Orfield & Lee, 2005); severe constriction in the educational pipeline (Haney et al., 2005); intensified tracking, even in the face of osten- sible de-tracking policies (Oakes, 1985; Yonezawa & Wells, 2005); increased stratifica- tion in higher education through the emergence of a more highly segmented system of colleges and universities—a segmentation that is also linked to stratification in outcomes of college attendance (Brint & Karabel, 1989; Hearn, 1984; Karen, 2002; Oakes, Rogers, Lipton & Morrell, 2002); as well as what counts as "official" knowledge (Apple, 2004; Bernstein, 1990; Bourdieu, 1979; Bourdieu & Passeron, 1970) are all tied to the produc- tion of unequal class outcomes. The linkage between race and class is particularly apparent in the concentration of African-American and Latino students in hyper segre- gated and high poverty schools in the northeast USA, a situation which has been exacer- bated by the repeal of desegregation court orders (Orfield, 2001; Orfield & Lee, 2005).

Taking Gamoran's point seriously means that we need to focus specifically on the ways in which parents and children of varying social class background and across race/ ethnicity experience and interact with family and educational institutions from pre-K through post-graduate school, as well as moving carefully to understand the ways in which such produced outcomes work in nations positioned differently in relation to globalizing culture and capital. This is obviously an ambitious project, one that cannot be accomplished in any single volume. *The Way Class Works* is intended to be an important step in this direction, holding as its main goal the re-centering of social class as a key analytic lens through which social life, particularly that related to family, schools, and schooling, must be understood and interrogated.

This volume is divided into four sections, each named with active verbs, symbolizing both that social class is actively constructed, created, and protected in relation to school, family, and the economy, and simultaneously that scholars must actively complicate notions of class by focusing on class, race, and gender intersections. The volume is comprised of twenty-four essays by distinguished scholars, each followed by questions for further reflection to encourage student discussion.

Section 1, *Thinking/Living Class*, offers a range of essays on the ways in which scholars conceptualize and research class formation and associated class practices. Essays in this section interrogate the economic basis of class re-alignment (Reich); explore the continuing importance of class analysis in a moment when its very relevance is being debated (Wright); focus on the production and maintenance of class through housing (Low); and analyze the ways in which class operates, alongside race, at the conjoined levels of public discourse and subjectivity in the lives of pregnant low income girls (Luttrell). To close this section, Aronowitz adds an interesting complement/contrast to these pieces through his use of autobiography.

Section 2, *Parenting Class*, focuses specifically on the ways in which a range of parenting choices and practices in both the United States and the UK are linked to class formation and associated educational outcomes. Essays focus on the ways in which white middle-class parents in the UK continue to reap the benefits of their classed and raced position in spite of the fact that they intentionally send their children to under resourced schools (Reay); assess the ways in which upper middle-class parents draw on their social networks to locate the best academic schools for their children (Devine); analyze the extent to which there are fundamental differences in child rearing practices by social class (essays by Lareau, and Maier, Ford, and Schneider); and, in discussion with points raised by Lareau, focus on what social class means for immigrant groups in the United States as they raise and educate the next generation (Li).

Section 3, *Schooling Class*, re-visits, extends, and/or challenges important findings in the literature on education and class formation, offering an assemblage of essays which focus on the linkage between social class and educational outcomes—what it looks like empirically, how it is impacted by what goes on within the school, and ways in which such relationship can be challenged by consumers, specifically middle-class parents. Essays in this section look closely at the relationship between class and outcomes of schooling (Gamoran); put forward a strong economic argument for greater educational equality for black males (Levin); focus on the ways in which school knowledge is differentially distributed in relation to student social class (Anyon); and assess the relationship between student social class and school track location (Kelly). Essays also locate the ways in which poor and working-class youth of color view the distributive injustices of the California public school system (Fine, Burns, Torre, and Payne); argue that equitable schooling actually benefits middle-class children (Brantlinger); and, with a specific focus on tertiary level education, interrogate the ways in which the field of education, particularly teacher education, is developing its own problematic discourse around class (Dimitriadis); and explore the ways in which the destabilization of the middle class in the

United States is linked to a reorganization of the opportunity structure of higher education (Thomas and Bell).

The final section, Section 4, *Complicating Class, Race, and Gender Intersectionality*, focuses specifically on the nested nature of race, class, and gender, suggesting that, while class is a key node of difference, it is often constitutive of race and/or gender dynamics, as tied to both national and local context. Essays in this section explore changes in the US white working class in the final quarter of the twentieth century (Weis); the ideological blackening of Hmong American youth which puts them at greater risk for school failure (Lee); the ways in which Bernstein's code theory enables us to understand the intersections between race and class in school outcomes at a highly successful public school for low income students (Sadovnik); the relationship between social space and social exclusion among male and female disadvantaged youth in Canada (Dillabough, Kennelly, and Wang); the linkages between class, race, and gender in the production of identifications, desires, and inequalities among Australian youth in differentially positioned schools (McLeod and Yates); and the ways in which the new global context (movement and migration, the internet, popular culture, new international division of labor, among others) eclipse former notions of social class, thereby demanding new ways of understanding the way class works (Logue and McCarthy).

A central tenet of this volume is that social class must re-claim a central position in discussion and debate around issues of social inequality. In so doing, we must join with our friends and colleagues internationally both to focus on the "way class works" in the twenty-first century—how it is constructed, nested in other nodes of difference, struggled over, and protected—as well as the ways in which we can use schools, in particular, to create a more just and equitable world. The deepening inequalities in evidence in the United States and elsewhere ought to be of concern to all of us, as, in the long run, the intensification of social inequalities in evidence across the globe benefits only the very wealthy. Our scholarship and practice must look toward a more just set of social arrangements.

Notes

This introduction has benefited from discussion with Michelle Fine, Greg Dimitriadis, Yoshiko Nozaki, Sheila Slaughter, and Scott Thomas.

1. Economists Piketty and Saez (2003) have done outstanding work on the growth of income inequality, empirically tracking such inequality in the United States since 1913. Data are clear that there has been rapid growth in income inequalities and that wage and salary growth has been weak during recent economic recovery, while corporate profits are exceptionally strong. Highlights as reported by Aron-Dine and Shapiro (2006) are as follows:

   - From 2003 to 2004, the average incomes of the bottom 99 percent of households grew by less than 3 percent, after adjusting for inflation. In contrast, the average incomes of the top 1 percent of households experienced a jump of more than 18 percent, after adjusting for inflation.
   - The top 1 percent of households (those with annual incomes above about $315,000 in 2004) garnered 53 percent of the income gains in 2004.
   - This disparity produced an exceptional jump in income concentration in 2004. The share of the pre-tax income in the nation that goes to the top 1 percent of households increased from 17.5 percent in 2003 to 19.8 percent in 2004. Only five times since 1913 (the first

year that this data set covers) and only twice since World War II has the top 1 percent's share risen by as much in a single year (in percentage point terms). Each percent point of income is equivalent to $69 billion in 2004.

- The share of total US income that the top 1 percent of households received in 2004 was greater than the share it received in any prior year since 1929, except for 1999 and 2000.

2. Dennis Carlson and Greg Dimitriadis (2003, pp. 18–21) do an outstanding job of "troubling" notions of identity, focusing carefully on what is "fiction" and what is "real." Lois Weis and Michelle Fine (2004) and Michael Apple (2006) take up this issue as well (see Weis, McCarthy & Dimitriadis, 2006, Afterword).

References

Anyon, J. (1981a). Social class and school knowledge. *Curriculum Inquiry, 11*(1), 3–42.

—— (1981b). Elementary schooling and the distinctions of social class. *Interchange, 12*(2–3), 118–32.

Apple, M. (2004). *Ideology and curriculum* (3rd ed.). New York: Routledge.

—— (2006). Afterword: Critical education, politics and the real world. In L. Weis, C. McCarthy & G. Dimitriadis (Eds.), *Ideology, curriculum and the new sociology of education* (pp. 203–19). New York: Routledge.

Arnot, M. (2002). *Reproducing gender? Essays on educational theory and feminist politics.* London: RoutledgeFalmer.

Aron-Dine, A., & Shapiro, I. (2006). *New data show extraordinary jump in income concentration in 2004.* Washington, DC: Center on Budget and Policy Priorities. Retrieved March 31, 2007 from www.cbpp.org/7-10-06inc.pdf

Bensman, D., & Lynch, R. (1987). *Rusted dreams: Hard times in a steel community.* Berkeley, CA: University of California Press.

Bernstein, B. (1990). *The structuring of pedagogic discourse.* New York: Routledge.

Bourdieu, P. (1979). *La distinction, critique sociale du jugement.* Paris: Editions de Minuit.

Bourdieu, P., & Passeron, J. C. (1970). *La Reproduction: Eléments pour une théorie du système d'enseignement.* Paris: Editions de Minuit.

Brint, S., & Karabel, J. (1989). *The diverted dream: Community colleges and the promise of educational opportunity in America, 1900–1985.* New York: Oxford University Press.

Carlson, D., & Dimitriadis, G. (Eds.). (2003). *Promises to keep: Cultural studies, democratic education, and public education.* New York: RoutledgeFalmer.

Centrie, C. (2004). *New lives, new freedoms: The identity formation of Vietnamese immigrant youth in an American high school.* New York: LJB Scholarly Press.

Crenshaw, K. (1989). *Demarginalizing the intersection of race and sex: A black feminist critique of antidiscrimination doctrine, feminist theory, and anti-racist politics* (pp. 139–67). Chicago, IL: University of Chicago Legal Forum.

Davis, M. (1986). *Prisoners of the American dream.* London: Verso Press.

Everhart, R. (1983). *Reading, writing and resistance.* Boston, MA: Routledge and Kegan Paul.

Fine, M., Weis, L., Powell, L., & Wong, M. (1997). *Off white: Readings on race, power and society.* New York: Routledge.

Fine, M., Weis, L., Pruitt, L., & Burns, A. (2004). *Off white: Readings on power, privilege and resistance.* New York: Routledge.

Gamoran, A. (2001). American schooling and educational inequality: A forecast for the 21st century. *Sociology of Education, Special Issue, Current of Thought: Sociology of Education at the Dawn of the 21st Century, 74,* 135–53.

Gaskell, J. (1992). *Gender matters from school to work.* Philadelphia, PA: Open University Press.

Giroux, H. (1997). Rewriting the discourse of racial identity: Towards a pedagogy and politics of whiteness. *Harvard Educational Review, 67*(2), 285–320.

Halle, D. (1984). *America's working man.* Chicago, IL: University of Chicago Press.

Haney, W., Abrams, L., Madaus, G., Wheelock, A., Miao, J., & Gruia, I. (2005). The education pipeline in the United States, 1970–2000: Trends in attrition, retention, and graduation rates. In L. Weis & M. Fine (Eds.), *Beyond silenced voices: Class, race and gender in United States schools, revised edition* (pp. 21–46). Albany: State University of New York Press.

Hearn, J. C. (1984). The relative roles of academic, ascribed, and socio-economic characteristics in college destinations. *Sociology of Education, 57,* 22–30.

Hogan, D. (1982). Education and class formation: The peculiarities of the Americans. In M. Apple (Ed.), *Cultural and economic reproduction in education* (pp. 32–78). London: Routledge and Kegan Paul.

——— (1985). *Class and reform: School and society in Chicago, 1880–1930.* Philadelphia, PA: University of Pennsylvania Press.

Karen, D. (2002). Changes in access to higher education in the United States: 1980–92. *Sociology of Education, 75*(3), 191–210.

Katz, M. (2001). *The price of citizenship.* New York: Metropolitan Books.

Kefalas, M. (2003). *Working-class heroes. Protecting home, community, and nation in a Chicago neighborhood.* Berkeley, CA: University of California Press.

Kelley, R. (1994). *Race rebels: Culture, politics and the black working class.* New York: Free Press.

Kincheloe, J., et al. (Eds.). (1998). *White Reign: Deploying whiteness in America.* New York: St. Martin's Press.

Lamont, M. (2000). *The dignity of working men: Morality and the boundaries of race, class and immigration.* Cambridge: Harvard University Press.

Lather, P. (1991). *Getting smart: Feminist research and pedagogy within the post-modern.* New York: Routledge.

Levin, H., & Rumberger, R. (1987). Education requirements for new technologies: Visions, possibilities, and current realities. *Educational Policy, 1*(3), 333–54.

Li, G. (2005). *Culturally contested pedagogy.* Albany: State University of New York Press.

London, H. (1978). *The culture of a community college.* New York: Praeger.

Marable, M. (1997). *Black liberation in conservative America.* Boston, MA: South End Press.

Massey, D., & Denton, N. (1993). *American apartheid: Segregation and the making of the underclass.* Cambridge: Harvard University Press.

McCarthy, C. (1988). Marxist theories of education and the challenge of a cultural politics of non-synchrony. In L. Roman, L. Christian-Smith & E. Ellsworth (Eds.), *Becoming feminine: The politics of popular culture* (pp. 185–204). Philadelphia, PA: The Falmer Press.

——— (1990). *Race and curriculum.* Philadelphia, PA: The Falmer Press.

——— (1993). Beyond the poverty of theory in race relations: Non-synchrony and social difference in education. In L. Weis & M. Fine (Eds.), *Beyond silenced voices: Class, race and gender in US schools* (pp. 325–46). Albany: State University of New York Press.

McRobbie, A. (Ed.) (1978). Working class girls and the culture of femininity. In Women's Studies Group, *Women take issue.* London: Hutchinson.

Mullings, L. (1997). *On our own terms: Race, class and gender in the lives of African Americans.* New York: Routledge.

Oakes, J. (1985). *Keeping track: How schools structure inequality.* New Haven, CT: Yale University Press.

Oakes, J., Rogers, J., Lipton, M., & Morrell, E. (2002). The social construction of college access: Confronting the technical, cultural and political barriers to low-income students of color. In W. G. Tierney & L. S. Hagedorn (Eds.), *Increasing access to college: Extending possibilities for all students* (pp. 105–21). Albany: State University of New York Press.

Oliver, M., & Shapiro, T. (1995). *Black wealth/white wealth: A new perspective on racial inequality*. New York: Routledge.

Orfield, G. (2001). *Schools more separate: Consequences of a decade of resegregation*. Cambridge, MA: Civil Rights Project, Harvard University.

Orfield, G., & Lee, C. (2005). Segregation 50 years after Brown: A metropolitan change. In L. Weis & M. Fine (Eds.), *Beyond silenced voices: Class, race and gender in United States schools, revised edition* (pp. 3–20). Albany: State University of New York Press.

Piketty, T., & Saez, E. (2003). Income inequality in the United States: 1913–98. *Quarterly Journal of Economics*, February.

—— (2006). *Income inequality in the United States, 1913–2002*. Oxford University Press.

Reich, R. (1991). *The work of nations: Preparing ourselves for 21st-century capitalism*. New York: Alfred A. Knopf.

—— (2001). *The future of success*. New York: Alfred A. Knopf.

Roman, L., & Christian-Smith, L. (Eds.). (1988). *Becoming feminine: The politics of popular culture*. Philadelphia, PA: Falmer Press.

Rubin, L. (1976). *Worlds of pain*. New York: Basic Books.

Sennett, R., & Cobb, J. (1972). *The hidden injuries of class*. New York: Vintage Books.

Spelman, E. (1988). *Inessential woman*. Boston, MA: Beacon Press.

Valli, L. (1986). *Becoming clerical workers*. Boston, MA: Routledge and Kegan Paul.

Walkerdine, V., Lucey, H., & Melody, J. (2001). *Growing up girl: Psychosocial explorations of gender and class*. New York: New York University Press.

Weiler, J. (2000). *Codes and contradictions: Race, gender identity, and schooling*. Albany: State University of New York Press.

Weis, L., & Fine, M. (2004). *Working method: Research and social justice*. New York: Routledge.

Weis, L., McCarthy, C., & Dimitriadis, G. (Eds.). (2006). *Ideology, curriculum and the new sociology of education*. New York: Routledge.

Willis, P. (1977). *Learning to labour: How working class kids get working class jobs*. Farnborough, UK: Saxon House Press.

Yonezawa, S., & Wells, A. (2005). Reform as re-defining the spaces of schools: An examination of detracking by choice. In L. Weis & M. Fine (Eds.), *Beyond silenced voices: Class, race and gender in United States schools, revised edition* (pp. 47–62). Albany: State University of New York Press.

Section 1

Thinking/living class

Chapter 1

Why the rich are getting richer and the poor, poorer

*Robert B. Reich**

"[T]he division of labour is limited by the extent of the market."
Adam Smith, *An Inquiry into the Nature and Causes of the Wealth of Nations* (1776)

Regardless of how your job is officially classified (manufacturing, service, managerial, technical, secretarial, and so on), or the industry in which you work (automotive, steel, computer, advertising, finance, food processing), your real competitive position in the world economy is coming to depend on the function you perform in it. Herein lies the basic reason why incomes are diverging. The fortunes of routine producers are declining. In-person servers are also becoming poorer, although their fates are less clear-cut. But symbolic analysts—who solve, identify, and broker new problems—are, by and large, succeeding in the world economy.

All Americans used to be in roughly the same economic boat. Most rose or fell together, as the corporations in which they were employed, the industries comprising such corporations, and the national economy as a whole became more productive—or languished. But national borders no longer define our economic fates. We are now in different boats, one sinking rapidly, one sinking more slowly, and the third rising steadily.

* * *

The boat containing routine producers is sinking rapidly. Recall that by mid-century routine production workers in the United States were paid relatively well. The giant pyramid-like organizations at the core of each major industry coordinated their prices and investments—avoiding the harsh winds of competition and thus maintaining healthy earnings. Some of these earnings, in turn, were reinvested in new plant and equipment (yielding ever-larger-scale economics); another portion went to top managers and investors. But a large and increasing portion went to middle managers and production workers. Work stoppages posed such a threat to high-volume production that organized labor was able to exact an ever-larger premium for its cooperation. And the pattern of wages established within the core corporations influenced the pattern throughout the national economy. Thus the growth of a relatively affluent middle class, able to purchase all the wondrous things produced in high volume by the core corporations.

* Robert B. Reich has served in three national administrations, most recently as Secretary of Labor under President Bill Clinton.

But, as has been observed, the core is rapidly breaking down into global webs which earn their largest profits from clever problem-solving, problem-identifying, and brokering. As the costs of transporting standard things and of communicating information about them continue to drop, profit margins on high-volume, standardized production are thinning, because there are few barriers to entry. Modern factories and state-of-the-art machinery can be installed almost anywhere on the globe. Routine producers in the United States, then, are in direct competition with millions of routine producers in other nations. Twelve thousand people are added to the world's population every hour, most of whom, eventually, will happily work for a small fraction of the wages of routine producers in the United States.[1]

The consequence is clearest in older, heavy industries, where high-volume, standardized production continues its ineluctable move to where labor is cheapest and most accessible around the world. Thus, for example, the Maquiladora factories cluttered along the Mexican side of the US border in the sprawling shanty towns of Tijuana, Mexicali, Nogales, Agua Prieta, and Ciudad Juárez—factories owned mostly by Americans, but increasingly by Japanese—in which more than a half million routine producers assemble parts into finished goods to be shipped into the United States.

The same story is unfolding worldwide. Until the late 1970s, AT&T had depended on routine producers in Shreveport, Louisiana, to assemble standard telephones. It then discovered that routine producers in Singapore would perform the same tasks at a far lower cost. Facing intense competition from other global webs, AT&T's strategic brokers felt compelled to switch. So in the early 1980s they stopped hiring routine producers in Shreveport and began hiring cheaper routine producers in Singapore. But under this kind of pressure for ever-lower high-volume production costs, today's Singaporean can easily end up as yesterday's Louisianan. By the late 1980s, AT&T's strategic brokers found that routine producers in Thailand were eager to assemble telephones for a small fraction of the wages of routine producers in Singapore. Thus, in 1989, AT&T stopped hiring Singaporeans to make telephones and began hiring even cheaper routine producers in Thailand.

The search for ever-lower wages has not been confined to heavy industry. Routine data processing is equally footloose. Keypunch operators located anywhere around the world can enter data into computers, linked by satellite or transoceanic fiber-optic cable, and take it out again. As the rates charged by satellite networks continue to drop, and as more satellites and fiber-optic cables become available (reducing communication costs still further), routine data processors in the United States find themselves in ever more direct competition with their counterparts abroad, who are often eager to work for far less.

By 1990, keypunch operators in the United States were earning, at most, $6.50 per hour. But keypunch operators throughout the rest of the world were willing to work for a fraction of this. Thus, many potential US data-processing jobs were disappearing, and the wages and benefits of the remaining ones were in decline. Typical was Saztec International, a $20-million-a-year data-processing firm headquartered in Kansas City, whose US strategic brokers contracted with routine data processors in Manila and with US-owned firms that needed such data-processing services. Compared with the average Philippine income of $1,700 per year, data-entry operators working for Saztec earn the princely sum of $2,650. The remainder of Saztec's employees were US problem-solvers and problem-identifiers, searching for ways to improve the worldwide system and find new uses to which it could be put (Maxwell Hamilton, 1989).

By 1990, American Airlines was employing over one thousand data processors in Barbados and the Dominican Republic to enter names and flight numbers from used airline tickets (flown daily to Barbados from airports around the United States) into a giant computer bank located in Dallas. Chicago publisher R. R. Donnelley was sending entire manuscripts to Barbados for entry into computers in preparation for printing. The New York Life Insurance Company was dispatching insurance claims to Castleisland, Ireland, where routine producers, guided by simple directions, entered the claims and determined the amounts due, then instantly transmitted the computations back to the United States. (When the firm advertised in Ireland for twenty-five data-processing jobs, it received six hundred applications.) And McGraw-Hill was processing subscription renewal and marketing information for its magazines in nearby Galway. Indeed, literally millions of routine workers around the world were receiving information, converting it into computer-readable form, and then sending it back—at the speed of electronic impulses—whence it came.

The simple coding of computer software has also entered into world commerce. India, with a large English-speaking population of technicians happy to do routine programming cheaply, is proving to be particularly attractive to global webs in need of this service. By 1990, Texas Instruments maintained a software development facility in Bangalore, linking fifty Indian programmers by satellite to TI's Dallas headquarters. Spurred by this and similar ventures, the Indian government was building a teleport in Poona, intended to make it easier and less expensive for many other firms to send their routine software design specifications for coding (Gupta, 1989).

* * *

This shift of routine production jobs from advanced to developing nations is a great boon to many workers in such nations who otherwise would be jobless or working for much lower wages. These workers, in turn, now have more money with which to purchase symbolic–analytic services from advanced nations (often embedded within all sorts of complex products). The trend is also beneficial to everyone around the world who can now obtain high volume, standardized products (including information and software) more cheaply than before.

But these benefits do not come without certain costs. In particular the burden is borne by those who no longer have good-paying routine production jobs within advanced economies like the United States. Many of these people used to belong to unions or at least benefited from prevailing wage rates established in collective bargaining agreements. But as the old corporate bureaucracies have flattened into global webs, bargaining leverage has been lost. Indeed, the tacit national bargain is no more.

Despite the growth in the number of new jobs in the United States, union membership has withered. In 1960, 35 percent of all non-agricultural workers in the United States belonged to a union. But by 1980 that portion had fallen to just under a quarter, and by 1989 to about 17 percent. Excluding government employees, union membership was down to 13.4 percent (US Government Printing Office, 1989). This was a smaller proportion even than in the early 1930s, before the National Labor Relations Act created a legally protected right to labor representation. The drop in membership has been accompanied by a growing number of collective bargaining agreements to freeze wages at current levels, reduce wage levels of entering workers, or reduce wages overall. This is an important reason why the long economic recovery that began in 1982 produced a smaller rise in unit labor costs than any of the eight recoveries since World War II—the low rate of unemployment during its course notwithstanding.

Routine production jobs have vanished fastest in traditional unionized industries (autos, steel, and rubber, for example), where average wages have kept up with inflation. This is because the jobs of older workers in such industries are protected by seniority; the youngest workers are the first to be laid off. Faced with a choice of cutting wages or cutting the number of jobs, a majority of union members (secure in the knowledge that there are many who are junior to them who will be laid off first) often have voted for the latter.

Thus the decline in union membership has been most striking among young men entering the work force without a college education. In the early 1950s, more than 40 percent of this group joined unions; by the late 1980s, less than 20 percent (if public employees are excluded, less than 10 percent) (Katz & Revenga, 1989). In steelmaking, for example, although many older workers remained employed, almost half of all routine steelmaking jobs in the United States vanished between 1974 and 1988 (from 480,000 to 260,000). Similarly with automobiles; during the 1980s, the United Auto Workers lost 500,000 members—one-third of their total at the start of the decade. General Motors alone cut 150,000 US production jobs during the 1980s (even as it added employment abroad). Another consequence of the same phenomenon was that the gap between the average wages of unionized and non-unionized workers widened dramatically—from 14.6 percent in 1973 to 20.4 percent by the end of the 1980s.[2] The lesson is clear. If you drop out of high school or have no more than a high school diploma, do not expect a good routine production job to be awaiting you.

Also vanishing are lower- and middle-level management jobs involving routine production. Between 1981 and 1986, more than 780,000 foremen, supervisors, and section chiefs lost their jobs through plant closings and layoffs (US Department of Labor, 1986). Large numbers of assistant division heads, assistant directors, assistant managers, and vice presidents also found themselves jobless. GM shed more than 40,000 white-collar employees and planned to eliminate another 25,000 by the mid-1990s (*The Wall Street Journal*, 1990). As the United States' core pyramids metamorphosed into global webs, many middle-level routine producers were as obsolete as routine workers on the line.

As has been noted, foreign-owned webs are hiring some Americans to do routine production in the United States. Philips, Sony, and Toyota factories are popping up all over—to the self-congratulatory applause of the nation's governors and mayors, who have lured them with promises of tax abatements and new sewers, among other amenities. But as these ebullient politicians will soon discover, the foreign-owned factories are highly automated and will become far more so in years to come. Routine production jobs account for a small fraction of the cost of producing most items in the United States and other advanced nations, and this fraction will continue to decline sharply as computer-integrated robots take over. In 1977 it took routine producers thirty-five hours to assemble an automobile in the United States; it is estimated that by the mid-1990s, Japanese-owned factories in the United States will be producing finished automobiles using only eight hours of a routine producer's time (International Motor Vehicles Program, 1989).

The productivity and resulting wages of US workers who run such robotic machinery may be relatively high, but there may not be many such jobs to go around. A case in point: In the late 1980s, Nippon Steel joined with the United States' ailing Inland Steel to build a new $400 million cold-rolling mill fifty miles west of Gary, Indiana. The mill was celebrated for its state-of-the-art technology, which cut the time to produce a coil of steel from twelve days to about one hour. In fact, the entire plant could be run by a small team of technicians, which became clear when Inland subsequently closed two of its old cold-rolling mills, laying off hundreds of routine workers. Governors and mayors take note: your much-ballyhooed foreign factories may end up employing distressingly few of your constituents.

Overall, the decline in routine jobs has hurt men more than women. This is because the routine production jobs held by men in high-volume metal-bending manufacturing industries had paid higher wages than the routine production jobs held by women in textiles and data processing. As both sets of jobs have been lost, US women in routine production have gained more equal footing with US men—equally poor footing, that is. This is a major reason why the gender gap between male and female wages began to close during the 1980s.

＊

The second of the three boats, carrying in-person servers, is sinking as well, but somewhat more slowly and unevenly. Most in-person servers are paid at or just slightly above the minimum wage and many work only part time, with the result that their take-home pay is modest, to say the least. Nor do they typically receive all the benefits (health care, life insurance, disability, and so forth) garnered by routine producers in large manufacturing corporations or by symbolic analysts affiliated with the more affluent threads of global webs.[3] In-person servers are sheltered from the direct effects of global competition and, like everyone else, benefit from access to lower-cost products from around the world. But they are not immune to its indirect effects.

For one thing, in-person servers increasingly compete with former routine production workers, who, no longer able to find well-paying routine production jobs, have few alternatives but to seek in-person service jobs. The Bureau of Labor Statistics estimates that, of the 2.8 million manufacturing workers who lost their jobs during the early 1980s, fully one-third were rehired in service jobs paying at least 20 percent less (US Department of Labor, 1986). In-person servers must also compete with high school graduates and dropouts who years before had moved easily into routine production jobs but no longer can. And if demographic predictions about the US work force in the first decades of the twenty-first century are correct (and they are likely to be, since most of the people who will comprise the work force are already identifiable), most new entrants into the job market will be black or Hispanic men, or women—groups that in years past have possessed relatively weak technical skills. This will result in an even larger number of people crowding into in-person services. Finally, in-person servers will be competing with growing numbers of immigrants, both legal and illegal, for whom in-person services will comprise the most accessible jobs. It is estimated that between the mid-1980s and the end of the century, about a quarter of all workers entering the US labor force will be immigrants (Federal Immigration and Naturalization Service, 1986, 1987).

Perhaps the fiercest competition that in-person servers face comes from labor-saving machinery (much of it invented, designed, fabricated, or assembled in other nations, of course). Automated tellers, computerized cashiers, automatic car washes, robotized vending machines, self-service gasoline pumps, and all similar gadgets substitute for the human beings that customers once encountered. Even telephone operators are fast disappearing, as electronic sensors and voice simulators become capable of carrying on conversations that are reasonably intelligent, and always polite. Retail sales workers—among the largest groups of in-person servers—are similarly imperiled. Through personal computers linked to television screens, tomorrow's consumers will be able to buy furniture, appliances, and all sorts of electronic toys from their living rooms—examining the merchandise from all angles, selecting whatever color, size, special features, and price seem most appealing, and then transmitting the order instantly to warehouses from which the selections will be shipped directly to their homes. So, too, with financial transactions, airline and hotel reservations, rental car agreements, and similar contracts, which will be executed between consumers in their homes and computer banks somewhere else on the globe (Deutsch, 1989).

Advanced economies like the United States will continue to generate sizable numbers of new in-person service jobs, of course, the automation of older ones notwithstanding. For every bank teller who loses her job to an automated teller, three new jobs open for aerobics instructors. Human beings, it seems, have an almost insatiable desire for personal attention. But the intense competition nevertheless ensures that the wages of in-person servers will remain relatively low. In-person servers—working on their own, or else dispersed widely amid many small establishments, filling all sorts of personal-care niches—cannot readily organize themselves into labor unions or create powerful lobbies to limit the impact of such competition.

In two respects, demographics will work in favor of in-person servers, buoying their collective boat slightly. First, as has been noted, the rate of growth of the US work force is slowing. In particular, the number of younger workers is shrinking. Between 1985 and 1995, the number of eighteen- to twenty-four-year-olds will have declined by 17.5 percent. Thus, employers will have more incentive to hire and train in-person servers whom they might previously have avoided. But this demographic relief from the competitive pressures will be only temporary. The cumulative procreative energies of the postwar baby-boomers (born between 1946 and 1964) will result in a new surge of workers by 2010 or thereabouts (Johnson & Packer et al., 1987). And immigration—both legal and illegal—shows every sign of increasing in years to come.

Next, by the second decade of the twenty-first century, the number of US aged sixty-five and over will be rising precipitously, as the baby-boomers reach retirement age and live longer. Their life expectancies will lengthen not just because fewer of them will have smoked their way to their graves and more will have eaten better than their parents, but also because they will receive all sorts of expensive drugs and therapies designed to keep them alive—barely. By 2035, twice as many Americans will be elderly as in 1988, and the number of octogenarians is expected to triple. As these decaying baby-boomers ingest all the chemicals and receive all the treatments, they will need a great deal of personal attention. Millions of deteriorating bodies will require nurses, nursing-home operators, hospital administrators, orderlies, home-care providers, hospice aides, and technicians to operate and maintain all the expensive machinery that will monitor and temporarily stave off final disintegration. There might even be a booming market for euthanasia specialists. In-person servers catering to the old and ailing will be in strong demand.[4]

One small problem: The decaying baby-boomers will not have enough money to pay for these services. They will have used up their personal savings years before. Their Social Security payments will, of course, have been used by the government to pay for the previous generation's retirement and to finance much of the budget deficits of the 1980s. Moreover, with relatively fewer young Americans in the population, the supply of housing will likely exceed the demand, with the result that the boomers' major investments—their homes—will be worth less (in inflation-adjusted dollars) when they retire than they planned for. In consequence, the huge cost of caring for the graying boomers will fall on many of the same people who will be paid to care for them. It will be like a great sump pump: in-person servers of the twenty-first century will have an abundance of healthcare jobs, but a large portion of their earnings will be devoted to Social Security payments and income taxes, which will in turn be used to pay their salaries. The net result: no real improvement in their standard of living.

The standard of living of in-person servers also depends, indirectly, on the standard of living of the Americans they serve who are engaged in world commerce. To the extent that *these* Americans are richly rewarded by the rest of the world for what they contribute, they will have more money to lavish upon in-person services. Here we find the only form of "trickle-down" economics that has a basis in reality. A waitress in a town whose major factory has just been closed is unlikely to earn a high wage or enjoy much job security; in a swank resort populated by film producers and banking moguls, she is apt to do reasonably well. So, too, with nations. In-person servers in Bangladesh may spend their days performing roughly the same tasks as in-person servers in the United States, but have a far lower standard of living for their efforts. The difference comes in the value that their customers add to the world economy.

* * *

Unlike the boats of routine producers and in-person servers, however, the vessel containing the United States' symbolic analysts is rising. Worldwide demand for their insights is growing as the ease and speed of communicating them steadily increases. Not every symbolic analyst is rising as quickly or as dramatically as every other, of course; symbolic analysts at the low end are barely holding their own in the world economy. But symbolic analysts at the top are in such great demand worldwide that they have difficulty keeping track of all their earnings. Never before in history has opulence on such a scale been gained by people who have earned it, and done so legally.

Among symbolic analysts in the middle range are US scientists and researchers who are busily selling their discoveries to global enterprise webs. They are not limited to US customers. If the strategic brokers in General Motors' headquarters refuse to pay a high price for a new means of making high-strength ceramic engines dreamed up by a team of engineers affiliated with Carnegie–Mellon University in Pittsburgh, the strategic brokers of Honda or Mercedes–Benz are likely to be more than willing.

So, too, with the insights of the United States' ubiquitous management consultants, which are being sold for large sums to eager entrepreneurs in Europe and Latin America. Also, the insights of the United States' energy consultants, sold for even larger sums to Arab sheikhs. US design engineers are providing insights to Olivetti, Mazda, Siemens, and other global webs; US marketers, techniques for learning what worldwide consumers will buy; US advertisers, ploys for ensuring that they actually do. US architects are issuing designs and blueprints for opera houses, art galleries, museums, luxury hotels, and residential complexes in the world's major cities; US commercial property developers market these properties to worldwide investors and purchasers.

Americans who specialize in the gentle art of public relations are in demand by corporations, governments, and politicians in virtually every nation. So, too, are US political consultants, some of whom, at this writing, are advising the Hungarian Socialist Party, the remnant of Hungary's ruling Communists, on how to salvage a few parliamentary seats in the nation's first free election in more than forty years. Also at this writing, a team of US agricultural consultants are advising the managers of a Soviet farm collective employing 1,700 Russians eighty miles outside Moscow. As noted, US investment bankers and lawyers specializing in financial circumnavigations are selling their insights to Asians and Europeans who are eager to discover how to make large amounts of money by moving large amounts of money.

Developing nations, meanwhile, are hiring US civil engineers to advise on building roads and dams. The present thaw in the Cold War will no doubt expand these opportunities. US engineers from Bechtel (a global firm notable for having employed both Caspar Weinberger and George Shultz for much larger sums than either earned in the Reagan administration) have begun helping the Soviets design and install a new generation of nuclear reactors. Nations also are hiring US bankers and lawyers to help them renegotiate the terms of their loans with global banks, and Washington lobbyists to help them with Congress, the Treasury, the World Bank, the IMF, and other politically sensitive institutions. In fits of obvious desperation, several nations emerging from communism have even hired American economists to teach them about capitalism.

Almost everyone around the world is buying the skills and insights of Americans who manipulate oral and visual symbols—musicians, sound engineers, film producers, makeup artists, directors, cinematographers, actors and actresses, boxers, scriptwriters, songwriters, and set designers. Among the wealthiest of symbolic analysts are Steven Spielberg, Bill Cosby, Charles Schulz, Eddie Murphy, Sylvester Stallone, Madonna, and other star directors and performers—who are almost as well known on the streets of Dresden and Tokyo as in the Back Bay of Boston. Less well rewarded but no less renowned are the unctuous anchors on Turner Broadcasting's Cable News, who appear daily, via satellite, in places ranging from Vietnam to Nigeria. Vanna White is the world's most watched game-show hostess. Behind each of these familiar faces is a collection of US problem-solvers/identifiers, and brokers who train, coach, advise, promote, amplify, direct, groom, represent, and otherwise add value to their talents.[5]

There are also the insights of senior US executives who occupy the world headquarters of global "American" corporations and the national or regional headquarters of global "foreign" corporations. Their insights are duly exported to the rest of the world through the webs of global enterprise. IBM does not export many machines from the United States, for example. Big Blue makes machines all over the globe and services them on the spot. Its prime US exports are symbolic and analytic. From IBM's world headquarters in Armonk, New York, emanate strategic brokerage and related management services bound for the rest of the world. In return, IBM's top executives are generously rewarded.

* * *

The most important reason for this expanding world market and increasing global demand for the symbolic and analytic insights of Americans has been the dramatic improvement in worldwide communication and transportation technologies. Designs, instructions, advice, and visual and audio symbols can be communicated more and more rapidly around the globe, with ever-greater precision and at ever-lower cost. Madonna's voice can be transported to billions of listeners, with perfect clarity, on digital compact disks. A new invention emanating from engineers in Battelle's laboratory in Columbus, Ohio, can be sent almost anywhere via modem, in a form that will allow others to examine it in three dimensions through enhanced computer graphics. When face-to-face meetings are still required—and videoconferencing will not suffice—it is relatively easy for designers, consultants, advisers, artists, and executives to board supersonic jets and, in a matter of hours, meet directly with their worldwide clients, customers, audiences, and employees.

With rising demand comes rising compensation. Whether in the form of licensing fees, fees for service, salaries, or shares in final profits, the economic result is much the same. There are also non-pecuniary rewards. One of the best-kept secrets among symbolic analysts is that so many of them enjoy their work. In fact, much of it does not count as work at all, in the traditional sense. The work of routine producers and in-person servers is typically monotonous; it causes muscles to tire or weaken and involves little independence or discretion. The "work" of symbolic analysts, by contrast, often involves puzzles, experiments, games, a significant amount of chatter, and substantial discretion over what to do next. Few routine producers or in-person servers would "work" if they did not need to earn the money. Many symbolic analysts would "work" even if money were no object.

* * *

At mid-century, when the United States was a national market dominated by core pyramid-shaped corporations, there were constraints on the earnings of people at the highest rungs. First and most obviously, the market for their services was largely limited to the borders of the nation. In addition, whatever conceptual value they might contribute was small relative to the value gleaned from large scale—and it was dependent on large scale for whatever income it was to summon. Most of the problems to be identified and solved had to do with enhancing the efficiency of production and improving the flow of materials, parts, assembly, and distribution. Inventors searched for the rare breakthrough revealing an entirely new product to be made in high volume; management consultants, executives, and engineers thereafter tried to speed and synchronize its manufacture, to better achieve scale efficiencies; advertisers and marketers sought then to whet the public's appetite for the standard item that emerged. Since white-collar earnings increased with larger scale, there was considerable incentive to expand the firm; indeed, many of the United States' core corporations grew far larger than scale economics would appear to have justified.

By the 1990s, in contrast, the earnings of symbolic analysts were limited neither by the size of the national market nor by the volume of production of the firms with which they were affiliated. The marketplace was worldwide, and conceptual value was high relative to value added from scale efficiencies.

There had been another constraint on high earnings, which also gave way by the 1990s. At mid-century, the compensation awarded to top executives and advisers of the largest of the United States' core corporations could not be grossly out of proportion to that of low-level production workers. It would be unseemly for executives who engaged in highly visible rounds of bargaining with labor unions, and who routinely responded to government requests to moderate prices, to take home wages and benefits wildly in excess of what other Americans earned. Unless white-collar executives restrained themselves, moreover, blue-collar production workers could not be expected to restrain their own demands for higher wages. Unless both groups exercised restraint, the government could not be expected to forbear from imposing direct controls and regulations.

At the same time, the wages of production workers could not be allowed to sink too low; lest there be insufficient purchasing power in the economy. After all, who would buy all the goods flowing out of US factories if not US workers? This, too, was part of the tacit bargain struck between US managers and their workers.

Recall the oft-repeated corporate platitude of the era about the chief executive's responsibility to carefully weigh and balance the interests of the corporation's disparate stakeholders. Under the stewardship of the corporate statesman, no set of stakeholders— least of all white-collar executives—was to gain a disproportionately large share of the benefits of corporate activity; nor was any stakeholder—especially the average worker— to be left with a share that was disproportionately small. Banal though it was, this idea helped to maintain the legitimacy of the core US corporation in the eyes of most Americans, and to ensure continued economic growth.

But by the 1990s, these informal norms were evaporating, just as (and largely because) the core US corporation was vanishing. The links between top executives and the US production worker were fading: An ever-increasing number of subordinates and contractees were foreign, and a steadily growing number of US routine producers were working for foreign-owned firms. An entire cohort of middle-level managers, who had once been deemed "white collar," had disappeared; and, increasingly, US executives were exporting their insights to global enterprise webs.

As the US corporation itself became a global web almost indistinguishable from any other, its stakeholders were turning into a large and diffuse group, spread over the world. Such global stakeholders were less visible, and far less noisy, than national stakeholders. And as the US corporation sold its goods and services all over the world, the purchasing power of US workers became far less relevant to its economic survival.

Thus have the inhibitions been removed. The salaries and benefits of the United States' top executives, and many of their advisers and consultants, have soared to what years before would have been unimaginable heights, even as those of other Americans have declined.

Questions for discussion

1. Give examples of products and/or services that you use which have been directly or indirectly produced in a country other than the one in which you reside. How can one relate this to Reich's discussion in the beginning of his chapter, about US companies moving their routine production to other countries?
2. Reich argues that the gender gap in wages began to close during the 1980s. What is the current status of this gender gap—and what does this mean for questions of gender identity formation?
3. Discuss the correlation between routine production jobs and high school level education in the 1980s. Compare and contrast the contemporary social and

economic climate with that of the 1980s relative to the relationship between the job market and one's education level.

4. How much of Reich's discussion on social security holds true today? How has the social security system in the US changed in recent years, and with what implications?

5. Reich argues that in-person servers will be competing with growing numbers of immigrants, both legal and illegal, for whom in-person services will comprise the most accessible jobs. How has this contributed to the various debates and policy decisions in the US in recent years?

6. How has the globalization of US corporations affected stakeholders and workers around the world? What is the nature of the power dynamics between the various countries in this phenomenon?

7. Do you agree with Reich's comment, "All Americans used to be in roughly the same economic boat?" Give reasons for your answer.

8. Expanding on Reich's analysis of nations emerging from communism, how have these nations' educational system been impacted by the trends of capitalism?

This chapter is from the *Work of Nations* by Robert Reich, copyright © 1991 by Robert Reich. Used by permission of Alfred A. Knopf, a division of Random House, Inc.

Notes

1. The reader should note, of course, that lower wages in other areas of the world are of no particular attraction to global capital unless workers there are sufficiently productive to make the labor cost of producing *each unit* lower there than in higher-wage regions. Productivity in many low-wage areas of the world has improved due to the ease with which state-of-the-art factories and equipment can be installed there.

2. US Department of Commerce, Bureau of Labor Statistics, "Wages of Unionized and Non-unionized Workers," various issues.

3. The growing portion of the US labor force engaged in in-person services, relative to routine production, thus helps explain why the number of Americans lacking health insurance increased by at least 6 million during the 1980s.

4. The Census Bureau estimates that by the year 2000, at least 12 million Americans will work in health services—well over 6 percent of the total work force.

5. In 1989, the entertainment business summoned to the United States $5.5 billion in foreign earnings—making it among the nation's largest export industries, just behind aerospace. US Department of Commerce, International Trade Commission, "Composition of US Exports," various issues.

References

Deutsch, C. H. (1989). The powerful push for self-service. *The New York Times*, section 3 (April 9): 1–6.

Federal Immigration and Naturalization Service (1986, 1987). *Statistical yearbook*. Washington DC: US Government Printing Office.

Gupta, U. (1989). US–India satellite link stands to cut software costs. *The Wall Street Journal* (March 6): B2.

International Motor Vehicles Program (1989). MIT.

Johnson, W., & A. Packer, et al. (1987) US Bureau of the Census Current Population Reports

Series P23/138, tables 2.1, 4.6. In *Workforce 2000: Work and workers for the 21st century*. Indianapolis: Hudson Institute.

Katz, L., & Revenga, A. (1989). Changes in the structure of wages: The US versus Japan. In *Calculations of current population surveys*. National Bureau of Economic Research, September.

Maxwell Hamilton, J. (1989). A bit player buys into the computer age. *The New York Times Business World* (December 3), p. 14.

The Wall Street Journal (1990). February 16: A5.

US Department of Labor, Bureau of Labor Statistics (1986). Re-employment increases among displaced workers. *BLS News* (October 14): 86–414, table 6.

US Government Printing Office Statistical Abstract of the United States (1989). Washington, DC, 416, table 684.

Chapter 2

The continuing importance of class analysis[1]

*Erik Olin Wright** *

The concept of class is one of the most contested within sociology. Not only is there considerable debate over precisely how this concept should be defined and elaborated, there is also considerable debate over its very relevance for contemporary sociology. It is perhaps ironic that in an era of deepening inequality and economic polarization within US society, some sociologists confidently proclaim the "Death of Class," or even argue that we are rapidly becoming a "Classless Society."[2] What is particularly striking is that these claims are not being made mainly by political conservatives, but by sociologists who broadly identify with progressive politics and ideal.

In this essay I will systematically engage one of the most interesting pieces in these discussions of the declining relevance of class, Jan Pakulski and Malcolm Waters' 1996 essay, "The Reshaping and Dissolution of Social Class in Advanced Society." While the core arguments they present are not new, as they themselves emphasize, they marshal those arguments in a more systematic way than most critiques of class analysis, and defend a particularly stark bottom line conclusion—that contemporary class analysts "manufacture class where it no longer exists as a meaningful social entity."[3] Defenders of class analysis should engage these arguments in the spirit of a healthy and serious inter- rogation of foundational concepts and their empirical relevance. Just as feminists need to take seriously, rather than dismiss out of hand as absurd, the claim that gender oppres- sion is withering away, so class analysts of both Marxist and Weberian inspiration need to take seriously the arguments that we are moving rapidly towards a classless society, or at least a society within which class has "dissolved" as a salient explanatory category.[4] I hope to show in this essay that Pakulski and Waters' arguments and evidence are not persuasive, but I believe a dialogue with their arguments can be productive for clarifying the nature of class analysis, the status of its explanatory claims, and the tasks it faces.

In the following section I will set the stage for a defense of class analysis by reviewing some of the key components of the concept of class in the Marxist and Weberian tradi- tions of class theory. Obviously the answer to the question "Does class still matter?" depends in part on precisely what one means by "class." In particular, it is important to understand what distinguishes "class" from other forms of social division, and why this form of social division is thought to be consequential (i.e., what causal mechanisms are identified by the concept of class). I endorse Pakulski and Waters' insistence that "class is fundamentally an economic phenomenon. It refers principally to differences in the ownership of property . . . and to differential market capacity, especially labor-market

* Vilas Distinguished Professor of Sociology at the University of Wisconsin.

capacity."[5] In order to assess the explanatory reach of class analysis it is necessary to elaborate in greater detail the specific mechanisms by which these economic phenomena are thought to generate consequences.

Following this clarification of conceptual foundations, I will briefly discuss four general propositions which Pakulski and Waters argue define the core commitments of class analysis. As I will try to show, their characterization of most of these commitments amounts to insisting that class analysis requires a generalized belief in class primacy, whereas I will argue that class primacy is not an essential component of class analysis. In the final section I will then examine a range of empirical evidence which indicates, I believe, the enduring importance of class divisions for understanding contemporary capitalist societies.

Class in the Marxist and Weberian traditions[6]

The contrast between Marx and Weber has been one of the grand themes in the history of sociology as a discipline.[7] Most graduate school programs have a sociological theory course within which Marx versus Weber figures as a central motif. However, in terms of class analysis, posing Marx and Weber as polar opposites is a bit misleading because in many ways Weber is speaking in his most Marxian voice when he talks about class.[8] The concept of class within these two streams of thought share a number of important features:

- Both Marxist and Weberian approaches differ from what might be called simple gradational notions of class in which classes are differentiated strictly on the basis of inequalities in the material conditions of life.[9] This conceptualization of class underwrites the common inventory of classes found in popular discourse and the mass media: upper class, upper middle class, middle class, lower middle class, lower class, underclass. Both Marxist and Weberian class analysis define classes relationally, that is, a given class location is defined by virtue of the social relations which link it to other class locations.
- Both traditions identify the concept of class with the relationship between people and economically relevant assets or resources. Marxists call this "relation to the means of production"; Weberians refer to "Market capacities." But they are both really talking about very similar empirical phenomena.
- Both traditions see the causal relevance of class as operating, at least in part, via the ways in which these relations shape the material interests and lived experiences of actors. Ownership of the means of production and ownership of one's own labor power are explanatory of social action because these property rights shape the strategic alternatives people face in pursuing their material wellbeing. What people have imposes constraints on what they can do to get what they want. To be sure, Marxists tend to put more weight on the objective character of these "material interests" by highlighting the fact that these constraints are imposed on individuals, whereas Weberians tend to focus on the subjective conditions, by emphasizing the relative contingency in what people want. Nevertheless, it is still the case that at their core, both class concepts involve the causal connection between: (a) social relations to resources, and (b) material interests via (c) the way resources shape strategies for acquiring income.

How then do they differ? The pivotal basis for the contrast is captured by the contrast between the favorite buzz-words of each theoretical tradition: life chances for Weberians, and exploitation for Marxists. The reason why production is more central to Marxist than to Weberian class analysis is because of its salience for the problem of exploitation; the reason why Weberians give greater emphasis to the market is because it so directly shapes life chances.

The intuition behind the idea of life chances is straightforward. "In our terminology," Weber writes,

> "classes" are not communities; they merely represent possible, and frequent, bases for communal action. We may speak of a "class" when (1) a number of people have in common a specific causal component of their life chances, in so far as (2) this component is represented exclusively by economic interests in the possession of goods and opportunities for income, and (3) is represented under conditions of the commodity or labor markets. [These points refer to "class situation," which we may express more briefly as the typical chance for a supply of goods, external living conditions, and life experiences, in so far as this chance is determined by the amount and kind of power, or lack of such, to dispose of goods or skills for the sake of income in a given economic order. The term "class" refers to any group of people that is found in the same class situation.] . . . But always this is the generic connotation of the concept of class: that the kind of chance in the market is the decisive moment which presents a common condition for the individual's fate. "Class situation" is, in this sense, ultimately "market situation."[10]

In short, the kind and quantity of resources you own affects your opportunities for income in market exchanges. "Opportunity" is a description of the feasible set individuals face, the trade-offs they encounter in deciding what to do. Owning means of production gives a person different alternatives from owning credentials, and both of these are different from simply owning unskilled labor power. Furthermore, in a market economy, access to market-derived income affects the broader array of life experiences and opportunities for oneself and one's children. The study of the life chances of children based on parents' market capacity is thus an integral part of the Weberian agenda of class analysis.

Within a Weberian perspective, therefore, the salient issue in the linkage of people to different kinds of economic resources is the way this confers on them different kinds of economic opportunities and disadvantages and thereby shapes their material interests. Within a Marxist framework, in contrast, the feature of the relationship of people to economic resources which is at the core of class analysis is "exploitation." Both "exploitation" and "life chances" identify inequalities in material well-being that are generated by inequalities in access to resources of various sorts. Thus both of these concepts point to conflicts of interest over the distribution of the assets themselves. What exploitation adds to this is a claim that conflicts of interest between classes are generated not simply by what people have, but also by what people do with what they have.[11] The concept of exploitation, therefore, points our attention to conflicts within production, not simply conflicts in the market.

Exploitation is a complex, and contentious, concept. At its core is the idea that the economic well-being of the exploiter depends, in part, upon the ability of exploiters to appropriate the labor effort of the exploited. More specifically, exploitation exists when three conditions are met:

(i)   The material welfare of one group of people causally depends on the material deprivations of another.
(ii) The causal relation in (i) involves the asymmetrical exclusion of the exploited from access to certain productive resources. Typically this exclusion is backed by force in the form of property rights, but in special cases it may not be.
(iii) The causal mechanism which translates exclusion (ii) into differential welfare (i) involves the appropriation of the fruits of labor of the exploited by those who control the relevant productive resources.[12]

The second of these conditions, and perhaps a muted version of the first, is present in the Weberian analysis of class and market capacities; the third defines the distinctive issue in Marxist class analysis: the welfare of "advantaged" classes depends not simply on their monopoly of economically salient resources, but also upon the effort of the exploited.

Understood in this way, the key implication of exploitation is that it generates an antagonistic interdependency of material interests between exploiters and exploited. Exploitation does not merely define a set of statuses of social actors, but a pattern of ongoing interactions structured by a set of social relations, relations which mutually bind the exploiter and the exploited together. Exploiters need the exploited, and this dependency of the exploiter on the exploited gives the exploited a certain form of power, since human beings always retain at least some minimal control over their own expenditure of effort. Social control of labor which relies exclusively on repression is costly and, except under special circumstances, often fails to generate optimal levels of diligence and effort on the part of the exploited.[13] As a result, there is generally systematic pressure on exploiters to moderate their domination and in one way or another to try to elicit some degree of consent from the exploited, at least in the sense of gaining some level of minimal cooperation from them. Paradoxically perhaps, exploitation is thus a constraining force on the practices of the exploiter. This constraint constitutes a basis of power for the exploited.

This contrast between the Marxist and Weberian traditions of class analysis is summarized in Figure 2.1. Weberian class analysis revolves around a single causal nexus that works through market exchanges. Marxist class analysis includes the Weberian causal processes, but adds to them a causal structure within production itself, as well as an account of the interactions of production and exchange. For example, as I have argued in detail elsewhere (Wright, 1985, 1997), a central feature of the class location of managers concerns the "loyalty rent" which managers receive by virtue of their position within the authority structure of production. This reflects the way in which location within the organization of production and not simply within market relations affects the "life chances" of managers. Similarly, as Bowles and Gintis and others have argued, the level of the social wage received by workers through the state affects their market capacity in ways which influence the capacity of capitalists to extract labor effort within production.[14] The Marxist concept of class directs our attention both theoretically and empirically towards these interactions.

A Weberian might reply that there is nothing in the Weberian idea of market-based life chances that would prevent the analysis of the extraction of labor effort within

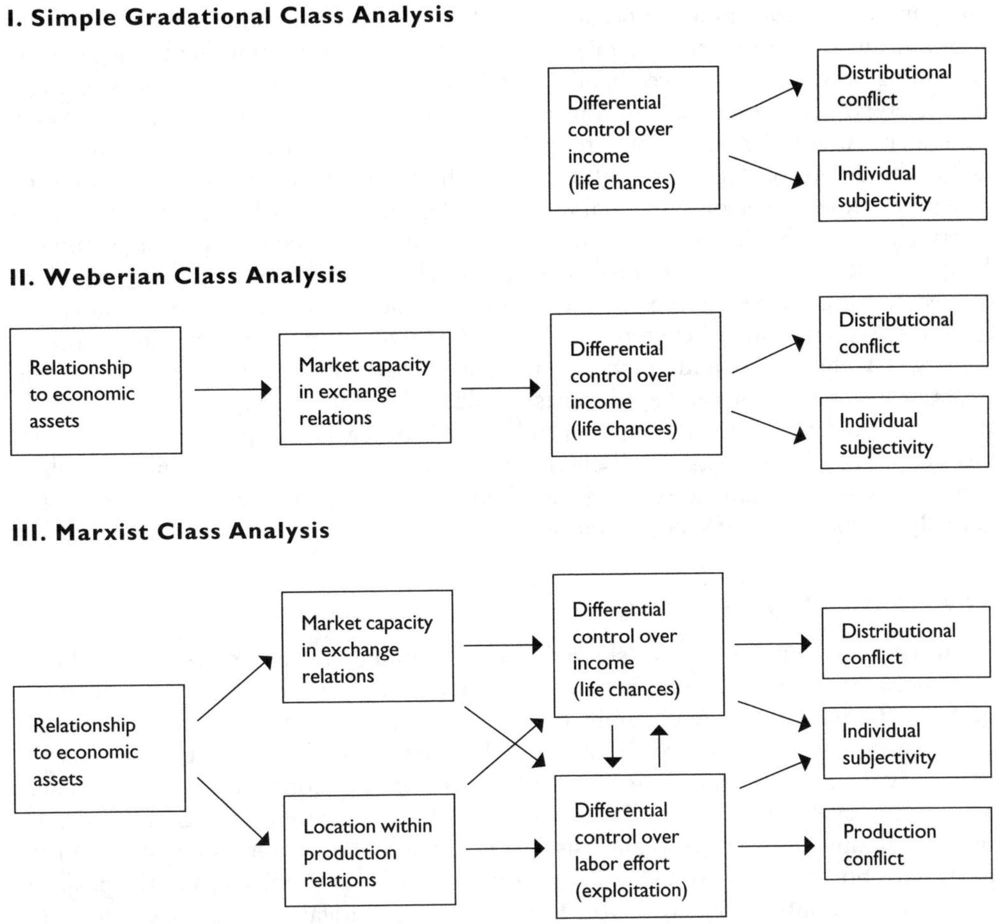
I. Simple Gradational Class Analysis
Differential control over income (life chances)
Distributional conflict
Individual subjectivity
II. Weberian Class Analysis
Relationship to economic assets
Market capacity in exchange relations
Differential control over income (life chances)
Distributional conflict
Individual subjectivity
III. Marxist Class Analysis
Relationship to economic assets
Market capacity in exchange relations
Location within production relations
Differential control over income (life chances)
Differential control over labor effort (exploitation)
Distributional conflict
Individual subjectivity
Production conflict

Figure 2.1 Three models of class analysis.

production. A good and subtle Weberian class analyst could certainly link the analysis of market capacities within exchange relations to power relations within the labor process, and thus explore the causal structures at the center of Marxist class analysis. In systematically joining production and exchange in this way, however, the Weberian concept would in effect become Marxianized. Frank Parkin, in a famous gibe, said, "Inside every neo-Marxist there seems to be a Weberian struggling to get out."[15] One could just as easily say that inside every left-wing Weberian there is a Marxist struggling to stay hidden.

This elaboration of the concept of exploitation has underwritten my efforts at reconstructing the Marxist concept of class in ways which would enhance its explanatory capacity for complex, developed societies. Specifically, it has provided the basis for defining concrete class "locations" in terms of a multidimensional view of how people are linked to the mechanisms of exploitation in capitalist economies. This facilitates studying the more complex ways in which people's lives are concretely embedded in class relations.[16]

For both Marxists and Weberians, classes would cease to be relevant for social analysis if either of two conditions occurred: (1) Everyone owned and controlled the same economically relevant assets—that is, everyone had the same relationship to the income-generating productive resources (land, capital, skills, information, labor power, etc.) of the society; (2) People owned and controlled different assets, but the ownership of assets no longer mattered for material interests. On the basis of these two conditions one could define the degree of "classness" of a society: the more egalitarian the distribution of assets and the less a person's material well-being depends upon their relationship to those assets, the lower the classness of a society.[17] The first of these conditions can potentially be approached through various processes that equalize capital ownership and education; the second through such things as unconditional basic income grants that significantly loosen the relationship between income and individual participation in economic activity.[18] Weberians would emphasize the ways in which these changes equalize the material life chances of people; Marxists would add to this an emphasis on how these changes would transform the interdependencies between laboring effort and material welfare. For both Marxists and Weberians, as long as these inequalities in ownership/control of assets exist and are consequential for the lives of people, class would remain a causally salient feature of social organization.

The death of class thesis

From the vantage point of Pakulski and Waters' critique of class analysis, these differences between the Marxist and Weberian currents of class analysis seem relatively unimportant. Their claim is not simply that the classical Marxian preoccupation with capitalist exploitation has become irrelevant, but that it is no longer the case that classes defined with respect to the ownership and control of any economically relevant assets matter very much. They build this argument around four core propositions about the theoretical foundations of class analysis which they term the proposition of economism, the proposition of group formation, the proposition of causal linkage, and the proposition of transformative capacity. Before looking at the empirical evidence, it will be useful to examine briefly the four propositions which Pakulski and Waters claim define the basic theoretical structure of class analysis. To facilitate the discussion I will number the sentences in their statement of each proposition.

The proposition of economism

(1)   Class is fundamentally an economic phenomenon.
(2)   It refers principally to differences in the ownership of property, especially productive property with an accumulation potential, and to differential market capacity, especially labor-market capacity.
(3)   Moreover, such economic phenomena as property or markets are held to be the fundamental structuring or organizing principles in societal organization.

Statements 1 and 2 in this proposition are on target. While some class analysts argue that class is as much a cultural and political concept as it is an economic concept, the core of both the Marxist and Weberian traditions of class analysis revolves around the economic content of the concept. The problem in this proposition enters with the third statement, specifically with the use of the definite article "the" before "fundamental." While class analysts may in general subscribe to the view that class is a fundamental structuring principle, no Weberian would consider class to be the fundamental principle, and many contemporary Marxists would also shy away from such a categorical claim, especially when it is specified with respect to an *explanandum* as vague and encompassing as "societal organization." To be sure, there is a strand of classical Marxism revolving around the "base/superstructure" metaphor in which the "base" is identified with class structure, the "superstructure" is everything else in society, and the base is seen as explaining the superstructure. Many, perhaps most, Marxists engaged in class analysis today reject such explanatory pretensions.[19] In any case, for class analysis to constitute a research program worth pursuing it is sufficient that it identify important causal mechanisms; it is not necessary that class be the most important or fundamental determinant of social phenomena.[20]

The proposition of group formation

(1)   Classes are more than statistical aggregates or taxonomic categories.
(2)   They are real features of social structure reflected in observable patterns of inequality, association, and distance.
(3)   So deep and fundamental are these cleavages that they form the principal and enduring bases for conflict and contestation.

Again, the first two of these statements correctly identify commitments of most class analysts, at least those of a nonpostmodernist bent. Most Marxists and Weberians are generally "scientific realists," seeing their concepts as attempts at understanding causal mechanisms that exist in the world, and thus both believe that if class relations matter they should generate observable effects. The third statement, however, would be rejected by virtually all Weberian class analysts from Weber to the present. Many contemporary Marxist class analysts would also demur from the statement in this unqualified and categorical form. While Marxists generally believe that class relations constitute an enduring basis for conflict, much of the thrust of contemporary Marxism has been towards understanding the conditions under which class compromises are formed and class conflict is displaced from center stage. While most Marxists would argue that even when class formation and class struggle have been contained there will continue to be effects of class relations on other forms of conflict, this does not imply the stronger claim that class cleavages constitute the principal basis for all conflict. To claim enduring and even pervasive effects is not to claim class primacy.

The proposition of causal linkage

(1)   Class membership is also causally connected to consciousness, identity, and action outside the arena of economic production.
(2)   It affects political preferences, lifestyle choices, child-rearing practices, opportunities for physical and mental health, access to educational opportunity, patterns of marriage, occupational inheritance, income, and so on.

This proposition is sound since Pakulski and Waters do not assert here that class must be the primary causal determinant of each of the *explananda* listed under (2). The proposition does not even insist that class be a direct cause of these *explananda* since the expression "causally connected to" encompasses indirect and mediated effects of class on phenomena outside of economic production. All the proposition therefore asserts is that access to economically relevant assets has a systematic effect (direct or indirect) on these kinds of phenomena. I would only add one caveat. As specified in this proposition, the list of phenomena on which class is claimed to have effects is almost completely open-ended. Most class analysts would qualify the "proposition of causal linkage" by saying that class matters more for some phenomena than others, and that for certain *explananda*, class might have negligible effects. Furthermore, the extent to which class matters for various *explananda* may itself be contingent upon various other variables— that is, there may be strong interactive effects between the micro-level effects of class location and various macro-level processes. Class analysis would not disappear as a legit-imate research program if for some of these *explananda* it turns out that class determi-nants were weak.

The proposition of transformative capacity

(1)   Classes are potential collective actors in economic and political fields.
(2)   Insofar as they consciously struggle against other classes, classes can transform the general set of social arrangements of which they are a part.
(3)   Class therefore offers the dynamic thrust that energizes society.
(4)   Classes are the principal collective actors that can make history.

Statement (1) accurately characterizes most forms of class analysis. Few class analysts deny that class is the basis for potential collective action. The second statement, because of the conditionality of the expression "insofar," would also be acceptable to most strands of class analysis so long as the word "transform" is taken to include something like "modifications in the rules of the game" and not simply "revolutionary ruptures in the game itself." The third and fourth statements are much more contentious because of the assertion of class primacy. While classical Marxism certainly affirmed the thesis that "class struggle was the motor of history," most contemporary Marxists would qualify such claims by stressing the importance of a variety of enabling conditions which make it possible for collectively organized class forces to have such system-shaping effects. Few Marxists believe that the collective capacity for radical transformations is automatically produced by the "contradictions of capitalism."[21]

Overall, then, Pakulski and Waters do accurately identify some central strands in class analysis in these propositions, but they consistently slide from a reasonable description of propositions that affirm the relevance of class to much stronger and contentious claims about class primacy. Indeed, they seem to believe that without the claim of class primacy, there would be no point at all to class analysis. In commenting on what they describe as weaker forms of class analysis, they state: "in order to distinguish itself from sociological analysis in general, this enterprise must necessarily privilege economically defined class over other potential sources of inequalities and division, as well as accept the principle of causal linkage. There would otherwise be little point in describing the activity as class analysis—a class analysis that can find no evidence of class is clearly misnamed" (p. 671). The final clause in this statement is clearly correct: if there was "no evidence of class," then there would be no point to class analysis. But the previous sentence is not: class analysis need not universally privilege class over all other social divisions in order to justify its research program.[22] Class analysis is premised on the view that class constitutes a salient causal structure with important ramifications. As I will show in the next section of this chapter, there is abundant evidence to support this claim. It is an additional, and much more contingent, claim that class processes constitute the most important cause of particular social phenomena, and a far more contentious (and implausible) claim that they constitute the most important cause of everything.

Evidence

As an explanatory concept, class is relevant both to macro-level analyses of social systems and micro-level analyses of individual lives. In both contexts, class analysis asserts that the way people are linked to economically relevant assets is consequential in various ways. In what follows we will explore a range of evidence that such consequences are an enduring feature of contemporary society.

Have class boundaries disappeared?

One way of exploring this question is to investigate what I have called the "permeability" of class boundaries.[23] Permeability refers to the extent to which the lives of individuals move across different kinds of social boundaries. One can study permeability of any kind of social boundary—race, gender, class, occupation, nationality—and one can study such boundary-crossing permeability with respect to a wide range of life events—mobility, friendship formation, marriage, membership in voluntary associations, etc. In my own research I have focused on three kinds of events—intergenerational class mobility, cross-class friendship formation, and cross-class household composition—and studied the extent to which these events occur across the different kinds of boundaries within a class structure.

The class structure concept I have used in my research sees class relations in capitalist societies as organized along three underlying dimensions—property, authority, and expertise (or skills). For purposes of studying class boundary permeability, I trichotomize each of these dimensions: the property dimension is divided into employers, petty bourgeois (self-employed without employees), and employees; the authority dimension into managers, supervisors, and nonmanagerial employees; and the skill/expertise dimension into professionals, skilled employees, and nonskilled employees.[24] I then define permeability as a boundary-crossing event that links the poles of these trichotomies. Friendships between employers and employees, for example, would count as an instance of permeability across the property boundary, but a friendship between a worker and a petty bourgeois or between a petty bourgeois and an employer would not. The empirical problem, then, is to explore the relative odds of permeability events across these three class boundaries, as well as the odds of events between different specific locations within the class structure. Without going into detail, some of the basic findings of this research are roughly as follows:

(1) The property boundary is generally the least permeable of the three boundaries for all three kinds of events (mobility, friendships, and household composition), followed by the skill/expertise boundary and then the authority boundary. With

some minor exceptions, this rank-ordering of relative permeability holds for the four countries I have studied—United States, Canada, Sweden, and Norway.

(2) The odds of mobility between a working class location (i.e., nonmanagerial, nonskilled, employee) and an employer location is about 25 percent of what it would be if the link between these two locations was random; the odds of a close personal friendship between these two locations is about 20 percent of what it would be if these events were random; and the odds of a two-earner household containing an employer married to a worker are about 10 percent of the random association.

(3) The odds of events linking workers and the petty bourgeoisie, on the other hand, are generally only modestly different from random for all three kinds of events. The class boundary between workers and petty bourgeois is therefore three to six times more permeable than the boundary between workers and employers.

None of these results demonstrate that class boundaries are the least permeable of all social boundaries in capitalist societies. Undoubtedly in the United States racial boundaries are less permeable to household composition than are class boundaries, and in some countries, religious affiliation may be a much less permeable boundary than class for certain kinds of events. But these results unequivocally indicate that class boundaries have not disappeared: the coefficients for events across the property and the expertise/skill boundaries are significantly negative (at p < .001 level in nearly all cases) in all countries.

Have inequalities in the distribution of capital declined to the point in recent years that it no longer matters much for people's lives?

Pakulski and Waters are correct that, compared to fifty years ago, there is a more egalitarian distribution of wealth in most capitalist countries. This does not, however, imply that the distribution has equalized to the point that the basic nexus between class and capital asset-holding has been broken. In 1983, the richest half of 1 percent of US households owned 46.5 percent of all corporate stock, 44 percent of bonds, and 40 percent of net business assets. The next .5 percent richest owned 13.5 percent of stock, 7.5 percent of bonds, and 11.5 percent of net business assets. The richest 1 percent of US households therefore own fifty to sixty times their per capita share of these crucial capitalist assets.[25] Of course, unequal ownership of these assets may not matter much for people's lives. The claim of class analysis is not simply that there is an unequal distribution of ownership and control of economic assets, but that this inequality in assets is consequential for people. In 1990 the average family income of the top 1 percent of income earners in the United States was just under $549,000. On average over $278,000 of this—more than 50 percent of the total—came directly from capital assets (not including an additional $61,000 from self-employment earnings). In contrast, the average family income of the bottom 90 percent of the population in the United States was only about $29,000 in 1990, of which, on average, less than 10 percent (about $2,400) came from capital assets.[26] The inegalitarian distribution of capital assets is clearly consequential.

The direct impact on household income is only one of the salient consequences of unequal distributions of capital assets. Equally important is the way the distribution of ownership rights in capitalist production affects the stability and distribution of jobs.

One would be hard pressed to convince a group of newly unemployed workers from a factory that has closed because the owner moved production abroad that their lack of ownership of capitalist assets has no significant consequences for their lives. If the workers themselves owned the firm as a cooperative, or if it were owned by the local community, then different choices would be made.[27] The same international pressures would have different consequences on the lives of workers if the distribution of capital assets—that is, in the class relations within which they lived—were different.

An objection could be raised that I have grossly exaggerated the levels of inequality in distributions of assets, since pension funds of various sorts are among the biggest holders of stock and other financial assets. Shouldn't those workers covered by pension funds be considered quasi-capitalists by virtue of their connection to these assets? Doesn't this effectively erode the class distinction between workers and employers?

The experience of conflict in Sweden in the 1970s over the proposal to create a "wage-earners fund" sheds light on the nature of the class relations linked to pension funds. In Sweden, like in many other countries, large pension funds exist for union members. Strict rules govern the nature of these pension fund investments, ostensibly to avoid risky investments and insure the continuing stream of income for future pensioners. In the 1970s a proposal in Sweden known as the Meidner Plan was made, initially by the left of the labor movement and the Social Democratic Party, which would have enabled pension funds to be used by unions to gradually gain ownership control of Swedish corporations. Corporations would have been forced by law to give stock to these funds as part of the benefits package for workers, and over time this would have resulted in a shift of real ownership from the Swedish capitalist class to the unions. All of this would have been done at real market prices, so there was no question of confiscation. The Swedish bourgeoisie massively and vigorously opposed this proposal. The original form of the Meidner Plan represented a fundamental shift from pension funds being a source of forced savings available for investment, to those funds being used to transform the governance structure of Swedish industry and thus, ultimately, the class structure.[28] The turmoil over this proposal led in part to the defeat of the Social Democratic Party, and in the end, the proposal was watered down to the point where it no longer posed any kind of threat. What this episode reflects is the fact that the various forms of indirect "ownership" of assets represented by such things as pension funds do not in fact constitute a significant erosion of the class relations of ownership and control of productive assets.

Is the extraction of labor effort no longer a problem in capitalist firms?

At the core of Marxist conceptions of class is the problem of extracting labor effort from producers who do not own the means of production. This problem has also emerged as a central theme in transactions cost economics under the rubric of principal/agent problems within capitalist firms. The economics version of the argument states that under conditions of information asymmetries (employees have private information about their work effort which is costly for employers to acquire) and a divergence of interests between principals and agents (employers want workers to work harder than the workers voluntarily want to work), there will be a problem of enforcement of the labor contract.

A range of consequences are generated by this principal/agent problem as employers adopt strategies which try to align the behavior of agents to the interests of principals.

One of the results is an "efficiency wage" in which workers are paid more than their reservation wage in order to raise the cost of job loss, thus making them more hesitant to shirk.[29] Another consequence will be the erection of an apparatus of monitoring and enforcement within firms. A third consequence is that employers make technological choices partially in terms of the effects of alternative technologies on monitoring and social control. This does not imply, of course, that the class dimensions of technical choice is always the most important, or even that it is always significant, but simply that employers are not indifferent to the effect of alternative technologies on their capacity to monitor and extract labor effort.[30] Considerable empirical evidence exists for each of these effects. Most economists do not use the language of class analysis in discussions of this principal/agent problem because they take the distribution of property rights within the capitalist firm for granted, yet this distribution of property rights is a central dimension of class structure. Making the class character of the problem explicit has the advantage of focusing attention on the ways in which variations in the class relations of production might affect the principal/agent problem. Consider two examples: worker-owned firms, and capitalist firms within which it is difficult to fire workers because they have enforceable employment rights.

In the case of cooperatives, Bowles and Gintis have argued that if workers were the residual claimants on the income generated within production (i.e., if they were the owners of the assets), the problem of monitoring and enforcement of work effort would be dramatically transformed.[31] The problem of extracting labor effort would not disappear because there would still be free rider problems among the worker-owners, but since in workers cooperatives there are stronger incentives for mutual-monitoring than in conventional capitalist firms, and since the motivations of actors are likely to strengthen anti-free rider norms, the costs of monitoring should go down and thus productivity would increase. Employees in an employee-owned firm are embedded in a different set of class relations than employees in a conventional capitalist firm, and this variation affects the labor extraction process.[32]

Capitalist firms within which workers have effective rights to their jobs are also a case of a transformation of class relations within production. In this case workers are not residual claimants to the income of the firm (i.e., they do not "own" the capital assets), but the employers have lost certain aspects of their property rights—they no longer have the full right to decide who will use the means of production which they "own." Such a situation poses specific problems for the employer. On the one hand, by making it harder to fire workers, strong job rights reduce the efficiency of monitoring and make shirking easier. But this constraint on firing also makes the time horizons of workers with respect to their place of employment longer and may make them identify more deeply with the welfare of the firm. Which of these two forces is stronger depends upon the details of the institutional arrangements that regulate the interactions of employers and workers. The research on the implications for cooperation and productivity of strong job rights in Japanese and German capitalism can be considered instances of class analyses of principal/agent problems.[33]

It is, of course, possible to discuss the effects of workers cooperatives or job rights on principal/agent problems without ever mentioning the word "class." Nevertheless, the theoretical substance of the analysis still falls within class analysis if the causally salient feature of these variations in firm organization centers on how workers are linked to economic assets.

Does class location no longer systematically affect individual subjectivity?

Pakulski and Waters are on their strongest ground when they argue that class is not a powerful source of identity, consciousness, and action. My own research on class structure, class biography, and class consciousness in the 1980s indicates that, in most of the countries I studied, class-related variables were only modest predictors of values on the various attitude scales I adopted. However, "modest" is not the same as "irrelevant." In Sweden, individual class location by itself explained about 16 percent of the variance in a class consciousness scale,[34] while in the United States the figure was only 9 percent and in Japan only 5 percent. When a range of other class-linked variables were added—including such things as class origins, self-employment experiences, unemployment experiences, and the class character of social networks—this increased to about 25 percent in Sweden, 16 percent in the United States, and 8 percent in Japan. In all three countries these class effects were statistically significant, but not extraordinarily powerful.

What should we make of these results? First of all, at least in the United States and Sweden, the explained variances in these equations are not particularly low by the standards of regressions predicting attitudes. In general, it is rare for equations predicting attitudes to have high explained variances unless the equations include as independent variables other attitudes (e.g., predicting views on specific policy issues by self-identification on a liberalism/conservatism scale). Part of the reason for this is undoubtedly the pervasive problem in adequately measuring attitudes; a significant part of the total variance in measured attitudes may simply be random with respect to any social determinants. And part of the reason for the low explained variance in attitude regressions is that the causes of individual attitudes are often irreducibly idiographic—it is hard to imagine a multivariate regression rooted in social structural variables that would "predict" that Engels, a wealthy capitalist, would be a supporter of revolutionary socialism. In any case, class often performs as well or better than other social structural variable in predicting a variety of aspects of attitudes.

The second thing to note in these results is the very large cross-national variation in the explanatory power of class variables for predicting individual attitudes. What is more, on a more fine-grained inspection, there are interesting variations in the specific ways class location and attitudes are linked in the three countries. Without going into any real detail here, if we define "ideological coalitions" as sets of class locations that are more like each other ideologically (as measured by these attitude questions) than they are like other locations, then we find three quite distinct patterns in these three countries. In Sweden, the class structure is quite polarized ideologically between workers and employers, and there is a fairly large "middle class coalition" that is ideologically quite distinct from the bourgeois coalition and from the working class coalition. In the United States, the class structure is less ideologically polarized and the bourgeois ideological coalition extends fairly deeply into the structurally defined "middle class": managers and professionals are firmly part of this coalition. In Japan there is a third configuration: ideological polarization is much more muted than in either of the other two countries and the ideological divisions that do occur fall mainly along the expertise dimension rather than the authority dimension of the class structure.

These patterns of variation demonstrate that the linkage between class location and individual subjectivity is heavily shaped by the macro-social context within which it occurs. Class locations do not simply produce forms of subjectivity; they shape subjectivity in interaction with a range of other processes—institutional arrangements within firms; political strategies of parties and unions; historical legacies of past struggles, and so on. These complexities certainly do undercut any simple minded class analysis that asserts something like "class determines consciousness." But they do not undermine the broader project of investigating the ways in which class, in interaction with other social processes, has consequences.

Conclusion

If the evidence we have discussed above is correct, then it certainly seems premature to declare the death of class. Class may not be the most powerful or fundamental cause of "societal organization," and class struggle may not be the most powerful transformative force in the world today. Class primacy, as a generalized explanatory principle across all social explananda, is implausible. Nevertheless, class remains a significant and sometimes powerful determinant of many aspects of social life. Class boundaries, especially the property boundary, continue to constitute real barriers in people's lives; inequalities in the distribution of capital assets continue to have real consequences for material interests; capitalist firms continue to face the problem of extracting labor effort from nonowning employees; and class location continues to have a real, if variable, impact on individual subjectivities.

In denying the significance of these kinds of empirical observations, Pakulski and Waters seem to be mistaking the increasing complexity of class relations in contemporary capitalist societies with the dissolution of class altogether. While it was never true that a simple, polarized, two-class model of capitalism was sufficient to understand the effects of class on consciousness and action in concrete capitalist societies, there were times and places when perhaps this was a reasonable first approximation. For most purposes this is no longer the case, and a variety of forms of complexity needed to be added to class analysis:[35]

- "Middle class" locations need to be given a positive conceptual status. In my work I have argued that middle class positions within the class structure should be viewed as what I call "contradictory locations within class relations." By this I mean the following: Class relations are composites that weave together distinct kinds of social relations. In particular, capitalist class relations involve a relation of *exploitation* combined with a relation of *domination*. In these terms capitalists occupy both the dominating and exploiting location within these two relations and workers the dominated and exploited locations. Managers, on the other hand, occupy a contradictory location: they are both dominating and dominated, and—often—both exploiting and exploited. This gives their class location a specific kind of complexity.
- The location of individuals within class structures needs to be defined not simply in terms of their own jobs (direct class locations) but also in terms of the ways they are linked to mechanisms of exploitation through family structure (mediated class locations).
- Class locations have a specific temporal dimension to them by virtue of the ways in which careers are organized. This temporal dimension means that to the extent that career trajectories have a probabilistic character to them, some class locations may have an objectively indeterminate character.

- The diffusion of genuine ownership of capitalist assets among employees, if still relatively limited, creates additional complexity in class structures since some people in managerial class locations, and even some in working class locations, can simultaneously occupy locations in the capitalist class as passive stock-owners. This constitutes a special form of "contradictory location within class relations."

Class analysis needs to incorporate these, and other, complexities. The reconstruction of class analysis in these ways, however, does not imply the dissolution of the causal processes which class theory identifies. The relationship of people to the pivotal economic assets of the capitalist economy continues to shape life chances and exploitation, and these in turn have wide ramifications for other social phenomena. These complexities may lead to a conceptual framework which is less tidy, and which perhaps evokes less fiery passions. But in the end, the contribution of class analysis to emancipatory projects of social change depends as much on its explanatory capacity to grapple with the complexity of contemporary capitalist society as on its ideological capacity to mobilize political action.

Questions for discussion

1. Why is the concept of class contested in the social sciences?
2. Why does the author endorse the argument of Pakulski and Waters that "class is fundamentally an economic phenomenon?" What do you think about this claim? What are the other social phenomena that influence the construction of the concept of class?
3. What are the commonalities and differences of the concept of class between Marx and Weber? What are the popular buzz-words of each tradition? Why are they central to their class analysis? How does the Weberian concept of class become Marxianized?
4. What are the four general propositions that were used by Pakulski and Waters to define the core commitments of class analysis? What is the author's take on these propositions?
5. How does class permeability work in terms of the three boundaries (property, authority, and expertise) for all three kinds of life events (mobility, friendship, and household composition)? Which of the class boundaries are the most and the least permeable and why?
6. Why do Pakulski and Waters argue that "class is dead?" How would it be to live in a classless society? What kinds of evidence does the author display to support the idea that class boundaries have not disappeared? If class boundaries had disappeared, what would it mean for social justice and social mobility?
7. According to the author, what are the salient consequences of unequal distribution of capital assets? Why is the distribution of capital assets unequal? Who benefits from this? What would be the possible ways of transforming this unequal process? What would the role of schools be in this transformation?
8. What is meant by contradictory location within class structure? Who is located there and why?

Acknowledgment

This chapter: Copyright © 1996 "Theory and Society, the Continuing Relevance of Class Analysis" by Erik Olin Wright. Reproduced by permission of Springer.

Notes

1. Sections of this paper originally appeared in Wright (1996) and Wright (2002).
2. See Pakulski and Waters (1996) and Kingston (2000).
3. Pakulski and Waters (1996, p. 667).
4. As often happens in these kinds of polemics, there is a natural tendency for the rhetoric to become more extreme and polarized than perhaps even the authors would actually believe. Statements of the form "social class is in the process of dissolving" tend to drift into statements like "social class has dissolved." This kind of slippage occurs frequently in the Pakulski and Waters paper. For example, they argue that the downward shift in the distribution of property "blurs traditional class divisions"—which suggests that the division is still present, but less sharply drawn—while immediately after they state that the "downward distribution of property . . . makes impossible the establishment of any boundary between classes on the basis of property"—which suggests not simply that the class division is blurred, but that it has disappeared entirely. The temptation in defending class analysis against their arguments is to focus on these extreme statements. It is, after all, much easier to find evidence which simply demonstrates that class divisions exist and have consequences, than to show that these divisions remain causally powerful. In my judgment, the real guts of their argument does not ride on these most extreme formulations, but on the weaker claim that class is no longer a powerful or salient explanatory category. It is on the weaker claim that I will therefore focus in this discussion.
5. Pakulski and Waters (1996, p. 670).
6. This section draws on chapter 1 of Wright (1997).
7. For discussions of the contrast between Marxist and Weberian class analysis, see, for example, Parkin (1979); Burris (1988); Giddens (1973); Wright (1979, Chapter 1).
8. For a more extended discussion of the convergences between Marx's and Weber's class analysis, see Wright (2002).
9. The contrast between "gradational" and "relational" concepts of class was first introduced into sociology by Ossowski (1963). For a more extended discussion of gradational concepts of class, see Wright (1997).
10. Weber (1924 [1958], pp. 181–82).
11. The conceptual distinction between life chances and exploitation being argued for here runs against the arguments of John Roemer who insists that exploitation is strictly a way of talking about the injustice of the effects of what people have (assets) on what people get (income). In this sense, he collapses the problem of exploitation into the problem of life chances and thus dissolves the distinction between Marxist and Weberian class analysis. The notion of the extraction of labor effort disappears from his analysis of exploitation. See Roemer (1986).
12. The expression "appropriation of the fruits of labor" refers to the appropriation of that which labor produces. It does *not* imply the value of those products are exclusively determined by labor effort, as claimed in the labor theory of value. All that is being claimed here is that a surplus is appropriated—a surplus beyond what is needed to reproduce all of the inputs of production—and that this surplus is produced through labor effort, but not that the appropriate metric for the surplus is labor time. For a discussion of this way of understanding the appropriation of the fruits of labor, see Cohen (1988, pp. 209–38).
13. For an extended discussion of the dilemmas faced by exploiters in effectively extracting labor effort, see Bowles and Gintis (1990) and Wright (1994, Chapter 4).
14. See Bowles and Gintis (1990).
15. Parkin (1979).
16. Pakulski and Waters mischaracterize the approach to class analysis which I advocate when they write: ". . . whereas twenty years ago students had to decide whether there were two or

three classes, they now have to decide whether there are seven or twelve" (1996, p. 667). My framework of class analysis postulates a distinction between the locations of individuals within class structures and class formations. There is an indeterminate number of distinguishable "locations." For example, depending upon the explanatory problem at hand, it might be necessary to produce a very fine-grained map in which one distinguishes between direct locations (locations determined by individuals' jobs) and mediated locations (locations within class relations determined by membership in households). For other purposes, a distinction between the class of wage-earners and the class of capitalists might be sufficient. The important point is that the class structure is defined by a set of causal processes, and class locations identify how individual lives are linked to those processes. Pakulski and Waters are correct when they conclude somewhat sarcastically that "One would look rather silly mounting a barricade armed with Wright's twelve class scheme," but this misrepresents the analytical status of the scheme itself. One "mounts the barricade" armed with a critique of capitalist exploitation and its consequences; the heterogeneity of material interests within the class formation mobilized around that critique reflects the complexity of class locations in contemporary capitalism. It would be "rather silly" to imagine that this complexity did not exist.

17. The classical normative ideal for social change within the Marxist tradition is captured by the image of a "classless" society. This utopian vision was theoretically grounded in the Marxist theory of historical trajectory—historical materialism—which postulated classlessness as an immanent alternative to capitalism generated by the contradictions within capitalism itself. While classlessness may be useful as a regulative ideal, it should probably be replaced with "less classness" as the pragmatic goal of radical egalitarians. For a discussion of the shift from classlessness to less classness, see Wright (1994, pp. 245–47).

18. For a discussion of how universal basic income is a move towards less classness, see Van Parijs and Van der Veen (1986).

19. As G. A. Cohen has convincingly argued, even in classical Marxism the idea of the "superstructure" was not so all-encompassing as to include everything other than the base. Instead, historical materialism generally takes the form of what Cohen calls "restricted historical materialism" (as opposed to "inclusive historical materialism"), in which the superstructure consists only of those noneconomic social phenomena which have reproductive effects on the base (i.e., effects which tend to stabilize and preserve the economic structure of society). According to Cohen, the thesis of restricted historical materialism is that superstructural phenomena defined in this way are functionally explained by the base. See Cohen (1988, Chapter 9).

20. As I have argued in detail elsewhere, it is extremely difficult to establish claims that some cause is the most important or most fundamental unless there is a very clear specification of the explanandum and the range of variation for which the claim applies. See Wright, Levine, and Sober (1992, Chapter 7).

21. For an extended discussion of the conditionality and contingency of the development of the capacity for transformative class struggles, see Wright, Levine, and Sober (1992, Part I).

22. In the context of their argument, I take the word "privilege" to imply "causally more important." There is a much weaker sense in which class analysis inherently does "privilege" class, namely that it focuses on class and its effects. In this sense an endocrinologist "privileges" hormones over other causal processes, but this hardly implies that endocrinology implies that hormones are universally more important than other causes. If Pakulski and Waters simply mean that class analysis focuses on class, then there is nothing contentious about their claims.

23. The research discussed here is reported in detail in Wright (1997).

24. Details of the strategy of analysis and operationalizations can be found in Wright (1985, Chapter 5 and Appendix II).

25. These data are from Mishel and Frankel (1991, p. 154).

26. Mishel and Frankel (1991, p. 34).

27. In a neoclassical model of the capitalist economy with perfect information and complete markets (including complete futures markets), property rights would make no difference. In such a world, if it were profit-maximizing for the capitalist to move a factory abroad then, even if the workers themselves owned the factory, it would be profit-maximizing for them to do the same thing. They would simply choose to unemploy themselves, move the factory abroad, and

hire workers there. In such a world workers would not be credit-constrained to obtain loans to buy the firms in which they worked, since with perfect information (including perfect information about the behavior of the workers) banks would not hesitate to make loans to workers. But we do not live in such a world, and it is precisely the pervasive information asymmetries and the absence of perfect futures markets that transforms the atomistic domination-free interactions of the Walrasian market into the power-laden, exploitative class relations of real capitalist societies. Also, it must be added, that in calculating the "costs" and "benefits" of alternative investment possibilities, worker-owners would be likely to include a range of issues around how they wish to live their lives which could not enter the calculation of capitalist-owners.

28. For a discussion of a model of transformation of pension funds into instruments of social control over capital, see Blackburn (2005).
29. For evidence on the costs of job loss, see Bowles and Schor (1987).
30. For an extended discussion of this model of extracting labor effort, see Bowles and Gintis (1990). For evidence on the role of monitoring and social control in technical choice, see Noble (1978) and Bowles (1988).
31. For an extended discussion of the effects on monitoring and efficiency of cooperative forms of ownership, see Bowles and Gintis (1998).
32. A variety of studies support the claim that productivity is higher in worker-owned firms than in comparable capitalist firms. For a review of the evidence see Levine and Tyson (1990).
33. David Gordon presents evidence that there is a strong inverse relation between the degree of cooperation in the labor management relations of a country and the weight of its administrative and managerial employment: the correlation between an index of cooperation and the percentage of administrative and managerial employment was –.72 for 12 OECD countries. Cooperative labor management relations are closely linked to strong job rights and other arrangements which increase the effective rights of workers within production. See Gordon (1996).
34. The class consciousness scale combined a number of simple strength of agreement/disagreement items concerning people's attitudes towards class conflict, corporations, employee participation in decision making, strikes, and related matters. For details see Wright (1997, Chapter 14).
35. For an extended discussion of these complexities, see Wright (1997).

References

Blackburn, R. (2005). The global pension crisis: From grey capitalism to responsible accumulation. *Politics & Society, 34*(2), 135–86.

Bowles, S. (1988). Social institutions and technical choice. In *Technological and social factors in long term economic fluctuations*, edited by M. DeMatteo, A. Vercelli, and R. Goodwin. Berlin: Springer Verlag.

Bowles, S., & Gintis, H. (1990). Contested exchange: New microfoundations for the political economy of capitalism. *Politics & Society, 18*(2), 165–222.

—— (1998). Recasting egalitarianism: New rules for communities, states and markets. In *Volume III of the Real Utopias Project*, edited by Erik Olin Wright. London: Verso.

Bowles, S., & Schor, J. (1987). The cost of job loss and the incidence of strikes. *Review of Economics and Statistics, LXIX*, 4, 584–92.

Burris, V. (1988). The neo-Marxist synthesis of Marx and Weber on class. In *The Marx-Weber debate. Key issues in sociological theory volume 2*, edited by Norbert Wiley. Newbury Park: Sage Publishers, 43–64.

Cohen, G. A. (1988). The labour theory of value and the concept of exploitation. In *History, labour and freedom*, edited by G. A. Cohen. Oxford: Clarendon Paperbacks, 209–38.

Giddens, A. (1973). *The class structure of the advanced societies*. New York: Harper and Row.

Gordon, D. (1996). *Fat and mean: Corporate bloat, the wage squeeze and the stagnation of our conflictual economy*. New York: Martin Kessler Books at the Free Press.

Kingston, P. (2000). *The classless society*. Stanford: Stanford University Press.

Levine, D., & Tyson, Lara d'Andrea (1990). Participation, productivity and the firm's environment. In *Paying for productivity*, edited by Alan Binder. Washington, DC: Brookings Institution, 183–244.

Mishel, L., & Frankel, D. (1991). *The state of working America*. New York: M. E. Shape.

Noble, D. (1978). Social choice in machine design. *Politics & Society, 8*, 3–4.

Ossowski, S. (1963). *Class structure in the social consciousness*. London: Routledge and Kegan Paul.

Pakulski, J., & Waters, M. (1996). *The death of class*. London/Thousand Oaks, CA: Sage.

Parkin, F. (1979). *Marxism and class theory: A bourgeois critique*. New York: Columbia University Press.

Roemer, J. E. (1986). Should Marxists be interested in exploitation? In *Analytical Marxism*, edited by John E. Roemer. Cambridge: Cambridge University Press.

van der Veen, R., & van Parijs, P. (1986). A capitalist road to communism. *Theory and Society, 15*(5), 635–55.

Wright, E. O. (1979). *Class structure and income determination*. New York: Academic Press.

—— (1985). *Classes 1985*. London: Verso.

—— (1994). *Interrogating inequality*. London: Verso.

—— (1996). The continuing relevance of class analysis—comments. *Theory and Society, 25*, 693–716.

—— (1997). *Class counts*. Cambridge: Cambridge University Press.

—— (2002). The shadow of exploitation in Weber's class analysis. *American Sociological Review, 67*, 832–53.

Wright, E. O., Levine, A., & Sober, E. (1992). *Causal aysmmetries, reconstructing Marxism*. London: Verso.

Chapter 3

Behind the gates

Social splitting and the "other"

*Setha Low** *

Visiting my sister in San Antonio

On our first visit to my sister's new home in San Antonio, Texas, my husband, Joel, and I are amazed to find two corral gates blocking the entrance to her development. I push an intercom button on the visitors' side. Getting no response, I hit the button repeatedly, finally rousing a disembodied voice that asks who we want to see. I shout Anna and Bob's last name. The entrance gate swings open, and we accelerate through onto a divided drive enclosed by a six-foot wall covered with bougainvillea and heavenly bamboo.

Once inside, large homes loom beside small vacant lots with "for sale" signs. The houses are mostly Southwestern stucco painted Santa Fe colors with terracotta tile roofs and a sprinkling of brick colonials with slate shingles and wood trim. Uniformly attractive, with neat lawns and matching foundation plantings, the street looks like a set from the movie *Pleasantville*. It is not just peaceful, wealthy, and secure, but unreal, like a doll's house or a planned development in Sim City.[1] Everything looks perfect.

Desire for safety, security, community, and "niceness," as well as wanting to live near people like themselves because of a fear of "others" and of crime, is not unique to this family, but expressed by most residents living in gated communities. How they make sense of their new lives behind gates and walls, as well as the social consequences of their residential choices, are the subjects of this chapter. The emergence of a fortress mentality and its phenomenal success is surprising in the United States, where the majority of people live in open and unguarded neighborhoods. Thus, the rapid increase in the numbers of Americans moving to secured residential enclaves invites a more complex account of their motives and values. Like other middle-class Americans, residents of gated communities are looking for a place where they feel comfortable and secure, but this seemingly self-evident explanation reflects different underlying meanings and intentions. And collectively, their individual decisions are transforming the American dream of owning a suburban home in a close-knit community with easy access to nature into a vision that includes gates, walls, and guards.[2]

Based on eight years of ethnographic research in gated communities in New York City, suburban Long Island, New York, and San Antonio, Texas, I present the stories of residents' search for security, safety, and community in a globalizing world. Parents with

* Professor of Environmental Psychology, Anthropology, and Women's Studies, and Director of the Public Space Research Group at the Graduate Center, City University of New York.

children, young married couples, empty-nesters, singles, widows, and retirees recount the details of living in recently constructed gated developments. Their residential histories and daily experiences highlight the significance of this growing middle- and upper-middle-class lifestyle and the conflicting values embodied in its architecture.

One explanation for the gated community's popularity is that it materially and metaphorically incorporates otherwise conflicting, and in some cases polarized, social values that make up the moral terrain of middle-class life. For example, it reflects urban and suburban tensions in the United States regarding social class, race, and ethnicity and at the same time represents the perennial concern with creating community. The gated community's symbolic power rests on its ability to order personal and social experience.

Architectural symbols such as gates and walls also provide a rationale for the moral inconsistencies of everyday life. For instance, many residents want to feel safe in their homes and argue that walls and gates help keep out criminals; but gated communities are not safer than nongated suburban neighborhoods, where crime rates are already low.[3] Instead, the logic of the symbolism satisfies conventional middle-class understandings of the nature of criminal activity—"it makes it harder for them to get in"—and justifies the choice to live in a gated community in terms of its moral and physical consequences— "look at my friends who were randomly robbed living in a nongated development."

Living in a gated community represents a new version of the middle-class American dream precisely because it temporarily suppresses and masks, even denies and fuses, the inherent anxieties and conflicting social values of modern urban and suburban life. It transforms Americans' dilemma of how to protect themselves and their children from danger, crime, and unknown others while still perpetuating open, friendly neighborhoods and comfortable, safe homes. It reinforces the norms of a middle-class lifestyle in a historical period in which everyday events and news media exacerbate fears of violence and terrorism. Thus, residents cite their "need" for gated communities to provide a safe and secure home in the face of a lack of other societal alternatives.

Gated residential communities, however, intensify social segregation, racism, and exclusionary land use practices already in place in most of the United States, and raise a number of values conflicts for residents. For instance, residents acknowledge their misgivings about the possible false security provided by the gates and guards, but at the same time, even that false security satisfies their desire for emotional security associated with childhood and the neighborhoods where they grew up. Living in a gated development contributes to residents' sense of well-being, but comes at the price of maintaining private guards and gates as well as conforming to extensive homeowners association rules and regulations. Individual freedom and ease of access for residents must be limited in order to achieve greater privacy and social control for the community as a whole. These contradictions—which residents are aware of and talk about—provide an opportunity to understand the psychological and social meaning-making processes Americans use to order their lives.

Defining the gated community

A gated community is a residential development surrounded by walls, fences, or earth banks covered with bushes and shrubs, with a secured entrance. In some cases, protection is provided by inaccessible land such as a nature reserve and, in a few cases, by a guarded bridge.[4] The houses, streets, sidewalks, and other amenities are physically enclosed by these barriers, and entrance gates are operated by a guard or opened with a key or electronic identity card. Inside the development there is often a neighborhood watch organization or professional security personnel who patrol on foot or by automobile.

Gated communities restrict access not just to residents' homes, but also to the use of public spaces and services—roads, parks, facilities, and open space—contained within the enclosure. Communities vary in size from a few homes in very wealthy areas to as many as 21,000 homes in Leisure World in Orange County, California—with the number of residents indexed to the level of amenities and services. Many include golf courses, tennis courts, fitness centers, swimming pools, lakes, or unspoiled landscape as part of their appeal; commercial and public facilities are rare. Gated communities are different from other exclusive suburban developments, condominiums, cooperatives, and doorman apartment buildings found throughout the United States. At the level of the built environment, the walls and gates are visible barriers that have social and psychological as well as physical effects. In practical terms, gated communities restrict access to streets and thoroughfares that would otherwise be available for public as well as for private transportation. And in some cases, gated communities limit access to open space and park land donated by the developer to the municipality or town in exchange for building higher-density housing than allowed by local zoning. Such land is designated as in the public domain, but is available only to people who live within the development.

The number of people estimated to be living in gated communities in the United States increased from four million in 1995, to eight million in 1997, and to sixteen million in 1998. By 1997, it was estimated that there were in excess of twenty thousand gated communities with more than three million housing units. A recently released census note by Tom Sanchez and Robert E. Lang, however, provides more accurate demographic statistics based on two new questions on gating and controlled access that were added to the 2001 American Housing Survey.[5] They found that 7,058,427, or 5.9 percent of households reporting that they live in communities, live in those surrounded by walls or fences, and 4,013,665 households, or 3.4 percent, live in communities where the access is controlled by some means such as entry codes, key cards, or security guard approval. The percentages varied by region with the West having the highest number of households living in walled or gated communities (11.1 percent), followed by the South (6.8 percent), the Northeast (3.1 percent), and the Midwest (2.1 percent). The metropolitan areas of Los Angeles, Houston, and Dallas have over one million walled residential units.[6] These figures correspond to the original estimates that approximately 16 million people live in gated communities (16,234,384 based on the census, assuming 2.3 persons per average household) and that most are located in the Sunbelt.[7] Sanchez and Lang also found two distinct kinds of gated communities: those comprised of mostly white, affluent homeowners, and those comprised of minority renters with moderate incomes. They also found that African-Americans were less likely to live in a gated community than Hispanics or whites.

But it is not just a US phenomenon—gated communities are proliferating in Latin America, China, the Philippines, New Zealand, Australia, post-apartheid South Africa, Indonesia, Germany, France, the former communist countries of Eastern Europe, urbanizing nations of the Arab world such as Egypt, Lebanon, and Saudi Arabia, and tourist centers along the Spanish coastline and the Côte d'Azur. In each context, gated communities serve different purposes and express distinct cultural meanings. For example, they house expatriate workers in Saudi Arabia, replicate socialist *datcha* housing in Moscow, provide a secure lifestyle in the face of extreme poverty in Southeast Asia, protect residents from urban violence in South Africa, create exclusive compounds for emerging elites in Bulgaria and China, and offer exclusive second homes or industry-sponsored housing in Western Europe. Gated communities are found at every income level throughout Latin America and take various forms, including upgraded housing complexes, retrofitted older neighborhoods, upscale center-city condominiums, small suburban developments, and large-scale master planned communities. Gating is a global trend drawing upon US models but also evolving from local architecture and sociohistorical circumstances, and is always embedded within specific cultural traditions.[8]

Fear of others

> Against whom was the Great Wall to serve as a protection? Against the people from the north. Now, I come from the southeast of China. No northern people can menace us there. We read of them in the books of the ancients; the cruelties they commit in accordance with their nature make us sigh in our peaceful arbors. The faithful representations of the artist show us the faces of the damned, their gaping mouths, their jaws furnished with great pointed teeth, their half-shut eyes that already seem to be seeking out the victim which their jaws will rend and devour. When our children are unruly, we show them these pictures, and at once they fly weeping into our arms. But nothing more than that do we know about these northerners. We have not seen them, and if we remain in our villages we shall never see them, even if on their wild horses they should ride as hard as they can straight towards us—the land is too vast and would not let them reach us; they would end their course in the empty air.
>
> Franz Kafka, "The Great Wall of China"[9]

My husband and I have reservations about going to a Fourth of July party, but my sister coaxes us with the promise of margaritas and sinful desserts, finally winning us over. Dressed in New York chic, we cross the street to enter an imposing Santa Fe-style house decorated with Mexican furniture and colorful textiles, full of people talking, children racing about, and our hosts serving drinks and dishing out enormous quantities of food. My husband wanders out to the pool, while I stay inside where it is air-conditioned. My choices are watching television with the older men or sitting with our hosts' teenage son and his friends. I sit down with the teenagers, and I am soon involved in a spirited discussion.

"Should we go downtown after dinner to see the fireworks along Riverwalk?" the hosts' son asks. Riverwalk is the commercially successful development that revitalized the center of San Antonio.

"Will there be many Mexicans there?" a tall, gangly boy in a Nike T-shirt and nylon running shorts asks.

"It'll be mobbed with Mexicans; I'm not sure I want to go," a girl with heavy blonde bangs responds.

I am struck by how they used the word *Mexican*. Yesterday I toured the local missions where the complex history of Spanish conquest and resettlement of indigenous peoples is inscribed in the protective walls of the church compounds. Surely, these young people learn about Texas history in school.

I interrupt the flow of conversation and ask them what they mean by "Mexican." A young man in baggy khakis and a baseball hat worn backwards looks at me curiously. "Why, the Mexicans who live downtown, on the south side of the city."

"What makes you think they are Mexican?" I ask, frowning a bit. "Because they speak Spanish?"

"They are dangerous," a young woman in a tennis skirt asserts, "packing knives and guns. Our parents don't allow us to go downtown at night."

They decide to stay and watch the fireworks from the golf course—at least they would not be with their parents—and wander off to find their other friends.

I remain at the table, my mind racing to bring together scattered bits of the history and culture of the region. Texas was originally part of Mexico, colonized by the Spanish. The majority of people who live in Texas identify themselves as descendants of the Spanish and/or Mexicans who settled the area. "Mexicans" can refer to the founding families of San Antonio, hacienda owners and other landholders, who make up a significant part of the political elite and upper class. "Mexicans" also can mean visiting Mexican nationals who maintain summer houses in the region and this neighborhood. There are people who legally immigrated to Texas but retain strong ties to their birthplace and call themselves "Mexicans." Finally, there are the "Mexicans" that the teenagers mentioned, a stereotyped group of what some locals think of as poor, undocumented workers who speak Spanish but who in fact come from all over Latin America.

The teenagers' discussion of "Mexicans" reminds me of T. C. Boyle's novel about a gated community in southern California. In one passage the protagonist is arguing with the president of the homeowners association about a decision to add gates to their walled suburban housing development.

> ". . . the gate thing is important—probably the single most important agendum we've taken up in my two years as president."
>
> "You really think so? To me, I say it's unnecessary—and, I don't know, irresponsible somehow. . . . I lean more to the position that we live in a democracy. . . . I mean, we all have a stake in things, and locking yourself away from the rest of society, how can you justify that?"
>
> "Safety. Self-protection. Prudence. You lock your car, don't you? Your front door? . . . I know how you feel . . . but this society isn't what it was—and it won't be until we get control of the borders."
>
> "That's racist, Jack, and you know it."
>
> ". . . Not in the least—it's a question of national sovereignty. Did you know that the US accepted more immigrants last year than all the other countries of the world combined and that half of them settled in California? And that's legal immigrants people with skills, money, education."[10]

Does Boyle capture what these teenagers are feeling? Are they reflecting local attitudes about immigration and the permeable boundary between Mexico and Texas that lies just a two-and-a-half-hour car ride away?

But it is not just in Texas and California that residents of gated communities regard immigrants as a source of fear. In New York as well residents identify "ethnic changes" and a changing socioeconomic environment as potentially threatening.

Carol and Ted—It's ethnic changes

Elena, one of my graduate students, and I arrive at Manor House earlier than expected, so we stop and talk with the guard at the gate. He is a young African-American man with short hair, wearing a conservative uniform—blue shirt and navy slacks. He is quite cordial, and invites us into his small room. This is his second job in a gated community. He likes working here, but feels that the residents sometimes expect too much: "after all, we are not police." He had worked at the Homestead where the residents complained that the guards were not doing their jobs. At Manor House it's better, but residents still do not want their rights infringed on. Elena asks him if he feels that living in a secure environment affects the residents in any way. He responds that it makes them more demanding and not very responsible. They expect the guards to relieve them of all obligations and problems, and to "jump to the rescue" even though the guards have no real power.

As Elena continues to converse with him, I reflect on how nice it is to have her with me on this interview. Elena was born in Romania, and has never been inside a US suburban home. In contrast to my experience, she is amazed that a couple with only one child would choose to live in such a large house. She provides her own cultural perspective and compares everything she sees to her life in Eastern Europe.

"Did you ask everything you wanted to?"

"It's great," she replies enthusiastically. "He feels that residents are too dependent on him, which will ultimately lead to problems. I'm not sure what kind of problems, but I can talk to him again later."

He waves us on, and we pass through the visitors' gate. It is a beautiful day, sunny and breezy. We drive along the winding road, passing a number of just-completed houses, all painted in pale colors, with shutters, porches, and landscape planting. There is subtle variation in style and design, but nonetheless the houses look remarkably similar to one another. Each is placed back from the curb with shrubs, grass, and flowers arranged in neat beds between the house and the street. The interviewee's vineyard model has a garage and driveway tucked away on the side of the house, allowing ample room for a wraparound porch in front. We arrive on time, park the car, and walk up the driveway.

Carol and Ted Corral are waiting for us at the door. They are both in their early fifties, casually dressed in tan slacks and matching polo shirts. Ted is a large, red-faced man with a loud voice, while Carol is pale with blond-gray hair, more soft-spoken and gentle. When they learn that we drove out from the city, they invite us to sit outside to enjoy the sunshine on the patio. We decline because the noise from airplanes overhead and the ongoing construction would interfere with tape-recording.

They have been living at Manor House for eight months, and had previously lived in Great Neck for the past twenty-eight years. Ted admits that it was "traumatic" to move, but they "made it," and he is now trying to minimize the impact of the move on their lives.

Carol tells me that they were attached to their previous home because they brought up their children there and because it had been built for them. Prior to Great Neck, they had lived in Brooklyn. "A long time ago," Ted adds, implying that he couldn't really remember.

Elena asks about their life in Great Neck. Ted replies that it's a great community socially, and that the children had a good school. It's an affluent community and offers lots of benefits. Carol adds that most of her friends were made there when her children were small. Great Neck had everything, so they did not have to leave for entertainment, restaurants, or even adult education courses. "It's almost like living in the city," Carol says, "but better."

Ted describes the community as "very, very educated. . . . You know, so everyone goes on to college, and it stressed the role of family, and you know, it's just a wonderful community. But it's changing, it's undergoing internal transformations."

Carol says, "It's ethnic changes."

And Ted repeats: "It's ethnic changes; that's a very good way of putting it."

Carol agrees and adds that it started to happen "in the last, probably, seven to eight years." The changing composition of the neighborhood made them so uncomfortable they decided to move.

I ask about their prior residence in Brooklyn. Ted shrugs his shoulders. I say that I would like to know about why they left for comparison purposes, and finally Carol answers. She tells me they had moved from Brooklyn to bring up their children in a better environment. The school system was changing, and they did not want their children to go to school with children from lower socioeconomic backgrounds who were being bused into their Brooklyn neighborhood.

"Those kids were wild," she says, "and had a different upbringing." She wanted to protect her children from exposure to the kinds of problems these kids might cause. The neighborhood was still comfortable, but the school system was not "desirable," as she tactfully put it. They had both grown up in Brooklyn, but the neighborhood changed, so they decided to build their own home in the suburbs.

Elena asks how they found Manor House. Ted answers, "driving by." Carol says there had been an announcement in the newspaper, and people were discussing that it had gone bankrupt and then had reopened under new ownership. I ask how they decided to move here, and Ted answers that they were looking for something that would suit their lifestyle better. He adds that they chose a gated community because they wanted a secure lifestyle with no hassles and no responsibilities.

I ask whether they would consider living in the city again and they both agree that moving back to the city would be out of the question. They had lived there for twenty-five years, but when they moved to the suburbs they had done so for a reason. They would never go back. Carol says the city was so different now compared to when she was growing up. "You're always on guard when you're walking." She still loves the city, but does not want to live there. She wants to come home to tranquility.

*　*　*

Dualistic thinking is a form of social splitting used to cope with anxiety and fear. It over-simplifies and dichotomizes cultural definitions and social expectations to differentiate the self from the other Anglos, from "Mexicans," whites from illegal immigrants, or whites from "ethnic others." The concept of splitting draws upon psychoanalytic relational theory, particularly Melanie Klein's work on the development of object relations. According to Klein, psychological splitting is the process of disassociation between "good" and "bad" representations beginning when the infant differentiates external and internal relationships by splitting the mother into good and bad, incorporating the good mother who can be identified with, and rejecting the bad. It is a psychological means of dealing with contradictory and often conflicting feelings.[11]

Psychological splitting can be used as a form of denial and resistance, providing a means of distancing oneself from an undesirable self-image and projecting it onto another. Social splitting is often used to project social fears onto a more vulnerable group, such as the Jews during World War II, or the homeless on the streets of present-day New York City. It also helps to explain the kind of us-versus-them thinking employed by the gated community residents to rationalize their fears of those outside the gates.

During periods of economic decline and social stress, middle-class people become anxious about maintaining their social status—what is referred to in these interviews as "the good life"—and seek to identify the reasons that their environment and social world is deteriorating. Social splitting offers a strategy that is reinforced by cultural stereotypes and media distortions, allowing people to psychologically separate themselves from people who they perceive as threatening their tranquility and neighborhood stability. The walls and gates of the community reflect this splitting physically as well as metaphorically, with "good" people (the good part of us) inside, and the "bad" remaining outside.

Advertisements for gated communities evoke this social splitting and even go a step further in envisaging what is being defended against. For example, the developer of Sanctuary Cove, Australia's first gated community, told reporters, "The streets these days are full of cockroaches and most of them are human. Every man has a right to protect his family, himself and his possessions, to live in peace and safety." Based on his study of gated communities in Australia, Matthew Burke found that the solidifying of perimeter barriers led to a greater sense of residents being "insiders," and reinforced the reverse process that "designates those beyond the walls as 'outsiders' [as] inevitable."[12]

Gating also involves the "racialization" of space in which the representation and definition of "other" is based on human biological characteristics, particularly racial categories. In the past, overt racial categorization provided the ideological context for restrictive immigration laws and discriminatory deed restrictions and mortgage programs. More recently, phenotypical characteristics are used to justify social prejudice and unfounded fears.[13] The thinking of one gated community resident in Sun Meadow, Texas, highlights how race still plays a dominant role in eliciting fear of the other in contemporary society.

Helen—Seeking privacy from someone at the door

Helen answers the doorbell after two rings, as I wait outside admiring her elaborately carved door with cut-glass panels. Through the glass I can see an atrium, two stories high, and an adjoining living room. It is a tan Scottsdale house with a red tile roof, similar in style to others on the street, but set at an angle on a corner lot to give it a distinctive flair. As Helen opens the door her fox terrier jumps out and runs down the driveway, barking at the children rollerblading by. She waves to her son as he catches the dog by the collar, and then invites me inside.

Helen is in her mid-forties, plump with brown hair and hazel eyes. She is dressed for golf in yellow shorts and matching shirt. Helen and her husband, Ralph, are avid golfers and active members of the Sun Meadow Club. They purchased their home from the original developer before he went bankrupt, and have lived here for over ten years. They were one of the first families to move in. Helen, her husband, and son lived in a number of different cities before moving here, because of her husband's varied businesses. She is a stay-at-home mother considering starting a business when her son finishes high school.

They originally moved to Sun Meadow for the golf course, but now would only consider living in a gated community. When I ask her why, she replies, "Because after seeing that there are so many beautiful neighborhoods that are not [in] a secure area, [and] that's where burglaries and murders take place. It's an open door [saying] to people, come on in. Why should they try anything here when they can go somewhere else first? It's a strong deterrent, needless to say."

She feels that there is less crime in gated developments than in San Antonio in general. She knows people living in equally nice nongated neighborhoods who have had their homes broken into and who have been assaulted with weapons. The worst that has happened in Sun Meadow is that a few cars have come through and "messed things up." She thinks that it was probably kids. Only a few families have been robbed or burglarized.

Helen feels that her community is different because it is secured. Without the gates, she thinks, anybody could come knocking on your door and put you in a compromising situation. She illustrates her point by telling me what happened to a friend who lives "in a lovely community" outside of Washington, DC: "She saw this fellow come to the door and she was very intimidated because she was white, and he was black, and you didn't get many blacks in her neighborhood. She only bought it [what he was selling] just to hurry and quickly get him away from the door, because she was scared as hell. That's terrible to be put in that situation. I like the idea of having security."

Helen and Ralph put on their burglar alarm every time they leave, although she thinks they may be overly cautious. She also keeps her doors locked, because she has had people walk in her front door thinking her house was for sale.

I ask her if she is concerned about crime in Sun Meadow. She answers, "No, not here, but in San Antonio." She goes on to explain that San Antonio, like any major city, has problems:

> There are gangs. People are overworked, they have families, they are underpaid, the stress is out of control, and they abuse their children. The children go out because they don't like their home life. There's too much violence everywhere. It starts in the city, but then the kids get smart enough and say, "Oh, gee, I need money for x, y, or z, but it's really hot in the city, let's go out and get it someplace else." We're the natural target for it. So being in a secure area, I don't have to worry as much as another neighborhood that doesn't have security.

She cannot imagine any city in the United States that does not have to worry, because so many people in the city live in poverty. She tells me about her friends living in a wealthy suburb who had their car stolen at gunpoint. They were going to move out of the neighborhood, which did not have gates or security, to a small town outside of San Antonio. When they investigated further, however, they learned that the small town had just as much crime as San Antonio. Helen concludes that it does not matter whether it is the city or the suburbs, you have to live in a gated community, or at least have enough property to have a dog, a security system on your house, and warning signs on your door.

Ironically, Helen's concern with crime developed after she moved into Sun Meadow, but living there reinforces the importance of having gates and guards for personal security. She is more concerned about someone walking into her house than with crime in general, yet she is one of the few residents who specifically cites an example in which racial difference triggered a sense of fear. Like Ted and Carol Corral, who moved because of "ethnic changes," Helen alludes to her friend's experience as the kind of thing that she is frightened of. "She was scared as hell," Helen comments. Her story—although displaced on her friend—suggests how Helen would feel if a black person came to her door. It is also unclear in the first vignette whether the Corrals are referring to racial or cultural differences in Great Neck. They could be referring to the large influx of Iranian Jews into their suburban neighborhood or the increasing number of Latino immigrants on Long Island. In both cases, however, these interviews conflate racial and ethnic differences with an increased potential for crime.

Racist fears about the "threat" of a visible minority, whether it is blacks, Latinos, "Orientals," or Koreans, are remarkably similar. This is because many neighborhoods in the United States are racially homogeneous. Thus, the physical space of the neighborhood and its racial composition become synonymous. This "racialized" spatial ordering and the identification of a space with a group of people is a fundamental aspect of how suburban landscapes reinforce racial prejudice and discrimination.[14]

Why should Helen's friend feel fearful just because a stranger comes to her door selling things? In Brooklyn and any urban neighborhood or integrated suburb, this would happen all the time. Think of how many times religious groups distributing pamphlets and recruiting converts knock on doors in all but the most isolated settings. Except for gated communities and other kinds of communities with secured, restricted entrances, such as military bases, prisons, boarding schools, doorman apartment buildings, or special hospitals, contact with people soliciting, selling, proselytizing, and campaigning is commonplace. In most neighborhoods the streets and the sidewalks are still public, and cross-cultural and cross-racial contact is still possible and even encouraged.

Another aspect of "fear of other" to consider is how the talk about the "other," the "discourse of fear," is used by residents to explain why gates are important. One example from Long Island (post-9/11) illustrates this point.

Linda—Separating ourselves from the great unwashed

Linda is a young mother of two boys, ten and twelve years old, in her early thirties. She is trim and keeps fit by running daily. She is a little nervous at being interviewed, but she is able to think about her surroundings and reflect on what her experiences have been there. Divorced, she lives in her recently deceased mother's house. It is a three-bedroom house, well furnished, although it is showing some signs of age. The entrance to the house is up a winding path, and the entry porch is set parallel to the road, making it feel very private even though it is an attached townhouse. Linda moved to Pine Hills two years ago, but her mother bought the house over fifteen years ago, when it was first built.

Her mother had moved to Pine Hills because she wanted to be in a setting where there would be neighbors close by, and to have the safety of the gate. Linda laughs and says:

> The security of the gate. Five dollars an hour, when they're asleep. I don't know how much security the gate is worth. Some of the guards just let you fly right in. The others have to strip-search you. It really depends. I guess that has been my experience with coming in. Some of them are okay, others want your fingerprints.
>
> [For her mother] it was just basically being less isolated on a big piece of property, and a couple of years before that we had something [happen]. There were helicopters

flying over this area. I mean, this may be going back ten years. I don't remember specifically when, but some inmate, they were looking for someone who had escaped who had a murder record. That was quite freaky. You would look out in the backyard and there'd be woods out there, and you'd wonder who is out there.

Linda goes on to say that she tries not to get a false sense of security:

Because, you know . . . people can come in here on foot. There's a golf course right behind us, and anyone could be wandering around on there, and decide to traipse through here.

Honestly I don't know how useful the gate is. The gate is useful in preventing vehicles from getting in; that is, if the person at the gate is alert and competent. Most of the time I do get a call if somebody's coming. What can I say about the gate? We did have same robberies here some years ago. I'll try to summarize this: [it's] good in preventing robberies whereby, you know, somebody would need a vehicle to load a whole lot of loot into a car or a van or whatever. But as far as preventing people on foot, it's ridiculous. You know, if anyone would have an interest in coming into this community and causing some kind of havoc or whatever, I think there are many ways they could get in.

Linda tells the following story to illustrate her point:

One time, one of my neighbor's boys, the little one, was missing. And this woman, I mean, she was white as a sheet, and she was really going to have a nervous breakdown. And we couldn't find him. He was actually in another neighbor's house with his friend, playing. I had called that house to find out, not realizing they were away, and there was a workman in the house. And these boys didn't know the workman. The workman just walked in there, went into the kid's room, and started working. So she wasn't at ease [because it was so easy for the workman to walk in without any adults being home, and that her boy was there with a strange workman].

You know, we are not living in very secure times now. . . . I can tell you that after a couple of robberies some of the older residents here felt comfortable with hiring a security car for patrolling the grounds. So they did try to do that.

To get in there is a password. I generally don't give mine out, unless it's a close friend or somebody that I know, or somebody who has my key and needs to get in. Usually, the people at the gate, they know you and they just let you in. A lot of people have automatic openers for the gate. Actually, I don't have one of those, I have a card that I can just slip in, and get in.

But Linda thinks that it is more than just security:

This is my theory: Long Island is very prestige-minded. And I think the very fact of having a guard at the gate is akin to living in Manhattan in a doorman building versus a three-flight walk-up type of thing. There's a certain "pass through the gate" of it. You know, other than the safety issue, just a kind of separating ourselves from the great unwashed, shall we say.

And I think with the gate thing, there is an increasing sense of insecurity all over the place. I think people are beginning to realize they are not really safe anywhere in Middle America. We have had so much violence occurring, the school shootings, you know. That could be part of it.

In this interview Linda tells a story about a workman who walks into a house, without anyone even noticing. This occurs in conjunction with a mother's fear that her youngest child is missing. Again an outsider is feared, even when he had nothing to do with the incident. Just his presence evokes comment.

Whether it is Mexicans, black salesmen, workers, or "ethnic changes," the message is the same: residents are using the walls, entry gates, and guards in an effort to keep perceived dangers outside of their homes, neighborhoods, and social world. Contact incites fear and concern, and in response they are moving to exclusive, private, residential developments where they can keep other people out with guards and gates. The walls are making visible the systems of exclusion that are already there; now the walls are constructed in concrete.

Social splitting, purified spaces, and racialization help to explain how this kind of dualistic thinking develops and becomes embedded in local culture. Residents talk about their fear of the poor, the workers, the "Mexicans," and the "newcomers," as well as their retreat behind walls, where they think they will be safe. But there is fear even behind the walls. There are workers who enter the community every day, and residents must go out in order to buy groceries, shop, or see a movie. The gates provide some protection, but residents would like more. Even though the gates and guards exclude the feared "others" from living with them, "they" can slip by the gate, follow your car in, crawl over the wall, or, worse, the guard can fall asleep. Informal conversations about the screening of guards and how they are hired, as well as discussions about increasing the height and length of the protective walls as new threats appear, are frequent in the locker room of the health club, on the tennis court, and during strolls in the community in the evening.

The discourse of fear encompasses many social concerns, about class, race, and ethnic exclusivity and gender.[15] It provides a verbal component that complements—and even reinforces—the visual landscape of fear created by the walls, gates, and guards. By matching the discourse of the inhabitants with the ideological thrust of the material setting, we enrich our understanding of the social construction and social production of places where the well-to-do live.

Gated community residents use gates to create the community they are searching for. But their personal housing decisions have had unintended societal consequences. Most important, they are disruptive of other people's ability to experience "community": community in the sense of an integration of the suburb and the city, community in terms of access to public open space, and community within the American tradition of racial and ethnic integration and social justice.

Architecture and the layout of towns and suburbs provide concrete, anchoring points of people's everyday life. These anchoring points reinforce our ideas about society at large. Gated communities and the social segregation and exclusion they materially represent make sense of and even rationalize problems Americans have with race, class, and gender inequality and social discrimination. The gated community contributes to a geography of social relations that produces fear and anxiety simply by locating a person's home and place identity in a secured enclave, gated, guarded, and locked.[16]

One of the striking features of the world today is that large numbers of people feel increasingly insecure. Whether attributed to globalization and economic restructuring, or the breakdown of the traditional institutions of social control, it has become imperative that governments and neighborhoods respond.[17] The threat of terrorism in the United States following the attack on the World Trade Center deepened Americans' fears. Yet to date the only solutions offered are increased policing in the public sector, and walling and gating, surveillance technologies, and armed guards in the private. These are inadequate solutions for what is actually a complex set of issues ranging from profound concerns about one's continued existence and emotional stability to everyday problems with economic survival and maintaining a particular way of life. Gated community residents then, like many Americans, are also searching for security.

The reasons people give for their decision to move to a gated community vary widely, and the closer you get to the person and his or her individual psychology, the more complex the answer. At a societal level, people say they move because of their fear of crime and others. They move to secure a neighborhood that is stable and a home that will retain its resale value. They move in order to have control of their environment and of the environment of those who live nearby. Residents in rapidly growing areas want to live in a private community for the services. And retirees particularly want the low maintenance and lack of responsibility that come with living in a private condominium development.

At a personal level, though, residents are searching for the sense of security and safety that they associate with their childhood. When they talk about their concern with "others," they are splitting—socially and psychologically—the good and bad aspects of (and good and bad people in) US society. The gates are used symbolically to ward off many of life's unknowns, including unemployment, loss of loved ones, and downward mobility. Of course, gates cannot deliver all that is promised, but they are one attempt to resurrect aspects of the American dream that many people feel they have lost.

My sister and her family are visiting us as I complete this work. Anna complains about the length of time it takes her to drive out of her gated community in the morning to take Alexandra to high school. Dust, ditches, and a never-ending string of angry drivers snake slowly past the main artery outside their gate. All other available routes also detour around impassable gates and feed onto this single road that is limited to two lanes by endless construction projects. She has to wait for a stranger to wave and let her into the line of traffic.

"The irony is that we are trapped behind our own gates," Anna says, "unable to exit. Instead of keeping people out, we have shut ourselves in."

Questions for discussion

1. What, according to Low, is the purpose of the gated community? What are the limits on one's "individual freedom" when living inside a gated community? What does the desire to accept such limits on "individual freedom" say about people's desire to shield themselves from "others" of different race and class backgrounds?

2. Discuss Klein's notion of "psychological splitting." How does this affect the residents' views of their decision to live in the gated community? How does this affect the residents' views of classed, raced "others?"

3. Two of the respondents cited "ethnic changes" as the reason that they were so uncomfortable that they left their suburban neighborhood to live in a gated community. Discuss the ways in which the ethnic isolation of the gated community may breed increasing discomfort among its residents. What then becomes the role of the ethnic "others" who work for and serve the residents? What does this say about the borders between the city and the suburbs?

4. What kind of symbolic logic has been adopted by the gated communities? How is it justified? How is it related to the tension between urban and suburban in terms of social class, race, and ethnicity?

5. Gated communities are a class phenomenon. What are some other examples of class phenomena and how do they work to reproduce class? In what ways are the notions of luxury and prestige associated with living in gated communities linked to class reproduction and mobility?

6. As Low pointed out, a "discourse of fear" runs throughout the narratives of her interviewees. How have you seen this "discourse of fear" work in your own community, school, or family? What role does the media play in perpetuating and/or heightening this fear?

7. Low stated that, "The walls are making visible the systems of exclusion that are already there; now the walls are constructed in concrete." Theorize around the systems of exclusion that Low is referring to and what the concrete walls symbolize.

8. In discussing gated communities and the "unintended societal consequences" of community isolation and segregation, Low stated that we have an "American tradition of racial and ethnic integration and social justice." In reflecting on the quote, discuss the extent to which racial integration and social justice are an American tradition.

Notes

1. A computer game that allows players to create simulated houses, neighborhoods, and cities.
2. Hayden 2003.
3. Atlas 1999.
4. Frantz 2000–2001.
5. Sanchez and Lang 2002. My sincere thanks to Haya El Massar who alerted me to the release of these figures and to Robert Lang and Tom Sanchez for allowing me to use their census note for this chapter.
6. Sanchez and Lang 2002, based on their text and table 2 on the top ten metropolitan regions.
7. Blakely and Snyder 1997 for original estimate, and Sanchez and Lang 2002 for census totals.
8. Carvalho, George, and Anthony 1997; Dixon and Reicher 1997; Jaillet 1999; Paquot 2000; Caldeira 2000; Frantz 2000–2001; Connell 1999; Burke 2001; Wehreim 2001; Lentz and Lindner 2002; Glasze and Alkhayyal 2002; Dixon et al. 2002; Webster et al. 2002; Giror 2002; Webster, Glasze, and Frantz 2002; Waldrop 2002; see also Cabrales Barajas 2002 for the recent Latin American work.
9. Kafka asserts through the voice of a Chinese narrator that the real purpose of the wall was not to serve as protection from ravaging hordes but to give people a sense of unity in their separate and isolated villages.

10. See T. C. Boyle, *The Tortilla Curtain* (New York: Viking, 1995), 100–03.
11. Klein 1963; Silver 2002.
12. Burke 2001 (147).
13. Ngin 1993.
14. Ray, Halseth, and Johnston 1997.
15. Kevin Birth also suggests that age may play a role in structuring these communities, especially the age of those who are feared. Personal communication.
16. Massey 1994; Martin and Talpede 1986.
17. Tulchin and Golding forthcoming.

References

Atlas, R. (1999). Designing safe communities and neighborhood. Proceedings of the American Planning Association.

Blakely, E. J., & Snyder, M. G. (1997). *Fortress America: Gated communities in the United States.* Washington, DC: Brookings Institute.

Burke, M. (2001). The pedestrian behavior of residents in gated communities. Paper presented at *Walking the 21st Century.* Perth, Western Australia, February 20–22.

Cabrales Baragas, L. F. (2002). Latinamérica: Paises abiertos, ciudades cerradas. Coloquio. Guadalajara, Jalisco, Mexico, July 17–20.

Caldeira, T. P. R. (2000). *City of walls: Crime, segregation, and citizenship in São Paulo.* Berkeley: University of California Press.

Carvalho, M., George, R. V., & Anthony, K. H. (1997). Residential satisfaction in *condominios exclusivos* in Brazil. *Environment and Behavior, 29*(6), 734–68.

Connell, J. (1999). Beyond manilla: Walls, malls, and private spaces. *Environment and Planning A, 31,* 417–39.

Dixon, J., Dupuis, A., Lysnar, P., & Mouat, C. (2002). Body corporate: Prospects for private urban governance in New Zealand. Paper presented at the International Conference on Private Urban Governance. Institute of Geography, Johannes Gutenberg Universität, Mainz, June 5–9.

Dixon, J. A., & Reicher, S. (1997). Intergroup contact and desegregation in the new South Africa. *British Journal of Social Psychology, 36,* 361–81.

—— (2000). "Whiting out" social justice. In *Addressing cultural issues in organizations,* edited by R. T. Carter, pp. 35–50. Thousand Oaks, CA: Sage.

Frantz, K. (2000–2001). Gated communities in the USA: A new trend in urban development. *Espace, Populations, Societes,* 101–13.

Giroir, G. (2002). The purple Jade Villas (Beijing): A golden ghetto in Red China. Paper presented at the International Conference on Private Urban Governance. Institute of Geography, Johannes Gutenberg Universität, Mainz, June 5–9.

Glasze, G., & Alkhayyal, A. (2002). Gated housing estates in the Arab world: Case studies in Lebanon and Riyadh, Saudi Arabia. *Environment and Planning B: Planning and Design, 29,* 321–36.

Hayden, D. (2003). *Building American suburbia: Green fields and urban growth, 1820–2000.* New York: Pantheon Books.

Jacobs, J. (1961). *The death and life of great American cities.* New York: Random House.

Jaillet, M.-C. (1999). Pent-on parler de secession urbaine a propos des villes européenes? *Revue Esprit, 258,* 145–67.

Klein, M. (1975). On the sense of loneliness. In *Envy and gratitude and other works, 1946–1963,* pp. 300–13. New York: Delta.

Lentz, S., & Lindner, P. (2002). Social differentiation and privatization of space in post-socialist Moscow. Paper presented at the International Conference on Private Urban Governance. Institute of Geography, Johannes Gutenberg Universität, Mainz, June 5–9.

Martin, B., & Talpade, C. (1986). Feminist politics: What's home got to do with it? In *Feminist studies/critical studies*, edited by T. de Lauretis, pp. 191–212. Bloomington: Indiana.

Massey, D. (1994). *Space, place, and gender*. Minneapolis: University of Minnesota Press.

Ngin, C. (1993). A new look at the old "race" language: "Race" and exclusion in social policy. *Explorations in Ethnic Studies, 16*(1), 5–18.

Paquot, T. (2000). Villas privées. *Urbanisme, 312*, May/June, 60–85.

Ray, B. K., Halseth, G., & Johnson, B. (1997). The changing "face" of the suburbs. *International Journal of Urban and Regional Research, 21*(1), 75–99.

Sanchez, T., & Lang, R. L. (2002). Security versus status. The two worlds of gated communities. *Census Note* 02: 02. Alexandria, VA: Metropolitan Institute at Virginia Tech.

Silver, C. (2002). Construction at deconstruction des identités de-genre. *Cahier du Genre, 31*, 185–201. Paris: Caisse National d'Assurance Vieillesse.

Tulchin, J. S., & Golding, H. A. (forthcoming). Citizen security in global perspective. In *Crime and violence in Latin America*, edited by H. F. Ehrlich and J. S. Tulchin. Washington, DC: Woodrow Wilson Center.

Waldrop, A. (2002). Fortification and class relations: The case of a New Delhi colony. Paper presented at the American Anthropological Association Annual Meeting, New Orleans, November 20–24.

Webster, C., Glasze, G., & Frantz, K. (2002). Guest editorial. *Environment and Planning B: Planning and Design, 29*, 315–20.

Wehrheim, J. (2001). Surveillance and spatial exclusion in German cities. Paper presented at the American Anthropological Association annual meeting. Washington, DC, November 28–December 2.

Chapter 4

The two-in-oneness of class

*Wendy Luttrell**

Introduction

This edited volume sheds much needed light on the different ways in which class works. In this chapter I argue that class works at two *levels*—the levels of public discourse and at the level of individual subjectivities; and in two *directions*—from the outside in and the inside out. I refer to this process as the *two-in-oneness* of class. This process has implications for the way we conceptualize the formation of subjectivity, which I refer to in the concluding section of the chapter.

In the field of cultural categories of social difference, the "pregnant teenager" offers an uncanny example through which to illustrate the two-in-oneness of class. Here, I bring the racialized, class-blind, gender muted, and stigmatizing public representations/ discourses about teenage pregnancy and young motherhood (i.e., the level of public discourse) into dialogue with how individual girls make their pregnancies their own (i.e., the level of individual subjectivites). By moving back and forth between these two levels and directions, the hidden life of class becomes more visible. I draw on examples from a five-year ethnographic study of the Piedmont Program for Pregnant Teens (PPT) and the perspectives of fifty low-income girls who were enrolled in it (Luttrell, 2003) to make my point.

Class splits: dignity, worth, and respectability

Ever since Sennett and Cobb (1972) published their path-breaking book, *The Hidden Injuries of Class*, scholars have searched for a blueprint that explains the *experience* of working-class-ness. One such template distinguishes between "respectable" and "unrespectable" life styles that has characterized many ethnographies of working-class culture in both white and black communities; there are the "settled" versus the "hard-living" families (Howell, 1973; Rubin, 1976; Weis, 2004); the "routine seekers" and the "action seekers" (Gans, 1962); the "good people," and the "trash" (Hannerz, 1969); those who are "doing something with their lives" and the "no-goods" (Anderson, 1990). Sherry Ortner might explain this phenomenon as the "tendency for working- or lower-class culture to embody within itself the split in society between the working and the middle class" (Ortner, 1991, p. 173). This same class split can be found within the middle class,

* Aronson Associate Professor, Human Development and Education, Harvard Graduate School of Education.

expressed as the "fear of falling"—an anxiety about losing their (unearned) advantages that Barbara Ehrenreich says preoccupies members of the professional middle class who worry that they have only educational credentials to ensure their economic security (1989). Meanwhile, as Katherine Newman argues in her book, *Falling From Grace*, those who have experienced downward mobility cope with "what their losses reveal about their moral character" (1988: *x*). In both cases, the meaning of "middle-class-ness" is associated with moral fitness, while "lower-class-ness" is equated with moral weakness. Thus, it is no surprise that the vast majority of Americans identify themselves as "middle class," and are much more likely to recognize the power of personal initiative than the power of social class in determining social success or failure.

That US class discourse is racially tinged is also well documented. "Whiteness" is to middle-class-ness as "blackness" is to lower-class-ness. Lois Weis contends that, "More than any other group, the identity and material position of white, working-class America is carved in relation to blacks, both discursively and materially" (2004: 7). And Sherry Ortner makes the point:

> African-Americanness carries a more or less automatic lower-class identity in the eyes of others; this much we know. But it also apparently carries a lower-class identity in terms of self-image: the same study that shows that Jews think of themselves as middle class even when they are factory workers also shows that African Americans tend to think of themselves as lower class, even when they are in high-status occupations: "Black managers with college degrees more often assert a working-class identity than equivalent white managers."
> (Vanneman & Cannon, 1987, p. 218; 1998, p. 13)

The same racially tinged class split that divides people into categories of worthiness, dignity, and respectability is found in cultural forms that make up American girlhood and womanhood. Indeed, historians have argued that the making of the US middle class was founded on principles of the "cult of true womanhood," an ideology that valorized (white) women's domesticity, virginity, heterosexual marriage, and elevated her to a figure of moral fortitude. Despite two waves of feminism, this ideology persists wherein "good" girls are pitted against "bad" girls in the race for respectability. Contemporary feminist literature on the role of class, race, and culture on girls' and women's self and identity formation is full of examples (Bettie, 2003; Brown, 1998; Brumberg, 1998; Collins, 1990; Holland & Eisenhardt, 1990; Holland et al., 1990; McRobbie, 1991; Skeggs, 1997; Steedman, 1986; Tolman, 1996, 2002; Walkerdine, Lucey, & Melody, 2001, to name a few). My own research emphasizes how poor and working-class girls live within and interpret the class split, at times embracing it and at times pushing against it (1997, 2003). For example, I found that while recounting their childhood memories of schooling, both black and white, working-class women type-cast "teachers' pets" as the "good"/"nice" girls who won teachers' approval set against the "bad"/"disobedient" girls like themselves (1992, 1997). Whereas some of the white, working-class women said they had actively chosen to reject the terms of the teachers' pet contest, refusing to align with the "middle-class" side of the class split (i.e., they wouldn't "act cutesy" to win teachers' approval), this was not an option for the black, working-class women. The black women believed their black teachers placed more value and gave more attention to well-dressed, lighter-skinned girls; as darker-skinned girls with "country ways," they felt themselves unable to compete in the teachers' pet contest. Similarly, as I will describe in more detail, the pregnant girls I interviewed sought to disassociate themselves from the "type" of girl who gets pregnant, and to defend against the stigma of being deemed a "bad"/"unfit" mother (2003). In both of my ethnographic studies, I argue that the duality of class pits women against each other as well as against those parts of *themselves* that don't align with dominant discourses of femininity.

Still, there are multiple and changing social conditions and cultural forms that give shape to class identities, affinities, and solidarities; class-ness is always being made and remade within different contexts (families, schools, workplaces, communities) and through racial and gendered boundaries that are created and enforced by these social institutions (Weis, 2004; Willis, 1977).[1] My argument in this chapter is that in the realm of discourse—the ways in which people talk and feel about themselves and others, and in the ever-so-subtle and everyday ways that people are oriented to understand their own success or failure—*the power of social class is hidden in notions of and feelings about individual worth, dignity, and respectability*. At the level of public culture, the hidden-ness of class means that the discourse is muted or missing, which helps to explain why social class is considered less credible than virtually every other kind of claim about what social position one holds (Lareau, 2003; Ortner, 2003). With respect to subjectivity, the hidden-ness of class means that complex feelings of ambivalence and anxiety about success and failure, possibility and constraint, entitlement and exclusion, longing and loss are not open to self-examination. Investigating competing public discourses about teenage pregnancy, and considering the ways in which individual girls contend with the stigma associated with it, helps to draw out the *embodied, social, cultural, and deeply affective* ways in which class works.

Stigma wars

Since colonial America, pregnant, unwed young women have served as scapegoats for America's social ills (Luker, 1996). But the official "war against teenage pregnancy" dates back thirty years when the Allan Gutmann Institute released a report entitled "11 Million Teenagers: What Can be Done About the Epidemic of Adolescent Pregnancies in the United States?" Ironically, this epidemic logic occurred during a time when birth rates to young women were actually at their lowest. What was different was that the teen population itself (and the number of teenage girls) had grown, and the social context had changed (Vinovskis, 1988). The most notable of these changes, according to Lawson and Rhodes (1993), was that the racial gap was closing between white women and women of color regarding sexuality, unmarried motherhood, and single parenting—and *white* girls were reported to be increasingly sexually active outside of marital relationships. This new social context created a perception that teenage pregnancy was a serious problem.[2]

Despite the decrease in adolescent pregnancies, sociologist Deirdre Kelly (1996, 2000) characterizes the continuing "war against pregnancy" as a *stigma contest*. Kelly identifies four groups, each with a different perspective on the problem: bureaucratic experts and their "wrong-girl" perspective; oppositional movements, including feminism and their "wrong-society perspective"; teen mothers' own perspective that the "stigma-is-wrong"; and social, religious, and economic conservatives, and their "wrong-family perspective."

According to Kelly, the "wrong-girl" discourse is dominant in that it holds the most sway in public understandings of the phenomenon of teenage pregnancy. It is also the most complicated to unravel because there are so many variations on the same theme.[3] Generally speaking, the "wrong-girl" discourse focuses attention on pregnant teens' motivations, as distinct from older (and especially *married*) women's, asking "why would a girl do that?" Underlying the question is a middle-class paradigm for a "normative" life trajectory—that is, finish school, get a job, find a male partner, marry, and have children. Making life choices that stray from this pattern, no matter what one's *actual* economic status might be, jeopardizes a woman's respectability and claims to "middle-class-ness."

By contrast, the "wrong-society" frame, first presented by feminists, identifies class inequality as the root cause of teenage pregnancy. Rosalind Petchesky (1984), noted for being one of the first to articulate a feminist position on teenage pregnancy, took issue with the individualistic notion of "choices," arguing that sexual conduct and reproductive decisions are highly contingent on girls' access to material resources, including opportunities for sex, birth control methods, and delivery systems. Researchers Arlene Geronimus and Sanders Korenman (1992) took this argument a step further, arguing that for young black girls living in poverty, having children when they are young may be an effective adaptation to economic deprivation. Younger girls who are in better health, with greater access to nutrition and social support, may be better equipped to become mothers than their older counterparts whose health and well-being has been compromised by living more years in poverty.

Kathryn Edin and Maria Kefalas (2005) offer a variation on this same theme, explaining that poor women put motherhood before marriage, not because they do not value the middle-class marriage model, but because they revere it and have less faith in their prospects of having a "good" marriage than their prospects of being "good" mothers. With respect to subjectivity, we could argue that for poor, young women marriage is a site of ambivalence—something they both long for but fear they will lose. We could also argue that marriage is a site of resistance, exemplified by poor women's keen awareness of men's desire to control (i.e., "I wanna have a baby by you," the phrase used by men in the "game" of heterosexual romance that was identified by the young women in Edin and Kefalas's study and by the pregnant girls with whom I worked).

In these studies, teenage mothers are invested with agency and positioned as architects of their lives. This stance underscores teen mother's own "stigma-is-wrong" discourse that stresses the positive and empowering aspects of their situations. Kelly found that teen mothers reject stigmas associated with teenage motherhood including "messages that portray them as victims, childlike, welfare abusers or morally tainted." I will discuss this discourse at more length in the next section.

For the proponents of the "wrong-family" discourse, teenage pregnancy *should* be stigmatized. Pregnant girls *should* be excluded from public settings to ensure that the moral fabric of adolescents unravels no further than it already has. Constance Nathanson's (1991) book, *Dangerous Passage: The Social Control of Sexuality in Women's Adolescence*, is still the most comprehensive discussion of how sexual categories and sexual social movements shape current understandings of teenage pregnancy as a social problem. She distinguishes between the morally tinged, wrong-family discourses from the racialized wrong-family construction, which casts *black teenage women on welfare* (which is a distortion of demographic evidence) as the "problem."[4] This racialized construction dates back to the 1960s and the characterization of "the black family" and its matriarchal household structures as the cause of poverty. This controversial hallmark of the Moynihan Report sparked a flurry of scholarship about the strengths and adaptability of African American family life.[5] What Nathanson calls the Neo-Moynihan analysis of teenage pregnancy introduces new class language—the black "underclass," a category of people who are cast as outsiders to the American dream. According to Nathanson, this new research has had a "profound legitimizing effect, converting 'the black family' from a political albatross to a permissible focus of media and programmatic interest by white as well as black individuals and organizations" (p. 68).

Most recent constructions of teenage pregnancy have shifted from being a "black, wrong-family" problem to being a "welfare" problem (which does not mean that racialized images of and stereotypes about pregnant teenagers no longer hold sway). The Personal Responsibility Act and welfare reform legislation (e.g., Title I-Block Grants for Temporary Assistance for Needy Families Public Law 104–93 [August 22, 1996]) targets "young women 17 and under who give birth outside of marriage." There is no mention of abortion or adoption or of its provision—both highly controversial issues—in this welfare reform legislation. For at the heart of the wrong-family stigma is a political agenda of "reprivatization"—a retreat from governmental provision for basic needs, especially those needs related to raising children. Unmarried women of means who have the resources to raise their children on their own (without being dependent upon the state) can escape the intense scrutiny of being a "wrong-girl" or part of a "wrong-family" form. Those "other," "undeserving" mothers who are dependent upon others (which is how pregnant teens are viewed) are those who are stigmatized.

Paralleling the trend toward reprivatization is the contemporary, broad-based, bipartisan marriage movement, supported by both religious and political leaders and increasingly found in sex education programs (Fine & McClelland, 2006). While marriage does not guarantee that individuals, especially children, will escape poverty,[6] it does establish one's association with respectability and the "middle-class" side of the class split.

The stigma contest illustrates the different ways in which the class split gets expressed through the social differences of gender, race, sexuality, and marital status: that "right" girls follow normative/middle-class life trajectories; that "good" girls show their "worth" by "waiting" until marriage to have sex (as in, "I'm worth the wait"); that "right" families are self-sufficient with no need for government supports or provisions—all key ingredients in the making of middle-class-ness.

The stigma-is-wrong

Over the course of my ethnographic research (1992–97), I met with fifty girls enrolled at the Piedmont Program for Pregnant Teens (a pseudonym) located in a southeastern, small industrial city. The girls were at different stages of their pregnancies and, over the course of each academic year, a few girls would give birth and return to the program as young mothers. Of the fifty girls, forty-five are black, three are Mexican-American, and two are white. All grew up in poor and working-class families and most of the girls were between fourteen and fifteen when we met. I have wrestled with how best to describe the girls. Whereas I might have referred to them as "young women," they called themselves girls. Whereas I would have referred to the majority of the girls as "African-American," they called themselves black. Whereas I might have referred to three of the girls as recent Mexican immigrants, the daughters of migrant workers who have settled in this southeastern city, they called themselves "Mexican and American." And whereas I have chosen to refer to two of the girls as white, this was not a label I heard them use to describe themselves. Meanwhile, their black classmates referred to them as "the white girl" but not in their presence. I have also wrestled with how best to describe myself in relation to the girls: as a mother; as a middle-class, middle-aged, university professor; as a self-consciously white woman in an educational setting with predominantly black students, teachers, and administrators.

Of course these labels are problematic and incomplete. Social categories of difference and belonging are elusive and fluid, made, remade, and contested in everyday contexts. Indeed, one goal of my research was to take readers inside one such social category of difference—the pregnant schoolgirl—to get up close and examine what it is like to both live inside it and try to push back against it.

Throughout my time at the PPPT, the "stigma contest"—as a larger discursive field from which the girls drew to talk about themselves and others—was played out in everyday, embodied, and deeply affective ways. The PPPT was housed on the second floor of a deteriorating annex building of what was once the largest city high school; it was in its seventeenth year of existence when I began my study. It had taken me eighteen months to gain access and secure permission; a set of negotiations that tell a story of their own about enduring racial conflicts and distrust that divide white and black city and country school officials, teachers, parents, and students in "Centerville" (a pseudonym).

On my first day of fieldwork at the school, two bulletin boards grabbed my attention—"Education is the Key to Combat Teen Pregnancy" and "Safe Sex or No Sex is the Only Key to Combat Teen Pregnancy." Alongside these "official" messages were six graffiti messages that appeared to be written in response:

"It's a choice of one's own mind."
"It's a choice of a gift, a life, another You."
Then in small, but bold letters is the statement, *"PPPT only hides you. Be proud, stay with the regular team."*
To the left of these messages is a big, scrawled X underscored by the even more rebellious message, *"This is a bunch of crap."*
And below this in eloquent cursive handwriting, *"don't be ashamed of your kids cause you weren't ashamed of having sex!"*

The official bulletin board messages didn't surprise me—education holds one key to "combat" teen pregnancy (I noticed the warlike language). The other key "safe sex" or "no sex" took for granted a host of assumptions about decision-making, agency, intentionality, and alternatives. I thought it was ironic that these messages were out of sync with the girls in the program who were already pregnant, had already decided to bring their pregnancies to term, and to remain in school. The graffiti, on the other hand, named the problem differently—encouraging the girls to defend against their stigma, marginalization, and feelings of shame: "PPPT only hides you. Be proud, stay with the regular team." "Don't be ashamed of your kids cause you weren't ashamed of having sex!" The other two graffiti messages speak to the girls' agency—"It's a choice of one's own mind." "It's a choice of a gift, a life, another You."

I was lost in these thoughts when playful voices filtered up the stairwell. The stairwell door swung open and I recognized Ms. Nelson who ushered me into room 310, saying,

"Girls, Ladies, quiet down, I want to introduce you to Dr. Luttrell. She's going to tell you about herself and her project; I have to speak with Ms. Washington and will be back in ten minutes."

There were six girls, all speaking at once.

"Yeah, you better go talk to Ms. Washington."

"If she spoke to me like how she spoke to Shanille, my mother would be up here cussing her out."

"She has a real attitude."

One girl stood up—she placed one hand on her hip, and with the other she shook her finger in another girl's face, "You don't bring the form, you don't come back," she said in a squeaky, high-pitched voice. I assumed she was mimicking Ms. Washington (who I later learned served as the program's counselor). I glanced at Ms. Nelson who seemed to be fighting back a smile.

"Ms. Washington is a teacher; you better show respect," Ms. Nelson said sternly.

Again six responses called out at once; I could only clearly hear two.

"She's no teacher."

"You are just taking up for Ms. Washington, but we don't have the same trouble with you. She's all about rules."

Ms. Nelson put an end to the conversation. Later, in the afternoon, I learned what happened between Shanille and Ms. Washington. Shondra volunteered to tell the story, squeezing herself out of the too-small wooden desk chair, "I'll tell it cause I saw it." Ms. Nelson took a seat, looked toward Shanille, who nodded approvingly.

Shondra stuffed her backpack under her shirt, swinging her newly extended belly from side to side which made the girls laugh before beginning her narration.

"She's walking down the hallway, minding her own business and scratching her belly." (*Shondra enacts these motions, then turns and throws the backpack on the desk, taking up Ms. Washington's part, speaking in a high shrill voice and waving her finger.*)

"What are you doing scratching your belly like that in school? You wouldn't carry yourself like that at church or on the street."

(*Shondra turns and puts the backpack under her shirt, again taking up Shanille's role.*)
"You never seen me at church or on the street."

The back and forth switching of characters continued. Ms. Washington said, "Don't talk to me like that." Shanille said, "I wouldn't have to if you didn't talk to me like a dog in a pound." Ms. Washington said, "Well, that's where you belong."

Several other girls joined in the storytelling, explaining that after the hallway exchange, Ms. Washington stormed into class, telling Ms. Nelson, "I don't know what is wrong with that girl." She turned to Shanille and said, "I don't know what is wrong with you, girl."

"Then Shanille starts cussin' Ms. Washington out. There was a lot of language and confusion."

Later, out of the girls' earshot, Ms. Nelson put this incident into a larger context— what she called "politics in the black community."

My first day at the PPPT shifted the ground under my researcher feet. I was struck by the adversarial "official" messages of the PPPT and the not-so-subtle everydayness of regulation. Something as ordinary as expecting the PPPT girls to sit in too-small wooden desks sent the subtle message that they had not only done something wrong by being pregnant, but that they themselves are wrong, "misfits" who didn't belong in school. But it was the way in which the subtle force of institutional discipline and punishment became painfully personal during the exchange between Ms. Washington and Shanille that struck me most. Their dispute over "proper" manners of deportment, how one should carry oneself in church, on the street, and in school illustrates the way class works: that class-ness is carried in the body, lived within punishing social practices and sites; and it is also lived through a set of defenses to avoid the sting of being accused of being on the wrong side of the class divide. Moreover, it was futile to parse out what role gender, race, and sexuality had to do with this conflict over worthiness, dignity, and respectability.

Conflicts over the proper way to "carry oneself" especially when a girl started "showing" were a recurring source of tension between some PPPT teachers and the girls, illustrating again and again through ordinary interactions that there is no female sexual category/conduct that isn't already infused with the class split. Teachers routinely tried to regulate the girls' behavior through class-coded language about respectability, especially in the public domain. They discussed accommodations the girls needed to make once they "started to show," including less sexualized attire and deportment, but especially before field trips when the girls were reminded that they would be seen as public representatives of the program. Meanwhile, the girls fought back by using their bodies (often enhanced in playful performance like Shondra's) to mock a teacher behind her back. The girls seemed to know just how to move their bodies in a way that would provoke a negative reaction.

Classroom discussions about the girls' deportment and conduct put me in mind of Karla Holloway's analysis of racial codes of conduct, which, she argues, fragments black girls' and women's sexual subjectivities (1995). She writes about her grandmother's warning that "nice" black girls should not wear red dresses as part of her "ongoing lecture series to me and my sisters on morality, values, and proper conduct for young Negro girls. . . . I am still conflicted about the intersection between public and private, and ever aware of the subtext of my grandmother's intimate awareness about public bodies—dark skinned, daringly colored, and female" (1995, pp. 16–17). The same subtext was being passed on by the black, PPPT teachers who sought to protect the girls by insisting they uphold their honor. But, as Holloway argues, this protection takes its toll on black women's minds, hearts, and bodies. Speaking again of her grandmother's admonition, "when she warned us away from red, she reinforced the persistent historical reality that black women's bodies are a site of public negotiation and private loss" (1995, p. 21). I want to emphasize that the class split is spoken between the lines of this warning (i.e., at the level of public discourse about "proper" conduct for black women), and buried within individual subjectivities. Black women's bodies are a site of public negotiation of middle- and lower-class-ness (regardless of one's *actual* class position) and private negotiation of the feelings this evokes—anger, pain, loss, and longing. The keen, intimate awareness of fragmentation about which Holloway writes, and the PPPT girls made visible through their daily interactions with teachers, is what I came to call "bodysmarts"—an intelligence (as in, "smarts") born of pain (as in, it smarts or hurts).[7]

Whatever can be said about the PPPT teachers' warnings, protectiveness, and differential treatment toward the girls' "showing," it was clear that the teachers were aware that the girls faced problems of stigma and isolation. Ms. Nelson pointed out the ironies of the program—that at the same time that it was designed to protect the girls from undue harassment in the "regular" school and to provide special encouragement to continue their education, the program isolated the girls from needed educational resources and thus stigmatized them in another way.

Indeed, special programs for pregnant teens that tend to target one segment of students (often low-income, urban girls of color) can serve to re-stigmatize those who enroll.[8] This reinforces the public perception that teen pregnancy/teen parenthood is a poor and "minority" problem and constructs a dynamic of self selection into and out of programs (Nathanson, 1991). Meanwhile, families with resources are likely to seek (and are often encouraged to do so) less stigmatized educational options for their daughters (Nash & Dunkle, 1989; Weatherly, Perlman, Levine, & Klerman, 1985, 1986; Zellman, 1981). And, it is "given" that teenage pregnancy programs target girls and not boys; thus allowing boys' adolescent sexual conduct to exist apart from public scrutiny.

When I asked about the racial imbalance of the PPPT, I was offered varying explanations, according to who was responding. Some teachers expressed hesitancy or suspicion about why I was asking. Ms. Peterson responded to my question by asking why I wanted to know—"why would that be an issue? Black people have run schools for black students for a long time, it is part of a tradition of education." Ms. Nelson, on first reflection, said she thought it had to do with the fact that the program was part of the city (as opposed to the county) school system, which was populated by predominantly low-income black students and controlled by predominantly middle-class black educators. Thus, the program was no different than any other city school in its identification as a "black" school. Later, however, she added that she thought "white people think about teenage pregnancy differently," because there was no similar program available for white students in the (predominantly white) county system. Meanwhile, PPPT girls had their own varying explanations, including one girl who observed that "white girls who get pregnant don't want to be associated with us" and another girl who noted that all the white girls she knew who got pregnant dropped out of school.

Ricki Solinger (1992) puts this racial segregation into a larger context, and describes the differences between the treatment and education of black and white pregnant girls from the 1950s to the 1970s. She points out that white girls during this time were treated as if they had a psyche—their deviance could be cured, and thus they were sent away to "homes for unwed mothers" to be reformed. Black girls, on the other hand, were not treated as if they had psyches or inner lives. Rather, their deviant motherhood was said to stem from their unruly and unredeemable sexual conduct. Twenty years later, in this particular local school context, pregnant white, working-class girls were still being educated separately from working-class girls of color.[9] The two white girls who were enrolled in the PPPT during the five years I was there ended up in the "homebound program"—a program in which girls were assigned a tutor who would bring course work to their home and provide guidance, and the work would be graded by the teacher in whose class the girl was enrolled. This option was used by girls enrolled in the PPPT when they were "put on bed rest by their physicians," according to Ms. Nelson. The homebound tutors I interviewed told me that the majority of the girls with whom they worked were white. The two white girls enrolled at the PPPT switched to the homebound program because they had been put on bed rest; but in the words of their black classmates, they "went missing."[10]

I want to draw attention to how the duality of class is embodied by the pregnant white, working-class girls going "missing," and thus hidden from view. Here, in negotiating the intersection between public and private space, the white, working-class girls'

bodies are also sites of "public negotiation and private loss." The subtext of their intimate awareness about their sexualized bodies (bodies that "show") is that they must
ward against being seen and feeling themselves to be the "wrong" side of working-class-
ness. In this instance, as in Holloway's grandmother's advice, women's bodies carry the
class split in society between lower and middle-class-ness. In both cases, the guarding
against being viewed on the wrong side of the class divide is anxiety-ridden, and comes at
a psychic cost that one will be found wanting.

That teenagers are "bad"/unfit mothers is another stigma against which the PPPT girls
felt they had to fight. When I asked the girls to complete the following sentences, "What
others think they know about me is –"; and "What I know about myself is –," the overwhelming response was to fill in the first blank with "that I will be a bad mother" (80
percent of the girls). And somewhat fewer (70 percent) filled in the second blank with
some variation on the statement "that having a baby is going to make me a better
person."[11] Often times noting the demands placed on them to shoulder domestic and
child-minding responsibilities, many of the PPPT girls said they were as likely to be
prepared, if not more so, than women who "did not know how to do for themselves."
Indeed, this was one of the PPPT girls' biggest complaints about how they were viewed
by others—that given the adult responsibilities they had been forced to assume at young
ages, they viewed the "bad mother" stigma and the "babies having babies" rhetoric as
out of touch with the realities of their lives, and indeed, the reality of many girls' lives.[12]
As one girl put it, "You don't have to be young to be a bad mother—you can be a bad
mother at any age, taking drugs, drinking, only thinking of yourself."

The PPPT girls took up the "stigma-is-wrong" discursive frame by emphasizing that
their pregnancy was, in fact, changing them for the better. The same student (Marisa)
went on to explain:

> I know I can't be thinking only of myself now. The good thing about being pregnant
> is that it has made me change some bad habits, including eating better and taking
> vitamins, getting more sleep.

Other girls talked about "cleaning up" and how being pregnant gave them "more
reasons to finish school, to work hard, and keep on track."

Again the tendency to embody the split *within* themselves between what is and is not
respectable (between middle and lower-classness) can be traced within the girls'
discourse. Their conversations resonated with Martha McMahon's (1995) research
about what distinguishes working-class from middle-class motherhood. Despite their
obvious differences, the PPPT girls echoed many of the same sentiments about pregnancy
and motherhood, as did the older working-class mothers in McMahon's study. Most
similar was the notion that motherhood is a pathway to maturity, an opportunity to
become a better person by taking on the responsibility of motherhood.[13] According to
McMahon:

> Whereas middle-class women indicated they felt they had to achieve maturity *before*
> having a child, working-class women's accounts suggest that many of them saw
> themselves as achieving maturity *through* having a child.
>
> (1995, p. 91; my emphasis)

McMahon argues that "moral reform" is a centerpiece of white, working-class motherhood, akin to Edin and Kefalas's reference to poor women's "moral hierarchy" that places motherhood above marriage. That pregnancy can serve as a motive to reform a life, to revise bad habits for the baby's sake, including either staying in or doing better in school, was a view held in the highest regard by the PPPT girls. If we take all these accounts seriously, we can see how class works through the denaturalization of marriage as a means to secure moral worthiness in favor of the naturalization of motherhood as a "promise I can keep"—a site and social practice that engenders deeply moral and affective ties between women and their children.

From outside in and inside out

At the level of individual subjectivities, we can understand the embodiment of the class split in society through the psycho-dynamics of pregnancy, which presents a girl or woman with the unique challenge of becoming conscious of two people living under one skin. I like the way Joan Raphel-Leff, in her book *Pregnancy, the Inside Story*, puts it:

> In pregnancy, there are two bodies, one inside the other—a strange union that recalls gestation of the pregnant woman herself in the uterus of her own mother many years earlier. When so much of life is dedicated to maintaining our integrity as distinct beings, this bodily tandem is an uncanny fact. Two-in-one body also constitutes a biological enigma, as for reasons we do not quite understand, the mother-to-be's body suppresses her immunological defenses to allow the partly foreign body to reside within her. I suggest that psychologically too, in order for a woman to make the pregnancy her own, she has to overcome threats posed by conception.
>
> (1995, p. 8)

Raphel-Leff calls this the inside story of pregnancy and argues that it differs for each pregnancy; every mother (no matter what her age) infuses the experiences of pregnancy with her personal feelings, hopes, memories, and powerful unconscious mythologies.

Meanwhile, there are external, "public" interests that also infuse the meanings an individual woman attaches to this two-in-one relationship between herself ("woman") and inside other ("fetus"). Indeed competing meanings of pregnancy continue to be debated within the law, especially regarding women's reproductive rights. Regardless of one's position on these issues, the point is that there are interests beyond the individual pregnant woman that mediate and make sense of her pregnancy. And whether she is consciously aware of it or not, these "outsider" interests affect her "insider" experiences. Is the pregnancy "legitimate or illegitimate," "planned or unplanned," "wanted or unwanted," "natural or inseminated," "within or outside of wedlock?" In short, we are not "free" as individual girls or women to forge our own distinct relationships with the other we carry. My challenge in *Pregnant Bodies, Fertile Minds* was to both elicit and recount the "inside stories" of teenage pregnancy—fifty girls, fifty stories. But the pattern of pregnancy as a site of bodily tandem, duality, and of both loss and longing was unmistakable.

As a kind of thought experiment, let us apply this doubleness—the inside and outside stories of pregnancy, and the blurred boundaries between self and inside other—to an understanding of how class works. Each person holds images, ideals, associations, and worries about worthiness, dignity, and respectability that are unique to her/him alone *and* that are part of a system of regulation and social control. Perhaps it is the two-in-oneness of the way class works that suppresses our defenses and allows lower-class- and middle-class-ness to reside within us, at both the personal/individual level and at the public/structural level. At the level of public discourse several ideologies converge to deny the class split—ideologies of meritocracy, individualism, and a belief that, regardless of social class, every individual has an equal opportunity to secure worth, dignity, and respectability. One strategy/defense for overcoming the (social) threat imposed by a collective recognition of systemic inequality is to disavow its existence. Another strategy/defense is to create moral boundaries, achieved effectively through the stigma wars.

What I saw on the first day at the PPPT, and what I heard from the girls I listened to over time, was their effort to wrestle with their anxiety-ridden circumstances and to answer back. Alisha's reflection on her experience echoed many that I heard:

> I think I was in denial about being pregnant. My friends kept saying to me, are you pregnant? You know how people get into your business, people talk but nobody could believe that I would get pregnant. I am so quiet. I am not the type who gets pregnant. After a few days, I wrote my mother a letter and left it on the ironing board and went on to school.

She goes on to describe the letter and her parents' reaction, including her mother's deep disappointment and sorrow. Alisha sounded defensive as she explained that she is "not the type of girl who gets pregnant"—as if she is in dialogue with those who would accuse her of being so. In this inner dialogue about what "type" of girl one is, Alisha grapples with pain, loss, and longing. For example, Alisha described her mother as being "devastated" with a forceful certainty, as if she had taken on her mother's feelings as her own. At the same time, Alisha believes change and mistakes are a natural part of life ("people change, people make mistakes"). Later, she seeks to clarify her feelings:

> I wasn't in love with my boyfriend, I mean we love each other, but we weren't in love. I don't regret getting pregnant, I regret having sex when I did. It should be special and it wasn't.

Just as she does not wish to be seen (or to see herself) as the "type" of girl who gets pregnant, Alisha longs for sex that is "special" (which, by extension, confirms her value and worth). Here again we see that female sexuality embodies the class split. Alisha's regrets are well matched with the continuing "missing discourse of desire" for young girls, where, despite whatever progress has been made, girls and women are not "free" to explore a full range of sexual pleasures and desires without it questioning their worthiness or respectability. Indeed, within the discourse available to her, it is "natural" or even "inevitable" that Alisha might be ambivalent about having had sex. But holding regrets towards one's baby—harboring ambivalent feelings toward the "other" one carries—might be more than she could bear. Recognizing such ambivalences would consign her to the especially uncomfortable category of being a "bad"/unfit mother. After a long silence where she looks like she is concentrating hard on what she is going to say, Alisha ends our conversation saying:

If you asked me "Did you want to have a baby?" I would say no. But since it happens, and if you are having sex, you have to know that it could happen. You have to know that there are consequences.

Alisha has read her social audience correctly because this *is* the prevailing question asked of pregnant teenagers; it is seemingly the *only* question being asked. As a result, the all-important question about what resources and support "lower-class" and poor young mothers need in order to raise healthy, successful children goes un-asked. Still, I worry that Alisha's audience can neither hear nor tolerate the complexity—the two-in-oneness of her answer. The hidden-ness of class means that her complex feelings of ambivalence and anxiety about the stigma wars (shame and blame), entitlement and exclusion, longing and loss are not open for her self-examination.

Conclusion

I have argued that class works at two levels—at the level of public discourse and at the level of individual subjectivities. I have suggested that class works in two directions—from the outside in and inside out in ways that are carried in bodies and in "bodysmarts"; enforced through socially and culturally set boundaries of morality; and with psychological defenses that help individuals ward against the "hidden injuries" (ambivalence, pain, loss, longing) of class. The two-in-oneness of class keeps it more hidden than other cultural categories of social difference, and requires, according to Ortner, "more intellectual archaeology" than race, ethnicity, and gender (1998, p. 13). I would extend this to say that class-ness requires more psychological theorizing before its power as a social force of attribution can be fully realized. What I have in mind starts with reconfiguring how we understand the formation of subjectivity as the "strange union" of outsideness and inside-ness (the intermingling of the social world and the inner world). This intermingling presents the subject with the unique challenge of becoming conscious of two (or three, or four) in oneness—a challenge that is fraught with ambivalence. It is the psychological working through of ambivalence (both consciously and unconsciously) that, in my view, could prove most useful in deepening our understanding of how class works.

Questions for discussion

1. In what ways might teenage pregnancy be argued to be a class issue? In what ways does class restrict access for some groups to contraception and moral discourse on teenage sexuality?
2. In what ways do the elite and middle class activate their social, cultural, and economic capital to avoid, limit, hide, or attempt to justify elite/middle-class teenage pregnancy?
3. Luttrell argues that "'whiteness' is to middle-classness as 'blackness' is to lower-classness." To what extent do you agree with this statement and what does it reveal in relation to Weis's argument (in this volume) that race and gender are nested in class?
4. Luttrell gives teenage pregnancy as an example of the intersection between

moral discourse and middle-class values. What other examples can you identify? How do they perpetuate class division?

5. What is the classed relationship that Luttrell identifies between public discourse
   and individual subjectivity? What are the links between class discourse and
   individual agency in the context of teenage pregnancy?

6. In the description of the encounter between Shandra and Ms. Washington,
   Luttrell shows how class is carried in the body. What discourses from each class
   are embodied in the body? How do clothing, body adornment, posture, and the
   like reflect class location?

7. What are the social discourses that have rendered fathers invisible in discussions
   about teenage pregnancy? In what ways does this reflect moral discourse and
   class positionality? Why is discourse so prevalent in developing and maintaining
   class division?

8. If, as Luttrell argues, class works at two levels—public discourse and individual
   subjectivity—what does this mean for other socially constructed concepts like
   race, gender, and sexuality?

Notes

1. Different cultural forms of masculinity are also wedded to the class split (Weis, 2004; Willis,
   1977). For example, Weis makes the argument that the white, working-class men in her longitudinal ethnographic study who cling to traditional masculinity associated with the "old industrial economy" and who are unwilling to associate with schooling or jobs that are
   "traditionally coded as feminine" are less likely to enjoy economic stability in the new service
   economy (p. 90). Her account shows how the class split between the "settled" and the "hard
   livers" is gendered.

2. Vinovskis notes several other reasons why policymakers embraced the epidemic logic of teen
   pregnancy, including the rising cost of early childbearing, varied political interests converging
   around the issue of teenage pregnancy as an alternative to the more controversial topic of abortion.

3. Also see R. Kenzel (1993) who writes about the development of a "wronged-girl" discursive
   frame that the Evangelical movement adopted which she compares to a psychoanalytic
   discourse that social workers used in their professionalization project.

4. See Luker (1996) for her discussion of the demographics of teenage pregnancy.

5. For example, see Ladner (1971); Stack (1974).

6. "In 1999, 4.3 million of America's 10.9 million poor children lived in married-couple families.
   Shifting from the official poverty measure to a more realistic 'self-sufficiency' income standard
   (roughly 200 percent of the poverty level), we find that 14.0 million of the 25.3 million children in families that were not self-sufficient lived in married-couple families" (Brown &
   Beeferman, 2001).

7. I adapt and extend this phrase used by Carla Massey (1996).

8. These students are tainted because of pregnancy and, then again, because of "special" education and its associated isolation.

9. Wanda Pillow (1997, 2004) reports discrepancies between program provision and opportunity
   with urban schools serving a majority of African-American girls (which she says follow a deficit
   model of treatment) and suburban schools serving white girls (which follow a reform model).

10. Girls use teen pregnancy programs differentially, with African-American and Latina teens
    having the highest rate of returning to school when pregnant (Manlove, 1998).

11. Deirdre Kelly found this same resentment about being pre-judged as bad mothers among the
    girls she studied (2000).

12. This has also been shown to be a common complaint among urban, poor, adolescent students
    who, in light of their adult responsibilities, view the school setting and school rules as

infantilizing (Burton, Obeidallah & Allison, 1996). I also heard this resentment from the white and black working-class women I interviewed (1997).
13. The in-depth interview data collected for McMahon's study were gathered in 1988–89, from fifty-nine mothers living in the metropolitan Toronto area. All the women in the sample were white and had only been educated in Canada (immigrant women were not included in the sample). McMahon makes a point to emphasize that her study was limited to investigating the "identity and the meaning of motherhood under specific social circumstances. The findings do not apply to all women or all stages of motherhood. As social circumstances change, so do identities and meanings" (1995, p. 31). She also notes that "race relations are often implicit in many cultural representations of motherhood and in public discourses about who should or should not have children. 'Other' women's motherhood provides shadow images that shape the dominant meanings of motherhood and thus the experience of motherhood among the white women in this study" (p. 32). Like McMahon, my study focuses on the meanings of motherhood for the PPPT girls and should not applied to all pregnant teenagers.

References

Alan Guttmacher Institute (1976). *11 million teenagers: What can be done about the epidemic of adolescent pregnancies in the United States?* New York: Alan Guttmacher Institute.

Anderson, E. (1990). *Streetwise: Race, class and change in an urban community.* Chicago and London: University of Chicago Press.

Bettie, J. (2003). *Women without class: Girls, race, and identity.* Berkeley, California: University of California Press.

Brown, J. L., & Beeferman, L. W. (2001). What comes after welfare reform?, in *Boston Review*, December 13. Accessed from: www.bostonreview.mit.edu/BR26.6/brown.html

Brown, L. M. (1998). *Raising their voices: The politics of girls' anger.* Cambridge, Massachusetts: Harvard University Press.

Brumberg, J. J. (1998). *The body project: An intimate history of American girls.* New York: Vintage Books.

Burton, L. M., Obeidallah, D. A., & Allison, K. (1996). Ethnographic insights on social context and adolescent development among inner-city African-American teens, in R. Jessor, A. Colby, and R. A. Shweder (Eds.), *Ethnography and human development: Context and meaning in social inquiry* (pp. 395–418). Chicago: University of Chicago Press.

Collins, P. H. (1990). *Black feminist thought: Knowledge, consciousness and the politics of empowerment.* London: HarperCollins Academic.

Edin, K., & Kefalas, M. (2005). *Promises I can keep: Why poor women put motherhood before marriage.* Berkeley, California: University of California Press.

Ehrenreich, B. (1989). *Fear of falling: The inner life of the middle class.* New York: Pantheon Books.

Fine, M., & McClelland, S. I. (2006). Sexuality education and desire: Still missing after all these years, in *Harvard Educational Review, 76*(3), 297–338.

Gans, H. (1962). *The urban villagers: Group and class in the life of Italian Americans.* New York: Free Press.

Geronimus, A. T., & Korenman, S. (1992). The socioeconomic consequences of teen childbearing reconsidered. *Quarterly Journal of Economics, 107*(4), 1187–1214.

Hannerz, U. (1969). *Soulside.* New York: Columbia University Press.

Holland, D., & Eisenhart, M. A. (1990). *Educated in romance: Women, achievement, and college culture.* Chicago: University of Chicago Press.

Holland, J., Ramazanoglu, C., & Scott, S. (1990). *Sex, risk, danger: AIDS education policy and young women's sexuality.* London: Tufnell.

Holloway, K. (1995). *Codes of conduct: Race, ethics and the color of our character.* New Brunswick, New Jersey: Rutgers University Press.

Howell, J. T. (1973). *Hard living on Clay Street.* Garden City, NY: Anchor Books.

Kelly, D. (1996). Stigma stories: Four discourses about teen mothers, welfare, and poverty, in *Youth and Society, 27*(4), 421–49.

—— (2000). *Pregnant with meaning: Teen mothers and the politics of inclusive schooling.* New York: P. Lang.

Kenzel, R. G. (1993). *Fallen women, problem girls: Unmarried mothers and the professionalization of social work, 1890–1945.* New Haven: Yale University Press.

Ladner, J. A. (1971). *Tomorrow's tomorrow: The black woman.* Garden City, New York: Doubleday.

Lareau, A. (2003). *Unequal childhoods: Class, race and family life.* Berkeley, California: University of California Press.

Lawson, A., & Rhode, D. L. (Eds.) (1993). *The politics of pregnancy: Adolescent sexuality and public policy.* New Haven: Yale University Press.

Luker, K. (1996). *Dubious conceptions: The politics of teenage pregnancy.* Cambridge, Massachusetts: Harvard University Press.

Luttrell, W. (1992). "The teachers, they all had their pets": Concepts of gender, knowledge, and power, in *Signs: Journal of Women in Culture and Society, 18*(3), Spring.

—— (1997). *Schoolsmart and motherwise: Working-class women's identity and schooling.* New York and London: Routledge Press.

—— (2003). *Pregnant bodies, fertile minds: Gender, race and the schooling of pregnant teens.* New York and London: Routledge Press.

Manlove, J. (1998). The influence of high school dropout and school disengagement on the risk of school-age pregnancy. *Journal of Research on Adolescence, 8*(2), 187–200.

Massey, C. (1996). Body-smarts: An adolescent girl thinking, talking, and mattering, in *Gender and Psychoanalysis, 1*(1), 75–102.

McMahon, M. (1995). *Engendering motherhood: Identity and self-transformation in women's lives.* New York: Guilford Press.

McRobbie, A. M. (1991). *Feminism and youth culture: From* Jackie *to* Just Seventeen. Boston: Unwin Hyman.

Nash, Margaret A., & Dunkle, M. C. (1989). *The need for a warming trend: A survey of the school climate for pregnant and parenting teens.* Washington, DC: Equality Center.

Nathanson, C. A. (1991). *Dangerous passage: The social control of sexuality in women's adolescence.* Philadelphia: Temple University Press.

Newman, K. S. (1988). *Falling from grace: Downward mobility in the age of affluence.* Berkeley, California: University of California Press.

Ortner, S. (1991). Reading America: Preliminary notes of class and culture, in *Recapturing anthropology: Working in the present,* edited by Richard Fox. Santa Fe, New Mexico: School of American Research Press.

—— (1998). Identities: The hidden life of class. *Journal of Anthropological Research, 54*(1), 1–17.

—— (2003). *New Jersey dreaming: Capital, culture and the class of '58.* Durham, NC: Duke University Press.

Petchesky, R. (1984). *Abortion and woman's choice: The state, sexuality and reproductive freedom.* New York: Longman.

Pillow, W. (1997). Exposed methodology: The body as a deconstructive practice, in *International Journal of Qualitative Studies in Education, 10*(3), 349–63.

—— (2004). *Unfit subjects: Policy and the teen mother.* New York and London: Routledge.

Raphael-Leff, J. (1995). *Pregnancy, the inside story.* Northvale, New Jersey, and London: Jason Aronson, Inc.

Rubin, L. (1976). *Worlds of pain: Life in the working-class family.* New York: Basic Books.

Sennett, R., & Cobb, J. (1972). *The hidden injuries of class.* New York: Vintage Books.

Skeggs, B. (1997). *Formations of class and gender.* London and Thousand Oaks, CA: Sage Publications.

Solinger, R. (1992). *Wake up little Susie: Single pregnancy and race before Roe V. Wade*. New York and London: Routledge Press.

Stack, C. (1974). *All our kin: Survival strategies in a black community*. New York: Harper & Row.

Steedman, C. (1986). *Landscape for a good woman: A story of two lives*. London: Virago.

Tolman, D. L. (1996). Adolescent girls' sexuality: Debunking the myth of the urban girl, in *Urban girls: Resisting stereotypes, creating identities*, edited by Bonnie J. Ross Leadbeater and Niobe Way. New York: New York University Press.

—— (2002). *Dilemmas of desire: Teenage girls talk about sexuality*. Cambridge, Massachusetts: Harvard University Press.

Vanneman, R., & Cannon, L. W. (1987). *The American perception of class*. Philadelphia: Temple University Press.

Vinovskis, M. (1988). *An "epidemic" of adolescent pregnancy? Some historical and policy consideration*. New York: Oxford University Press.

Walkerdine, V. H. L., & Melody, J. (2001). *Growing up girl: Psychosocial explorations of gender and class (qualitative studies in psychology)*. New York: New York University Press.

Weatherly, R. A., Perlman, S. B., Levine, M., & Klerman, L. V. (1985). *Patchwork programs: Comprehensive services for pregnant and parenting adolescents*. Seattle: Center for Social Welfare Research, School of Social Work, University of Washington.

—— (1986). Comprehensive programs for pregnant teenagers and teenage parents: How successful have they been? *Family Planning Perspective, 18*(3), 73–78.

Weis, L. (2004). *Class reunion: The remaking of the American white working class*. New York and London: Routledge Press.

Willis, P. (1977). *Learning to labor: How working class kids get working class jobs*. New York: Columbia University Press.

Zellman, G. (1981). *A title IX perspective on the schools' response to teenage pregnancy and parenthood*. Santa Monica, California: Rand.

Chapter 5

Reflections on class and educational reform

Stanley Aronowitz[*]

Prologue

I never knew my maternal grandmother. She died when my mother was twelve years old, an event that was to materially as well as psychologically shape her life. When my grandfather remarried two years later, his new wife did not want her around so my mother was sent to live with his sister, her husband, and child. My mother's family—women as well as men—were garment workers. They came to the United States to escape the brutal Tzarist regime in Russia and Poland. Most of them were revolutionary socialists who were subject to imprisonment and exile. In a wrinkle on the usual Jewish working-class immigrant story they were skilled workers who moved up the US class ladder—but without the benefit of school credentials. My grandfather was a highly skilled tailor who worked as a cutter in the men's clothing trade and eventually elevated himself to manage other workers. His sister Lily was a sewer of the whole garment in the high-end section of the dress industry. She sewed very expensive dresses by hand, a craft that has virtually disappeared. Her husband Zelig began as a machine operator, but became a writer and labor reporter for the *Jewish Daily Forward* which, under the leadership of Abraham Cahan, its editor until World War II, was a real power among immigrant Jews. My grandmother's brother, a founder of the Cloak and Suit local of the International Ladies Garment Workers' Union, was also a machine operator of ladies' coats and suits who, at the end of his life, became a small landlord with properties in the mostly black communities of the Bronx.

These were educated people who read and spoke several languages, revered "classical" music, but acquired their knowledge mostly in the course of life rather than in schools. Probably the one exception was that some of them went to union-sponsored citizenship courses where they acquired knowledge of some US history. And the union also ran English language courses, using labor and socialist texts, novels, and daily newspapers. My great uncle Zelig had a fairly large library of English and Yiddish language books. I couldn't read the Yiddish but the English language books included contemporary works of American and European history, political commentary, the novels of Dostoevsky, Mann, and Kafka, among others. My mother attended high school in the Bronx until she was fourteen years old but was forced to drop out and go to work. She spent the next twenty-five years selling boys' clothing in several department stores,

[*] Distinguished Professor of Sociology at CUNY Graduate Center and Director of Center for the Study of Culture, Technology, and Work.

eventually becoming an assistant buyer at Klein's, one of the premier discount department stores in New York. For more than twenty-five years before retirement at age sixty-
seven, she worked in union wholesale textile shops as an assistant bookkeeper. It was
only after retirement that she fulfilled a life-long aspiration to return to school, first
earning her GED and then attended community college but left for the Center for Worker
Education, a bachelor's degree program for union members and other working adults at
City College of New York, where she graduated cum laude in 1987 at age seventy-four.

What my mother gained from schooling was no career, but a bibliography and the
chance to participate in discussions with fellow students about literature and politics, her
two favorite subjects. She had always been a voracious reader, musician, and painter
throughout her life but, except for the arts, never had the chance to share her literary
insights with others. That, rather than career preparation, was the main value of school.
Like her aunt and uncle she was mostly self-taught except, perhaps, her exquisite
command of the English language which, since Yiddish was the lingua franca of her
parental and adopted households, probably required the drills that took place in PS 57
and Junior High School 45 in the Bronx.

I come from a family of unschooled but highly educated members of the "labor aris-
tocracy." Their example, probably emulated unconsciously, prompted me to leave school
in my freshman year of college, an event that upset both of my parents. But like them (my
father did graduate high school but left college after his first year), I felt that further
schooling was superfluous to my intellectual development. Certainly after more than
twelve years of schooling, I had come to the end of my tolerance for boredom and did not
return to get a degree for fifteen years, and it was only after I entertained the idea of
leaving full-time union work—a job that required no advanced degrees—that I re-entered
undergraduate school on condition I would not be required to attend classes. Instead,
placed in the charge of a mentor, with whom I met once or twice during the academic
year, I wrote a long paper and was duly certified as a bachelor of arts by the New School.
In order to make this arrangement I agreed to attend its PhD program in sociology. After
a stunning first semester sitting in classes taught by the likes of Jurgen Habermas, Iring
Fetscher, and Adolph Lowe I ran out of Germans and, faced with the prospect of
studying with US sociologists schooled in the post-war shadow of the leading figures of a
non-critical, positivist social science, Talcott Parsons and Robert Merton, I left school
once more in the middle of the second semester, and found a way to earn my PhD by
other means, again without the obligation to take classes. Beginning with some observations in my first book *False Promises*, for more than thirty years I have written about and
commented on schooling, almost always in the context of considering the system from
the vantage point of workers.

The rocky road to educational reform

My general disenchantment with schooling "as we know it" led me to participate in the
founding of various types of alternative schools. The first, New York's Free University,
was a non-degree granting institution that was started by a group of radicals who
believed that traditional schools had mostly ruined the passion for learning among young
people and that they/we deserved another shot at getting a critical education. Founded in
1965 the school was one of a kind. In contrast to "socialist" schools of later vintage that
were linked to specific political organizations and Marxist ideology, the Free University

invited teachers with diverse knowledge and intellectual orientations who shared only the disdain for bureaucratic state institutions. The anarchist philosopher Murray Bookchin taught, as did market libertarian, economist Murray Rothbard. Marxian leftists like James Weinstein, a historian and radical entrepreneur, was also a founder, and Alan Krebs, a defector from college teaching whose inspiration it was to gather the original faculty and organizers and later an ardent Maoist, offered classes, as did the poet Susan Sherman. I taught there as well. Among my "students" were Robert Christgau and Ellen Willis, both in the process of inventing rock criticism, and Tuli Kupferberg, a member of the satiric singing group The Fugs. The school flourished in an environment of cultural revolution and political dissent that attracted people from literally all walks of life: workers and students, lawyers, physicians, artists, and, of course, lower east siders intent on reinventing the lost art of bohemianism. When the conditions that supported the school faded—the protest movements of the 1960s, cheap rent, and relatively carefree youth—so did the Free University and all but a handful of its emulators.

Five years later I accepted a chance offered by a group of East Harlem and Yorkville parents to help organize an "experimental" public high school—the first since World War II—which would combine occupational and academic learning and be directed, primarily, to working class white, black, and Puerto Rican kids. Financed in part by the Ford Foundation which was in the midst of its brief moment of fomenting educational innovations, and a reluctant New York City's Board of Education, Park East High School opened in fall, 1970 with eight full-time teachers and one hundred and fifty students drawn from both neighborhoods. Its first home was the basement of the local Catholic church; subsequent to the initial faculty among the teachers was a nun from a local convent and the others, chosen by a committee of parents, were recruited from among licensed teachers of the Board.

We began with no principal. Some of those duties were temporarily shared by the two full-time staff members responsible for organizing the school pending the selection of a licensed principal drawn from the official list. We had no problem with the requirement, imposed by the teachers' union—a representative of which sat on the governing committee—to hire from the official list, because in a cohort of twenty thousand high school teachers we were bound to attract a handful of talented educators who really wanted to do something new. Selecting a principal from the approved list was another matter. In the first place the pool of candidates was very small. More to the point by the time a person attains high administrative rank she or he has been a part of the system for decades, learned its bureaucratic practices, and is likely to internalize its values and intellectual orientation. We wanted a teacher/director but the Board and the Supervisors' union would not hear of it. It turned out to be the eventual undoing of the school's aspiration to break away from the usual, dismal character of nearly all state schools, especially the mostly dysfunctional high schools that littered New York City's neighborhoods.

Of course the first two years were glorious. Student and teacher enjoyed a degree of freedom to invent new ways of learning. Consistent with the best work of developmental psychology classroom practice was more than supplemented by extensive use of the vast resources of the city. For example, our biology teacher, who had studied at Indiana University with an eminent geneticist, was an ardent ecologist, so Central Park became a laboratory and our private bestiary. We commandeered a lab from a nearby hospital, while IBM came in and donated and set up a state of the art computer lab right in the basement. Of course, they had to send an instructor because none of the teachers or the administrators knew the first thing about them. We all learned along with the students. Students were asked to suggest course electives and chose science fiction, Puerto Rican literature, and the history of civil rights, and the staff scrambled to fulfill these desires. I, myself, taught the science fiction course to a class of twelve eager participants, while the course in Puerto Rican literature was taught by a neighborhood writer. For more than a few of the students, Park East was nothing short of a savior; years later a grateful parent met me at a Greenwish Village bar and refused to let me buy drinks. He claimed I had saved his son from committing suicide. Others among the first cohort went on to become intellectuals, political activists, top technical professionals. Thirty-five years later, I am occasionally in touch with them.

Needless to say this cornucopia came to an end with the arrival of the "real" principal who convinced members of the governing committee—parents, community activists, and union officials—that the standard curriculum was best suited to ensure that students could gain access to colleges, a claim some of us disputed but to little avail. Within a few years after my, and my colleagues', departure (we had two- and three-year contracts to plan and execute the basic organization of the school but not to run it), Park East expanded to six hundred students, acquired a real school building, and took its place among New York City high schools. It is still a relatively decent place but hardly the reform bastion it set out to be.

In late spring of 1972 I interviewed for a job at Staten Island Community College's experimental school, a mélange of programs that had been encouraged by Bill Birenbaum, its president, which, as he later confessed, was his way of working around the largely vocational and professional emphasis of the rest of the institution. To accomplish this objective he needed to raise "soft" money—funds that were not provided by the city and state budgets. On the heels of the '60s penchant for doing new things, it was not too difficult to fund unconventional curricula. After a year of teaching in the experimental school my niche turned out to be a mandate to organize a "youth and community studies" associate's degree as a transfer to a parallel program at SUNY Stonybrook which offered a bachelor's degree in the subject. I was given a second teaching line to fill and I hired David Nasaw, then a newly minted PhD in History from Columbia University. Nasaw was pleased to have the job at a time when history rivaled philosophy for the lack of full-time opportunities for even the products of the leading universities. We were foolish, so we took the program into three communities as well as a site on the SICC campus: Bedford Stuyvestant, the Lower East Side, and Flatbush. We held classes in the storefronts and lofts of community organizations which, as late as the early 1970s, were still funded by city, state, and federal money. Our students were community outreach workers and, in the case of Flatbush, young adults who had had drug problems and wanted to go back to school. What course we could not teach was handled by adjuncts, most of who were people with extensive experience in community organizing and eager to try their hand at classroom instruction.

Then came the New York City fiscal crisis of 1976 to the present, and with it a huge wet blanket descended over public education. That event signaled the end of the brief period of educational and other social reforms. It was the precursor of the so-called Reagan revolution during which neo-liberal policies dominated public life. For the past thirty years we have been fed with a steady diet of market-driven concepts, the policy analogue of which is that the private sector can do it better. The only new ideas that received any hearing were those having to do with cost-cutting, administrative control of teachers and students, crime prevention, and the concept that schooling was about job preparation for private business. Government must now obey "bottom-line" criteria as if any service were to be considered a commodity. Many professors and administrators still spouted the rhetoric of critical thinking, saw education as a preparation for "life," but as colleges and universities hired more adjuncts and fewer full-time teachers, and workloads steadily increased, by the 1990s it became brutally apparent that the gulf between schooling and education had so widened that even the most optimistic among us no longer denied that state schools had, for the most part, become credential mills. In many four-year as well as community colleges corporations virtually seized the curriculum and instructors increasingly taught by the numbers. All resistance to these self-evident rules had to go underground.

Go to college or die

Ours is the era when "higher education" credentials have become the new mantra of public schooling. The rationale for the need for credentials is the technological imperative, the material basis of which is deindustrialization. The days, it seems, are long gone when a teenager could drop out from high school and get a decent paying factory job or go into retailing or wholesaling with the prospect of eventually earning enough to support self and family with dignity. Now, we are told, from retailing to computer services and administration, everyone needs a degree. Whereas my family and I required none of the trappings of post-secondary schooling, today anyone possessing merely a high school diploma is consigned to low waged jobs or, if black or Latino, often none at all.

But earning a degree does not an education make. On the contrary, as Peter McLaren and many others have noted, schooling is most often a ritual performance, both for the teacher and the student. For one thing, many kids leave high school without adequate preparation for college-level work. "College-level" here means the ability to perform research and write a lengthy paper. While many upper middle-class students have learned these "skills" already, most public high schools serving working-class students do not require serious academic performance as a criterion for graduation. At a time when politicians and their supplicants sing the praises of science and mathematics as necessary prerequisites for technical jobs, many schools lack science laboratories or, if they have the space, do not supply up-to-date equipment so that students can perform even the most routine experiments in chemistry and biology. And systems are chronically short of qualified science and math teachers, the result of which is that many courses cannot be offered to meet entrance requirements of research universities and many private colleges. For another, as we have learned, environments for facilitating learning—books in the home, parents who can help teach their children how to use libraries, or even neighborhood libraries that have the materials and the staff to assist research—are not the norm. In short, in this richest and technologically most advanced society in the world, illiteracy in both its crude and more sophisticated forms is rampant.

Ask any teacher working in a third-tier state or private college or university. They normally have overcrowded classes of thirty-five or more, not only at the community colleges but at most of these institutions. In fact, some private colleges are the beneficiaries of students who have been refused admission in public colleges and universities where the pressure to maintain higher academic admission standards has reduced the number of working class, especially black and Latino students. In some cases middle-class whites are forced to seek private colleges because their high school records are simply not good enough for public schools. I know that this assertion seems counterfactual to the usual perception that the private schools are "better." This may be true of the three hundred elite colleges and universities where class sizes are smaller and faculty is always at students' disposal. But the third tier story is quite different, at least in the northeast where these institutions are numerous. Of these students, many of my colleagues report that perhaps a fifth of their classes—seven or eight students—are minimally prepared to address the tasks of the course and far fewer are on top of the subject matter. Writing good papers is the exception, even among these students. For most of their classes, the ability of most students to read the assignments is always in doubt. The quality of their oral class participation usually exceeds their written work and, where tests are required, the results are typically disheartening because, even where their reading is good enough, they have never been schooled in effective test-taking let alone acquire the cultural capital their peers accumulate in private or upscale suburban public schools. Of course, given the fact that admissions offices at some schools still give more weight to the various scholastic "aptitude" tests than grade point averages or recommendations, for upper middle-class kids attending a test-taking course given by a private tutorial company is de rigueur.

No doubt earning a post-secondary credential has become mandatory for the world of services and, in some cases, even for qualification for apprenticeships in union-sponsored highly skilled manual trades such as electrician and plumber. But as I have implied in this essay, the credential is incommensurate with the requirements of the job; its ubiquity is due, chiefly, to the widespread recognition that post-secondary credentials are absolutely necessary for qualification for the new world of work. And, except for the professions, the credential does not signify necessary knowledge, but the willingness of the student to submit to the controls that have been imposed by the chronic shortage of good paying jobs.

In fact, we know that many graduates of elite schools feel impelled to seek a graduate degree because the bachelor's credential is widely regarded as merely a stepping stone. The liberal arts graduate interested in the arts—writing, journalism, editing, film, or music composing or performance—is discovering the limits of their cultural capital. The once possible freelance career has almost vanished because the venues of newspapers, magazines, are gone and the on-line publications offer a budding writer no way to make a living. Print media, including book publishing, are experiencing a sea change in their ability to stay alive. The entry level job of assistant editor is disappearing as publishers pile more and more on harried editors; if there are editorial assistants, their pay is so low they are likely to quit within the first year. And once prosperous record companies that offered jobs to studio musicians, technicians, and entrepreneurial administrators are either folding or cutting their staffs to the bone. Aspiring filmmakers find that they may have all the necessary skills and knowledge to make movies, but unless they go to a prestigious film school for their master's degree and get social capital—a fancy term for contacts and networks—their chance of catching on in any capacity within the industry—technical or artistic—is almost nil. Even the ambiguous title of management "trainee" often requires an MBA where once the bachelor's was sufficient. School systems and state agencies increasingly deny certification for elementary and secondary school teachers unless the master's has been presented. They may be granted temporary credentials that permit them to teach but not tenure. And in the health professions, now the sector of choice for many working-class men as well as women because of the rapid growth of hospitals, nursing homes, and the key profession of nursing, where once an associate's degree was enough, now, credentially, agencies and employers are requiring a minimum of a bachelor's in nursing and, frequently, make clear their preference for the master's. The poorly paid jobs in social work, especially in schools and medical institutions, nevertheless have followed the credential inflation that marks most of the other sub-professions (jobs that do not require the PhD). As a consequence, hundreds of thousands of professionals are finding that their qualifications are outdated. Again, it is not that education schools and nursing schools, for example, offer "advanced" knowledge. It is simply a matter of control. Institutions want you to demonstrate your subordination by taking more and more courses and acquiring more credentials.

The class system in schooling has taken a new and disturbing turn. There is less education and more time spent in class. The vaunted US mobility system, always a partial truth, has all but collapsed. Students know that getting credentials is simply an endurance test and most have no expectation of receiving a critical education. The problem is that in our profoundly anti-intellectual culture, it is hard to know where working-class young people can find education. With the decline of the labor movement and the Left, once the best sources of critical thought, they are on their own, and until a real youth movement re-emerges, chances are slim that things will change in this respect. The unions resemble not so much a movement for which the intellectual and political developments, as well as interests of their members and the working class, are paramount, but service organizations, best described as engaged in the business of survival. Their members are scarcely participants in the affairs of the union and do not and cannot expect to receive an alternative education. And the Left, disorganized and dispirited, is at best a mélange of single issue movements and electoral machines for which the aspiration of providing an alternative education for its activists, let alone its potential constituents, is simply not on the agenda.

So where can a bright, intellectually ambitious young person turn? Perhaps inspiration and support comes from the occasional teacher, perhaps from a fellow worker, perhaps from a chance encounter with ideas. What is certain is that in our profoundly anti-intellectual culture, it won't come from schools or the media. What is equally sure is that without an articulate and culturally motivated Left, the powerless will remain at the mercy of the system of control and subordination.

Questions for discussion

1. How did the author's deep history and life experiences shape his direction toward educational reform?
2. Aronowitz charges colleges and universities as having become credential mills. Do you view institutions of higher education in this way? What seems to have influenced such a strong claim? What are the consequences of this accusation?
3. If indeed "the credential does not signify necessary knowledge, but the willingness of the student to submit to the controls that have been imposed by the chronic shortage of good paying jobs," how are we to view our own educational endeavors? Is it "simply a matter of control?"
4. How have the content of curriculum, the dissemination of knowledge, and academic standards changed over the past several years? What are your predictions for higher education?

Section 2

Parenting class

Chapter 6

Class out of place

The white middle classes and intersectionalities of class and "race" in urban state schooling in England

*Diane Reay**

Introduction

As Weis (2004) asserts, with the growing ascendancy of neo-liberalism accompanied by an intensification of social inequalities in the USA (Apple, 2003; Katz, 2001; Reich, 2001), the UK (Blanden & Machin, 2004; Blanden, Gregg & Machin, 2005; Galindo-Rueda et al., 2004; Seager & Milner, 2006), and more widely (Freeman-Moir & Scott, 2003; McLeod & Yates, 2006) the need for serious class-based analyses could not be more pressing. However, the focus of much social justice work has traditionally been on the working classes (Reay, 2006; Sennett & Cobb, 1972; Skeggs, 1997; Weis, 1990; Willis, 1977). In contrast, the research that I am currently engaged in is part of a small but growing trend in the UK to focus on the privileged in society (Ball, 2003; Power et al., 2003; Vincent & Ball, 2006). While most of this work emphasizes class as the most salient aspect of identity my research specifically concentrates on the intersections of class and race through a focus on white, middle-class identity.

Historically white middle-class identity in the UK has been an idealized one held up for its "others," the working classes, to aspire to. Just as whiteness continues to serve as an invisible norm, the unraced center of a racialized world (Wray & Newby, 1997), so middleclassness has long held the privileged place of classed normativity (Bourdieu, 1984). And certainly in the late 2000s the white middle classes, and particularly the white middle classes as they are inscribed in policy discourses, best fit the ideal of the democratic citizen, individualistic, responsible, participatory, the active chooser; these are the prevailing conceptions of the white middle classes. Traditional notions of "the bourgeois self" have prioritized individuality, self-interest, and self-sufficiency (Mills, 1968). It has recently been argued that developing market forms in education and the wider public sphere are producing new kinds of moral subjects (Sayer, 2005). Yet, the contemporary educational markets in both the UK and the USA also draw upon classical liberal views underpinned by a political and economic liberalism which is deeply embedded in modern Western societies (Chubb & Moe, 1990). The individualized self-interested and self-sufficient self remains the ideal.

Market policies have not only valorized choice and consumerism, they have also eroded communal well-being and a sense of solidarity (Jonathan, 1997; Nash, 2003). There has been a retrenchment and a withdrawal from the social across class as capitalist restructuring and processes of privatization begin to threaten both middle and working-class

* Professor of Education in the Faculty of Education, University of Cambridge, UK.

ways of life. Recent research on social class and whiteness both here in the UK and in the USA point to some of the disquieting aspects of such global trends for white middle-class identities. In the UK we have Tony Giddens' (2000) excluding and exclusive white middle classes, Butler and Robson's (2003) isolationist non-mixers, Stephen Ball's (2003) strategic, self-interested profit maximizers, and George Alagiah's (2006) cautionary tale about the white middle classes fleeing rather than embracing diversity. Similarly, in the USA, there is Barbara Ehrenreich's (1997) anxious paranoid middle classes with their over-inflated fear of falling socially and Ellen Brantlinger's (2003) affluent professionals with their liberal rhetoric and conservative neo-liberal practices. As Berking (1996) argues, processes of privatization and social protectionism appear to have generated a society whose assets in solidarity have been exhausted. The contemporary cultures of individualization and privatization have eroded commitments and investments in the public sphere, the reduction of graduate jobs at the same time as the rapid expansion of higher education has resulted in middle-class anxiety and a loss of certainty, while the growing gap between the rich and the poor has exacerbated class divisions (Anyon, 2000).

It is against this social and conceptual terrain that the Economic and Social Research Council funded project on identities, educational choice, and the white urban middle classes in England is being conducted. Together with Gill Crozier and David James, I am looking at the white middle classes who still send their children to socially mixed, urban state schooling; those middle classes who can be seen to be "acting against self-interest" educationally. Our project then has been an optimistic one, its intention to explore middle-class identities that are grounded in sociality and a commitment to "the common good," and the ways in which these might work against, and disrupt, normative views of what it means to be "middle class" at the beginning of the twenty-first century. So we are focusing on those white middle classes who are still actively embracing diversity, those middle classes who retain a commitment to class and ethnic mixing, in other words a socially inclusive middle class as opposed to Giddens' socially exclusive middle class. They also trouble powerful contemporary discourses; those which couch middle-class self-interest as a universal good, as well as moral discourses of "doing the best for your child" that are tied to notions of rational choice (Brighouse, 2002). As one of our parents, a political party official, asserted: "I believe doing the best thing for my child, and for most children on the whole, is to go to a school where they meet a whole wide range of people." However, this is not what is commonly understood as "doing the best for my child" and, as a consequence, attending schools with a wide ethnic and social class mix is not normative white middle-class behavior either in the USA or the UK.

The research study

We felt the best place to try and find these middle classes is in ethnically diverse inner city comprehensives—to research the educationally integrationist middle class—what we might see as the educational equivalent of the participatory democratic citizen within three urban conurbations in very different areas of England—London, Riverton, a prosperous city in the West of England with 7 percent of school pupils from ethnic minority communities. and Norton, a northern English city with a sizeable working class but only 4 percent ethnic minorities. The research study employs in-depth qualitative research methods to document and understand the contribution principled choice and ethical dispositions make to such white, middle-class identity formation. Using choices in relation to urban schooling, it examines the social actions, and the orientations, commitments, and motivations underlying them, of white middle-class parents faced with dilemmas of ethical choice in relation to their children's schooling when their local state schools are ones that most white middle-class parents shun. While much research has examined normative choice-making among the middle classes (Ball, 2003; Vincent & Ball, 2006) our research deliberately set out to examine those white middle classes who choose schools that are normally seen by their peers as "not for the likes of us." The aim is to investigate how such practices are related to a wider sense of identity and identification and the extent to which these are influenced by class fraction and white ethnicity.

Our sample includes approximately 120 white middle-class families. Overall, we conducted 240 interviews. This chapter is based on the London sample and draws on the analysis of interviews with parents in the 63 families we have interviewed, a total of 32 fathers and 63 mothers. Although there are quotations from only a small number of these interviews, the themes they raise are saturated in the data and can be found to varying degrees in both Norton and Riverton as well as the London data (see Reay et al., 2007).

Slightly over half of our sample were self-identifiers, responding to an article in a leftwing broadsheet newspaper, *The Guardian*, about the research project which specified that its focus was the white middle classes. However, we also assessed middleclassness conventionally using the Registrar General classification scheme (social classes 1 and 2) to identify households as middle class, as well as gathering information about both parents' educational levels. In all the families subjective class definition matched objective socio-economic categorization and in only one of our families were neither parents graduates (a household where the father is an actor and the mother a choreographer). However, conventional approaches to social class are simply a starting point for a methodology that analyzes and understands middle-class identity in terms of practices and processes (Reay, 1998; Skeggs, 2004). Ethnographic interviewing practices (Brewer, 2000) that allow for a judicious mix of open-ended questioning and careful prompting and probing have been employed to elicit, not only individuals' deeply held values and commitments, but also ambivalences, fears, and anxieties about acting in contradiction to normative white middle-class behavior. In order to capture these more psycho-social aspects of identity we followed the analytic approach outlined in Hollway and Jefferson (2000). Our intention is to develop theoretical understandings of the ways in which social privilege is both maintained and challenged in the context of multicultural urban schooling.

The pleasures and perils of white middle-class privilege

As I have argued elsewhere (Reay et al., 2007) white middle-class subjects who can be seen to be "acting against self-interest" are split, divided between the acquisitive self-interested self and a more altruistic, public spirited self and have to live with the tensions generated through the contradictory interplay of cooperation and competition, consumerism and welfarism (Miller, 1993). Brantlinger (2003) has a similar analysis of the educated middle classes in the USA who, she asserts, have divided minds—a public rejection of hierarchies behind which lurks a personal desire for them. Such tensions, between a desired inclusivity and a socialized exclusivity, were particularly apparent among our sample of white middle-class parents. They are dealing at first hand with the tensions between new civic ideals of social diversity and the resurgent demand for the pursuit of educational excellence (Poynting & McQueen, 2003).

The predominant educational experience for the white middle classes is to fit seamlessly into schooling, finding places where there are "people like me," and as Bourdieu (1989, p. 43) points out, "when habitus encounters a social world of which it is the product, it finds itself 'as a fish in water,' it does not feel the weight of the world and takes the world about it for granted." However, our white middle classes were deliberately choosing schooling where they were "fish out of water"; an experience that, for many of them, generates a habitus divided against itself. This process of being divided Bourdieu (1999, p. 511) describes as "doomed to duplication, to a double perception of self." The white middle classes opting for ethnically diverse comprehensive schooling are positioned in an uncomfortable space on the boundaries of two very different cultures and ways of being, between elite, predominantly white middle-class social networks and the predominantly working-class multiethnic social spaces of school and locality. As a consequence they have to engage in psychic, intellectual, and interactive work in order to maintain their contradictory ways of being, their dual perceptions of self. They had deliberately eschewed trying to get "the best" educationally for their children in terms of high achieving and selective schooling, while still wanting the best for their children in terms of educational achievement and attendance at elite universities. Tessa, a psychotherapist, was representative of almost all our parents when she said:

> Academic achievement is very important to me definitely. I care obsessively really and I want them to do well. I don't see why I should compromise but really I don't see why they shouldn't do just as well here.

The seductions of privilege, these parents' ability to mobilize resources of cultural, social, and economic capital, unavailable to the majority of families whose children attend their schools, jostle uncomfortably alongside political and moral commitments to comprehensivization and more equitable ways of being and interacting.

However, there was also an openness to difference and a recognition of the benefits in attending multiethnic comprehensive schools, and all our parents pointed these out. A knowledge and understanding of different cultures was emphasized by both parents and children. For Dan Adkin attending a working-class multiethnic comprehensive has given his daughter a familiarity and understanding of cultural difference:

> Emily, for example, goes to a school where predominantly it's a kind of working-class environment, a lot of children come from difficult, yes difficult, disadvantaged domestic situations. And it's roughly 50 percent non-white. And so she's got this kind of middle-class background and goes on middle-class holidays with a middle-class family, and has got reasonably wealthy grandparents who have left an inheritance for her kind of thing. And she goes and spends several hours a day with people who come from very different backgrounds, so she's exposed to both and is totally comfortable with both.
>
> (Dan Adkins, teacher)

Similarly Ollie, the son of two teachers, emphasizes the knowledge he has gained of working-class places and lives in contrast to the students at the more elite sixth form college he moved to at age sixteen:

> Unlike them I did know the kind of world of Denton and the estates and all of that stuff. Obviously I have not lived there and I've not really experienced it, I am not going to pretend to have that kind of empathy, but I certainly know them and I know it is there. In a way that a lot of people just don't seem to.

Less prevalent was the ability to fit readily and easily into very different social milieux to those of family and friends As Sally Rouse admits: *"I don't think my kids' social networks in the school are very wide. They stick to like basically but at least they have experience of different sorts of people in school."* Issues of fear, anxiety, security, and safety are all embedded in choices of sameness over difference and Julie Hextell hints at some of the reasons for that in her interview. For a few of the parents, including Julie, this is a disappointment. Their children are not availing themselves of the multicultural resources on offer in their schools. As Julie Hextell says: *"I know a lot of parents get very upset that they seem to have only white friends."* She goes on to talk about her concern when her own daughter only seemed to have white friends, lamenting that *"there is very little point in sending her to such a school if she is not taking advantage of what it offers."* In all of this it is difficult to retrieve a sense of middle-class altruism, a civic commitment to "giving back" to society, or even of inadvertently adding value to the educational experiences of working-class students whatever their ethnicity. Julie Hextell demonstrates that intertwined with a focus on discovering something intrinsically valuable in multiethnic schooling is an emphasis on difference as a resource that might bring their children some advantage.

So, despite varying degrees of social mixing with the classed and racialized other across the sample, nearly all the white middle-class young people remain firmly and primarily anchored in white middle-class networks. The white middle-class interest in difference and otherness can thus be understood not only as a recognition and valuing of "the other," but also as a project of cultural capital acquisition through which these white middle-class families seek to display their liberal credentials and secure their class position (Bourdieu, 1984; May, 1996). As a consequence, the ability to move in and out of spaces marked as "other" becomes part of the process through which this particular fraction of the white middle classes come to know themselves as both privileged and dominant (Razack, 2002).

We can see further evidence of this in the reflections of a number of parents who raise the issue of the "value-added" gained in terms of confidence and self-esteem that comes through attending schools where many of the children are far less privileged:

> The funny thing is, something I didn't realize is, I think it is very good for their self-esteem, I mean we are free loading in a way, partly because they have got all these opportunities and a lot of them are cheap and/or free, but also they are top of the tree academically at a school like that and if they went to another school they would be average. . . . But I think they think they are great and so that is very good for their self-esteem. It's very good for their self-esteem being top in lots of subjects.
>
> (Sally Rouse, secondary school teacher)

And:

> Bryony has come out very confident because she was top of the pile as well in that
> school and she overcame all her fears and worries at the beginning and has come out
> extremely well adjusted socially and emotionally, very confident and knows where
> she wants to go.
>
> (Julian Drew, senior arts manager)

In both these quotes the profits accruing to the white middle classes are fore-grounded
but it is much harder to see what the gains might be for the black and white working-
class children who make up the majority in these schools. Hester, who went to an East
London comprehensive and is now at a high status university, makes some telling
comments about the consequences for such students in which she emphasizes problems
rather than profits for the working-class majority:

> It is really difficult because I think in some ways it is quite idealistic to say that every
> school should have a perfect mixture of different classes and different races. I think it
> does cause problems. I don't think by sticking lots of different people together in one
> place it doesn't get rid of the difference, it just intensifies the conflict. I think it just
> makes people from like unfortunate backgrounds I don't think they appreciate
> having other people that have come from more privileged backgrounds. I don't think
> they think "oh that's really good of them to come and mix with us." I think it is
> almost as if it is rubbed in their faces.

Hester uses the term "difference" but, as becomes evident later in the quote, she really
means privilege and its lack. And the bringing together of intractable differences of
advantage and disadvantage in educational spaces, reputedly characterized by an egalitarian ethos, generates discomforts of both resentment and a sense of inferiority on the
part of the disadvantaged and defensiveness and a sense of superiority on the part of the
advantaged. As Paula, a financial consultant, comments in relation to her daughter's
experience at a predominantly multiethnic working-class comprehensive:

> Victoria was deemed too posh and not streetwise enough. . . . She said they don't
> want to have anything to do with me and quite frankly I don't want to have anything
> to do with them.

In both Hester and Paula's words we gain a powerful sense of the resulting tensions and
conflicts for those "from unfortunate backgrounds"; those whom Hester sees as having
privilege "rubbed in their faces." This is the tension and discomfort generated when there
is social mix with little social mixing. Too often what the white middle classes bring to
the "common" school is an "out-of-place" exclusivity, or what Chris, an investment
manager, terms "a sense of feeling extra":

> He was very bright and he wasn't getting enough stimulation and he was feeling
> extra all the time if you know what I mean because he always knew the answers and
> the other kids didn't and so you know he felt excluded. And the school was fantastic,
> he got extra lessons, they celebrated his "extraness" if you like within the class.

It is difficult but unavoidable to see what "extra," with its connotations of "better" and "superior," means in this context. It is little wonder that Hester's "unfortunates" feel resentful.

The gains and losses of being and doing difference

However, this is but part of the tale. It is important to remind ourselves that these are the white middle classes who, because of their commitment to compehensivization, are confronting an unfamiliar field with all the attendant discomforts of difference and the exposure of their white middle-class privilege. For Bourdieu, field is the context in which practices take place. He argues that the relation between habitus and field operates in two ways:

> On one side, it is a relation of conditioning: the field structures the habitus, which is the product of the embodiment of the immanent necessity of the field (or of a hierarchy of intersecting fields). On the one side, it is a relation of knowledge or cognitive construction: habitus contributes to constituting the field as a meaningful world, a world endowed with sense or with value, in which it is worth investing one's energy.
>
> (Bourdieu in Wacquant, 1989, p. 44)

As Bourdieu (1999) makes clear, when habitus and field do not accord there are inevitable conflicts and disjunctures. For the white middle-class families in our sample such misfits between field and habitus were frequently manifested in a complex array of difficult emotions. The liberal-left, white middle classes may feel compelled to protect and safeguard their children's advantages but many of them also simultaneously feel guilty and awkward about their privilege. Ben, a barrister, conveys some of the difficulties embedded in making non-normative middle-class choices:

> It is difficult sending your children to inner city comprehensives when you are a middle-class professional because it looks so patronizing and it looks like a mini experiment for your kid and I am conscious that it would be misinterpreted like that. Rather like shopping around for the best kind of differences.

Such conflicted feelings are further aggravated by a nagging sense of anxiety that such choices may result in children "under-achieving" educationally.

Stephen Ball argues (2003, p. 162) that for the middle classes concerns and anxieties about getting it right and doing the right thing are engendered and reinforced with social networks. If white middle-class parents, in part, become moral subjects by learning and acquiring behaviors and attitudes from others in their class setting then when those others opt for private and selective state sector parents like those in our sample are often left with a sense of abandonment and righteous indignation, but also anxiety and guilt. There is no reassurance of community. Instead we have a language of panic in which the psychic costs of principled choices becomes very evident. Unsurprising then that anxiety, guilt, and contradictory responses permeated our interviewees' responses. In the quote below we can see powerful conscious and unconscious conflicts cutting through Vicky's narrative:

They are very seductive the private schools, they sort of, you know, into thinking they're the best and I think it's, yeah you could say it's racism, it's classism at the start, but it's fear, it's fear that you're sending your child into a lesser environment, somewhere where they're not going to be able to do as well.

(Vicky, charity worker)

Vicky's emphasis on state schools as "lesser" places is telling. If class is internalized for the working classes as "an intimate form of subjectivity experienced as knowledge of always not being 'right'" (Skeggs, 1997, p. 90), how is class internalized for the middle classes especially when the internal fears and defenses of white middle-class parents like Vicky are supported in the wider social world through discourses which themselves contain enduring phantasies about the inferior intellectual capacities of the working classes (Carey, 1992)? There are a number of references to "children who hold the bright ones back" but more common, as the quotes have already shown, are the references to how bright and extra their own children are. Daniel, a journalist, has two sons who attend a comprehensive that has a 90 percent Asian intake, predominantly Bangladeshi and Pakistani students. Unlike Asian students in the US context and other categories of Asian students in the UK, Bangladeshi and Pakistani students are underperforming relative to the white English majority. Talking about his oldest son, Daniel explained:

He's in the Gifted and Talented program, but more than that, he's in the top 2 percent, I mean he's off the scale. And we are members of the National Association for Gifted Children so I mean we've seen other gifted children, it's a bit like an elephant, once you've seen one you recognize it.

The benefits of social mix in state schooling can be undermined by white middle-class dispositions to feel both socially and intellectually superior to the working classes. And it would appear from our data that even this progressive fraction of the middle classes sometimes bring their sense of being right and being "extra" into educational spaces populated by those who have far less social and educational confidence. Unsurprising then, as we have seen in earlier quotes, that the white middle classes, dealing with the unusual situation of being a minority, often do not view the majority working-class white and ethnic minority students in their schools as people they can easily or comfortably fit in with.

You know also he was the only, he was alone, he didn't have a single mate, he didn't know anybody, he was by himself, whereas virtually everybody else came up with a peer group, so he was sitting by himself and you know he is very white and he's very middle class. So looking round, all the groups are mixed, there isn't a sort of "white middle-class group" he could go and slot himself into, it doesn't work like that, you've got the group from this primary school, and that primary, they're already mixed up. . . . So I think he found it really difficult. I know he did, it was horrible, we used to walk to school and it was a nightmare. The first term I just felt sick, the whole time. I would like it to be the norm for people to go to their local school and not to be scared in the way that I was scared. I would like people like me to send their children to Petersdale and not be scared. I think a lot of my fear was irrational. I'm sure it was. I didn't even go and look at the school, so how rational can this be?

(Vicky)

Within private and selective schools the middle classes are one of a social group or collective of individuals that offers "the two fold blessing of being someone and not having to be alone in doing it (Berking, 1996). For our families, and particularly those choosing the lowest performing schools, that is not the case. We can see this very clearly in Vicky's description of Marcus' isolation.

Caught within multicultural capitalism

It is important for critical social science, on the one hand, to identify hidden instrumental strategies and power relations behind apparently innocent and disinterested action and, on the other hand, to uncover genuinely unintended advantages deriving from ethical behavior (Sayer, 2005). Initially our project was a naïve one in that we hoped to find in the white middle classes sending their children to urban comprehensives a fraction of the middle classes characterized by altruism and a sense of civic responsibility. We did find those qualities in our sample, but as we can see clearly in what parents say about their children their altruism and sense of civic responsibility was tempered by a degree of anxiety and defensiveness. There were also aspects of acquisitiveness and elitism we had not anticipated. Writing of her American white middle-class neighbors bell hooks argues that:

> They may believe in recognizing multiculturalism and celebrating diversity . . . but when it comes to money and class they want to protect what they have, to perpetuate and reproduce it—they want more. The fact that they have so much while others have so little does not cause moral anguish, for they see their good fortune as a sign they are chosen, special, deserving.
>
> (hooks, 2000, p. 3)

While most of the white middle-class parents in our study did not make claims about their children's "extraness," their specialness, their white middle-class privilege becomes particularly apparent in the multiethnic, working-class schools they chose to send their children to. Our white middle-class families come to see themselves as privileged in predominantly working-class, multiethnic educational spaces, but alongside complex, mixed feelings of empathy and guilt are more utilitarian practices of capitalizing on privilege. In fact most of the parents, while distancing themselves from the more exclusivist white middle-class majority, continued to deploy their greater economic, social, and cultural capital to get more educationally for their own children. Despite their best intentions class is always at work, continuing to trump these parents' more egalitarian politics. Brantlinger (2003) argues that prevalent images of the educated middle classes in the USA depict them as liberal, progressive, empathetic, generous, and attuned to the best interest of working-class, lower-income people. However, as Brantlinger (2003, p. 192) goes on to argue, "on subconscious and unspoken levels we eschew both equitable distribution of resources and substantial inclusion of others into our exclusive communities." However, such processes of eschewing are far from static and fixed. Rather, class privilege reasserts itself into these families' educational experiences despite parents' intentions to act in more equitable ways.

The white middle classes we have been researching are certainly not isolationist non-mixers (Butler & Robson, 2003), and unlike Alagiah's picture of the white middle classes they are actively seeking out diversity. However, running alongside an openness to difference there are still shades of elitism. They may not be an excluding white middle class but they still retain elements of both exclusivity and self-interest. While sometimes choice of ethnically mixed state schooling was accompanied by a commitment, and even practices, to improve educational resources for other less privileged children, on the whole actively seeking to enhance the common good was not normative for this group of white middle-class parents either. Like Butler and Robson's (2003) London middle classes these parents constitute "a class in and for itself." Theirs was a multicultural, but only rarely a socialist, egalitarianism. While they were anxious not to refuse or misrecognize cultural others they do not seem to understand the injuries of class (Sennett & Cobb, 1972).

Conclusion

In our research the most powerful intersectionality we have been dealing with is the interface between whiteness and middleclassness. We are trying to make sense of a confusion of heterogeneity—there are many shades of whiteness (Reay et al., 2007) and a multitude of middle-class positionings even among this diminishing fraction of the middle classes. However, what the data has highlighted clearly is that as many, if not more, white middle-class practices are directed at maintaining social privilege as dissolving it. As Mike Savage and his colleagues (2005, p. 43) found in relation to their Northern English white middle-class sample, there is a profound paradox at the heart of liberal, progressive middle-class dispositions and inclinations. The celebration of diversity and multiculturalism acts "as a means of self-reinforcement, a form of self-congratulation" for avoiding what they see to be the narrowness and bigotry of more conventional, white middle-class educational choices. So while at one level difference is celebrated and welcomed, the embracing of diversity only goes so far, and rarely far enough to jeopardize and put at risk children's educational achievement. In particular, white middle-class privilege is brought into strong relief against the backdrop of the social and educational disadvantage that makes up much of the landscape of urban comprehensives in England. There is often an intensification of privilege as children are "naturally" placed in top sets, gifted and talented programs, and receive private tuition to compensate for what parents perceive to be inadequate teaching standards in key subject areas (Reay, 1998). Twenty-five years ago Bob Connell and his colleagues (1982) wrote about the ways in which class, race, and gender can either conflate, contradict, or work against each other. Despite the varied shades of whiteness and perfusion of middleclassness (Reay et al., 2007) the dominant theme throughout our data is the ways in which race and class privilege compound rather than undermine each other among this liberal "left-leaning" fraction of the white middle classes. We are left with the question of whether middleclassness can work against white privilege, and the uncomfortable reflection that even for this group of progressive, pro-welfare middle classes, self-seeking, acquisitive individualism remains in constant tension with more egalitarian, community-based motivations.

Questions for discussion

1. Why is middle class perceived to be the norm in terms of class division? What are the limitations of centralizing middle-class experiences and rendering elite and working-class experiences to the periphery?
2. Why are many conceptions of social class emphasized as the most salient aspect of identity? What could be other components of this identity?
3. Why are middle-class ideas and aspirations portrayed as universal? In what ways do moral discourses like "doing the best for your child" reflect middle-class aspirations?
4. From the chapter we can see a visible conception of middle class that appears to be in opposition to "normative white middle-class behaviors." How does this conception work to reinforce middle-class advantaged position in the long run?
5. Why do you think that "despite varying degrees of social mixing with the classed and racialized other across the sample, nearly all the white middle-class young people remain firmly and primarily anchored in white middle-class networks?" How can this be associated with the notions of recognition and valuing of "others?"
6. Reay states that bringing together those from unfortunate backgrounds and those having privilege generates tension and reinforces class reproduction. How can we create safe educational spaces of systematic contact?
7. This chapter suggests middle-class families are seeking out schools which appear to be ethnically diverse and offer multicultural resources. Consider additional factors affecting school choice. Do these other factors reflect egalitarian impulses and the image of a more democratic educational institution? Might these factors also reveal the same troubling conclusions as suggested by the author? Explain.
8. If you were a middle-class parent of school children, where would you send your children (inner city school or middle-class school)? Why might you have similar dilemmas that participants of this study experienced?

References

Alagiah, G. (2006). *A home from home: From immigrant boy to English man.*
Anyon, J. (2000, April 25). *Political economy of an affluent school suburban school district: Only some students get the best.* Paper presented at the American Educational Research Association Conference. New Orleans.
Apple, M. (2003). *The state and the politics of knowledge.* New York: Routledge.
Ball, A. (2003). *Class strategies and the education market: The middle classes and social advantage.* London: RoutledgeFalmer.
Berking, H. (1996). Solitary individualism: The moral impact of cultural modernisation in late modernity. In S. Lash, B. Szerszynski & B. Wynne (Eds.), *Risk, environment and modernity* (pp. 189–202). London: Routledge.
Blanden, J., & Machin, S. (2004). Educational inequality and the expansion of UK higher education. *Scottish Journal of Political Economy, 51*(2), 230–49.
Blanden, J., Gregg, P., & Machin, S. (2005). *Intergenerational mobility in Europe and North America.* London: Centre for the Economics of Education, London School of Economics.

Bourdieu, P. (1984). *Distinction*. Cambridge: Polity Press.

—— (1989). In Wacquant, L. Towards a reflexive sociology: A workshop with Pierre Bourdieu. *Sociological Theory, 7*(1), 26–63.

—— (1990). *In other words: Essays towards a reflexive sociology*. Cambridge: Polity Press.

—— (1999). *"The contradictions of inheritance" in the weight of the world*, Pierre Bourdieu et al. Cambridge: Polity Press.

Brantlinger, B. (2003). *Dividing classes: How the middle class negotiate and rationalize school advantage*. New York: RoutledgeFalmer.

Brewer, J. (2000). *Ethnography*. Buckingham: Open University Press.

Brighouse, H. (2002). *School choice and social justice*. Oxford: Oxford University Press.

Butler, T., & Robson, G. (2003). *London calling: The middle classes and the re-making of inner London*. Oxford: Berg.

Carey, J. (1992). *The intellectuals and the masses*. London: Faber and Faber.

Chubb, J., & Moe, T. (1990). *Politics, markets and American schools*. Washington, DC: Brookings Institution.

Connell, R., Ashenden, D., Kessler, S., & Dowsett, G. (1982). *Making the difference: Schools, families and social division*. Sydney: George Allen and Unwin.

Ehrenreich, B. (1997). *Fear of falling: The inner life of the middle classes*. New York: HarperPerennial.

Freeman-Moir, J., & Scott, A. (Eds.). (2003). *Yesterday's dreams: International and critical perspectives on education and social class*. Christchurch, NZ: Canterbury University Press.

Galindo-Rueda, F., Marcenaro-Gutierrez, O., & Vignoles, A. (2004). *The widening socio-economic gap in UK higher education*. London: Economics of Education, London School of Economics.

Giddens, A. (2000). *Runaway world: How globalization is reshaping our lives*. London: Routledge.

Hollway, W., & Jefferson, T. (2000). *Doing qualitative research differently*. London: Sage.

hooks, b. (2000). *Where we stand: Class matters*. New York: Routledge.

Jonathan, R. (1997). *Illusory freedoms: Liberalism, education and the market*. Oxford: Blackwell.

Katz, M. (2001). *The price of citizenship*. New York: Metropolitan Books.

May, J. (1996). Globalization and the politics of place: Place and identity in an inner London neighbourhood. *Transactions of the Institute of British Geographers, 21*(1), 194–215.

McLeod, J., & Yates, L. (2006). *Making modern lives: Subjectivity, schooling and social change*. New York: State University of New York Press.

Miller, T. (1993). *The well-tempered self: Citizenship, culture and the postmodern self*. Baltimore, MD: Johns Hopkins University Press.

Mills, J. S. (1968). *Utilitarianism, liberty, representative government*. Dent, London: Everyman's Library.

Nash, R. (2003). Dreaming in the real world: Social class and education in New Zealand. In J. Freeman-Moir & A. Scott (Eds.), *Yesterday's dreams: International and critical perspectives on education and social class*. Christchurch, NZ: Canterbury University Press.

Power, S., Edwards, T., Bagnell, G., & Whitty, G. (2003). *Education and the middle class*. Buckingham: Open University Press.

Poynting, S., & McQueen, K. (2003). In J. Freeman-Moir & A. Scott (Eds.), *Yesterday's dreams: International and critical perspectives on education and social class*. Christchurch, NZ: Canterbury University Press.

Razack, S. (Ed.). (2002). *Race, space and the law: Unmapping a white settler society*. Toronto: Between the Lines Press.

Reay, D. (1998). Rethinking social class: Qualitative perspectives on gender and social class. *Sociology, 32*(2), 259–75.

—— (2006). The zombie stalking English schools: Social class and educational inequality. *British Journal of Educational Studies, 54*(3), 288–307.

Reay, D., et al. (2007, forthcoming). A darker shade of pale: Whiteness, the middle classes and multi-ethnic inner city schooling. *Sociology*.

Reich, R. (2001). *The work of nations: Preparing ourselves for 21st century capitalism*. New York: Alfred A. Knopf.

Savage, M., Bagnall, G., & Longhurst, B. (2005). *Globalization and belonging*. London: Sage.

Sayer, A. (2005). *The moral significance of class*. Cambridge: Cambridge University Press.

Seager, A., & Milner, M. (2006). Gap between the richest and poorest workers widens. *The Guardian*, 3 October, p. 26.

Sennett, R., & Cobb, J. (1972). *The hidden injuries of class*. New York: Vintage.

Skeggs, B. (1997). *Becoming respectable: An ethnography of white working-class women*. Cambridge: Polity.

—— (2004). *Class, self, culture*. London: Routledge.

Strauss, A., & Corbin, J. (1990). *Basics of qualitative research: Grounded theory procedures and techniques*.

Vincent, C., & Ball, S. (2006). *Childcare choice and class practices: Middle class parents and their children*.

Weis, L. (1990). *Working class without work: High school students in a de-industrialising economy*. New York: Routledge.

—— (2004). *Class reunion: The remaking of the American working class*. New York: Routledge.

Willis, P. (1977). *Learning to labour*. Farnborough: Saxon House.

Wray, M., & Newby, A. (1997). *White trash*. New York: Routledge.

Chapter 7

Class reproduction and social networks in the USA

*Fiona Devine**

While many Americans consider the USA to be a "land of opportunity," especially in comparison to Western European countries, there is increasing awareness and greater evidence to suggest this is not the case. As the correspondents of *The New York Times* noted in *Class Matters* (2005), class has a significant impact on all aspects of US life. Class, for example, has more of an influence on who goes to elite four-year colleges than it did in the past. That is to say, the effect of social background on life-chances has grown stronger in recent years. From the end of World War II until the mid-1970s, there was considerable upward social mobility and the trend was towards a decline of the effects of family background on educational and occupational attainment (Hout, 1988; Hout et al., 1993). This period was characterized by considerable affluence, the growth of higher education, the upward shift of the occupational structure towards more high-level professional and managerial jobs, and a collective commitment to equality, especially equality of opportunity. Since the late 1970s, however, the evidence suggests that upward social mobility has evened out and may even be declining (Bradbury & Katz, 2004; Scott & Leonhardt, 2005; see also Morgan et al., 2006). This period has been noted for economic troughs and accompanying redundancy and unemployment, the growth of low-level jobs in the service sector such as in retail and personal services, growing income inequality between rich and poor, and a commitment to the operation of a free market rather than alleviating inequalities. Thus, in a society where intergenerational upward social mobility may be halting, or even declining, the ways in which class inequalities are reproduced are crucial to understand.

In this more recent era, the importance of schooling in the process of class reproduction has become more important. Brint (2006) powerfully argues that rather than provide opportunities for social mobility—as was the case in the post-war period—it is now apparent that the field of education is where class inequalities are reproduced. The influence of social background and cognitive ability on educational attainment has actually increased over generations. Data from the General Social Survey (GSS) indicate that the chances of a son or daughter—born between 1946 and 1960 to a father in a professional occupation—completing college were 38 percent compared with 19 percent for the son or daughter born in the same period of a father in unskilled blue-collar employment. For sons and daughters born between 1955 and 1971, these figures shifted to 59 percent and 19 percent respectively with the difference between them growing from

* Professor of Sociology at the University of Manchester, UK.

26 percent to 40 percent (Brint, 2006, pp. 176–77). Brint (2006, p. 187) concludes that "the United States has become less a beacon of opportunity than a colossus of inequality." If this is so, a key issue is how these class inequalities are reproduced over time and space. What are the processes that link social background, educational attainment, and occupational outcomes? These macro-level questions can to be answered with reference to micro-level family strategies (Erikson & Goldthorpe, 1993). Families are crucial here. Specifically, how do advantaged upper-middle and middle-class families transfer their resources from one generation to the next? The aim of this chapter is to consider how these parents mobilize their economic, cultural, and social resources to ensure their children's educational and occupational success. The ways in which inequalities of class and race are linked in these processes of reproduction are also considered.

The first section considers different theoretical explanations for the persistence of class inequalities and educational outcomes. The similar way in which Goldthorpe and Bourdieu discuss the pivotal role of parents in mobilizing economic, cultural, and social resources/capitals is noted. They both only make passing reference to the importance of social resources/capitals (social networks) in the reproduction of advantage, although the work of Granovetter and Coleman is helpful here. The second section describes how the empirical research on predominately white upper-middle and middle-class families—involving interviews with 86 parents with 116 children between them—in the USA and the UK was conducted. Drawing on the US interview material, the third section focuses on how parents mobilize their social resources—their social networks—to their children's advantage during the years of compulsory schooling. It also considers how parents use these social networks as their children enter higher education and the labor market. It will be seen that parents draw on their social networks for information and advice about the best schools to send their children to ensure academic success. Close and loose ties are a shortcut to information and advice so they can exercise choices and make decisions. This information is personalized information and, given it is knowledge shared by other people like themselves—namely: highly educated professional people—it is information and advice they can trust. A crucial component of the use of social networks is that middle-class children socialize with the children of other middle-class professional parents who value educational and occupational success. The role of parents in the formation of their children's homogenous advantaged social networks is thereby noted. The conclusion gives further consideration to the role of social networks in the reproduction of class inequalities and how they are interwoven with race inequalities too.

Explaining the persistence of class inequalities

There are two competing theoretical explanations for the stability of class relations. One theory is associated with Goldthorpe (1980, 1987, 2000) who is famous for his work on social mobility in the UK and later comparative research with Erikson (Erikson & Goldthorpe, 1993). His empirical research showed that while the overall or absolute levels of upward mobility changed from the 1940s, relative rates of upward mobility (the relative changes of people coming from different classes ending up in the middle class) remained unchanged. He argued these continuities should be understood with reference to the desirability, advantages, and barriers associated with different class positions.[1] In relation to the relative advantages of different class positions, he distinguished between three types of resources: (i) economic resources (including wealth, income, and other forms of capital); (ii) cultural resources (which refer to the importance attached to life-long education within the family); and (iii) social resources (involvement in social networks that can serve as channels of information and advice). The relative barriers of different classes derive from the lack of resources outlined above. Most importantly, members of the middle class are keen to hold on to their advantages and they have the power—via the resources they command—to do so. Economic resources are the most important resource because they are exclusive goods that can be easily transmitted from one generation to another in comparison to cultural and social resources that are inclusive goods that are less easily transmitted. Thus, economic resources, for example, explain differential rates in access to higher education and, thereby, levels of educational and occupational success overall.[2]

The other theory that seeks to explain the stability of class relations in time and space is associated with the work of Bourdieu. Bourdieu's theoretical ideas about the role of cultural capital in the reproduction of educational inequalities established his earliest reputation in the sociology of education. This notion of capitals was later extended to his famous study of distinction and taste (Bourdieu, 1984) and an analysis of class (Bourdieu, 1986, 1987). Classes, he argued, are clustered around different types of capitals: economic capital (income and money derived from employment, self-employment, the ownership of businesses, etc.), cultural capital (dispositions, tastes, values, and cultural distinctions), and social capital (advantaged networks useful for information and advice).[3] Those in positions of power (namely, the upper and middle classes) exploit these capitals to ensure their superiority over others and to do so legitimately. Unlike Goldthorpe, Bourdieu stressed the importance of cultural capital in the reproduction of class differences. It is the conversion of economic capital into cultural capital in its institutionalized or objectified form—including educational credentials—that is all-important. He argued that "cultural capital has its own structure of value . . . independent of income and money" (Bourdieu, 1984, p. 62). Cultural capital is created out of struggles between social classes that attempt to legitimate their own culture. Hence, cultured upper and middle-class parents pass their cultural capital on to their children via educational qualifications. This is how educational and wider societal inequalities are produced.

While Goldthorpe and Bourdieu are often seen as rival theorists in their approach to class analysis, their explanations for the persistence of class inequalities share many similarities which often get overlooked. Despite their different approaches, for example, they talk about the same processes when they refer, in Goldthorpe's case, to the "mobilization of resources" and, in Bourdieu's case, to the "exploitation of capitals." The terminology might be different but they are talking about much the same thing. Moreover, both of them focus on three types of resources/capitals, economic, cultural, and social, which they define in remarkably similar ways. While they might emphasize the importance of different capitals, Goldthorpe (2000, pp. 241–42) also works with a theory of cultural capital of sorts while Bourdieu (1987, p. 326) has never denied the importance of the economic in his work. They both, however, fail to fully elaborate on the importance of social resources/social networks—which they both define in terms of social networks—in the reproduction of advantage or domination. Goldthorpe, for example, argues that social resources are important only when academic success is not forthcoming. Parents turn to family, friends, and other contacts to help their children into decent jobs. Bourdieu (1987, p. 364) also notes that those in positions of dominance "have all sorts of ways of evading scholastic verdicts" and that the "effects of social capital (a helping hand, 'string pulling,' the 'old boy network') tend to correct the effect of academic sanctions." Social networks are considered only when investments in other capitals have not yielded results. Neither of them, in other words, considers the ways in which social networks might be mobilized in the pursuit of academic success in all its dimensions.

The concept of social networks is most closely associated with the work of Granovetter (1973/1995, 1985) who noted the role of informal social contacts, for information and advice, in getting a job.[4] The person who has considered social networks in the pursuit of education credentials, of course, is Coleman (1988, 1994). He described the part played by social capital in the creation of human capital: namely, the skills and capabilities that influence people's life-chances. He also defined social capital in terms of social networks although he went on to explore "how interpersonal relationships generate feelings of trust, establish expectations and reinforce norms" (Coleman, 1988, p. 1779). He suggests that social capital is a resource that can be mobilized to advantage in that parents can use it to help their children be successful in school. Social capital includes wider community relationships and points to the ways in which local communities, including organizations like the church for example, influence young people's expectations and monitor and guide their everyday behavior by rewarding success and punishing failure.[5] Social capital is, in effect, a form of social support to parents. It reinforces the cultural values and practices (i.e., cultural capital) of the family inside the home. It also acts as a social sanction if they try to stray from their parents' path. Drawing on this wider consideration of the role of social networks in the reproduction of educational advantage, this chapter considers how the predominately white, upper and middle-class parents of my research drew on their social networks for information and advice about good schools to send their children, and a significant dimension of what constitutes a good school is that children will be socializing with other, mostly white, middle-class children whose parents place a high value on educational and occupational success.

The empirical research in the USA and the UK

Intensive interviews were undertaken with upper middle-class parents in Manchester in the UK (between 1996 and 1997) and Boston, Massachusetts in the USA (between 1998 and 1999) (Devine, 2004a, 2004b, 2005).[6] In total, interviews were conducted with eighty-six parents who had one hundred and sixteen children between them (see Table 7.1). Knowing middle-class reproduction is closely associated with occupations with particular mobility trajectories (Grusky & Weeden, 2006), a decision was made to interview people from two middle-class professions—medicine and teaching—and their partners who were employed in a wide range of occupations. Physicians (or doctors as they are more liked to be called in the UK) were chosen as an example of an established profession known for its high level of occupation inheritance and social closure. In the recent past, it was a very male dominated profession too, although this situation is now changing (Bianchi, 1995). The interviewees occupied a range of positions in hospital settings in both nations and in Community Health Centers in the USA and in General Practices in the UK. Some of them were married to fellow medics although husbands and wives were also social workers, engineers, opticians, teachers, and so on. Teachers (or educators as Americans sometimes say) were chosen as an example of a less established semi-profession known to welcome women. It remains female dominated (Bianchi, 1995;

Table 7.1 The sample of American and British interviewees

	Interviewees	Number of children
American Physicians	12	
American Partners	9	27
American Educators	12	
American Partners	8	28
British Doctors	12	
British Partners	12	33
British Teachers	12	
British Partners	9	28
Total	86	116

Goldin, 1990; Mare, 1995). Interviews were conducted with teachers in state or public schools and in charter schools in the USA and state and private schools in the UK. Again, some of them were married to fellow teachers, although partners were bank lending officers, customer service supervisors, accountants, journalists, and so forth.

The eighty-six interviewees in the USA and the UK were a diverse group of men and women. Most of the US informants were born in the USA including four African-Americans. The sample also included first-generation immigrants/migrants from Puerto Rico, Japan, Sri Lanka, and Britain. Some of the interviewees were second or third generation of families from Ireland and (former) East European countries. It also became apparent during the interviews that a number of the informants were Catholic or Jewish. Most of the UK interviewees were born in Britain although there were also first-generation immigrants/migrants from Ireland, Jamaica, India, and South Africa. Some of them were the second or third generation of families from Ireland, Russia, and former East European countries like Hungary. Again, many of the UK interviewees were Catholic or Jewish. The interviewees from each country, in other words, were quite an ethnically and racially diverse group of people (Chiswick & Sullivan, 1995; Coleman & Salt, 1996; Harrison & Bennett, 1995; Peach, 1996). They were also diverse in their class backgrounds. Some came from long established upper middle-class families whose grandparents were also middle class. Other interviewees came from families new to the middle class in that their parents had enjoyed upward mobility from the working class into professional and managerial jobs. Others still were from working-class backgrounds themselves who had enjoyed long-range social mobility into medicine, teaching, and various other occupations. The heterogeneity of the middle class(es), noted in nationally representative quantitative research, was certainly to be found here (Erikson & Goldthorpe, 1993).

The interviewees had one hundred and sixteen children between them. Most of the families in both countries comprised two or three children. The fifty-five US children ranged in age between six months to twenty-nine years and each interviewee had at least one child currently making their way through the education system. Thus, they were attending public or private elementary schools, middle schools, high schools, universities, liberal arts colleges, and local community colleges. The sixty-one UK children ranged in age between one and thirty-four years although, again, each interviewee had at least one child making their way through the education system. They were to be found in state or private primary schools, secondary schools, sixth form colleges, colleges of further education, and universities. In both countries, some of the older children were trying to establish themselves in the labor market while others were well established in their careers already. There were examples of young people who were in high-level professions like medicine, law, accountancy, and so forth. There were others in lower-level non-manual jobs like youth workers, hotel managers, athletics trainers, travel agents, and billboard designers. Some of the interviewees' children—often the sons and daughters of medics and their partners—were already in the upper middle class. Other young people, invariably the sons and daughters of teachers and their partners, were in the lower levels of the middle classes.

The interviews were conducted either at the interviewees' home or at their workplace. They lasted, on average, approximately two hours. They took the form of life history interviews in which the interviewees were asked about family and childhoods, educational experiences, and work histories. Then the discussion moved on to children, education, and, where applicable, work histories. By talking to the interviewees about their early lives first of all, it was possible to get a sense of how they had *drawn* on family resources before they entered the labor market. The interviewees were, in effect, "children" in these stories reflecting back on how their parents had helped them do well in the education system and enter good jobs in the labor market. It was important to hear about their experiences of education and employment first, and how various opportunities and constraints had shaped their lives. These experiences influenced, in some way, how they now assisted their children. The interviewees then became "parents" as they described how they were *applying* their resources to help their children navigate their way through the school system into employment. For the purposes of this chapter, attention will focus on the US interviewees and how they sought to help their children do well in school and the labor market with particular reference to how they applied their social resources—social networks—in the pursuit of the educational and occupational success of their offspring.

Social networks and US education

The US interviewees drew on their social networks of family, friends, neighbors, and colleagues from work for information and advice about the best academic schools to send their children. They drew on such advice at every stage of their children's education although, unsurprisingly, this advice was most important as children transferred to different schools at various points in their education and choices could be exercised. A number of the medics sent their children to expensive private pre-schools—often Montessori schools—from the age of about three until they were ready for kindergarten at six.[7] Invariably, these informants heard of such schools from their circle of friends who, of course, had the economic resources to send their children to these private pre-schools and shared the same cultural capital regarding their aspirations for their children's early education. Jane Bennett spoke of how,

> We had heard of it [the pre-school] from a number of people, including some people who had twenty-year-old children who had been to that school a long time ago, and they just were very excited about it.

Similarly, Susan Pearson explained,

> My son went to the Montessori school. My daughter went to a co-operative nursery
> school where one parent came in every day to assist. It was excellent. How do you
> choose? You talk to your friends and neighbors who know about it. You jockey for
> position. It's just like trying to get your kids into the Blue Coats or Dulwich. You put
> their name down on the list and you play the game.[8]

With such information and advice being passed around among contacts, it was no
wonder that competition to get into such schools was tough.

Some of the interviewees sent their children to private elementary schools and they
drew on their social networks for advice about school choices. It was the way in which
they established the academic reputation and status of schools. Those who had grown up
in Boston could draw on their childhood knowledge about local schools. They could also
call on the recommendation of siblings and old friends and their experiences of educating
their children at such schools. The interviewees described how they spoke to their friends
and acquaintances about the education of their children. Judy Kennedy and her husband,
who grew up in Boston, clearly sought the help of friends and neighbors in making the
anguished decision to send their sons to private school. As George Marshall said,

> I have friends who have gone through the public school system and most people
> found it very difficult for themselves and their kids. The teachers in the schools were
> pretty uneven and at that time there was a fair amount of violence in the schools. I
> had a friend who did it and she ended up spending a huge amount of time getting
> involved in the schools, to know the schools, to know the teachers, to know which
> school was good for third grade, to know which school was good for fourth grade,
> that kind of thing. Among other things, we didn't have the time to do that.

Under time pressures (Hochschild, 1999; Schor, 1992), it was by talking to other people
about such experiences that they developed a sense of the choices and decisions ahead of
them. The emphasis was on how they were not alone in confronting the "big disarray" of
the public school system.

Of course, the interviewees who sent their children to public elementary schools also
called on the advice of friends and acquaintances in their choice of schools. Indeed, such
help was especially important given variations in the quality of education provided under
the auspices of the public school system in the USA (Brint, 2006; Cookson & Persell,
1985; Kozol, 1991). Close ties and loose connections were important although loose
connections were often most important for the geographically mobile (Fischer, 1982;
Granovetter, 1973/1995). Daniel Lewis, for example, moved from the West Coast to
Boston just before he sent his daughter to kindergarten. As he explained,

> The choice of public schools is based upon where you live and the truth of the matter
> was we looked very carefully as to where we wanted to live as to how the public
> schools were. In fact, one of the physicians I worked with, her brother was teacher at
> a public school in [N] so I talked to him and he was actually wonderful. He said buy
> whatever house you like because all the public schools are excellent here in [N]. So
> he was actually very helpful and that being said, we looked for a house we could
> afford in the neighborhood we liked but we wanted to be some place where we were
> pretty sure of the public schools.

For the mobile in Boston, colleagues from work were an important information source too. Charles Khan spoke of how he acquired information,

> By chatting in the coffee room and most people in medicine, and generally for professionals in this country, they move to suburbia to supposedly the better places for the better schools and better security. The urban violence is a fact of life.

The effect of this advice was that the medics, in particular, were clustered into the most affluent white residential communities in Boston and surrounding cities, educating their children among an elite population in schools with high academic reputations that they ascertained from their various contacts. Indeed, many of the interviewees commented on the fact that their local (overwhelmingly white) neighbors and friends had high aspirations for their children and there was a high level of involvement in schools. Patrick Dutton, for example, explained how his daughter was participating in an experimental school plan in the small affluent town in which they lived and he noted, "It is quite amazing how so many of our friends' children who had the same ethos and drive in education that we did got into that class." Similarly, his wife, Susan, noted,

> There are a lot of committed parents particularly in this district. This is a middle-class white professional town. Go up to [W] and its blue collar and the school system is not so good. It's totally about parent commitment.

It is interesting to note how parent commitment was regarded as the key to success! There were some, however, who were uncomfortable living in this white elite, residentially segregated population (Massey & Denton, 1993). Missing the ethnic and cultural diversity of the West Coast, Anna Gray disliked the predominately white area in which she lived. There were a few high-achieving Asians from India or Sri Lanka who were not seen as "people of color" (Lee, 2005) while African-Americans and Latinos—historically disenfranchised groups of course—were hard to find. She also described how,

> The parents are all motivated and much more involved in the classroom than either of us. . . . There are a lot of women in this area who had major positions who were CEOs of corporations and they have stopped all this to become mommies and they are people who are type A high power. They have got to focus their energy somewhere. They focus it on their kids.

Of course, information and advice about good schools from social networks was also important for those interviewees, primarily the educators and their families, who could not afford to live in such affluent areas. It was a neighbor, for example, who supplied Bernice Hughes with crucial information about a private bussing scheme (Eaton, 2001) that allowed her children to be educated in the suburbs rather than the city. Similarly, Don and Elisabeth Danson lived in his family home in South Boston and their children went to the local elementary school. He explained how his wife had talked to lots of people about the school, her sister had sent her children to the school, and she had been very happy with their education. Finally, Don mentioned,

> They get a good education as it seems that the kids from [T] do better when they first

get to middle school. It seems that way. One of our friends' teachers at one of the other middle schools said if she had it all to do again, she wished she'd sent her kids to [T]. That's always nice to know.

Contacts with fellow teachers, either well known or only known through others, were a crucial source of reassuring information and advice. Indeed, they could provide inside information about schools and their expert knowledge was highly valued because it was personalized and came from friends or friends of friends that they knew and trusted. Interestingly, Elizabeth emphasized the value she and her husband placed on the ethnic and cultural diversity of the schools her children attended and made reference to other middle-class friends who were somewhat afraid of such diversity. She was aware of the ways in which class and race were linked in relation to school choice as has long been noted by Orfield (Kugler & Orfield, 2002).

Social networks were clearly mobilized when the interviewees were confronted with choices of schools as the children progressed from elementary to middle school and/or high school. Again, many of the interviewees observed what their family and friends were doing around them and, more often than not, followed their lead. They shaped their expectations as to what they would do and were a guide as to how to act. Jack Poole, himself privately educated, spoke of how most of "the people I know, they have all sent their children to private high schools." Not surprisingly, he envisaged doing the same, although he and his family lived in one of the most affluent communities with the best high schools in the state. Similarly, his wife, Jane, spoke of how,

> Many people, I think, probably in my position would expect to send their children to private school from beginning to end. The majority of my colleagues, all their children are in private schools.

Interestingly, Jane had enjoyed a good public school education in which she excelled. She appreciated it very much. Nevertheless, she was aware that her husband had been "educationally and academically challenged" at his private school "in a very positive way." She added,

> Now there's no doubt that people meet people of influence in places like private schools and so financially if we are feeling comfortable at that point, it is going to be very tempting to afford them the opportunity that he felt to be very good.

That such schools might facilitate such social networks among their children did not go unrecognized.

The wider, social effects of sending children to particular schools, therefore, were understood and appreciated. Ken Bailey, for example, made some general observations about how the public school system worked in the USA as well as some particular comments about his son's education. At the general level, he was well aware of how the system worked and he knew how to work the system, although he neither emphatically endorsed existing institutional arrangements, nor enthusiastically embraced what he had to do to ensure his children's educational success. As Ken explained,

> It's my firm belief that the town of [L], it's a self-fulfilling prophecy in that families

who are interested in education, who themselves are well educated, who are going to push their kids in school and make sure they do fine, all live in [L]. . . . The kids are basically from families of folks who are doing well professionally and value education.

He also noted that such towns attracted immigrants from South and East Asia—India, Sri Lanka, Korea, and China—who valued education even more and they "leaned" on their children heavily. More specifically, his son had Asian friends who came from highly disciplined households. As he suggested,

> These are the kids that my son plays with. They say "I guess I should do homework." [He thinks] "they're all doing homework, maybe my parents aren't so crazy." If all your friends are watching TV and playing Nintendo, your parents are the crazy ones and they go, "Well, Jimmy's outside, how come I can't play?" Instead, my son goes, "Cheers. I'm glad I'm not doing as much as he is," so it's all compared to your circumstances the way I view it.

It is interesting to note here how Ken drew on stereotypical views of Asians as both disciplined and too disciplined (Lee, 2005, p. 5). This discipline was seen as a positive aspect of their character. Being too disciplined is often seen in a negative light of course. In this context, however, this trait was seen as a virtue rather than a vice. Ken's son saw Ken as a reasonable rather than strict parent and their relations over homework were good as a consequence.

Drawing on their experiences at work, many of the teachers were conscious of the importance of their children socializing with other children whose parents occupied a similar socio-economic status and who valued education and tried to inculcate these values into their children. Linda Chapman, for example, spoke of how,

> You want your kids to be around other kids that are right for them and have the same values because they work very hard. You really want your children to be in a place where other parents value education and they have similar kinds of backgrounds and interests.

Some of the teachers lived in relatively affluent suburbs where they could increase the probability of their children socializing with other such children while others did not. There were downsides, however, to placing your children in the more affluent environments. Ray Chapman was greatly concerned about the limited economic diversity. He spoke of how,

> There are hardly even people that are like the people I grew up with and that makes me nervous for them I think. . . . In fact, one of the things Linda and I find a challenge and work consciously to do is to have them interact with people from a lower social class than we are because I am a little bit worried about attitudes that are drifting in because of the [N] community about what it means to be working class. I kind of self-identify having working-class roots so a respect for people in the trades or who have craft skills that not necessarily involve college. I don't know whether

that lesson will take. I'm more worried about the Mercedes that you get at age sixteen. That's the value gone.

Turning to higher education, all of the interviewees expected their children to go to college and, especially, in the case of medics, to go to some of the top schools including the Ivy League schools. First and foremost, they wanted their children to get into the top schools so that they would enjoy a top-level education that would place them well in the job market. Academic success, in this respect, was crucial. That said, the interviewees also remembered the importance of being around other "high caliber undergraduates, learning from them and socializing with them." They wanted their children to enjoy such "exposure" to other bright people who would go into jobs of importance and become people of importance (i.e., with power). The advantages that might accrue from this resource were appreciated. Don Danson spoke of the importance of friends and contacts met at college or university. As he suggested,

> With a lot of people, you are sort of setting yourself up for life. This doesn't sound quite right but if you make the right contacts it will carry you on through your life.

At the same time, Don acknowledged that the importance of social networks could not be overstated. He pulled back from saying it was the crucial resource in people's lives. As he said,

> OK, I went to [S]. Say, I happen to interview and the guy that interviewed me, maybe, he was alumni [S], he might try to give me a little bit better of an advantage because I am an alumni and then the other guy maybe went to another school down the street. It's that way it would help, but if someone is smart enough or if they get into the right situation, they are going to do well no matter what.

Be that as it may, some of the interviewees' children had expressed a desire to go to an Ivy League or other top school even though some of them were incredibly young to do so. That they knew family and friends that went to such institutions made it familiar rather than a distant aspiration. Gillian Wolkowitz talked about how her daughter, Tina, aged thirteen, was considering such places as Harvard, Brown, and Dartmouth. As she explained,

> She is also interested in Dartmouth because we have a cousin who graduated from Dartmouth, well, a couple of them, but one that she is very close to who is now sailing around the world who really impresses her and has talked oodles about Dartmouth and we went to his graduation.

Her husband, Roy, talked about how their friends acted as "role models" to their daughter. Their friends had influenced Tina's career aspirations to go into law. He said,

> My wife's best friend is a very wealthy lawyer who has a couple of back-to-back beach houses on Long Island. That's where we spend our summers so she gets a first hand look at the lifestyle. She now knows what it takes to go to school and college and to become a lawyer. She has a chance to see what the rewards bring. They have

two big houses. They have a boat, a couple of boats actually. They have cars. They had round the clock help and their idea of summer work is they will come out and spend a week and they will have their faxes and telephones and they do all this business. She's there and hears all this and it's very exciting. Arranging to meet clients and judges from the beach. I think she thinks this is what all lawyers do.

These were the people they socialized with who, in turn, influenced their daughter's high social world and high aspirations.

The interviewees' social networks and their children's emerging networks had a powerful influence, therefore, in shaping their hopes and plans. They were powerful in applying negative as well as positive social pressures, however (Lareau, 1989, 2000, 2003). Financial considerations loomed large for David and Sarah Neale as the eldest daughter, Katy, prepared to go to college. They could not afford the fees to send her to the more prestigious colleges so less reputable institutions had to be considered instead. In the end, Katy successfully obtained a full athletics scholarship at a university in the Mid West. Sarah recalled her daughter's friends "kind of belittled it" because they had not heard of the university and it was not close by on the East Coast. Sarah was "really proud" of how Katy dealt with the situation and delighted that her daughter was now traveling the country and enjoying a variety of experiences. David Neale also spoke of the social pressures on his daughter and how she desperately wanted to follow her friends to some of the more prestigious colleges on the East Coast. He explained,

It was very hard for her. She was really upset about it. [B] is so affluent or whatever. It doesn't look like it's affluent around here and it is not but a lot of her friends are going to great schools or very expensive schools and she was really cognizant of that and there is so much pressure to go to the best school.

This example certainly captured the impact of friends and acquaintances in shaping the expectations and pressures to follow certain educational and occupational pathways on the interviewees' children.

Interestingly, whether as a virtue of necessity or otherwise, David adopted a critical perspective on the social pressures to go to the top schools. He acknowledged the advantages of going to elite institutions like Harvard. That said, he also believed that it was possible to do well elsewhere without spending so much money. David said, "I am the champion of the smaller university. Learn what you can and then challenge those people." Other interviewees adopted a critical stance to the status of such schools. Ken Bailey, again, was of the view that it is "the person that makes the career and not the school you went to." Reputations, after all, were often overrated and should not be accepted unquestioningly. Similarly, many of the interviewees, like Nadia Khan, wondered whether such places offered the best education because it was research fellows and not professors that taught people. The professors certainly did not get to know (and, it followed, not care about) their students. Yet, returning to David Neale, he felt confident about the decision he had to make for his daughter because he could draw on his social networks for reassurance. As he explained,

I'm from the Mid West and I think she has a great opportunity at [K] and she had some good opportunities that are reasonably priced so I think she is better off where she is. I certainly made an executive decision like you are going there but I knew [K]. I knew the school when I worked at [P] because their chemistry department was outstanding and I worked with maybe five or six people who had gone to the university of [K] so I knew it was an outstanding school and good value.

A number of the interviewees' children had gone or were making their way through universities and college courses. None of the teachers' children had attended the most prestigious Ivy League schools, although some had gone to other reputable institutions (such as one of the Seven Sisters women-only colleges) or small private colleges that had a "very decent name." The interviewees talked about how their children choose their university or colleges. Of utmost importance, to be sure, were entry requirements and likely SAT scores. It was, of course, academic credentials that dictated entry to such schools. In addition, the interviewees made reference to the importance they attached to the status or standing of colleges, of particular departments, courses, and so on. Again, the issue of status—academic or otherwise—was established by talking to their friends and acquaintances. Their children did the same. Thus, the social world in which they lived, and the social networks in which parents and children were connected to others, influenced their choices, decisions, and actions. Finally, it should be noted that among the small number of young people finding their feet in the labor market, the influence of social networks—including immediate and extended family and old and new friends—in finding entry-level jobs and temporary work after graduation in difficult labor market conditions was readily apparent. Academic credentials were only part of the story of occupational success.

Conclusion

This chapter has considered the reproduction of class inequalities—and the intersection of class and race inequalities—by addressing the way in which upper middle-class and middle-class parents mobilize their social resources—their social networks of family, neighbors, work colleagues, and friends—to their children's advantage as they make their way through school into the labor market. The focus on the processes by which families mobilize their social resources provides important insights into how class and race inequalities are reproduced over time and space. The empirical material has shown that (predominately white) privileged parents draw on their social networks for information and advice about the best schools to send their children to ensure academic success. Close and loose ties are a shortcut to information and advice so they can exercise choices and make decisions. This information is personalized information and, given it is knowledge shared by other people like themselves—namely: highly educated professional people—it is information and advice they can trust. A crucial component of the use of social networks is that upper middle-class and middle-class children socialize with the children of other such parents who value educational and occupational success. The role of parents in the formation of their children's homogenous advantaged social networks is thereby noted. Overall, the role of social resources—social networks—is crucial to the reproduction of class and race inequalities. It is not a resource of last resort since it is integral to the ways in which parents ensure their children's educational and occupational success. It is also crucial, of course, to the accompanying social distance (Bottero,

2004) that characterizes relations between classes and races in the USA and the UK today.

Questions for discussion

1. What role did schooling play in making the United States a colossus of inequality in the post-1980s era?
2. In Devine's theoretical discussion, she mentions that cultural and social resources are less easily transmitted than economic resources. What is your opinion? Use examples to support your position.
3. Use the concepts—economic, cultural, and social resources/capitals—to reflectively analyze your own life history, particularly by focusing on those relevant to your schooling and occupation.
4. Why is children's socialization with children of similar class backgrounds integral to class reproduction? In what ways are friendship patterns important in life's classed journey? Give examples from your own life.
5. How do the upper-middle and middle-class parents operate their social capital to ensure their children's academic achievement? Compare the cases in this chapter with your own experiences.
6. Why does Devine disagree with Goldthorpe and Bourdieu that social networks are considered only when investments in other capitals have not yielded results?
7. Use the case mentioned by Devine to explain how social networks can reinforce the cultural capital of the family.
8. Is it possible to elevate one's class position through social networks? Or, is it only effective in shaping hopes and future plans?

Notes

1. It is a great shame that the social desirability of old and new professions and occupations is no longer part of class analysis as it was in the past.
2. These theoretical ideas were explored by himself (Goldthorpe, 1996) and with Breen (1999, 2005). Their analysis of class differences in higher education also refuted Saunders' (1995) claims about the UK being a meritocracy. Saunders was much influenced by Herrnstein and Murray's *The Bell Curve* (1994) which was, of course, seriously undermined by the work of Fischer et al. (1996).
3. Bourdieu also talked about a fourth capital: namely, symbolic capital. When the other forms of capital are considered as legitimate, they take the form of symbolic capital. As Skeggs (1997, p. 8) explains with regard to Bourdieu's thinking, "Legitimation is the key mechanism in the conversion to power. Cultural capital has to be legitimated before it can have symbolic power. Capital has to be regarded as legitimate before it can be capitalized upon."
4. It is interesting to remember that Granovetter's study of social networks was originally a study of luck in that he was curious about the debates surrounding Jencks' and his colleagues (1972) study of the impact of socio-economic background on income and their conclusion that luck, not social background, was the key to a high income. This position was subsequently revised to acknowledge the considerable impact of social background on income (Jencks et al., 1979). The huge importance of Granovetter's work on social networks—and the importance of loose over close ties—for understanding the social embeddedness of economic life has been much appreciated since (Granovetter, 1985, 1995).

5. There is, in fact, considerable overlap in the ways in which Bourdieu and Coleman define cultural and social capital. Coleman's discussion of social capital in the family is remarkably similar to Bourdieu's concept of cultural capital (Bourdieu & Coleman, 1991). Swartz (1997) and Swartz and Zolberg (2004) provide an excellent discussion of Bourdieu's work on class as does Weininger's (2006) recent work.
6. The way in which the British and Americans talk about class is quite different and I have considered this issue elsewhere (Devine, 2004b). Briefly, the British usually define themselves as working class or middle class. Americans rarely use the term working class and call themselves middle class although they make distinctions between the lower middle class, middle class and upper middle class. The British would consider both doctors and teachers as middle class, while Americans would consider physicians as upper middle class and educators as middle class. For the purposes of this chapter, where I focus on the US interviewees, I refer to the middle and upper middle classes.
7. Montessori schools—originating from the work of Maria Montessori, a medical doctor who taught disadvantaged children in Rome, Italy in the late nineteenth and early twentieth centuries (Standing, 1998)—were highly regarded by a number of the interviewees. These informants subscribed to the Montessori philosophy of fostering the full potential of children with its specific focus on the needs of each individual child. They subscribed to Montessori's theory of child development and its child centered approach. What was especially valued was the emphasis on freedom and self-development within a planned and structured environment to produce confident and capable children well equipped to meet the demands of the future. There is a certain irony that a model of child development and education arising out of research with disadvantaged children has been taken with such gusto by parents of advantaged children.
8. Dulwich College, which is now an expensive independent private boys' school in South London, was established in 1619 to educate a small number of poor boys to realize their potential. Designed for the poor, it has become a highly sought after school by the rich. Similarly, the UK's system of Blue Coat schools, which are scattered around the country, was designed for children from modest homes who could be educated in ways to make them well-rounded personalities who could cope with life's challenges. Again, these schools have been especially popular with privileged parents anxious for their children to enjoy the philosophy of learning and knowledge that underpins the educational principles of these schools.

References

Bianchi, S. M. (1995). Changing economic roles of women and men. In R. Farley (Ed.), *State of the union: Volume one: Economic trends*. New York: Russell Sage Foundation.

Bottero, W. (2004). *Stratification: Social division and inequality*. London: Routledge.

Bourdieu, P. (1984). *Distinction*. London: Routledge.

—— (1986). The forms of capital. In J. E. Richardson (Ed.), *Handbook of theory of research for the sociology of education*. London: Tavistock.

—— (1987). What makes a social class?: On the theoretical and practical existence of groups. *Berkeley Journal of Sociology, 32*, 1–8.

Bourdieu, P., & Coleman, J. S. (Eds.). (1991). *Social theory for a changing society*. Boulder, CO: Westview Press.

Bradbury, K., & Katz, J. (2004). *Wives' work and family income mobility*. Federal Reserve Bank of Boston Series, Paper No. 04–3.

Breen, R. (2005). Why did class inequalities in educational attainment remain unchanged over much of the twentieth century? In A. F. Heath, J. Ermisch & D. Gallie (Eds.), *Understanding social change*. Oxford: Oxford University Press.

Breen, R., & Goldthorpe, J. H. (1999). Class inequality and meritocracy: A critique of Saunders and an alternative analysis. *British Journal of Sociology, 50*, 1–27.

Brint, S. (2006). *Schools and societies* (2nd ed.). Stanford, CA: Stanford University Press.

Chiswick, R. R., & Sullivan, T. A. (1995). The new immigrants. In R. Farley (Ed.), *State of the union: Volume two: Social trends*. New York: Russell Sage Foundation.

Coleman, J. (1994). *Foundations of social theory*. Cambridge, MA: Harvard University Press.

Coleman, J. S. (1988). Social capital in the creation of human capital. *American Journal of Sociology, 94*, 95–120.

Coleman, J. S., & Salt, J. (Eds.). (1996). *Ethnicity in the 1991 census, volume 1*. London: OPCS.

Cookson, P. W., & Persell, C. H. (1985). *Preparing for power*. New York: Basic Books.

Correspondents of *The New York Times* (2005). *Class matters*. New York: Henry Hold and Company.

Devine, F. (2004a). *Class practices: How parents help their children get good jobs*. Cambridge: Cambridge University Press.

—— (2004b). Talking about class in Britain. In F. Devine & M. C. Waters (Eds.), *Social inequalities in comparative perspective*. Oxford: Blackwell Publishing.

—— (2005). Middle-class identities in the United States. In F. Devine, M. Savage, J. Scott & R. Crompton (Eds.), *Rethinking class, culture, identities and lifestyles*. Basingstoke: Palgrave.

Eaton, S. E. (2001). *The Other Boston Busing Story*. New Haven, CT: Yale University Press.

Erikson, R., & Goldthorpe, H. E. (1993). *The constant flux*. Oxford: Clarendon Press.

Fischer, C. S. (1982). *To dwell among friends*. Chicago: University of Chicago Press.

Fischer, C. S., et al. (1996). *Inequality by design*. Princeton, NJ: Princeton University Press.

Goldin, C. (1990). *Understanding the gender gap*. New York: Oxford University Press.

Goldthorpe, J. H. (1980) (in collaboration with C. Llewellyn and C. Payne). *Social mobility and class structure in modern Britain*. Oxford: Clarendon Press.

—— (1987) (in collaboration with C. Llewellyn and C. Payne). *Social mobility and class structure in modern Britain* (2nd ed.). Oxford: Clarendon Press.

—— (1996). Class analysis and the reorientation of class theory: The case of persisting differentials in educational attainment. *British Journal of Sociology, 47*, 481–505.

—— (2000). *On Sociology*. Oxford: Oxford University Press.

Granovetter, M. (1973). *Getting a job*. Chicago: University of Chicago Press.

—— (1985). Economic action and social structure: The problem of embeddedness. *American Journal of Sociology, 91*, 481–510.

—— (1995). *Getting a job* (2nd ed.). Chicago: University of Chicago Press.

Grusky, D. B., & Weeden, K. (2006). Does the sociological approach to studying social mobility have a future? In S. L. Morgan, D. B. Grusky & G. S. Fields (Eds.), *Mobility and inequality*. Stanford, CA: Stanford University Press.

Harrison, R. J., & Bennett, C. E. (1995). Racial and ethnic diversity. In R. Farely (Ed.), *State of the union: Volume 2: Social trends*. New York: Russell Sage Foundation.

Herrnstein, R. J., & Murray, C. (1994). *The bell curve*. New York: The Free Press.

Hochschild, A. R. (1989). *The second shift*. New York: Avon.

Hout, M. (1988). Expanding universalism, less structural mobility: The American occupational structure in the 1980s. *American Journal of Sociology, 93*, 1358–1400.

Hout, M., Raftery, A. D., & Bell, E. O. (1993). Making the grade: Educational stratification in the United States: 1925–89. In Y. Shavit & H.-P. Blossfeld (Eds.), *Persistent inequalities: Changing inequalities in 13 countries*. Boulder, CO: Westview.

Jencks, C., et al. (1972). *Who gets ahead?* New York: Basic Books.

—— (1979). *Inequality*. New York: Basic Books.

Kozol, J. (1991). *Savage inequalities*. New York: Crown Publications.

Kugler, E. G., & Orfield, G. (2002). *Debunking the middle-class myth: Why diverse schools are good for all kids*. London: Rowan and Littlefield.

Lareau, A. (1989). *Home advantage*. New York: The Falmer Press.

—— (2000). *Home advantage* (revised ed.). New York: Rowman and Littlefield.

—— (2003). *Unequal childhoods: Class, race and family life*. Berkeley, CA: University of California Press.

Lee, S. J. (2005). *Up against whiteness: Race, school and immigrant youth*. New York: Teachers College Press.

Mare, R. D. (1995). Changes in educational attainment and school enrolment. In R. Farley (Ed.), *State of the union: Volume 1: Economic trends*. New York: Russell Sage Foundation.

Massey, D. S., & Denton, N. A. (1993). *American apartheid*. Cambridge, MA: Harvard University Press.

Morgan, S. L., Grusky, D. B., & Fields, G. S. (Eds.). (2006). *Mobility and inequality*. Stanford, CA: Stanford University Press.

Peach, C. (Ed.). (1996). *Ethnicity in the 1991 census, volume 2*. London: OPCS.

Saunders, P. (1995). Might Britain be a meritocracy? *Sociology, 29*, 23–41.

Schor, J. B. (1992). *The overworked American*. Cambridge, MA: Harvard University Press.

Scott, J., & Leonhardt, D. (2005). Class in America: Shadowy lines that still divide. *The New York Times*, May 15, p. A1 ff.

Skeggs, B. (1997). *Formations of class and gender: Becoming respectable*. London: Sage.

Standing, E. M. (1998). *Maria Monetessori: Her life and work*. New York: Penguin.

Swartz, D. L. (1997). *Culture and power*. Chicago: Chicago University Press.

Swartz, D. L., & Zolberg, V. L. (Eds.). (2004). *After Bourdieu: Influence, critique, elaboration*. Dordrecht: Kluwer Academic Publishers.

Weininger, E. B. (2006). Foundations of Pierre Bourdieu's class analysis. In E. O. Wright (Ed.), *Approaches to class analysis*. Cambridge: Cambridge University Press.

Chapter 8

Watching, waiting, and deciding when to intervene

Race, class, and the transmission of advantage

Annette Lareau[*]

The intersection of race and class is an important, but somewhat vexing, subject for sociologists. While it is widely agreed, for example, that members of the black middle class draw on their class resources in confronting the experience of racial discrimination, the actual benefit that class confers has often been presumed. There are few studies that demonstrate how class works in the rituals of daily life.

In this chapter, I use data collected using ethnographic methods, including family observations, to argue that while black middle-class families face unique problems in child rearing, in the sense that they face problems that are not confronted by white middle-class families in raising children, they draw on a set of *generic* class resources in the management of these problems. In particular, I suggest that black *and* white middle-class families draw on a similar set of generic class resources. In their interactions with institutions, there are three important ways that social class appears to matter: first, middle-class parents presume that they are entitled to have the institution accommodate to their child's individualized needs. Second, middle-class parents feel comfortable voicing their concerns with people in positions of authority. Third, middle-class parents across race appear to be willing and able to climb the hierarchy of authority to pursue their interests. Due to the response of professionals working in these institutions, in some instances there are signs that the class resources of parents produce profits, although the actual long-term implications can only, in this particular study, be a matter of speculation.

My book *Unequal Childhoods* (2003) identifies the largely invisible but powerful ways that parents' social class impacts children's life experiences.[1] It shows, using in-depth observations and interviews with middle-class (including members of the upper-middle-class), working-class, and poor families, that inequality permeates the fabric of the culture. In *Unequal Childhoods*, I argue that key elements of family life cohere to form a cultural logic of child rearing. As professionals have shifted their recommendations from bottle-feeding to breast-feeding, from stern approaches to warmth and empathy, and from spanking to time-outs, it is middle-class parents who have responded most promptly.[2] Moreover, in recent decades, middle-class children in the United States have had to face the prospect of "declining fortunes."[3] Worried about how their children will get ahead, middle-class parents are increasingly determined to make sure that their children are not excluded from any opportunity that might eventually contribute to their

* Annette Lareau teaches in the Department of Sociology at the University of Maryland, College Park.

advancement. Middle-class parents who comply with current professional standards and engage in what I call a pattern of "concerted cultivation" deliberately try to stimulate their children's development and foster their cognitive and social skills.

This chapter, then, seeks to highlight the importance of class resources in the lives of middle-class black children. It would be a mistake, however, to suggest that race did not matter in children's lives. There were important aspects of daily life that were profoundly shaped by race including racial segregation in the housing of their neighborhoods as well as street encounters, i.e. where black fathers reported receiving insults in interpersonal exchanges. Nevertheless, the role of race was less powerful than I had expected. In terms of the areas focused on in *Unequal Childhoods*—how children spend their time, the way parents use language and discipline in the home, the nature of the families' social connections, and the strategies used for intervening in institutions—white and black parents engaged in very similar, often identical, practices with their children.[4] As the children age, the relative importance of race in their daily lives is likely to increase.[5] In fourth grade (the targeted grade in this study), however, in very central ways, race mattered less in children's daily lives than did their social class.

In the theoretical language of Pierre Bourdieu, both black and white middle-class parents, and mothers in particular, routinely scanned the horizon for opportunities to activate their cultural capital and social capital on behalf of their children.[6] By shrewdly framing their interventions in ways that institutions such as schools and public and private recreational programs found compatible with their organizational processes, parents could gain important advantages for their children. By teaching their daughters and sons how to get organizations to meet their individualized needs, white and black middle-class mothers pass along skills that have the potential to be extremely valuable to their children in adulthood. These are class-based advantages.

Methodology of *Unequal Childhoods*

The larger study presented in *Unequal Childhoods* is based on intensive "naturalistic" observations of twelve families (six white, five black, and one interracial) with children nine and ten years old. With the help of white and black research assistants, I carried out interviews first with the mothers and then with many of the fathers of these children from middle-class, working-class, and poor families (Table 8.1). To better understand the expectations that professionals had of parents, I also interviewed the children's classroom teachers and other school personnel. Emerging from this data are class-based patterns in the pace and behaviors of everyday life. Although this chapter centers almost exclusively on a discussion of middle-class families, *Unequal Childhoods* tells us that working-class and poor families have very different relationships to institutions: relationships that are characterized by distance, distrust, and dependence.[7] In great contrast to middle-class families in this study, when working-class and poor children confronted institutions they generally were unable to make the rules work in their favor, nor did they obtain capital for adulthood; however, because of patterns of legitimization, children raised according to the logic of concerted cultivation can gain advantages, in the form of an emerging sense of entitlement. In *Unequal Childhoods* I demonstrate the cultural logic of childrearing that tends to differ according to families' social class positions (Table 8.2). In contrast to many, I suggest that social class does have a powerful impact in shaping the daily rhythms of family life.

Methodological Overview of Study

Interview study

- Classroom observations in three public schools (one predominantly white suburban school in the northeast, one racially mixed city school in the northeast, and one midwestern school in a small city)
- In-depth interviews with mothers and fathers of 88 children whose children were nine and ten
- Most of the families came from three schools; the remaining children (especially white poor and black middle-class) came from social service programs or informal networks
- Most of the data collected 1993–1995 but some earlier and later
- Interviews with educators and other school personnel

Family observations of 12 families

- Usually 20 visits, usually *daily* in the space of one month
- Most visits lasted two to three hours but sometimes longer
- One overnight visit
- Families were paid, generally $350, at the end of the study
- Worked in racially diverse teams of two or three, sharing visits to the families
- Nine of the 12 families (but neither of the black middle-class families) came from the classrooms where we did observations; response rate of people we asked was 61% (i.e., we asked 19 to get 12)

Doing the fieldwork

- No question that we were disruptive but families adjusted
- Yelling and cursing increased, especially on the third and tenth days
- Went with families to children's organized activities and other events
- Children generally liked our visits, said it made them feel "special"
- We often carried tape recorders with us, used in writing fieldnotes
- Research assistants usually spoke with me (or in a few cases a project manager) after every field visit to provide support and guidance in writing up field notes

---

It is from this larger study that I provide details on one black middle-class family to present a small piece of the overall argument, but the steps that this family took to activate their middle-class resources and intervene in their children's lives through institutions were very similar, in some ways indistinguishable, from the actions of other middle-class families, whether white or black. To offer just one example, the Kaplan family, a white middle-class family where the mother is a psychologist and the father is a doctor, were upset about the lyrics in a school holiday song. Early in the fall of their son's fourth grade year, Mr. and Ms. Kaplan learned that the school choir would be singing a Christian song entitled "Glad Tidings" which included the line, "come let us bow and worship Him now." This line offended the Kaplans (who happened to be Jewish), not for religious reasons, but because these lyrics seemed to blur the distinction between church and state.[8]

The Kaplans activated a formidable array of class resources over this matter. First, Ms. Kaplan spoke with the choir teacher about it, but the choir teacher did not take it seriously and, instead, stressed the diversity of the choir program (which included a Hanukkah song). Second, not dissuaded, Ms. Kaplan took her concern to the principal who also rebuffed her, noting that it "was only a song." Still, the educators offered to have their son sit it out. But the Kaplans were not satisfied with this response since they felt it singled out their son unfairly. They subsequently wrote a letter to the Superintendent asking for a district review of policies on this matter. The Superintendent

Table 8.1 Distribution of children in the study by social class and race

Social class	White	African-American	Total
Middle class[1]	Garret Tallinger Melanie Handlon	Alexander Williams	
	Study total: 18	Study total: 18	Study total: 36
Working class[2]	Wendy Driver Danny Yanelli	Jessica Irwin[4] Tyrec Tayor	
	Study total: 14	Study total: 12	Study total: 26
Families in poverty[3]	Katie Brindle Karl Greeley	Tara Carroll Harold McAllister	
	Study total: 12	Study total: 14	Study total: 26
Total	Study total: 44	Study total: 44	Study total: 88

Notes

Study total figures for each cell include the children named in the cell.

[1] Middle-class children are those whose households have at least one parent who is employed in a position with a significant amount of occupational autonomy, usually in a professional or managerial position, and who has a college degree.

[2] Working-class children are those whose households have at least one parent who is employed in a position with limited occupational autonomy, usually in a skilled or semi-skilled position. Parents' educational level may be high school drop-out, high school graduate, or may include some college courses, often at a community college. This category includes lower-level white collar workers.

[3] Poor children are those whose households have parents who are on public assistance and do not have steady participation in the labor force. Most of these parents are high school drop-outs or high school graduates.

[4] Child is biracial.

consulted the district lawyer and, in the end, wrote them a letter reporting back that he "counseled" the principal on the matter. No one heard "Glad Tidings" that holiday season. In taking these three steps—feeling entitled to request the school make an accommodation to their child's individualized need, challenging people in positions of authority, and pursuing the matter up the hierarchy of command—the Kaplans drew on resources directly connected to their class position, including their educational background and occupational conditions.

It is these social class resources that, as I show in the case of the Marshall family, also appear to be of value to black middle-class parents as they monitor and intervene in their children's experiences in institutions outside the home.

Spinning profits from capital

Mr. and Ms. Marshall and their two girls, Fern (12) and Stacey (10), live (along with two guinea pigs, Scratch and Tiny) on a very quiet, circular street lined with large, recently built, two-story suburban homes with a market value of about $200,000 each.

Ms. Marshall is a college graduate and also holds a Master's degree in computer science. Employed full time in the computer industry, she telecommutes one day per week. Like his wife, Mr. Marshall has a college degree and was very active in his

Table 8.2 Typology of differences in childrearing

	Childrearing approach	
	Concerted cultivation (middle-class families)	Accomplishment of natural growth (working-class and poor families)
Key elements	Parent actively fosters and assesses child's talents, opinions, and skills	Parent cares for child and allows child to grow spontaneously
Organization of daily life	– multiple child leisure activities orchestrated by adults	– child "hangs out" particularly with kin
Language use	– reasoning/directives – child contestation of adult statements – extended negotiations between parents and child	– directives – rare for child to question or challenge adults – general acceptance by child of directives
Interventions in institutions	– criticisms and interventions on behalf of child – training of child to take on this role	– dependence on institutions – sense of powerlessness and frustrations – conflict between childrearing practices at home and at school
Consequences	Emerging sense of entitlement on the part of the child	Emerging sense of constraint on the part of the child

fraternity as an undergraduate. He is employed as a civil servant. Although the Marshalls' income is around $100,000 per year, the family, especially Ms. Marshall, often worries about money and being downsized as some of her colleagues have been.

The Marshalls' well-to-do, racially integrated, suburban neighborhood constitutes a transitional area. It is near the boundary with the central city and with a large, all-black middle-class area; on the other side lies a predominantly white residential area. The racial balance of the girls' daily lives (and of their parents' lives, as well) varies across settings. Stacey and Fern attend a local public school that is part of a district known for having good schools; most of the families in the district are white but about one-quarter are black, and there is a sprinkling of Asian and Hispanic families. During the school year, Stacey and Fern spend much of the day in classes for gifted students, the majority of whom are white.[9] The beauty parlor where the girls go on many Saturdays is all black. The church the family attends is all black. But most of the children and adults in the girls' organized activities, including gymnastics and summer camp, are predominantly white.

The family is busy. The hectic pace of their lives is similar to other middle-class families we observed as well as to signs of an increase in organized activities from national data. Not unlike other middle-class families in the study (Table 8.3), the Marshalls' lives are frenetic as is demonstrated in the girls' list of activities (Table 8.4).

Stacey is active in gymnastics. Fern is active in basketball. Both girls attend Sunday school; Stacey is in the church youth choir, which rehearses on Friday nights and performs every third Sunday. Both girls are "junior ushers" at church. Each girl often has three or four events per week during the school year. During the summer, the girls move

Table 8.3 Participation in activities outside of school: Boys

	Activities organized by adults	Informal activities
Middle class		
Garrett Tallinger (white)	Soccer team Traveling soccer team Baseball team Basketball team (summer) Swim team Piano Saxophone (through school)	Plays with siblings in yard Watches television Plays computer games Overnights with friends
Alexander Williams (black)	Soccer team Baseball team Choir Church choir Sunday school Piano (Suzuki) School plays Guitar (through school)	Restricted television Plays outside occasionally with two other boys Visits friends from school
Working class		
Billy Yanelli (white)	Baseball team	Watches television Visits relatives Rides bike Plays outside in the street Hangs out with neighborhood kids
Tyrec Taylor (black)	Football team Vacation bible school Sunday school (off/on)	Watches television Plays outside in the street Rides bike with neighborhood boys Visits relatives Goes to swimming pool
Poor		
Karl Greeley (white)	Goes to swimming pool Walks dogs with neighbor	Watches television Plays Nintendo Plays with siblings
Harold McAllister (black)	Bible study in neighbor's house (occasionally) Bible camp (1 week)	Visits relatives Plays ball with neighbor children Watches television Watches videos

Table 8.4 Participation in activities outside of school: Girls

	Activities organized by adults	Informal activities
Middle class		
Melanie Handlon (white)	Girl Scouts Piano Sunday school Church Church pageant Violin (through school) Softball team	Restricted television Plays outside with children in the neighborhood Bakes cookies with mother Swims (not on swim team) Listens to music
Stacey Marshall (black)	Gymnastics lessons Gymnastic teams Church Sunday school Youth choir	Watches television Plays outside Visits friends from school Rides bike
Working class		
Wendy Driver (white)	Catholic education (CCD) Dance lessons School choir	Watches television Visits relatives Does housework Rides bike Plays outside in the street Hangs out with cousins
Jessica Irwin (black father/ white mother)	Church Sunday school Saturday art class School band	Restricted television Reads Plays outside with neighborhood children Visits relatives
Poor		
Katie Brindle (white)	School choir Friday evening church group (rarely)	Watches television Visits relatives Plays with Barbies Rides bike Plays with neighborhood children
Tara Carroll (black)	Church Sunday school	Watches television Visits relatives Plays with dolls Plays Nintendo Plays with neighborhood children

from one elaborate summer camp to another (e.g., gymnastics camp, basketball camp, and horseback riding camp). Finding out about activities, assessing their suitability, meeting enrollment deadlines, and coordinating transportation is a time-consuming act of labor. In most homes, it is mothers, not fathers, who do this work. Although Mr. Marshall will share in the driving if requested, Mr. and Ms. Marshall agree that it is overwhelmingly Ms. Marshall who handles the girls' lives and their activities, as well as any complaints about Fern's or Stacey's institutional experiences.

Interventions in institutions

Social class seemed to make a difference in how parents, primarily mothers, managed children's complaints about institutions. Middle-class mothers were often very interventionist, assertively intervening in situations. Sometimes parents were successful, and sometimes they were not. But in the process, they directly taught their children how "not to take no for an answer" and to put pressure on persons in positions of power in institutions to accommodate their needs.

As the children went through their lives, problems surfaced. Stacey, for example, was not admitted to the gifted program (she missed the cut-off by two points). Fern enjoyed basketball camp but did not have anyone to sit with at lunch. Unlike working-class and poor parents, who tended to grant their children autonomy in these settings, Ms. Marshall—along with other white and black middle-class parents—took an energetic and active role in overseeing her daughters' lives. In small, brief, but instrumental encounters, Ms. Marshall shepherded her daughters through institutions. For the gifted program, for example, she found out that the school district would accept scores from private testing, located someone to do the testing, paid $200, took the scores back to the district, and, even though Stacey still was just below the cut-off for admission, talked to the administrator about it. Stacey was admitted to the gifted program. Ms. Marshall's belief that she has the right and the responsibility to intervene in the classroom is widely shared by middle-class parents, mothers in particular. At Swan, the middle-class, predominantly white suburban school where the research assistants and I carried out classroom observations, the teachers noted that parents frequently came barging into school to complain about minor matters. For example, a scheduling conflict that resulted in some third-graders not getting a chance to perform a skit for their peers in the other third-grade classrooms prompted three different mothers to come in to school the very next morning to let the teacher know how disappointed their children were and to inquire into exactly why some children had gotten the opportunity to perform and others had not.

Not unlike other middle-class parents then, when Ms. Marshall becomes aware of a problem, she moves quickly, drawing on her work and professional skills and experiences to remedy a perceived inequity. She displays tremendous assertiveness, doggedness, and in some cases effectiveness in pressing institutions to recognize her daughters' individualized needs. Stacey's mother's proactive stance reflects her belief that she has a duty to intervene in situations in which she perceives that her daughter's needs are not being met. This is clear in the way she handles Stacey's transition from her township gymnastics classes to the private gymnastic classes at Wright's. Stacey had been very successful in a township gymnastics program and, at the encouragement of her instructor, and as a result of her mother's search efforts, she enrolled at a private gymnastic club called

Wright's. Yet, Stacey's transition from her township gymnastics classes to the private classes at Wright's was not easy: the first session at the club was rocky, as Ms. Marshall describes:

> The girls were not warm. And these were little . . . eight and nine-year-old kids. You know, they weren't welcoming her the first night. It was kinda like eyeing each other, to see, you know, "Can you do this? Can you do that?"

More importantly, Ms. Marshall reported that the instructor is brusque, critical, and not friendly toward Stacey. Ms. Marshall cannot hear what was being said, but she could see the interactions through a window. A key problem is that Stacey does not know specific terms for skills since her previous instructor had not taught them to her. As Ms. Marshall says,

> Suddenly, the first day in [gymnastics] class, everything that Stacey did, you know, uh, . . . Even, even though she was doing a skill, it was like, "Turn your feet this way," or . . . "Do your hands this way." You know, nothing was very, very good or nothing was good, or even then just right. She [Tina, the instructor who Ms. Marshall believes to be of Hispanic descent] had to alter just about everything [Stacey did]. I [Ms. Marshall] was somewhat furious. . . .

When the class ends and she walks out, Stacey is visibly upset. Her mother's reaction is a common one among middle-class parents: She does not remind her daughter that in life one has to adjust, that she will need to work even harder, or that there is nothing to be done. Instead, Ms. Marshall focuses on Tina, the instructor, as the source of the problem, as Ms. Marshall says:

> We sat in the car for a minute and I said, "Look, Stac," I said. She said, "I—I," and she started crying. I said, "You wait here." The instructor had come to the door, Tina. So I went to her and I said, "Look." I said, "Is there a problem?" She said, "Aww . . . she'll be fine. She just needs to work on certain things." Blah-blah-blah. And I said, "She's really upset. She said you-you-you [were] pretty much correcting just about everything." And [Tina] said, "Well, she's got—she's gotta learn the terminology."

Ms. Marshall acknowledges that Stacey isn't familiar with specialized and technical gymnastics terms. Nonetheless, she continues to defend her daughter in her discussion with the gymnastics instructor:

> I [Ms. Marshall] do remember, I said to her, I said, "Look, maybe it's not all the student." You know, I just left it like that. That, you know, sometimes teaching, learning and teaching, is a two-way proposition as far as I'm concerned. And sometimes teachers have to learn how to, you know, meet the needs of the kid. Her style, her immediate style was not accommodating to—to Stacey.

Here Ms. Marshall is asserting the legitimacy of an individualized approach to instruction. She frames her opening remark as a question ("Is there a problem?"). Her purpose, however, is to alert the instructor to the negative impact she has had on Stacey ("She's really upset"). Although her criticism is indirect ("Maybe it's not all the student . . ."), Ms. Marshall makes it clear that she expects her daughter to be treated differently in the future. In this case, Stacey does not hear what her mother says, but knows that her wishes and feelings are being transmitted to the instructor in a way that she, as a young girl, could not do herself.

Moreover, in what is a common procedure in the Marshall home, Stacey's mother pursued the problem. The very next morning she called the gymnastics school and spoke with the owner. She asked (having first checked with Stacey) that her daughter be moved to the Advanced Beginner class. That class, however, was already full. In many organizations, Stacey would have had to stay in the intermediate class. In this case, the owner accommodated the mother and daughter, assigning a second instructor to the Advanced Beginner class so that Stacey could join that group. So, through this series of institutional interactions, Stacey Marshall gets access to a gymnastics class better suited to her skill and experience level. In another instance, construction was taking place in the gym where the gymnastics summer camp was being held; as a result, the space was reduced and safety concerns were raised. Ms. Marshall called the regional office of the YMCA to inquire if there were any standard guidelines on the matter and ended up speaking with the director. In other areas, however, Ms. Marshall was much more hesitant. During the period of our observations, Ms. Marshall was agonizing over the proper gymnastics setting for Stacey. Stacey had left Wright's recently and was planning to take part in a Y program but that program turned out to be less attractive than originally believed. Ms. Marshall appeared to turn this problem over in her mind (i.e., should Stacey go back to Wright's or go to another township program even further away). She toured the facilities with Stacey and generally fretted about what to do. Thus, as with other problems that I discuss below, sometimes Ms. Marshall watched, waited, and wondered what to do before deciding upon a course of action. Ms. Marshall is a conscientious role model for Stacey, deliberately teaching her daughter strategies for managing organizational matters. Although it is hard to know how much Stacey absorbs her mother's lessons in how to deal effectively with people in positions of power in organizations, or how much she might draw on those lessons in the future, exposure to such learning as a child has the potential to be a tremendous lifelong asset.[10]

All families interact with an array of institutions. For middle-class mothers, the boundaries between home and institutions are fluid; mothers cross back and forth, mediating their children's lives. When Ms. Marshall discovered how unhappy Stacey was after her first gymnastics class in a private program, she did not hesitate to intervene. Almost seamlessly, the daughter's problem became the mother's problem. Ms. Marshall firmly believed that it was her responsibility as a parent to ensure that Stacey's activities provided an opportunity for positive, self-affirming experiences. Like other middle-class mothers we observed, Ms. Marshall acted like a guardian angel, hovering over her children, closely monitoring their everyday lives, ever ready to swoop down to intervene in institutional settings such as classrooms, doctors' offices, or day camps.

Middle-class parents' interventions on behalf of their children can produce a twofold advantage. The children's interactions with teachers, health-care professionals, and camp counselors become more personalized, more closely tailored to meet their specific needs. Just as important, the children expect this individualization, and they begin to acquire a vocabulary and orientation toward institutions that will be useful in the future, when they come to extract advantages on their own behalf.

Transmission of advantage to children

The benefits that Stacey gains are not, however, simply in the experiences she has in these settings. Instead, she also learns by observing her mother's actions that it is reasonable to expect organizations to accommodate the specialized needs of an individual. And, her mother directly trains her.

Problems continued to surface with the coaching staff at Wright's Gymnastic Club. Stacey, although quite talented in her gymnastics, has been unable to execute one key movement on the parallel bars called a kip, which is seen as a major impediment to her advancement. The last straw came when Stacey, arriving home from the gym on a day when her father has picked her up, announces, "She [Tina] told me I'm lazy." This leads Ms. Marshall and Stacey to decide that Stacey should decline the invitation she received to be part of the club's elite gymnastics team. In so doing, Ms. Marshall teaches Stacey that she has the right to turn down such a coveted spot. Moreover, she explicitly trains her daughter, in a way that a manager might prepare for an important meeting, to think through her response to Tina ahead of time:

> Before Stacey went to the next class, I said, "What are you gonna to say to them, if they ask you why?" And she said, "I'm . . ." You know, I said, "I think you better sit down and think about it." 'Cause, I said, "They might ask you." And sure enough, they did. Um . . . 'cause, and we talked about it. I said, I said, "It might be feasible for you to just say that you just decided that you weren't ready for it." You know. And leave it at that.

The response from the instructor to Stacey's prepared statement serves to further antagonize Ms. Marshall:

> I remember Stacey came out that night from class, and she—she got in, crying. She said, "You were right. She did ask me." And I said, "Well, what did you say?" She said, "We told 'em that I just didn't think I was ready for it." And I said, "Well, what did they say?" She said, "Tina just went Humm" [said in a disdainful, haughty voice]. You know, like that. And here I'm thinking to myself, well, I don't really think that was appropriate.

Ms. Marshall was dissatisfied with how the coach handled the matter. Thus she was unable to avoid difficulties in the institutional experience of her daughter. What she did do, however, was transmit to Stacey and Fern a sense of entitlement in their encounters. She taught them to strategize, rehearse their replies in advance, and critically assess the stance of people in positions of authority. Other middle-class families we observed, and interviewed, appeared to take similar stances.

Too often, sociologists focus on the presence or absence of resources. This approach, however, fails to acknowledge that individuals are strategic in their use of valuable, and scarce, resources. In the families in this study, middle-class parents often had many more concerns than they raised with adults working with their children. Put differently, they were *selective* in their activation of capital. Ms. Marshall reflected on the possibility that subtle forms of discrimination were in play, including the gymnastic club and in Fern's summer camp, but did not intervene; in an instance with Art the bus driver, however, she watched and waited but then ultimately did call the district office to complain.

Selective activation of capital: Watching, waiting, and deciding to intervene

Ms. Marshall grew up in a southern community where, for example, swimming pools were racially segregated when she was a child. She knows from personal experience that "subtle forms of discrimination are always present" and says,

> Any time something happens, with my kids, you know, . . . on a sports team or whatever, in the classroom. I have to kinda grapple with . . . is, well, is race an issue?

Because the *potential* for racial discrimination is always present, isolating race as the key factor in a specific situation can be hard. In some instances, as with the Wright gymnastic program, Ms. Marshall worried about it privately but in a complicated mixture of ambivalence, second guessing, and insecurity did not come to any resolution:

> [if] she's [Tina] [is saying things to Stacey] because this is a little black kid. You know, that . . . she's not gonna do it [become a star performer]. However . . . they [have] had minority kids who had risen to the top there. So it's not an issue of the entire team is white [or that] my kid would never get on it. That's not true. If my kid was good enough, I—I think they would, I—I'm pretty sure that they'd let her on it. You know, primarily because the goal is to win. You know, and if you're black, red, yellow, green, they would put their kid on the team . . . because they want to win.

Similarly, when Fern feels excluded from the camaraderie at her basketball camp (where she is the only black child among about one hundred girls), Ms. Marshall again hesitates, pondering what the best response might be.

> Fern came home one day and she was talkin' to Stacey about it. She . . . I said, "How are things?" She said, "Fine," she said, "except for lunch." I said, "Who'd you eat with?" "Myself." [deep sigh from Ms. Marshall]

Fern sees it as a racial issue:

> Fern said, "You know." I said, "Well, did you talk to 'em?" She said, "Yeah, I talked to them." . . . Apparently there was dialogue . . . about who scored in the game . . . and they were doing things, but when it came time for lunch—she ended up at a table by herself. . . . The staff [members] are other kids—high school kids, girls on the team. . . . So to some extent . . . maybe there's not another adult that's taking the lead to, like, pull Fern into a lunchtime group. I said to her, "Do you want me to say something?" She said, "No." And part of it is because it's just a week. [Fern's camp lasts one week.]

Ms. Marshall had only one brief telephone chat with the coach before she enrolled Fern, and then she had said hello to him when she dropped her daughter off on the first morning. She noted that the coach "was not out-going" and that she did not "have a relationship" with him that would provide a framework "to have a dialogue." She considered, but ultimately decided against, speaking to him.

In some cases, though, she does intervene, usually after a period of watchful scrutiny. She described a particularly difficult situation that arose with the girls' school bus driver when both of her girls complained that Art, the bus driver, was, in Fern's words, "racist" and directed black children where to sit, "picked on them" for example by not letting them open the windows, and inconsistently enforced district policies of not letting children bring a friend on the bus without a note.

> Fern had shared with me last year. She said, "Art's racist. He makes all the black kids sit on the back of the bus and he only yells at us. . . ." And blah-blah-blah. Again, in that, you know, I'm listening to this and I'm thinking, "Well, is this just a child, you know, being overly sensitive, or—or what?"
> When Stacey started riding the bus this year, she started saying the same thing. She says, "Art's, Art only picks on us." She says, "He won't even let us open the windows." Policies seemed to be upheld differently for the different races. Apparently there was, on one day, a little white boy was bringing a friend home, and didn't have a note [from his parents]. The boy was allowed to ride the bus. A few days later, a little black girl was riding home with a friend and she was not permitted on the bus.

Although aware of her daughters' concerns, Ms. Marshall did not immediately launch an intervention or share the girls' observations with school staff. Instead, she kept her eye on the situation:

> I never just leave 'em at the bus stop. The bus picks them up at the end of the corner here. I will always stay there in the car, and I began to watch. You know, just kind of look and see where kids are on the bus.
> Near the end of the school year, there was a discussion in Fern's class and other children—including white students . . . spoke up and said they saw it too. You know. And a couple of other black kids are in the class, who also ride the bus, [and they] said, "Yeah, Art does this."

The white children's validation helped Ms. Marshall overcome her hesitancy about complaining. She called the district's administrative offices and spoke to a staff person:

> So I called over and I spoke to the guy who is in charge of transportation services over there. . . . He said, you know, "We don't, we don't stand for that."

Ms. Marshall not only had an idea about the nature of the problem, she also had in mind the proper organizational solution.

> His approach was a bit different than what I told him I thought he should have taken. He said, "Well," he said, "If you were calling earlier, we could have put a

camera on the bus." I said, "I'm not asking you to put a camera on the bus; I'm asking you to let this man know that the children perceive something and that parents, at least one parent, is aware of something that he said." He went into the fact that our school district subcontracts the busing service. . . . [This meant that, legally, the district could not speak directly to the driver.] I said, "Well, next thing you do is call the supervisor." (emphasis added)

While the district administrator was preoccupied by the possibility of putting a camera on the bus (the following school year since it was too late for this school year), Ms. Marshall felt the proper intervention was for the administrator to talk to the bus driver directly, something that was not possible given the sub-contract the district had with the bus service. In the fall, Ms. Marshall plans to call the transportation administrator before school starts to find out who will be driving the school bus. In the meantime, she seems distressed and somewhat at a loss as to what to say when Stacey and Fern continue to express concerns about Art but stressed that, "you've got to judge a person as a person." But still, her children knew, and observed, her complaining to people in positions of power on their behalf.

Black middle-class parents, mothers especially, undertook more labor than did their white middle-class counterparts, as they worried about the racial balance and the insensitivity of other children, and framed appropriate responses to their own children's reactions. From time to time, children and parents both encountered difficult and painful situations, such as the one the Marshall girls faced when they rode the school bus. Though race seemed a constant worry for the Marshalls and resulted in intermittent interventions—watching, waiting, and deciding when and if to intervene—there is little difference among black and white middle-class families (mothers in particular) in demonstrating for their children a strategic way of activating capital.

Discussion

So, what are we to make of these patterns? Had I been studying older children, I am convinced that the patterns would have been different and that racial patterns would have been more distinctly powerful for adolescents than for children nine and ten years of age. In key aspects of daily life, including racial segregation in residential housing, interpersonal dynamics that adults experienced on the street, and complications in occupational settings, black middle-class families experienced powerful racial dynamics. Indeed, among middle-class families, race played a role, not in terms of whether or how parents intervened in their children's organizational lives, but rather, in the kinds of issues that they kept their eyes on and in the number of potential problems parents and children faced. Middle-class black parents—whose children tend to spend a large part of their daily lives in predominantly white environments—were attuned to issues of racial exclusion and insensitivity on the part of other children as well as adults. Still, in the United States, as in the social sciences, the power of class resources can be shrouded, and at times obscured, by the visibility of race. Other times the power of social class is widely presumed but rarely demonstrated.

In this chapter, I have sought to demonstrate the power of social class in shaping the interventions in children's lives. As I have discussed, Ms. Marshall, along with other black and white middle-class parents, intervened in many aspects of her children's life, including in trying to modify the actions of the gymnastic coach. She also intervened when she was concerned about her children experiencing racial discrimination, as when her children complained about Art, the bus driver. Once she drew the conclusion that there was a problem, there appeared to be little difference in the strategies she used intervening over non-racial matters (that is to say the gymnastic coach being too critical of her daughter) and racial matters (her concerns about Art, the bus driver).[11] Nor, for that matter, were there striking differences in how black and white middle-class parents intervened in institutions on behalf of their children. Instead, middle-class parents, black and white, displayed striking similarities in appearing to directly help create a robust sense of entitlement in their children through their interactions with people in positions of authority.

While black middle-class families face unique problems, even if tied specifically to racially lived issues, they draw on a set of *generic* class resources in the management of these problems, a set of generic class resources that are shared by both black and white parents. In this chapter I have stressed three aspects of middle-class perceptions: that first, parents presume that they are entitled to have the institution accommodate to their child's individualized needs; second, they feel comfortable voicing their concerns with people in positions of authority; and third, they are willing and able to climb the hierarchy of authority to pursue their interests.

Since the children were only in fourth and fifth grade, it is difficult to measure consequences. Indeed, I cannot even be certain as to how much the children absorbed and internalized their parents' instruction. Yet Stacey clearly had experiences, such as the gifted program and a more individualized gymnastics program, that she would not have had without her mother's intervention. In addition, the parallels with the world of work are striking, as when Ms. Marshall has Stacey carefully prepare for a difficult encounter. Overall, the profits yielded by these class interventions seem to be individually insignificant but potentially cumulatively important.

Finally, however, there is a long and rocky road between the definition of a concern and the activation of class-based resources to intervene in institutions. They are not one and the same. Yet this process has not been sufficiently studied; instead, possession is confounded with activation. By studying the process of framing a concern for intervention, the importance of class-based resources in the efforts by parents to transmit advantages, and the ways in which children are directly trained in, and then clearly enact, these class-based resources, sociologists stand to help to further untangle the complex relationship between race, class, and inequality in institutions, thereby contributing to one of the most visible, and pressing, questions of the day.

Questions for discussion

1. Discuss Lareau's use of cultural and social capital in the lives of black and white middle-class families. Do black and white middle-class families pass along cultural and social capital to their children in similar ways? Explain your response.
2. As Lareau noted, Stacey and Fern spent their academic (school) and organized activity time with mostly white children, while their non-academic, less structured time was spent among blacks. What role does race play in shaping the

classed activities of these girls? What might this say about black middle-class families in the larger context?

3. Across the black and white middle-class families, it is the mothers rather than the fathers who attend to most of the children's enrichment. Discuss the role of gender in these middle-class parenting practices. What might be the significance of seemingly constant gender roles across racial groups?

4. What, in your opinion, are the "generic class resources" used by middle-class parents? Discuss what Lareau names as the "three important ways that social class appears to matter" in regard to parenting styles, namely around education and positioning. What role might parents' educational backgrounds play?

5. Lareau asserts that there are times when the power of social class is widely presumed but rarely demonstrated. What does she mean by this? Further your explanation with examples.

6. In reflecting on the explicit lessons that Ms. Marshall tried to teach her daughter Stacey, what implicit messages might Stacey also gain from such teachings? What messages might Stacey receive about those who have similar and different race and class backgrounds?

7. In several incidents Ms. Marshall, despite education and social class status, hesitated to intervene on her daughters' behalf where race was involved. What does it say about the power of race in the lives of black middle-class people? What does it say about racial stratification that Ms. Marshall waited until she received confirmation from white children that the bus driver, Art, had behaved in a racist manner? Why might she, as a black middle-class woman, hesitate to name racism?

8. Lareau states that, for the black children, race did not seem to play a consistent, significant role in their day-to-day lives. How might race impact Stacey and Fern (and middle-class black children more broadly) as they enter into different types of personal (seeking partners, colleagues) and professional (seeking employment) relationships in their adult lives? Do you think that Ms. Marshall's teachings have prepared them to negotiate their raced, classed adult lives?

Notes

This chapter contains selections from *Unequal Childhoods: Class, Race, and Family Life* (University of California Press, 2003). The author gratefully acknowledges the financial support of the Spencer Foundation as well as additional funding from the Alfred P. Sloan Foundation, the National Science Foundation, Temple University, and the University of Maryland. Numerous colleagues and graduate students patiently provided feedback on earlier versions of these ideas. Katherine Mooney, Erin McNamara Horvat, and Elliot Weininger warrant special mention. Amy Stich and Lois Weis generously edited the paper. All errors, of course, are the responsibility of the author.

1. Annette Lareau, *Unequal childhoods: Class, race, and family life*, Berkeley: University of California Press, 2003.
2. See Urie Bronfenbrenner's article, "Socialization and social class through time and space," pp. 362–77 in *Class, status and power*, edited by R. Bendix and S. M. Lipset. New York: The Free Press, 1966.

3. Katherine S. Newman, *Declining fortunes: The withering of the American dream*, New York: Basic Books, 1994 as well as Donald L. Bartlett and James B. Steele, *America: What went wrong?*, Kansas City: Andrews and McMeel Publishers, 1992.

4. In this study there were also, in some contexts, differences in sociolinguistic terms (including special words for white people). For a more general discussion of this issue see Mary Patillo-McCoy, *Black picket fences: Privilege and peril among the black middle class*, Chicago and London: The University of Chicago Press, 2000 as well as Douglas Massey and Nancy Denton, *American Apartheid*, Cambridge: Harvard University Press, 1993.

5. See Ellis Cose, *The rage of a privileged class*. New York: HarperCollins Publishers, 1993 and Mary C. Waters, *Black identities*, New York: The Russell Sage Foundation, 1999.

6. See Pierre Bourdieu, *Distinction*, Cambridge: Harvard University Press, 1984, David Swartz, *Culture and power: The sociology of Pierre Bourdieu*, Chicago: University of Chicago Press, 1997, and Annette Lareau and Elliot B. Weininger, "Cultural capital in educational research: A critical assessment," *Theory and Society*, 32, 5/6, 567–606.

7. Although beyond the scope of this chapter, let me just note that the working-class and poor families we studied did not demonstrate comparable displays. One black mother, Tara Carroll's mother, for example, seemed annoyed that the teacher kept pronouncing her daughter's name incorrectly but she whispered the proper pronunciation under her breath when the teacher got up to get a piece of paper during the parent/teacher conference. She did not appear to feel entitled to demand that the teacher use the proper pronunciation or to confront the teacher, let alone the principal, on this or other matters.

8. The song is titled "Glad Tidings," words and music by Natalie Sleeth, written for a two-part choir. Copyright © 1978 by Hinshaw Music Inc., PO Box 470, Chapel Hill, NC 27514. The full line containing the phrase that irked the Kaplans is "The babe was foretold by prophets of old, and greeted with treasures of silver and gold, so come let us bow and worship Him now, no heart unaware of His worth."

9. Some teachers were "all up in arms" when Fern began spending more and more time with her black girlfriends, who were not in the gifted program. The teachers complained to Ms. Marshall that Fern was "not associating with the right children," not spending time with girls "who are at her level." Ms. Marshall worried that, as a student, Fern was being judged on the basis of her friendships rather than on the basis of her own academic achievement (she was an honor roll student).

10. It is also possible, of course, that children could learn helplessness and dependence upon their parents to fix life problems for them.

11. As other scholars have noted, Ms. Marshall did display some forms of hesitancy and feelings of ambiguity in coming to a decision as to whether the problems her children faced were linked to racial discrimination (see, for example, Joe Feagin and Melvin P. Sikes, *Living with racism: The black middle-class experience*, Boston: Beacon Press, 1994). Still, Ms. Marshall also displayed ambivalence and hesitancy over her interventions in non-racial matters, such as the choice of an appropriate gymnastics program for Stacey, where the matter weighed heavily on her mind as she tried to reconcile conflicting priorities including distance, cost, quality of training, and opportunities for competition. Thus it is hard to say if she was more ambivalent and hesitant in racially charged matters than in other matters.

Chapter 9

Are middle-class families advantaging their children?

*Kimberly S. Maier, Timothy G. Ford, and Barbara Schneider**

Introduction

Within the domain of research on families—particularly with regard to how parents transfer class advantages to their children—there is skepticism as to whether or not class can adequately account for distinctions found in the everyday actions and behaviors of parents and their children. As Kingston (2000) argues, ". . . class distinguishes neither distinctive parenting styles or [sic] distinctive involvement of kids" in specific behaviors (p. 134). On the other hand, there are family researchers who favor understandings of inequalities among families that are based on social class, and in some cases, these researchers have found sharp class distinctions in areas such as parenting style and practices (Lareau, 2002, 2003). Examining data from the 500 Family Study, an extensive study of middle-class dual-earner couples and their children, this chapter explores whether there are cultural lifestyle choices consistent with dominant middle-class parenting practices, or if the patterns of parenting are so diverse that the concept of a middle-class home advantage may be overstated.

Social class and life choices

The recent resurgence of the class analysis debate has rekindled questions as to the utility of social class as a concept used to describe and/or explain social inequality or conflict (Clark & Lipset, 1991; Grusky & Sørensen, 1998; Grusky & Weeden, 2001; Kingston, 2000; Pakulski & Waters, 1996; Weeden & Grusky, 2005). Critics in this debate argue that class is no longer an effective tool in understanding current trends in stratification, due to the increased influence of individual identity and choice in making lifestyle decisions (Grusky & Weeden, 2001). This debate has found application in many subfields of sociology, including research in family life.

Traditional conceptions of social stratification are predicated on the belief that people can be hierarchically distinguished on the basis of one or more criteria into distinct

* Kimberly S. Maier is Assistant Professor of Measurement and Quantitative Methods and affiliate of Educational Policy in the College of Education at Michigan State University. Timothy G. Ford is a doctoral student in the Curriculum, Teaching, and Educational Policy program at Michigan State University and a Research Associate at the Data Research and Development Center. Barbara Schneider is the John A. Hannah Distinguished Professor in the College of Education and the Department of Sociology at Michigan State University.

groups or classes (Clark & Lipset, 1991). These criteria are often defined in socioeconomic terms, with researchers choosing factors such as income, occupation, and/or education to draw class distinctions. Once established, these distinctions provide a framework in which to understand inequality in society at large. While it is difficult to argue against the existence of social inequalities in greater society, many social scientists are unsure whether or not these inequalities can be meaningfully explained or theorized in social-class terms (Kingston, 2000).

One area where social-class explanations of inequality become potentially problematic is at the level of the family. Recent increases in the numbers of dual-earner families have resulted in major shifts in parental roles and attitudes, with an increasing emphasis on the role of the father in child rearing and a more balanced, equitable division of labor in the household (Clark & Lipset, 1991). The demands of the workplace are influencing parents' interactions with their children, and the outcomes of these interactions often are associated with the level of autonomy and challenge parents perceive that their jobs afford them (Christensen, 2005; Kohn & Schooler, 1983). Among middle-class parents, the types of jobs mothers and fathers hold vary significantly, as individuals are more likely to identify themselves as middle-class regardless of their occupation or income. Despite the variation in occupations among middle-class parents, recent research shows that working families experience considerable stress and strain in their personal lives that they attribute to overworking. The perceived need to work long hours to simply "keep up" is negatively affecting the relationships working parents have with their children and their partners (Schneider & Waite, 2005). As the demands of work steadily encroach on the amount of time parents have to spend with their children, so too comes the potential for cross-class convergence. Working parents from dual-earner households in all strata cope with similar day-to-day household maintenance and child-rearing challenges, and experience similar pressures to balance work and home demands, especially when it comes to ensuring their children's success and future life chances (Griffith & Smith, 2005).

Social class, parenting practices, and advantage

Nevertheless, there are some scholars who believe social class is a useful tool for understanding how differences in child-rearing practices translate into advantage in terms of life chances and future social position (Kusserow, 2004; Lareau, 2002, 2003). Lareau (2002, 2003) has found significant class distinctions with regard to parents' child-rearing practices. She identifies two different "cultural logics of child rearing," which are distinct along social-class boundaries. Middle-class parents' child-rearing practices are characterized as "concerted cultivation," while working-class and poor parents' practices are labeled "accomplishment of natural growth."

"Concerted cultivation" as an approach to child rearing emphasizes a child's participation in structured activities outside the home and a focus on language development, as well as parents' active role in their children's education. In contrast, "the accomplishment of natural growth" is a more passive approach to child rearing, in which children are given a wide berth to structure and manage their own leisure time, leaving respect and deference to authority as one of the few concepts to be actively taught by working-class and poor parents. It is Lareau's (2002, 2003) contention that the values and beliefs embedded within these different practices are differentially treated by institutions. Thus, the middle-class practice of cultivation is an effective transmitter of social advantage, due to its congruence with the expectations of schools.

One of the major critiques of the use of social class as a macro-level construct is the concern that among any of the "big class" (e.g., "middle-class") specifications there are likely to be distinct practices and values associated with individualized lifestyles. Critics often suggest that taking a more micro-level approach to the study of social class can better identify these distinctions, leading to greater macro-level explanations (Weeden & Grusky, 2005). The relationship between social class and parenting seems to be somewhat limited in its operational definitions, and we suspect that among the middle-class there are functional group differences in parenting styles. Parents choose to allocate the time they spend with their children in different ways, and these allocations need to be understood as a socialization process that is influenced in part by the communities to which they belong and the experiences they themselves had as children (Snyder, in press).

While there can be little doubt that the family plays a critical role in the transmission of values, morals, and life choices—which may or may not translate into advantage for children—the mechanisms by which this occurs are less evident. The 500 Family Study data provide an opportunity to add to our understanding of the nature of middle-class parenting, especially as it pertains to the concept of middle-class advantage. This chapter, in its exploration of the lives of middle-class parents and their children, seeks to deepen our understanding of the existence and extent of social-class differences with regard to parenting.

Method

The questions in this investigation are examined using data from the 500 Family Study, conducted by the Alfred P. Sloan Center on Parents, Children, and Work at the University of Chicago. The 500 Family Study contains rich, detailed information on over 500 middle-class, dual-earner families in eight communities across the USA. For this analysis, data were obtained from parent surveys and the Experience Sampling Method (ESM).[1] The parent survey included a number of items used in other national studies of families, including extensive information on parents' occupation and work experiences as well as parents' involvement in household chores, childcare, and other parenting activities. The ESM is a unique method of obtaining information on the experiences of individuals at the moment they occur. Developed by Csikszentmihalyi and colleagues (Csikszentmihalyi & Larson, 1984; Csikszentmihalyi, Larson, & Prescott, 1977), the ESM is administered over the course of a week during which participants wear a wristwatch programmed to beep randomly in two-hour blocks. When signaled, participants fill out a self-report form consisting of several open-ended and scaled responses which capture how they are feeling, where they are and with whom, and what they are doing. Research examining the ESM has established it as a reliable and valid instrument for measuring time use and emotional well-being.[2]

Sample

As this study is concerned with how middle-class parents interact with their children, a sub-sample of parents with children who responded to at least fifteen ESM signals was selected for analysis. The cases were further reduced from this initial subset by selecting only those cases where parents reported being with their child in a place other than work.[3] These selection procedures resulted in a final sample of 723 parents, consisting of 434 mothers and 289 fathers yielding a total of 6,491 total ESM observations, 4,416 for mothers and 2,075 for fathers. It is important to note that the 500 Family Study focused on families with either adolescents, young children, or both. For this analysis we have included all of these types of families.

The members of the 500 Family Study are quite diverse; 18 percent of its participating families earn $50,000 per year or less, and over half earn more than $100,000 per year—25 percent of which earn over $150,000 per year. Some families have only one parent who graduated from college, while in other families both parents are professionals. It is important to note here, however, that this is not a representative sample of all families in the USA.

Measures

Primary and secondary activities.   A unique feature of the ESM is that it captures respondents' primary and secondary activities when they are beeped. On the ESM form, participants respond to the questions "What was the main thing you were doing?" and "What else were you doing at the same time?"—their open-ended responses resulted in over four hundred distinct activity codes for the 500 Family Study. For the purposes of our analyses, these activity codes were recoded into ten categories: leisure, chores, childcare, talking with children, talking with family, helping with homework, personal time, personal care, eating, and other.[4] From these categories, a series of dummy variables were created to indicate when a parent was engaged in a particular activity; participants were assigned a value of 1 if they were engaged in an activity, or 0 otherwise. These dummy variables were then used to estimate the amount of weekly time parents spend in a certain activity,[5] as well as to obtain measures of how parents feel while engaged in those activities.

Emotion measures.   In order to capture the emotive states of parents while engaged in activities, positive and negative affect measures were constructed. These measures are composite variables, each containing several separate emotion items from the ESM data. Choices on which separate measures should constitute both positive and negative affect were based on composite measures used in prior research. Positive affect was based on scales constructed by Csikszentmihalyi and Larson (1984), Csikszentmihalyi, Rathunde, and Whalen (1993), and Koh (2005), whereas negative affect was based on scales used by Koh (2005). The positive affect composite variable used in this analysis contains ESM items including: feeling happy, cheerful, friendly, and relaxed (Cronbach's alpha = .83). The negative affect composite variable includes the items: feeling angry, frustrated, irritated, strained, and stressed (α = .87).[6]

Results

How much time do parents spend with their children?

It has been suggested that parents today are investing considerable time in their children (Sayer, Bianchi, & Robinson, 2004). Using data from the ESM, Figure 9.1 shows the

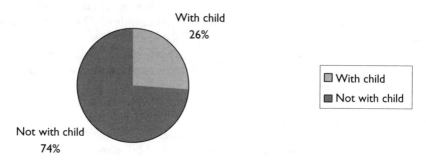

Figure 9.1 Proportion of parents' weekly time outside of work spent with child. Total number of parents reporting not at work (*n* = 747 parents based on 24,944 beeps). Total number of parents reporting being with their child outside of work (*n* = 723 parents based on 6,491 beeps).

proportion of time per week parents spend with their children outside of work.[7] As shown in Figure 9.1, parents report spending approximately one-quarter of their waking time outside of work with their children, leaving a substantial block of time outside of work that is spent either alone or with their spouse, relatives, or other children.[8] Considering that the proportion of time spent, as shown in the figure, is based on responses outside of work—time most likely to be spent in the company of one's children—it is somewhat surprising to note that, in these instances, only a small portion of a parent's time is spent with their child.

Figures 9.2 and 9.3 show the proportion of time mothers and fathers spend per week with their child. Together these two figures indicate that, while mothers had nearly twice as many ESM responses as fathers, the proportion of time spent with child between mothers and fathers does not differ markedly. In fact, these data show that mothers and fathers spend a nearly equal proportion of their time outside of work with their child.

What activities do parents do with their children?

Given that mothers and fathers spend strikingly similar amounts of time with their children outside of work, the question becomes: What are parents doing while with their

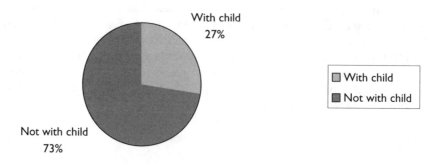

Figure 9.2 Proportion of mothers' weekly time outside of work spent with child. Total number of mothers reporting not at work (*n* = 444 mothers based on 16,116 beeps). Total number of mothers reporting being with their child outside of work (*n* = 434 mothers based on 4,416 beeps).

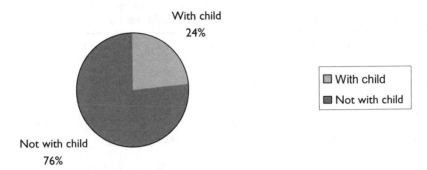

Figure 9.3 Proportion of fathers' weekly time outside of work spent with child. Total number of fathers reporting not at work (*n* = 303 fathers based on 8,828 beeps). Total number of fathers reporting being with their child outside of work (*n* = 289 fathers based on 2,075 beeps).

child and how much time are they spending weekly in those activities? Table 9.1 shows the average weekly hours parents (as well as mothers and fathers disaggregated) spend engaged in various activities while with their children. Means are reported for both primary and secondary activities.

Table 9.1 shows parents spend the most time engaged in leisure and chores as primary activities while with their children, averaging about 4.28 and 4.10 hours per week respectively. Of particular note are the talking categories. The table shows parents report being engaged in talking either with their child or with other family members for a substantial amount of time per week—an average of 7.50 hours; this activity accounts for approximately 21 percent of the time parents spend with their children outside of work. If one considers the ratio of time spent talking with children or family as a primary or secondary activity, talking is reported three times more as a secondary activity than a primary. This suggests that talking with children is more likely to occur when parents are focused on a central task, such as doing chores.

Looking at differences between mothers and fathers, we see that fathers spend fewer hours per week doing chores and engaging in childcare activities than mothers. Fathers also spend less of their weekly time talking (both to their children and other family members) than mothers. Finally, mothers spend nearly twice as much time helping their children with homework than fathers. These data show that mothers continue to shoulder the primary responsibility for childcare and chores; the weekly time that fathers spend in these two activities is nearly half of what mothers, on average, spend. These findings are consistent with Lee (2005) who found gender differences with regard to time spent engaged in household chores, with wives spending consistently more time than husbands.

With respect to childcare, the differentials in time spent between mothers and fathers found here is consistent with Sayer, Bianchi, and Robinson (2004). They concluded that, while fathers are spending more time in childcare than in the past, mothers' still do the lion's share of childcare activities. Using independent samples t-tests conducted on the differences between mothers' and fathers' average weekly time spent in various activities with child, we found that the differences between mothers and fathers in time spent on childcare, chores, talking with children, and homework (among others) were all statistically significant.

Table 9.1 Mean weekly hours spent in activities by parents with their children outside of work and independent samples t-tests of mother and father differences[a]

Activity category	Parents (n = 723)		Mothers (n = 434)		Fathers (n = 289)		
	Mean (hours/wk)	Standard deviation	Mean (hours/wk)	Standard deviation	Mean (hours/wk)	Standard deviation	t-statistic[b] (p-value)
Leisure							
Primary	4.28	4.53	4.35	4.53	4.17	4.52	.535 (.593)
Secondary	3.24	3.80	3.36	4.03	3.07	3.43	1.00 (.317)
Chores							
Primary	4.10	4.52	4.91	4.96	2.87	3.43	**6.54 (.000)**
Secondary	1.85	2.88	2.38	3.27	1.07	1.92	**6.77 (.000)**
Childcare							
Primary	2.88	4.17	3.55	4.71	1.87	2.93	**5.92 (.000)**
Secondary	2.21	4.05	2.80	4.68	1.33	2.62	**5.40 (.000)**
Talking w/Children							
Primary	0.96	1.86	1.11	2.00	0.72	1.59	**2.92 (.005)**
Secondary	3.42	3.75	4.13	4.03	2.35	2.98	**6.84 (.000)**
Talking w/Family							
Primary	0.78	1.50	0.82	1.51	0.71	1.46	.982 (.326)
Secondary	2.34	3.02	2.37	2.95	2.30	3.14	.326 (.744)
Homework							
Primary	0.34	1.04	0.42	1.19	0.22	0.74	**2.82 (.005)**
Secondary	0.15	0.63	0.19	0.72	0.09	0.46	**2.18 (.030)**
Personal Time							
Primary	1.23	2.26	1.40	2.50	0.99	1.84	**2.57 (.010)**
Secondary	1.15	2.21	1.36	2.37	0.83	1.90	**3.31 (.001)**
Personal Care							
Primary	0.61	1.50	0.79	1.70	0.35	1.09	**4.21 (.000)**
Secondary	0.24	0.86	0.30	0.96	0.15	0.69	**2.38 (.018)**
Eating							
Primary	2.63	2.86	2.52	2.78	2.79	2.97	1.25 (.209)
Secondary	0.95	1.70	0.97	1.67	0.91	1.74	.493 (.622)
Other							
Primary	0.45	1.18	0.58	1.32	0.24	0.88	**4.21 (.000)**
Secondary	0.52	1.28	0.57	1.31	0.43	1.23	1.41 (.159)

Notes

All significant t-test results ($p < .05$) are in bold.

a   These hours are based on 56 beeps administered during the week, or 8 beeps per day including the weekend, for all participants. Beeps were scheduled to over-sample the time spent before families went to work and when they returned home in the evening.

b   Independent samples t-tests were conducted on mean differences in weekly hours spent in activities between mothers and fathers. T-statistics are listed and their corresponding p-values are in parentheses. Statistically significant results to $p < .05$ in bold.

Also reported in this table are the variations in the average time that parents spend in activities outside of work (standard deviations). What is important here is that there is substantial variance in types of activities parents do with their children.[9] This suggests families are quite dissimilar with respect to the types of activities they choose to engage in with their children.

How do parents feel when with their children?

Another important dimension to understanding the experience of parents spending time with their children is how they feel while engaged in these various activities. Table 9.2 shows the average scores of positive affect for parents while engaged in activities with their child. Overall, parents' reports of affect tend to be quite positive, suggesting that they enjoy the time they spend with their children, regardless of the types of activities in which they are engaged. However, there are differences. Fathers' reports of

Table 9.2 Parents' positive affect (7-point scale) while engaged in activities with child and independent samples t-tests of mother and father differences[a]

Activity category	Mothers		Fathers		
	Mean	Standard deviation	Mean	Standard deviation	t-statistic (p-value)
Leisure					
Primary	5.17	1.08	5.36	1.07	**1.98 (.049)**
Secondary	5.11	1.05	5.30	1.03	1.92 (.055)
Chores					
Primary	4.48	1.14	4.73	1.03	**2.41 (.016)**
Secondary	4.63	1.21	4.89	1.09	1.76 (.078)
Childcare					
Primary	4.66	1.21	4.96	0.96	**2.28 (.023)**
Secondary	4.56	1.06	5.00	1.11	**3.06 (.002)**
Talking w/Children					
Primary	5.17	1.24	5.12	1.41	.240 (.810)
Secondary	4.86	1.16	5.22	0.97	**3.29 (.001)**
Talking w/Family					
Primary	5.33	1.33	5.26	1.26	.337 (.737)
Secondary	5.01	1.18	5.41	1.10	**3.28 (.001)**
Homework					
Primary	4.58	1.42	4.60	1.13	.050 (.960)
Secondary	4.47	1.48	4.53	1.40	.109 (.913)
Personal Time					
Primary	4.89	1.37	5.12	1.19	1.29 (.196)
Secondary	4.85	1.28	5.03	1.01	1.04 (.300)
Personal Care					
Primary	4.42	1.28	5.04	1.30	**2.38 (.019)**
Secondary	4.61	1.18	4.98	1.12	1.07 (.288)
Eating					
Primary	5.30	1.16	5.39	1.03	.823 (.411)
Secondary	5.10	1.29	5.34	1.17	1.35 (.177)
Other					
Primary	5.67	1.10	5.44	0.89	.903 (.369)
Secondary	5.45	1.29	5.47	1.16	.101 (.920)

Notes
All significant t-statistics (p < .05) in bold.
a The composite variable positive affect is comprised of the following variables from the ESM data: feeling happy, cheerful, friendly, and relaxed (Cronbach's α = .83). The cheerful, friendly, and relaxed variables, which are on a four-point scale (0 to 3), were recoded to match the happy variable which is on a seven-point scale (1 to 7). Details on the construction of this scale can be found in Chapter 6, Psychometrics of ESM data, in Hektner, Schmidt, and Csikszentmihalyi (2007).

positive affect, although not statistically significant in all cases, are generally higher than those of mothers, regardless of activity, with only a few exceptions. Negative affect demonstrates the same patterns—albeit in the opposite direction—with fathers reporting lower average affect than mothers.[10, 11] One possible interpretation of these findings is that there are gender-based differences in the reporting of these feelings, with fathers tending to give higher ratings of positive affect and lower ratings of negative affect.

Looking more closely at individual activities, however, there are several differences of note. First, mothers' overall mean positive affect is considerably lower than fathers' both in primary and secondary chores and childcare. This suggests that mothers, in shouldering a disproportionately large measure of the duties in these areas, may be, over time, adversely affected by the demands of household maintenance, especially since these mothers are also employed outside the home. These negative feelings may be compounded by a mother's frustration in not being able to devote more of her time to simply being with her child.[12]

Mothers' mean positive affect scores for talking with children as a primary activity lend some credence to this assertion. Mothers' positive affect while talking with their children is high relative to their scores in other activities, with the exception of the eating and "other" categories, which are high regardless of parent. One possible explanation for mothers' high average affect in these particular activities is that they reflect instances when a mother's focus is more squarely on her child, potentially enhancing the mother–child connection and thus increasing overall affect. This contrasts with instances in which talking is secondary to other, more pressing tasks (e.g., washing dishes or doing laundry). The sharp decline in mean positive affect from primary to secondary "talking with child" seems to support this position.

One activity that both mothers and fathers find particularly stressful is helping with homework. The responses on helping with homework show the highest negative affect of all activities with a measure of 0.50 and 0.46 primary and secondary for mothers and 0.48 and 0.49 for fathers. These findings suggest that this activity is a particularly stressful and frustrating one for parents.[13]

How do these activities vary among middle-class families?

To investigate the relationship between time spent in activities by parents and socioeconomic status (SES), correlations between parents' hours spent in activities with their children and income and highest degree attained were examined. As Table 9.3 shows, there is some evidence of stratification with more affluent families being less likely to engage their children in household chores. Moreover, these parents are more likely to engage in conversations with their children.[14] Other analyses (see, for example, Lee, 2005) show that nobody enjoys household tasks, and we suspect that these particular families are socializing their children early on to avoid tasks they perceive as drudgery.

We further explored whether parents with more resources and education were more likely to have their children participate in activities. Overall, the average time that this middle-class sample of parents spent taking their children to activities was between one and five hours per week. There was, however, no observed relationship in this regard. Correlations between income and highest education and time spent taking children to such activities were negligible, with the only statistically significant value being between highest education and time spent taking kids to activities ($r = 0.09$, $p < .01$).

Table 9.3 Spearman correlations of parents' weekly hours spent in activities by income and education

Primary activities

	Leisure	Chores	Child-care	Talk family	Talk child	Home-work	Personal time	Personal care	Eating	Other
Income	−.043	−.117*	−.011	.031	−.064	.036	−.058	−.119*	.100*	.065
Highest degree	−.074	−.117**	−.026	−.042	−.068	.054	−.054	−.094*	.086*	−.041

Secondary activities

	Leisure	Chores	Child-care	Talk family	Talk child	Home-work	Personal time	Personal care	Eating	Other
Income	−.109*	−.058	.014	.219**	−.088	−.075	−.063	−.075	.029	.081
Highest degree	−.089*	−.130**	−.038	.058	−.078*	−.010	−.035	−.074	.015	.045

Notes
*p < .05; **p < .01 (2-tailed).

Discussion

In this chapter, we have argued that shifts in parental roles and attitudes brought on by increases in the number of dual-earner families make understanding parenting practices in social-class terms problematic at best. It is our suspicion that, among middle-class families, there are likely to be functional group differences in parenting styles associated with individualized lifestyles. Looking across our results, claims of distinct middle-class parenting practices are, for this diverse sample, mixed. On a very broad level, it would appear that middle-class parents are spending only a small fraction of their overall time outside of work in the company of their children. This particular finding seems to support Lareau (2002, 2003) who found sharp class differences regarding time use, with middle-class households often spending little time together as a family due to the disproportionate number of resources leveraged towards the support of children's activities outside the home.

Regarding time use, however, this is where the similarities stop. Our findings indicate that middle-class parents are not spending large amounts of time supporting children's activities outside of the home. Moreover, the number of hours parents invest in these activities has no observable relationship to socioeconomic factors, suggesting that middle-class families are quite diverse in the amount of time they invest in support of their children's activities, with some spending considerably fewer hours than others.

Examining more closely the types of activities parents engage in with their children, the results are less straightforward. It seems that parents are, despite the demands of work, household maintenance, and childcare, able to find time to relax, watch television, play sports, or otherwise engage in leisure activity with their children. Talking also seems to play a significant role in middle-class family life, although it seems clear that the disparate demands of parenting result in talk being an activity that usually accompanies a more central task such as childcare or chores. There is evidence, however, that middle-class parents are not as similar with regard to the nature of the time they spend with their children as these overall findings would lead us to believe. In fact, we found evidence of substantial variation across families with regard to how parents allocate their time across categories of activities.

If any middle-class distinctions based on income and education are discernible with regard to activities, it seems to be in the avoidance of chores and in increased opportunities for communication. There is marginal evidence that wealthier, highly-educated parents tend towards avoiding tasks they perceive as drudgery. This may also be due, in part, to dual-earner families having considerably less time to spend on household maintenance, owing to the fact that mothers—on whom it is clear the onus of childcare and chore-related activity continues to fall—are working outside of the home in greater numbers. As a result, middle-class parents are, in many cases, using a portion of the disposable income they enjoy as a result of having two incomes to purchase household services (Hochschild, 1989). Additionally, there is some evidence to indicate that wealthier middle-class families talk more. This suggests that some aspects of "concerted cultivation" may be occurring; however, the socioeconomic diversity of the families studied here clearly shows that there is considerable variation in how talk is being used across what we code as middle class.

Parents' feelings while engaged in activities with their children also shed some light on the competing spheres of work and home among dual-earner families. Mothers clearly feel good when they are simply talking with their children, and feel generally less so when that talking is done while attending to household chores or the minutiae of childcare. There is an overall sense, however, that parents enjoy being with their children, regardless of the activity. The question then becomes: if parents enjoy time spent with their children so much, why do they spend so little of their available time with them? Could this be one of the personal costs of having to work long hours?

Conclusion

Taken together, our findings suggest that, with regard to parent/child interaction, claims of a coherent logic of child-rearing practice among middle-class families—and the corollary advantage it provides—are somewhat overstated. Time use, while small with regard to time spent with children, is otherwise highly variable among middle-class families. Leisure time, which Lareau (2002, 2003) suggests is absent in middle-class families due to the constant demands of children's activities, is clearly a healthy part of average middle-class family life—at least in this sample of 500 families. Furthermore, our data show that parents' practices did not necessarily reflect any underlying philosophy regarding their children's participation in activities outside the home. While the middle-class model of child rearing that is "concerted cultivation" clearly attributes a high degree of cultural capital to parents' over-scheduling of their children's time, we found very little evidence of this among the middle-class families in our study. In fact, parents spent a very small portion of their overall time with their children taking them to and from activities.

Despite these conclusions, we found evidence—albeit weak—which suggests the possible existence of a coherent logic of child-rearing practice, not among middle-class families *per se*, but one which may be emerging among *upper* middle-class families.[15] We did find marginal evidence that wealthier, highly-educated families talk more and tend to avoid chores and other tasks which they perceive as drudgery. One possible explanation for these findings could be that parents who may be considered "upper middle class"— that is, those with an annual income over $100,000 or more—may be using their

disposable income in strategic ways with their child
among middle-class families towards the commo
example, could be viewed as a parenting strategy de
valuable free time outside of school for the purposes ot
will more directly impact school performance and, therefoi

Although our overall findings suggest wider, more divers
among middle-class families, we acknowledge that our work i.
tions. Although the 500 Family Study data, and especially the ESM,
of information about the daily occurrences of parents and children, .
the dynamics of family life are extremely complex, and so too are the oi
which parents transfer social-class advantages to their children. Clearly,
research may have advantages in being able to tease out what are often cov
nisms of reproducing existing social stratification (e.g. Lareau, 2003; Kusserov
What our work and the work of these researchers have in common is the belief th
family and parents' child-rearing practices play a critical role in the transmission
values, morals, and life choices. Further research should continue to focus on attempting
to understand and tease out the mechanisms by which this occurs.

Questions for discussion

1. How do Maier, Ford, and Schneider describe the relationship between parents,
   parenting style, and class?
2. Why do Maier, Ford, and Schneider argue that the coherent logic of middle-
   class child-rearing practices is overrated?
3. Maier, Ford, and Schneider suggest that the "middle-class practice of cultivation is an effective transmitter of social advantage, due to its congruence with
   the expectation of schools." What practices do elite and lower classes employ?
   What resources does each group draw upon to successfully negotiate institutions like schools?
4. Reflect on the notion that mothers who work outside the home shoulder most
   of the household maintenance. What might this tell us about the way gender is
   intertwined with class? Does this resonate with your own family structure (past
   or present) or those that you are familiar with?
5. Maier, Ford, and Schneider argue that critics of the saliency of class in determining life chances advocate that "class is no longer an effective tool in understanding current trends in stratification, due to the increased influence of
   individual identity and choice in making lifestyle decisions." In what ways does
   individual agency negate class division?
6. In which category would you put your parents' parenting style? How did it
   affect your life chances? What would be different if your parents had treated
   you in other ways?
7. Dual-income families are increasingly common in the current economic context.
   In what ways could this be described as a classed phenomenon? What are the
   economic realities that families in different classes must negotiate? What
   perception might this lead those in different classes to have in relation to neo-
   liberalism, capitalism, and globalization?

hat are the advantages and disadvantages of using macro- and micro-level approaches to studying social class? Which approach do you think is most useful and why?

tes

1. The 500 Family Study also included interviews with mothers, fathers, and their children which lasted approximately an hour per subject. In addition, young children were interviewed and home visits with the families were conducted. For a full description of the multiple data collections used in this study, see Schneider and Waite (2005).

2. For an in-depth examination of issues related to the validity and reliability of the ESM as a method as well as the data it produces, please refer to Hektner, Schmidt, and Csikszentmihalyi (2007), Jeong (2005), and Mulligan, Schneider, and Wolfe (2005).

3. There are two designations in the 500 Family Study data for whether a parent was with a child when they were beeped. If a parent has multiple children, being "with child" means that the parent was either with a child other than the focal child, or was with the focal child. The ESM variable "with target" makes the distinction between the focal child and other children in the family. This study chose to look specifically at parent interaction with the focal child, so cases were selected based on the designation "with target" only.

4. The categories chosen were based on categories used in other ESM studies, specifically those employed by Larson and Richards (1994), and Graesch et al. (2006). While some of the activities contained within some of these categories may seem obvious—helping with homework or talking with children, for example—others require more explanation. "Personal time" includes activities such as thinking, praying, meditating, and sleeping/napping. "Personal care" includes activities such as grooming, getting dressed, receiving health care, and taking medication. "Leisure" includes playing sports, watching television or movies, joking, singing or dancing, and playing with children or pets. "Childcare" includes helping children with personal care, taking children somewhere, watching and waiting for children, and reprimanding or guiding a child. To establish face-validity for the activity codes, Larson was consulted; he generally concurred with the number and types of categories we constructed and made a few suggestions for some modifications which we incorporated.

5. Beginning with the assumption that beeps are randomly distributed across the week, we approximate hours per week spent in various activities by taking the total signaling period for the week (16 waking hours per day × 7 = 112 hours) and multiplying this number by the proportion of time spent in each activity. This proportion is calculated by dividing total number of beeps engaged in the activity by total number of beeps for each person. For example, a person who was engaged in leisure activities for 15 percent of their week would equal 16.8 hours per week (.15 × 112 hours = 16.8 hours). For further discussion of these conversions, see Hektner, Schmidt, and Csikszentmihalyi (2007).

6. Koh's (2005) negative affect composite variable is actually composed of eight individual measures, three of which were excluded from this analysis for their relatively low inter-correlation with other variables in the measure. Thus, for this analysis, the five variables with the highest inter-correlations were selected for inclusion in the negative affect variable.

7. In order to capture as many instances when parents would likely have an opportunity to interact with their children, we chose to look at all responses when parents were not at work (as opposed to only those at home). This choice makes it possible to capture instances where parent and child interact outside of the home, including, for example, driving in the car, shopping at the mall, and meeting at the child's school. Additionally, this choice provides for a clearer picture of how much time parents actually spend with their children due to the exclusion of workplace responses, which seldom include instances of parent and child together (only n = 52 out of n = 33,095 or 0.1 percent of total responses). Considering that a significant portion of parents' time is spent at work—n = 8,151 or approximately 25 percent of total time for this sample—including these additional responses would only distort our understanding of how much time parents are spending with their children. In this case, then, parents' time spent with their children reflects the actual time spent in proportion to *total opportunities* to be together.

8. In this study, one of the children in the family was designated as the focal child. This child was either a teenager or aged five to six. This calculation indicates the number of hours the mother and father spent with the focal child. It is important to note that, in some instances, while there was another child in the household—the average for the sample being one additional child per family—that sibling was sometimes at college, or otherwise not living at home. In the instance when there were multiple children close in age or younger than the focal child, the time spent with these children was calculated separately. The average amount of time spent with other children outside of the focal child was relatively small—approximately 2,600 beeps, or 10 percent of parents' total time outside of work.

9. The variance of a number is a measure of how spread out a set of numbers are; the variance is the average of the squared deviations from the mean: $s^2 = \Sigma(x_i - \mu)^2/(n-1)$.

10. A similar analysis was also conducted for the negative affect composite variable—which is not the inverse of the positive affect composite variable—see the emotion measures section. By having lower scores, this means that fathers report having less negative affect than mothers.

11. The differences between the two across the various activities were not statistically significant, with the exception of one secondary activity, talking with child. Since the differences in negative affect between mothers and fathers are not significant, we have excluded that table here. It is available from the authors upon request.

12. The high participation of mothers in the area of chores and childcare is seen in the numbers of parents reporting having been engaged in these activities. For instance, 75 percent (323 out of 434) of mothers report doing chores as a primary activity and 49 percent (211 out of 434) as a secondary activity. On the other hand, 58 percent (168 out of 289) of fathers report doing chores as a primary activity and 30 percent (88 out of 289) as a secondary activity. Similarly, 54 percent of mothers (236 out of 434) report being engaged in childcare activities as a primary activity, and 41 percent as a secondary. Conversely, fathers report childcare activities 39 percent as a primary and 28 percent as a secondary activity.

13. We acknowledge, of course, that we must remain skeptical of these results given that the sample sizes for the homework activity are quite low.

14. We must emphasize here that the resultant effect sizes of these particular correlations are, according to Cohen (1988), characterized as negligible to small.

15. Indeed, of the families in Lareau's (2002, 2003) study which served as exemplars of "concerted cultivation," a substantial proportion could be classified as "upper middle class."

References

Christensen, K. E. (2005). Achieving work-life balance: Strategies for dual-earner families. In B. Schneider & L. J. Waite (Eds.), *Being together, working apart: Dual-career families and the work-life balance* (pp. 449–57). New York: Cambridge University Press.

Clark, T. N., & Lipset, S. M. (1991). Are social classes dying? *International Sociology, 6*, 397–410.

Cohen, J. (1988). *Statistical power analysis for the behavioral sciences* (2nd ed.). Mahwah, NJ: Earlbaum.

Csikszentmihalyi, M., & Larson, R. (1984). *Being adolescent: Conflict and growth in the teenage years.* New York: Basic Books.

Csikszentmihalyi, M., Larson, R., & Prescott, S. (1977). The ecology of adolescent activities and experiences. *Journal of Youth and Adolescence, 6*, 281–94.

Csikszentmihalyi, M., Rathunde, K. R., & Whalen, S. (1993). *Talented teenagers: The roots of success and failure.* New York: Cambridge University Press.

Graesch, A. P., Broege, N., Arnold, J. E., Owens, A., & Schneider, B. (2006). *Family activities, uses of space, and emotional well being: A collaborative merging of time diary and ethnoarchaeological data.* Working Paper No. 44: UCLA Sloan Center on Everyday Lives of Families.

Griffith, A. I., & Smith, D. E. (2005). *Mothering for schooling.* New York: RoutledgeFalmer.

Grusky, D. B., & Sørensen, J. B. (1998). Can class analysis be salvaged? *The American Journal of Sociology, 103*, 1187–234.

Grusky, D. B., & Weeden, K. A. (2001). Decomposition without death: A research agenda for a new class analysis. *Acta Sociologica, 44*(3), 203–18.

Hektner, J. M., Schmidt, J. A., & Csikszentmihalyi, M. (2007). *Experience sampling method: Measuring the quality of everyday life.* Thousand Oaks, CA: Sage.

Hochschild, A. (1989). *The second shift: Working parents and the revolution at home.* New York: Avon Books.

Jeong, J. G. (2005). Obtaining accurate measures of time use from the ESM. In B. Schneider & L. J. Waite (Eds.), *Being together, working apart: Dual-career families and the work-life balance* (pp. 461–82). New York: Cambridge University Press.

Kingston, P. (2000). *The classless society.* Stanford, CA: Stanford University Press.

Koh, C. Y. (2005). The everyday emotional experiences of husbands and wives. In B. Schneider & L. J. Waite (Eds.), *Being together, working apart: Dual-career families and the work-life balance* (pp. 169–89). Cambridge: Cambridge University Press.

Kohn, M. L., & Schooler, C. (1983). *Work and personality: An inquiry into the impact of social stratification.* Norwood, NJ: Ablex Publishing Corporation.

Kusserow, A. (2004). *American individualisms: Child rearing and social class in three neighborhoods* (1st ed.). New York: Palgrave Macmillan.

Lareau, A. (2002). Invisible inequality: Social class and childrearing in black families and white families. *American Sociological Review, 67,* 747–76.

—— (2003). *Unequal childhoods: Class, race, and family life.* Berkeley: University of California Press.

Larson, R., & Richards, M. H. (1994). *Divergent realities: The emotional lives of mothers, fathers, and adolescents.* New York: Basic Books.

Lee, Y. S. (2005). Measuring the gender gap in household labor: Accurately estimating wives' and husbands' contributions. In B. Schneider & L. J. Waite (Eds.), *Being together, working apart: Dual-career families and the work-life balance* (pp. 229–47). Cambridge: Cambridge University Press.

Mulligan, C., Schneider, B., & Wolfe, R. (2005). Non-response and population representation in studies of adolescent time use. *Electronic International Journal of Time Use Research, 2*(1), 33–53.

Pakulski, J., & Waters, M. (1996). The reshaping and dissolution of social class in advanced society. *Theory and Society, 25,* 667–91.

Sayer, L. C., Bianchi, S. M., & Robinson, J. P. (2004). Are parents investing less in children? Trends in mothers' and fathers' time with children. *American Journal of Sociology, 110*(1), 1–43.

Schneider, B. L., & Waite, L. J. (Eds.). (2005). *Being together, working apart: Dual-career families and the work-life balance.* Cambridge: Cambridge University Press.

Snyder, K. A. (in press). "A vocabulary of motives": How parents understand quality time. *Journal of Marriage and Family.*

Weeden, K. A., & Grusky, D. B. (2005). The case for a new class map. *The American Journal of Sociology, 111,* 141–212.

Chapter 10

Parenting practices and schooling

The way class works for new immigrant groups

*Guofang Li**

Introduction: The issue

There is a consensus in sociological and educational research that social class is intricately implicated in the relation between parenting practices and a child's academic development (Bornstein & Bradley, 2003; DeGarmo, Forgatch & Martinez, Jr., 1999; Hughes, Jr. & Perry-Jenkins, 1996). Social class, the hierarchical social distinctions between individuals or groups in a given society or culture (traditionally defined by parental occupation, education, income, and private ownership), is believed to influence parents' ways of raising and educating a child, which in turn affects the child's socio-cognitive and academic development. For example, middle-class parents (mostly European Americans) are reported to be more responsive to their children's needs, more communicative to their children at home, and are more likely to use inductive reasoning and authoritative parenting (clear setting of standards and firm enforcement of rules, and encouragement of independence and individuality, etc.) than their working-class and poor counterparts. They often engage in a process of concerted cultivation in which children's talents are cultivated early on in life through organized activities such as music lessons and sports; this concerted, deliberate cultivation usually fosters a sense of entitlement that helps negotiate more class advantages when interacting with schools (Lareau, 2003). In addition, middle-class parents are also reported to be more involved in their children's education in school and at home. They are more likely to be more directly involved in school than low SES parents. In Lareau's (2000) study, for example, the upper-middle-class parents influence their children's school programs through requests for teachers and for placement in specialized programs, and through direct intervention of classroom instructional practices in subjects such as spelling and math. They also take a more assertive role than working-class parents in shaping the promotion and retention decisions (Lareau, 2000, 2003). These childrearing and parental involvement practices are reported to inculcate more positive attitudes in children toward school and help form better study habits, reduce absenteeism and dropping out, and therefore promote more positive academic outcomes.

In contrast, working-class or poor parents, on the other hand, are reported to rely more on commands and directives in parenting rather than reasoning, and are more authoritarian (i.e., obedience- and status-oriented, and expecting their orders to be

* Associate Professor of Second Language and Literacy Education in the Department of Teacher Education, Michigan State University.

obeyed without explanation) (Baumrind, 1991). They tend to undertake a childrearing process that is characterized as the accomplishment of natural growth in which parents see a clear boundary between adults and children, and children are often left to have control over their own free time and leisure activities. These kinds of childrearing practices are often found to result in a sense of constraint in their interactions in institutional settings (Lareau, 2003). In terms of parental involvement, working-class (and poor) parents are said to hold the idea of separate responsibilities between school and home, whereas middle-class parents see themselves as having shared responsibilities with school in the education process of their children (Lareau, 2000). They tend to view the academic development of the student as a function of the school, and the role of home and school should not interfere with each other (Chavkin & Gonzalez, 1995; Heath, 1983). These parenting practices are believed to be less inductive to positive attitudes toward school and often correlate with lower school achievement.

Though the literature provides strong evidence for the effects of social class on parenting and child development, the research has focused largely on European-American and African-American populations. Several studies have found that when similar measurements are used for immigrant populations, the results are often varied and sometimes contradictory to the mainstream findings. For example, in terms of parenting styles and strategies, Asian immigrant parents (regardless of social class) tend to be authoritarian rather than authoritative; they are more demanding and less responsive and they also pay less attention to emotional support in childrearing (Chao, 1996). However, in comparison with other groups, they experience a higher rate of academic success. Other studies on Asian parenting practices (such as Blair & Qian, 1998; Steinberg et al., 1994) found that parental control was positively related to children's school performance. Research on other immigrant groups such as the Hispanics also suggests different findings. Similar to the Asian groups, Cardona, Nicholson, and Fox (2000) found that middle-class Hispanic mothers reported a higher frequency of discipline and a lower frequency of nurturing with their very young children than Anglo-American mothers and there were no differences in expectations between the two groups. On the contrary, Sampson (2003) found that some poor Latino families demonstrated many middle-class values and childrearing practices described above. Their limitations, however, were language and culture, rather than social class differences. Other researchers such as Li (2005) conclude that when understanding social class influences on immigrants, the locality (e.g., urban vs. suburban) of their settlement also matters as different SES neighborhoods often exert qualitatively different parental involvement patterns.

These contradictory findings suggest that traditional socio-economic indicators may not have the same meaning for immigrant families as they do for American-born families as the social class index alone cannot adequately explain the interrelations between immigrant parenting practices and school achievement. As the US population becomes increasingly multicultural and multiethnic, it is necessary to have a more contextualized approach to understand how social class implicates parenting and schooling among immigrant groups. The goal of this chapter is to discuss from this perspective what social class means and how it works for immigrant groups when they raise and educate their next generation. In the pages that follow, I will first reconceptualize what social class means for immigrant groups; I then discuss how some contextual factors such as culture and ethnicity, and community characteristics, affect immigrants' parenting practices.

Finally, I illustrate the complex workings of social class on parenting through examining one immigrant family's parenting practices and schooling in an inner city neighborhood.

The meaning of social class for new immigrants in the USA

Social class is not only a gradational concept constructed from the social organization of economic relations and defined by social relations of production but also a sociological process through which people live their lives (Anyon, 1980; Li, 2005; Walkerdine, Lucey & Melody, 2001). The former sees social class as affecting the allocation of persons to different positions in the production process, as well as the allocation of materials and other rewards and disadvantages to groups categorized within the class boundaries established by the dominant mode of production (Anyon, 1980). The latter sees social class as lived social practices through which ordinary people live, survive, and cope (Walkerdine, Lucey & Melody, 2001; Weis, 2004). Social class is therefore not simply a static construct but a developing one that can be changed through one's socialization process. As Anyon (1980) summarizes, social class in this sense involves "a complex of social relations that one develops as one grows up—as one acquires and develops certain bodies of knowledge, skills, abilities, and traits, and as one has contact and opportunity in the world" (p. 71).

Wright (1997, 2003) theorizes these two faces of social class as objective and subjective class locations. Objective class location answers to the question "how are people objectively located in distribution of material inequality?" It is usually defined in terms of material standards of living usually indexed by income or wealth, that is, how people earn their money and how much of it they have (Hout, 2006; Wright, 2003). Subjective class location answers to the question of how people locate themselves and others within a social structure of inequality. This aspect of social class is contextually dependent upon how individuals understand class distinctions and position themselves in relation to these distinctions within a social institution. To some extent, this class location is very much related to what people do with their income or wealth—their lifestyles, occupation, culture, and ethnicity; and it can vary considerably across time and space (Hout, 2006; Wright, 2003).

The objective and subjective aspects of social class are important to understanding the new immigrant groups who often transition across time, space, and different social systems. Due to the process of change in their lives, their subjective and objective class locations may not match. As a result, many may be situated in contradictory class locations. Fuligni and Yoshikawa (2003) point out that since many of the socio-economic features of immigrant families were developed in their countries of origin, their socialization and behavior patterns are therefore more closely tied to their native cultural backgrounds than to the norms of contemporary US society. Therefore, immigrant groups' objective class location in the USA may not reflect their subjective class location (and vice versa) due to their dual frame of references in two countries and two class systems. For example, in terms of parental education, due to the differential availability of education around the world, even though many immigrants (e.g., those from Mexico, Africa, or Southeast Asia) may have lower levels of education in comparison to US norms, they are ranked as "middle class" or higher in their native countries. They are likely to bring their educational values to the USA and these values will continue to influence what and how they shape their children's education in the USA. The discrepancy between their subject and objective class locations may in part influence immigrant parents' understanding of the meaning of what being well-educated means in the USA. Parents with high school education in their native countries may perceive their aspiration for their children to attain a high school education as high or satisfactory. Other parents who come from higher educational backgrounds may have higher expectations and aspirations for their children and hence their achievement in the USA.

Similar contradictory class locations can also be found in relation to immigrants' occupations and income levels. Due to the discrepancy between immigrants' native countries and the norms in US society, many immigrants experience a decline or drop in terms of occupation status in the host society (Chiswick, Lee & Miller, 2003; Kochhar, 2005). Though the decline occurs across all levels, it is found to be steepest for the higher skilled occupations such as managers and administrators. This means immigrants who were middle class in their native countries may now work in low-status (and/or low-wage) professions that require minimal educational attainment and skills (and/or English language abilities) due to the immigration policies and the existing class structure in the US society (Fuligni & Yoshikawa, 2003). Among the Mexican immigrants, for example, though their educational attainment may be high in their native country, they tend to work in concentrated non-professional, service occupations, such as the building trades, cleaning and maintenance, and food preparation and serving. In addition, their occupational status continues to lag further behind and their representation in management and professional occupations demonstrates further decline in comparison to that of whites despite the record economic expansion in the USA in the 1990s and the emergence of an information economy (Kochhar, 2005). In fact, as Reich (2000) points out, in what seems to be a period of unprecedented prosperity between 1990 and 2000, the US economy had gone through a major restructuring and decentralization that had resulted in greater disparities between people at the bottom of the economic ladder and those at the top. As a result, many immigrants, though they had a middle-class background in their countries of origin, often have to start at the bottom of the economy and work longer and harder simply to make ends meet. They have become the new "middle-class poor people" in the USA (Sampson, 2003, p. 124).

In terms of income level and wealth, new immigrant groups are found to fare comparatively less well than their US-born counterparts. For example, the 1990 census data show that median immigrant incomes lag about $3,700 for families and about $1,800 for households in comparison to the total US population (Portes & Rumbaut, 1996). If the factor of income packaging (i.e., assembling of income from multiple extended family members and combining formal and informal sources of income) is considered, the median income of immigrants can be even lower (Tienda & Raijman, 2000). Even though many immigrants may have lower economic standing in the USA, due to foreign currency exchange and the economic situations in their native countries, their current income level in the USA is a substantial absolute increase in comparison to what they would have been receiving in their native countries. It is very common for immigrants (regardless of their levels of income) to send portions of their income as remittances to their relatives in their native countries. The World Bank officially estimates that, in 2005, immigrants from developing countries who live in developed countries sent home more than $223 billion to their families in developing countries—a figure more than twice the level of international aid (The World Bank Group, 2006). The unique patterns of immigrants' financial capital suggest that expected associations among parent income, parenting, and children's development, based on traditional national measurement, may not apply to immigrant families (Fuligni & Yoshikawa, 2003).

Though immigrants' unique financial pattern may make them seem even lower in income level, this, however, is by no means a straightforward indicator of their subjective class location or what they do with their income and how they support/invest in their children's education. In fact, research has shown that, despite their low income, many immigrants manage to provide a quality home environment, buy books and/or computers, and pay for tutoring classes (Li, 2002; Sampson, 2003). Many have also relied on co-ethnic networks (Lew, 2006) and/or government programs (Fuligni & Yoshikawa, 2003) as social and cultural resources to support their children's education. Like middle-class parents, many low-income immigrants are able to facilitate "concerted cultivation" with limited resources. They are also willing to be actively involved in school settings when opportunities are provided and structural barriers are removed (Fine, 1993; Delgato-Gaitan, 1990).

The discrepancy between immigrants' subjective and objective class locations in the USA (i.e., related to parents' education, occupation, and income) can be both an underestimate and an overestimate of what takes place within the families. According to Fuligni and Yoshikawa (2003), it can be an underestimate because the parents' objective class location may reflect a belief in the value of education and a level of parental involvement and support that surpasses that of a US equivalent. This is evident in numerous research studies which suggest that immigrants with lower educational backgrounds both have high aspirations and expectations for their children and that many immigrant children achieve higher educational attainment in the USA than their US-born peers of similar class backgrounds. The discrepancy can also be an overestimate of what they can do with their children at home because they usually are less proficient in the English language and less knowledgeable about US schools and instruction. Therefore, to fully understand how social class mediates the impact of immigrants' parenting practices on their children's schooling, it is important to situate their current class standings within the families' specific socio-cultural contexts.

Understanding social class and immigrants' parenting practices: Contextual factors

In addition to the factors discussed above, two contextual factors are also important mediators of social class and parenting practices among immigrants: the culture and ethnicity factor and the school and community factor.

The culture and ethnicity factor

In terms of culture and ethnicity, it is widely accepted that culturally determined child and adult characteristics drive parenting behavior and hence their ways of educating their children (Kotchick & Forehand, 2002; Ogbu, 1981). Though research on culturally specific parenting styles among different ethnic groups has not been conclusive, some generalizations can be made in terms of childrearing values and specific parenting strategies. For example, several researchers have argued that Latinos have a culturally specific approach to education that is characterized as a collective orientation toward childrearing (Bempchat, 1998; Grossman, 1995; Harwood et al., 2002). In this approach, parents stress individual academic achievement but at the same time they stress the importance of group and the extended family. Children are taught to be cooperative and group-oriented rather than competitive and individualistic. They are also taught to value the sacrifices their parents made in their pursuit of a good education (Sampson, 2003). Similarly, several studies have found that Asian immigrant parents (i.e., mothers) have different beliefs from Caucasian parents about their specific roles in their children's education. They not only place greater value on education and are willing to invest more in their children's education, but also use a more direct intervention approach (e.g., through teaching and tutoring at home) to their children's schooling and learning and convey a much stronger belief that they can play a significant role in their children's school success (Chao, 1996; Li, 2002, 2006a, 2006b). They tend to moralize more often, emphasize a greater sense of family obligation, value grades more than general cognitive achievement, are less satisfied with a child's accomplishments, and believe more in effort and less in innate ability as a factor in school success (Hidalgo, Siu & Epstein, 2004). These culturally specific childrearing practices are, at times, in conflict with school practices that are often based on the values and beliefs of middle-class European Americans. Due to the compounding effects of social class and cultural differences, several studies of low-income immigrant families (e.g., Hyslop, 2001; Li, 2003; Sampson, 2003) found that immigrant parents are often unaware of practices essential to helping their children develop academic skills and are confused about what the school expects from their children, often feeling uncertain about how to help their children. Therefore, in addition to language barriers, immigrant children may also experience a cultural mismatch between school and home (Li, 2003, 2006b). Thus, in addition to the language factor, it is also important to consider how social class interacts with cultural beliefs to shape immigrant parenting practices.

The school and community factor

Another factor, the community and school context, is also believed to be significant in mediating immigrants' parenting practices. As I alluded to earlier, working-class and poor immigrants tend to settle in impoverished inner-city neighborhoods while middle-class immigrants often choose to stay in suburbs. It is common knowledge that communities with better SES status tend to have better schools than those of poor neighborhoods (Knapp & Woolverton, 2004; Li, 2005). High SES schools possess more physical capital—they attract better-qualified teachers, receive more resources and funding, are better equipped with technology, and are generally in a safer and more orderly environment. On the contrary, schools that serve low-income students receive fewer resources, experience greater difficulties attracting qualified teachers, and face many more challenges in addressing students' needs (Lee & Burkman, 2002). Suárez-Orozco and Suárez-Orozco (2002) discovered in their research on effective schools for immigrant children that schools the children typically attend range from high-functioning schools with a structure of high expectations and a focus on achievement to catastrophic institutions characterized by ever-present fear of violence, distrust, low expectations, and institutional anomie. The latter kinds of schools, what they call "fields of endangerment," are usually located in neighborhoods troubled by drugs, prostitution, and gangs, often focusing on survival, not learning.

These social and physical characteristics of communities and schools often contribute to the decisions parents make about the way they structure and regulate their children's activities (Kotchick & Forehand, 2002). Gutman, McLoyd, and Tokoyawa (2005) suggest that neighborhood characteristics are important mediators between economic hardship and parent and child behaviors. Higher neighborhood stresses often lessen parents' ability to share positive activities with their children or to be actively involved in their children's learning at home. For low-income parents living in inner-city communities, they may emphasize more parental control and higher expectations for obedience and respect for authority. On the contrary, attendance at higher-SES schools (and residence in those communities) is found to increase immigrant students' academic performance and the positive effect of parents' SES (Portes & MacLeod, 1996). In a multilevel analysis, Beyers and co-authors (2003) found a significant association between neighborhood structure and mothers' parental monitoring that affects adolescents' externalizing behavior. Similarly, in a study on the influence of social environment on Mexican immigrant youths, Eamon (2005) concludes that lower-quality neighborhoods provide lower levels of cognitive stimulation and lead to more parent–youth conflict, and therefore have a negative effect on the youths' reading achievement. In fact, research has suggested that, in high-risk communities, neighborhood danger (such as violence, drugs, and crime) may exert a much stronger influence than culture and ethnicity on parenting. Pinderhughes and co-authors (2001), for example, conducted a comparative analysis of parenting between African-American and European-American parents in rural and urban contexts. They discovered that initial race differences in parental warmth, appropriate and consistent discipline, and harsh interactions disappeared between the two groups of parents in urban high-risk communities. On the contrary, cultural differences in parental behaviors between the two groups were found to be apparent in lower-risk suburban communities. These findings suggest that when considering the effect of social class on immigrants' parenting practices, it is important to consider the locality and neighborhood characteristics as these factors play an important role in shaping how immigrants interact with their children.

How social class works on parenting practices: Profile of one immigrant family

As discussed above, social class works differently on parenting practices among immigrant families who often have dual frames of reference for social mobility (Ogbu, 1983). When analyzing the interaction between social class and immigrants' parenting practices, it is necessary to consider their values and class locations prior to immigration as well as their objective class locations in the USA. In addition, it is important to consider the contextual factors such as language and culture differences, locality of residence, and neighborhood characteristics. That is, immigrants' parenting practices must be understood from an ecological theory of nested contextual influences including personal history, language and culture, schools, and communities, all of which influence parenting (Bronfenbrenner, 1986). Since research on parenting practices and social class has been predominantly quantitative and does not illustrate how parents translate the impact of social class into their everyday living and parenting, in the following, drawing on a larger two-year ethnographic study conducted between 2004 and 2006 in an inner-city community in Western New York State, I provide a detailed picture of how class works in one immigrant family's parenting practices in their day-to-day life (for a detailed description of the methodology, see Li, in press).

The Torkeri family: The middle-class poor people

The Torkeri family originally came to the USA from a southern city of Sudan called Juba in 1999. There are six children in the family: Owen (15 years of age), Nina (13), Fred (11), Irene (6), Jude (3), and Igma (8 months). Owen goes to an inner-city high school; and Nina and Fred (who is a special needs student) go to a public school designated for refugee children, Rainbow Elementary. The family of eight lives in an upper level two-bedroom apartment of a two-story house in an inner-city neighborhood known for its high crime rates, drugs, and alcohol problems. The mother, Anne, stays home to take care of the children while the father, Tifa, works as a welder for forty hours a week to support the family. He earns about $11.79 per hour. He sleeps about four hours a day and rises very early every morning to fix some used cars to make extra money. In addition to supporting the family in the USA Anne and Tifa send about $100 a month to Anne's mother and sister who are taking refuge in Egypt.

At first glance, their occupation and income make them one of the lowest in the US economic ladder. When looking at their immigrant history, it is apparent that they came from middle-class backgrounds in Sudan. Anne was raised in a well-off Christian family in Sudan and attended a private missionary high school called a "comboni" school. After marriage and motherhood, she studied for a BA in Sudan for which she took courses in education, clinical psychology, and women's studies, but did not finish the internship training. Tifa studied law in Egypt as a foreign student and he also wanted to become a medical doctor. He left Egypt to immigrate to the USA before he completed his studies. Because of their educational backgrounds and their English training after immigration, they are both fluent in English in addition to speaking their mother tongues and Arabic.

Having traveled from Sudan to Egypt and then to the USA, Anne and Tifa are very excited about the new opportunities they have in the USA. They have very high expectations and aspirations for their children's education. Like many other immigrant parents who come to the USA to seek better opportunities for their children, Anne stressed the importance of the "chances" that her children can get in the USA. She compared what they had in Sudan with what is available for their children in the USA and believed that their children should make use of the opportunities that they have in the States. She expects them to become responsible citizens and be successful in the future: "I want them [to] go to college, go to university. If they want to do further study, that's good, because there are chances here." Tifa, who also expects the children to go to university, has more specific goals for his children: "Irene is always studying because she wants to be a doctor. One day she will be a doctor. . . . Owen like fixing things, so when I ask him, he said he want to be an engineer. Nina is always talking about, I think, she like to be a teacher, but she didn't say that, you can tell from how she always act. I don't know . . . Fred want to be a policeman." He feels very proud that his children are working hard to achieve what he could not in the USA and he tries his best to support them "because what I didn't achieve . . . if they did it, that will be good for me . . . I'm doing [work] like this to help them to achieve what they are dreaming. I try my best."

Dealing with the inner-city neighborhood

Anne and Tifa do not like where they live. Anne has been particularly unhappy about the neighborhood, "You see kids outside, you hear loud music and all . . . oh my goodness, these neighbors . . . all out drinking; people coming in and out . . . you can see the women that there's something going on. I don't want my kids to go out and play . . ." In order to move out of here, they participate in the Habitat for Humanity program in which Anne and Tifa provide five hundred hours of community service to secure a house in a better neighborhood. "Even now and then, I'm under stress because I'm just thinking if I could just get the place right away, we'll leave."

The neighborhood characteristics have had significant influences on how they discipline their children. Since they live in a neighborhood with lots of drugs, alcohol, and crime, Anne and Tifa have to enforce much stricter rules on their children. They cannot allow them to play outside or visit their neighbors or friends as freely as they would in Sudan. For example, to prevent Owen from joining gangs in school, he is not allowed to play on their basketball team, but is allowed to play on the church basketball team. Anne explains:

> If they go to school, I don't know what they are doing there, like if they have friends, I want to know who are they . . . who are their parents and how do they behave, all these stuff. I'm more concerned about that because my elder son, he got a friend from Philippine, and most of the time, sometimes he stay with his friend . . . I told him I'm not happy . . . to be very strict with you or like telling you not go with friends and all this stuff. But you're still very young that I want to know whom do you go with. Is he staying with his parents or staying lonely, all this stuff, I mean. One day, I said I want to go and meet [the friend's mother] and he said okay. The following day, he came with the mother of the boy. . . . So I said it's good, and one day I took my son and I went to see the house of his friend to make sure that he was in the good place.

Anne and Tifa find that in the USA everyone is too independent and there is not a safe and responsible community to socialize their kids as people do not interfere with other people's business even if they see children are not behaving. "Here they don't do that . . . [they'd say], 'you're not supposed to talk to my kids like that. Who are you? . . . I don't know you and all.' But at home nobody will say that." This kind of indifferent environment was even more difficult for them to raise the girls as danger seems to be everywhere and no adults would interfere if anything goes wrong, especially when the girls are out with their friends. Anne reasons:

> This is more difficult to me. . . . The custom in this country is not like ours. There I can trust anybody, and I can let her go. But here, I can't trust anybody. [Nina] got friends like, sometimes she want to go, I said, "No, no, no. Don't go to anybody's home. Don't enter the home completely. You can play at the porch outside. But don't enter the home." Because if something happen to you, the first thing the police will ask me, why did you let your son or your daughter go there? And you are not there, even if she tell me the story, if I relate the same story to the police, they will not believe me because you are not there.

Race, culture, and ethnicity

One important dimension of their life in the USA is dealing with their Sudanese identity in relation to the "Afro-Americans" (what Anne and Tifa call African-Americans). In most cases, Anne and Tifa found that although they were categorized together with the African-Americans, they clearly differentiate *themselves* from them. Tifa commented, "The way how we look at things, me and Anne and the kids will be different, the value here and the values in Sudan, the different place."

Anne notes that the differences are historical: "The difference between us and them, we know where we come from. We know our generation; we know our elder grandpa and all this stuff . . . have a language that you can speak and you know where you come from." In her view, discrimination exists in the USA, but it exists in many countries. The important thing, in her view, is to value education and struggle for the chances that one has. This is precisely the difference between "Afro-Americans" and Sudanese people and why she thinks that Sudanese people are better in this respect: "There are things like that happening. But is still there is chance. Why do you give up that like for education? They have a lot of chances here." Tifa believed that to combat the bad images of being black in the USA is through doing good things. His philosophy is that "you cannot force somebody to love you; you have to do something good."

Tifa and Anne tried their best to instill this kind of outlook in their children. Tifa reasons that it all depends on how you act and interact with people: "It depend on the way how you are dealing with people. Like me now, I am a big guy, sometimes if I'm going on the street, and they will stop like this way, they are afraid of me. You know, then they will run away from me, but if I smile to people, people will instead come close to me. You know, like that." He himself has been stopped by the police several times, but every time he was respectful so he never got into trouble with them and his record is clean. These positive experiences make him believe that being respectful and doing good things is the key to change people's perceptions of black people. He hopes that his children will also learn these lessons.

For Anne and Tifa, a significant part of being Sudanese is to educate their children in Sudanese ways. To follow their Sudanese culture, they have to educate their children to have more respect and obedience for elders. As Tifa illustrated, "There in Sudan, we have to respect the elder . . . respect a lot of things, we have to respect everybody who is older than you. . . . That's our [culture], it's very important for us . . ."

Another cultural way is to follow the gender roles in their country. Owen, for example, is not required to do many household chores or take care of the younger children, as Nina is, because in Sudan "men are not allowed to do anything." However, Anne believed that children should adopt some American ways, so she occasionally asked Owen to wash dishes. But being the eldest child, Owen is expected to set a good role model for the young ones by doing something good and being responsible and he is under tremendous pressure to be the role model. He remarked, "Mom doesn't want me to do things that are bad so they [younger siblings] don't follow." Compared to Owen, Nina takes on many more household chores—she helps Anne take care of the babies whenever Anne needs to run errands or do community service; she also helps with cooking and cleaning up.

Another cultural way of educating their children is through story-telling. Anne often tells them stories about her life in Sudan—how she grew up there, the schools she attended, and how she listened to her parents. She hopes that they can learn to listen to her and appreciate her advice:

> I always like to tell them the story about our country, how we have been . . . I said, we are now in a different country, with different cultures. . . . If you learn the positive things, it will be good for the future. But if you learn the negative things, it will destroy you. . . . But now, you have been hearing that a lot of stories that kids are misbehaving; they don't listen to their parents, they call police for their parents, and all this. So, this is not our culture. I said, "You should listen. Don't say that 'Oh because we are in America, and free, I can do whatever.'" Because there is too much freedom here for the kids. When I was in school . . . I always listen to what [my parents] said. That's why I reach up to this country. If I don't listen to my parents, I will not even finish my school at that time.

Inner-city schools and parental involvement

Because Anne and Tifa highly value education, they pay close attention to the differences between schools in the USA and in Sudan. The biggest concern for them is the safety of the schools. They were shocked to learn that "even in the primary schools here, they have a lot of crimes." Anne comments: "This is more advanced country. But still there is a lot of crime because there are other crimes that I have never seen in my country." Tifa attributed the crime to the lack of discipline in US schools: "Here they allow kids even to say bad words about their teachers . . . it will never happen in my country as we have high respect for teachers." In terms of curriculum and instruction, they believe that although US schools have more material resources, they are less rigorous than schools in their native country. Comparing to her own schooling experiences, Anne believed that the schools her children attend in the USA are "too loose" and "they learn less in the primary . . ." as they felt that US schools lacked adequate instruction in what they call "general knowledge" which includes math, geography, and history.

Another big concern they have is the ESL (English as a Second Language) programs in the schools. According to Anne, their two sons, Owen and Fred, were the most affected by the ESL programs. By New York State regulations, ESL students are assessed and then pulled out from regular class for small group English language instruction. Anne believed that such pullout programs were detrimental to ESL students like her children. Anne was particularly worried about Owen who is in the eleventh grade and who needs good grades if he wants to go to college. She observed that pulling Owen out of his mainstream classes caused problems in his performance in the content areas of his mainstream classes. His teacher did not make up for him what he missed while he was attending the ESL classes; however, he was graded the same as the regular class students. Sometimes he was not aware that there were assignments while he was in the ESL classes; therefore, he sometimes failed to submit the assignments. Fred, who is in Rainbow Elementary, had a similar experience. As a special needs student, he was pulled out of mainstream classes for three programs: ESL, Physical Therapy, and Occupational Therapy that he had to attend during school hours. Anne thought that if he could attend the mainstream classes instead of being pulled out for the ESL class, he would do much better.

In order to fight for their children to get the same education as US-born children, for three years Anne has repeatedly taken the issue to the teachers and schools. She went to

Owen's high school to complain and she went and talked to Fred's teachers and principal in the international school. She even went to some school meetings, including PTA meetings, to raise the issues, but the schools "insist that the kids should take the ESL . . . and it's according to the system, [the schools] can't change anything. It [depends] on the government . . ."

Realizing that they have to fight the "system," Anne actively finds ways to work the system. Her frustration with the ESL programs in the two schools made her realize the importance of school choice for her children. After a couple of attempts to change schools for her children, Anne learned that Owen, Nina, and Fred, who were not born in the USA, had no choice but to go to the schools designated for refugee children. She decided that her younger children who either grew up or were born in the USA would not attend those schools. She also learned from her Sudanese friends that "the magnet school, usually, you go to the City Hall, and then they do it through lottery. If you fill the paper and . . . if they pick one of your kids, then if they are siblings, they can go through." She describes how she first enrolled Irene in a different school:

> I would like to apply for my daughter [Irene], but I don't want her to go to Rainbow Elementary . . . because she starts here. That means, she don't have any problem with the language. . . . My idea is I want her either [to] go to the charter school, or either to go to the magnet schools. And they said, magnet school, they will not allow her to go there unless you have to apply at the City Hall also. That's the same obstacles. But the charter school sent me a letter and I took all the paper they needed, document that they needed, and now she got the acceptance.

Since Jude also did not have any prior schooling experiences in Sudan or Egypt, Anne managed to send her to the same charter school that Irene attended—a school that gives more reading assignments and homework every day. When Irene and Jude finished preschool and kindergarten, Anne managed to enroll them in a school outside the city.

Anne and Tifa also learned that Nina has different options for middle school. Nina did not want to become a teacher, as Tifa had observed. She wants to become an artist, and her school counselor advised her to go to an art academy. Since they really wanted Nina to go to university, they decided she should apply for a more academically oriented school even though they knew that they were forcing her to do things that she did not like and there was a possibility that she might not do well. Although getting the information about the school and sending in their application was difficult and worrisome, and they even missed their first orientation, Nina was eventually accepted. Knowing that there are differences in schools and programs, Anne expressed that she would continue to struggle for her children. "But you have to struggle for yourself. If you didn't struggle, you are not able to [get ahead] from where you start . . ."

Concerted cultivation at home

Anne and Tifa's perception of school differences makes them more vigilant about their children's studies at home. They realized that "here, if the parents didn't pay attention, after some time the teacher will stop paying attention too. . . . They don't care." Since Tifa works most of the time, Anne takes up most of the responsibility of checking the children's homework. With limited English and limited understanding of the American school system, it is a tremendously difficult task for her. ✓

Every day when the children come back from school, Anne asks them about what happened in school and checks their backpacks to see what kinds of homework they have. The children usually watch TV or play on their old computer while she gets supper ready. Owen usually goes to a nearby after-school program to tutor young children for a couple of hours to make some extra money. After supper, Anne asks everyone to clean up the dining table and their coffee table to do their homework. When they study, no eating or drinking is allowed because it might ruin their books and notebooks. Anne believes that it is important to "do one thing at a time."

While the older children do their homework, Anne helps the younger ones (Irene and Jude) with reading and writing and practice spelling. She also plays card games with them to teach numbers, colors, animals, and fruits, and Scrabble to increase their vocabulary. Sometimes, they invent games to play. After this, Anne tries to do the same thing with Fred, who is required to read twenty minutes a day for his school assignment, but it is very tough to get him to read. Because of his disability, Fred "easily gets mad." In addition to writing, Anne also helps Fred with math. For Owen and Nina, who are older, Anne just "let[s] them do it by themselves" first and then checks later "if they are doing it right or wrong."

Although most of the time Anne enlists Owen's help with difficult words or math problems, she tries her best to be actively involved in his homework as well. She is not happy that he does not pay attention to his handwriting and spends too much time playing basketball. She knows that she can't keep him studying all the time, but she has to remind him that he should not "put basketball like the major thing." She tries to review his major assignments before he hands them in. When reviewing some of his essays, she teaches him that how he writes should be different from how he speaks, and she also points out some spelling errors and asks him to check dictionaries. Her active involvement at times saves Owen from unfair penalization from the school. One time, Owen's teacher called and said that Owen did not submit his essay assignment. Anne told him that she just reviewed it the night before and corrected it for him.

This incident reinforced her belief that it is very important for her to be actively involved in her children's education. When the children have a test, Anne usually helps them prepare for it. She lets them study first and then she tests them: "First of all, you study by yourself and then, if you know yourself that you learn them all by heart and you come and then, I will do the test for you." Her children joked, "Mom, you are pretending that you are a teacher."

In addition to being closely involved in homework, concerted cultivation for the children's development in the Torkeri home is also reflected in the activities into which Anne and Tifa actively involve the children through searching out a variety of resources and community organizations such as the church. For example, since Nina and Fred are interested in music and art, Anne and Tifa actively involve them in the church activities where Fred can play drums and Nina can participate in dancing and singing. Through the church activities, Anne also signed up Nina and Fred for many summer camp activities that were free or very low-cost. Since Fred and Owen like sports such as soccer and basketball and the city schools do not offer these extracurricular activities in the summer, Anne was looking to other community resources for these activities. In sum, the Torkeri family's concerted cultivation of their children's education and upward social mobility occurred in multiple immigrant "free spaces" crossing both private and public spheres (Centrie, 2000, p. 81). By doing so, they instilled in their children high expectations for learning and strong desires for success in America.

Conclusion

The Torkeri family's story of parenting in inner-city USA suggests that their income level and their current occupation, that is, their objective class location, is not a determinant factor that shapes immigrants' parenting practices. Instead, it is the complex workings of the family's current class location, their prior class location, their cultural practices, as well as the neighborhood and school conditions, that influence how the parents educate their children and get involved in their schooling. As their story shows, the family's middle-class background shapes their high expectations for their children and their knowledge base as to what schools should be like. Their middle-class background also afforded the parents ability to search for different resources to facilitate their children's extra-curriculum activities (though in a more limited way), and to fight with the school about ESL programs and other school policies. The cultural values, those that emphasize discipline and respect for elders, shape how they expect their children to behave in school and home and how they educate their children to combat the racism against African-Americans or black people in general. However, their efforts were clearly shadowed by the poor and unsafe neighborhood and school conditions. In order to keep them safe and protected, they have to enforce strict discipline and parental control of their children's whereabouts. They also made a more conscious effort to get involved in their schoolwork at home. More important, they managed to create multiple "free spaces" (Centrie, 2000) and (re)work the school system in order to overcome negative school conditions.

The family's parenting practices within their socio-cultural contexts suggest that traditional class analysis that focuses exclusively on parental education, occupation, and income does not work for immigrant families. Rather, a more contextualized approach that emphasizes immigrants' family history, race, culture, and locality will be more appropriate in understanding how social class works for immigrant groups. Without this broad lens of analysis, we will stop short of understanding how immigrant families really operate (Kotchick & Forehand, 2002).

Conceptualizing parenting within a family's social, economic, and cultural context has important implications for educational policy. First, it is important to break the established binary positions concerning parental practices between working-class/poor and middle-class parents (e.g., those discussed in the beginning of this chapter). As the Torkeri family's story demonstrates, poor families may hold middle-class values, attitudes, and worldview and adopt the childrearing practice of concerted cultivation, all of which are important to the children's educational process (Sampson, 2003). As other research has demonstrated, poor children from many poor families do achieve success in school. Therefore, it is necessary to avoid the family deficit model and situate the family's parenting practices and schooling within their specific socio-cultural and socio-historical contexts.

Second, it is necessary to look beyond the family to focus on school and community factors that also contribute to immigrant children's underachievement. As the family's story suggests, though the family works hard to educate their children at home through their own cultural values and childrearing practices, the structural barriers from the inner-city schools that reproduce the poverty cycle, and the immigration system that devalues their prior experiences, have significantly affected what the family can do with their children's schooling outside home. Following Bourdieu's (1990) argument that schools transmit middle-class "cultural capital" from one generation to the next, thus ensuring the dominance of the ruling class, inner-city poor schools seemed to have functioned as a mediation agency that helps "filter out" poor immigrant minorities' own cultural capital, though it may also be middle class in its own right. As the Torkeri family's stories suggest, this is often processed *"against their will"* through language, examinations, and certifications or, in Bourdieu's terms, Pedagogical Actions (PA) (Bourdieu, 1990, p. x, original italics). These pedagogical actions are seen as symbolic violence that arbitrates the space of social positions among different cultural groups. Therefore, to understand new immigrants' parenting practices in inner-city contexts, it is necessary to crystallize how and what pedagogical actions the schools take to mediate/regulate how social class works for these groups of newcomers and the next generation, often against their will.

Questions for discussion

1. Are childrearing practices culturally specific or are they universal? Do they conflict with school practices? If so, how? Discuss this by drawing from your own or your classmates' experiences in schools and colleges.
2. What is meant by objective and subjective class locations? How does an understanding of these concepts contribute to the field of immigrant/diaspora studies?
3. How has the development of a contradictory class location been exacerbated by the contemporary US economy? Predict the potential consequences of this development on both a national and global scale.
4. Why is the immigrant's unique financial pattern not a straightforward indicator of their subjective class location? How are they able to facilitate "concerted cultivation" with limited resources?
5. Based on Li's discussion of Asian immigrants and Hispanic parents, discuss the extent to which our current understanding of race and class are limited to a black–white binary. What lessons can be learned from a more culturally and ethnically inclusive look at class?
6. Drawing from the example of the Sudanese family, how does Li's chapter contribute to our understanding of the interaction between social class and educational systems in other countries?
7. Why should the US educational system address the needs of immigrant communities? Can these concerns, regarding immigrant needs, be addressed by educational policies? Might these issues be discussed and potentially alleviated (or needs fulfilled) outside of traditional educational contexts? Discuss your answers.
8. Li advises that schools must think about what pedagogical actions they could take to mediate/regulate how social class works for immigrant groups. What are these possible pedagogical actions, and how can they be implemented in the classroom?

References

Anyon, J. (1980). Social class and the hidden curriculum of work. *Journal of Education, 162*(1), 67–92.

Baumrind, D. (1991). The influence of parenting style on adolescent competence and substance use. *Journal of Early Adolescence, 11*(1), 56–95.

Bemchat, J. (1998) *Against the odds: How "at-risk" students exceed expectations.* San Francisco: Jossey-Bass.

Beyers, J. M., Bates, J. E., Pettit, G. S., & Dodge, K. A. (2003). Neighborhood structure, parenting processes, and the development of youths' externalizing behaviors: A multilevel analysis. *American Journal of Community Psychology, 31*(1–2): 35–53.

Blair, S. L., & Qian, Z. (1998). Family and Asian students' educational performance. *Journal of Family Issues, 19,* 355–74.

Bornstein, M. H., & Bradley, R. H. (Eds.). (2003). *Socioeconomic status, parenting, and child development.* Mahwah, NJ: Lawrence Erlbaum Associates.

Bourdieu, P. (1990). Introduction. In P. Bourdieu & J. Passeron (Eds.), *Reproduction in education, society and culture* (1970). Trans. Richard Nice. London: Sage Publications.

Bronfenbrenner, U. (1986). Ecology of the family as a context for human development: Research perspectives. *Developmental Psychology, 22,* 723–42.

Cardona, P. G., Nicholson, B. C., & Fox, R. A. (2000). Parenting among Hispanic and Anglo-American mothers with young children. *The Journal of Social Psychology, 140*(3), 357–65.

Centrie, C. (2000). Free spaces unbound: Families, community, and Vietnamese high school students' identities. In L. Weis & M. Fine (Eds.), *Construction sites: Evacuating race, class, and gender among urban youth* (pp. 65–83). New York: Teachers College Press.

Chao, R. K. (1996). Chinese and European American mothers' beliefs about the role of parenting in children's school success. *Journal of Cross-Cultural Psychology, 27*(4), 403–23.

Chavkin, N., & Gonzalez, D. L. (1995). Forging partnerships between Mexican-American parents and the schools. Washington, DC: Office of Educational Research and Improvement (ERIC Document Reproduction Service No. ED 388 489).

Chiswick, B. R., Lee, Y. L., & Miller, P. W. (2003) Patterns of immigrant occupational attainment in a longitudinal survey. *International Migration, 41*(4), 47–68.

DeGarmo, D. S., Forgatch, M. S., & Martinez, C. R., Jr. (1999). Parenting of divorced mothers as a link between social status and boys' academic outcomes: Unpacking the effects of socioeconomic status. *Child Development, 70*(5), 1231–45.

Delgado-Gaitan, C. (1990). *Literacy for empowerment: The role of parents in children's education.* New York: Falmer Press.

Eamon, M. K. (2005). Social-demographic, school, neighborhood, and parenting influences on the academic achievement of Latino young adolescents. *Journal of Youth and Adolescence, 34*(2), 163–74.

Fine, M. (1993) [Ap]parent involvement: Reflections on parents, power, and urban public schools. *Teachers College Record, 94*(4), 682–710.

Fuligni, A. J., & Yoshikawa, H. (2003). Socioeconomic resources, parenting, poverty, and child development among immigrant families. In M. H. Bornstein & R. H. Bradley (Eds.), *Socioeconomic status, parenting, and child development* (pp. 107–24). Mahwah, NJ: Lawrence Erlbaum Associates.

Grossman, F. (1995). *Special education in a diverse society.* Boston: Allyn and Bacon.

Gutman, L. M., McLoyd, V. C., & Tokoyawa, T. (2005). Financial strain, neighborhood stress, parenting behaviors, and adolescent adjustment in urban African-American families. *Journal of Research on Adolescence, 15*(4), 425–49.

Harwood, R. H., Leyendecker, Carlson, V., Asecio, M., & Miller, A. (2002). Parenting among

Latino families in the US. In M. H. Bornstein (Ed.), *Social conditions and applied parenting* (pp. 47–58). Mahwah, NJ: Lawrence Erlbaum.

Heath, S. B. (1983). *Ways with words: Language, life, and work in communities and classrooms.* New York: Cambridge University Press.

Hidalgo, N., Siu, S.-F., & Epstein, J. (2004). Research on families, schools and communities: A multicultural perspective. In J. A. Banks & C. A. M. Banks (Eds.), *Handbook for research on multicultural education* (2nd ed.) (pp. 631–55). San Francisco: Jossey-Bass.

Hout, M. (2006). *How class works: Objective and subjective aspects of class since the 1970s.* Paper presented at the conference "How Class Works," New York University (April 21, 2006), New York.

Hughes, R., Jr., & Perry-Jenkins, M. (1996). Social class issues in family life education. *Family Relations, 45*(2), 175–82.

Hyslop, N. (2001). Hispanic parental involvement in home literacy. *ERIC Digest D158.*

Knapp, M. S., & Woolverton, S. (2004). Social class and schooling. In J. A. Banks & C. A. M. Banks (Eds.), *Handbook of research on multicultural education* (2nd ed.) (pp. 656–81). New York: Jossey-Bass.

Kochhar, R. (2005). *The occupational status and mobility of Hispanics.* Washington, DC: Pew Hispanic Center.

Kotchick, B. A., & Forehand, R. (2002). Putting parenting in perspective: A discussion of the contextual factors that shape parenting practices. *Journal of Child and Family Studies, 11*(30), 255–69.

Lareau, A. (2000). *Home advantage: Social class and parental intervention in elementary education* (2nd ed.). New York: Rowman & Littlefield Publishers.

—— (2003). *Unequal childhoods: Class, race, and family life.* Los Angeles: University of California Press.

Lee, E. V., & Burkman, D. T. (2002). *Inequality at the starting gate: Social background differences in achievement as children begin school.* Washington, DC: Economic Policy Institute.

Lew, J. (2006). *Asian Americans in class: Charting the achievement gap among Korean American youth.* New York: Teachers College Press.

Li, G. (2002). *"East is east, west is west?" Home literacy, culture, and schooling.* New York: Peter Lang.

—— (2003). Literacy, culture, and politics of schooling: Counter narratives of a Chinese-Canadian family. *Anthropology & Education Quarterly, 34*(2), 184–206.

—— (2005). *Asian-American education across the class line: A multi-site report.* Buffalo, NY: GSE Publications, SUNY Press.

—— (2006a). What do parents think? Middle-class Chinese immigrant parents' perspectives on literacy learning, homework, and school–home communication. *The School Community Journal, 16*(2), 25–44.

—— (2006b). *Culturally contested pedagogy: Battles of literacy and schooling between mainstream teachers and Asian immigrant parents.* Albany: SUNY Press.

—— (in press). *Culturally contested literacies: America's "rainbow underclass" and urban schools.* New York: Routledge.

Ogbu, J. U. (1981). Origins of human competence: A cultural-ecological perspective. *Child Development, 52,* 413–29.

Pinderhughes, E. E., Nix, R., Foster, E. M., & Jones, D. (2001). Parenting in context: Impact of neighborhood poverty, residential stability, public services, social networks, and danger on parental behaviors. *Journal of Marriage and Family, 63* (November): 941–53.

Portes, A., & MacLeod, D. (1996). Educational progress of children of immigrants: The roles of class, ethnicity, and social context. *Sociology of Education, 69,* 255–75.

Portes, A., & Rumbaut, R. G. (1996). *Immigrant America: A portrait* (2nd ed.). Berkeley, CA: University of California Press.

Reich, R. (2000). *The future of success: Working and living in the new economy.* New York: Vintage.

Sampson, W. A. (2003). *Poor Latino families and school preparation: Are they doing the right things?* Lanham, MD: Scarecrow Press.

Steinberg, L., Lamborn, S. D., Darling, N., Mounts, N. S., & Dornbusch, S. M. (1994). Overtime changes in adjustment and competence among adolescents from authoritative, authoritarian, indulgent, and neglectful families. *Child Development, 65,* 754–70.

Suárez-Orozco, C., & Suárez-Orozco, M. M. (2002). *Children of immigrants.* Cambridge, MA: Harvard University Press.

The World Bank Group (2006). *First world development indicators.* Retrieved on October 27, 2006 from http://devdata.worldbank.org/wdi2005/Cover.htm.

Tienda, M., & Raijman, R. (2000). Immigrants' income packaging and invisible labor force activity. *Social Science Quarterly, 81,* 291–310.

Walkerdine, V., Lucey, H., & Melody, J. (2001). *Growing up girl: Psychosocial explorations of gender and class.* New York: New York University Press.

Weis, L. (2004). *Class reunion: The remaking of the American white working-class.* New York: Routledge.

Wright, E. O. (1997). *Class counts: Comparative studies in class analysis.* Cambridge: Cambridge University Press.

—— (2003). Social class. In G. Ritzer (Ed.), *Encyclopedia of social theory.* Thousand Oaks, CA: Sage.

Section 3

Schooling class

Chapter 11

Persisting social class inequality in US education

Adam Gamoran[*]

For the "millennium" issue of *Sociology of Education*, I had the opportunity to offer a forecast for the future of US educational inequality during the twenty-first century (Gamoran, 2001). After reviewing past trends and available evidence about the causes of educational inequality, I reached two conclusions: First, I predicted that the next hundred years would witness a substantial decline in racial inequality in educational outcomes. Second, I argued that social class inequality would persist through the next century at about the same level as it had in the previous.

My first conclusion has received critical attention, enough to raise doubts about the optimistic forecast of declining racial inequality (Alexander, 2001; Gosa & Alexander, 2007; Long, Kelly, & Gamoran, 2005). My second, more pessimistic conclusion regarding persistent social class inequality has received less attention in the literature. The purpose of this chapter is to re-examine that conclusion in light of evidence that has come to light since 2000, and in recognition of new policies and programs designed to reduce inequality of educational opportunity. To foreshadow my current findings, the updated evidence and new policies do not provide a basis for overturning the earlier conclusion that the outcomes of US education will continue to be stratified by social class.

The stratification of opportunity in US education

I provided six reasons to support my conclusion that social class inequality will persist through the twenty-first century. (When I wrote of social class inequality, I referred to socioeconomic differences, that is, differences in educational achievement and attainment associated with parents' education, occupation, and income.) The first, and perhaps most compelling, argument is that the differences, which are substantial, have persisted at steady levels throughout the twentieth century. Evidence on achievement inequality came from Campbell, Hombo, and Mazzeo's (2000) trend analyses of the National Assessment of Educational Progress (NAEP) over three decades. In contrast to race differences in test scores, which discernibly narrowed particularly from about 1970 to 1988, the trends showed that achievement differences by parents' education hardly wavered. Moreover, differences in attainment by socioeconomic background have been similarly stubborn in their persistence. Despite the dramatic expansion of US education over the course of the twentieth century, relative differences in levels of schooling attained by

* Professor of Sociology and Educational Policy Studies at the University of Wisconsin-Madison.

persons from varied social class origins were largely preserved (Hout, Raftery, & Bell, 1993).

Second, a compelling theory has emerged that helps explain the persistence of educational inequality. According to "maximally maintained inequality," persons in positions of privilege strive to pass on their advantages to their offspring (Raftery & Hout, 1993; Shavit & Blossfeld, 1993). When new opportunities arise (e.g., in the form of educational expansion), the privileged classes are often better positioned to grasp the new opportunities than are their disadvantaged counterparts. As a metaphor for the process of educational expansion with persisting inequality, one may think of educational allocation as an expanding pie: each group's piece of the pie becomes larger, but the relative differences among pieces are preserved. According to maximally maintained inequality, only when a level of attainment is saturated for the privileged group—that is, when nearly all the members of the privileged class have attained some level of schooling—do members of the lower class have a chance to catch up. Yet in the case of the USA, Hout, Raftery, and Bell (1993) found that members of disadvantaged social classes are not closing the gap in high school completion, even though almost all members of the middle class now complete high school. This suggests that educational inequality in the USA has been powerfully maintained despite expansion.

Findings of past inequality might say little about future inequality if the underlying conditions that supported inequality were to change. However, this has not occurred, so a third reason to expect persisting social class inequality is that the same broader social conditions that supported educational inequality in the twentieth century are still operating in the twenty-first. US education is still largely supported by property taxes, so that wealthier communities have more resources to support education. The USA is still a society stratified by social class and race; indeed schools today exhibit more black–white segregation than at any time in the past forty years (Gamoran & Long, 2007). Recent tax policies and income trends appear to have widened inequalities of family resources (Krugman, 2004). This is particularly important because, even if school resources were equalized, the reduction in educational inequality would be modest, as inequality by social background is more closely linked to students' home resources than to the resources available in their schools (Coleman et al., 1972; Hanushek, 1996; Jencks et al., 1972; Rothstein, 2004). Moreover, recent federal policies designed to equalize opportunities for students of different social backgrounds will be limited in their impact because, among other reasons, only about 10 percent of education funding derives from federal sources (more about current federal policy appears below). Culturally, schools are still more aligned with middle-class families than with those of less privileged origins, and middle-class families have a sense of entitlement about their schools that disadvantaged families often do not share (Lareau, 1989, 2003). Overall, differences in school performance are rooted in inequalities that lie outside the school, and the persistence of inequalities outside school portends similar persistence in inequality of educational outcomes (Rothstein, 2004).

The final three reasons are more political than sociological. Unlike race, social class is not constitutionally protected: there is no guarantee of equal opportunity on the basis of income in the USA. Moreover, the USA has witnessed essentially no political mobilization on the part of the poor, in contrast to the crucially important mobilization activities of race, ethnic, language minority, and gender movements. Finally, and corresponding to the preceding, whereas many social programs have been directed at enhancing opportunities for minorities and women, educational programs directed at those who are economically disadvantaged have been far fewer. Of course, many voices have been heard in support of the education of poor children, including calls in the late twentieth century for economic school integration (Kahlenberg, 1996, 2001), but there are as yet few signs that such programs are taking hold.

For all these reasons, I concluded that the levels of inequality in achievement and attainment, which had remained at steady rates as long as they had been monitored during the twentieth century, would persist through the twenty-first.

New evidence, theories, and policies on educational inequality

Has any recent evidence come to light that bears on the forecast of persisting inequality? Achievement trend data have become available for a few more years. In addition, new analyses have been conducted of the twentieth-century trends in attainment. These analyses and findings tend to reinforce my earlier conclusions. Similarly, new explanations and policies concerning educational inequality fail to overturn my previous conclusion.

Update on trends in achievement and attainment

NAEP trends are now available for reading and mathematics through 2004, and the most recent trends for social background largely confirm the patterns through 1999: test score differences among students whose parents obtained different levels of education have been largely stable since the 1970s (Perie, Moran, & Lutkus, 2005). I focus mainly on the trends for thirteen-year-olds, because the trends for seventeen-year-olds are affected to an unknown degree by fluctuations in the population of students who are still enrolled in school at that age. Among thirteen-year-olds, the gap in reading achievement between students whose parents dropped out of high school and those whose parents completed college narrowed very slightly (and non-significantly) between 1980 and 2004, from 34 points to 32 points. The gap was narrowest in 1988 (29 points), but now it is about as large as it was twenty-five years ago. The trends are more positive in mathematics, as the gains of the 1980s have not all been given up: what was a 39 point difference in 1978 now stands at 30 points, a statistically significant improvement. Most of this improvement, however, occurred between 1978 and 1982, when the gap was measured at 31 points. Since 1990, NAEP mathematics scores have risen at all levels of parental education, but the gaps have been preserved.

The evidence available on trends in educational attainment has not changed much over the past five years, but fresh analyses have been conducted that shed new light on patterns of inequality by social class. In particular, analyses of three waves of national surveys by the National Center for Education Statistics (NCES)—the National Longitudinal Study of the High School Class of 1972, the High School and Beyond Study (base year 1980), and the National Educational Longitudinal Study (base year 1988)—have been scrutinized for differences in attainment among the three cohorts. As with earlier (mainly census-based) studies, socioeconomic differences are persistent—and substantial. For example, Grodsky (in press) reported that having college-educated parents rather than high school-educated parents was worth as much scoring 88 points higher on the SAT. Similarly, Roksa, Grodsky, Arum, and Gamoran (2007, p. 180) reported that "in the 1990s, individuals whose parents graduated from college had approximately five times the odds of entering both baccalaureate and elite baccalaureate institutions as individuals whose parents graduated from high school, all else equal." Even after controlling for high school achievement, the children of college-educated parents have an advantage of 2.5 times (any four-year college) to 4 times (elite college) compared to the offspring of parents with high school educations. Father's occupation also contributed to stratified educational attainment, but the effects were less salient. In the cases of both parental education and father's occupation, levels of inequality were no smaller in the 1990s than they had been in the 1970s.

These findings of stability across three cohorts of high school graduates also emerged in new analyses by Turley, Santos, and Ceja (in press), which focused on variation among students from different social origins in applications to college during the senior year of high school (and the following summer and fall). As the first step towards college enrollment, the application process sheds light on differential expectations as well as serving as the link between expectations and enrollment. Focusing on parents' education and income, the authors noted the same general patterns of stability in social class stratification that other analysts have found with respect to class differences in college enrollment. The pattern of stability for social class differences held for applications to any college, applications to four-year colleges, and applications to the most selective four-year colleges. Income differences tended to fluctuate somewhat, but the gaps in applications between income categories were no smaller for the class of 1992 than they had been for the class of 1972. Gaps by parents' education were consistently stable, with one exception: Rates of applications among persons whose parents were college graduates grew even farther ahead of those whose parents were high school graduates in 1982 and 1992 compared to 1972. For example, the former were 1.96 more times likely than the latter to apply to a four-year college in 1972, 2.95 times more likely in 1982, and 2.71 times more likely in 1992. Thus, any departure from stability found in these data reflected *increases* rather than decreases in social class inequality in educational attainment.

New explanations for persisting inequality

According to the theory of maximally maintained inequality, when a transition becomes saturated in the privileged class (that is, nearly all members of the privileged class reach a given level of education), inequality in the attainment of that level will decline. In the US, however, despite educational expansion, that has not occurred, even at the levels of high school completion and college enrollment, which are overwhelmingly accomplished by the middle classes. Why has inequality not diminished at these levels? One explanation is that when most students reach a given level of schooling, inequality re-emerges through differentiation within that level. For example, as high school became a mass institution, separate tracks (academic, general, vocational) emerged that tended to be stratified by social class (e.g., Gamoran, 1987). Similarly, the rise of community colleges may be seen in part as an effort to introduce further levels of stratification within the US education system as higher education becomes more and more prevalent (e.g., Brint & Karabel, 1989). Lucas (2001) coined the term "effectively maintained inequality" to describe this process of qualitative distinctions preserving inequalities even as quantitative differences fade. He provided evidence to support this pattern for the USA, as did Ayalon and Shavit (2004) for Israel. The findings of Turley, Santos, and Ceja (in press) on unequal probabilities of college applications to two-year, four-year, and highly selective four-year colleges also reflect effectively maintained inequality in the differentiation of opportunities for higher education.

New evidence on policies to reduce inequality

Recently, evidence has come to light that suggests that policies about affirmative action and financial aid may have the result of exacerbating rather than ameliorating inequality by social class. Whether federal and state programs to reduce inequalities in test scores and high school completion will have their intended effects is also very much open to question.

Class inequality in higher education

In his research on trends in inequality by race and class, Grodsky (in press) found that elite universities have exhibited a preference for minority students—reflecting affirmative action policies—but not for students from disadvantaged economic circumstances, controlling for race. On the basis of findings like these, critics have charged that race-based affirmative action leaves out the students who need it most: economically disadvantaged minority students (Kahlenberg, 1996). Although affirmative action may continue to reduce racial gaps in college enrollment, it does little to reduce social class inequality.

Financial aid policies would seem likely candidates for reducing economic inequality in access to higher education. In the USA, unlike many other countries, most of the cost of higher education is borne by students and their families (although tuition charges are becoming more prominent around the world as other nations move towards the US model of privately-funded higher education; see Heller & Rogers, 2006). One might expect, therefore, that the provision of financial aid for needy students would be an effective mechanism for reducing inequality that results from unequal family resources. The current trend in US higher education, however, is away from need-based financial aid and towards merit-based financial aid, that is, towards financial aid that is awarded on the basis of students' accomplishments during high school (Heller & Rogers, 2006). Since high school achievement is stratified by social class, merit aid tends to exacerbate inequalities (Heller, 2006; Heller & Rogers, 2006). Even when merit aid is means-tested—that is, provided to the most meritorious of a disadvantaged group—it is not likely to reduce inequality much because the highest achievers within a disadvantaged group tend to be relatively advantaged within that group (e.g., low-income students with relatively more educated parents; see Heller & Marin, 2004). Only need-based aid for all those who meet the admission standards of a given institution is likely to reduce class inequality, and programs of this sort are becoming less prevalent. This trend also points towards persisting class inequality, if not growing class-based inequality, in higher education enrollments. It is the sort of policy that may underlie findings reported by Turley, Santos, and Ceja (in press), that the offspring of the most educated parents are more likely to apply to college, and to the most prestigious colleges, compared to those who have parents with less education.

Class inequality in K-12 education: No child left behind?

At the K-12 level, US education has been subjected to a series of standards-based reforms since the 1980s. The most recent of these federal initiatives, the No Child Left Behind Act of 2001 (NCLB, 2002), is distinctive in its emphasis on inequality. Reducing achievement gaps is a central goal of NCLB, and is the main reason it has received strong support from congressional Democrats as well as Republicans (Loveless, in press). Several elements of NCLB support the aim of reducing inequality, so in theory at least, this is a policy that could help reduce stratification by social class.

NCLB requires states, as a condition of receiving federal education funding, to set standards for student performance and to assess students annually in reading and mathematics in grades 3 through 8 and once in high school. Each state sets a cut point on its achievement tests that identifies students as "proficient." The fraction of students that are required to reach the proficiency threshold increases over time, towards the goal of 100 percent proficient by 2013–14. All districts and schools are held accountable for bringing increasing proportions of students to proficiency. Most significant for inequality is that these proportions are assessed not just for students overall, but for students in population subgroups, including race/ethnic groups, students on free and reduced-price lunch, students with disabilities, and English language learners. (Population subgroups must reach a certain size to be counted; the group size varies by state and subgroup but around forty is typical.) This feature of NCLB means that schools cannot hide their low-achieving subgroups behind overall high averages. Nor can schools artificially boost scores by holding out students from taking the test, or by designating students as having special needs: testing at least 95 percent of students is another NCLB standard, and no more than 3 percent of students can take an alternative assessment for special needs students. English language learners must also be assessed, first in English language competence and then, beginning in their second year in the USA, in subject areas.

Reporting scores for students on free and reduced-price lunch is a major step forward towards highlighting the achievement gap for students from economically disadvantaged families. In a society where race and ethnicity tend to be recognized social categories but economic status is not, this feature of education policy stands apart from past reforms. Of course, it is one thing to identify achievement gaps and quite another to remedy them. NCLB includes several potential remedies, which sound promising in principle but whose early implementation has been problematic.

Under NCLB, a school whose students do not reach the required proportion proficient in a given year is labeled as not making "adequate yearly progress" (AYP). A school that does not make AYP for two successive years is required to develop an improvement plan, offer professional development to teachers, and allow students to transfer to another, more successful school. After three years, schools are required to offer free tutoring to students. More punitive sanctions begin with the fourth year, ultimately leading to the reconstitution of schools. If these sanctions result in inducing improvements in the schools of poor children, and/or in providing better learning opportunities to children from disadvantaged circumstances, then NCLB would help close the social class achievement gap. Who could argue with free tutoring, one of the most proven strategies for improving achievement of struggling students? NCLB also contains supplemental funds for schools to use research-proven strategies for teaching reading, in a program known as

Reading First. Adopting proven strategies for children from poor families seems to take direct aim at social class inequality in education.

Finally, NCLB requires states to place a "highly qualified teacher" in every classroom, meaning a teacher who has a college degree, teaching certification, and has demonstrated subject-matter competence. Because prior research has uncovered inequality in teacher qualifications across schools serving different populations (e.g., Oakes et al., 1990), the highly qualified teacher requirement could also lead to more equal learning opportunities than currently prevails.

While NCLB has been effective at identifying achievement gaps, its strategies for improvement have yet to yield the desired results. NAEP scores do not show declines in achievement gap among children from more and less educated parents, but it is too soon to judge NCLB by NAEP scores. More troubling is that many of the strategies are flawed in their design or implementation. Most important, the approach to measuring AYP is likely to mix up effective and ineffective schools. As reviewed above, student achievement reflects many conditions, of which the school is but one, and often not the most important. Yet under NCLB, schools are held fully accountable for bringing a designated fraction of students to an absolute achievement target. In reality, many schools with high achievement levels can take partial credit at best for that accomplishment, since it depends on many other conditions, so reaching the target does not necessarily mean the school is particularly effective. Moreover, schools that do not reach the target may in fact be highly effective in improving scores relative to students' starting points. Thus, the AYP calculation fails to distinguish between effective and ineffective schools and may lead to misapplication of sanction and inefficient use of resources. It is not hard to envision that the AYP sanctions could lead to schools that are among the most effective in improving test scores for low-achieving students being dismantled because they have not met an achievement target that fails to consider non-school factors as partially responsible for test scores.

Remedies proffered by NCLB have thus far not met expectations. School choice and tutoring have contributed little because few students have availed themselves of these opportunities. In an incisive review of tutoring programs under NCLB, Farkas and Durham (in press) identified two main reasons why tutoring as required by NCLB is not meeting expectations. First, only about 20 percent of eligible students are receiving the tutoring. Moreover, many tutoring programs experience serious problems of student attendance, so that even among those who receive some tutoring, many may not receive enough to boost their achievement. Second, the quality of tutoring programs is uncertain; they are unregulated, and most do not exhibit the characteristics of highly effective programs. For example, the research on tutoring supports one-on-one tutoring, but the tutoring offered in response to AYP sanctions tends to have groups as large as six to eight students. Farkas and Durham conclude by calling for research on the tutoring programs, and argue they are unlikely to close achievement gaps if they do not meet quality standards and serve a greater portion of the nation's needy students.

Whereas Reading First was supposed to allow schools to bring new resources to bear on the problems of struggling readers using scientifically tested reading programs, revelations have emerged indicating the program was more about promoting a particular ideology of reading instruction—and particular companies whose products fit this ideology—than about allowing states, districts, and schools to make decisions about how to improve children's reading (Manzo, 2006; Office of the Inspector General, 2006). A national evaluation of the effects of Reading First is currently under way, but already the program has been called into question.

It is too soon to judge the implementation of the highly qualified teacher provision of NCLB, because it is just beginning to be enforced, but the relevant evidence from past reforms is mixed. On the one hand, greater subject matter competence (as demonstrated by college degrees or test scores) is modestly associated with higher student achievement (e.g., Monk & King, 1994). On the other hand, a variety of past accountability measures such as assessment standards, sanctions for failing schools, and availability of resources for improvement have had inconsistent effects on teacher qualifications (Desimone, Smith, & Frisvold, in press).

Based on the performance of NCLB to date, it is difficult to have confidence in its prospects for reducing the achievement gap. It is unique in its bipartisan support, and in its focus on the disadvantages of low-income students, and these may be regarded as important first steps. Improvement, however, will come only if effective schools can be supported instead of sanctioned, and if the approaches aimed at improving learning opportunities for children from disadvantaged families can be implemented in meaningful and effective ways.

Conclusions

In 2001, I predicted that educational stratification by social class would continue at current levels throughout the twenty-first century. Nothing that has come to light in the last five years has led me to change this prediction. Trends in test scores and attainment have held steady. Sociological research has improved our understanding of these trends, but has provided no new reasons to think they will be altered.

My prediction implies that No Child Left Behind will not reach its goal of overcoming the achievement gap between students on free and reduced-price lunch and other students. I do not think failure is inevitable. However, my review of the evidence and my understanding of the sources of existing inequalities suggest that success is unlikely, and will only come if NCLB is implemented very differently in the future than it has been thus far.

Questions for discussion

1. Discuss the six reasons Gamoran provides to support his conclusion that social class inequality will persist through the twenty-first century. Specifically, what does he mean by "maximally maintained inequality?" Why are the final three reasons more political than sociological?

2. What is the No Child Left Behind Act of 2001 (2002)? What have been its major supporting arguments? What have been its major points of contention?

3. According to Gamoran, why does the NCLB Act seem unlikely to eliminate class divisions between schools and between the students attending these schools?

4. Why do some scholars argue that elite universities have exhibited a preference for minority students (for affirmative action policies), but have not done so for

students from disadvantaged economic circumstances? What is your opi about such policies?

5. Discuss reasons as to why the author argues that affirmative action policies and financial aid may exacerbate inequality among institutions of higher education.

6. Perhaps it seems reasonable to argue that the schools of some parents' children should have greater subsidies because these parents pay more in property tax, but how does this particular tax and subsidy system create social inequality? How does this system work for and against people of varying social class relative to education?

7. Educational expansion within the USA is supposed to provide everyone with greater opportunities to obtain education. To what extent does such expansion create opportunities for every social group? Give examples from your own experience.

8. Should the rights of lower classes (at the level of income, for example) be defined and protected by the constitution in ways similar to race, gender, and ethnicity? Why or why not?

Note

Work on this chapter was supported by a grant from the William T. Grant Foundation.

References

Alexander, K. L. (2001). The clouded crystal ball: Trends in educational stratification. *Sociology of Education, Extra Issue*, 169–77.

Ayalon, H., & Shavit, Y. (2004). Educational reforms and inequalities in Israel: The MMI hypothesis revisited. *Sociology of Education, 77*, 103–20.

Brint, S., & Karabel, J. (1989). *The diverted dream: Community colleges and the promise of educational opportunity in America 1900–1985*. New York: Oxford University Press.

Campbell, J. R., Hombo, C. M., & Mazzeo, J. (2000). *NAEP trends in academic progress: Three decades of school performance*. NCES document No. 2000–2469. Washington, DC: US Department of Education.

Coleman, J. S., Campbell, E. Q., Hobson, C., McPartland, J. M., Mood, A. M., Weinfield, F. D., & York, R. L. (1972). *Equality of educational opportunity*. Washington, DC: US Government Printing Office.

Desimone, L., Smith, T., & Frisvold, D. (2006). Has NCLB improved teacher and teaching quality for disadvantaged students? In A. Gamoran (Ed.), *Standards-based reform and the poverty gap: Lessons for "No Child Left Behind."* Washington DC: Brookings Institution Press.

Farkas, G., & Durham, R. (in press). The role of tutoring in standards-based reform. In A. Gamoran (Ed.), *Standards-based reform and the poverty gap: Lessons for "No Child Left Behind."* Washington DC: Brookings Institution Press.

Gamoran, A. (1987). The stratification of high school learning opportunities. *Sociology of Education, 60*, 135–55.

—— (2001). American schooling and educational inequality: A forecast for the 21st century. *Sociology of Education, Extra Issue*, 135–53.

Gamoran, A., & Long, D. A. (2007). Equality of educational opportunity: A 40-year retrospective. In R. Teese, S. Lamb, & M. Duru-Bellat (Eds.), *International studies in educational inequality: Theory and policy*. New York: Springer Press.

Gosa, T., & Alexander, K. L. (2007). Family (dis)advantage and the educational prospects of African-American youth: How race still matters. *Teachers College Record, 109*.

Grodsky, E. (in press). Sponsored mobility in higher education. *American Journal of Sociology*.

Hanushek, E. A. (1996). School resources and student performance. In G. Burtless (Ed.), *Does money matter? The effect of school resources on student achievement and adult success* (pp. 43–73). Washington, DC: Brookings Institution Press.

Heller, D. E. (2006). *Merit aid and college access.* Paper presented at the Symposium on the Consequences of Merit-Based Student Aid, Wisconsin Center for the Advancement of Postsecondary Education, University of Wisconsin-Madison, Madison, WI.

Heller, D. E., & Marin, P. (Eds.). (2004). *State merit scholarship programs and racial inequality.* Cambridge, MA: Harvard Civil Rights Project.

Heller, D. E., & Rogers, K. R. (2006). Shifting the burden: Public and private financing of higher education in the United States and implications for Europe. *Tertiary Education and Management, 12*, 91–117.

Hout, M., Raftery, A., & Bell, E. O. (1993). Making the grade: Educational stratification in the United States, 1925–89. In Y. Shavit & H.-P. Blossfeld (Eds.), *Persistent inequality: Changing educational attainment in thirteen countries* (pp. 25–49). Boulder, CO: Westview Press.

Jencks, C. L., Smith, M., Acland, H., Bane, M. J., Cohen, D. K., Gintis, H., Heyns, B., & Michelson, S. (1972). *Inequality: A reassessment of the effects of family and schooling in America.* New York: Basic Books.

Kahlenberg, R. (1996). *The remedy: Class, race, and affirmative action.* New York: Basic Books.

—— (2001). *All together now: Creating middle class schools through public school choice.* Washington, DC: Brookings Institution Press.

Krugman, P. (2004). *The great unraveling: Losing our way in the new century.* New York: W. W. Norton & Company.

Lareau, A. (1989). *Home advantage: Social class and parental intervention in elementary education.* New York: Falmer Press.

—— (2003). *Unequal childhoods: Class, race, and family life.* Berkeley, CA: University of California Press.

Long, D. A., Kelly, S., & Gamoran, A. (2005). *Whither the virtuous cycle? Trends in the black–white gap in educational attainment.* Paper presented at the annual meeting of the American Sociological Association, Philadelphia.

Loveless, T. (in press). The peculiar politics of "No Child Left Behind." In A. Gamoran (Ed.), *Standards-based reform and the poverty gap: Lessons for "No Child Left Behind."* Washington, DC: Brookings Institution Press.

Lucas, S. R. (2001). Effectively maintained inequality: Education transitions, track mobility, and social background effects. *American Journal of Sociology, 106*, 1642–90.

Manzo, K. K. (2006). Scathing report casts cloud over "Reading First." *Education Week*, October 4, pp. 1, 24–25.

Monk, D. H., & King, J. R. (1994). Multi-level teacher resource effects on pupil performance in secondary mathematics and science: The role of teacher subject matter preparation. In R. Ehrenberg (Ed.), *Contemporary policy issues: Choices and consequences in education.* Ithaca, NY: ILR Press.

No Child Left Behind Act of 2001, Pub. L. No. 107–10, 115 Stat. 1425 (2002).

Oakes, J., Ormseth, T., Bell, R. M., & Camp, P. (1990). *Multiplying inequalities: The effects of race, social class, and tracking on opportunities to learn math and science.* Santa Monica, CA: RAND.

Office of the Inspector General, US Department of Education (2006). *The Reading First program's grant application process: Final inspection report.* Washington, DC: US Department of Education. Retrieved January 10, 2007 from www.ed.gov/about/offices/list/oig/aireports/i13f0017.pdf

Perie, M., Moran, R., & Lutkus, A. D. (2005). *NAEP 2004 trends in academic progress: Three decades of academic performance in reading and math*. NCES document no. 2005–2464. Washington, DC: US Department of Education.

Raftery, A. E., & Hout, M. (1993). Maximally maintained inequality: Expansion, reform, and opportunity in Irish education, 1921–75. *Sociology of Education, 66*, 22–39.

Roksa, J., Grodsky, E. S., Arum, R., & Gamoran, A. (2007). Changes in social stratification and higher education in the United States. In Y. Shavit, R. T. Arum, and A. Gamoran, with G. Menahem (Eds.), *Stratification in Higher Education: A Comparative Study*. Stanford, CA: Stanford University Press.

Rothstein, R. (2004). *Class and schools: Using social, economic, and educational reform to close the black–white achievement gap*. Washington, DC: Economic Policy Institute.

Shavit, Y., & Blossfeld, H.-P. (Eds.). (1993). *Persistent inequality: Changing educational attainment in thirteen countries*. Boulder, CO: Westview Press.

Turley, R. N. L., Santos, M., & Ceja, C. (in press). Social origin and college opportunity expectations across cohorts. *Social Science Research*.

Chapter 12

The social cost of inadequate education of black males

*Henry M. Levin**

Introduction

Although there is a general concern about levels of educational achievement and attainment in the USA, the educational situation of black males is particularly worrisome. At almost every grade level black males are about one standard deviation below the non-Hispanic, white student population in test measures of student achievement—about at the 16th percentile relative to the 50th percentile for the overall population. A recent study estimates that African-American males had a rate of graduation after four years of high school of about 48 percent in contrast with a 74 percent rate for white males and a 70 percent graduation rate for the overall population (Greene & Winters, 2006). The comparable figures for African-American females and for white females were 59 percent and 79 percent respectively.[1] Gaps between graduation rates for black and white males among the states are also large and differ considerably among the different states (Holzman, 2006). For example, Florida and Nevada are reported to graduate less than one-third of their black males on schedule, and the graduation rates for black males are particularly low in the large cities.

Sadly, students from families with less education and income and who are members of minorities show lower student achievement even in their pre-school years. That is, they start behind other children academically and are unlikely to catch up without major educational interventions on their behalf (Fryer & Levitt, 2004; Lee & Burkam, 2002).

It is widely recognized that unequal educational outcomes lead to unequal economic consequences for individuals. In particular, those individuals with the lowest educational attainments and the poorest quality education—these often overlap—can expect to face inferior employment prospects, low wages, poor health, and greater involvement in the system of criminal justice (Neal, 2006). This situation has important consequences for society and for the government sector as well as we will see below. To create fairer educational outcomes, government must invest in effective educational strategies that will help black males and other minority groups to experience greater educational success. Yet, there has been a reluctance to provide the school resources that might more nearly equalize and raise educational outcomes for low-income and minority students in the USA and for black males in particular. This reluctance is not costless to any society that must finance such investments because there are social consequences of such educational neglect.

* William Heard Kilpatrick Professor of Economics and Education at Teachers College, Columbia University and Director of the National Center for the Study of Privatization in Education.

At its heart, the issue of educational inequality emanating from socioeconomic disadvantage is a moral issue rather than an economic issue. That is, it is a challenge to the fairness of a democracy or social justice in a society in which education is the major public instrument for more nearly equalizing life's opportunities. The cost of such a social injustice is twofold. It creates a society that violates its most basic social and political precepts that underlie its democratic claims. It is also an economic issue for society because poor education of individuals leads to large social costs in the form of lower societal income and economic growth, lower tax revenues, and higher costs of such public services as health, criminal justice, and public assistance. In this respect, it is possible to view efforts to improve educational outcomes for at-risk populations as a public investment in which there are costs and returns to that investment.

Thus, public benefits of improved education in the form of higher graduation rates for black males can be evaluated in terms of higher tax revenues and reductions in the costs of public services that these educational improvements can confer. These benefits can be compared with the costs of providing the necessary educational interventions that will raise high school graduation rates of black males to ascertain what the public receives on such an investment. The purpose of this chapter is to report on an original, empirical study addressing the returns to public or government investments in the education of black males (Levin et al., 2006). The bottom line appears to be that such public investments yield public returns considerably in excess of the costs of the investments. Although this finding is a very important one justifying increased investment in educational approaches that will raise the graduation rates of black males, it is important to continue to emphasize the justice or fairness criterion for improving the education of black males and other minority groups rather than just the economics. Nevertheless, the economic imperative is an important supporting argument for a social policy that is ethically defensible.

In the next section I will provide a bit of historical background for the investment and benefit–cost approach that is reviewed here. The following sections will denote the costs and benefits of educational investment in black males. The final section will provide a summary of the results and their policy implications.

Previous studies

In 1970 the US Senate formed the Select Senate Committee on Equal Educational Opportunity to explore a federal role that might build on the delayed movements to integrate the US Public Schools. Despite the famous Supreme Court decision in Brown vs. Topeka in 1954 and its 1955 clarification of "all deliberate speed," the actual shift towards desegregating schools by race did not proceed in any substantial way until about 1968. The Select Senate Committee on Equal Educational Opportunity under Senate Walter Mondale represented an attempt to hold hearings on that progress and to use social science and expert witnesses to support this direction as well as to seek new ways of improving the education of minority and economically disadvantaged students.

Mondale's concern was that expert testimony frequently referred to the costs of incarceration and public assistance associated with a poorly educated population, but no one was able to provide the Committee with concrete estimates of those costs. Accordingly, the Committee decided to commission a study which might provide at least an approximate estimate of the magnitudes of the public costs of not educating students adequately.

If these costs could be avoided by educational investments, they would be considered the public benefits of such policies.

The Committee decided to commission a study of the "Costs to the Nation of Inadequate Education" (Levin, 1972). It should be noted that the availability of information and the capacity of computers to statistically analyze the data were far more limited some four decades ago than they are today. This study attempted to derive specific estimates of such social costs by evaluating the failure to attain a minimum of high school completion for the 25–34-year-old male age group in 1970. Using lifetime income patterns by race and education level, and adjusting for the presumed, lower "ability" of high school dropouts, simulations were made to estimate the additional earnings associated with greater numbers of high school completers (as well as for those who might then undertake some post-secondary education). Based upon this analysis it was estimated that $237 billion in lifetime income (1970 dollars, or about $1.2 trillion in 2004 dollars) was lost by the failure to attain a minimum of high school completion; of this sum, about $71 billion (about $350 billion in 2004 dollars) in government revenues was lost. Assessments were also made of costs of inadequate education in public assistance and crime and criminal justice as well as presentations of information on reduced political participation, intergenerational mobility, and higher health costs. However, data shortcomings meant that though these were informative, they were far more speculative.

It was assumed that educational investments in compensatory resources would have to increase by 50 percent for every year of schooling, elementary through high school, a very generous increase in costs, in order to provide the resources that would lead to graduation. The overall cost of providing these additional resources for the dropout cohort that was analyzed was estimated at about $40 billion in 1970 dollars (about $200 billion in 2004 dollars). When these were compared with just the benefits of higher tax revenues from increased high school completion of those who were dropouts, the benefits would have been almost twice the costs.

Ramirez and del Refugio Robledo (1986) replicated this type of analysis for the cohort of Texas ninth graders in 1982–83 who were projected to drop out before their anticipated graduation in 1986. They estimated the benefits of a dropout prevention program as those attributable to savings in public assistance, training and adult education, crime and incarceration, unemployment insurance and placement, and higher earnings associated with the additional high school graduates. Such benefits were calculated at $17.5 billion, and the costs to eliminate dropouts for this cohort were estimated at slightly less than $2 billion, for a cost–benefit ratio of nine to one. The specifics of this investment were unclear and the assumptions underlying it. Estimates of additional tax revenues were 2.5 times greater than the costs to taxpayers.

Catterall (1987) undertook a similar analysis of children who dropped out of high schools in Los Angeles for all students in the class of 1985. He concluded that, because of the dropouts, the Los Angeles class of 1985 was likely to generate over $3 billion *less* in lifetime economic activity than if all of its members had graduated. Catterall suggested that the cost of investing successfully in dropout reduction would be a mere fraction of this amount. Furthermore, he found that Los Angeles was addressing the dropout problem with specific programs that were spending the equivalent of only about $50 per dropout, or less than one-half of 1 percent of school spending, even though 40 percent of its students were not graduating.

Recent studies using longitudinal data sets have concluded that high quality pre-school experiences for African-American populations are a good public investment. Such pre-school interventions have been shown to improve later student achievement and ultimate educational attainments and to reduce public costs of special education, grade repetition, public assistance, and crime. These studies have found that the public benefits are four to seven times as great as the costs (Belfield et al., 2006; Masse & Barnett, 2002; Reynolds et al., 2002). But the question that we wished to address was a more specific one, whether using these and other interventions to increase black male graduation rates would provide public benefits that exceeded public costs. In what follows I will provide a non-technical presentation of the public costs and benefits of increasing black male graduation. Technical details can be found elsewhere (Levin et al., 2006).

Public costs of producing more graduates

It may appear that the cost of increasing high school graduation is straightforward, but that is not the case. In order to obtain costs, one must begin by finding programs that have been rigorously evaluated and have shown success. An extensive review of the literature comprising more than two hundred articles and reports yielded only five interventions with such evidence. These included two preschool programs (Belfield et al., 2006; Reynolds et al., 2002); smaller class size (Finn, Gerber & Boyd-Zaharias, 2005); higher teacher salaries (Loeb & Page, 2000); and a high school program that emphasized small learning communities, instructional improvement, and teacher advocacy for each student (Quint et al., 2005)

Total costs of each program were estimated using a resource-based approach (Levin & McEwan, 2001) and divided by the numbers of additional graduates induced. These were added to the costs of the additional years of schooling to graduation as well as the additional costs for those who are likely to continue into post-secondary education. Total public investment costs for each additional graduate by age twenty were calculated to be compared with the value of benefits.[2] Cost per additional black male graduate for the five interventions varied from about $59,000 for the high school intervention of First Things First, $68,000 for the Chicago Pre-School Centers, $91,000 for the Perry Preschool Approach, $97,000 for Class Size Reduction, and about $120,000 for the Teacher Salary Increase. What appears to be a high cost is due primarily to inflating schooling investments below the age of twenty to their present value at age twenty as well as inclusion of the cost of additional years of schooling for the added graduates and the fact that the spending on interventions must be applied to a much larger group of students to yield additional graduates. That is, the total cost must be divided among only the additional students who graduate, not those who would have graduated without the intervention. Bear in mind that about half of black males graduate in four years even without extra investment. The cost of the intervention for every one hundred at-risk students yields three to nineteen additional graduates, so the cost for each one hundred students must be divided only over this smaller number of additional graduates. Despite what appears to be a high investment cost, the key question is how these costs compare with the public benefits conferred by additional black male graduates.

Public benefits of more high school graduates

Public benefits were derived by estimating additional tax revenues and reductions in the costs of public health and crime resulting from improved numbers of black males attaining high school completion.[3] A brief picture of each follows.

Additional tax revenues

Black males who graduate from high school as well as those who continue on to college have higher rates of labor force participation, employment, and wages than those who drop out of high school. For example, among 21–35-year-old black males about two-thirds of high school graduates are employed compared with about half of high school dropouts. Annual earnings of the high school graduates are almost twice those of high school dropouts. These increases in earnings translate into large increases in government tax revenues over a lifetime, a difference of about $168,000 over a lifetime when calculated as a present value at age twenty. What is noteworthy is that the additional tax revenues alone outweigh the investment costs of producing additional high school graduates in the black male population. But, what of the public cost-savings for health and crime when black males experience greater educational success?

Reduced costs of public health

The lower educational levels of black males contribute to less-healthy lifestyles and poorer health status that lead to considerably shorter life expectancy than for white males. Arias and co-authors (2003, p. 116) report that in 2001 black males lived to about sixty-nine years compared to seventy-five years for white males. Because of inferior job prospects and low incomes, black male high school graduates are unlikely to have private health care coverage. Therefore, they must rely upon publicly or philanthropically financed care. Such care is found largely under Medicaid, the state program with federal assistance for providing health care to low-income families and individuals. If they experience disability before age sixty-five, funding is provided by Medicare, even though that program is primarily aimed at those sixty-five and over. Finally, local governments and charities also subsidize the health and medical care of the poor. The relation between education and subsidized care is a very substantial one. Muennig (2006) reported that 81 percent of African-American males with less than nine years of education received publicly reimbursed care, but only 28 percent of college graduates. Careful analysis of the incidence of public health treatment of black males by educational level and its cost analysis show high cost burdens on the public health system for less-educated persons. Using detailed records of public costs of health care, it appears that African-American males who did not graduate from high school had publicly reimbursed health costs that were almost $34,000 greater over their lifetimes (calculated in present value at age twenty) than graduates.

Reduced costs of crime

Likewise, high school graduates show a steep reduction in crimes relative to high school dropouts (Lochner & Moretti, 2004). Black males, in particular, show high overall involvement in the criminal justice system that is associated with their education levels. Among black males, 18–65 years of age, 19 percent of high school dropouts have been incarcerated in comparison with 8 percent of high school graduates and 1 percent of college graduates (Raphael, 2004). Among younger black males, those 18–25, the rates are even higher with almost a quarter of high school dropouts experiencing incarceration (Harrison & Karberg, 2003). Rates of incarceration for black males are six to eight times as great as for white males (Pettit & Western, 2004, p. 164).

Belfield (2006) has estimated the public costs of crime by first calculating the incidence of crime for black males with different educational levels. About 80 percent of crimes are included in his analysis, those for which there are data by race, gender, and educational level. Associated public costs are calculated for the following cost categories: criminal justice system operation (especially police and courts); costs of incarceration including parole and probation; public restitution to victims; and crime prevention activities.

Based upon these procedures, the minimum public costs for criminal justice that would be saved by converting a high school dropout to a high school graduate would be almost $56,000 in present value at age twenty. This amount is actually understated because we could not account for the public costs for 20 percent of the crimes due to a lack of data availability by education, race, and gender. Moreover, we do not include any of the costs prior to age twenty, even though juvenile crimes and their associated costs are substantial.[4]

Is it worth it?

The central question asked in this study is whether the public benefits exceed the costs of educational investments devoted to improving rates of high school graduation and post-secondary education among those who continue. When we evaluated systematically the public costs of the five different interventions using a resource cost approach (Levin & McEwan, 2001), it was found that the value of the investment that would be incurred for each additional high school graduate produced varied from just under $60,000 to $120,000. In contrast, the combined benefits in terms of additional tax revenues and reductions in public costs of services for health and criminal justice were about $257,000 in present value at age twenty. This means that the benefits exceeded the costs of the lowest cost intervention by almost $200,000 per new graduate and the highest cost intervention by about $137,000 per new graduate. When placed in terms of ratios of benefits to costs, the benefits varied from $2 for each dollar of cost to $4 of benefits for each dollar of cost. These are very healthy returns for social investments.

We conclude that beyond the ethical argument for greater educational equality for black males, there is a strong economic argument. Successful investments in raising black male graduation rates have a strong economic payoff for society. For each public dollar invested, the returns are several-fold. If we were just to equalize high school graduation rates between black and white males for the twenty-year-old age group, we estimate a net benefit (benefits minus costs) to society of between $3 to 5 billion. If we apply this to subsequent cohorts of students, the amount would be comparable and the cumulative totals of net benefits to society could easily exceed $100 billion. What is unique is that an economic argument is consistent with one of justice for those born into less advantaged circumstances. Both for the sake of fairness and efficient resource allocation, there is a strong imperative for obtaining educational equality for black males.

Questions for discussion

1. Is denying education a moral question, and a social injustice? If so, why, and what are the consequences of this deprivation?
2. What are the current debates around the issue of academic achievement? How does this intersect with notions of race, class, and gender?
3. What might be the implicit and/or explicit dangers associated with framing educational equality for black males as an economic issue? Why do you think the author chooses to frame the issue in this way?
4. Do you agree that unequal educational outcomes lead to unequal economic consequences for individuals? How do notions like cultural and social capital contribute to this relationship?
5. What was the central issue in Brown v. Board of Education of Topeka, Kansas? In your opinion, what is the current status of desegregation in the USA?
6. If the educational inequality experienced by black males is a moral issue as well as an economic one, will economic benefits be enough to realign and level out the statistics between and among minority groups and those of white males? In a social context which allows for such inequalities to persist, is it possible for monetary benefits to change the patterns of injustice?
7. Looking at financing for higher education, who do you think must pay for the cost of education—the government, the student, and/or the family? Give reasons for your response.
8. Do you imagine that an increase in the graduation rates of African-Americans from institutions of higher education would alter negative associations based upon stereotypes of black youth? Would this alteration be perceived as having complied with "whitened standards of life?" What might be the implications of such a phenomenon?

Notes

1. Statistics on high school completion depend upon both definitions (e.g., inclusion of high school equivalency such as passing the General Education Development exam or GED) as well as the age at which data are collected. A recent report with much higher estimates of high school graduation rates using different methods and data sources for estimation is Mishel and Roy (2006). Even when including the less demanding criterion of the GED and allowing more years for completion, black males lag the other populations considerably in high school completion.
2. More technical versions of this research are available from www.cbcse.org. A published version is Levin, Belfield, Muennig, and Rouse (2006) where more detail can be found. Present value calculations are appropriate when investments have different time patterns between when costs are incurred and benefits received. In this case, most of the costs of investment are incurred before the age of twenty with some starting as early as the pre-school years. The flow of benefits begins at age twenty and continues over a lifetime. To make these differing time patterns of costs and benefits comparable, it is necessary to convert them to common values at a point in time, so-called present value. A discount rate of 3.5 percent was used. For more detail on these types of calculations see Levin and McEwan (2001). For justification of the 3.5 percent discount rate see Moore et al. (2004).
3. Most of the estimates are based upon the cost and benefits that prevailed from 2000–2005. Some might question whether the benefits from additional tax revenues for high school graduates might be driven down by the additional supply of high school graduates. This is unlikely

because, with a 50 percent dropout rate, the additional black males with a high school credential would constitute only 3 to 4 percent of the labor market. In fact, by the age of twenty it
appears that about 75 percent of black males have completed high school or have obtained a
GED credential according to the Current Population Survey of March 2005 of the Bureau of the
Census of the US Department of Commerce. Of these, a significant portion of new high school
completers would be distributed across the lower levels of post-secondary education. So the
impact on the overall supply of high school graduates would be limited. Further, the increase in
the demand for more educated groups has generally been greater, the higher the level of education, meaning that the earnings gap between dropouts and graduates is likely to be sustained or
even increase.
4. Our reason for including benefits starting at age twenty is due to the fact that figures on high
    school completion at earlier ages do not include those who take longer to obtain their high
    school credential. By choosing age twenty as a baseline we understate earlier benefits, but have
    a more accurate picture of high school completion.

References

Arias, E., Anderson, R., Kung, H., Murphy, S., & Kochanek, K. (2003). Deaths: Final data for
2001. *National Vital Statistics Reports, 52.*

Belfield, C. R. (2006). *The consequences of raising the graduation rate for black males: The effects
on crime.* Working Paper. Teachers College, New York.

Belfield, C. R., Nores, M., Barnett, S. W., & Schweinhart, L. J. (2006). The High/Scope Perry
preschool program. *The Journal of Human Resources, 41*(1), 162–90.

Catterall, J. (1987, October–November). On the social costs of dropping out of school. *High
School Journal, 71,* 19–30.

Finn, J. D., Gerber, S. B., & Boyd-Zaharias, J. (2005). Small classes in the early grades, academic
achievement, and graduating from high school. *Journal of Educational Psychology, 97,* 214–23.

Fryer, R. G., & Levitt, S. D. (2004). Understanding the black–white test score gap in the first two
years of school. *Review of Economics and Statistics, 86,* 447–64.

Greene, J. P., & Winters, M. A. (2006). *Leaving boys behind: Public high school graduation rates,
48.* New York: Manhattan Institute.

Harrison, P. M., & Karberg, J. (2003). Prison and jail inmates at midyear 2002. *Bureau of Justice
Statistics Bulletin,* NCJ 198877. Washington, DC: US Department of Justice.

Holzman, M. (2006). *Public education & black male students: The 2006 state report card.* Boston:
Schott Foundation for Public Education.

Lee, V. E., & Burkam, D. T. (2002). *Inequality at the starting gate: Social background differences
in achievement as children begin school.* Washington, DC: Economic Policy Institute.

Levin, H. M. (1972). *The costs to the nation of inadequate education.* Select Senate Committee on
Equal Educational Opportunity, 92nd Congress. Washington, DC: US Government Printing
Office.

Levin, H. M., & McEwan, P. (2001). *Cost-effectiveness analysis: Methods and applications.* Thousand Oaks, CA: Sage.

Levin, H. M., Belfield, C., Muennig, P., & Rouse, C. (2006). The public returns to public educational investments in African-American males. *Economics of Education Review* (forthcoming).

Lochner, L., & Moretti, E. (2004). The effect of education on crime: Evidence from prison inmates,
arrests, and self-reports. *American Economic Review, 94,* 155–89.

Loeb, S., & Page, M. E. (2000). Examining the link between teacher wages and student outcomes:
The importance of alternative labor market opportunities and non-pecuniary variation. *The
Review of Economics and Statistics, 82,* 393–408.

Masse, L., & Barnett, S. (2002). A benefit-cost analysis of the abecedarian early childhood intervention. In H. M. Levin & P. McEwan (Eds.), *Cost-effectiveness and educational policy.* Larch-
mont, NY: AEFA Handbook: Eye on Education.

Mishel, L., & Roy, J. (2006). *Rethinking high school graduation rates and trends.* Washington, DC: Economic Policy Institute.

Moore, M. A., Boardman, A. E., Vining, A. R., Weimer, D. L., & Greenberg, D. H. (2004). Just give me a number! Practical values for the social discount rate. *Journal of Policy Analysis and Management, 23,* 789–812.

Muennig, P. (2006). *The consequences of inadequate education for black males: The effects on health.* Working Paper. Teachers College Equity Symposium.

Neal, D. (2006). Why has black–white skill convergence stopped? In E. Hanushek and F. Welch (Eds.), *Handbook of the economics of education.* Elsevier: New York.

Pettit, B., & Western, B. (2004). Mass imprisonment and the life course: Race and class inequality in US incarceration. *American Sociological Review, 69,* 151–69.

Quint, J., Bloom, H. S., Rebeck Black, A., & Stephens, L. with Akey, T. M. (2005). *The challenge of scaling up educational reform: Findings and lessons from first things first.* New York: Manpower Development Research Corporation.

Ramirez, D., & del Refugio Robledo, M. (1986). *Texas school dropout survey project: A summary of findings.* San Antonio: Intercultural Development Research Association.

Raphael, S. (2004). *The Socioeconomic status of black males: The increasing importance of incarceration.* Working Paper. University of California-Berkeley.

Reynolds, A. J., Temple, J. A., Robertson, D. L., & Mann, E. A. (2002). Age 21 cost-benefit analysis of the Title I Chicago child–parent centers. *Educational Evaluation and Policy Analysis, 24,* 267–303.

Chapter 13

Social class and school knowledge

*Jean Anyon**

When Max Weber and Karl Marx suggested that there were identifiable and socially meaningful differences in the educational knowledge made available to literati and peasant, aristocrat and laborer, they were of course discussing earlier societies. Recent scholarship in political economy and sociology of knowledge has also argued, however, that in advanced industrial societies such as Canada and the USA, where the class structure is relatively fluid, students of different social class backgrounds are still likely to be exposed to qualitatively different types of educational knowledge. Students from higher social class backgrounds may be exposed to legal, medical, or managerial knowledge, for example, while those of the working classes may be offered a more "practical" curriculum (e.g., clerical knowledge, vocational training) (Bowles & Gintis, 1976; Karabel, 1972; Rosenbaum, 1976). It is said that such social class differences in secondary and postsecondary education are a conserving force in modern societies, an important aspect of the reproduction of unequal class structures (Apple, 1979; Karabel & Halsey, 1977; Young & Whitty, 1977).

The present chapter examines data on school knowledge collected in a case study of five elementary schools in contrasting social class settings in two school districts in New Jersey. The data suggest, and I will argue, that while there were similarities in curriculum topics and materials, there were also subtle as well as dramatic differences in the curriculum and the curriculum-in-use among the schools. The study reveals that even in an elementary school context, where there is a fairly "standardized" curriculum, social stratification of knowledge is possible. The differences that were identified among the schools suggest as well that, rather than being simply conserving or "reproductive," school knowledge embodies contradictions that have profound implications for social change. The reproductive and non-reproductive possibilities of school knowledge involve theoretical implications of the data and will be delineated after the data have been presented.

Methodology

Data on the nature and distribution of school knowledge were gathered in an investigation of curriculum, pedagogy, and pupil evaluation practices in five elementary schools

---

* Jean Anyon teaches Education and Social Policy in the Doctoral Program in Urban Education at the City University of New York.

differentiated by social class.[1] The methods used to gather data were classroom observation; informal and formal interview of students, teachers, principals, and district administrative staff; and assessment of curriculum and other materials in each classroom and school. Classroom data to be reported here are drawn primarily from the fifth and second grades in each school. All schools but one departmentalize at the fifth-grade level, and with the exception of the school that does not, where only one fifth-grade teacher agreed to be observed, in all schools two or three fifth-grade teachers and two second-grade teachers were observed and interviewed. All but one of the teachers in the study had taught for more than four years. The fifth grade in each school was observed by the investigator for ten three-hour periods, and the second grade was observed for two three-hour periods. Formal interviews were carried out during lunchtime, and before and after school. Data were gathered between September 15, 1978, and June 20, 1979.

For purposes of this study, social class is considered as a series of relationships to several aspects of the process in society by which goods, services, and culture are produced. The terminology defining social classes and differentiating the schools in this study is to be understood in a technical sense, as reflected in the process by which the sample of schools was selected. Thus, the schools in this study were differentiated not only by income level as an indicator of parent access to capital, but also by the kind of *work* that characterized the majority of parents in each school.[2]

The first three schools were in a medium-size city district in northern New Jersey, and the final two were in a nearby New Jersey suburban district. In each of the three city schools, approximately 85 percent of the students were white. In the fourth school, 90 percent were white, and in the last school, all were white. The first two schools are designated *working-class schools*, because the majority of the students' fathers (and approximately one-third of their mothers) were in unskilled or semiskilled occupations, with somewhat less than one-third of the fathers being skilled workers. Most family money incomes were at or below $12,000 during the period of the study, as were 38.6 percent of all US families (US Bureau of the Census, 1979, p. 2, table A). The third school is designated the *middle-class school*, although because of residence patterns the parents were a mixture of highly skilled, well-paid blue collar and white collar workers, as well as those with traditional middle-class occupations such as public school teachers, social workers, accountants, and middle-managers. There were also several local doctors and town merchants among the parents. Most family money incomes were between $13,000 and $25,000 during the period of the study, as were 38.9 percent of all US families (US Bureau of the Census, 1979, p. 2, table A).

The fourth school is designated the *affluent professional school*, because the bulk of the students' fathers were highly paid doctors such as cardiologists; television or advertising executives; interior designers; or other affluent professionals. While there were a few families less affluent than the majority (e.g., the families of the superintendent of schools and of several professors at nearby universities, as well as several working-class families), there were also a few families who were more affluent. The majority of family money incomes were between $40,000 and $80,000 during the period of the study, as were approximately 7 percent of all US families.

The final school is called the *executive elite school*. The majority of pupils' fathers in this school were vice presidents or more advanced corporate executives in US-based multinational corporations or financial firms on Wall Street. Most family money incomes were over $100,000 during the period of the study, as were less than 1 percent of US families (see Smith & Franklin, 1974).

Despite several similarities in curriculum among the schools in this study (indeed, all schools were subject to the same state requirements), there were substantial differences in knowledge among the schools. The following sections of this chapter present and discuss data on these differences. Data from each social setting include significant information on the school, the teachers, and the community; what school personnel said, in interviews, about school knowledge; evidence from the curriculum and the curriculum-in-use in several content areas (e.g., math, science, social studies); and what students expressed concerning school knowledge and its meaning for them. A dominant theme emerged in each social setting, and these are also presented and briefly discussed.

Working-class schools

What school personnel said about school knowledge

I asked the two fifth-grade and two second-grade teachers in each school what knowledge was most appropriate for the children in their classes. Most spoke of school knowledge in terms of facts and simple skills. One fifth-grade teacher said, for example, "What these children need is the basics." When I asked her what the basics were, she said, "The three Rs—simple skills." When I asked why, she responded, "They're lazy. I hate to categorize them, but they're lazy." A fifth-grade teacher in the other school said she did social studies by putting notes on the board which the children then copied. I asked why she did that, and she said, "Because the children in this school don't *know* anything about the US, so you can't teach them much." A second-grade teacher when asked what was important knowledge for her students said, "Well, we keep them *busy*."

Evidence from the curriculum and the curriculum-in-use

Mathematical knowledge was often restricted to the procedures or steps to be followed in order to add, subtract, multiply, or divide. All schools in the district use the same math text. It has numerous pages which are explicitly intended as departures from the mechanics of such skills as adding and subtracting. These pages call for mathematical reasoning, inference, pattern identification, or ratio setup, for example. One of the fifth-grade teachers called these pages "the thinking pages" and said she "rarely" uses them. "They're too hard." She concentrates, she said, "on the basics." That is, "how you multiply and divide." The fifth-grade math teacher in the other working-class school said, "These pages are for creativity—they're the extras." A common feature of classroom mathematics in both working-class schools was that the children were largely asked to carry out procedures, the purposes of which were often unexplained, and which were seemingly unconnected to individual thought processes or decision making.

Teachers in each school in the district are given a choice of the social studies text they want to use. The texts chosen by the fifth-grade teachers in the working-class schools contained less information, fewer inquiry or independent research activities, and more of an emphasis on social studies knowledge as facts to be remembered than the texts used in any other school under consideration. In one of the working-class schools the fifth-grade teachers chose a text intended for "low ability students . . . who often exhibit environmental deficiencies . . . and social and emotional problems" (teacher's guide, p. 3). A striking characteristic of the textbook is the paucity of information. The book is intended as a year's work; it is divided into sixteen "lessons." There are one to four paragraphs of history in each lesson, a vocabulary drill, and a review and skills exercise in each to check "recall and retention." The teacher's guide explains the sparsity of information by saying that an important criterion of teaching materials for "educationally deficient students" is that "[e]xtraneous subject matter and excessive details should be eliminated in order to present subjects and concepts that are important and also within the[ir] comprehension range . . ." (p. 39).

The social studies knowledge in these schools was the least "honest" about US society. There was less mention of potentially controversial topics than in other series in other schools. Both texts refer to the economic system as a "free enterprise" system. There are five paragraphs on minority and women's rights and history in one text and ten in the other. (As we will see, this is considerably less than discussions of these topics in books used in other schools in this study.) As in most US history texts, however (Anyon, 1979b; FitzGerald, 1979), there is contained in both texts the history of powerful groups—political parties and leaders, military systems, business, technology, industry. There is little information on the working class in either book—four pages in one book and two in the other discuss labor history. Neither text attempts to identify interests workers have in common, nor discusses the situations of economic and social conflict in which workers exist.

Social studies instruction commonly involved carrying out tasks such as copying teacher's notes, answering textbook questions, or coloring and assembling paper cutouts. For example, in the school where the second book was available, the fifth-grade teacher had purchased a supplemental booklet from Instructo entitled *The Fabulous Fifty States*. Each day she put information from the booklet in outline form on the board and the children copied it. The type of information did not vary: the name of the state, its abbreviation, state capital, nickname of the state, its main products, main business, and a "fabulous fact" (e.g., "Idaho grew 27 billion potatoes in one year. That's enough potatoes for each man, woman, and . . .").

What students said about knowledge

To get some impression of what the children thought about school knowledge, I interviewed ten students in the fifth grade in each working-class school (and twenty fifth-grade children in each of the other schools). After discussing with them what they did in school, I asked each child to tell me what knowledge is (not school knowledge, just knowledge in the general sense). Most children in the working-class schools had some difficulty interpreting my question. Many asked, "What?" or "What do you mean?" It seemed that my question was not meaningful to them. I said, "What do you think of when I say the word 'knowledge?'" They gave the following answers: "To know stuff?" "The skills to do the work." "A chance to make a better world?" "Skills." "Ability—you have ability to do things." "Doing pages in our books and things." "To remember things?" Six children said they did not know.

I then asked them, "Where does knowledge come from?" Six said, "[It comes from] teachers." Other answers were, "Books." "The Board of Ed." "Scientists." "Dictionary." "Your mind?" "Your personality?" "From learning." Seven said they did not know.

I asked if they could *make* knowledge, and if so, how. After some discussion of what I meant, in which I said, "Can you make it, or is it already made?" "Could you make it yourself or could somebody else?" "What would you have to do to make knowledge?" Fifteen children said no (you can't make knowledge). One girl said, "No, because the Board of Ed makes knowledge." I asked her how, and she said, "Oh, just by listening to stuff."

It should be noted that during discussions of school knowledge not a single child in either working-class school used words such as "think," or "thinking." Most spoke in terms of behaviors or skills, and only one mentioned the word "mind." About half the children appeared uncomfortable during the interview, even though they knew me and were quite friendly in the playground and in class. Most of their answers were short, and they did not elaborate without prodding, and often not even then. They, more than the children in any other school, seemed to be trying to guess what it was I wanted them to say rather than to reflect on their own experience.

During my interviews with the children, I also asked them if they thought they would go to college. All but three of the children in these working-class schools said no, they didn't think they would. Two said that they might not have the money, and eleven said their grades wouldn't be good enough. I asked what they wanted to be when they grew up, and then if they could "be anything they wanted"—if, for example, they could "get any type of job" they wanted. Sixteen said no. The reasons they gave were that they weren't "smart enough," or they "didn't have the skills," or "if it's hard I couldn't do it." Three children mentioned there might not be enough jobs. It should be noted that most responses to these last questions suggest that many of these children already "know" that what it takes to get ahead is being smart, and that they themselves are *not* smart.

Resistance as a dominant theme

A dominant theme that emerged in these two schools was student *resistance*. Although some amount of resistance appeared in every school in this study, in the working-class schools it was a dominant characteristic of student–teacher interaction. In the fifth grades there was both active and passive resistance to teachers' attempts to impose the curriculum. Active sabotage sometimes took place: someone put a bug in one student's desk; boys fell out of their chairs; they misplaced books, or forgot them; they engaged in minor theft from each other; sometimes they rudely interrupted the teacher. The children also engaged in a good deal of resistance that was more passive. They often resisted by withholding their enthusiasm or attention on occasions when the teacher attempted to do something special. Passive resistance can also be seen on some occasions when the children do not respond to the teacher's questions.

It seems to be the case that what counts as school knowledge in these two working-class schools is not knowledge as concepts, cognitions, information, or ideas about society, language, math, or history, connected by conceptual principles or understandings of some sort. Rather, it seems that what constitutes school knowledge here is (1) fragmented *facts*, isolated from context and connection to each other or to wider bodies of meaning, or to activity or biography of the students; and (2) knowledge of "practical" rule-governed *behaviors*—procedures by which the students carry out tasks that are largely mechanical. Sustained conceptual or "academic" knowledge has only occasional, symbolic presence here.

Middle-class school

What school personnel said about school knowledge

When I asked teachers what knowledge was appropriate for their students, most of them directly or indirectly referred to what was in the books they were using. One teacher said, "What they need for high school and maybe college." She nodded at the social studies textbook and said, "It's a little hard for them. It's on a sixth-grade level. But my goal is understanding." The language arts teacher said, "You could say knowledge is what they need for daily life." This teacher suggested the major role the textbook played in her instruction. After she had given a homework assignment a child asked, "Is it in the book?" The teacher said, "Of *course* it's in the book. Did I ever give you anything that's *not* in the book?" "No," said the child. (The English textbook she used is the 1969 edition of *Language for Everyday Life*.) Part of the attitude that knowledge is what is in textbooks seems to be the feeling that knowledge is made by experts and consists of standard rules and "content." This content is perceived as more important or legitimate than what one discovers or attempts to define for oneself.

Evidence from the curriculum and the curriculum-in-use

In this school I observed more flexibility regarding procedures in math than in the working-class schools. For example, there is sometimes a choice: one may do two-digit division the long way or the short way, and there are some math problems that can be done "in one's head." Moreover, in contrast to the teacher's explanations in the working-class schools, when this teacher explained how to do math or what to do next, there was usually a recognition that a cognitive process of some sort was involved: rather than simply lead the children through a series of steps, she usually gave several ways to do a problem, and then said, "I want to make sure you understand what you're doing." She often asked a child to say how he "did" a problem.

Social studies knowledge in this school was more "conceptual" than in the working-class schools in that there was less emphasis on retention of facts and development of simple "skills" and more emphasis on children's *understanding* of the generalizations and other content of the books. The social studies textbook chosen for use in the school is *Let Freedom Ring* (1977), a US history text that is part of Silver Burdett's "discipline centered" social studies series. One purpose of the text is to introduce fundamental concepts from the various disciplines of the social sciences. The authors say, "The curriculum must identify the basic social science concepts and generalizations that are to be developed" (teacher's guide, p. 4). The textbook itself contains repeated statements about the value of reform, such as the need for continued improvement in providing civil rights for minorities. In addition, there is an emphasis throughout on cultural pluralism and the value of ethnicity: Indeed, of nine units, one entire unit, "Investigating Cultural Plurality," focuses on pluralism and on various ethnic groups in US society.

Social studies activity commonly involved reading the text and listening to the teacher's explanations, answering the teacher's questions or those in the text, and occasionally doing a report (e.g., "getting information" on an Indian tribe). Classroom activity rarely involved sustained inquiry into a topic. The fifth-grade social studies teacher said she did not use the text's "Using the Main Idea" activities very often. She said she didn't have time. She said that she has "enough to do to get them to understand the generalizations." "They read it [the text], I explain, and sometimes I give them a quiz."

What students said about knowledge

When I asked the children what knowledge was, seventeen gave me the following responses: "To remember." "You go to a museum." "You learn facts and history." "You study about your ancestors." "To study things we need to know." "It's smartness." "It means you're intelligent." "Remembering." "Knowledge is something you learn." "To know things." "It's studying. What you do is store facts in your head like cold storage until you need it later for a test, or your job." Three children said they didn't know what knowledge was; perhaps they did not understand my question.

When I asked where knowledge comes from, I got the following answers: Two said, "From the teacher." "From the old times." "From old books." "From scientists." Two said, "From libraries." Three students said, "From encyclopedias." Three children said, "From books." "From my mother—she tells me what to do." "From movies or TV?" "From *Sesame Street*." "Knowledge comes from everywhere." "From Latin?" "You hear other people talk with the big words." It should be noted that these responses have to do mostly with knowledge being "out there," existing in books and libraries, not resulting from one's own activity.

When I asked the children in the middle-class school if they or someone else could make knowledge, nine said no and eleven said yes. The children who said yes gave responses like the following (when I asked them how knowledge would or could be made): Three said, "I'd look it up." "You can make knowledge by listening and doing what you're told." Two said, "I'd go to the library." "By doing extra credit." It should be noted that these responses do not suggest a particularly active relationship to the production of knowledge; rather, knowledge is "given" and not made by themselves.

"Possibility" as a dominant theme

What emerged as a dominant theme in this school was the sense of *possibility*. While I saw in all schools bulletin boards or lesson plans announcing observance of national holidays such as Columbus Day and Lincoln's Birthday, there was, in the middle-class school, an increased amount of this kind of holiday and patriotic activity, more than in any other school in this study. Education in particular seems to be accepted as important, indeed vital, to one's ability to get a job or enter college. There was the feeling that if one works *hard* in school (and in life), one will go far. A prominent attitude expressed by the children in interviews and elsewhere was anxiety about tests and grades. All but two said that yes, they were going to go to college, although they did not know where they would go.

It seems to be the case that knowledge in this school is more conceptual than in the working-class schools in that it is less a matter of facts and skills and more a matter of traditional bodies of "content." It is, in this sense, understanding and information from socially approved sources. Information, facts, and dates can be accumulated and exchanged for good grades and college or a job. Knowledge here, however, is not usually connected to biographies or exploratory activities of the learners, and is thus divorced from processes of personal discovery (as indeed it is in the working-class schools as well).

There is, however, in this school, the sense of possibility: school knowledge has real value, if one has "enough" of it.

Affluent professional school

What school personnel said about school knowledge

Most of the personnel I interviewed in this school referred to school knowledge as involving either individual discovery and creativity, "important ideas," or personal activity on the part of the student (as in the use of science or math equipment). In response to my question of what knowledge is most appropriate for her students, one of the two fifth-grade teachers said, "My goal is to have the children learn from experience. I want them to think for themselves." She also expressed the wish that they "try to make sense of their experience."

I asked the other fifth-grade teacher (who did not agree to be observed) what was most important in social studies education (her specialty). She told me, "It's learning to think. I use questioning techniques [to get them to think]." The principal said that the students should not just "regurgitate" facts, but should "immerse themselves in ideas." He said that "creativity and personal development" are important goals for the children in his school.

Evidence from the curriculum and the curriculum-in-use

Mathematical knowledge is supposed to come from discovery and direct experience. Activities I observed in the teaching of math included the use of geoboards, making and producing an 8 mm film on the metric system, measuring perimeters of their own drawings and generating questions for others to answer about the drawings, collecting data in surveys, and carrying out other empirical investigations with objects such as cubes and scales. The teacher says she does "all" the pages in the math book which concern mathematical patterns. She told me the publisher has supplemental dittos for those pages, and she does "a lot of those."

Scientific knowledge in her class is also intended to result from children's experience and attempts to discover for themselves. All fourth, fifth, and sixth grades use the *Elementary Science Study* (ESS) where typical problems in the fifth grade ask the children to experiment in their own ways with materials such as aluminum and copper and glass rods in order to discover properties of the materials (e.g., which one heats the fastest).[3] The teacher said the value of the ESS approach to science is that they can "think about what they do." She said, "It gives them a hands-on experience so they can make sense of it. It doesn't matter whether it [what they find] is right or wrong, I bring them together and there's value in discussing their ideas." In the fifth grade I observed, the teacher often responded to children's questions of "I don't get this" or "How should I do this?" or "What does this mean?" with "*You* decide"; "What do you *think*?"; "Test it to see if it's right"; "Does that make *sense*?"; and "You can figure that out for yourself."

Although knowledge, thus, is intended as resulting from personal activity, thought, and creativity, there are multiple constraints on this. The teacher, for example, often asks for the "right answer" especially in math, where "right answers" are part of the system of manipulating numbers. And in science and math, one's work must fit empirical reality (e.g., one must measure accurately, and one's answers must lie in the accuracy of the fit between one's own measurements and the physically observable reality—what is measured).

Another type of constraint appears in the published reading programs for individualized instruction which form the basis of reading programs above fourth grade in this school (and in the executive elite school). A boxed set of each of the following programs was available and used consistently in the fifth grade that I observed: EDL *Listen and Think* series; SRA *Power Builder*; SRA *Reading Laboratory*; *Reading for Concepts*; and *The Yearling*.[4] While most of these reading programs do attempt to engage the children in conceptual thinking of one sort or another (i.e., analyzing stories, reading for main ideas) all of them are highly systematized and there are almost always "right answers."

The social studies series used in this school (and in the executive elite school) is Allyn and Bacon's *Concepts and Inquiry Program*. It emphasizes what it calls "higher concept" learning. Unlike the series in the working-class and middle-class schools, it discusses at length such topics as social class, the power of dominant ideas, and "competing world views." The district fifth-grade curriculum is intended to cover ancient civilization (e.g., ancient Greece and Rome) and Latin America. This fifth grade spent eight of ten months on ancient civilization. The teacher's guides to the series emphasize repeatedly that "conceptual learning should never degenerate into rote memorization followed by boring, parrot-like regurgitation of facts" (*Ancient Civilization*, p. 3). This guide lists thirty "performance objectives" for fourth- and fifth-grade social studies. Although called "performance" objectives, almost all are conceptual rather than behavioral.

Classroom social studies in the fifth grade that I observed involved some discussion of the text, but the teacher's emphasis was on artistic, graphic, dramatic, and written elucidation of cultural artifacts and ideas of Sumerians and Ancient Greeks. The teacher said she used the books "basically as a resource." She has the children "read it, and outline it," and uses it as a guide for inquiry activities and discussion. But, she said, most of her ideas for craft activities come from other sources. The class baked clay cuneiform replicas, wrote stories and plays, and created murals on the division of labor in ancient societies. Such activities were supported and facilitated when several families took their children to see the Tutankhamun exhibit and when one boy who had seen a different version of this exhibit in Paris brought in catalogues so the class could compare the two exhibits.

What students said about knowledge

When asked about what knowledge is, the children gave the following responses: "The way you think. Yes, the way you think." "Ideas and, um, smart people can find a lot of problems. They can think about them and they can realize them [sic]. When there is something wrong, they can realize what's wrong with it." "You think up ideas and then find things wrong with those ideas." "I don't know." "Being smart." "Knowing a lot of subjects." "It's when you know something—you can be a great scientist." "When you know something really well." Two said they weren't sure.

I asked them "Where does knowledge come from?" and got the following responses: "People and computers." "Your head." "People—what they do." "Something you learn." "From your brain; if you don't know about it at the start and you don't understand, but if you really work hard at it you will." "Your brain, you make it up in your brain." (Two other children also said that "their brains did the work.") "From reading and learning." "From going places." Four children said, "From reading." "When you learn in school." "You learn it in schools and college and high school." "Anybody, if they're willing to really learn something, can really go far in that subject—be a scientist, study craters. You could study ancient times or be a geologist." (Three said they didn't know.)

When I asked "Can you make knowledge?" sixteen children said yes; only four said no. They said that making knowledge involved the following: "Work hard, doing your best." "Albert Einstein studied very hard, and the first time he flunked out of college, but then he studied very hard and made it to the top." "You can make knowledge if you invent something." "If I were making knowledge, I'd take it step by step." "If you discover something." "I'd think of something to discover, then I'd make it." "I guess you could make some, but you have to be willing to learn and work hard." It should be noted that many of these answers reveal a rather active approach to the acquisition, if not creation, of knowledge.

Narcissism as a dominant theme

A dominant theme in this school was what I call *narcissism*, or extreme individualism. This emerges, for example, in the emphasis in the classroom on thinking for oneself, on externalizing, in creative projects of all sorts, what is internal in the attempts to individualize instruction, in the personal discovery intended by the science and math programs, and in the principal's and teachers' stated emphasis on personal development and creativity as important goals of education.

In addition to the stress in this school on individual development and expression, there was a stress on (or minor theme of) what I will call "humanitarianism" or "liberal ideals." The principal closes the morning intercom announcement each day with "do something nice for someone today." There is a "Good Deed Box" in the office and a certificate distributed on Fridays for a child who has done the nicest thing for "somebody who needs something nice." As in the executive elite school, there are clothing and food drives "for the poor." The social studies series attempts to be honest about society, recognizing, as it does, social classes, controlling ideas, and class conflict. It is also the most "liberal". Because of the recognition of social conflict, for example, there appear to be good reasons for social struggle, labor unions, and civil rights legislation. There is an entire fourth-grade textbook devoted to discussion of (and entitled) *Prejudice and Discrimination*.

Many of these children of affluent professionals are not at all sure they can be anything they want when they grow up, and their futures seem less than certain to them. Only half of them thought they could be anything they wanted, although all but one were sure they were going to college. Almost all wanted to go to a "good college." They all told me that to be anything you want "You really have to try hard" and "You have to go to the right college."

It seems to be the case that knowledge in the affluent professional school is not only conceptual but is open to discovery, construction, and meaning making; it is not always given. Knowledge is often concepts and ideas that are to be used to make sense, and that thus have personal value. Although knowledge may result from personal creativity and independent thinking, there are constraints and directives on what count as answers.

Knowledge has individualistic goals, but it also may be a resource for social good. It is analytical and more realistic about society than knowledge in the middle-class and working-class schools. The children are also getting a good dose of two dominant social ideologies: that the system itself will be made more humane by expressions of concern for the less fortunate, and that individuals, not groups, make history.

Executive elite school

What school personnel said about school knowledge

When I asked the two fifth-grade and two second-grade teachers in this school what knowledge was important for their students, most referred to intellectual processes such as reasoning and problem solving. One said, "They'll go to the best schools, and we have to prepare them." Another said, "It's not just academics; they need to learn to think. They will have important jobs, and they need to be able to think things through." When I asked a second-grade teacher who I was observing what was appropriate knowledge for her students, she said, "They need to learn the basics, we're going back to that now." "The basics?" I asked. "Yes, to think and write properly." Referring to science, a fifth-grade teacher said, "I try to get them to create an environment where they can solve problems—they manipulate variables and solve a problem."

The superintendent of schools, who has an EdD from Harvard University, is attempting to institute a "Philosophy for Children Program" in the school, the purpose of which would be "to teach children to think and reason correctly, and to come up with valid conclusions."[5] The fifth-grade teachers in this school said they have been instructed by the superintendent to develop an "Olympics of the Mind"—a competition of "open-ended questions" for which there are no "set answers."

Evidence from the curriculum and the curriculum-in-use

The fifth-grade teacher who teaches math said that her goal in this subject is the development of mathematical reasoning. She said the "demands" of "getting through the curriculum" do not leave her time to have the children "explore" with manipulables such as geoboards. She said she also tries to teach math as a "decision-making process." She usually asks the children to explain why their answers are right or wrong, to explain how they know or how they found out an answer.

Science is another subject in which an intellectual process such as reasoning was stressed. The principal said that all teachers in the school are "required" to use a science program. The fifth- and sixth-grade teachers used the ESS. According to the principal, the rest of the teachers in the school use *Science—A Process Approach* (SAPA). SAPA was designed to present instruction that is "intellectually stimulating and scientifically authentic." It focuses on the processes involved in scientific reasoning, and there is a "progressive intellectual development with each process category." The children are expected to learn such things as how to infer internal mechanisms of plants, how to make and verify hypotheses about animal behavior, and how to perform experiments on the actions of gases.[6]

While this school used the same social studies series as the affluent professional school, social studies instruction in the classes I observed here was more academically (rigorously) organized than in the affluent professional school, followed more closely the discussion questions posed by the text, and involved a large amount of independent library research but very little creative or artistic project work. The fifth-grade social studies teacher said she based her instruction on discussion questions in the text and district study guides, and on activities provided by ten "individual study packets."

Social studies knowledge was more sophisticated, complex, and analytical than in other schools. The social studies teacher I observed said she tried to have the children tackle the "important concepts." The following are examples of questions from the children's text that I heard discussed in class: "Greek comedies often poked fun at popular leaders. Would this be possible in a society that was not free? Can you think of any bad effects this might have? Any good effects?" "Look up the word 'imperialism.' What are some good and bad effects of imperialism?" (p. 41).

Social studies knowledge in this school also involved an explicit recognition of social class in ancient history. For example, the text identified, and the students discussed, what the text calls a "ruling class" in ancient society. In every chapter but two in the text on Greek and Roman civilization, there is the heading "Classes in Society" (with relevant concepts identified). Not only textbooks but the individual study packets as well included an explicit recognition of social class. There were two fifth-grade packets for independent study of Latin America. One was on geography, and the other was called "Class and Culture."

Scattered throughout the teacher's guide are references to other social classes, for instance "the lower classes," "the common classes." For example, "Rule by the ignorant and easily swayed lower classes led to grave errors in judgment like the Syracusan expedition" (teacher's guide, *Greek and Roman Civilization*, p. 55). (Interestingly, however, while the series is quite explicit about classes in ancient Greece and Rome [and Sumer], and a sixth-grade text called *The Challenge of Change* is quite explicit about the social class divisions in European history, the textbook series does not discuss class in this fashion in the US history textbook it provides for fourth grade, and there is no division there of US society into social classes.)

While classroom social studies knowledge tends to be *analytical*, neither text nor most social studies discussions were *critical* of the social class structure or distribution of wealth and power; rather, they gave it high value and a "naturalness," or "timelessness," going back, indeed, to ancient Greece. There were occasions, however, in the classroom of the fifth-grade teacher who teaches math, science, and health but not social studies, when class discussions were "almost" critical; that is, the teacher often asked the children *why* things were done or happened in a certain way, when that way appeared to be *irrational*. Discussions like this and indications that such discussions may go on in other rooms (e.g., intricate bulletin board displays of designs for home heating with solar power; school clothing and food drives; stories written about families who are poor and black; and district-run affirmative action and sexism awareness workshops for teachers) indicate that the school may play a politically liberalizing role in the children's upbringing.

What students said about knowledge

When I asked them what knowledge was, the children in this executive elite school gave the following answers: "Knowing certain things." "You have to really figure it out." "Thinking." "Knowing something that not too many people know; deep down, that's your knowledge. You have your opinion and then you know inside for sure, but the other person's never heard it before." "What you're *expected* to know." "What you're supposed to know." "It's being able to know and answer questions." One child said, "It depends on how you use it [the word]. There are two kinds of knowing: information knowing and wise knowing. Information knowledge, that's what you learn in school. Wise knowing is moral knowing, it's maturity. You learn that in life. . . ." "You have to be able to figure out things sensibly." "Knowing more than anybody." "Being the best." Three others said, "Knowing things." "When someone asks you a question you can answer it without any trouble—like I've been answering yours—only thinking for a minute."

The answers of the children in this school seem to speak less to creativity or thinking independently or making "sense," as did the answers given by many affluent professional children. Rather, these children spoke of the need to know *existing* knowledge and to do well, to understand, explain, and answer correctly (and quickly). The answers of many of these children were, without prodding on my part, longer than those of most others in other schools, and some were conceptually more sophisticated. Most of these children were quite tense during the interviews. They listened closely, tried to answer precisely and quickly, and were somewhat stiff, very formal, and polite.

When I asked where knowledge comes from, more than half (thirteen of twenty) said "from past experience," or from "tradition" or "other people." Only three mentioned that knowledge comes from one's brain or what one does. Several answers that call forth tradition were "How are you using that [the word knowledge]?" I say, "information knowing." He says, "Well, actually it began long ago—as accidents. Like fire, supposedly the Greeks . . . Somebody learned it, say, two pebbles and two stones, that's four. They figured it out, and now it's been passed down and everybody knows it, or most people."

When I asked "Can you make knowledge?" ten said yes, nine said no, and one said, "That's a ridiculous question!" When I asked "How could you make knowledge?" five said, "Learning—when other people teach you." "If you find something." "If I do an experiment in school I can find out if something is true or false." "If you invented something." "If you wanted to figure something out—whether if no one knew that two plus two is four, you could go out and figure it out." The rest said, "It depends." For example, "It depends. You could learn *some* stuff by yourself, but you could never learn to *talk* by yourself. Yes, that's a good example." "Not really," said one girl, "you can make computers, and they make knowledge. But you can get it, or have it and put it in something." These children, as compared to the affluent professional children, took a somewhat more passive attitude toward the creation of knowledge. For many, it comes from tradition, it is "out there," in what is known and expected of you, and you must learn it and know it.

One boy, who said he wants to be "a well-known lawyer like my father," told me, "You don't know you're the best until you've beaten the best." Seventeen of the twenty children said, without hesitation, yes they could be whatever they wanted when they grew up. Most (14), however, did not have any clear idea of what they wanted to be. They spoke of how good they were at soccer, skiing, swimming ("better than most kids my age," said one boy). Another said, "I'm interested in so *many* things that I can make something good out of anything." One boy said, "I could be the president if I wanted, but that doesn't turn me on." When I asked what being anything they wanted to be would depend on, they said, "It depends on how hard you try," "on having self-confidence," and "on going to the right school." The schools they mentioned were (in declining order of number of times mentioned): Harvard, Yale, Princeton, Notre Dame, Lehigh, Columbia, "Harvard graduate school for business," and "MIT graduate school in science."

Excellence as a dominant theme

Emerging from the executive elite school was a theme of excellence—the necessity of preparation for being the best, for top-quality performance. This does not allow for narcissistic coddling, but demands a great deal of "toeing the line," and self-discipline.[7] For example, the academic pace was much brisker here than in any other school. The teachers often told the children that they alone were responsible for themselves, for "keeping up," and for their work. This was the only school in the study in which the children were required to be doing schoolwork *before* the late bell rang to start the day. The principal, referring to his teachers, said, "We have no laggards in this school." He issued numerous memos regarding "quality instruction," "making use of every moment," and the importance of high student achievement scores. In April a fifth-grade teacher said to me, "The teachers are panicked. There's so much of the curriculum to get through before the end of the year." Many children in the school, it appeared to me, were more intense in competition and performance than most children in other schools. Indeed, some of them defined school knowledge in terms of their ability to perform well, for example to answer my questions.

The data suggest that knowledge in this executive elite school is academic, intellectual, and rigorous. There is an attempt to teach more, and more difficult, concepts than in any other school. Knowledge results not from personal activity or attempts to make sense, but from following rules of good thought, from rationality and reasoning. In many cases, knowledge involves understanding the internal structure of things: the logic by which systems of numbers, words, or ideas are arranged and may be rearranged. There is a sense and a practice that the rationality of logic and math is the model of correct and ethical thinking, and living. Intimately connected to what counts as knowledge for most children in this school is the perceived pressure to perform, to excel, to get into the "best" schools. Although highly privileged, many of these children are working *very* hard to keep what they have.

Conclusion and implications

The following assessment will focus on the profound differences in the curriculum and the curriculum-in-use as related to reproductive and non-reproductive aspects of knowledge in each social-class setting. "Reproductive" will refer to aspects of school knowledge that contribute directly to the legitimation and perpetuation of ideologies, practices, and privileges constitutive of present economic and political structures. "Non-reproductive" knowledge is that which facilitates fundamental transformation of ideologies and practices on the basis of which objects, services, and ideas (and other cultural products) are produced, owned, distributed, and publicly evaluated. The present definition of social change as fundamental transformation transcends the goals of, but does not deny the importance of, humanitarian efforts and practices in institutions such as the school.

As we shall see, however, the genesis of truly transformative activity is in the contradictions within and between social settings.

In the working-class schools there are two aspects of school knowledge that are reproductive. First, and quite simply, students in these schools were not taught their own history—the history of the US working class and its situation of conflict with powerful business and political groups, for example its long history of dissent and struggle for economic dignity. Nor were these students taught to value the interests which they share with others who will be workers. What little social information they were exposed to appears to provide little or no conceptual or critical understanding of the world or of their situation in the world. Indeed, not knowing the history of their own group—its dissent and conflict—may produce a social amnesia or "forgetting" (Jacoby, 1975), resulting in quietistic implications. A second reproductive aspect of school knowledge in these working-class schools was the emphasis in curriculum and in classrooms on mechanical behaviors, as opposed to sustained conception. These working-class children were not offered what for them would be *cultural capital*—knowledge and skill at manipulating ideas and symbols in their own interest, for example historical knowledge and analysis that legitimates their dissent and furthers their own class in society and in social transformation.

On the other hand, however, there is a major contradiction in school knowledge in these working-class schools, and from this may emerge a situation that is potentially socially transformative. Teacher control of students is a high priority in these schools, as in other schools. What the teachers attempted, in these two working-class schools, however, was *physical* control. There was little attempt to win the hearts and minds of these students. Now, our own era in history is one in which social control is achieved primarily through the dominant ideology and the perceived lack of ideological alternatives. But the working-class children in the schools studied here were taught very little of the ideology that is central to stable reproduction of the US system.

The absence of traditional bodies of knowledge and ideology may make these children vulnerable to alternative ideas; the children may be more open to ideas that support fundamental social change. Indeed, some of the children were already engaged in struggle against what was to them an exploitative group—the school teachers and administrators. They were struggling against the imposition of a foreign curriculum. The children's struggle, however, was destructive to themselves. Really *useful* knowledge for these students, for example honest "citizenship" education, would authenticate students' own meanings and give them skills to identify and analyze their own social class and to transform a situation that some already perceive is not in their own interest.

In the middle-class school, the children I observed were not taught the history of workers or of dissent, nor were they instructed to unify around common interests they will have as wage earners in a system in which many middle-class jobs are becoming increasingly like industrial and clerical jobs—mechanical and rote. There were, however, distinguishing characteristics of knowledge in this middle-class school that are important primarily because of the social-class location of the families. For example, the notion of knowledge as originating in external and externally approved sources, as generated and validated by experts, may yield a passive stance before ideas and ideology and before the creation or legitimation of new ideas. This, of course, has implications of intellectual passivity, and ideological quietude. Moreover, school knowledge in the middle-class school was highly commodified. The reification of ideas and knowledge into given facts and "generalizations" that exist separately from one's biography or discovery contributes to the commodification of knowledge. In the social-class position of the present middle-class school the teachers and students perceive the knowledge to have market value: there is a perceived chance that if one can accumulate facts, information, and "generalizations," one can exchange them for college entrance or for a white-collar (perhaps even professional) job. Commodification of knowledge in the middle-class school is reproductive in part because it helps to legitimize and reproduce the ideology of production for consumption, for example production of knowledge and other cultural products for the market rather than for personal use or for social transformation.

There is a second aspect of knowledge in the middle-class school that is reproductive. This is also a part of the apparent acceptance or belief in the possibility of success for oneself. It is a social fact of major importance that the US middle class is a group whose recent history has shown rapidly decreasing economic stability for individual families. There is, thus, material reason for the reification of knowledge into accumulatable form and for the anxiety which the children manifest concerning tests, college, and jobs. For example, the amount of attention one must pay to "getting ahead" not only leaves little interest or time for critical attention, but it also actively fosters and strengthens belief in the ideologies of upward mobility and success.

In the affluent professional school there are several aspects of school knowledge that are reproductive. First, the children are taught what is, for most of them, their own history—the history of the wealthy classes. They are taught that the power of their own group is legitimate. They are, as well, taught ways of expressing and using such ideas— that ideology—in their own interests. They are being provided with cultural capital. Indeed, the fact that the knowledge of their own group is socially prestigious knowledge enhances the exchange value of their knowledge as capital. Moreover, because many affluent professional jobs still require conception and creativity and independent thought, many of the children in this school will be in the privileged position of having the *use* value of their knowledge (for personal creativity, for example) be at the same time its *exchange* value (for example, they will get paid for doing creative, conceptual work).

A second aspect of school knowledge that is reproductive here is its nascent empiricism (by empiricism I refer to the emphasis in adult science on basing knowledge on experience and on appearances, on observable data this experience produces). As the basis for knowledge or explanations, empiricism is socially reproductive when it provides a framework for allegedly independent thought. Empiricism uses characteristics of observable data and characteristics of the observed relationships between data for its explanations; empiricism eschews explanations and analyses which are based on transcendent and non-empirical knowledge (see Bernstein, 1978). This mode of inquiry thus uses categories and explanations that are confined to what already exists, to what can be observed. This mitigates against challenges to the necessity or naturalness of these categories and of what exists. School science programs and math manipulables make a small contribution, then, to the legitimation of empiricism as a way of seeking and testing knowledge, and to the acceptance of what is, as opposed to what could be. The programs are, in this case, a potential invisible boundary of the social thought of these children.

Accompanying the nascent empiricism in this affluent professional school is the emphasis on individual development as a primary goal of education (as opposed, for example, to the development of the priority of collective goals). A priority on personal expression, personal "meaning making," and the "construction of reality" mitigates against collectivistic values and meanings and solutions; it is thereby reproductive of values important to an individualistic, privately owned, and competitive economy. Finally, the emphasis in the curriculum and classrooms on active use of concepts and ideas by students, as opposed to a stress on mechanics or rote behaviors, facilitates the perpetuation of an unequal division of labor in US society, where some (these children?) will plan and others (working-class and middle-class children?) will have jobs that entail carrying out the plans.

There are, however, basic contradictions apparent in the school knowledge of these affluent professional children. In these conflicts one can see powerful implications for social transformation. For example, the contradiction between attempting as a student, and making sense as an adult, presumably later in one's professional creative labors, in a society where many things do *not* make sense and are irrational is a conflict which may generate political radicalism. Such a conflict may lead to intellectuals who are highly critical of the system and who attempt to persuade others by disseminating their own views. Or, it may lead to political activism, to overt attempts to take physical action against perceived political and economic irrationalities. It is probably true that the conflict inherent in attempting to make sense in a world that is in many ways irrational is present for all children in all schools and social classes. What makes the conflict a potentially powerful force in the affluent professional school, however, is first the social-class position of these children, their cultural capital, and future access to information, power, and further cultural capital afforded to them by their social position. A second factor important here is the nature of their schooling. These children were told, and encouraged, more than the children in any other school to be creative, to think for themselves, and to make sense. It is indeed because of such encouragement to the young that the increasingly ideological notions of freedom and democracy can be turned back upon the economically and politically powerful and made into truly transformative demands.

Another contradiction to the school knowledge of these children that is non-reproductive is the contradiction between the value placed on creativity and personal decision making, and the systematic, increasingly rationalized nature of school and professional work in US society. This conflict, already apparent in the use of science and reading programs in this school, is a contradiction that suggests possible later conflicts between the use and exchange values of knowledge in adult work, for example between one's own creativity and the increasing rationalization and control of professional work by technology, bureaucratic trends, and centralization. It also suggests class conflict between affluent professionals, with their own interests and skills and relative power in the bureaucracy on one hand, and the capitalists, who are their "bosses" and who hold the purse strings, on the other. It is, then, important to provide the children of the affluent professional class with school knowledge that is not just conceptual, analytical, and expressive, but that is also critical and collective. Such knowledge would foster responsiveness not only to the needs of individual "meaning making" and development, but to the development of a wider social collectivity that, not coincidentally, would affirm the needs of the working and middle classes as well.

School knowledge in the executive elite school was the most "honest" about society, US social problems, and social irrationalities. It was sometimes expressive of liberal concerns, as well. Indeed, it came the closest to being socially critical. The children were given analytical and unsentimental insight into the system. Whereas, for example, middle-class children might see a pluralism of equal or competing ethnic cultures, the children of the executive elite might perceive social class and economic conflict. Thus, these children may be less ideologically mystified than, for example, the middle-class students. The executive elite students—in different and more socially profitable ways than the working-class students—may see more clearly through the rhetoric of nationalism and equal opportunity to the raw facts of class and class conflict.

There is a potential contradiction here in the "clarity" of understanding the system that may, in the particular context of the social-class position of these children, have transformative possibilities. This is the contradiction for them between the use and exchange values in their knowledge: the contradiction between using knowledge for pleasure and enjoying one's class privilege, for example, and the exchange value of knowledge when it must be used to maintain that privilege. Two particular characteristics that empower this contradiction for these children (because the contradiction does appear in weaker forms in other schools) are, first, that extreme pressure is necessary, and excruciating struggle is demanded in a capitalist political democracy to actually maintain one's position of economic power and privilege. To grow up in the modern capitalist class is not only to enjoy travel, luxury, good schools, and financial wealth; it is also to have to maintain power in the face of others competing with you, within an irrational economic system that is increasingly difficult to predict, manage, and control—not only in the US but in a rebellious Third World, as well. To be the "best," one must continually "beat the best." This is severe pressure. Second, to be a powerful capitalist, one must cause suffering and actually exploit others. Indeed, one's wealth and power are possible only because there are others (e.g., a reserve "pool" of workers) who do not have power and resource. These two "facts of life" of "being a capitalist" mean that if one is not ideologically secured, one may reject these demands. In contrapuntal fashion, the pressures, the irrationalities, and the exploitative characteristics of one's role in the system may one day cause the system to be perceived as the enemy—to be destroyed, rather than exploited. While such efforts at social transformation are violent and irrational and are not condoned, they must be acknowledged as non-reproductive in intent.

By situating school knowledge in its particular social location, we can see how it may contribute to contradictory social processes of conservation and transformation. We see the schools reproducing the tensions and conflicts of the larger society. It becomes apparent as well that an examination of only one social site may blur the distinctions and subtleties that a comparative study illuminates. That is, a social phenomenon may differ by social class; and indeed similar (or the same) phenomena may have different meanings in different social contexts. This study has suggested, as well, that there are class conflicts in educational knowledge and its distribution. We can see class conflict in the struggle to impose the knowledge of powerful groups on the working class and in student resistance to this class-based curriculum. We can see class conflict in the contradictions within and between school knowledge and its economic and personal values, and in attempts to impose liberal public attitudes on children of the rich.

Class conflict in education is thus not dormant, nor a relic of an earlier era; nor is the outcome yet determined. No class is certain of victory, and ideological hegemony is not secure. Those who would struggle against ideological hegemony must not confuse working-class powerlessness with apathy, middle-class ideology with its inevitability, or ruling-class power and cultural capital with superior strength or intelligence. Just as blacks were not the happy-go-lucky fellows of former stereotypes, so the working class is not dull or acquiescent, and the rich are not complacent or secure. Indeed, perhaps the most important implication of the present study is that for those of us who are working to transform society, there is much to do, at all levels, in education.

Questions for discussion

1. Reflecting upon the differences in teachers' attitudes toward and expectations regarding students' abilities based on the collective class background of the student population in each of the four schools, discuss the potential consequences of these differences on a societal level.

2. Compare the schools within Anyon's study to determine the differences between attitudes of school personnel regarding school knowledge. To what might we attribute these differences? To what does Anyon attribute these differences? This shortened version of her classic piece was written in the early 1980s. To what extent do you think you would find the same results if you did the study today? Why or why not?

3. What do the author's findings reveal about student perceptions and those of school personnel regarding the curriculum and the curriculum-in-use? Discuss the relationship between perceptions of students and school personnel. To what extent does one reinforce or depend upon the other?

4. What is the difference between cultural and social capital? How do these concepts work either to impede or benefit students of varying social class?

5. How does Anyon distinguish between reproductive and non-reproductive aspects of knowledge? In comparing these school settings, which allows for the greatest potential to generate alternatives to dominant ideologies?

6. According to the author, "In each of the three city schools, approximately 85 percent of the students were white, in the fourth school, 90 percent were white, and in the last school, all were white." Why do you suppose the last school (the elite school) is composed of a racially homogeneous student body? Do you suspect this study would have similar findings if these schools had been more diverse? How does race complicate issues of class?

7. Consider Anyon's definition of social class within the text. Is this definition sufficient for assessing class divisions today? Is attempting to define such a complex and nebulous term problematic? If so, in what ways?

8. Is school knowledge different from other forms of knowledge? If so, how are other forms of knowledge distinctive from knowledge that is produced and disseminated within schools? Is school knowledge more valuable than knowledge produced within other contexts (i.e., popular culture, museums, etc.)? In what situations and under what conditions is it more or less valuable?

Notes

I would like to thank Michael Apple, Stewart Bird, Henry Giroux, Nancy King, James Scott, Roger Simon, Bob Tabachnick, Philip Wexler, and Geoff Whitty for their encouragement, critical comments, and editorial advice during various phases of the work involved in producing this chapter.

1. The study was funded by two grants from Rutgers University Research Council, whose generous support is hereby acknowledged.
2. For further discussion of social class in these terms, see Anyon (1980).
3. Stated goals of the *Elementary Science Study* are to encourage children to use science materials to find answers to their own questions in their own ways. The emphasis is not on the teaching of a series of science concepts or on the creation of scientific prodigies, but on relatively unstructured experiences that emphasize "active involvement, freedom to pursue one's own interests, imagination and individuality." The materials are aimed at "developing self-directing, autonomous, and self-actualizing individuals." See accounts by Hal (1972) and also Educational Development Center (1971).

   In some second- and third-grade classrooms I noticed *Science—A Process Approach* (SAPA) materials on shelves. Five of the eight teachers in K-3 said that they didn't use these materials, that they did science "on their own," or "informally"; the other three reported that they did use the SAPA materials.
4. Reading in the working-class and middle-class schools was not individualized at any level (they did, however, use a *programmed* reading series [Sullivan Programmed Readers] in the early grades). None of the boxed reading programs mentioned as used in the affluent professional school was in any of the working-class or middle-class schools except for SRA. An SRA kit was available in all classrooms I visited. The teachers in the working-class schools said they did not use it. A teacher in one of the working-class schools said she didn't use it "because the kids cheat." In the middle-class school, one teacher used her SRA *Power Builder* and another skills kit from SRA that she got because she lied, by telling the state "comp ed" person that she had more students eligible than she did. She says she has the kids use the kits once a week because "it's fun, and they like it"; also, "so I don't miss any skills." I asked four other teachers in the fourth and fifth grades in the middle-class school, and they said they did not use their SRAs; one teacher stated, "It's too much trouble."
5. See Hugh Munby's (1979) critique of the program which appeared in *Curriculum Inquiry* 9(3).
6. The quote and descriptions are taken from Mayor's (1972) account. See also American Association for the Advancement of Science (1972).
7. It is at this point that I would make sure that it is understood that I do not intend the themes reported in the schools to be monolithic; no theme purports to include every child. There were subcultures or groups in all of the schools (e.g., there were children in the working-class schools who did not resist, and children in the middle-class school who did resist and who were cynical about their "possibilities"). It is not possible here, however, to include all data and all interpretations. I must choose what is most representative, or what appears to be significant for some other reason. In the executive elite school, however, there was a noticeable competing subculture of resistance within the fifth grade, which appears to me to have significance because it was so strong and yet involved a clear minority of children.

References

American Association for the Advancement of Science (1972). *Science—a process approach: Purposes, accomplishments, expectations* (AAAS Miscellaneous Publication no. 67–12, September 1967). Lexington, MA: American Association for the Advancement of Science.

Anyon, J. (1979a). Education, social "structure" and the power of individuals. *Theory and Research in Social Education, 7*(1), 49–60.

—— (1979b). Ideology and United States history textbooks. *Harvard Educational Review, 49*(33), 361–86.

—— (1980). Social class and the hidden curriculum of work. *Journal of Education, 162*(1), 67–92.

Apple, M. (1979). *Ideology and curriculum*. Boston: Routledge and Kegan Paul.

Bernstein, R. (1978). *The restructuring of social and political theory*. Philadelphia: University of Pennsylvania Press.

Bowles, S., & Gintis, H. (1976). *Schooling in capitalist America: Educational reform and the contradictions of economic life*. New York: Basic Books.

Educational Development Center (1971). *A working guide to the elementary science study*. Newton, MA: Educational Development Center.

Fitzgerald, F. (1979). *America revised*. Boston: Little, Brown.

Hal, C. (1972). Elementary science study. In D. Lockard (Ed.), *The eighth report of the national clearinghouse on science and mathematics curricular development*. Baltimore, MD: University of Maryland.

Jacoby, R. (1975). *Social amnesia*. Boston: Beacon Press.

Karabel, J. (1972). Community colleges and social stratification. *Harvard Educational Review 42*(4), 521–62.

Karabel, J., & Halsey, A. H. (1977). *Power and ideology in education*. New York: Oxford University Press.

Mayor, J. (1972). Science—a process approach. In D. Lockard (Ed.), *The eighth report of the national clearinghouse on science and mathematics curricular development*. Baltimore, MD: University of Maryland.

Munby, H. (1979). Philosophy for children: An example of curriculum review and criticism. *Curriculum Inquiry, 9*(3), 229–49.

Rosenbaum, J. (1976). *Making inequality: The hidden curriculum of high school tracking*. New York: Wiley.

Smith, J., & Franklin, S. (1974). The concentration of personal wealth, 1922–69. *American Economic Review, 64*(4), 162–67.

US Bureau of the Census (1979). Money income in 1977 of families and persons in the United States. In *Current population reports*, Series P-60, no. 118. Washington, DC: United States Government Printing Office.

Young, M., & Whitty, G. (1977). *Society, state and schooling*. Sussex, England: Falmer Press.

Zinn, H. (1980). *A people's history of the United States*. New York: Harper and Row.

Chapter 14

Social class and tracking within schools

*Sean Patrick Kelly**

When James Rosenbaum conducted his seminal case study of tracking in the early 1970s, he found that the track structure at Grayton High could be described using the metaphor of a "tournament" (Rosenbaum, 1976). Rather than low-track courses presenting an opportunity for students to work hard and eventually move into college-preparatory classes, upward mobility at Grayton was practically non-existent. For the cohort of students Rosenbaum observed, not a single student left the general or business track in the ninth grade to move up into the college track by twelfth grade (Rosenbaum, 1976, table 3.4). Meanwhile, high-track students had to work quite hard to maintain their place in the curricular hierarchy, or they would soon find themselves in regular-track courses where the likelihood of going to a competitive university was much lower. Rosenbaum studied a single school, and subsequent research on the educational trajectory of students has found substantially more movement, both up and down the track hierarchy, than did Rosenbaum. In most schools, the curriculum is not literally organized as a single-elimination tournament, as it appeared to be at Grayton. Nevertheless, only a small proportion of low-track students actually move into college-preparatory classes during high school and stay there. Lucas (1999) found that about 12 percent of students in mathematics and 21 percent of students in English had a net upward movement over the last two years of high school.[1] A student who begins secondary school in low-track classes will likely finish high school in low-track classes.

For important methodological reasons, Rosenbaum selected Grayton High because it served a student body that was almost entirely white and predominantly working class. If he had walked into a more diverse school and conducted an in-depth analysis of high- and low-track classrooms, he would have found a strong relationship between the social class of the students and their track locations. Thus, even when attending the same schools, students from different social class backgrounds have very different educational experiences because in actuality they are not exposed to the same instructional environments. Students from middle- and upper-middle-class backgrounds spend their middle and high school years in college-preparatory classrooms with mostly other advantaged students, while lower-class students are relegated to low-track classrooms more often than not. In the educational tournament, to use Rosenbaum's terminology, students from disadvantaged backgrounds often fail to make the high-track cut.

---

* Assistant Professor of Sociology at the University of Notre Dame, and a researcher at the Center for Research on Educational Opportunity.

The official rationale behind the practice of tracking is that by matching high and low performing students to instructional environments specifically tailored for their current level of achievement, all students will benefit. Contrary to this logic, four decades of research has led to the conclusion that low-track classrooms do not offer as rich an educational environment as high-track classrooms; high-track students benefit the most from the practice of tracking. The experiences of disadvantaged students in low-track classrooms are neither ephemeral or inconsequential; indeed, being a low-track student affects nearly every aspect of their lives as students, from test scores (Carbonaro, 2003), grades (Farkas et al., 2005), educational aspirations (Hotchkiss & Dorsten, 1987), self-esteem (Oakes, 1985), and friendship patterns (Kubitschek & Hallinan, 1998), to their likelihood of going to college (Lucas, 2001). Family background and test scores being equal, a student in the college-preparatory track is three times as likely to attend college as a student taking regular or vocational track courses (Erigha & Carbonaro, 2006). Thus, the practice of tracking tends to increase educational inequality rather than decrease it (Gamoran & Mare, 1989).

In this chapter I begin by presenting some estimates of how likely students of differing social class backgrounds are to be found in high- and low-track classrooms. The consistency of these estimates is quite striking; socially advantaged students are much more likely to be found in high-track classrooms. I then turn to examining why social class is so tightly connected with students' track locations. Evidence suggests that students themselves, families, and schools all have an important influence on the track location of students.

The course-taking gap among students of differing social class backgrounds

Table 14.1 presents the descriptive relationship between social class and track locations in several nationally representative educational databases spanning the 1960s, 1970s, and 1980s. The robust conclusion is that students from disadvantaged backgrounds are much more likely to be in low-track classrooms than students from middle-class and upper-middle-class families. Expressed as correlation coefficients, the relationship between social class and tracking in these studies is between .23 and .39, somewhat less than the correlation between achievement and track location in the same studies (between .41 and .67).[2] It can be difficult to grasp the significance of correlation coefficients though, especially when they express the relationship between categorical variables.[3]

Kelly (2004) provides a more detailed breakdown of students' track locations in mathematics by levels of parental education in the National Educational Longitudinal Survey (NELS), which surveyed tenth graders in 1990. Track placements in mathematics have a particularly strong influence on students' educational trajectories. Math track placement has a large effect on achievement growth, perhaps the most of any of the core subjects (Gamoran, 1987), and colleges and universities look at mathematics course taking as a strong indicator of readiness for quantitative areas of study such as engineering, computer science, and the like . . . (Adelman, 1998). Moreover, as a subject in secondary schools, mathematics is typically characterized by a high level of differentiation among courses, with both the pace and content of the curriculum differing across courses. Kelly's data, taken from students' freshman and sophomore year transcripts, shows how

Table 14.1 Descriptive relationship between social class and track location, 1960–1990

Correlation between academic track and social class[a]

Database (study)		Notes[b]
20 school sample, 1964–65 (Alexander & McDill, 1976)	.23	N = 3,699, 12th grade
EEO Urban High school sub-sample, 1965 (Heyns, 1974)	.26	N = 15,384 12th grade
Youth in Transition Study, 1966 (Wiatrowski et al. 1982)	.39	N = 1,886, 11th grade
NLS, 1972 (Rosenbaum, 1980)	.36[c]	N = 16,683, 12th grade
HS&B, 1980 (Lee & Bryk, 1988)	.30, .35[d]	Public schools, N = 1,883, 10th grade

Probability of track location by categories of parent's highest education (N = 13,548, 9th & 10th grades)

NELS, 1988 (Kelly, 2004)[e]	≤ High school	≥ College degree
≥ Algebra II & Geometry	1.8%	10.3%
Algebra II & Geometry	6.3%	23.8%
Algebra II or Geometry but not both	31.0%	44.5%
Algebra I	30.2%	14.5%
≤ Algebra I	30.7%	6.9%

Notes

a Social class measures typically include composite scales of father's and mother's education, and earnings. When scales are not available, correlations are reported with father's education. The most common measure of track location is student reported overall track location, dichotomized as a (0,1) variable indicating academic (college-prep) vs. non-academic (regular, remedial, and vocational) track location.

b Databases are nationally representative, or originally sampled to be so, with the exception of the Alexander and McDill (1976) study.

c School record indicator of track location (0,1) college, non-college bound.

d Advanced course taking in Mathematics.

e Kelly (2004) analyzed sequences of mathematics courses using transcript data on course taking in the 9th and 10th grades.

likely students with parents of differing educational attainment are to be found in each of five mathematics sequences. The lowest sequence represents students who had not yet enrolled in Algebra I by their sophomore year, while the highest sequence represents students that had completed Algebra II and Geometry and were currently enrolled in a more advanced mathematics course. Students with a parent who had completed a college degree were about four times as likely to be enrolled in one of the highest two math tracks than were students whose parents had completed only high school or less. Less than 2 percent of students whose parents had never enrolled in college were in the highest mathematics sequence. Students from advantaged family backgrounds were also much *less* likely to be enrolled in the lowest tracks.

Why are disadvantaged students so much more likely to end up in low-track classrooms?

The prominent role of achievement in the track placement process

In most high schools, track assignments are formally based on objective criteria such as test scores and classroom grades. Longitudinal studies of students in the transition from middle to high school show a strong connection between students' grades, test scores, and their track location. In two nationally representative studies of secondary schooling conducted by the US Department of Education—High School and Beyond (base-year 1980) and NELS (base-year 1988)—test scores are the single strongest predictor of track location (Gamoran & Mare, 1989; Kelly, 2004).[4] It makes perfect sense that schools should establish test score or grade cut-offs for placement into a given track. The point of tracking in the first place is to establish classrooms where students' levels of achievement are relatively homogeneous, and thus, teachers can concentrate on teaching material appropriate to his or her students' current knowledge and skills. Of course, the test information that a school uses to inform track placement decisions will depend on when standardized tests are administered in their district or state, and on the content of the specific test selected for use. For example, some but not all language arts tests include an essay component. Since the mid 1990s the use of standardized tests has increased greatly, with many districts and states now testing students each year in grades six through eight.

Unfortunately, differences in the achievement levels of students of different social class backgrounds are quite large even when students enter school (Entwisle & Alexander, 1990) and grow quickly during the early years of school (Entwisle & Alexander, 1992). For example, data from the 2005 National Assessment of Educational Progress (NAEP) shows that fourth graders who are eligible for free lunch, a rough proxy of a family's income, scored about 23 points lower on the mathematics assessment than students who are not eligible for free lunch (NCES, 2006).[5] Thus, by the time students reach middle or high school where curriculum differentiation begins, lower social class students are at a substantial disadvantage on these objective track placement criteria.

While most students' track placements are strongly influenced by their level of achievement, there is still some variability in track placements even for students of very similar levels of achievement, as measured by standardized tests for example. Indeed, Hallinan (1992) documented a substantial overlap in the achievement distributions of adjacent track levels. Track placements are heavily influenced by achievement, but many students in schools' regular-track classrooms are higher achieving than the students in the same schools' high-track classrooms. Hallinan's findings lead us to ask the question, why might one student end up in a high-track course, and another a low-track course, when they are equally qualified?

Studies of social class and track placement have shown that even if test scores and grades are equivalent for two students, the lower social class student is more likely to be placed in a low-track class than the student from an advantaged background (Gamoran & Mare, 1989; Kelly, 2004; Lucas, 1999). Kelly (2004) estimated that, holding test scores and grades constant, having a parent with a college degree makes a student almost 20 percent more likely to be in one of the top two math sequences. Gamoran and Mare's (1989) analysis suggests an even stronger effect of social class. They found that "students who miss one-quarter of the questions [on a comprehensive test of mathematics achievement] but come from advantaged backgrounds had as much chance of being in the college track as the impoverished students who answered *every* question correctly."[6] Although most of the social class differences in track location can be accounted for by differences in achievement manifested in elementary school, or even before children begin formal schooling, a large residual effect of social class remains.

The occasional influence of parental interventions

A student's success in school depends on making a solid academic effort in class, as well as making the right behavioral choices outside of class that support cognitive development, such as completing homework and getting a good night's rest. Parents can have powerful effects on a student's chances of success by being involved with their child's education. From monitoring homework completion, to making sure their child gets to school well-rested, parents support school readiness and success in the classroom. These types of involvement are likely to have an impact on students' track locations, because of their influence on student achievement. In addition, highly educated parents may go beyond the general oversight of their children's education, overtly intervening on behalf of their students during the track placement process. Stating this hypothesis bluntly, highly educated parents may essentially "demand" that their student be placed in a high-track course. If that were the case, social class might have a clear and direct impact on students' track locations. This hypothesis was borne out in Baker and Stevenson's (1986) case study of a school that allowed significant parental agency in the track placement process, and also in a study by Gamoran (1992) of five school districts with diverse approaches to tracking. In Gamoran's analysis, interventions by high SES parents primarily occurred when an average achieving student missed the school's cut-off point for honors placement. In that case, the parent felt that their child should be enrolled in the honors class and worked with the school on their student's behalf.

Whether or not parents intervene on behalf of their children may be affected by social class differences both in familiarity with a school's track structure and even in their understanding of the profound importance of tracking (Baker & Stevenson, 1986; Gamoran, 1992). Lower social class parents may not be aware that they should, or can, demand that their child be enrolled in college-preparatory classes. In a study of two school districts, Useem (1991) found that more highly educated parents were more involved in a host of school matters. Parent–Teacher Associations and other voluntary school organizations help parents develop an understanding of the school's track structure and the nature of their student's school experience compared to other students. Useem found that middle-class parents' knowledge about tracking was further bolstered by interacting with other middle-class parents. Schools portray high-track courses as having demanding work loads and posing a greater risk of failure than regular- or low-track courses. Social networks provide middle-class parents with examples of success in high-track classes, making them more confident in pursuing a high-track placement for their own children. The insider knowledge of more educated parents gives them an edge in dealing with the school (Useem, 1991). Indeed, from the perspective of school personnel, middle-class parents sometimes take involvement in their children's schooling a step too far. It is one thing to try to override teacher and administrator's authority to make track placements, but quite another when parent involvement encroaches on diverse matters of curriculum and instruction. When that happens, teachers and school administrators in middle-class communities must struggle to maintain the professional autonomy they see as necessary to carry out their work in the school (Lareau, 2000).

Even if the *level* of parental intervention is similar among parents of differing social classes, parents of higher social class may be more successful in working with schools to tailor their children's educational experience (Lareau, 2000; McNeal, 1999). Parents from all social class backgrounds value education and want the best possible opportunities for their children. However, social status is an important resource in dealing with school personnel. Less-educated parents may find negotiating with more highly educated school personnel difficult. The language of the school curriculum is quite technical, and less educated parents may have difficulty with the educational rhetoric school personnel marshal in support of their decisions. Moreover, while less-educated parents want to advocate on behalf of their children, they may also feel a tendency to be deferent towards school personnel who hold relatively high status occupations.

Are the kinds of parental interventions found by Baker and Stevenson, Useem, and others widespread, and how much difference do they really make in a student's track location? Subsequent research by Kelly (2004) has failed to confirm the hypothesis that parental intervention is largely responsible for the differences in track locations of students from high and low social class backgrounds. In the hundreds of schools included in his analysis, Kelly found that parents did sometimes intervene on behalf of their students, securing for them a higher-track location. But most schools do not completely allow parents to determine course placements, as they did in the Baker and Stevenson study, and a relatively small number of parents intervene directly in the track placement process. The agency of middle- and upper-middle-class parents is sometimes responsible for a student's track location, but this occasional practice does not explain the large differences in track location related to social class.

Internalized expectations of school success among middle-class students

By the time students reach middle school, they are beginning to have well-formed *educational aspirations*, the level of education they hope to achieve, and *expectations* of educational success, practical thoughts on what s/he is likely to achieve. In a comprehensive high school, some students take for granted that they are college bound, envisioning their future lives in professional occupations, while other students see their educational situation as more precarious. Both kinds of students, those with high expectations and those with more modest expectations, are in essence competing for slots in the school's high-track classes.

It is true that the average student has quite high expectations of their future educational attainment. Barbara Schneider and David Stevenson (1999) conducted a study of the changing educational expectations of US youth since the 1950s. Overall, they found that expectations of attending college and graduate school have risen sharply in recent decades. By the standard of the jobs that are actually available today, today's teens even seem a bit unrealistic in their expectations. For example, many more teens aspire to careers in engineering, architecture, and the sciences than positions currently exist in those occupations. However, another segment of today's teenagers see high school as the end of the educational line. They hope to secure good jobs in occupations that do not require post-secondary education. As with other elements of schooling, social class has a profound effect on educational expectations. Students whose parents do not have college degrees are more than twice as likely not to expect to go to college than students who have a parent with a college degree (Hoogstra, 2000).

Educational aspirations (Lee & Byrk, 1988) and expectations (Gamoran, 1992) have strong effects on students' subsequent track locations. For a student who does not plan to attend college, taking "college-preparatory" coursework might seem like extra work, with little pay-off. There is also the issue of a sense of social belonging. Students who take for granted the fact that they will attend college will be more likely to feel that they *belong* in upper-track courses with other students who are similarly inclined, who share their future. Tyson, Darity, and Castellino (2005) found that, in choosing to take a lower-track course, students are not necessarily disregarding the importance of school success, but seeking out the setting in which they have friends and feel comfortable.[7]

The relationship between educational expectations and track location helps explain why students from lower social class backgrounds are less likely to take college-preparatory courses, even if they have the grades and test scores that indicate an upper-track course would be a good fit for their knowledge and skills. Kelly (2004) estimates that, once differences in achievement are taken into account, about one-fifth to one-quarter of higher social class students' remaining course-taking advantage can be accounted for by differences in students' expectations of their future educational attainment.

Summary

Students from middle- and upper-middle-class families have a decisive advantage over lower social class students in gaining access to college-preparatory learning environments. While it is beyond the scope of this chapter to closely detail the profound effect this has on students' lives, clearly high-track learning environments are effective ones, both in the sense that achievement gains are large, and in so far as students are best prepared for further education after high school. There is no single explanation for why students from socially advantaged homes more often make their way into upper-track courses than other students. Middle- and upper-middle-class parents sometimes intervene on behalf of their children, securing a high-track placement for a student who might otherwise be in the regular track, or a placement in the regular track when guidance counselors and teachers recommend a remedial placement. But this type of intervention is an occasional occurrence. The fact that socially advantaged students arrive at middle school with stronger verbal and mathematics skills is the main reason they are positioned in upper-track courses. Beyond achievement differences, middle- and upper-middle-class students also have an advantage because they have internalized expectations of educational success.

Variation in tracking systems across schools

In 1970, Aage Sorrenson argued that tracking is not a uniform phenomenon across schools. Instead, tracking systems are likely to vary on several important dimensions. In this section I discuss variation across schools on two dimensions that are likely to impact the track locations of students from high and low social class backgrounds, the *inclusiveness* of a school's tracking system and the objectivity of a school's placement criteria. Unfortunately, only a small amount of research on specific school policies is available from which to draw conclusions. Nevertheless, two conclusions seem warranted. First, students from socially advantaged backgrounds are better able to seek out and benefit from schools that emphasize a college-preparatory curriculum, and this contributes to their better odds of being in high-track courses. Second, within schools, when placement criteria are objective, low-track students will have better chances of gaining access to a college-preparatory curriculum.

Differences in inclusiveness: An emphasis on a college-preparatory curriculum for all students

The inclusiveness of a school's track structure refers to the extent to which a school's college-preparatory courses are highly selective, allowing only a small percentage of the school's students to enroll, or inclusive, encouraging as many students as possible to take a college-preparatory curriculum. Even if two schools had students of identical average levels of achievement, Sorensen (1970) argued, don't expect them to have the same proportion of these students enrolled in the college track. Michael Garrett and Brian Delany's (1988) study of differences in inclusiveness across four schools showed just how disparate schools' approaches to tracking can be. At the time of their study, college-bound students in their district enrolled in geometry in the tenth grade. In the most inclusive school they studied, high achieving math students (those who were at the seventy-fifth percentile in the state as a whole) had a 56 percent chance of taking geometry as sophomores. In the least inclusive school, less than 5 percent of the high achieving math students were enrolled in geometry as sophomores. Garrett and Delany showed in vivid detail that tracking systems are not universal. Which school a student attends can have as much or even more of an impact on track placement than her or his level of achievement.

Are middle- and upper-middle-class families more likely than lower social class families to send their children to schools with a college-preparatory focus, like the inclusive school Garrett and Delany studied? Two factors make this likely to be the case. First, the increased wealth and earnings of middle- and upper-middle-class parents means they have much greater flexibility in choosing schools for their children. Financial stability gives them the opportunity to send their children to private schools or to reside within the district or school boundaries of the public schools that they choose. The advent of "magnet" schools, which draw diverse students from throughout a district by offering a special curricular focus (the arts, sciences, etc. . . . .), has increased opportunities for choice in many school districts. But financial resources are sometimes needed to overcome obstacles in taking advantage of new opportunities, such as arranging for transportation to send a student to a magnet school. Second, middle-class parents find it easier to gather information about local schools than do lower social class parents. Middle-class parents typically have a larger social network outside of their immediate family and neighborhood. In addition, they are often better able to navigate the educational rhetoric of schools with can sometimes be confusing. It seems likely that students from socially advantaged backgrounds are well positioned to benefit from school-to-school differences in inclusiveness by seeking out schools which emphasize a college-preparatory curriculum. In studies of social class and tracking, researchers find that, indeed, higher social class students attend schools that are more inclusive than do lower social class students (Kelly, 2004; Spade, Columba & Vanfossen, 1997).

The objectivity of placement criteria

It is difficult for guidance counselors or other school personnel to know for certain which of the several levels of courses offered will be the best match for a particular student. This is because how a student responds to a class depends to a large extent not on the innate ability of that student, but on how engaged he or she is. If a student is ready to put forth their best effort, s/he can usually succeed even in the most rigorous high school course.

Then again, school personnel have to be realistic. The necessary level of effort for a student of borderline achievement to succeed in an advanced class may or may not be forthcoming.

What criteria does a school use, then, to sort students into the system of tracked courses they have created? Many schools subscribe to a "contest" model of education (Turner, 1960). Under a contest model, schools emphasize chances for upward mobility in the creation of track placement policies. Thus, choice plays a prominent role in the placement process, allowing for the possibility that highly motivated low-track students will want to move into college-track courses. However, while the course selection process involves some amount of student choice, counselors still employ criteria in providing guidance to students, and schools develop rules governing the track placement process. The realization of contest norms is tempered by the concurrent goal of making the best possible matches between students of differing achievement levels and the available curricular options.

Table 14.2 summarizes the results of three studies of tracking, which provide some insight into the range of criteria used by schools in the track placement process. Despite the prevalence of a contest ideology, it is readily apparent from Table 14.2 that it is highly unusual for a school to allow students complete discretion in choosing courses. In Kelly's (2007) study of course guides in North Carolina, not a single school showed evidence of a completely open system where students were free to enroll in any level of course. Many schools claim to have an "open enrollment" policy, and yet they have a number of criteria, which can include pre-requisite courses, co-requisite courses in other subjects, minimum standardized test score or grade requirements, and teacher recommendations.

Beyond the amount of choice students have in the placement process, schools differ in the objectivity of their placement criteria. No criterion is completely free from bias. Even standardized tests occasionally contain questions that are easier for certain students to answer correctly. However, standardized tests, or even grades, are somewhat more objective than teacher or guidance counselor recommendations. Really, it is surprising that schools so often use teacher recommendations, considering that teachers' evaluations of their students are already contained in the students' grades.

In Kelly's (2007) study of course-taking policies in North Carolina, he found that many schools relied on placement criteria that were highly subjective indeed.[8] Consider, for example, the following requirements for enrollment in honors English at Cedar Grove High School:[9]

- mastery level of basic skills in language and mechanics;
- high level of self-motivation;
- high level of independent thinking and insight;
- inquisitive mind—reluctant to accept facts and information as purely memory work to regurgitate;
- high level of oral communication skills;
- high level of composition skills;
- exemplary past scholastic record.

These requirements are highly subjective because they do not specify how something like "inquisitiveness" or "insight" is to be measured or what constitutes a "high level."

Table 14.2 Three studies of course placement criteria

Spade, Columba, & Vanfossen, (1997). Main criteria for assignment to mathematics and science course described by school staff in six schools.[a]

	Teacher recommendations	*Test scores & grades*
School W$_A$	Weak	Weak
School W$_E$	Weak	Strong
School M$_A$	Weak	Strong
School M$_E$	Weak	Strong
School A$_A$	Strong	Strong
School A$_E$	Strong	Strong

Gamoran (1992). Main criteria for assignment to honors English courses described by school staff in five communities.[b]

	Tests	*Teacher recommendations*	*Student/parent preferences*
District A	√	√	
District B		√	
District C		√	√
District D	√	√	
District E	√		

Kelly (2003). Frequency of grade, test score, and teacher recommendation requirements listed in official course guides from 92 North Carolina high schools, 1997–98 school year. Column A indicates course guide listed criteria as "required." Column B indicates course guide listed criteria as "recommended."

	Grade policy		*Test score policy*		*Teacher recommendations*	
	A	*B*	*A*	*B*	*A*	*B*
English	27 (29%)	8 (9%)	21 (23%)	11 (12%)	40 (43%)	12 (13%)
Math	27 (29%)	8 (9%)	19 (21%)	2 (2%)	36 (39%)	19 (21%)
Science	27 (29%)	6 (7%)	8 (9%)	1 (1%)	46 (50%)	5 (5%)
Social Studies	19 (21%)	6 (7%)	0	0	36 (39%)	3 (3%)

Notes
a An "average" and an "excellent" school were selected from each of three communities with schools serving working-class, a middle-class, and affluent families. Schools are labeled accordingly (e.g., Me for Middle-Excellent). Data taken from Spade, Columba, and Vanfossen's text description of placement criteria.
b Data from Gamoran (1992; table 1).

In some instances, schools require students to submit a writing sample for placement in advanced English courses. This writing sample is no doubt evaluated on some of the above criteria. A writing sample is a tangible piece of student work that multiple parties can simultaneously evaluate though. Who is to say if a student has a more "inquisitive" mind than another student, and just how inquisitive does that mind have to be? Most of the time these highly subjective placement requirements were listed in conjunction with more concrete requirements, such as grades and test scores, but fifteen schools in the sample listed *solely* vague placement requirements for enrollment in English courses.

When one is confronted with a set of vague requirements for course placement, it may feel as if gaining entry into courses is like gaining entry into an elite country club. At Jefferson High, for example, students could not just register for certain honors courses; they had to be "invited into this class."

If teacher recommendations and other subjective criteria were used to make exceptions for admitting students into higher tracks that ordinarily would not be, then they might serve to reduce the inequality in course taking among students from different social class backgrounds. This use of subjective criteria would be consistent with a contest model of tracking. In practice though, teacher recommendations are frequently used additively, to *reduce* the amount of entry into high-track courses. This use of subjective placement criteria could be part of the reason that large residual differences in track placements among students of differing social class remain, even when students' grades and test scores are equivalent. If course placement decisions were based more heavily on standardized tests and grades, the gap in the track positions between students from different social class backgrounds would likely be reduced. Broaded's (1997) study of educational tracking between schools in Taiwan provides an example of a system in which strict adherence to the results of entrance exams reduces social class disparities in access to the nation's rigorous academic high schools. In Taiwan, socially advantaged and disadvantaged students with similar test scores have the same chances of being admitted to an academic course of study. Standardized tests are not infallible though; they can also be misused. For example, it would be inappropriate to place a student with a history of good grades in a remedial class because of low scores on a single test. The appropriate use of standardized tests for track placements and other "high stakes" decisions is to identify students who will benefit from a program of study, not as stand-alone criteria used to exclude students from courses they would benefit from taking (Heubert & Hauser, 1999). Also, many educators are likely to find a policy that relies heavily on standardized tests and grades unattractive because it eliminates student choice in the placement process. Under the contest model, choice—even if it is not as much choice as one might think—is seen as a desirable element of tracking systems.

Conclusion

The great contradiction of education in the modern era is that it is both an avenue for upward mobility, as well as the main social institution in which social status is reproduced from one generation to the next. To examine systems of curricular tracking is to see this contradiction at work. The most important determinant of a student's curricular track is their level of academic achievement. A student who shows promise, regardless of their social class background, is likely to find their way into an academic curriculum where they can prepare for further education at a college or university. But the educational tournament does not exactly occur on a level playing field. Students from advantaged social class backgrounds have greater access to an academic curriculum. Social status is reproduced as academic course taking leads to college enrollment and eventually to jobs in high status occupations for those from advantaged homes.

Most of the social class advantage in academic course taking stems from the fact that, when students begin school, there are already large differences in achievement along social class lines, and these differences grow throughout elementary school. When students make the transition to middle school, and again in high school, middle- and upper-middle-class students are at a distinct advantage. Socially advantaged students also benefit from internalized expectations of success, and occasionally, from pushy parents who act on their behalf.

The social class advantage occurs within the context of a school's track structure which differs in important ways from school to school. A great deal more is left to learn about the specific school policies that create the context for unequal access to tracked learning environments. Here too, it is easy to be overly optimistic that the right changes in school policy might level the playing field. Schools are complex social organizations; predicting the effect of a policy initiative on educational inequality is difficult. Ideas that might seem promising can be undermined in the implementation process, and unforeseen negative consequences are common. Nevertheless, certain elements of school policy seem likely to improve access to the academic track for socially disadvantaged youth. These policy elements include objective track placement criteria, or restricted use of subjective criteria to promote inclusion in high-track courses, and an emphasis on including a greater number of students in the academic track in schools which serve poor and working-class families.

Questions for discussion

1. According to Kelly, schools, families, and students all have an impact in the track placement process. How do schools create a "context" in which social class influences course taking?

2. Which systems or structures deny low-class students access to high-track courses? In what ways do high-/middle-class students benefit disproportionally from tracking?

3. Given the discouraging evidence provided by the author, why do you suppose the practice of tracking is so prevalent? Whose interest does this serve? In formulating your answer, consider the diverse set of actors that influence educational policy, including teachers, administrators, parents, the business community, and students themselves.

4. Tracking is the practice whereby students of similar achievement levels are grouped together in order that instruction is more suited to their level. Yet, tracking is almost an exact replication of class divisions, with high-class students in high-track classes and low-class students in low-track classes. Why is this? What is the relationship between class, tracking, and educational success?

5. Tracking is "one piece in the puzzle" that ensures relatively high social position and income for already privileged students. What other "pieces" exist that ensure the replication of class positions? Which "piece," in your opinion, is most influential?

6. In what ways can class be considered a system of codes about educational aspirations and expectations that translate into high-track placement and educational success?

7. What might be the outcome if tracking was abolished in an attempt to improve the quality of teaching, learning, and resources for lower-class students? Do you

think abolishment of tracking would lead to greater educational success for low-class students? Why?

8. Given Kelly's argument that tracking is detrimental to lower-class students, which system would you suggest might improve schooling outcomes for these students? Which programs or policies might schools enact in order to foster high expectations for disadvantaged students?

Notes

1. These estimates include movement between the "college-preparatory" and "non-college-preparatory" tracks, as well as movement from not taking a course in a given subject (HS&B database).
2. Of course, track location is a *cause* of achievement differences, especially by 10–12th grade.
3. Correlation coefficients describe the strength of association between two variables using a common metric ranging from 0 to 1, where 0 equates to "no association whatsoever" and 1 equates to "perfect correspondence" between two phenomena. Thus correlation coefficients provide a useful way of summarizing the strength of a relationship which can be compared across studies or outcomes. Track placements are a categorical outcome though; a student is either enrolled in a college preparatory course or they are not. Thus, the strength of association between a student characteristic such as social class and course taking can be readily expressed in terms of different students' chances or odds of being in a given course. This is a more intuitive approach than using correlation coefficients.
4. NCES administered achievement tests to participating students covering the areas of reading comprehension, mathematics, science, and history/citizenship/geography. The test content was developed by content area specialists and each battery of questions provides a reliable estimate of achievement in the general content areas (NCES, 1991). However, only so much content can be covered in a single testing session, so certain domains of knowledge or skills are likely to be omitted in the NCES data.
5. The standard deviation in the 2005 NAEP fourth-grade math assessment was 28 points.
6. Quotation from Fischer et al. (1996), adapted from Gamoran and Mare (1989). Gamoran and Mare's (1989) estimates are not directly comparable to Kelly's (2004) because of measurement discrepancies. Kelly used transcript data to measure course taking, and a more rigorous criteria for courses being "upper track." But, stated in a more similar metric to Kelly's interpretation, they found that higher social class students were about 36 percent more likely to be in the college track.
7. Tyson et al. examined racial differences in course taking, but I present that as evidence of a more general social process.
8. In this study I conducted a content analysis of curriculum guides in ninety-two high schools in North Carolina. Using Sorensen's (1970) organizational dimensions of tracking as an initial framework, I investigated the policies used to determine course placements. There are no overarching tracking systems in North Carolina that formally determine placement in all subjects simultaneously. However, a web of policies ensured a well-developed tracking system was in place. The well-elaborated system of policies included rules linking placement in one subject (e.g., math) to placement in other subjects (usually science, but occasionally unrelated subjects like English) and rules establishing criteria for enrollment in upper-track courses, which reduced the number of students in a college-preparatory curriculum. A high level of differentiation also existed with many schools having five or more distinct tracks in some subjects. At the time of the study, over half of the schools also engaged in "occupational course sequencing," a guidance system encouraging students to enroll in groups of tracked courses. Since, the fall of 2000 in North Carolina, occupational course sequencing has become an official state policy, with graduation requirements organized around different sequences of study. Although this study presents data from only one state, this portrait of tracking in the late 1990s suggests that the "de facto" tracking Lucas (1999) observed in data from the early 1980s is not de facto at all, but generated by specific school policies.
9. School names are pseudonyms.

References

Adelman, C. (1998). *Women and men of the engineering path: A model for analyses of undergraduate careers.* Washington, DC: US Department of Education, Office of Educational Research and Improvement.

Alexander, K. L., & McDill, E. L. (1976). Selection and allocation within schools: Some causes and consequences of curriculum placement. *American Sociological Review, 41,* 963–80.

Baker, D. P., & Stevenson, D. L. (1986). Mother's strategies for children's school achievement: Managing the transition to high school. *Sociology of Education, 59,* 156–66.

Broaded, C. M. (1997). The limits and possibilities of tracking: Some evidence from Taiwan. *Sociology of Education, 70,* 35–53.

Carbonaro, W. (2003). Track effects on student learning: Examining learning gains across discrepant classes. Paper presented at the 2003 meeting of the International Sociological Association's Research Committee on Social Stratification and Mobility (RC28), New York University, August.

Entwisle, D. R., & Alexander, K. L. (1990). Beginning school math competence: Minority and majority comparisons. *Child Development, 61,* 454–71.

—— (1992). Summer setback: Race, poverty, school composition, and mathematics achievement in the first two years of school. *American Sociological Review, 57,* 72–84.

Erigha, M., & Carbonaro, W. (2006). *Who goes to college? Linking tracking to post-secondary enrollment.* Center for Research on Educational Opportunity: Unpublished manuscript.

Farkas, G., Wilkinson, L., Schiller, K., & Frank, K. (2005). Teacher grading practices within school social contexts: Do they disadvantage lower SES and ethnic minority students? A presentation at the Center for Research on Educational Opportunity's Examining Educational Inequalities conference, April 29, 2005.

Gamoran, A. (1987). The stratification of high school learning opportunities. *Sociology of Education, 60,* 135–55.

—— (1992). Access to excellence: Assignment to honors English classes in the transition from middle to high school. *Educational Evaluation and Policy Analysis, 14,* 185–204.

Gamoran, A., & Mare, R. D. (1989). Secondary school tracking and educational equality: Compensation, reinforcement, or neutrality. *American Journal of Sociology, 94,* 146–83.

Garet, M. S., & DeLany, B. (1988). Students, courses, and stratification. *Sociology of Education, 61,* 61–77.

Hallinan, M. (1992). The organization of students for instruction in the middle school. *Sociology of Education, 65,* 114–27.

Heubert, J. P., & Hauser, R. M. (1999). *High stakes: Testing for tracking, promotion, and graduation.* Washington, DC: National Academy Press.

Heyns, B. (1974). Social selection and stratification within schools. *American Journal of Sociology, 79,* 1434–51.

Hoogstra, L. (2000). The design of the study: Sample and procedures. In Csikszentmihalyi & Schneider (Eds.), *Becoming adult.* New York: Basic Books.

Hotchkiss, L., & Dorsten, L. (1987). Curriculum effects on early post high school outcomes. In R. G. Corwin (Ed.), *Sociology of education and socialization* (pp. 191–219). Greenwich, CT: JAI Press.

Kelly, S. (2004). Do increased levels of parental involvement account for the social class difference in track placement? *Social Science Research, 33,* 626–59.

—— (2007). The contours of tracking in North Carolina. *The High School Journal, 90,* 15–31.

Kubitschek, W. N., & Hallinan, M. T. (1998). Tracking and students' friendships. *Social Psychology Quarterly, 61,* 1–15.

Lareau, A. (2000). *Home advantage.* Lantham: Rowan and Littlefield.

Lee, V. E., & Bryk, A. S. (1988). Curriculum tracking as mediating the social distribution of high school achievement. *Sociology of Education, 61*, 78–94.

Lucas, S. R. (1999). *Tracking inequality: Stratification and mobility in American schools.* New York: Teachers College Press.

—— (2001). Effectively maintained inequality: Education transitions, track mobility, and social background effects. *American Journal of Sociology, 106*, 1642–90.

McNeal, R. B. (1999). Parental involvement as social capital: Differential effectiveness on science achievement, truancy, and dropping out. *Social Forces, 78*, 117–44.

National Center for Education Statistics (NCES). (1991). Psychometric report for the NELS: 88 base year test battery. US Department of Education, NCES 91–468.

—— (2006). *The condition of education, 2006.* US Department of Education, NCES 2006–071.

Oakes, J. (1985). *Keeping track: How schools structure inequality.* New Haven: Yale University Press.

Rosenbaum, J. E. (1976). *Making inequality.* New York: Wiley.

—— (1980). Track misperceptions and frustrated college plans: An analysis of the effects of tracks and track perceptions in the national longitudinal survey. *Sociology of Education, 53*, 74–88.

Schneider, B., & Stevenson, D. (1999). *The Ambitious Generation.* New Haven: Yale University Press.

Sorensen, A. (1970). Organizational differentiation of students and educational opportunity. *Sociology of Education, 43*, 355–76.

Spade, J. Z., Columba, L., & Vanfossen, B. E. (1997). Tracking in mathematics and science: Courses and course-selection procedures. *Sociology of Education, 70*, 108–27.

Turner, R. H. (1960). Sponsored and contest mobility and the school system. *American Sociological Review, 25*, 855–67.

Tyson, K., Darity, W., & Castellino, D. (2005). Black adolescents and the dilemmas of high achievement. *American Sociological Review, 70*, 582–605.

Useem, E. L. (1991). Student selection in course sequences in mathematics: The impact of parental involvement and school policies. *Journal of Research on Adolescence, 1*, 231–50.

Wiatrowski, M. D., Hansell, S., Massey, C. R., & Wilson, D. L. (1982). Curriculum tracking and delinquency. *American Sociological Review, 47*, 151–60.

Chapter 15

How class matters

The geography of educational desire and despair in schools and courts[*]

Michelle Fine, April Burns, María Elena Torre, and Yasser A. Payne[**]

> Every day, every hour, talented students are being sacrificed. . . . They're [the schools]
> destroying lives.
>
> Maritza, college student, speaking about her urban high school

> Obviously there's no there's . . . there are not enough books [and] there's overcrowding
> . . . *I'm expected to teach a class of forty-eight to forty-six students with only thirty-
> six books with only thirty-six chairs. If those conditions don't improve, education
> can't improve.* Again, go to any other school—and of course you're going to see better
> academic program because more resources for more children, more one on one interac-
> tion with student to teacher. And again, I'm only one person. I don't have a TA. I don't
> have any assistance in the classroom except the other kids. . . . Overcrowding . . . *we're
> expected to perform miracles*, part a Red Sea, if you will.
>
> Educator, Joel Vaca

In so many buildings we call public schools, the spirits of poor and working-class urban youth of color, and their educators, are assaulted in ways that bear academic, psychological, social, economic, and perhaps, also, criminal justice consequence. We write on the devastation wrought by *alienating public schools* (Delpit, 1995; Hilliard, 1990, 2002; Kohl, 1994; Kohn, 2000; Woodson, 2000, reprinted). Theorizing within and beyond reproduction theory (Anyon, 1983; Aronowitz & Giroux, 1993; Bowles & Gintis, 1976), we seek to understand the psychological and social devastation incited by buildings that are structurally damaged, educators who are under credentialed, and institutions with neither intellectually nor politically enticing projects for youth to undertake.

This essay seeks to expose not simply the material conditions that poor and working-class students contend with in their schools; not simply the testing regimes that injure the spirit of teaching and learning. Instead, we venture in this essay to study how *class consciousness* comes to be inscribed on and embodied by poor and working-class youth, through their schools. While we have no illusions that schools alone convey these

---

[*] A longer version of this chapter originally appeared in Fine, M., Burns, A., Payne, Y., & Torre, M. E. (2004). Civics lessons: The color and class of betrayal. *Teachers College Record, 106*, November, 2193–223.

[**] Michelle Fine is Distinguished Professor of Social Psychology, Women's Studies, and Urban Education at the Graduate Center, CUNY. April Burns is a doctoral student in Social-Personality Psychology at the City University of New York, Graduate Center. María Elena Torre is Chair of Education Studies at Eugene Lang College of The New School. Yasser A. Payne is Assistant Professor in the Black American Studies Program at the University of Delaware.

insidious messages or that schools alone could dismantle the gross racial and class ineq-uities that characterize our nation (see Anyon, 2005; Lareau, 2003; Rothstein, 2004), we do know that schools—as a public institution—whisper intimately the words, that land on and saturate the souls of youth.

As an expert witness, Michelle was invited into the *Williams v. California lawsuit*, brought by a class of California youth attending severely under-resourced schools. We report here on focus group and survey material we gathered from more than one hundred students and graduates of these schools, about the conditions of their schools and the consequences. The data are compelling on a simple point: schools are public institutions that convey unequivocally to poor children and youth their fundamental disposability.

In these places we call schools, poor and working-class youth, often times immigrants, come to see how class fundamentally organizes our nation; how hollow the promise of meritocracy is; how vast and enduring social inequities are; and how written off they and their peers have become.

As the public sphere realigns so that state dollars increasingly finance prisons and mili-tary recruiters, testing industries and zero-tolerance measures in schools, poor and working-class youth of color are *reading* these conditions of their schools as evidence of public betrayal. Not simply incorporating the messages, these boys and girls/young women and men critically analyze social arrangements of class and race stratification and their "place" in the social hierarchy. Like children who learn to love in homes scarred by violence, they are being asked to learn in contexts of humiliation, betrayal, and disrespect. It would be inaccurate to say that youth are learning nothing in urban schools of concentrated poverty. Neither fully internalizing this evidence nor fully resisting it, these children are learning their perceived worth in the social hierarchy. This profound civics lesson may well burn a hole in their collective souls.

In the early part of the twenty-first century, schools of poverty and alienation trans-form engaged and enthused youth into young women and men who believe that the nation, adults, and the public sphere have abandoned and betrayed them, in the denial of quality education, democracy, the promise of equality. Were that not enough, California marks the "cutting edge state" in which historic commitments to Affirmative Action in higher education have been retrenched, wrenching even dreams of college and university out the imaginations of generations of African-Americans and Latinos. Youth know that the blades of race, class, and ethnicity cut the cloth of public resources, to determine who receives, and who is denied, a rich public education.

Many have written eloquently on this perverse realignment of the public sphere to satisfy and engorge elite interests; that is, to gentrify the public sphere. But few have interrogated how poor and working-class youth of color witness, analyze, critique, and mobilize in the face of this State realignment. This is the project we ended up docu-menting the critical class consciousness of US youth, specifically how they view material injustices, procedural injustices, and what Iris Marion Young calls the (in)justice of being denied recognition (Young, 2002).

We take the California schools in question to be emblematic of a growing set of public schools, located in communities of poverty and communities of color, increasingly segre-gated and obsessed with testing and classification; in which facilities are in desperate disrepair, faculty are under credentialed and turning over at alarming rates, and instruc-tional materials are fully inadequate to the task of educating for rigor and democracy. These schools are not simply reproducing race and class inequities. Far worse, these schools educate poor and working-class youth, and youth of color, away from academic mastery and democracy, toward academic ignorance and civic alienation.

Methodology

To prepare our expert report, we collected data from a broad range of students attending schools in the "plaintiff class." Jury research firms were hired to conduct random digit dialing in affected neighborhoods, in order to generate the survey and focus group samples. Four criteria were specified: respondents needed to be current students, not dropouts; respondents need to be reached via random digit dialing, no friendship or snowball nominations; respondents should not be connected to, or made explicitly aware of, the litigation until after the interview; and parental consent is essential. Approximately four hundred calls were placed to generate each focus group of ten to twelve young adults. Interviewed students were educational "survivors" (not dropouts), randomly identified, and not selected from within peer or friendship patterns.

A multi-method research design was undertaken: *surveys* were completed anonymously by eighty-six middle and high school focus group members, prior to their involvement in the focus group discussion; *eleven focus groups* were facilitated with one hundred and one youth attending plaintiff schools in the San Francisco, Oakland, and Los Angeles areas, as well as a group (of peers) in Watsonville; and *eleven telephone interviews* were held with graduates of California schools that fall within the plaintiff class. All of these graduates are currently in attendance at college.

Survey-based gender and race/ethnicity data on eighty-six students indicate: forty-four females and forty-two males; four students who identify White, one Biracial, twenty-five Latino/Hispanic, and fifty-six Black. Parental and student consent was obtained for all focus group participants. In a few cases in which there was no parental consent, participants were turned away.

Cumulative inequity: Schooling toward alienation

Counter to stereotype that poor youth don't care about education, the youth whom we interviewed were clear and insistent: they want high quality, demanding teachers. They are upset when such teachers leave their schools mid-year or after just one year, which is typical. The evidence from elementary, middle, high school, and college students—cross-sectional for sure—reveals, over time, how pride in self curdles to shame in mis-education; how yearning for quality educators warps to anger about denied access to such educators; and how local civic engagement shrinks away from national commitments to citizenship. These three institutional dynamics are central to this production of *schooling toward alienation.*

The longer students stay in schools with structural problems, high levels of uncertified teachers, teacher turnover, and inadequate instructional materials, the wider the academic gaps between White children and children of color, or wealthy children and poor children, grow to be, and the more alienated they become (Ancess, 2000; Boyd-Franklin & Franklin, 1999; Bryk & Driscoll, 1988; Elliott & Dweck, 1988; Fine, 1991; Meier, 1998; Valenzuela, 1999). Schools of alienation incite cumulatively a process which warps yearning into anger, pride into shame, and local engagement into civic alienation.

From yearning to anger

> Right now I have this one teacher that's like, he's my English teacher and *he's like really trying to help the students right now.* We're looking into colleges and stuff. He's really trying to help us, like learn things, because it's like, he'll pull you out of class for a reason. It will be like to learn the stuff.
>
> High school girl

These students know what good education looks like. And they want it. Across focus groups and surveys, the students were very clear that they want teachers who care and demand rigorous work. We asked the students, "What does a teacher who cares look like?" Students described a "good teacher" as someone who holds high standards and helps students reach those standards. Someone who listens, asks questions, and listens to student answers. Students were excited about teachers who want to know what students think. Some praised faculty who assign lots of homework, if they provide support and time to finish.

GIRL: Like he said, we got a lot of substitutes right now. . . . Some of them cap [put you down], some of them play football. That's not what we come to school for. So we got our teachers there that are pretty cool. But last year we had all our teachers. *I love the good teachers,* but the best ones are like . . .
BOY: *They change the whole school around.*
GIRL: They change the whole school.
BOY: *My favorite is all the good teachers.*

These students know the difference between "substitutes" who "play football" and teachers who "change the whole school around." They appreciate a caring teacher who is responsive when they are confused. A good teacher wants to know the students, and provides lots of red marks on their papers. Trouble is, few of these students encounter and enjoy "good" teachers on a regular basis. Most explain that they have had a range of teachers. Too many, however, have disappeared mid-year, are long-term substitutes, or don't know their content areas. In the plaintiff schools, the percentage of fully certified teachers ranges from 13 to 50 percent. In the State of California, the percent of under credentialed teachers is directly related to percent students of color and students eligible for free/reduced price meals, rising to an average of 24 percent non-credentialed teachers for 91 to 100 percent of students eligible for free/reduced lunch. Teacher turnover rates are reported by some principals to be as high as 40 percent in a matter of two to three years.

By high school, the yearning for quality educators bumps into the realization, by these youth, that they are being denied. At the bump, resignation blends with anger. The optimism of youth seems to drain by high school, when students describe "teachers only there for a pay check" or other adults who "know, they know, they just ignorant and don't care about us." By high school, the youth believe that they are being denied a fair share of educational resources for their education (Fine & Burns, forthcoming). At this point, the yearning converts to anger:

When I ask for help, and there's too many kids and I know the teacher can't pay attention to me, I'm ignored. *That makes me mad. They blame kids when they can't fix things.*

The structural conditions of their schools, combined with the belief that White and wealthy youth receive better, provoke a sense of anger voiced by many youth, particularly high school students whom we interviewed (Boyd-Franklin & Franklin, 1999). These young women and men express a cumulative and piercing sense of what Faye Crosby (Crosby, Muehrer & Loewenstein, 1986) and Iyer et al. (2004) call *relative deprivation*; a substantial discrepancy between what they believe they deserve and what they actually receive (Crosby, Muehrer & Loewenstein, 1986). Relative deprivation, with associated anger and grievance, derives when individuals experience a discrepancy between what they have and what they want; what they have and what they believe they deserve; what they don't have and others do.

It is important to be clear. It is not the case that these youths simply internalize the messages that the broader society is targeting at them. Nor is it the case that they simply resist these messages. In a complex montage of internalization, resistance, and transformation, these young women and men clearly and unambivalently read their social disposability and their political dispensability. They know they are viewed as unworthy. With the wisdom of "dual consciousness" (DuBois, 1990), and through the hazy gauze of meritocratic ideology and false promises, with the guillotine of high stakes testing overhead, they speak through dual registers of yearning and anger, pride and shame, engagement and alienation, fear and desire. They can, at once, critique the dominant ideologies about poor kids, urban youth, and pathology and mimic these same sentiments when asked to evaluate other students who are having difficulties. Perhaps the ultimate sign of their desire to belong, to be citizens with a place at the table, they are *critics*, *consumers*, and *producers* of a meritocratic ideology. And they are angry that despite their willingness to engage, they are denied.

GIRL: I'm in tenth grade. And what I like about my school, or what I don't like about my school, is *how they teach us like animals, like they cage us up and like they keep putting more gates and more locks and stuff and then they expect us to act like humans* and I feel like if you treat us like animals that's how we going to act. . . .

In a series of comments that are difficult to hear, the next set of students are concerned that educators "treat us like inmates" or think they are "coming in to teach killers." In the absence of a community of qualified educators and a rich, intellectually engaging school environment, most youth turn away from the academic and relational features of schooling with a blend of anger, resignation, or despair. Those who graduate feel little loyalty to their high schools and sometimes even what may sound like survivor guilt (Lifton, 1994).

Leaving my high school was sad but *I didn't do enough at [my high school]* to make it better. It pains me to see what my younger brothers and sisters go through at [my high school]. *I feel guilty about my opportunities, compared to others in my community, and seriously considered dropping out* of college several times. . . . You know, it's hard to know that I am getting an education while other people I know aren't. *I guess I'm the lucky one, given all of the students who couldn't beat the stacked odds.*

(Chantal, graduate, now in college)

The anger bleeds toward some educators, privileged youth from other communities, and the broken promise of democracy for all. Within these statements of anger, however, there is still pride, hope, and a yearning for something to change.

Pride to shame

Sitting beside the anger lay a complex geographic splitting of pride and shame. That is, the students speak with pride about themselves within their local communities, and then mumble quietly, with some shame, as they imagine themselves venturing beyond.

Across the focus groups with current students, and in individual interviews with graduates, the youth spoke with some confidence about self, family, and community. They told us they have "skills" that other youth don't have, developed, largely, through confrontation with adversity. "I think we have more life experience." "We have street knowledge." "We're smarter, we're not just all proper." "We know about struggling, trying to get to the top, and not just, you know bouncing right up there." Some of these same youth commented upon specific, positive aspects of their schools. A number recall fondly teachers who supported them in hard times.

To the extent that students spoke with strength and confidence, they were speaking about themselves *within* their communities. Once they discursively wandered beyond the borders of the local, shame, stigma, and fear peppered their talk (Bronfenbrenner, 1979; Davidson & Phelan, 1999; Eccles et al., 1993; Goffman, 1961; Lewis, 1992). At that point, they describe themselves as academically handicapped by opportunities denied, ill equipped to attend a "real" or "serious" college, embarrassed by limited vocabulary, math skills, and exposure.

As if characters in Sennett and Cobb's (1993) *The Hidden Injuries of Class*, these students spoke of the "lacks" that their education has instilled in them; as if they embodied the inferiority of their schooling. As one young woman told us:

> [If kids from a wealthy school came in here right now], I wouldn't talk because *they would be more sophisticated* or something, and understand words I don't know *and I don't want to be embarrassed.*
>
> (abbreviated quote in Fine's notes)

Students explain that they have been systematically mis-educated because people in government, throughout the State, and even some of their teachers *want* them to be ignorant. One focus group conversation was particularly chilling on this point:

> Yes, that be like *putting all the bad kids in one school, that's just like putting, you know, just like putting them in jail.* They going to be crazy . . .

It was painful to listen as some students explained that they believe that schools *want* students to feel ashamed or embarrassed, so that the students will leave and classes will become smaller, with no adult responsibility for the loss of student bodies. These interviews reveal a raw sense of social disposability, and as penetrating, the students' sense of helplessness to disrupt these conditions (Burhans & Dweck, 1995; Dweck, 2002; Dweck & Reppucci, 1973; Dweck & Wortman, 1982; Elliott & Dweck, 1988; Miller, 2001; Rholes et al., 1980; Stipek & Tannat, 1984). Michael Lewis argues that youth or adults who endure a prolonged experience of shame are likely to express anger, "an emotional substitute for unacknowledged shame . . . a reaction to a frustration of action . . . a reaction to an injury to self" (1992, p. 150).

Filth

Toward the end of each focus group we circled the room, asking each student to suggest one element of their "ideal school." It was striking when a young girl whispered, with some initial hesitation but then elegant simplicity: "If I could have my ideal school, I guess I would have *seats on the toilets and enough paper in the bathroom to clean your- self*" (abbreviated quote in Fine's notes, not transcript). "If you go to a dirty school, *you feel like you're dirty*, you know, not clean" (young man, focus group).

A second form of shame was narrated: the shame of being educated in contexts of filth and decay. Schools, like other contexts of childhood and adolescence, are not simply the places where development happens (Lerner & von Eye, 1998; Werner & Altman, 1998; Wolfe & Rivlin, 1987). They are intimate places where youths construct identities, build a sense of self, read how society views them, develop the capacity to sustain relations, and forge the skills to initiate change. These are the contexts where youth grow or they shrink. Environmental psychologists Werner and Altman (1998) argue: "[C]hildren are not separate from their actions or feelings, nor are they separate from other children or the physical, social and temporal circumstances that comprise unfolding events. They are so interconnected that one aspect can not be understood without the others. . . . The street . . . is not separate from its inhabitants" (p. 125).

Buildings in disrepair are not, therefore, merely a distraction; they are identity producing and self-defining. Since the early part of the twentieth century, psychologists and sociologists (Cooley, 1998; DuBois, 1935; Fanon, 1967; Goffman, 1961; Mead, 1988; Merton, 1987) have argued that children and youth develop a sense of self from the messages they gather from adults and peers, structures and institutions, around them. What the culture says about the child, his/her family, and community comes to be inter- nalized, in part, by that child. Children who are valued tend to be more positive in self- concept than those who are disparaged (DeLuca & Rosenbaum, 2001). This value may be communicated in what people say about and to them. But just as powerful, the quality of the contexts in which they are growing "speaks" to youth about how they are viewed and valued (Maxwell & Evans, 2000). If surrounded by decay, disrepair, and filth, and no adult intervenes to protect, a child may come to see him/herself as worthy of little more or at least that adults see him/her as unworthy.

Student Alondra Jones details the corrosive effects of a negative structural context on the developing selves of young students:

> It makes me, you know what, in all honesty, I'm going to break something down to you. *It make you feel less about yourself*, you know, like you sitting here in a class where you have to stand up because there's not enough chairs and you see rats in the buildings, the bathrooms is nasty, you got to pay. And then you, like I said, I visited

Mann Academy, and these students, *if they want to sit on the floor, that's because they choose to. And that just makes me feel real less about myself because it's like the State don't care about public schools*. If I have to sit there and stand in the class, they can't care about me. It's impossible. So in all honesty, it really makes me feel bad about myself.

A number of environmental studies demonstrate the specific psychological and physiological effects of environmental stressors such as crowding, noise, heat, and other structural factors on students' capacity to concentrate and produce academic work and to induce high levels of negative interactions and anger among and within the youth. Robert S. McCord, in a systematic analysis of schools in the San Francisco Unified School District, concludes, "The findings of my school facility appraisal reported in this Declaration point to a pattern of disparate facility conditions associated with the racial and ethnic identity of SFUSD schools. This pattern of disparate conditions is likely to convey the message of racial inferiority that is implicit in a policy of segregation" (2002, p. 12). Valkiria Duran (2002) found that structural building quality predicts students' attendance which, in turn, bears directly on academic achievement. The links are significant. The youth concurred. In one focus group, a series of comments reveals how overcrowding affects learning:

BOY: I just feel like it's deep—right now it's like five thousand people overcrowded. It's way overcrowded. And it's like, you know, *you don't even have to go there [inaudible], because basically they don't know if we go there*, you can just come on campus or whatever. Like right now, we got three different tracks, and they don't know, like, if you don't have an ID, you just, like, you can tell them you have to take your ID picture of whatever and just go on in, and they'll believe you, because they don't really know who go there, because they've got so many kids in that school.

INTERVIEWER: But how does that affect you as a student?

BOY: Because, like, they could let the wrong person on campus or whatever or, like [inaudible], and it's really too many people, just . . . last year, *I had forty-two kids in my algebra class*.

Saegert (1999) and Krenichyn and Saegert (2001) document the psychological and physiological impact of crowding and other environmental stressors on youth. Evans, Kliewan, and Martin (1991) report that youth blood pressure rises, concentration diminishes, and errors on difficult tasks multiply in the presence of noise. Edwards (1979) found that educational building conditions can hurt student performance, accounting for 5 to 11 percent of student performance on standardized tests.

These schools not only stress youth and educators. The evidence suggests that they also fail to buffer poor and working-class youth from stressors they experience outside of school (Ancess & Ort, 2001; Meier, 1998). As Lepore, Saegert, and others have documented, working and learning in conditions of environmental stress not only undermines the capacity to concentrate and complete difficult tasks, but may compromise students' and educators' abilities to adapt to the many stressors they confront.

"It's on me": Self-blame and academic troubles

Across the focus groups we could hear a fleeting, infrequent, but emotionally powerful discourse of self-blame for past mistakes. While most of these youth attribute their mis-education to structural inequities, a strong undercurrent of student blame pierced the focus groups.

GIRL: When I was in middle school, . . . I skipped that grade, went right to the ninth grade from seventh grade. I chose to mess that ninth grade year up. I chose to cut and shoot dice and be doing other things that I'm not supposed to do, you know. *So that was my mistake, my fault.* You know, in my tenth grade year, I destroyed it, you know. I made nothing of it all, nothing. I passed, I don't know how I passed, you know. So when I look at my transcript, I look at it and say *this is where I failed. I know I won't be able to make it into a university because of me, not because of what peer pressure or what this principal said or what this teacher was teaching me.*

While the students discussed, in the aggregate, structural problems of teacher turnover, overcrowding, absence of books, ineffective guidance counselors, etc. they also accepted much responsibility for their own behaviors. A whispered discourse flows through the groups, revealing self-blame for past behaviors. Students who offered such analyses typically asserted a very punitive perspective on their own biographies: past mistakes do and should dictate a life of impoverished educational, social, and economic opportunities.

Students who view educational difficulties as largely their own fault have little sense that school can/will help them achieve positive educational outcomes (Fine et al., 2002). Low expectations for adults convert into self-defeating attitudes by which students hesitate to ask for help they need. One young man expressed it well: "*I don't ask the teacher for nothing. I do it all on my own, or ask my friends for help.*" "I don't ask the teacher for nothing" is of course a defensive posture, rejecting educators' help before educators refuse his request. These students then convert this defense into an internalized and unrealistic belief in personal responsibility, which colludes with a larger social ideology about "their" fault. In the end, these students do not learn how to ask for or receive help, do not get the help, and, in the likely event of failure, they conclude that it is "my fault." Meritocracy triumphs again.

Perhaps most damaging with respect to future outcomes, some of the youth have elaborated a very punitive ideology that mistakes they have made in the past will and should predict negative future outcomes. These youths have committed what psychologists would call a "characterological personal attribution" or "fundamental attribution error" for past mistakes. When people attribute bad outcomes to a moral flaw in themselves, it tends to be difficult to shed the shame, change behavior, and/or believe yourself entitled to future, positive outcomes. They have internalized the broader societal message about poor youth: that they *deserve* bad outcomes from the time of their "mistakes" forward (Janoff-Bulman, 1992). Poor children, especially poor children and youth of color, in contrast, tend to be held personally accountable for "mistakes" for which other children are given "second chances" (see Lefkowitz, 1998; Poe-Yagamata & Jones, 2000), with dire consequences that can last a lifetime (see Ayers et al., 2001).

Giving back to the community, alienated from the State

In focus groups and surveys, the California youths express refreshing, deep, strong, and committed civic commitments *toward* family, community, and cultural groups. As Bowen and Bok (1998) demonstrate with youth of color who graduate from college, these are the very young adults most likely to display a commitment to give back to the community, to serve and model an ethic of community spirit. The poor and working-class youth who were interviewed described just such a spirit of citizenship.

While voicing strong local commitments, these young men and women simultaneously reveal a stinging anger at schools that spreads outward toward other governmental institutions and the nation. Their willingness to extend their caring and commitments to the country, to beliefs in democracy, and to a broad moral community called the USA has been jeopardized (Flanagan et al., 1998; Yates & Youniss, 1998). Frustrated, their alienation stretches from schooling denied, to governments which betray, to democratic promises that remain unfulfilled.

> *It's like what is the Board getting paid for* and they can't even come fix our bathroom. They can't even mop our halls. *So what they doing with that money?*

> * * *

> They *[government] fake* like they are [trying to change things]. Because they go to the board meetings and they talk to Willie Brown and everything. And one of my friends is on the committee. And all the [inaudible], Willie Brown says oh, this is what, we're going to do this and everything and he's always talking about how San Francisco is one of the cleanest cities. And *he's a wolf ticket seller. I mean, he lies, sorry.*

As these comments reveal, the youth want nothing more than what most adults ask for today: *public accountability.* They want someone to assure that the State and the adults will fulfill their legal obligations to educate. They want someone to monitor inequities, intervene, and remedy. The focus group and survey data suggest that students in California's most disadvantaged schools are being educated away from these "obligations of citizenship" and toward civic alienation. They are learning that their needs are irrelevant to policy makers and government leaders. They speak through a sophisticated discourse of public critique, but don't believe that anyone is listening.

The survey data reveal the suspicions these youths also hold of the economy and the government. Forty-two percent of the surveyed high school students and 25 percent of those interviewed from middle school believe that labor market prospects will *always* be hard for them and their families. Forty percent of the high school students and half of the middle school students believe that government is designed to serve the "rich." Only one-third of the high school students and 20 percent of the middle school students think they can make a change in the workings of government. Finally, while 65 percent of the middle school youth view the USA as "basically fair and everyone has an equal chance to get ahead," this figure drops to 23 percent by high school.

These youth reveal a broad based, sophisticated, and critical consciousness of class structures, the stability of inequity, the illusion of mobility and their "place."

Hearing problems: A violation of procedural justice

For years, critical scholars of education have heard poor youth and youth of color who attend inadequate public schools, who tell us of some teachers who don't care, schools that don't educate, and the resultant anger, shame, stress, and anxiety (Fine, 1990; Valenzuela, 1999; Wasley et al., 1999; Weis, 1991). These California youth were no exception. As one young man described his concern:

> Because before we had a teacher for like the first three weeks of our multi-culture class and then the teacher didn't have all her credentials so she couldn't continue to teach. And since then we've had like ten different substitutes. And none of them have taught us anything. We just basically do what we wanted in class. *We wrote letters, all the class wrote letters to people and they never responded. We still don't have a teacher.*

What was striking and distinct about the California focus groups was the powerful voice of institutional betrayal that these youths expressed to audiences who refused to listen. It was not simply the case that these youth, like so many youth across the USA in under-resourced schools, were denied adequate education and felt helpless. Many of the youth had, in the face of overwhelming odds, tried to secure help. They had spoken up, protested, asked for a "real" teacher, or raised an academic concern. What broke their hearts and their spirits was that few adults listened. Even fewer acted.

Students in a high school focus group were most agitated as they contrasted how their schools ignored their requests for quality education, but responded (if superficially) when the State investigated school policies and practices:

> *We all walked out,* 'cause of the conditions, but they didn't care. They didn't even come out. They sent the police. The police made a line and pushed us back in. *Don't you think the principal should have come out to hear what we were upset over? But when the state is coming in, they paint,* they fix up the building. They don't care about us, the students, just the state or the city.

These youth describe a doubled experience of disappointment and betrayal. Disappointed by the relative absence of quality faculty and materials, they feel helpless to master rigorous academic material and powerless to solicit effective help. Were that not enough, when these youth do complain, grieve, or challenge the educational inequities they endure, they confront a wall of silence, an institutional "hearing problem." On surveys, only 34 percent agreed or strongly agreed, "People like me have the ability to change government if we don't like what is happening." These schools are preparing a generation of youth who sustain ethical commitments to family, kin, and community but believe that the government and the nation view them as unworthy and disposable. In such settings, youth report high levels of perceived betrayal by, resistance to, and withdrawal from persons in positions and institutions of public authority (Fine et al., 2002). These schools are helping to blunt civic engagement and produce, instead, civic alienation.

Going to college?

As the surveys reveal, almost all of these youth expect to graduate from high school and attend college. A full 85 percent of surveyed high school students consider it likely that they will graduate from their present school, and 91 percent indicate that they would like to attend college after graduation. However, a full 50 percent feel that they are "less well" prepared for college than peers throughout the State of California. This represents a serious rise from the 15 percent of middle school students who report that they feel "less well prepared for college" than peers. The high school students appear to hold high aspirations for college, but are filled with legitimate anxiety about inadequate preparation.

In addition to the high school students who worried about under-preparation, a small group of graduates from these schools who are now attending college were interviewed. Given the high dropout rates of these schools and the few who go onto college, this sample of college-going students represents some of the most academically successful graduates of their schools. Most were surprised to feel less competent than peers. A number admitted to thoughts of dropping a course or dropping out of college.

> I kept thinking *they know more than I do*. It seems like I had to do more than them, like I have to go to a lot of tutorial classes. What [my school] has offered me has made my transition to college really difficult. I'm pretty much intimidated in college . . . I keep thinking, "*Am I going to make it?*"
>
> (Female graduate, now at UC Berkeley)

The reflections of these graduates reveal the academic and psychological consequences of academic under-preparation, even for the "stars" of these schools:

> High school didn't provide me with any AP or honors classes so I was never exposed to college level work. When I took calculus my first year in college, *I couldn't compete. I ended up having to drop* the class and take an easier math course. The expectations and standards at [school] were too low. Many students felt like they weren't being exposed to the education they needed. We could see what students at Lowell High were getting, all the AP classes and textbooks. But we had to share most of our books and some we couldn't even take home.
>
> (Male graduate, Class of 2000, at UC Berkeley)

These young women and men *thought* they were top students at their California high schools. Reflecting back on their high school years, these college students all admit that they were under-challenged. While they credit teachers and/or counselors who "really pushed me . . . taught me to keep an open mind and not to quit," all agree that teachers "could have given more work, they could have been harder on us." When asked "What did you get from your high schools?" these young women and men report that high school was a context in which they developed a sense of persistence, learning to beat the odds, to struggle, even when no one was in their corner. One young woman, now attending community college, explains, "In high school, *I didn't feel any support*, especially in terms of college going. I got some basics . . . but *I don't feel prepared for college*."

Civics lessons

The schools in question are educating youth toward intellectual mediocrity and alien-ation, and away from academic mastery and democracy. The youth whom we surveyed and interviewed are the academic "success stories" of impoverished neighborhoods. These are not young women or men who have dropped out. They are the survivors; the believers, whom we are slowly undermining.

Despite the fact that these poor and working-class youth are asking, desperately, for quality educators and challenging curriculum, the evidence suggests that the more years these youth spend in these schools, the more shame, anger, and mistrust they develop; the fewer academic skills they acquire; and the more our diverse democratic fabric frays. While class is traditionally considered a strong predictor of academic success, we have evidence here that academic (ine)quality is an equally strong predictor of class.

Given the political economy of the USA, the racial stratifications and the broad base of social inequities that confront poor and working-class youth, and youth of color, the question for this case asks to what extent do these schools reproduce broad social inequi-ties, worsen them, or reduce their adverse impact (cf. Anyon, 1983)? The evidence presented here suggests that these schools substantially worsen already existent social inequities with psychological, academic, and ultimately economic consequence. One may ask, further, isn't it the case that *all* public schools serving poor and working-class youth, and youth of color, suffer these conditions and produce these outcomes?

There is now a well established body of evidence of compelling, inquiry-based small schools in Philadelphia, New York City, Chicago, and elsewhere, designed for poor and working-class youth. A number of these schools designed for poor and working-class youth have fundamentally de-coupled the too typical correlation of class and academic success. Built with a commitment to what Lori Chajet (forthcoming) calls *institutional agency*, these schools are designed to resist the natural correspondence of class and schooling.

Studies demonstrate that these small public schools can be effectively organized to open opportunities, support strengths and needs, satisfy their yearnings for quality education, prepare for higher education, and cultivate a strong ethic of community engagement (see Fine et al., 2007). While the top-down proliferation of small schools in urban districts has become a troubling, quick-fix fad, that reflects all the ills of standard-ization, privatization, gentrification, and high stakes testing, there is substantial evidence that schools can mediate (not eliminate) the damage of larger social forces (see Ancess, 2000; Chajet, forthcoming; Cook & Tashlik, 2005; Fine, 2005; Fine et al., 2007. In poor communities, neither academic failure nor alienation are natural or healthy.

In contrast to the interviewed students in California, students in such schools learn about the possibilities and movements for social change and their responsibilities to participate in creating change (see Anand et al., 2002; Ancess, 2000; Fine et al., 2002). Their social critique moves to hope and action, not despair and alienation.

In the California schools in the plaintiff class, students are indeed getting a "civics lesson" in which they are learning to feel powerless, alienated, shameful, angry, and betrayed. The likelihood of democratic engagement by these youths and young adults is fundamentally threatened by their experiences in these schools (Flanagan et al., 1998). Even so, some have tried to speak out about these educational inequities, only to be ignored again. With this lawsuit, they are asking adults to be allies in the struggle for racial and class justice.

Coda

In 2004, Governor Arnold Schwarzenegger settled *Williams v. California*, acknowledging: "Today is a great victory that we celebrate here for California's neglected students. And I am here to tell you that we will neglect our children no more." A year later, a Rand Corporation report found ". . . continuing inequalities in the resources—both capital and human—available to schools in poor communities with large concentrations of African-American and Latino students."

During this same time period, the State of California instituted a high stakes exit examination which would deny a diploma to any students who couldn't pass. In 2005, the Human Resources Research Organization (2005) published the *Independent Evaluation of the California High School Exit Exam* where they found significant and disproportionate adverse impacts of CAHSEE, on youth of color and immigrant youth. By eleventh grade, only 35 percent of special education students, 51 percent of English language learners, 63 percent of African-Americans, and 68 percent of Latinos passed both parts of the exam. By the end of their junior year, nearly 100,000 members of the Class of 2006 had not passed the CAHSEE and up to half of these young people were expected to not satisfy the requirement prior to graduation, including "nearly half of English language learners and two-thirds of students with disabilities."

These demographic disparities reveal the stubborn institutional and political conditions in which failure has been produced. Poor students, students of color, immigrant youth, and economically disadvantaged students are highly concentrated in schools with lower pass rates and fewer credentialed educators. They disproportionately attend those schools with some emergency-certified math and language arts teachers. Students who receive special education services are *more* likely to be taught by educators credentialed in neither English Language nor math instruction; the rate of certified English Language teachers is far lower in schools with high concentrations of African-American students than district-wide.[1]

Despite a series of court decisions against the State, on May 24, 2006 the California Supreme Court reinstated the CAHSEE as a condition for graduation. All students in the Class of 2006—even those who have admittedly been deprived of a thorough and adequate education—will have to pass the examination in order to receive a diploma (see Valenciz, Valenzuela, Sloan & Foley, 2005; McNeil, 2005 for parallel analysis of Texas).

The children of California have been twice betrayed; disproportionately youth of poverty, youth of color, and immigrant youth struggling to persist in some of the worst schools in the nation.

Questions for discussion

1. Discuss the "three institutional dynamics" central to the production of schooling toward alienation. What is the process involved in the production of these dynamics? Who or what is responsible for their reversal?

2. Among the students in this chapter, how does the concept of meritocratic ideology contribute to turning feelings of yearning to anger?

3. Despite feelings of anger toward society (for example, the government), how do these students exhibit a strong sense of citizenship in relation to their local communities? Why do you suppose these feelings exist within local boundaries, but transform into feelings of anger when extended into schools and the larger social arena?

4. The authors describe the filth, decay, disrepair, and absence of adequate resources; how do these aspects of these students lived realities work on their psyches? How are filth and decay related to poor academic performance?

5. The authors mention: "there is substantial evidence that schools can interrupt the damage of larger social forces." What must be done to overcome persistent inequality, as modeled in schools in Philadelphia, New York City, and Chicago?

6. The authors state: "The longer students stay in schools with structural problems, high levels of uncertified teachers, teacher turnover, and inadequate instructional materials, the wider the academic gaps between White children and children of color, or wealthy children and poor children, grow to be, and the more alienated they become." What might the total outcome and impact on a societal level look like if this does indeed continue at the same rate, with equal measure? How will this projection (the continuance of these great disparities) affect college and university campuses within the USA, the overall economy, race relations, and so forth?

7. If you were to imagine a sample of participant schools that reflected wealth and "whiteness," what might these voices tell us about inequality? Are the students in this study the only voices capable of understanding and articulating severe disparity?

8. Researchers facilitated focus groups as one qualitative method (among their multi-method research design) for their analysis. In the case of this particular study, why do you suppose the authors chose to use focus groups? What are the strengths and weaknesses of this approach to social research?

Notes

This chapter has been funded, in part, by the Leslie Glass Institute, the Rockefeller Foundation, and the Spencer Foundation. Much appreciation to Morton Deutsch, Susan Opotow, Linda Powell, and Janice Steil for very helpful feedback.

1. A second lawsuit was launched because of a 1999 Legislative mandate for the State Board of Education to "study" alternatives to the exit exam, which the Superintendent and the Board have refused to undertake.

References

Anand, B., Fine, M., Perkins, T., & Surrey, S. (2002). *Keeping the struggle alive: Oral histories of school desegregation in the North*. New York: Teachers College Press.

Ancess, J. (2000). The reciprocal influence of teacher learning, teaching practice, school restructuring, and student learning outcomes. *Teachers College Record, 102*(3), 590–619.

Ancess, J., & Ort, S. (2001). *Making school completion integral to school purpose & design.* Paper presented at the conference, Dropouts in America: How severe is the problem? Sponsored by Achieve, Inc. and the Civil Rights Project, Cambridge, MA.

Anyon, J. (1983). Workers, labor and economic history, and textbook content. In M. Apple & L. Weis (Eds.), *Ideology and practice in schools* (pp. 37–60). Philadelphia: Temple University Press.

—— (2005). *Radical possibilities: Public policy, urban education, and a new social movement.* New York: Routledge.

Aronowitz, S., & Giroux, H. A. (1993). *Education still under siege* (2nd ed.). Westport, CT: Bergin & Garvey.

Ayers, R., Ayers, W., Dohrn, B., & Jackson, T. (2001). *Zero tolerance.* New York: The New Press.

Bowen, W. G., & Bok, D. (1998). *The shape of the river: Long-term consequences of considering race in college and university admissions.* New Jersey: Princeton University Press.

Bowles, S., & Gintis, H. (1976). *Schooling in capitalist America.* New York: Basic Books.

Boyd-Franklin, N., & Franklin, A. J. (1999). *Boys to men: Raising African American sons.* New York: Dutton.

Bronfenbrenner, U. (1979). *The ecology of human development.* Cambridge: Harvard University Press.

Bryk, A., & Driscoll, M. (1988). *The high school as community.* Madison, WI: National Center on Effective Secondary Schools.

Burhans, K., & Dweck, C. (1995). Helplessness in early childhood: The role of contingent worth. *Child Development, 66,* 1719–38.

Chajet, L. (forthcoming). The power and limits of small school reform: Institutional agency and democratic leadership in public education. In D. Carlson, Gause & Charles (Eds.), *Keeping the promise: Educational leadership and the promise of democracy in our time.* Boston: Peter Lang.

Cook, A., & Tashlik, P. (2005). Standardizing small. *Rethinking schools, 19*(4), 15.

Cooley, C. H. (1998). *On self and social organization.* Chicago: University of Chicago Press.

Crosby, F., Muehrer, P., & Loewenstein, G. (1986). Relative deprivation and explanation: Models and concepts. In J. Olson, M. Zanna & P. Hernan (Eds.), *Relative deprivation and assertive action. The Ontario Symposium, 4* (pp. 214–37).

Davidson, A., & Phelan, P. (1999). Students' multiple worlds. *Advances in Motivation and Achievement, 11,* 233–73. Greenwich, CT: JAI Press.

Delpit, L. (1995). *Other people's children: Cultural conflict in the classroom.* New York: New Press.

DeLuca, S., & Rosenbaum, J. (2001). *Are dropout decisions related to safety concerns, social isolation and teacher disparagement?* Paper presented at the Harvard University Civil Rights Project, Conference on Drop Outs, Cambridge, MA.

DuBois, W. E. B. (1935). Does the negro need separate schools? *Journal of Negro Education, 4,* 328–35.

—— (1990). *Souls of black folks.* New York: First Vintage Books.

Duran, V. (2002). *Building quality and student achievement: An exploratory study of 95 urban elementary schools.* Unpublished manuscript. Environmental Psychology Program, The Graduate Center, CUNY.

Dweck, C. S. (2002). Beliefs that make smart people dumb. In R. J. Sternberg (Ed.), *Why smart people do stupid things.* New Haven: Yale University Press.

Dweck, C. S., & Reppucci, N. D. (1973). Learned helplessness and reinforcement responsibility in children. *Journal of Personality and Social Psychology, 25,* 109–16.

Dweck, C. S., & Wortman, C. (1982). Learned helplessness, anxiety, and achievement motivation: Neglected parallels in cognitive, affective, and coping responses. In H. W. Krohne & L. Laux (Eds.), *Achievement, stress, and anxiety.* Washington, DC: Hemisphere.

Eccles, J. S., Wigfield, A., Midgley, C., Reuman, D., MacIver, D., & Feldlaufer, H. (1993). Negative effects of traditional middle schools on students' motivation. *The Elementary School Journal, 93*(5), 553–74.

Edwards, R. (1979). *Contested terrain.* New York: Basic Books.

Elliott, E., & Dweck, C. (1988). Goals: An approach to motivation and achievement. *Journal of Personality and Social Psychology, 54*, 5–12.

Evans, G., Kliewan, W., & Martin, J. (1991). The role of the physical environment in the health and well being of children. In H. Schroeder (Ed.), *New directions in health psychology assessment* (pp. 127–57). New York: Hemisphere.

Fanon, F. (1952, 1967). *Black skin, white masks.* New York: Grove Press.

Fine, M. (1990). The "public" in public schools: The social construction/constriction of moral community. *Journal of Social Issues, 4*(1), 107–19.

—— (1991). *Framing dropouts: Notes on the politics of an urban public high school.* Albany: State University of New York Press.

—— (2005). Not in our name. *Rethinking Schools, 19*(4), 11–14.

Fine, M., & Burns, A. (forthcoming). Class notes. *Journal of Social Issues,* special volume on social class and schooling.

Fine, M., Freudenberg, N., Payne, Y., Perkins, T., Smith, K., & Wanzer, K. (2002). "Anything can happen with police around": Urban youth evaluate strategies of surveillance in public places. In C. Daiute & M. Fine (Eds.), *Youth perspectives on violence and injustice. Journal of Social Issues.* Special volume.

Fine, M., Pedraza, P., Jaffe-Walter, R., Futch, V., & Stoudt, B. (2007). Swimming: On oxygen, resistance and possibility for international youth under siege. *Anthropology and Education Quarterly, 38*(1), 76–96.

Fine, M., Torre, M., Boudin, K., Bowen, I., Clark, J., Hylton, D., Martinez, M., Missy, Roberts, R., Smart, P., & Upegui, D. (2002). Participatory action research: From within and beyond prison bars. In P. Camic, J. E. Rhodes & L. Yardley (Eds.), *Qualitative research in psychology: Expanding perspectives in methodology and design.* Washington, DC: American Psychological Association.

Flanagan, C., Bowes, J., Jonsson, B., Csapo, B., & Sheblanova, E. (1998). Ties that bind: Correlates of adolescents' civic commitments in seven countries. *Journal of Social Issues, 54*(3), 457–75.

Goffman, E. (1961). *Asylums: Essays on the social situation of mental patients and other inmates.* New York: Anchor.

Hilliard, A. G. (1990). Rx for racism: Imperatives for America's schools. *Phi Delta Kappan, 71,* 593–600.

—— (2002). Introduction. In V. G. Morris & C. Morris (Eds.), *The price they paid.* TC Press.

Iyer, A., Leach, C., & Pedersen, A. (2004). Racial wrongs and restitutions: The role of guilt and other group based emotions. In M. Fine, L. Weis, L. Powell, Pruitt & A. Burns (Eds.), *Off white: Readings on power, privilege and resistance* (2nd ed.) (pp. 345–61). New York: Routledge.

Janoff-Bulman, R. (1992). *Shattered assumptions: Toward a new psychology of trauma.* New York: Free Press.

Kohl, H. (1994). *"I won't learn from you!": And other thoughts on creative maladjustment.* New York: New Press.

Kohn, A. (2000). *The case against standardized testing: Raising the scores, ruining the schools.* Portsmouth, NH: Heinemann.

Krenichyn, K., Saegert, S., & Evans, G. (2001). Parents as moderators of psychological and physiological correlates of inner city children's exposure to violence. *Applied Developmental Psychology, 22*(6), 581–602.

Lareau, A. (2003). *Unequal childhoods: Class, race and family life.* Berkeley: University of California Press.

Lefkowitz, B. (1998). *Our guys: The Glen Ridge rape and the secret life of the perfect suburb*. New York: Vintage Press.

Lerner, R., & von Eye, A. (1998). Integrating youth- and context-focused research and outreach. In D. Gorlitz, H. Harloff, G. Mey & J. Valsiner (Eds.), *Children, cities and psychological theories* (pp. 573–97). New York: Walter de Gruyter.

Lewis, M. (1992). *Shame*. New York: Free Press.

Lifton, R. (1994). *The protean self: Human resilience in an age of fragmentation*. New York: Basic Books.

Maxwell, L., & Evans, G. (2000). The effects of noise on preschool children. *Journal of Environmental Psychology, 20*, 91–97.

McCord, R. (2002). *Declaration of Dr. Robert S. McCord in San Francisco NAACP et al., vs. San Francisco Unified School District, et al.*

McNeil, L. (2005). Creating new inequalities: Contradictions of reform. *Phi Delta Kappan, 81*(10), 728–47.

Mead, G. W. (1988). *Mind, self and society*. Chicago: University of Chicago Press.

Meier, D. (1998, January). Can these schools be changed? *Phi Delta Kappan*, 358–61.

Merton, R. (1987). The focused interview and focus groups: Continuities and discontinuities. *Public Opinion Quarterly, 51*(5), 550–66.

Miller, D. (2001). Disrespect and the experience of injustice. *Annual Review of Psychology, 52*, 527–53.

Poe-Yamagata, E., & Jones, S. (2000, April). *And justice for some*. Washington, DC: Youth Law Center, Building Blocks for Youth Report.

Rholes, W., Blackwell, J., Jordan, C., & Walters, C. (1980). Understanding self and others. In E. Higgins & R. Sorrentino (Eds.), *Handbook of motivation and cognition, 2* (pp. 369–407). New York: Guilford.

Rothstein, R. (2004). *Class and schools: Using social, economic and educational reform to close the Black–White achievement gap*. Washington, DC: Economic Policy Institute.

Saegert, S. (1999). *Environment and children's mental health: Residential density and low-income children*.

Sennett, R., & Cobb, J. (1993). *The hidden injuries of class*. New York: W. W. Norton.

Stipek, D., & Tannatt, L. (1984). Children's judgments of their own and their peers' academic competence. *Journal of Educational Psychology, 76*, 75–84.

Valenciz, R., Valenzuela, A., Sloan, K., & Foley, D. (2005). The Texas accountability system. *Phi Delta Kappan, 83*(4), 318.

Valenzuela, A. (1999). *Subtractive schooling*. Albany: SUNY Press.

Wasley, P., Fine, M., King, S., Powell, L., Gladden, M., & Holland, N. (1999). *Small schools, great strides*. Report published by the Bank Street College of Education, New York.

Weis, L. (1991). *Working class without work*. New York: Routledge Publishers.

Werner, C., & Altman, I. (1998). A dialectical/transactional framework of social relations: Children in secondary territories. In D. Gorlitz, H. Harloff, G. Mey & J. Valsiner (Eds.), *Children, cities and psychological theories* (pp. 123–54). New York: Walter de Gruyter.

Wolfe, M., & Rivlin, L. (1987). Institutions in children's lives. In C. Weinstein & T. David (Eds.), *Spaces for children* (pp. 89–112). New York: Plenum.

Woodson, C. G. (2000). *The mis-education of the negro*. Chicago: African American Images.

Yates, M., & Youniss, J. (1998). Community service and political identity development in adolescence. *Journal of Social Issues, 54*(3), 495–512.

Young, I. M. (2002). *Inclusion and democracy*. Oxford, England: Oxford University Press.

Chapter 16

Playing to middle-class self-interest in pursuit of school equity

*Ellen Brantlinger**

"American schools are among the most unequal in the industrialized world" (Darling-Hammond, 2006, p. 13). Some doubt the possibility of progressive change (David, 2003). Apple (2000) claims that in "conservative restoration it is difficult to keep progressive visions alive and not slide into cynicism" (p. 145). To combat defeatism, it is necessary to find ways to bring about educational transformation. My research addresses school disparities, while seeking ways to reduce them. My first study focused on low-income parents (1985). At some point I turned my scholarly gaze upward to look at the middle class (1993, 2004, 2006). After "studying up," I concluded that school inequities do not result from unintended or uncontrollable forces, but rather from deliberate collaboration between an educated class responsible for determining the nature of schooling and capitalists with an interest in controlling the minds and actions of citizens[1] (Chomsky, 2002; Harvey, 2005; Leonardo, 2003; Molnar, 2005; Saltman, 2003, 2005). My study reports always culminated with the prognosis that the educated middle class would never reject meritocracies because they privilege children of their class.

Regardless of the reality of vast school inequalities, hegemonic ideologies circulate the message that equal opportunity exists in education and that subordinates are at fault for lesser outcomes. Although such deceptive ideas may be deliberately developed and spread by those who think they gain from inequitable schools, my studies indicate that discourses about Others' nature and needs are so socialized into middle-class people's thinking that they speak and live them without being conscious of the flaws in their perceptions or the damaging consequences of their words and actions (Brantlinger, 2004). For example, although middle-class people have little direct contact with low-income people, they glibly narrate stories about their deficiencies in intellect and work ethic. Without access to evidence to the contrary, they *know* in their gut that the playing field is level and that their version of *Others* is accurate. They find reasons to blame working-class and low-income people for class discrepancies and hold themselves up as models to emulate. Indeed, because such distorted views and current school advantages for the middle class are so entrenched, it is essential to ask whether elites can change. A pessimistic prediction is that dominant classes will always pursue self-interest in managing public life. Marxists have long noted that, even in supposed democracies, social institutions always serve the interests of dominant classes (Althusser, 1971; Ball, 1998; Freire, 1985, 2004). Gramsci (1971) warns that ruling classes never willingly give up advantage, therefore it is up to the working class to struggle to transform society.

* Retired from the Department of Curriculum and Instruction at Indiana University in 2004.

Everyone agrees that economic, political, and social equity are beneficial for subordinate classes, and hence that democratic reform is important for them. It makes sense that this class should rally—or be rallied—to work toward democratic initiatives in education and society. Yet, sociologists contend that due to being socialized as subordinates, working and unemployed classes rarely are positioned psychologically or in terms of wielding power to make change (Ball, 1998, 2006; Bowles & Gintis, 1976; Bourdieu, 1977; Fanon, 1961, 1967; Olssen, 2004). Spivak (1988) asked if the "subaltern could speak." She felt that subordinates were so persuaded by hegemonic messages, for example, that their inferiority was the cause of societal disparities, that they lost a voice in public affairs. Evidence of internalization of blame surfaced repeatedly in my interviews; however, like Apple and Buras (2006), I found that my low-income participants had considerable insight into the reasons for social class disparities and were angry at unfairness in the system (Brantlinger, 1985, 1993). What is disheartening in terms of possible subordinate activism is that they are overwhelmed by, and demoralized about, the vast inequalities in all of their life domains. Most are convinced that it is futile to try to bring about change because they wield so little power over the circumstances of public life. Given these realities, as well as the likelihood that educated classes will continue to control public institutions, an alternative is to turn to the educated class in pursuit of school transformation.

The status of the middle class and school meritocracy

Through recent years, pressured by neo-liberal ideologies about the economic purposes of schooling and under the watchful gaze of accountability gurus who espouse and enforce strict compliance to teaching abstract academics, professionals have collaborated with middle-class parents to design increasingly competitive and inequitable schools. In such meritocratic schools, students are required to compete with one another to earn the credentials that allow them to get ahead (of others) in life (Young, 2004). Meritocratic schools give middle-class students a monopoly of high status positions and exclusive access to quality educational resources. Such class- and race-based school input discrepancies give white, middle-class students an edge in reaching achievement goals (Darling-Hammond, 2006; Ladson-Billings, 2006).

After World War II, for a while the burgeoning ranks of the educated class and their relative prosperity coincided with economic and social gains made by a unionized working class. Despite the democratic rationale for enhancing equal educational opportunity and the temporary success of equitable school reform (Lee, 2002), according to sociologists Apple (2001) and Ball (1998), conservatives tightened control of the meritocratic system and coerced school personnel to abandon progressive reform. At the same time, regardless of espousing ideals about school equity, because getting the best for their children was a foremost concern, middle-class parents used their clout to create school advantage for their children (Brantlinger, 2004). The middle class got on board with this "real dominant class"[2] to intensify the pressures on children for testable academic achievement and on schools for stratifying systems to structure an unequal and competitive school world. It might be said that, with few interests in common, global capitalists and middle-class parents conspired to create meritocratic schools (Young, 2004).

Perhaps inspired by John F. Kennedy's call to voters to think of the good of the country rather than themselves and by Lyndon Johnson's plans for the Great Society, middle-class people became aware of ethical demands on them to attend to the needs of the poor. The strategies they developed, however, were counterproductive in terms of improving schools for subordinates. Professionals designed and implemented a range of compensatory and special education school arrangements for poor children and children of color (Ferri & Connor, 2006). These interventions relegated subordinates to school margins and created job opportunities for the educated class (Brantlinger, 2006). In comparison to that blame the victim approach, desegregation and detracking reform successfully reduced achievement (and resource) gaps between rich and poor children (Alvarez & Mehan, 2006; Lee, 2002). Sleeter (2000) argues that the effectiveness of multicultural and equitable reform in reducing class disparities in the 1980s and 1990s caused the neo-liberal backlash that pressured educators to focus solely on academics that could be measured on high-stakes gateway exams. It seems reasonable to conclude that appealing to the educated class's empathy for subordinates did not institute progressive reform over the long run. The loss of distinction and privilege was not supported by the educated middle class (Brantlinger, 2004).

In this chapter, I take a radically different approach in attempting to convince middle-class people to advocate for equitable schooling. This represents a change in my perspective regarding the chances for school transformation and the middle class's willingness to facilitate democratic change. Rather than subscribing to my usual rational pessimism, I dabble in what is probably an untenable optimism. Nevertheless, my tactic here is not to convince middle-class people of their own moral duty to subordinates, but rather to appeal to the middle class's own self-interest as the incentive for transforming schools. While continuing to blame the ravages of meritocratic schooling on the flawed thinking and self-centered actions of educated people,[3] I still turn to this class in pursuit of transformation to democratic schooling. Contrary to common sentiments, I argue that equitable schooling actually benefits middle-class children. To convince middle-class constituencies to support democratic change, I offer these "potentially persuasive" arguments: (1) highly stratified and competitive schooling is socially and emotionally damaging to all children, including the supposed middle-class winners in the system; (2) widening class disparities in school conditions and student outcomes—and, relatedly, large and increasing wage gaps between adults of dominant and subordinate classes—are not conducive to enabling democratic ideals or middle-class prosperity; and (3) supporting school inequity is inconsistent with middle-class ethics. I address how the middle class's current view that meritocratic schools benefit their children is naive and short-sighted. I point to dangers in current economic trends and, finally, suggest ways to accomplish equitable school reform.

Argument I: Problematic schooling for middle-class youth

My first persuasive argument is that highly abstract curriculum and rigid evaluation systems that intensify student stratification and competition are damaging to middle-class children. Most people concur that school is not a supportive place for low-income children. LeCourt (2004) writes: "Because I grew up in a working-class, inner-city neighborhood, school was not always a friendly place" (p. 2). The implication is that, unlike students in her social class, middle-class students have welcoming school surroundings. Based on Bourdieu's (1977, 1984) theories of similarities of perspectives and customs within a given class habitus, it does seem that teachers and middle-class students would understand each other and have much in common. Nevertheless, despite class similarities in the teachers and the taught, that schooling may not be friendly to middle-class youth is evident in: (1) the high rates of substance abuse, depression, and suicide among students at elite high schools—private and public—and universities (Currie, 2005); (2) the phenomena of being stressed out and anxious or giving up on school/life and dropping out among middle-class and high-achieving students (Burkett, 2001; Levesque, 2002; Newman, 2004; Pope, 2001; Webber, 2003); (3) the high incidence of bullying and ostracism in suburban schools (Eder, 1995; Garrett, 2003; Merton, 1994); and (4) the rage apparent in students involved in the rampage shootings at predominantly middle-class schools (Brown & Merritt, 2002). These realities illustrate that middle-class students do not live with one another in complete harmony, nor do they all necessarily weather the competitive school system well.

Noting that people construct their identity within certain structural limits, Bourdieu (1984) compares distinctions between each social class habitus. His research does not address the tensions produced by within-class competition. Anyone who has attended school can attest to the presence of a pecking order that results as students labor to distance and dissociate themselves from other classes and distinguish themselves from others in their own class. Students readily admit that all "peers" are not considered equal, but vary along a range of such characteristics as gender, race, family income, religion, attractiveness, athleticism, special talents, intelligence, and academic success. By the time adolescents reach secondary school—when identity and belonging become foremost in their minds—variation along these continua determine individuals' social status and sense of place in school. Identity is based on perceptions of self in relation to others and, sadly, on the subordination of Others (Morrow & Torres, 2003). Indeed, identity formation involves "learning to position oneself within historic struggles over power" (Dimitriadis & Carlson, 2003, p. 18). Self-perception of identity and portrayal of one's identity by others are linked to techniques of power, including the dynamics observed by Foucault (1979); that is, surveillance (endless monitoring), normalization, exclusion, classification, and regulation.

Psychologists (and the lay public) typically espouse the theory that individual student pathology, such as anger or withdrawal, is due to dysfunctional family life. Based on that theory, a puzzle remains as to why many violent, depressed, and stoned students come from "good," two-parent, middle-class families. In contrast to personal pathology theories, Wexler (1996) looks at the economic/structural level of school and societal circumstances to pinpoint the causes of individuals' problems. Wexler presents a classic Marxist analysis of student commodification, exploitation, and alienation. He claims that modern (meritocratic) schools have turned away from a socially relevant curriculum and an ethics based on the common good, and instead use abstract knowledge as a credential, capital, or commodity. In such competitive situations, students are pressured to do meaningless work to achieve individual goals. Wexler argues that students are exploited by this commodification, hence become alienated from their teachers, peers, parents, and selves. Alienation is debilitating, even toxic. It does not lead to productive social experiences or constructive outcomes for any student. By their secondary school years, many low-income students have disengaged from schooling, whereas their middle-class counterparts have largely bought into the meritocracy game. Hence, it may be the latter who are most seriously hurt by schools' "relentless ranking schemes" and "raging competitive forces" (Currie, 2005, pp. 70, 121). Wexler's first edition of *Critical Social Psychology*

(1977) was written before the neo-liberal legislation (Nation at Risk, 1983; America 2000; No Child Left Behind, 2001) ratcheted up within and between-school competition and toughened the sanctions for schools and students who were not up to par. Clearly, student and teacher commodification, exploitation, and alienation have intensified and curriculum has been rendered more inauthentic and meaningless. Undergirding school and societal competition is a Darwinian survival of the fittest mentality, rather than mutual recognition of human similarities and common goals.

It is reasonable to conclude that adolescents' private troubles reflect larger social issues (Currie, 2005). Their adjustment and sense of purpose and agency also affect future social milieus. Fuss (1995) argues that the "neurotic structure of colonialism itself" affects the mental state of citizens (p. 141). Mental pathologies are the direct product of oppression (Fanon, 1961, 1967). Oppression is not unique to subordinate classes, however; it also results from dominant class exploitation along gender, achievement, and sexual orientation lines. Oppression is evident in successful students if they do not judge their achievements to be in harmony with their deep personal desires and needs.

Performance theory is relevant to ideas about student commodification. People engage in habitual routines, which Butler (1993) calls performances. Students are lured into performing stylized repetitions of behaviors that are discursively established based on their purportedly being socially valuable. Goffman (1959) referred to these as "presentations of self in everyday life." Enacting ritual performances, in turn, influences students' understanding of social life; that is, performances function to naturalize political, moral, and legal conventions. Žižek (2002) notes that performativity always has a retroactive basis. Students' lifescripts are sedimentations of others' experiences (Alexander, 2006). Students internalize the "body-subject of pre-existing histories" that are "overpopulated with the intentions of others," hence students "are prisoners" of "immanent self-production" (McLaren, 2006, p. xvi). The "need to be constantly accountable increases [student] visibility and requires that [they] align [their] performances with external accountability criteria" (Anderson, 2006, p. 211). Ball (2001, in Anderson, 2006, p. 211) calls the requirement to perform for others "fabrication" or "fabricating performances." Gallegos (2006) points out that students "perform school in the shadow of imperialism" (p. 107). The implication of performance theory is that, in being required to re-enact inane, externally directed rituals, students lose purpose, agency, and even a sense of self as their personal needs and wishes are deemed irrelevant. Clark (2004) writes: "performance and image are the name of the [suburban school] game. Just below the sheen of coerced normality are the stress and strain of personal survival in a hostile world" (p. 19).[4]

In analyzing the interviews of forty low-income and thirty-six high-income adolescents for *The Politics of Social Class in Secondary Schools* (1993), I found that a few affluent youth never wavered from confidently narrating stories about their own superiority and entitlement. They maligned low-income youth and felt little connection to them. Others saw the interview as an opportunity to vent regarding the harmful personal impact of the intense pressures for unrealistic achievement by parents and teachers. Some admitted to dreading the future as they worried they would not live up to their own or others' expectations. A few high-achievers called themselves imposters, and anguished that they would not survive in college without parents' daily help with homework. Elaborating on friction with peers, many confessed to being insecure about their social standing in cliques. They felt they had no real friends because of tensions aroused by interpersonal social and academic competition. Regardless of their own advanced achievement, these respondents were envious and resentful of peers who did better or had "unfair" advantages.

In re-reading transcripts of my audiotapes, I found that more than half of those interviewed conveyed that they existed outside school norms or that their true feelings were not really known by others. At one time or another, almost all thirty-six affluent interviewees used an external evaluation system (e.g., in accelerated classes, 4.0 GPA, high scores on standardized tests) to assess their own worth. When I first analyzed interviews, perhaps because I was so alarmed by low-income students' descriptions of their depressing lives in and out of school, I failed to recognize the extent of high-income students' unhappiness. In some ways, high-income participants had a comparatively easy time; nevertheless, school for them was no bed of roses. In *Hurt: Inside the World of Today's Teenagers*, Clark (2004) writes, the "other side to the idyllic picture of suburban high schools" is "a landscape of internal fears, loneliness, and insecurities held in check, where friendships are generally shallow, and where performance and image are the name of the game" (p. 19).

Brooks Brown (2002) co-wrote *No Easy Answers: The Truth Behind Death at Columbine*. A friend of shooters Eric and Dylan (and for a while also a suspect), Brooks felt that it was the negative social scene in the accelerated learning program ("where all the kids were trying to one-up the others") that primarily accounted for Dylan being "messed up and angry" (p. 20). "Finding friends within the program was virtually impossible—classmates weren't friends; they were competitors, and it was a battle to make sure that nobody got too far ahead of anybody else" (p. 31). Brooks wrote that Dylan was a "smart kid who could see the injustices in the world clearly and was frustrated by them" (p. 20). Brooks dropped out of the accelerated program and, for him, the "debate team was a godsend, as was drama class" (p. 45). He implies that these activities created caring, intellectually engaging communities for him within a generally hostile school environment. Brooks recalled that when he was failing and was bothered by bullies, his parents did not attempt to understand him but instead tried to fix him by pushing him to buy into the system. In terms of his own interpretation of reasons for student violence, Brooks elaborates:

> What's the easier sell for a politician: to go out there and tell people that they've screwed up, that they need to take better care of their kids, that they've created an ugly, uncaring society for the next generation, and need to search out their souls for a solution? Or to just say that the evil entertainment industry is ruining our kids? It's easier to blame the entertainment industry.
>
> (p. 16)

In addition to social class conflict, tensions surrounding gender, race, ethnicity, and sexual orientation are rife in secondary schools. David (2003) writes: "Middle class girls all became very highly achieving academically but routinely saw their performances as ordinary and had great anxiety about balancing their cleverness with their femininity. They routinely saw themselves as 'not good enough'" (p. 149). There are a multitude of accounts of difficulties for GLBT youth (Sadowski, 2003) and for students of color (Lee, 2003; Noguera, 2003). Because the topic of this volume is social class, I do not address research covering these other cultural groups. It is important to note that social class is invariably intertwined with race, ethnicity, gender, and sexual orientation in influencing adolescents and schools. The point I want to emphasize here is that middle-class adults must wake up and notice the clear and compelling evidence of student discontent in meritocratic schools. They must also be aware that the present school system brings on dysfunction rather than reducing or eradicating it among youth. Middle-class professionals and parents may be so bewildered by neo-liberal ideologies that tout school's narrow economic purposes that they fail to notice these are not in their own class's best interests.

Argument 2: Consequences of the widening gaps between rich and poor

Conditions that result from huge and expanding income gaps between the rich and poor are referred to as "Brazilianization." Evidence of its consequences in the USA include the concerted attacks on public education and welfare, and subsequent reduction of public funds to these services. Labor unions have disappeared and the clout they once held to make gains for working classes has diminished. The minimum wage has not been raised in decades. At the same time, there have been substantial reductions in health care coverage and retirement pensions. Deregulation and industrial relocation abroad have substantially decreased wages, environmental and worker protections, and corporate taxes (Micklethwait & Woldridge, 2004). A reverse-progressive formula now exists, so the very wealthy pay few taxes. Due to tax reductions and military spending, the federal deficit has burgeoned. Such phenomena signal that the dynamics of Brazilianization are having a dangerous impact on life in the USA.

The disasters of impoverishment of the poor are widely recognized; however, the effects of extreme wealth distribution disparities on middle classes receive less attention. Nevertheless, an integral part of Brazilianization is the loss of middle-class jobs, particularly social service sector jobs. Due to decreased corporate taxes and revenues from the wealthy—as well as military expenditures—fewer funds are available to cover the government's domestic role of maintaining a supportive civil society. Responsibility for citizen welfare previously provided jobs for the educated middle class. Although this class has so far retained a living wage, it has witnessed a decline in financial and employment conditions. Therefore, instead of focusing solely on the situations of the poor, the middle class must think about how Brazilianization affects them. The reality of widening income gaps is that ruling classes do not support public sector professional jobs. Hacker (2006) refers to the steady decline in two-income families' economic security over the past thirty years as the "great risk shift."

One of the problems with class alignment in modern US society is that the perceived boundaries between elite, middle, and working classes are blurred because everybody believes they are middle class (Felski, 2002). I selected participants for my local studies (1985, 1993, 2004) based on residential location. I recruited "high-income" people from suburbs and "low-income" people from housing projects, trailer parks, and areas with diminished housing. Consistent with Felski's hypothesis, wealthier participants called themselves "middle class," with only a few adding "upper." Low-income respondents also identified as middle class, often comparing themselves to down and out acquaintances who they felt were "lower class." The demographic data collected from participants made it clear that "high-income" status equated with jobs requiring an advanced education and "low-income" status with service jobs or unemployment. Despite universal self-labeling as middle class, emotions roused by divisions between highly educated and less educated classes were glaring in the narratives. Respondents used such expressions as "haves and have nots," "preppies and grits," "respectable people or to-do's and the rest of us," or "ordinary children versus kids from dysfunctional families." High- and low-income informants described a dichotomous and antagonistic local class system in which each was each other's Other. A third tier—a genuine elite or ruling class—was not apparent in their mental schema of social class.

There is not space here to provide an adequate overview of the complex US class system; however, I draw briefly from Nance's (2003) *Gangs in America: The Rise of Corporate Power and the Disabling of Democracy* to make the case that through their successful negotiation for unregulated and unbridled power in the past several decades, the global corporate class has created enormous wealth for themselves while relegating the US working class, and many in the middle class, to poverty and declining conditions. These corporate owners compose the actual ruling class who own the means of produc- tion, control the nature and location of labor, and decide how wealth is distributed. While this real ruling class was overlooked and invisible in the narratives of my middle- and working-class informants, it is this corporate class and not the educated class that constitutes the indisputable Other to the oppressed and the declining middle classes. Similarly, global capitalists, rather than the working and unemployed classes, are Other to all middle-class people who do not own corporations or have large monetary assets.

Under current circumstances, low-income people's sense of self as middle class and the educated class—rather than a capitalist ruling class—as their antagonist surely mitigates against working-class loyalty or effective revolutionary spirit. That issue, however, is not the focus of my chapter. Instead, I address the problematic aspects of college-educated people's alignment with "haves" and their disparagement of the working class in their own class binary. The construct "false consciousness" has been criticized when applied to working classes. Yet, because the middle class has limited insight into actual class rela- tions and because their perception of their own class status is so out of kilter with the reality of a three-tiered class system, it is reasonable to accuse them of having a false consciousness. I return to this concept in the final section of this chapter, where I briefly describe "transformative pedagogy."

Wright (1985) calls the middle class a contradictory class in that it ties its interests to the ruling class but does not benefit from capitalism in the same way as elites—it does not control significant capital nor does it own the means of production. In the twenty years since Wright's book was written, trends indicate that it is even more problematic for middle-class people to align with the ruling classes whose interests are served by deni- grating and dismissing all levels of workers in order to keep salaries low and profits high (Hill, 2006). The war of elites has not only been on the working class, but also the middle class—neither has benefited from recent social, political, and economic trends (Hacker, 2006; Harvey, 2005; Jacobs, 2006). In terms of the confounding of classes, the "working poor" construct has dubious class connotations. It seems that "poor" has begun to include the middle class. Lou Dobbs (2006), prime time CNN news commentator, made it his mission to expose "the war on the middle class." The point here is that the ruling class (global capitalists and hereditary elites) does gain from people's un- and under- employment—if wages and benefits stay low, elites' profits soar. Then, too, capitalist- dominated governments can turn to the unemployed and underemployed to recruit a so-called voluntary military force to fight imperialist battles for resources and uncontested power. Such power and financial disparities benefit ownership classes. Besides the advantages entailed in being exalted to a position above the working class, it is not reasonable to believe that keeping laborers down and elite classes up is in the interests of educated classes.

A civil society based on laws, education of the young, care of the infirm and elderly, universal health care benefits, protection of collective land, just distribution of societal resources, enlightened self-interest, and social engagement of citizens is requisite to a democracy. With the exception of a petty bourgeois of managers and small business owners, the middle class is composed of people educated for work in civil society. During the second half of the twentieth century, jobs for an educated class have come from tax-based resources that flowed to sustain civil society. What the educated class should understand is that when untaxed profits stay with elite classes, resources for employing educated people in civic enterprises dissipate. Widening financial gaps threaten public services and middle-class employment. These gaps also jeopardize government based on a range of empowered citizens involved in deliberative democracy (Jacobs, 2006).

The key to professional civil servants' employment is education. This class is shaped and distinguished through schooling. Education as capital is rewarded with somewhat higher salaries than earned by those with less education. Yet the mutual animosity and social segregation caused by real or perceived attribute and reward disparities between middle and working classes creates a conflict with few gains for either class. School's function of educating democratic citizens is essential, whereas the stratifying role of education in producing differential amounts of social capital is divisive and unnecessary. Given the current trends of global capitalism, which include corporate deregulation and loss of corporate taxes that previously went to fund local and national institutions (including schools), for the educated class to prosper in the future, it must align itself with working rather than elite classes in pursuit of equity in schools and society. It is apparent that an upward trajectory for elite classes results not only in impoverishment of working classes, but in a downward trajectory for middle classes. Although middle-class people may feel that the increasingly disparate wage structure does not harm them, ultimately it puts this class in peril of losing employment. Hence, the educated class must question their loyalty to the capitalist ruling class and work collectively with working classes to secure a reasonable future for their offspring and themselves. These two subordinate classes can work together politically to (re)regulate corporations, reduce financial disparities, increase public services to citizens, and prevent further disappearance of middle- and working-class jobs.

Argument 3: Middle-class advantage is out-of-sync with their ethics and ideals

While being schooled as Americans, students daily recite, "with liberty and justice for all." They learn that "all people are created equal" and have "equal protection under the law." These sayings exemplify widespread beliefs about human equality and worth. While engaging in religious practices, people are exposed to versions of social reciprocity ethics. This moral code appears in most world religions: "What is hateful to you, do not to your fellow man. That is the entire Law; all the rest is commentary" (Judaism). "Hurt not others in ways that you yourself would find hurtful" (Buddhism). "No one of you is a believer until he desires for his brother that which he desires for himself" (Islam). "Do unto others as you would have them do unto you" (Christianity). "Blessed is he who preferreth his brother before himself" (Baha'i Faith). Certainly people are socialized in a number of important venues to espouse the social reciprocity morality as the grounding for their relationships and social actions.

Some scholars claim that social reciprocity morality is more than a socialized product, but rather has genetic origins. Drawing partly from research on primate behavior, Hauser (2006), a biologist, concludes that people are born with a moral grammar wired into their neural circuits. This moral code evolved because restraints on behavior are necessary for social living and also because humans are interdependent as they engage in daily life pursuits. While recognizing that moral codes are shaped by such external forces in people's lives as religious and ethical training, Hauser asserts that humans' concern for others—their altruism—is innate. Although currently people demonstrate different levels of this instinctive moral code, Hauser sees it as an obvious source to be drawn from in establishing equitable and humane social life. Similarly, Koggel (1998) recommends that instead of limiting thinking to what individuals need as independent, autonomous agents, a relationship approach asks what moral persons embedded in relationships of interdependency need for each other to flourish.

Brown (1991) did a meta-analysis of anthropological studies that he reports in *Human Universals*. He concludes that all human societies develop hierarchical status positions and differentiated resource distribution systems based on race, gender, and family traits. At the same time, to a greater or lesser extent, all people subscribe to the moral ideals of social reciprocity. On a rhetorical level, the social reciprocity morality seems to be widespread as it is expressed in world religions, radical humanism, and national constitutions. Nevertheless, middle-class Americans do not live in accordance with social reciprocity ideals when they structure schools. Whether willingly or not, educators have succumbed to the neo-liberal agenda to turn schools (and people) into compliant commodities that fuel the economic engine (Apple, 2000). Clearly neo-liberal ideologies and pressures from federal legislation have distracted empathetic students and teachers from a progressive use of agency.

Related to holding competing and mutually exclusive perspectives, my studies of high-income people reveal tensions surrounding the disconnect between morality and actions/beliefs. In *Dividing Classes* (2004), I counter the myth of middle-class support for equitable schooling by detailing how students, parents, school personnel, and board members continuously negotiate for school advantage. An interesting occurrence in the interviews was that middle-class people first responded to questions about schooling by espousing democratic ideals. After establishing themselves as liberals, they went on to insist on the need for advanced and separated schooling because their children were brighter, more academically prepared, and had stronger work ethics than children from working-class and impoverished families. The initial pro-equity speech allowed them to dissociate from conservatives who "did not care about the poor." When confronted with a situation that forced them to come out for or against school tracking and segregation, they emotionally objected to this "unrealistic" dilemma. "In theory," they would support detracking and desegregation, but felt they could not sacrifice their children's future by allowing them to be "held back by others." So, while waxing eloquently about the desirability of heterogeneous schools, middle-class parents anxiously demanded rank ordered, tightly academic schooling based on the rationale that their children needed this kind of schooling to survive in a competitive world. Middle-class respondents blamed the poor for class divisions and hierarchical classroom arrangements. Although practiced in verbally bridging the chasm between ethics and actions, when accused of being accountable for social class disparities, they squirmed. They saw their solutions for reducing disparities, which inevitably centered around compensatory interventions aimed at bringing the deficient subaltern up to par, as benevolent. Some seemed baffled, even insulted, when it was pointed out that such interventions served to intensify student segregation, deny equal access to high quality instruction, and relegate subordinates to inferior school status. Despite liberal and compassionate self-identification, my middle-class participants came down squarely on the side of keeping the playing field unequal and divided.

Given that the educated middle class has the power to structure schools, it is necessary to convince them of the urgency of restructuring for equity. The nature of current conditions may render it an ideal time to catch their attention. Brown (1991) claims that people tend to call upon social reciprocity ideals in times of crisis. Clearly, US citizens perceive the nation and world to be in extremely unsettled and stressful times as they witness the dramatic effect that capitalism has had on world economies. Some among the affluent are aware that a consumption-oriented lifestyle has a disastrous environmental impact, including the precipitation of global warming. Similar to Brown, Hunt (2000) contends that it is during difficult times or in periods of social upheaval that people are prone to endorse human rights ideals—to hold certain "truths to be self-evident." Given growing fears about the future, combined with the stress caused by desires being out-of-sync with ethics, the middle class might be persuaded to relinquish the privileges of status and power to realize ideals and long-term security. Again, it must be emphasized that equitable education must be presented as in the interest of the middle class rather than as a sacrifice made for Others.

The pedagogy of transformation

It is important for the middle class to look beyond immediate advantages and success in competition to more universal democratic values related to the directions of political, economic, and social life. Historically, the educated class has controlled social institutions, hence I identify them as agents best positioned to enable change. Yet, for democratic transformation to succeed, educators must support school (societal) reform based on social reciprocity ethics. This entails asking those who control schools to figure out what it means to align ethics and actions to work for truly democratic and socially responsive ideals. The educated class must become aware of the harmful consequences for subordinate children and *children of their class* caused by meritocratic school structure and the recent reform of academic intensification. They must interrupt persuasive ruling-class ideologies that suppress compassionate ethics, recognize that growing disparities between rich and poor threaten the livelihood of their class, and see the need for prompt action if they are to preserve a modicum of middle-class comfort. This influential class must admit to wielding power in politics and to controlling social institutions. To consider school reality, they need only listen to their children.

One hindrance to generating support for democratic schools is that school personnel with leftist instincts seem wary of expressing their views or getting "politically" involved, whereas conservatives glibly announce negative attributes of subordinates and elaborate support for neo-liberal politics (Brantlinger, 2004). That "political" (progressive) thought must be concealed is likely the residue of cold war politics and the witch hunt that McCarthy held to condemn leftists as unpatriotic traitors. Although I found considerable support for progressive agendas based on social reciprocity morality among teachers and administrators, a dilemma remains as to how these educators can become comfortable enough to be candid about preferences and secure in knowing that they will be protected from NCLB sanctions or retribution from wealthy parents who demand school advantage for their children.

The push for democratic change does not emerge in a vacuum. The middle class includes individuals who develop models for communitarian democracy based on social reciprocity ethics (Bellah, 1986; Dworkin, 2000; Gutmann, 1992; Rawls, 1971). School personnel can testify that many students' intellectual interests and civic actions are consistent with reciprocity morality. Indeed, among the youth perceived to have dropped out of the middle-class race for affluence and recognition, many engage as social activists who fervently challenge rightist agendas at local and national levels. Multicultural education spokespersons cite effective attempts to enhance the cultural awareness of dominant class students (Ladson-Billings, 2006; Leonardo, 2003). Earlier in the past century, democratic education was envisioned by prominent educators (Counts, 1932, 1934; Dewey, 1909, 1931, 1944).

For Freire (1985), emancipatory education for the oppressed involved raising awareness of social class conditions while providing literacy instruction. "Pedagogy is to be simultaneously grounded in an immediate social reality while also seeking to transcend and transform the confines surrounding the context" (Ewing, 2005, p. 6). "Developing consciousness is part of a humanizing pedagogy" (Freire, 2004, p. xx). In facilitating enlightenment, it is essential that educated constituencies be challenged to reconsider their support for meritocratic schooling and make constructive plans for structuring inclusive, democratic, and socially relevant schools. I previously referred to the middle class's false consciousness regarding its perceptions of its status in class hierarchy, class affiliation, and long-term interests. Following Freire's model of emancipatory instruction, efforts should be made to raise consciousness of class realities of dominant class students, parents, and professionals. Such instruction could be integrated into school curriculum and media venues using the same pedagogical techniques as Freire used with the oppressed. Although the flawed thinking and faulty class identification of the educated class is disheartening, perhaps it is their obvious discomfort regarding the dissonance between their choices and values that provides the greatest hope for them to change and become advocates, and activists, for democratic schools.

Reducing false consciousness requires relearning. Scholars recommend various effective strategies. In discussing critical literacy, Provenzo (2005) points out that learning "involves an essential process of dialogue, interaction, negotiation, and mutual understanding with all peoples and cultures," hence "democracy is not a fixed noun, but an active verb, as is culture an activity and not merely a thing" (p. 2). "People need the opportunity to exercise and preserve conscience whenever possible" (Arons, 1997, p. 54). Instruction should not be didactic or top-down, "participatory democracy requires a collective process of self-education" (Davies, 2004, p. 123). The ultimate goal is to help dominant middle-class groups understand and evaluate divisive and inequitable trends in schooling and in social life under unchecked and unrestricted global capitalism, and judge them to be contrary to their interests and ideals. In the process they should reconcile their desire for certain status and lifestyle attainment with their spiritual longings and recognize that their future lies with working classes rather than with global capitalists. The subordinate classes—middle and working—can collectively work to create a world in which peace, equity, and ecological protection are in the best interest of all. Aronowitz (2006) touts the need for solidarity to challenge the military and corporate interests that turn knowledge into the production of an exchange credential or commodity. To revisit performance theory, Butler (1993) informs readers that performances not only solidify rituals, but also are sites of resistance against the structure—what she calls "performative subversions." Gramsci introduces the idea of "organic intellectuals," an educated class whose affiliations and allegiances remain with working classes. Gramsci was hopeful that these liberated persons would gain insight into the problems of social inequality and be willing to rise against capitalist forces and engage in activism for change. Even Marx thought peaceful transition to socialism was possible (Davies, 2004, p. 53).

Questions for discussion

1. Brantlinger states that "US schools are among the most unequal in the industrialized world." How and why does this inequality occur?
2. The author offers three arguments to "convince middle-class constituencies to support democratic change." Which of these do you find most compelling and why? Which do you not find compelling and why?
3. The performance of learning requires students to repeat behavior that is deemed socially valuable. What different kinds of behaviors are valued by high, middle, and lower classes? Drawing on personal experience, how are these behaviors fostered in families and in educational contexts?
4. Brantlinger argues that "equitable schooling actually benefits middle-class children." What arguments can you construct to support and contest this statement? In light of the arguments you made (and have heard from other sources), do you agree with this statement and why?
5. Meritocracy is the fundamental principle underpinning the US school system. Is it the most appropriate principle to underpin education, and why might some groups claim that it is problematic?
6. The author offers a "pedagogy of transformation" which will ultimately facilitate change toward a more democratic education. But, what does a "truly democratic education" look like? Are the author's suggestions for change conceivable for the future of US education?
7. "The neo-liberal agenda to turn schools (and people) into compliant commodities that fuel the economic engine" is prevalent in schools. How does this agenda differ according to class position? In what ways is education used as a tool to procure the consent of the lower and/or middle class in their own oppression?
8. Given that significant disparities exist between classes, why do you think the class system continues to exist in countries claiming to be "democratic?"

Notes

1. Or, neo-liberals (a "hegemonic bloc of rightist forces") who define democracy in free market terms and refer to students as "consumers" and to knowledge as "educational products" (Apple & Buras, 2006, p. 6).
2. Social class terminology is rather ambiguous. It seems appropriate to refer to the educated middle class as "dominant" because of their control over social institutions. Yet, the corporate class is the real ruling class in that it owns the means of production and has disproportionate financial assets, thus can exert control over economic, political, and social life.
3. Lynn Davies (2004) points out that despite thinking of themselves as morally superior, highly educated people have been responsible for a host of major atrocities.
4. Similar to others who write about adolescent issues, Clark's solution is caring and nurturing adults. He does not suggest that the structure of schools and society be changed.

References

Alexander, B. K. (2006). Critically analyzing pedagogical interactions as performance. In B. K. Alexander, G. L. Anderson, & B. P. Gallegos (Eds.), *Performance theories in education: Power, pedagogy, and the politics of identity* (pp. 41–62). Mahwah, NJ: Lawrence Erlbaum.

Althusser, L. (1971). Ideology and the ideological state apparatus. In *Lenin and philosophy*. New York: Monthly Review Press.

Alvarez, D., & Mehan, H. (2006). Whole-school detracking: A strategy for equity and excellence. *Theory into Practice, 45*(1), 82–89.

Anderson, G. L. (2006). Performing school reform in the age of the political spectacle. In B. K. Alexander, G. L. Anderson, & B. P. Gallegos (Eds.), *Performance theories in education: Power, pedagogy, and the politics of identity* (pp. 199–220). Mahwah, NJ: Lawrence Erlbaum.

Apple, M. W. (2000). *Official knowledge: Democratic education in a conservative age* (2nd ed.). New York: Routledge.

Apple, M. W., & Buras, K. L. (Eds) (2006). *The subaltern speak: Curriculum, power and education struggles.* New York: Routledge.

Aronowitz, S. (2006). Subaltern paradise: Knowledge production in the corporate academy. In M. W. Apple & K. L. Buras (Eds.), *The subaltern speak: Curriculum, power and education struggles* (pp. 177–96). New York: Routledge.

Arons, S. (1997). *Short route to chaos: Conscience, community, and the re-constitution of American schooling.* Amherst: University of Massachusetts Press.

Ball, S. (1998). Educational studies, policy entrepreneurship and social theory. In R. Slee, G. Weiner, & S. Tomlinson (Eds.), *School effectiveness for whom? Challenges to the school effectiveness and school improvement movements* (pp. 70–83). London: Falmer.

Ball, S. J. (2006). *Education policy and social class: The selected works of Stephen J. Ball.* London: Routledge.

Bellah, R. N. (1986). *Habits of the heart: Individualism and commitment in American life.* New York: Harper & Row.

Bourdieu, P. (1977). *Outline of a theory of practice.* Cambridge: Cambridge University Press.

—— (1984). *A social critique of the judgment of taste.* Cambridge, MA: Harvard University Press.

Bowles, S., & Gintis, H. (1976). *Schooling in capitalist America.* New York: Basic Books.

Brantlinger, E. (1985). Low-income parents' perceptions of favoritism in the schools. *Urban Education, 20*, 82–102.

—— (1993). *The politics of social class in secondary schools: Views of affluent and impoverished youth.* New York: Teachers College Press.

—— (2004). *Dividing classes: How the middle class negotiates and rationalizes school advantage.* New York: RoutledgeFalmer.

—— (Ed.) (2006). *Who benefits from special education? Remediating (fixing) other people's children.* Mahwah, New Jersey: Erlbaum.

Brown, B., & Merritt, R. (2002). *No easy answers: The truth behind death at Columbine.* New York: Lantern.

Brown, D. E. (1991). *Human universals.* Philadelphia: Temple University Press.

Burkett, E. (2001). *Another planet: A year in the life of a suburban high school.* New York: Perennial.

Butler, J. (1993). *Bodies that matter: On the discursive limits of "sex."* New York: Routledge.

Chomsky, N. (2002). *Understanding power: The indispensable Chomsky.* New York: New Press.

Clark, C. (2004). *Hurt: Inside the world of today's teenagers.* Grand Rapids, MI: Baker Academic.

Counts, G. (1932/1978). *Dare the school build a new social order?* (Reprint) Carbondale, IL: Southern Illinois University Press.

—— (1934). *The social foundations of education.* New York: George Scribner's Sons.

Currie, E. (2005). *The road to whatever: Middle-class culture and the crisis of adolescence.* New York: Metropolitan Books.

Darling-Hammond, L. (2006). Securing the right to learn: Policy and practice for powerful teaching and learning. *Educational Researcher, 35*(7), 13–24.

David, M. E. (2003). *Personal and political: Feminisms, sociology and family lives.* Stoke on Trent, UK: Trentham Books.

Davies, L. (2004). *Education and conflict: Complexity and chaos.* New York: RoutledgeFalmer.

Dewey, J. (1909). *Moral principles in education.* Boston: Houghton Mifflin.

—— (1931). *Individualism, old and new.* London: George Allen & Unwin.

—— (1944). *Democracy and education: An introduction to the philosophy of education.* New York: The Free Press. (Original work published in 1916.)

Dimitriadis, G., & Carson, D. (Eds.) (2003). Introduction. *Promises to keep: Cultural studies, democratic education and public life* (pp. 1–35). New York: RoutledgeFalmer.

Dobbs, L. (2006). *The war on the middle class.* New York: Viking.

Dworkin, R. (2000). *Sovereign virtue.* Cambridge: Harvard University Press.

Eder, D. (1995). *School talk: Gender and adolescent culture.* New Brunswick, NJ: Rutgers University Press.

Ewing, E. T. (Ed.) (2005). *Revolution and pedagogy: Interdisciplinary and transnational perspectives on educational foundations.* New York: Palgrave.

Fanon, F. (1961). *The wretched of the earth.* New York: Grove.

—— (1967). *Black skin, white masks.* New York: Grove.

Felski, R. (2002). Why academics don't study the lower middle class. *The Chronicle of Higher Education,* p. B24.

Ferri, B. A., & Connor, D. J. (2006). *Reading resistance: Discourses of exclusion in desegregation and inclusion debates.* New York: Peter Lang.

Foucault, M. (1979). *Discipline and punish: The birth of the prison* (A. Heridan, trans.). New York: Vintage.

Freire, P. (1985). *The politics of education: Culture, power, and liberation.* S. Hadley: Bergin/Garvey.

—— (2004). *Pedagogy of indignation.* Boulder: Paradigm.

Fuss, D. (1995). *Identification papers.* New York: Routledge.

Gallegos, B. P. (2006). Performing school in the shadow of imperialism: A hybrid (coyote) interpretation. In B. K. Alexander, G. L. Anderson, & B. P. Gallegos (Eds.), *Performance theories in education: Power, pedagogy, and the politics of identity* (pp. 107–26). Mahwah, NJ: Lawrence Erlbaum.

Garrett, A. E. (2003). *Bullying in American schools: Causes, preventions, interventions.* Jefferson, NC: McFarland.

Goffman, E. (1959). *The presentation of self in everyday life.* New York: Doubleday.

Gramsci, A. (1971/1929–35). *Selections from the prison notebooks* (Q. Hoare & G. N. Smith, Eds.). New York: International Publishers (original work published in 1929–35).

Gutmann, A. (1992). Communitarian critics of liberalism. In S. Avineri & A. De-Shalit (Eds.), *Communitarianism and individualism* (pp. 134–54). New York: Oxford University Press.

Hacker, J. S. (2006). *The great risk shift: Assault on American jobs, families, health care, and retirement and how you can fight back.* Oxford: Oxford University Press.

Harvey, D. (2005). *A brief history of neoliberalism.* New York: Oxford University Press.

Hauser, M. D. (2006). *Moral minds.* New York: HarperCollins.

Hill, D. (2006, April 8). *Education, class, and capital in neoliberal globalisation: Some implications for social class analysis and analysts.* American Educational Research Association Annual Meeting in San Francisco.

Hunt, L. (2000). *Tracing the origins of human rights.* Patten Lecture: Indiana University, Bloomington.

Jacobs, L. R. (2006). *Inequality and American democracy: What we know and what we need to learn.* New York: Russell Sage.

Koggel, C. M. (1998). *Perspectives on equality: Constructing a relational theory.* Lanham, MD: Rowman & Littlefield.

Ladson-Billings, G. (2006). From the achievement gap to the education debt: Understanding achievement in US schools. *Educational Researcher, 35*(7), 3–12.

LeCourt, D. (2004). *Identity matters: Schooling the student body in academic discourse.* Albany: State University of New York Press.

Lee, J. (2002). Racial and achievement gap trends: Reversing the progress toward equity. *Educational Researcher, 31*(1), 3–12.

Lee, S. J. (2003). Model minorities and perpetual foreigners: The impact of stereotyping on Asian-American students. In M. Sadowski (Ed.), *Adolescents at school: Perspectives on youth, identity, and education* (pp. 41–50). Cambridge, MA: Harvard University Press.

Leonardo, Z. (2003). *Ideology, discourse, and school reform.* Westport, CT: Praeger.

Levesque, R. J. R. (2002). *Dangerous adolescents, model adolescents: Shaping the role and promise of education.* New York: Kluwer.

McLaren, P. (2006). Foreword. In B. K. Alexander, G. L. Anderson, & B. P. Gallegos (Eds.), *Performance theories in education: Power, pedagogy, and the politics of identity* (pp. xv–xix). Mahwah, NJ: Lawrence Erlbaum.

Merton, D. (1994). The cultural context of aggression: The transition to junior high school. *Anthropology of Education, 25*(1), 29–43.

Micklethwait, J., & Woldridge, A. (2004). *The right nation: Conservative power in America.* New York: Penguin.

Molnar, A. (2005). *School commercialism: From democratic ideal to market commodity.* New York: Routledge.

Morrow, R. W., & Torres, C. A. (2003). Series Editors' Foreword. In G. Dimitriadis & D. Carlson (Eds.), *Promises to keep: Cultural studies, democratic education, and public life* (pp. ix–xi). New York: RoutledgeFalmer.

Nance, T. (2003). *Gangs of America: The rise of corporate power and the disabling of democracy.* San Francisco: Berrett-Koehler.

Newman, K. S. (2004). *Rampage: The social roots of school shootings.* New York: Basic Books.

Noguera, P. A. (2003). Joaquin's dilemma: Understanding the link between racial identity and school-related behaviors. In M. Sadowski (Ed.), *Adolescents at school: Perspectives on youth, identity, and education* (pp. 19–30). Cambridge, MA: Harvard University Press.

Olssen, M. (Ed.) (2004). *Culture and learning: Access and opportunity in the classroom.* Greenwich, CT: Information Age Publishing.

Pope, D. C. (2001). *Doing school: How we are creating a generation of stressed out, materialistic, and miseducated students.* New Haven: Yale University Press.

Provenzo, E. F., Jr. (2005). *Critical literacy: What every American ought to know.* Boulder: Paradigm Publishers.

Rawls, J. (1971). *A theory of justice.* Cambridge, MA: Harvard University Press.

Sadowski, M. (2003). Growing up in the shadows: School and the identity development of sexual minority youth. In M. Sadowski (Ed.), *Adolescents at school: Perspectives on youth, identity, and education* (pp. 85–101). Cambridge, MA: Harvard University Press.

Saltman, K. J. (2003). *Education as enforcement: The militarization and corporatization of schools.* New York: Routledge.

—— (2005). *The Edison schools: Corporate schooling and the assault on public education.* New York: Routledge.

Sleeter, C. E. (2000, April 28). *Keeping the lid on: Multicultural curriculum and the organization of consciousness.* American Education Research Association Meeting in New Orleans.

Spivak, G. C. (1988). Can the subaltern speak? In C. Nelson & L. Grossberg (Eds.), *Marxism and the interpretation of culture* (pp. 271–313). Urbana: University of Illinois Press.

Webber, J. (2003). *Failure to hold: The politics of school violence.* New York: Rowman & Littlefield.

Wexler, P. (1996). *Critical social psychology, 2nd edition.* New York: Peter Lang. (First edition, 1977.)

Wright, E. O. (1985). *Classes.* London and New York: Verso.

Young, M. F. D. (2004). Preface. In M. Olsen (Ed.), *Culture and learning: Access and opportunity in the classroom* (pp. x–xi). Greenwich, CT: Information Age Publishing.

Žižek, S. (2002). *For they know not what they do: Enjoyment as a political factor* (2nd ed.). London and New York: Verso.

Chapter 17

Class, teachers, and teacher education

Greg Dimitriadis *

Introduction

Traditionally, schools of education have been seen in largely functional ways, as sites for training teachers. Our relationship to the more formal disciplines has been largely subordinate and functional. We have been seen as "handmaidens" to disciplines such as English, Math, and History. Our role, popularly conceived, has been to train teachers to effectively implement other people's curricula, typically de-contextualized sets of skills. This position of "gracious submission" has made us particularly vulnerable to recent politically motivated attacks (Pinar, 2004). Key here are the new accountability and testing logics which have largely dominated popular discussion around education. The most notable of these US movements, of course, has been the No Child Left Behind legislation. The effects of this legislation have been broad and deep—including the attenuation of the curricula, both in terms of substance and pedagogical practice—though they have been particularly profound on the most vulnerable of public schools. At the most basic level, a corporate language has overtaken school discourse, a language that implies clear inputs and outputs, assessments and measurements that can be correlated and compared across disparate sites. Knowledge itself has come to be treated like a perfectly transparent commodity, one that can be treated and dispensed independent of particular actors in context.

It should come as little surprise, then, that students who enter teacher training programs often echo such sentiments. Particularly with the rise of high stakes testing, students often want to know "what works" first and foremost. This is of course understandable. High stakes testing has all but colonized the complicated landscape new teachers must traverse. Even those critical of such testing regimes—and I would venture to say most are—recognize that it "is" the reality they must face, whether they like it or not. Such students often long for the "what to do on Monday morning" type of reference texts and pedagogies. This has led to an often de-contextualized approach to learning, an impulse which seems to move across individual subjects or content areas. More than anything, it has led to a particular approach to pedagogy—one of narrow "control" and "competence" on a terrain of material scarcity.

This press for a functional, practical curricula has been happening for some time now (Pinar, 2004). Yet, our moment is unique in one new, critical way. This press for immediately "practical" knowledge about learning, narrowly defined, is now all but mandated

---

* Associate Professor of Sociology of Education at the University at Buffalo, SUNY.

by the federal government. The Educational Science Reform Act of 2002 clearly prioritized experimental research as the "gold standard" for educational research—in particular, large-scale randomized experiments tied to "testable" subjects such as Math and Reading. Most important here are "replicable" studies that make "causal" connections between learning "variables." The goal is easily "generalizable" knowledge tied to a prefigured or defined set of measurable outcomes. This is now "real" or "hard" knowledge. Everything else is—at very best—a luxury. This is now considered the most relevant kind of knowledge.

To echo Maxine Greene, student educators are now asked to address "what is"—not "what can be." This full-scale assault on the pedagogical imagination can profoundly delimit the ways teacher-educators understand and interact with their students. Indeed, even notions of cultural difference have been caught up in this discourse of control and containment. On one level, we see this in the ways cultural knowledge is increasingly deemed as superfluous when set against these new measures of accountability. With student test scores tracked by race, class, and gender, difference is seen as a problem to be managed—not engaged. We see this press for easy, generalizable knowledge brought to bear on questions of difference on a broader level as well. As Cameron McCarthy and I have argued elsewhere, notions of "cultural competence" have provided school administrators with a managerial language which looks to contain difference, rather than engage it in productive ways. This is commonly evidenced in most reductive forms of "multicultural education." Working against what might be called the contemporary "tide of difference," many such educators have all-but ignored the world of multiplicity that flourishes in the everyday lives of youth outside of the school. Such approaches to difference insist on bringing the problems of multiplicity and difference into a technocratic framework of institutional control (Dimitriadis & McCarthy, 2001).

Over the past several years, I have tried to write "against the grain" of contemporary logics in education. With others, I have embraced the kinds of critical and multi-disciplinary paradigms that promise us closer rapprochement with the lives of young people. In this essay, I will reflect on the kind of scholarship I have conducted over the past few years and make a case for why I think such work can be of value to young teachers. In doing so, I will pay particular attention to the question of "class." As I will argue, challenging our students to wrestle with the complex worlds of young people necessarily raises issues of class—not to the exclusion of other modes of oppression but as inextricably intertwined with them. It also challenges us to think about how oppression works in systemic ways. I write against efforts to make "class" one more node of difference with which teachers must be "competent."

Class and pedagogy

Since coming to Buffalo in 1999, I have regularly taught a basic social foundations of education course to incoming teachers. This course is designed to help students think about the contexts within which schooling happens. While most teacher education courses take the classroom as the most basic unit of analysis, this course looks at young people's lives in more expansive and open-ended ways. The course is concerned with young people's lives as they unfold across myriad sites and settings, with "education" as it happens on the margins of formal institutions. The course takes great pains to understand the ways in which various social, cultural, and political contexts can radically circumscribe the kinds of encounters teachers have with students in the classroom. The course is designed to help students reflect on all the things that happen outside the classroom door.

I have sometimes taught my own work in these classes. In particular, I have assigned *Friendship, Cliques, and Gangs: Young Black Men Coming of Age in Urban America* (2003). This book is a deeply contextual look at the lives of two young people living in the urban Midwest over a six-year period, conducted at a community center which both attended. These two young men, Rufus and Tony, were extended family hailing from the same Southern hometown of Humbrick, Mississippi. As I demonstrate, these two youth occupy different places in the popular imagination about black youth—Rufus was "good" and Tony was "bad." Both attended a Midwest community center which was the loci for this work. While similar in many ways, both followed very different life courses. Rufus has stayed clear of trouble, forming close relationships with the club and its staff members. While he has not done particularly well in school, he has participated in many extracurricular activities such as football and has done well in them. A very well-liked teen, Rufus has received a number of awards at the club, including "Youth of the Year," as well as at school. Tony, however, has had a considerably more conflict-ridden life. As he stressed to me a number of times, he has had numerous problems at school with his teachers and with the law throughout his life. He spent nearly all his teen years on probation and was involved with gangs from age thirteen on.

The teens, however, were close friends—they called each other "cousins" even though they are not related by blood—and come from the same home town in Mississippi. Tony had a large family in this Midwest city, including numerous aunts and, most especially, cousins. Rufus, significantly, referred to all of Tony's cousins as his own. They are all roughly the same age and have been Rufus's primary group of friends for his entire life. This group, numbering roughly six, share a long history, even living together in the same house for a time growing up. This house, recently torn down in a city-wide renovation project, was at the center of their early lives, serving as a kind of home base for the group. When Rufus's mother moved up to this town from the South, she stayed in this house with Rufus until she got settled in her own home with the help of one of Tony's aunts—Rufus's godmother—who got her a job. This house was a first stop on the trip from Mississippi for many.

These claimed familial ties were crucial for both teens, as was their friendship generally. Tony looked up to Rufus as a person who could "kick it" or hang out with different groups of people without getting into the kind of trouble he often found himself in. In this Rufus is singular, as other members of the clique had trouble with the law and were also involved, in varying degrees, with gangs. He was also a comforting ear for Tony, who commented that Rufus was "like a counselor" to him, helping him through some particularly hard times. Finally—and perhaps most significantly—Rufus was a living connection to a Southern neighborhood and ethic that Tony prized above all else. In turn, Tony and his family provided Rufus, whose only blood relative in town is his mother, with a family of his own away from his home "down South." He noted: "Like up here, I really don't have no family. I just call Tony and then my cousins 'cause they the closest thing." This large familial network was very important to Rufus, providing him with a sense of solidarity as well as informal protection in the neighborhood. *Friendship, Cliques, and Gangs* detailed their friendship and the ways in which it challenged such reductive stereotypes about youth. The book does not aim for breadth or scope in terms of issues around youth. Rather, I look closely at their notions of friendship, the role of a local community center in their lives, and the ways they sought out relationships with valued older figures in the community. In addition, it traces my ever-evolving and deepening relationship with each.

Tony and Rufus's story grew unexpectedly out of my first book *Performing Identity/Performing Culture: Hip Hop as Text, Pedagogy, and Lived Practice* (2001), a long-term ethnography of young people and their uses of hip hop at a local community center. This book consisted of historical and theoretical commentary as well as three extended ethnographic case studies: the ways Rufus and Tony constructed notions of place through talk about Southern rap; the ways a group of youth constructed notions of history through watching the film *Panther*, a film they connected to hip-hop culture more broadly; and finally, the ways young people constructed notions of "self" through talk about the life, death, and "afterlife" of icon Tupac Shakur. I argued in this book that reception practices—how young people picked up and responded to these hip-hop texts—were unpredictable and became more so when moving from local social networks to individual biographies.

As I demonstrated in *Friendship, Cliques, and Gangs*, my relationship with Rufus and Tony deepened and grew during this period of research. In many respects, my focus on popular culture was derailed by the immediacies of their lives and the ways in which I was called on to be a part of their lives. Indeed, one of the most common questions I am asked when teaching this book is how I as a white man managed to get so close to these two young people. This question is often asked by young teachers who want to think about ways in which they can connect with students. The answer is one that I develop through the narrative of the book. My relationship with these youth deepened as I became a functional part of their lives, as they came to rely on me more and more for meeting their everyday material demands. I was one more resource to meet the myriad and often unpredictable demands that face young people at the margins.

For Tony, providing this support meant trips to McDonald's or rides to the store or work or copies of rap CDs. After he was assaulted and nearly killed for intervening in a conflict involving his cousin, it meant visits to the hospital with various goods or simple companionship when he was in fear of further retaliation from his rivals. According to Tony, a conflict had been building between his cousin and several other youth for some time. They agreed to fight it out, man-to-man, one-on-one. Tony showed up to make sure his cousin had a fair fight. For whatever reason, one of the other youth's friends thought he was a threatening presence and hit him in the head with a baseball bat. He was hospitalized for a time and immobilized for several months when he returned home. During this period, Tony needed personal and material support from those around him. For me, this meant constant visits, DVDs, magazines, trips to fast food places, etc.—anything to distract him from his pain. For Rufus, who lived with only his mom, providing this support meant hauling large bags of clothes to the laundromat, cashing social security checks, and going grocery shopping at discount stores out of town. It also included, when she became increasingly ill, constant trips back and forth with Rufus to the hospital, the nursing home, and the dialysis center. Mary had been diagnosed and mis-diagnosed with a variety of medical problems stemming from her diabetes. Her long spells in the hospital left Rufus on his own, having not only to tend to his own needs and the needs of their household, but to help navigate the Byzantine health and social services agencies in which his mother's life was enmeshed. All of this helped me understand the importance and immediacies of day-to-day survival for these teens. I could never predict quite what these would be. But they were always extremely particular and extremely immediate.

Meeting these needs allowed me to renegotiate my particular relationship with each of these teens and also the young people at the community center more broadly. Yet, the story was not a linear one, with my moving from simple "outsider" to "insider" status. As an older white male from the university, there were parts of their lives to which I could never have access. But the ways we connected around their immediate needs helped open up and deepen my relationship with each. I was always, as a result, negotiating and re-negotiating my own sense of whiteness as it was read and re-read through evolving everyday realities. In addition, I was always negotiating my class status. Growing up relatively privileged, class became more "visible" to me than it ever had been. In particular, it became clear to me how the most mundane of material pressures could radically alter and derail their lives. For example, Tony's glasses were broken in the fight mentioned above. While he was applying for assistance to replace them—a process which took several weeks—he was nearly blind. He could only listen to TV while he recovered from his injuries. He surely could not look for work until he had them. In addition, Rufus developed a severe toothache while his mother was in the hospital. He tried ignoring it, applying tubes of Ambisol to numb the pain. But it was unbearable and he spent many nights crying, couldn't concentrate in school, couldn't work, and eventually had to have several teeth removed. In both cases, the small problems of life—the kind that I would have handled or had handled for me growing up—could alter the course of their lives. Like other nodes of power, class is often invisible to those who benefit from its privileges. While I might have "known" this on some level going into the study, it took on a new resonance for me as this study unfolded.

In some respects, then, the move from *Performing Identity/Performing Culture* to *Friendship, Cliques, and Gangs* signaled a move from a focus on "culture" to one of "class." Yet, I would in the end resist such a reading. The lives of young people rarely allow us such comfortable hermeneutics. Indeed, the language of multi-cultural education has fostered what have been called "additive" or "interlocking" approaches to oppression. (The former implies that one becomes "more" oppressed as one adds various nodes of oppression—being a woman, a lesbian, poor, black, etc. The latter implies that one must look at particular situations to see how these oppressive forces interact.) While I am certainly more sympathetic with the latter approach, each implies that we can look at and separate race, class, gender, disability, sexuality, etc., as distinct axes of analysis. The work of James Banks (2005) and other multi-cultural educators often betrays an impulse to create neat taxonomies to help explain away young people's lives. One assumes that young people's experiences of their raced, classed, or gendered selves can be pulled apart for heuristic value—and then put back together again.

Our encounters with young people, however, typically exceed these distinctions in critical ways. As I argue here, embodied narratives such as these disrupt ideas about cultural competence. As we get closer and closer to the particularities of young people's lives, we see how they live in the middle of multiple, overlapping, and often contradictory modes of identification. It is very difficult in a study such as mine to offer simple "take away" lessons that can be applied in rote and unthinking fashion in other contexts. Rufus and Tony's lives were motivated by the immediate and pressing demands of being young, poor, and black. This complicated, particular nexus resists the kinds of heuristics that many multi-cultural educators offer. Such narratives put us in the middle of strug-gles that we can try to think through—not master or "solve" in ready-to-hand ways.

As we move into new and uncertain economic times, we must not let "class" fall into the easy managerial language that has so marked multi-cultural education. In this respect, economic class is the one mode of "difference" that has yet to be fully collapsed into this narrow technocratic language. While "class" is typically mentioned as a key node of difference in multi-cultural education, it has not lent itself to the kinds of "what to do on Monday morning" solutions that have tended to mark questions of "race." There is no simple "celebration of cultural difference" that can easily encompass class. And this is not a bad thing. I will look now at the broader debate about class and its possibilities and dangers. I will then look at one popular but extremely limited approach to teaching about class—the Ruby Payne industry. I will conclude with my own thoughts about how teacher-educators can take up such issues.

Class

While Americans are famously loath to talk about questions of class, the realities of economic inequality in this country can no longer be comfortably denied. On one level, we see this in our now well established move from an industrial to a post-industrial global economy. More and more young people will spend their lives working in service sector jobs that provide minimal income, no (or almost no) benefits, and little job secu-rity. On another, broader level, we see this in the ways that *all* labor is coming to operate under these logics. For example, as Simon Head (2003) points out, many of the so-called white collar job sectors (e.g., those of IT [Information Technology] and health care) have come to "manage" or "reengineer" the work of its employees in much the same way that Walmart and others do—segmenting job tasks into discrete units, "flexibly" farming them out to the cheapest possible workers. The net effect has been new, massive concen-trations of wealth into fewer and fewer hands—at every level.

Economic indices do not always adequately reflect these everyday realities. As Stanley Aronowitz writes in *Just Around the Corner* (2005), we are in the midst of what he calls a "jobless recovery." The economic growth often associated with big public spending projects (as outlined by Keynes) has served to spur some measures of economic growth, but their effects are not being felt by the majority of citizens. The spending on the Iraq war, a key example, has not fostered the kind of broad-based economic growth that spending on World War II did. Larger and larger sums of money are being spent on more intense weapons development projects that benefit smaller groups of people. Indeed, the cost of the war in Iraq, the National Priority Project estimates, is now over $340 billion. Clearly, this kind of spending is not benefiting poor or even middle-class US citizens. In fact, this kind of military spending has served to justify "belt tightening" domestically. As Francis Fox Piven has recently argued in *The War at Home* (2006), "war" overseas has served to justify wholesale pillaging back home—cuts in taxes to serve the very wealthy and large-scale industrial deregulation, for example. Again, we are at a moment of new, massive concentrations of wealth, with particular implications for the education and work worlds of those still in school.

As "class" has moved to the forefront of mainstream debate and discussion, I would argue, it has not yet settled comfortably into a dominant discourse. We are poised to address the question in any number of ways—some of which will keep us firmly in place, some of which might take us in new and more productive directions. I recall here the recent collection *Class Matters*, collected from the year-long series by the *New York Times*. The series was in many respects remarkable. It looked to talk about the massive divisions in wealth that have rapidly accelerated in this country over the past few years. The book discusses the often blind faith that US citizens have in their ability to transcend class—and the difficulty in so doing. As Janny Scott and David Leonhardt elegantly write in the book's first chapter, "Mobility is the promise that lies at the heart of the American dream" (p. 2). However, "new research on mobility, the movement of families up and down the economic ladder, shows that there is far less of it than economists once thought and less than most people believe" (p. 2). They go on to document the "extraordinary jump in income inequality" that has come to mark the last decades:

> The after-tax income of the top 1 percent of American households jumped 139 percent, to more than $700,000, from 1979–2001, according to the Congressional Budget Office, which adjusted its numbers to account for inflation. The income of the middle fifth rose by just 17 percent, to $43,700, and the income of the poorest fifth rose only 9 percent.
>
> (p. 19)

Clearly, we are at a moment when economic divisions are accelerating at a rapid pace—and the terms for discussion are largely up for grabs. We see this evidenced starkly in the range and type of contributions to this fine book. I would like to contrast two such articles in the book, each of which tells us very different things about "class"—"A Marriage of Unequals" by Tamar Lewin and "Life at the Top in America Isn't Just Better, It's Longer" by Janny Scott. Reading these articles in counter-distinction to each other allows us to see the ways questions of class can be taken up in different ways with different implications.

The first article, "A Marriage of Unequals," discusses the question of cross-class marriages. The author argues that the issues in cross-class marriages are often similar to the ones in cross-race marriages. The article is certainly interesting and informative. But it largely reduces class to a set of simple identity markers that can be isolated and mobilized. Lewin writes,

> Marriages that cross class boundaries may not present as obvious a set of challenges as those that cross the lines of race or nationality. But in a quiet way, people who marry across class lines are also moving outside their comfort zones, into the uncharted territory of partners with a different level of wealth and education, and often, a different set of assumptions of things like manners, food, child-rearing, gift-giving, and how to spend vacations. In cross-class marriages, one partner will usually have more money, more options, and, almost inevitably, more power.
>
> (pp. 53–54)

While the author gestures toward questions of power, we see class here largely reduced to a set of behavioral characteristics. The danger here is what Michael Apple calls the "gritty materialities" of class that get lost in discussions about social comportment, discussions which can remove questions of economic inequality from a powerful sense of history and social context.

In distinction, the latter article looks closely at the ways social class permeates all aspects of our lived, embodied practice—with life and death consequences. Here, the author looks closely at three different people who had heart attacks, and traces the consequences for each. This includes an elite architect, a solidly middle-class utility worker, and a working-class maid. Scott writes, "Architect, utility worker, maid: heart attack is the great leveler, and in those first fearful moments, three New Yorkers with little in common faced a single common threat. But in the months that followed, their experiences diverged" (p. 28). As the author demonstrates, one's class not only has implications for the kinds of medical care one can afford, but for the range of less visible variables. She continues,

> Class informed everything from the circumstances of their heart attacks to the emergency care each received, the households they returned to, and the jobs they hoped to resume. It shaped their understanding of their illness, the support they got from their families, their relationships with their doctors. It helped define their ability to change their lives and shaped their odds of getting better.
>
> (p. 28)

The article goes on to detail the ways in which this devastating phenomena had significantly different effects depending upon one's place in the class spectrum. We see class saturate every aspect of the lives of these patients, often in interlocking and deeply contextual ways.

A key example here is the question of "diet." Each of these patients has been given advice about what to eat and what not to eat. The wealthy architect, Jean Miele, has a stay-at-home wife who shops for healthy foods and takes time to make different and good tasting meals. Miele has a relatively easy time eating in healthy ways. Will Wilson, the middle-class African-American transportation worker, had a harder time. Largely wed to the kinds of foods he grew up with, fried chicken, pork chops, and macaroni and cheese, Wilson found it more difficult to eat the kinds of grains recommended by his doctor. He did make "lukewarm" efforts, however, as he and his wife attended more closely to his diet. Finally, Eva Gora, the Polish working-class maid, had the hardest time of all. Food was one of the only areas of her life she had control over. It was all but impossible to give up eating McDonald's and other kinds of fast food. She did not stick to her diet.

These notions of class are thick and deep. They saturate the lives of all social actors across the class spectrum, with life and death consequences. They cannot be reduced to a set of identity markers such as "assumptions of things like manners, food, child-rearing, gift-giving, and how to spend vacations." We see here what Apple calls the "gritty materialities" of class—the ways people are situated in unfair ways, with life options and chances doled out accordingly. As economic inequality comes to the forefront of popular consciousness, I argue, we must not lose a deep and passionate sense of class as a fully embodied experience that structures our lives in deeply unfair ways.

To return to the earlier discussion, my connection with the two youth in my study—clearly, poor youth at the margins—was around the specific material circumstances of their lives. Their lives were saturated and shot through with questions of class, tangled up in race and gender, and also a function of their individual personalities. Their friendship with each other, so critical to each at a key juncture in their lives, was not solely a function of their race, their class status, their gender, or even their individual stories. It was a function of all of these at once. Understanding how and why they resonated with a local community center and not school, for example, meant understanding all as they worked in deft unison. No one could be abstracted and mobilized to make school more "culturally relevant." Treating the lives of such youth in our classrooms is not easy business—nor should it be.

Class and education

The field of education is slowly developing its own discourse around issues of class—with attendant possibilities and dangers. I would like to look now at the latter of such danger, particularly as represented by the Ruby Payne industry which has built up over the past few years. Payne's company "aha! Process, Inc" offers a range of products and services, built upon the idea that one can discover the rules of middle-class life and teach them to working-class students. Her programs are designed to uncover these hidden rules and teach them to young people. We see here efforts to collapse questions of economic class into simple rules that can be learned and mastered. In this sense, class is "operationalized" as a kind of identity marker.

Payne's most popular book is undoubtedly *A Framework for Understanding Poverty* (2005). In this book, Payne provides a "user-friendly" guide for educators and other service providers, uncovering and exposing the ways in which cross-class difference is often about misunderstanding, about not understanding the "rules" of wealth. In fact, Payne seems loath to talk about structural class distinctions. Throughout the book, Payne refers to the class structure as one of "economic diversity." Never does she talk of this "economic diversity" as unfair—it is simply the case that "individuals are stationed all along the continuum of income; they sometimes move on that continuum as well" (p. 2). Underlying this "economic diversity" is a deep-seated code system. According to Payne, "Schools and businesses operate from middle-class norms and use the hidden rules of middle class. . . . for our students to be successful, we must understand their hidden rules and teach them the rules that will make them successful at school and work" (p. 3). These rules are various, largely revolving around issues of identity and comportment. For example, she discusses attitudes toward food. For those in poverty, quantity is important—"did you have enough?" For the middle class, the key question is that of quality—"did you enjoy it?" For the wealthy, presentation is important—"was it presented well?" (pp. 42–43). Other categories include clothing, time, language, and humor.

We see here an effort to reduce class (poverty, middle class, and wealth) to a handful of behavioral characteristics which can then be taught to young people to help traverse the class spectrum. The effort is of course reductive. The book's back cover, in fact, highlights as a selling point the book's many "helpful charts and summaries." The effort is also dangerously stereotypical at times. For example, in her discussion of the "hidden codes" of class, she charts the family structure of those in different class strata—those in poverty tend to have "matriarchal" families, those in the middle class tend to have "patriarchal" ones, and those with wealth tend to have structures dictated by "who has money" (pp. 42–43). In foregrounding class as an explanatory mechanism, Payne ignores all the ways gender can have its own autonomy and can intersect with class in new ways. Lois Weis's (2004) recent work comes immediately to mind. According to Weis, the young, working-class men who can survive in this new, economic terrain are the ones who can renegotiate their gender roles in flexible ways. They are the ones who, for example, can share childcare or can pool resources with partners as they take on jobs traditionally coded as "feminine" (e.g., nurses assistant). Weis came to this conclusion re-interviewing young adults from her earlier study. It came from a deep understanding of their narratives as they unfolded over time. Seen in this light, Payne's work can be dangerously reductive. It can take us away from people's lived lives and to the realm of hardened stereotype. As such, Payne's book echoes the managerial language of many reductive forms of multi-cultural education—the kind which tries to create "culturally relevant" pedagogies that often ignore the complex cultural lives of youth.

I argue here that we need to vigorously resist such efforts. In a moment where "quick fixes" dominate pedagogical common sense, we should struggle with our students toward more difficult kinds of knowledge. One might contrast, to return to the above, how "food" is discussed in Janny Scott's "Life at the Top in America Isn't Just Better, It's Longer" with how it is discussed in Payne's *A Framework for Understanding Poverty* (2005). Scott deeply contextualizes the choices the three heart attack patients make about what they eat. As she demonstrates, the wealthy architect's "good choices" are the result of a whole host of contextual forces and factors, including a stay-at-home wife who can buy and prepare pricey and tasty food for Miele. They include, as well, the fact that Miele's life choices and options allow him a "long view" on his health. In turn, the medi-ocre choices of Wilson, the middle-class African-American, reflect both his more limited circumstances and resources as well as his cultural investments in his foods of choice. Finally, the "poor choices" of Gora, the Polish working-class maid, reflect the ways in which she exercises her limited agency where she can find it—no matter how self-destruc-tive. For Gora, this means eating the unhealthy fast food she has grown to love—though it has consequences for her long-term well-being. As Scott notes, food is one of the very few areas of Gora's life that she feels some control over. Contrast these rich and textured accounts with Payne's simple delineation of how those along the "economic spectrum" feel about food—from "did you have enough?" to "was it presented well?"

I argue here for a "thick materiality" which will put us in touch with the ways in which class, culture, and biography intersect. To return to our earlier discussion, such texts do not often have easy "take away" lessons about learning or even youth more broadly. Such texts often work against the grain of contemporary logics in education which tend to stress facile notions of control and competency. Indeed, one of the most important lessons we can learn from young people is the limits of facile notions of peda-gogical competency. I am often asked, when teaching *Friendship, Cliques, and Gangs*, if I "helped" the youth in the study, if somehow my wiser perspective on their lives allowed them to see themselves in new ways. The answer, sadly, is "no." The material circum-stances of these youth, I argue, were always paramount. They did not need or want me to tell them that their decisions were good or bad ones. They continually faced specific, immediate, and overwhelming needs. I tried to meet them here, on this fraught terrain.

I was, however, able to challenge my own agendas and preconceptions about youth, opening up a richer space to think about the possibilities inherent in all pedagogical encounters. In many ways, the complexities of their lives forced me to always question any notion of easy and premature closure in my own thinking about education—where it happens, around what texts, and toward what ends. I try, in my own classes, to work with young people toward such "difficult knowledge"—with economic location a key node therein.

Toward a broader understanding of economic inequality: concluding thoughts

As I noted at the outset of this chapter, the push for a "functional" curricula tied to measurable "outcomes" now dominates school discourse—from federally mandated policy to everyday classroom practice. The "gold standard" here is "generalizable" findings generated from and tied to randomized experiments. This kind of work is often counter-posed with qualitative work which often seems small scale and not relevant beyond the particulars of individual studies. I would like to close this essay by challenging these assumptions, particularly as they relate to our understandings of class. Indeed, studies such as *Friendship, Cliques, and Gangs* are often criticized for the ways they draw on small "samples," for the ways they seem so particular to idiosyncratic, individual lives. The question is typically, "what does this tell us about the world outside of the experiences of these particular individuals?" The issue is complex. When we remove research from the terrain of replicable methods and approaches, we enter the realm of individual and collective narrative. The rich and detailed case studies which often result can be critical for students thinking through and imagining their own connections with youth. They should not be marginalized, nor seen as ancillary to "real" scientific work.

In fact, I have often heard students in my classes and others say "I know those kids!" or "I was that kid!" when reading my book. The response is not atypical—I know of many other qualitative researchers who have heard similar such responses to their work. Clearly, there is something in this narrative and others like it that resonate across our individual studies, challenging the ways in which we think about research and the relationship between research and pedagogy. Emerging from contemporary concerns with "generalizability," the preferred method for much teacher education is now influenced by what might be called a "power point" approach to pedagogy. The results of large-scale studies are mined for "useful tips" which can then be easily deployed in the classroom. I argue that our particular stories—stories like these or those in Weis's *Class Reunion* (2004), MacLeod's *Ain't No Makin' It* (1995), or Devine's *Maximum Security* (1995), among many, many others—give us another angle of vision on the question of generalizable knowledge.

As Michelle Fine notes, many social scientists have been overly "concerned with the technical specificity of empirical generalizability"—that is, the question of formally and technically replicating studies—at the same time we are "under concerned with generalizability of theory and action" (in press). According to Fine, the latter means talking in more open-ended ways about how our ideas and experiences evoke similar issues across different sites, pushing toward an intellectual rather than technical generalizability. This gets us closer to what Fine calls "theoretical generalizability"—a way to "deeply investigate what about [our] findings resonates (or not) in particular settings" (Fine, in press). Even more broadly, Fine takes us from this notion of "theoretical" to "provocative" generalizability. Echoing the work of Maxine Greene, she maintains that looking across sites allows us to "to move [our] findings toward that which is not yet imagined, not yet in practice, not yet in sight" (Fine, in press).

Looking at such similar stories across different contexts allows us to think simultaneously about the ways in which broad structural questions of class difference might be addressed. The charge here is paying attention to the specificity of individual experience in all its particularity while looking more broadly at how we are all situated by larger structures not "of our own choosing." In many ways, we need to work toward a language that gets us past a very old and very unhelpful set of dichotomies—between structure and agency, the general and particular, etc. I look toward a scholarship that is both intensely particular—documenting in brutal detail the ways in which economic inequality plays out in individual lives—and bold in its claims about broad resonance. Indeed, there is a reason these stories seem so familiar to people. It is because the brutalities of economic inequality structure people's lives in remarkably durable and similar ways. Finding a language to address both imperatives seems our contemporary charge, both in and out of the classroom.

Questions for discussion

1. Discuss the author's perceptions of the new accountability and testing logics dominating education today. How do these trends impact contemporary educational practices and social research?
2. Dimitriadis argues that the discourse and practice of "multi-cultural education" and the notion of "cultural competence" are problematic for understanding the everyday lives of youth. Why is the circulation of these notions considered problematic? How is social class related to this discussion?
3. The author suggests that teachers should not teach class-based distinctions in a managerial way, but should struggle with students to gain a more difficult knowledge of the "gritty materialities" of youth. What kinds of pedagogical strategies might be employed within the context of the classroom to initiate a turn away from the containment of difference?
4. The chapter concludes by counter-posing randomized experiments which offer "generalizable findings" with the nature of qualitative work. Based upon this discussion, how might the author's experimental discourse contribute to the contemporary debates surrounding qualitative research?
5. If class is one more node of difference in which teachers must be competent, what are the pragmatic/ethical issues that teachers will encounter when trying to "help" lower class students? Can class be taught? What are the implications of such teachings?
6. Discuss Dimitriadis's perspective on the Ruby Payne industry. What does this say about the US attitude toward class?
7. Today, if a teacher is willing to engage with young people, especially those who are disadvantaged, what kind of challenges will s/he face? While discussing this question, consider the recent movements toward accountability in the US educational system.
8. What are the various methodological dilemmas and issues that Dimitriadis, situating himself as the researcher, brings up in this chapter? How do they inform his research work discussed herein?

Note

I would like to thank Lois Weis for her helpful feedback on this chapter.

References

Aronowitz, S. (2005). *Just around the corner: The paradox of the jobless recovery*. Philadelphia: Temple University Press.

Banks, J. (2005). *Race, culture, and education: The selected works of James Banks*. New York: Routledge.

Devine, J. (1995). *Maximum security*. Chicago: University of Chicago Press.

Dimitriadis, G. (2001). *Performing identity/performing culture: Hip hop as text, pedagogy, and lived practice*. New York: Peter Lang.

—— (2003). *Friendship, cliques, and gangs: Young black men coming of age in urban America*. New York: Teachers College Press, Columbia University.

Dimitriadis, G., & McCarthy, C. (2001). *Reading and teaching the postcolonial: From Baldwin to Basquiat and beyond*. New York: Teachers College Press, Columbia University.

Fine, M. (in press). *Bearing witness: Methods for researching oppression and resistance*.

Head, S. (2003). *The new ruthless economy*. Oxford: Oxford University Press.

Lewin, T. (2005). A marriage of unequals. In *New York Times* Correspondents (Eds.), *Class matters* (pp. 63–72). New York: Times Books.

New York Times Correspondents (Eds.) (2005). *Class matters*. New York: Times Books.

Macleod, J. (1995). Ain't no making it: Aspirations and attainment in a low-income neighborhood. Boulder, CO: Westview Press.

Payne, R. (2005). *A framework for understanding poverty*. Highlands, TX: aha! Process Inc.

Pinar, W. (2004). *What is curriculum theory?* Mahwah, NJ: Lawrence Earlbaum Press.

Piven, F. (2006). *The war at home: The domestic costs of Bush's militarism*. New York: The New Press.

Scott, J. (2005). Life at the top in America isn't just better, it's longer. In *New York Times* Correspondents (Eds.), *Class matters* (pp. 27–50). New York: Times Books.

Scott, J., & Leonhardt, D. (2005). Shadowy lines that still divide. In *New York Times* Correspondents (Eds.), *Class matters* (pp. 1–26). New York: Times Books.

Weis, L. (2004). *Class reunion*. New York: Routledge.

Chapter 18

Social class and higher education

A reorganization of opportunities

*Scott L. Thomas and Angela Bell**

Introduction

Karabel's 2006 volume on admissions at America's most elite private colleges calls attention to the ways in which college admissions policies reflect the power relations among major social groups in the USA. It has been argued that subordinate social classes have long experienced these inequalities in part because they lack the political power for effective mobilization in order to call attention to such class-based differences (Karen, 1991). Karabel's work powerfully elucidates the sources of this relative powerlessness and ties it to the larger preoccupation by scholars, policy-makers, and the general public about inequalities among college participation rates.

Over the past decade, much attention has been directed toward understanding racial and gender inequalities in access, marking conditions of inequality and progress in the equalization in educational opportunity (e.g., Hurtado, Inkelas, Briggs & Rhees, 1997; Perna, 2000; St. John, 1991; St. John, Musoba & Simmons, 2003). More recently, new lines of inquiry have been opened to better understand the processes driving the significant and persistent lag in the college participation rates of students from subordinate social classes (e.g., Kane, 2001; McDonough, 1997; St. John et al., 2003). While much of this work has focused on rates of college participation generally, very little attention has been given to the wide variance in the qualitative aspects of that participation. College experiences, and the ultimate value of those experiences, vary widely and are often tightly bound to social class origins and future life course outcomes.

Through this chapter we evidence one aspect of the processes that perpetuate class-based inequalities within the higher education enterprise. We note that, while poor and minority students are entering colleges and universities in greater numbers, the US system of higher education threatens to evolve into a system of *de facto* segregation between these new entrants and those students from more privileged backgrounds who have traditionally participated in higher education as a "rite of passage" for the middle and upper classes.

The historical exclusivity and class-based inequalities in the elite private sector are well documented (e.g., Bowen & Bok, 1998; Bowen, Kurzwell & Tobin, 2005; Karabel, 2006) and are therefore of less interest to us than are the persistent and growing inequalities at the nation's increasingly elite public colleges and universities. Many of today's

* Scott L. Thomas is Associate Professor and Angela Bell a doctoral candidate at the Institute of Higher Education at the University of Georgia.

most notable emerging elite public universities were originally established as part of the Morrill Act of 1862 to "promote the liberal and practical education of the industrial classes in the several pursuits and professions in life" (Morrill Act of 1862, sec 4). It would be these very institutions that helped to fuel America's unparalleled economic growth through the turn of the twentieth century and into the "Gilded Age"—a period that was distinguished by both the fruits of tremendous economic growth and, somewhat ironically, punishing class inequalities in the USA.

But these too were the institutions that figured centrally in the contraction of those inequalities in the mid-twentieth century. Through a combination of the Great Depression, New Deal programs, World War II, and a dramatic opening of the US higher education system (largely through the Serviceman's Readjustment Act of 1944), what has been referred to as the *Great Compression*—a drastic reduction in the income gaps defining social and economic life of the Gilded Age—emerged (Goldin & Margo, 1992). Of course, inequality still existed in the middle part of the twentieth century, but the income gaps defining that era of Gilded Age America were powerfully reduced, enabling new opportunities for upward mobility and the emergence of a burgeoning middle-class society.

We suggest through this chapter that a more recent destabilization of the middle class has contributed to heightened status concerns that have, in turn, resulted in a reorganization of the opportunity structure within the US higher education system. This reorganization is serving to solidify the grasp of the middle classes on institutions that were previously much more downwardly class-inclusive. The twin structural barriers of unequal opportunity for academic preparation and increasingly unaffordable tuition and fee pricing are today systematically discouraging opportunities for enrollment at these institutions by members of subordinate classes. The cost of this reorganization may be measured in terms of diminished labor market positions for students from the lower and working classes and a subsequent attenuation of faith in the principle that higher education is a vehicle for socioeconomic mobility.

Over the past fifteen years a remarkable economic enrichment of the upper middle and upper classes has helped to fuel a hyper-competitive environment for admission to the nation's most selective colleges. A by-product of the intense demand for the slots at the more elite schools is a trickle-down in demand for spaces at schools at which the admissions process used to be much less competitive. Even with significant expansion at many of these relatively less selective schools, the crush of applicants from more affluent backgrounds can be seen as squeezing out students from less affluent backgrounds who, in turn, enroll in institutions even further down the prestige hierarchy.

There are two main drivers of this reorganization: (1) great differentials in the ability to prepare academically for college, and (2) spiraling costs of college attendance combined with shifts in financial aid that place a greater share of the increased financial responsibility on the shoulders of students and their families. First consider that academic preparation is powerfully connected to social class. Merit in the college admissions process is typically measured by a combination of high school GPA, the range of college preparatory courses taken, SAT exam scores, and class rank. Wealth brings well-documented advantages in K-12 schooling and extracurricular activities that factor directly into students' performance on these measures that are critical in the college admissions process (Oakes & Saunders, 2004; Orfield & Lee, 2005; Perna, 2003; Weis & Fine, 1993).

For many students from lower income backgrounds the opportunity to prepare academically is tied as much to the quality of the primary and secondary schools as it is to access to college preparatory classes that will qualify for consideration in the college admissions process at more selective schools. Also at issue is the relative lack of availability of knowledgeable college counselors to aid in academic strategies that will be viewed favorably by college admissions officers (McDonough, 1997; Perna, 2003). The children of more affluent parents, on the other hand, are more likely to attend schools with a breadth of college prep courses and ample staffing for college counseling (Perna et al., 2006). Moreover, many more affluent parents are better able to strategize and position their children for success through private tutoring, college counseling, and SAT preparation courses that are known to improve high school GPAs and performance on standardized admissions tests such as the SAT. All of these realities have a powerful influence on the ability of a student to appear more or less "meritorious" in the eyes of campus admissions officers. Lower SES students meanwhile have fewer resources (monetary, academic, and otherwise) at their disposal to translate their talents into competitive applications.

The other major factor in this reshaping of the opportunity structure is the dramatic increase in the cost of college attendance over the past decade. State higher education budgets have shrunk, leading public colleges and universities to increase tuition and student fee charges by almost 200 percent since 1981 (College Board, 2006a; Heller, 2002). Private college tuitions have increased roughly 150 percent in the same period. The National Center for Public Policy and Higher Education estimates that families in the bottom income quartile in 2005 would have to devote 73 percent of their annual income to cover the costs of attending the average public four-year institution for a single year (National Center for Public Policy and Higher Education, 2006). The economic impact of these increasing costs is compounded by shifts in institutional, state, and federal financial aid policies that place a greater weight on loans than grants and on "non-need" aid such as scholarships rather than forms of "need-based" aid that were much more commonplace a decade ago (College Board, 2006b; St. John & Asker, 2003). In sum, the financial costs of college are becoming prohibitive for many students from lower income families.

Simultaneously, many colleges, some more cash strapped than others and all more tuition reliant than in the past, recognized that a new market was emerging and began to reshape themselves to attract the more affluent students who are able to bear a greater share of the increasing cost of tuition. Some of these institutions became much more selective (as we will show below), moving into the market for "star" faculty, and offering amenities ranging from elaborate recreation centers to luxury dorms (Ehrenberg, 2002). In the private sector, complex forms of enrollment management and tuition discounting became important tools for managing admissions to ensure the maximization of increasingly precious tuition revenue (Davis, 2003; Redd, 2000, 2002). Schools offer significantly reduced tuition to highly qualified students in order to lure them from other institutions, increase the credentials of the entering class, and thereby increase the prestige of the institution. In some cases, former tacit agreements to maintain need-blind admissions have been undermined in order to increase the number of enrollees who do not need aid.

In the next section we provide a capsule history of the US higher education system in the middle and late parts of the twentieth century. This description of the evolution of the higher education system is important because we are interested in the processes by which this reorganization of institutions has occurred.

Massification and diversification of higher education

Unparalleled expansion has occurred in the US higher education system over the past sixty years, with total enrollments growing from 2.3 million students in 1947 to just over 17 million students in 2004 (Snyder, Tan & Hoffman, 2006). Much of this growth is attributable to direct government intervention in the form of the GI Bill, which provided funding of college opportunities for those returning from World War II, and the Civil Rights Act of 1965 which paved the way for the end of segregation in American schools and colleges. The rate of growth early in this period outpaced the system's physical capacity in many instances, a challenge that was eased through monumental government investment associated with the space race and the Cold War (Diamond & Graham, 1997; Geiger, 2004). Expenditures of all colleges and universities rose from 2.3 percent of the US GDP in 1949 to the current high of 4.7 percent (it has hovered between 3.7 and 4.7 percent since 1963).

A couple of items related to this expansion of higher education are particularly noteworthy. First, this growth truly represented an expansion of access as opposed to a simple accommodation of population growth. Consider that the population of those 18 to 24 years old (i.e., traditional college-going age) in 1947 was 16.4 million while in 2004 it stood at just over 29.1 million—a roughly 78 percent increase (US Census Bureau, 2006). So while the college age population increased by 78 percent between these two points, college enrollments grew by 639 percent (from above). Or consider that just over 45 percent of high school completers were enrolled in college within twelve months of leaving high school in 1960. By 2004, that enrollment rate had jumped to almost 67 percent (Snyder, Tan & Hoffman, 2006, table 182). Students attending on a part-time basis increased from 34 percent in 1959 to a high of 44 percent in 1992 before settling back to 39 percent by 2004 (Snyder, Tan & Hoffman, 2006, table 170). So by these and many other measures, new entrants to higher education thronged to college campuses around the nation.

In addition to overall growth in college participation, the racial/ethnic and gender diversification of the higher education system has increased markedly. By 1972, Black, White, and Hispanic recent high school graduates reported college enrollment rates of 44.6 percent, 49.7 percent, and 45 percent respectively (Snyder, Tan & Hoffman, 2006, table 181) (we note here however that the dramatically lower rate of Black and Hispanic high school completion rates mask larger structural problems in the racial diversification of our nation's campuses). Women, who in 1960 had a continuation rate of only 37.9 percent within twelve months of completing high school (compared to a 54 percent rate for men), began eclipsing the male enrollment rate by the mid-1970s. By the early part of the twenty-first century over three-quarters of women were continuing on to college within twelve months of completing high school (compared to 61 percent of men) eliciting alarm by many in the education community. Women represented 55 percent of all 18 to 24-year-old undergraduates in 2003 (Snyder, Tan & Hoffman, 2006, calculated from table 173).

A second noteworthy element of this expansion was the growth and shift of institutional types (see Tables 18.1A and 18.1B). Just after World War II, there were about

Table 18.1A Number and distribution of higher education institutions, 1949–2005

	1949–50	2004–05
Total institutions	1,851	4,216
4-year percent of total	72%	60%
2-year percent of total	28%	40%
Public institutions (percent of total)	641 (35%)	1,700 (40%)
4-year percent of publics	54%	38%
2-year percent of publics	46%	62%
Private institutions (percent of total)	1,210 (65%)	2,516 (60%)
4-year percent of privates	81%	75%
2-year percent of privates	19%	25%

Table 18.1B Higher education enrollments by control of institution

	1949–50	2004–05
Total institutions	2,444,900	17,272,044
Percent enrolled in publics	49%	75%
Percent enrolled in privates	51%	25%

Source: Snyder, Tan, and Hoffman, 2006.

1,850 colleges and universities in the USA with roughly twice as many private institutions as there were public. Two-year colleges constituted about 46 percent of public colleges and about 19 percent of private schools. Student enrollments were evenly split between the public and private sectors. By 2004, 75 percent of the total enrollment was to be found on public campuses. Private sector enrollments were now split into two categories—the traditional not-for-profit colleges and for-profit campuses, a relative newcomer. Public institutions (1,700) accounted for 40 percent of all degree granting colleges and approximately two-thirds of those (1,061) were community college campuses. In 2005, there were 2,516 private colleges and universities with about one-quarter (622) of those being two-year colleges. Two important trends here are the large increase in proportion of students attending public institutions (from 49 percent to 75 percent) and the simultaneous growth in the share of public institutions that are two-year colleges. A full 72 percent of the growth in the public sector over this time period can be accounted for by creation of two-year schools.

From one perspective, the American Dream—of which the opportunity for college access is a large part—is alive and well. There is greater diversity in college type and more students from a variety of social and religious backgrounds are attending college than ever before. Indeed, even the most elite campuses in the USA have diversified in notable ways across this sixty-year window. People of color, Jews, and women have all found their way to the nation's most prestigious campuses, rendering the white Anglo-Saxon Protestant male the minority. In short, gender and race gaps in postsecondary participation overall have considerably narrowed over the past fifty years.

But underlying these numbers are alarming realities that are, for many, quite at odds with the logical ends of that American dream. Consider first that despite the much heralded closure of gaps in the college enrollment rate, college completion rates (bacca-laureate or higher) of those 25 to 29 for those who enrolled in college after high school range from the mid-30 percent range for Hispanics and Blacks to 75.9 percent for Asians (about 53 percent of Whites complete by age 25 to 29) (Mortenson, 2006b). Men, on average, are completing at lower levels than women, thus compounding the disadvantage resulting from their declining enrollment rates over the past thirty years. With the esca-lating cost of college (College Board, 2006a) and breathtaking increases in the reliance on student loans to finance these costs, the economic penalties to the individual for not completing are greater than ever (Price, 2004).

Class stratification in higher education

While much attention has been paid to race and gender inequalities, systematic focus on class-based inequalities in higher education has proven more difficult due to a paucity of hard data on participation by class. Class, unlike other officially measured categories such as race, gender, or religion, is not carefully tracked in higher education or other social institutions in the USA. This is in part due to the US tendency of denying the power of class in everyday life, denial fostered by a belief that, at its core, US society is power-fully meritocratic. There is a pervasive belief that with hard work and persistence any reasonably intelligent person, regardless of his or her initial social station, can realize meaningful upward socioeconomic mobility. The counterpoint to this belief is, of course, that failure is a direct function of personal deficiency rather than structural circumstance. Belief in this idea is a driving force behind notions of "meritocracy" that help to preserve the social and political order in the USA. Karabel (2006) and Brint and Karabel (1989) offer thorough considerations of this logic highlighting the distinction between equality of opportunity and equality of condition.

Understanding how class maps onto contemporary college opportunities necessitates a brief consideration of the landscape of higher education. The array of colleges and universities in the USA has been defined in many different ways. In the current vernac-ular, this array is often referred to as the higher education marketplace, where customers (students) compare the costs and presumed benefits of institutions for which they are qualified. This vernacular reflects an important trend toward a largely private valuation of higher education with little or no direct regard for the value of higher education as a social good. The shift in emphasis on higher education as a private good is encouraged by rampant increases in tuition over the past twenty years, with increasing attention being called to the enhanced earning power enjoyed by college graduates as a rationalization for continued investment by the students and their families.

As offensive as this metaphor of the marketplace may be to some, it enables a powerful illustration of the "value" of goods in this market—a market that can be logically segmented in a number of ways. Zemsky offered one such segmentation scheme in 1997, arraying the distribution across a continuum from "Name Brand" (elite) institutions to the "Convenience/User Friendly" (open access) institutions. Through this segmentation scheme, Zemsky shows a remarkable pattern of consistent advantages enjoyed by students attending more selective institutions. The advantages of attending institutions at the name brand end of the spectrum include higher earnings, a greater likelihood of enrollment in post-graduate education, and greater levels of civic participation. Prestige-conferring institutions such as these are also those with the highest tuition and fee prices and among those with the greatest rate of growth in those prices over recent years.

Elite higher education opportunities cannot, by definition, be expanded in significant ways without reducing their value. The expansion of the past six decades therefore has largely taken place in sectors of lesser prestige such as the community college, state colleges and universities, and through the expansion of the public flagship research university. We provide data in the following section that illustrates the ways in which this expansion has impacted students from low-income families over the last decade.

Patterns defining the reorganization

One way of tracking this reorganization of higher education opportunity is to look at who is attending the selective institutions in the USA. While the continuation of low-income and non-traditional students on to college has climbed over the latter part of the twentieth century, attendance by these students at the more selective institutions has declined over the past ten years. Although higher education institutions are not required to report their enrollments by income background, data on the number of students who receive Pell Grants are available. The Pell Grant program is the federal government's first line of support for students from low-income families. These grants are modest in size with the average grant in 2006 being $2,354 (College Board, 2006b). The 2003–4 Federal Pell Grant Program End-of-Year Report indicates that 83 percent of dependent Pell Grant recipients at four-year institutions came from families with incomes equal to or below $40,000, and 78 percent of all Pell recipients had family income equal to or below $30,000. Table 18.2 shows the percent of enrollees at different types of institutions who are Pell Grant recipients as of 2001.

Rather than chipping away at the persistent class-based gap, the "best" institutions as defined by *US News & World Report* and even state flagship institutions in 2001 are serving far fewer low-income students than less selective institutions such as community colleges, two-year institutions, and the larger population of four-year schools. Not surprisingly, Historically Black Colleges and Universities (HBCUs), and Hispanic Serving Institutions (HSIs), are educating a disproportionate share of low-income students. These

Table 18.2 Distribution of Pell Grant recipients

Type of postsecondary institution	Percent of enrollees receiving Pell Grants in 2001	Percent change in Pell enrollees 1992–2001
All undergraduate	29.8%	+2.3%
51 best liberal arts colleges	13.0%	−0.8%
50 best national universities	17.9%	−0.3%
State flagship universities	20.7%	−1.3%
Community colleges	27.2%	+4.0%
Public universities	27.4%	+1.4%
All 2-years	27.8%	+4.1%
All 4-years	28.4%	+0.9%
Private 4-year colleges and universities	29.8%	−0.5%
Hispanic serving institutions	32.3%	+6.7%
Historically black colleges and universities	60.8%	+6.4%

Source: *Postsecondary Opportunity* (June, 2004).

2001 numbers are a product of a trend over the past ten years defined by decreasing numbers of low-income students at the most selective institutions and growing shares of low-income students at less selective institutions. The data show that 34 of the 51 best liberal arts colleges, 33 of the 50 best national universities, and 31 of the state flagship institutions saw a reduction in their number of Pell Grant recipient enrollees from 1992–93 to 2000–1 (Mortenson, 2004a, 2004b, 2004c). Similarly, the 50 most selective private institutions (with enrollments of more than 1,000 students) in 2003–4 had a 9.3 percent Pell Grant enrollee share and the 50 most selective public institutions in 2003–4 had a 15.4 percent Pell share as compared with 31.1 percent and 31.0 percent for all private and public four-year institutions (Mortenson, 2005b). This represented a .5 percent Pell enrollee share drop for the 50 most exclusive privates (which were serving very few low-income students to begin with) and a 1.6 percent drop for the 50 most exclusive publics over the preceding decade, despite increased public attention to equity and affordability.

While 10 to 15 percent of students at very selective institutions being on Pell might seem commendable, this share must be viewed in light of the fact that a third of students at four-year institutions overall are on Pell. Furthermore, 58 percent of the households in the USA as a whole fall in the income bracket that encompasses virtually all Pell recipients (< $60,000) (US Census Bureau, 2005; US Department of Education, 2004). Given that low-income students have been shown to be less likely to be academically prepared for college, it may be unreasonable to expect that proportions of Pell recipients at very selective schools mirror the number of poor households in the country. Nevertheless, these trends show us moving even further from that goal through changing admission standards, increasing challenges to affordability, and inequalities in ability to prepare.

The ultra-elite colleges and universities, whose prestige and talent-packed applicant pools are unassailable, by and large did not reduce their shares of Pell enrollees during this time period. They were at the top of the school rankings and stayed there. But a careful examination of many schools who managed to increase selectivity (through significant increases in applications and relatively stable growth in admissions) and climb the US News & World Report rankings reveals simultaneous losses in shares of Pell enrollees. For example, the University of Georgia, assisted in its retention of in-state high achieving scholars with the merit-based HOPE scholarship, was able to move from being a second quartile university in 1991 up to number 58 in the 2003 rankings of national universities and number 20 among all public universities. This movement was due in part to an acceptance rate that moved from 79 percent to 65 percent, the percent of its freshman class from the top 10 percent of its high school class rising from 33 percent to 46 percent, and the average SAT rising from 1,004 to 1,209. But these shifts were accompanied by a reduction from 15.9 percent of its freshmen being on Pell grants in 1992 to 14.0 percent in 2003. Bear in mind that state universities such as the University of Georgia are among the nation's largest campuses and that while a seemingly small drop in percentage share, 1.9 percent represents a loss of 475 low-income students on a campus of 25,000. And again, the share of Pell enrollees was low to begin with and is moving in the wrong direction.

Even without the leveraging effect of a state-wide merit-based scholarship, many large universities, especially in the Midwest and West, made gains over the last decade in the rankings while enrolling proportionally fewer students from lower income backgrounds. These changes in ranking are driven by increasing selectivity, as evidenced by acceptance rates, and the academic records of the freshman class as indicated by the share of freshmen from the top 10 percent of their high school class. Examples of these patterns are shown in Table 18.3.

And yet, it is not just the most selective institutions which are seeing lower numbers of low-income students. Low-income students are less likely to be in four-year institutions in general than they were a decade ago. Continuing the format of the earlier data, between 1992–93 and 2000–2001 there was a 2.9 percent drop in the enrollment share of Pell Grant recipients at four-year institutions across all states, with 48 of the states seeing a decline in their Pell enrollment shares (Mortenson, 2003). Conversely, during the same window of time, the Pell enrollment share at two-year public colleges increased by 1.2 percent (ibid.). This continues a much larger trend beginning in the 1970s of students receiving Pell Grants being more likely to opt to enroll at two-year institutions rather than at four-year schools. In 1974, 62.4 percent of Pell Grant recipients attended four-year schools. By 1994, the number was down to 48.3 percent and, in 2002, 46.2 percent of Pell recipients enrolled at four-year schools (Mortenson, 2006a).

Meanwhile Pell recipients attending two-year schools have risen from 37.6 percent in 1974 to 55.1 percent in 2002. Many have written critically about the structural role of the community college in the "cooling out" of student aspirations (Clark, 1960). Brint and Karabel (1989) provide one of the more cutting analyses of this criticism, linking these "open access" opportunities to notions of meritocracy and the broader class structure.

Table 18.3 Change in select university Pell share of freshman class and prestige, 1992–2004

Institution	Change in Pell share of freshman class 1992–2003	Change in acceptance rate 1992–2004	Change in % of freshman class from top 10% of high school class 1992–2004	Change in US News rankings
University of Georgia	−1.9%	79–65%	33–46%	2nd tier national university in 1994, to No. 58 national and No. 20 public in 2003
University of Missouri (Columbia)	−7.8%	73–89%	31–29%	2nd tier national university in 1994, to No. 73 national and No. 32 public in 2003
University of Nebraska (Lincoln)	−6.1%	93–76%	19–25%	3rd tier national university in 1994 to No. 107 in 2003
University of Oklahoma	−8.4%	86–88%	30–32%	3rd tier (Nos. 115–71) national university in 1994 to 2nd tier in 1998 to No. 117 in 2003
University of Tulsa	−4.6%	89–76%	43–60%	3rd tier national university in 1994 to No. 90 in 2004
University of Wisconsin	−3.6%	75–65%	33–55%	2nd tier national university in 1994 to No. 36 in 1998 to No. 32 in 2001

Sources: *US News & World Report*, America's Best Colleges, 1992, 1998, 2001, 2003, 2004 Editions; Pell Grant Shares of Undergraduate Enrollments in Postsecondary Institutions—1992, 2001, 2002, and 2003, from *Postsecondary Education Opportunity*, www.postsecondary.org/ti/ti_38.asp.

More recently, Dougherty and Kienzl (2006) show that students from lower socioeconomic backgrounds are at a great disadvantage relative to their more affluent peers in
terms of actually making it across the gap between those two-year institutions and the
four-year campuses from which they hope to earn a baccalaureate degree. As heightened
competition for spaces at more selective universities pushes those less well prepared and
less well capitalized farther down the prestige hierarchy, it becomes tempting to gener-
alize concerns expressed about the community college to the least well resourced of four-
year opportunities that many low-income students are more likely to experience.

Some of this downward shift in the four-year sector can be attributed to the increasing
selectivity among public four-year institutions. From 1986 to 2005, the share of four-
year institutions that classify themselves as highly selective or selective grew from 28.8
percent to 35.9 percent. The great bulk of institutions are considered "traditional," selecting
the top 50 percent of high school graduates with the middle 50 percent of admittees
having ACT of 20–23 or SAT of 950–1,270. This group's share of institutions grew from
39.5 to 44.8. But the share of institutions that characterize their admissions as liberal or
open shrank from 31.7 percent to 19.3 percent (Mortenson, 2005a). Even among public
four-year colleges, the share of selective institutions rose by 4.1 percent and traditional
institutions rose by 15.2 percent. This resulted in 14.6 percent and 3.1 percent drops in
the share of liberal and open access institutions in the public four-year college sector.

If Pell recipients are less well represented at selective institutions and four-year
colleges, then we may assume that more affluent students are taking their place. We
might infer this from the selectivity shifts outlined above and the knowledge that grades
and college admission test scores are correlated with income. This conclusion is also
borne out by survey data on the median estimated parental income of freshmen in post-
secondary institutions in 2002 (Table 18.4). Median parental income for students at all
two-year schools is just under $50,000 while that of students at all Bachelors granting
institutions is nearly $70,000. The median parental income of students at all universities
is almost $79,000. And within these broad categories of institutions, as selectivity

Table 18.4 Median estimated parental income of college freshmen, Fall 2002

| | Academic selectivity | | | | |
	Low	Medium	High	Very high	All
All Two-year					
Public					$49,680
Private					$49,680
All Bachelors					$69,504
Four-year					$64,778
Public	$52,581	$63,676	$76,099		$62,979
Private					$67,031
Nonsectarian	$57,845	$70,313	$73,038		$70,732
Catholic	$53,305	$59,481	$77,903		$67,441
Other religions	$52,000	$61,971	$85,583		$62,556
Universities					$78,834
Public	$66,900	$82,949	$86,326		$74,771
Private	$84,414	$106,699	$117,188		$97,007

Source: *The American Freshman: National Norms for Fall 2002.*

increases, the median parental income of the students rises also. For example, at public universities where the income level overall is about $75,000, the median parental income of students at low selectivity schools is about $67,000, medium selectivity is about $83,000, and high selectivity is about $86,000.

If there were equal returns for investment at all types of higher education, these concerns regarding the stratification of higher education by family income would be of less consequence. This is not the case, however. It is widely accepted that students entering two-year institutions, even if planning to obtain a bachelor's degree, are much less likely to do so than students who immediately enroll in a four-year institution. Even within four-year institutions, more selective schools, through advantages such as additional student support services and positive peer effects, have higher graduation rates than less selective schools. And, of course, it is the college degree which ultimately symbolizes completion of the rite of passage and provides the greatest opportunity for socioeconomic mobility.

There has been a great deal of research demonstrating labor market advantages associated with graduation from higher prestige undergraduate institutions (e.g., Behrman, Rosenzweig & Taubman, 1995; Brewer & Ehrenberg, 1996; Thomas, 2000, 2003). Other studies have looked at the payoff to a prestigious undergraduate degree in terms of the likelihood of enrolling in graduate school and the quality of that graduate school. Eide, Brewer, and Ehrenberg (1998), using the National Center for Education Statistics' National Longitudinal Study of the High School Class of 1972 and High School and Beyond, find that students from elite private institutions are more likely to go to graduate school and to attend a research institution when they do so. More recently, Zhang (2005) found that 18 percent of bachelor degree recipients from high prestige public universities were to go on to graduate programs within four to five years (prestige was determined by Barron's college selectivity rankings). Graduates from medium prestige public institutions enjoyed a similar 11 percent advantage. Zhang also showed that graduates from higher prestige institutions were more likely to enter doctoral programs directly, to enroll at more prestigious universities for that doctoral work, and more likely to finish their doctoral work within five years of entry. Thus, not only are students from more selective institutions more likely to finish their bachelor's degrees and earn higher wages in the labor market, they are also more likely to accrue even further human capital through attending and completing more prestigious graduate programs. This, in turn, can be connected back to heightened opportunities for social mobility.

While it is true that increasing numbers of students from all walks of life are engaging in higher education, the patterns shown here give us cause for concern as to equity in the quality of outcomes that students from subordinate classes will experience. As college costs rise and many institutions become more selective, low-income students are becoming increasingly channeled into two-year and lower-prestige four-year institutions. Their more affluent and better prepared peers, meanwhile, are able to solidify their hold on more selective, higher quality colleges and universities that better ensure opportunities for upward mobility and, ultimately, control over the very institutions that can preserve these class differences. While the shift over the past decade in percent of lower-income students attending the more selective institutions is small, it represents tens of thousands of students and is moving existing disparities in the wrong direction. These patterns are consistent with Karabel's (2006) suggestion that admissions policies reflect the power relations among the major social groups in the USA.

Questions for discussion

1. In funding higher education, how has the shift from grants and scholarships to loans impacted students from low-income families? How is this shift indicative of power relationships within the USA?
2. Drawing on the authors' discussion of the history of higher education within the USA, what are possible reasons for the growth of two-year public institutions? How are two-year institutions affected by changes among public four-year institutions?
3. Although the overall number of low-income students attending colleges has increased, the rate of enrollment in selective institutions has declined. How do you explain this discrepancy?
4. Discuss the existing and potential social implications of unequal college participation rates among social groups. Do you predict these figures will change over the next decade? If so, why and how might they change? If not, explain why you imagine these trends will continue.
5. What caused the shift from considering higher education as a public good to that of a private good? How does this logic impact students from various social class backgrounds?
6. Considering the social complexity of trends working to reproduce inequality, offer two factors obstructing the opportunity of low-income students to attend selective colleges. How do you suppose we might begin to reverse these trends?
7. How do notions of meritocracy contribute to the preservation of the social and political order in the USA? Consider how this discussion is associated with difficulties in measuring systematic class-based inequalities in higher education.
8. Under its current reorganization, it is argued that higher education is no longer the vehicle for socioeconomic mobility. Does this hold true in all cases, for all poor and working-class individuals aspiring for upward mobility? What does this movement mean for the mobility of the elite faction of the population? Will this reorganization produce a downward projection for individuals within the upper class?

References

Behrman, J. R., Rosenzweig, M. R., & Taubman, P. (1995). *Individual endowments, college choice, and wages: Estimates using data on female twins.* Revised paper for NSF/RESTATA Conference on School Quality and Educational Outcomes.

Bowen, W. G., & Bok, D. (1998). *The shape of the river: Long-term consequences of considering race in college and university admissions.* Princeton: Princeton University Press.

Bowen, W. G., Kurzweil, M. A., & Tobin, E. M. (2005). *Equity and excellence in American higher education.* Charlottesville: University of Virginia Press.

Brewer, D. J., & Ehrenberg, R. G. (1996). Does it pay to attend an elite private college? Evidence from the senior high school class of 1980. *Research in Labor Economics, 15,* 239–72.

Brint, S., & Karabel, J. (1989). *The diverted dream: Community colleges and the promise of educational opportunity in America, 1900–1985.* New York: Oxford University Press.

Clark, B. R. (1960). The cooling-out function in higher education. *American Journal of Sociology,* *65, 569–76.*

College Board (2006a). *Trends in college pricing.* Washington, DC: Author.

—— (2006b). *Trends in student aid.* Washington, DC: Author.

Davis, J. S. (2003). Unintended consequences of tuition discounting. Lumina Foundation for Education. Available at: http://www.luminafoundation.org/publications/tuitiondiscounting.pdf.

Diamond, H. D., & Diamond, N. A. (1997). *The rise of American research universities: Elites and challengers in the postwar era.* Baltimore, MD: The Johns Hopkins University Press.

Dougherty, K. J., & Kienzl, G. S. (2006). It's not enough to get through the open door: Inequalities by social background in transfer from community colleges to four-year colleges. *Teachers College Record, 108*(3), 452–87.

Ehrenberg, R. G. (2002). *Tuition rising: Why college costs so much.* Cambridge: Harvard University Press.

Eide, E., Brewer, D. J., & Ehrenberg, R. G. (1998). Does it pay to attend an elite private college? Evidence on the effects of undergraduate college quality on graduate school attendance. *Economics of Education Review, 17,* 371–76.

Geiger, R. (2004). *Knowledge and money: Research universities and the paradox of the marketplace.* Palo Alto, CA: Stanford University Press.

Goldin, C., & Margo, R. A. (1992). The great compression: The wage structure in the United States at mid-century. *Quarterly Journal of Economics, 107*(1), 1–34.

Heller, D. E. (Ed.). (2002). *Condition of access: Higher education for lower income students.* West Port, CT: Praeger.

Hurtado, S., Inkelas, K. K., Briggs, C., & Rhee, B. S. (1997). Difference in college access and choice among racial/ethnic groups: Identifying continuing barriers. *Research in Higher Education, 38,* 43–75.

Kane, T. J. (2001). *College-going and inequality: A literature review.* New York: The Russell Sage Foundation.

Karabel, J. (2006). *The chosen: The hidden history of admission and exclusion at Harvard, Yale, and Princeton.* New York: Houghton Mifflin.

Karen, D. (1991). The politics of class race and gender: Access to higher education in the United States, 1960–86. *American Journal of Education, 99*(2), 208–37.

McDonough, P. M. (1997). *Choosing colleges: How social class and schools structure opportunity.* New York: State University of New York Press.

Mortenson, T. (2003). Pell Grant Students in Undergraduate Enrollments by Institution Type and Control, 1992–93 to 2000–2001. *Postsecondary Education Opportunity, 138* (December). Oskaloosa, IA.

—— (2004a). Pell Grant Enrollment at State Flagship Institutions, 1992–93 to 2001–2. *Postsecondary Education Opportunity, 140* (February). Oskaloosa, IA.

—— (2004b). Pell Shares of Undergraduate Enrollments at the 50 Best National Universities 1992–93 and 2001–2. *Postsecondary Education Opportunity, 141* (March). Oskaloosa, IA.

—— (2004c). Pell Shares of Undergraduate Enrollments at the 51 Best National Liberal Arts Colleges 1992–93 and 2001–2. *Postsecondary Education Opportunity, 142* (April). Oskaloosa, IA.

—— (2005a). Segregation of Higher Education Enrollment by Family Income and Race/Ethnicity, 1980 to 2004. *Postsecondary Education Opportunity, 160* (October). Oskaloosa, IA.

—— (2005b). The Gated Communities of Higher Education: 50 Most Exclusive Public and Private Four-Year Institutions, 2003–4. *Postsecondary Education Opportunity, 162* (December). Oskaloosa, IA.

—— (2006a). Access to What? *Postsecondary Education Opportunity, 164* (February). Oskaloosa, IA.

—— (2006b). College Graduation Rates, 1947–2006. *Postsecondary Education Opportunity, 173* (November). Oskaloosa, IA.

National Center for Public Policy and Higher Education (2006). *Measuring up: The national report card on higher education.* Retrieved January 12, 2007, from www.higheredinfo.org/dbrowser/index.php?submeasure=75&year=2005&level=nation&mode=data&state=0.

Oakes, J., & Saunders, M. (2004). Education's most basic tools: Access to textbooks and instructional materials in California's public schools. *Teachers College Record, 106*(10), 1967–88.

Orfield, G., & Lee, C. (2005). *Why segregation matters: Poverty and educational inequality.* Cambridge, MA: Harvard University, Civil Rights Project.

Perna, L. W. (2000). Differences in the decision to attend college among African Americans, Hispanics, and Whites. *Journal of Higher Education, 71.* Ohio State University Press.

—— (2003). *Inequitable and inadequate school resources: A critical barrier to obtaining the academic preparation that is required to enroll in college.* Paper presented at the Institute for Higher Education's Conference on Higher Education Access and Opportunity. Athens, GA.

Perna, L. W., Rowan, H., Thomas, S. L., Bell, A., Anderson, R., & Li, C. (2006). *The role of college counseling in shaping college opportunity: Variations across high schools.* Unpublished manuscript.

Price, D. V. (2004). *Borrowing inequality: Race, class, and student loans.* Boulder, CO: Lynne Rienner Publishers.

Redd, K. E. (2000). Discounting toward disaster: Tuition discounting, college finances, and enrollment of low-income undergraduates. *New Agenda Series, 4*(2). Indianapolis: USA Group Foundation.

—— (2002). Funding and distribution of institutional grants: Results from the 2001 survey of undergraduate financial aid policies, practices, and procedures. *Journal of Student Financial Aid, 32*(2), 24–36.

Snyder, T. D., Tan, A. G., & Hoffman, C. M. (2006). *Digest of education statistics 2005* (NCES 2006–30). US Department of Education, National Center for Education Statistics. Washington, DC: US Government Printing Office.

St. John, E. P. (1991). What really influences minority attendance? Sequential analysis of the high school and beyond sophomore cohort. *Research in Higher Education, 32*(2), 141–58.

St. John, E. P., & Asker, E. (2003). *Refinancing the college dream: Access, equal opportunity, and justice for taxpayers.* Baltimore: Johns Hopkins Press.

St. John, E. P., Musoba, G. D., & Simmons, A. B. (2003). Keeping the promise: The impact of Indiana's twenty-first century scholars program. *Review of Higher Education, 27*(1), 103–23.

Thomas, S. (2000). Deferred costs and economic returns to college quality, major and academic performance: An analysis of recent graduates in Baccalaureate and beyond. *Research in Higher Education, 41*(3), 281–313.

—— (2003). Longer-term economic effects of college selectivity and control. *Research in Higher Education, 44*(3), 263–99.

US Census Bureau (2005). *Household income 1999.* Retrieved January 31, 2007, from www.census.gov/prod/2005pubs/c2kbr-36.pdf

—— (2006). *Current population survey (CPS), March 2006.* Washington, DC: US Census Bureau.

US Department of Education, Office of Postsecondary Education (2004). *2003–2004 Federal Pell Grant Program End-of-Year Report.* Washington, DC: Pearson Government Solutions.

US News & World Report (1992). *America's best colleges.* Author.

—— (1998). *America's best colleges.* Author.

—— (2001). *America's best colleges.* Author.

—— (2003). *America's best colleges.* Author.

—— (2004). *America's best colleges.* Author.

Weis, L., & Fine, M. (Eds.) (1993). *Beyond silenced voices: Class, race and gender in United States schools*. Albany: SUNY Press.

Zemsky, R. (1997). In search of a strategic perspective: A tool for mapping the market in postsecondary education. *Change Magazine*, November/December, 23–38.

Zhang, L. (2005). *Does quality pay? Benefits of attending a high-cost, prestigious college*. New York: Routledge.

Section 4

Complicating class, race, and gender intersectionality

Chapter 19

Toward a re-thinking of class as nested in race and gender

Tracking the white working class in the final quarter of the twentieth century

*Lois Weis**

> I wouldn't mind my wife working as far as secretarial work or something like that. Whatever she wanted to do and she pursued as a career. If there was children around, I'd like her to be at home, so I'd like my job to compensate for just me working and my wife being at home.
>
> Seth, 1985

* * *

> I want to go to college for four years, get my job, work for a few years and then get married . . . I like supporting myself. I don't want my husband supporting me. I like being independent. My dad [. . .] used to work at the strip mill; now he's not. Now everything's gone, benefits and everything.
>
> Judy, 1985

In 2001, Seth is Head of Maintenance at Freeway High; his wife is a secretary. Judy is a radiologic technician, married to a non-union construction worker. Both Seth and Judy hoped to leave Freeway when they were in high school. Neither they nor their spouses, also from Freeway, left the area.

It is twenty-one years since I first met Seth, Judy, and thirty-nine additional third-year white students as part of a full-scale ethnographic investigation of a white working-class high school located in Freeway—a then rapidly de-industrializing town in north-eastern USA. Spurred by work on the white working class inside a more robust economic context (Everhart, 1983; McRobbie, 1978; Willis, 1977), my intent was to probe identity formation processes among working-class youth, male and female, during times of severe economic dislocation.

The resulting volume, *Working Class Without Work* (Weis, 1990), is a study of identity formation among white working-class male and female students in relation to schools, economy, and family of origin, capturing the complex interconnections between and among secondary schooling, human agency, and the formation of collective consciousness within a radically changing economic and social context. I suggest in this volume that young women exhibit a "glimmer of critique" with regard to traditional

---

* State University of New York Distinguished Professor of Sociology of Education at the University at Buffalo, State University of New York.

gender roles in the working-class family and that young men are ripe for New Right consciousness given their strident racism and male dominant stance in an economy, like that immortalized in *The Full Monty* and the BBC serial *The Missing Postman*, which offers them little.[1]

Based on re-interviews in 2000–2001 with thirty-one of the original forty-one ethno-graphically embedded 1985–86 white students (who, at the time of the re-interview, were in their early thirties), I produced *Class Reunion* (Weis, 2004), an exploration, empirically and longitudinally, of the re-making of the US white working-class fraction in the latter quarter of the twentieth century.[2] Arguing that we cannot write off the working class simply because white men no longer have access to well-paying laboring jobs in the primary labor market (Edwards, 1979), jobs which spawned a distinctive place for labor in the capital–labor accord (Apple, 2001; Hunter, 1987), I track and theorize the re-making of this group *as a distinct class fraction*, both discursively and behaviorally inside radical, globally based economic restructuring (McCall, 2001; Reich, 1991, 2001; Rogers & Teixeira, 2000).[3]

In this context, Seth and Judy's stories are not unique, but rather suggestive of what has happened to a large portion of the white industrial proletariat in the USA, a proletariat that has been remade and, simultaneously, has re-made itself in the face of massive changes in the global economy. Reconstituting itself on a daily basis in homes, bars, hospitals, donut shops, gas stations, schools, warehouses, and the like, the white working-class fraction is effectively staging its own "class reunion"—a class reunion which, given the fundamentally altered world economy and the particular place of the industrial proletariat inside this new economy, embodies deep restructuring along gender lines, the long-term outcomes of which are markedly unclear. Demands for, and the very necessity of, women's independence in this newly minted class fraction exist inside a highly traditional patriarchal culture, one laced with and maintained at times by physical beatings. Ironically, though, it is this uneasy gendered realignment that is a necessary condition for the newly articulated "settled" white working class. As men and women of the new white working class simultaneously and collectively assert whiteness in relation to familiar groups of color in the USA, such as African-Americans, as well as, in this particular community, Yemenites, men and women reconverge. Splitting along gendered lines as shaped and ultimately propped up by heterosexuality, white working-class men and women reunite along race lines, producing, for the moment at least, a class fractional collective which both partially affirms, and simultaneously serves to challenge, globally driven demand for the neo-liberal subject.

In contrast to much previous (and excellent) work on social class then, work that was largely conducted inside a different historic/economic moment (Anyon, 1981; Bensman & Lynch, 1987; Everhart, 1983; Foley, 1990; Willis, 1977), wherein class is seen fundamentally (and wholly in many cases) to constitute itself in relation to *other classes*, I argue that the production of class, at least in the case of the white working class under consideration here, must be understood as deeply nested in race and gender. By nested, I mean that race and gender lie within class and class dynamics wherein both the production and movement of class can be understood only with serious and continued attention to the ways in which other key nodes of difference both wrap class and simultaneously serve to produce it. Class, then, is constructed thematically and practically around, and in relation to, gender and race rather than primarily in relation to other classes. Such "nested nodes" (class, race, and gender) cannot be understood, however, only in relation to one another, as they are themselves nested in political economy which, in the final quarter of the twentieth century, means neo-liberalism.

Ideological transformations

The new US white working-class fraction sits inside a worldwide press toward neo-liberalism. As Michael Apple (2001) argues, "If we were to point to one specific defining political/economic paradigm of the age in which we live it would be neo-liberalism" (p. 17). For Robert McChesney (1999):

> Neo-liberal initiatives are characterized as free market policies that encourage private enterprise and consumer choice, reward personal responsibility and entrepreneurial initiative, and undermine the dead hand of the incompetent, bureaucratic and parasitic government, that can never do good even if well intended, which it rarely is.
>
> (p. 7)

McChesney continues: "Instead of communities, [neo-liberalism] produces shopping malls. The net result is an atomized society of disengaged individuals who feel demoralized and socially powerless" (p. 11).

The production of neo-liberal subjects is a key component to such ideological transformation—subjects who are capable of "understanding themselves as autonomous agents, producers of their present and their future, inventors of the people that they are or may become" (Giddens, 1991). Such individuals are, by necessity, detached from community, operating autonomously as they author their lives: "If we think about the end of jobs for life and the production of a culture of uncertainty [the notion of] self-invention through a discourse of limitless choice provides a way to manage the government of potentially unruly and disaffected subjects," a project that "requires acceptance of a certain kind of psychological discourse as a true description of oneself . . . so if one is out of work, one has to transform oneself into the right kind of employable subject" (Walkerdine, Lucey & Melody, 2001, pp. 2–3). Rather than pressing toward individuals who are tightly bound to class and race/ethnic communities then, as was arguably the case under an industrial economy, neo-liberalism presses toward a cadre of "de-raced, de-classed and de-gendered individuals" (Apple, 2001, p. 39).

In light of these assertions, it is important to consider the extent to which the new white working-class fraction in the USA, as tracked ethnographically over a pivotal fifteen-year period (Weis, 2004), embodies these tendencies. As data snippets at the beginning of this chapter suggest, Freeway white working-class girls, fueled by a sense of power attached to an almost entirely unacknowledged (middle-class) women's movement and a simultaneous fear of the ravages of plant closings and accompanying divorce, began, in the mid-1980s, to re-shape themselves as the consummate neo-liberal subject—a subject of self-invention and transformation, one who is capable of surviving and perhaps even thriving in the new world order.

The ever-evolving capitalist economy, coupled with accompanying replacement of the older Keynesian welfare state with neo-liberal policies and practices in the latter quarter of the twentieth century, simultaneously demanded and enabled this move on the part of white working-class women. Given their "real" class location, however, it was not possible for the majority of women of the former industrial proletariat to create themselves as autonomous producers (and/or consumers) and manage to be much other than poor. Under the assumption of largely heterosexual coupling, all but one of the original young women in *Working Class Without Work* hooked up with men of similar class background, men with whom they could feel "comfortable" because they are "like them." By virtue of gender trajectories explored extensively in *Class Reunion*, in particular those associated with hegemonic white working-class masculinity and its lived out distancing from school knowledge and culture/mental labor (which are coded as feminine), such men were less apt than working-class white women to have made widespread moves toward becoming the self-invented subject under the new global economy, a self-invention which more often than not now demands tertiary level education. Such partnership liaisons were both desired *and at the same time necessary* if white working-class women and men were to accomplish what I call a newly articulated form of "settled" working-class life—in other words, life which exhibits the trappings of the formerly solid working class, such as home and car ownership, as well as health insurance coverage and pensions, although often in substantially reduced form or non-existent. While women were perhaps desirous of creating themselves as fully neo-liberal subjects while in high school—thereby living out what I call "the freedom dream"—this was, in reality, virtually impossible to enact, given both their "real" class location and their lived association with particular kinds of men, those with whom they share a class habitus of origin. This habitus, as I argue at length in the larger volume (2004), keeps Freeway women almost entirely connected to men of a specific class background: men who go to bars or donut/coffee shops frequented by the white working class, watch particular spectator sports in specific locations (local bars, homes, race sites), come from comparable working-class families and communities, possess skills and contacts deeply woven in the fabric of masculine working-class culture, and intersect with formal school knowledge in particular class coded and gender linked kinds of ways. Thus class re-emerges under neo-liberalism at the lived level, although in reconfigured form, serving to defeat, in part, the push toward "de-classing" evidenced in economic transformation. Quite bluntly, the 1985–86 young women, except for one who married a financial advisor (and even she is only a separation away from moving back to her parents' home and community of origin), partnered over time with men who were from working-class Freeway or communities exactly like Freeway. This is in spite of the fact that all except one of the 1985–86 young women, unlike the men, attended and/or completed college/university.

To be sure, the family is a unit of consumption, and the idea of the consumer is crucial here. Men and women of the new white working-class fraction in the early twenty-first century are happy with their lives largely because they can purchase (through extended credit at high interest rates) valued consumer goods and forms of entertainment and services—dirt bikes, large flat-screen televisions, homes in working-class white communities (although such communities are, in their terms, "under siege" and under constant self-surveillance to keep out "outsiders"), hockey tickets, trips to NASCAR races, and the like. But this is accomplished in ways that do not take dead aim at social class in quite the way proponents of neo-liberalism might like; men and women of the former industrial proletariat both have been "rearranged" in class terms due to the massive shift in the global economy, but they have also "rearranged" themselves so as to preserve a white working-class fraction—one which is distinct in key ways from what is arguably a larger working class now composed of men and women across race and ethnic group of color.

While neo-liberalism may demand the unmoored, de-raced, de-classed, and de-gendered subject, it is arguably the case that members of the former industrial proletariat are fighting back at their own lived level—insisting on *being classed*, and certainly *raced* in spite of the fact that they increasingly enter and remain attached to the economy as *individuals*. While not necessarily calling themselves working class (members of the US working class have exhibited a love–hate relationship with this signifier for decades), members of the former white industrial proletariat nevertheless carve out a distinct class fraction—one which rests upon uncomfortable, but necessary, gender realignment for men, and, as I suggest below, the simultaneous deep patrolling of race borders by both men and women. The press of neo-liberalism in this specific class fraction only reaches so deep, as the class fraction continues to constitute itself around key categories of class, race, and gender, thus contradicting at the *lived* level the full imperatives and implications of neo-liberalism.

Whiteness, gender, and the economy

There's beginning to be a lot of Arabians . . . Anywhere you go—just things they do. . . . And there is a lot of trouble with them in school now [her mother is a lunch monitor at Freeway High] . . . Arabians are now living on this side of town. On the corner, on the other street . . . they're all over now.

Sandy, age 31, 2001

Things have changed a lot [since I was in high school], you know. . . . There weren't as many Arabs as there are now. But I know there's a lot of them around here now. It's increasing. And they're buying up everything. Businesses, houses, everything . . . I know people who have gone as far as buying the house next to them, and they got nobody living there—just so they [Arabs] wouldn't buy it.

Clint, age 31, 2000

As men and women of the former industrial proletariat carve a new class fraction, they do so fully in relation to one another, in spite of the desire for "independence from men" expressed by Freeway teenage girls. This no doubt has a psychological component, one lived out within the strictures of heterosexuality, but it is also purely economic. Neither the men nor the women could live the life they desire if by themselves, as exemplified by what I call the "hard living" men in the 2004 volume, those who still live in relation to norms of hegemonic working-class masculinity, desirous of both the hard labor associated with the old industrial proletariat as well as the perks of such labor/wages linked to the domination of women. Freeway girls did not, therefore, compromise their dreams of "freedom" so much as enter into necessary domestic arrangements that would allow them to support both themselves and their children in concert with their men. Freeway boys did in fact compromise their dream of supporting their wives. Bill, who stated in 1985 that if he got a "good job" his wife would "stay home and be a regular woman," is now as much dependent on his wife's labor as his own. In 1985 Lanny asserted: "Before we had any kids, she'd be working; but if we had kids, she wouldn't work; she'd be staying home, taking care of the kids." In 2001 the unattached Lanny lives with his mother, as he does not earn enough money working at Deltasonic to make it on his own.

In point of fact, women's gendered trajectory is increasingly linked to the economy and men's gendered trajectory is increasingly tied to what is happening within the family. Men are de-moored from assumed economic space—a mooring that granted them certain rights in the home/family sphere in prior generations, at the same time as women are surging into the very sector that encourages so much of men's psychological distress. It is the crossing of home/family/wage earning borders by *both* men and women that enables this new class fraction to flourish (by this I mean they are relatively privileged; they are not poor), whether they like it or not. Fueled by a deeply rooted sense of possibility evident as far back as high school (as Carla, now an elementary school teacher married to a police officer, stated in 1985, "I want to get my schoolwork over with, get my life together, get a job . . . I want to be independent. I don't want to be dependent on him for money")—a sense of possibility borne of the struggles of the women's movement as well as the opening up of the economic sector to women—women now experience, at some level at least, the "freedom" they desired, perhaps encouraging them to carry the burdens of their gender/class on their shoulders.

In light of my earlier assertions regarding the nested nature of class production (class as nested in lived out/struggled over everyday realities of race and gender), the importance that race, racism, and raciality play in the making of the new white working-class fraction demands further attention, as does the unique role of the Yemenite community in this particular locale, a group which migrated to Freeway in the 1940s to work steel, albeit, as with African-Americans, in the lowest paid and dirtiest jobs. Although neo-liberalism presses toward the de-raced, de-classed, de-gendered subject, the industrial proletariat in the USA simultaneously and doggedly engages in the "fixing" of race—their own as well as that of the constructed non-white "other"—in this case, African-Americans and Yemenites. Such "fixing," paradoxically, occurs at one and the same time as racial identity is being de-stabilized at other levels (Dolby, 2001; McCarthy, Crichlow, Dimitriadis & Dolby, 2004). McCarthy (2003), for example, signals the end of the "auratic status" of race, arguing that

> [T]he notion of racial identity as residing in "origins," "ancestry," "linguistic" or "cultural unity" has been shattered, overwhelmed by the immense processes of hybridity, disjuncture, and re-narration taking place in what Arjun Appadurai (1996) calls the new techno, media, and ideoscapes now disseminated in ever-widening areas and spheres of contemporary life. Migration, electronic mediation, biometric and information technologies have separated culture from place. And, difference has become an abstract value that can be dirempted from specific groups and settings and combined and recombined in ways that allow, for example, clothing designer magnates like Tommy Hilfiger to appropriate elements of hip hop culture, to recombine semiotically these elements into new forms of clothing fashion, and then sell these new designs back into the inner city itself.
>
> (Hall, 1996, p. 4; as cited in McCarthy, 2003)

Catherine Cornbleth (2003) picks up on this moment of de-stabilization in racial/ethnic identities among US high school students. Based on ethnographic interviews, she argues that young people now de-construct racial identities rather than "fix" them as did earlier generations. If, however, we focus on high school students *as they take up adult-hood* as I do in the two volumes discussed in this chapter, it becomes clear that the white working-class project in the USA involves the *continual stabilization* of race at one and the same time as race becomes de-moored, or de-stabilized, by larger social forces.

The neo-liberal subject position as pursued with vengeance by the young Freeway women in the mid-1980s, a subject position both made possible and simultaneously demanded/encouraged by economic global realignment and accompanying worldwide press toward free market policies that encourage private enterprise, is only partially embodied and materialized as young women grow to adulthood. For the former white industrial proletariat, whiteness privileges at one and the same time as it enables the continued "fixing" of race at a time of simultaneous de-stabilization of race and class. With great respect for the writing of McCarthy, Crichlow, Dimitriadis, and Dolby, as well as that of Cornbleth, the ways in which whiteness is both celebrated and simultaneously fixes "others" of color should not be ignored and/or underestimated, as race, class, and gender are produced in particular locations *over time*. It is the "over time" element that I explore here, as it is the focus on the lived-out temporal dimension that enables us to understand fully the production of class, and, most fundamentally, the ways in which class production processes are linked, in the USA at least, to the nesting of race and gender. By way of example, although racial categories may be de-stabilized by "hybridity," re-narration, disjuncture, and so forth in ever widening arenas of contemporary life, part of the project of the white working class, as it stakes out a new form of white working-classness in the latter quarter of the twentieth century, is that it partially defeats, on its own lived-out cultural and psychological level, the intrusion of such re-narration around race. As race is de-stabilized in a wide set of arenas, then, the new white working-class fraction fights hard to *re-stabilize* it, thereby stabilizing, with the help of simultaneous gender realignment as noted above, class itself.[4]

Significantly, white working-class women join their men in this "fixing" at precisely the moment of motherhood/adulthood, although they did not exemplify racial "fixing" as teenagers, in sharp contrast to Freeway boys whose very identity was bound up with the negative fixing of race, particularly that of African-American males (Weis, 1990). Thus the same women, whose identity production in high school had little to do with racial fixing and/or categories (Weis, 1990), now demand, as do their men, largely white living space, arguing that Yemenites (who they call Arabians or "A-rabs"), in particular, are both fundamentally different from themselves, and at the same time largely responsible for de-stabilizing their community and associated way of life.[5] Most importantly for the overall class project examined here, women join their men in such racial fixing (their own as well as that of others) at precisely the moment when gender potentially acts to fracture necessary cohesion given practical demand for both men's and women's labor in and outside of the home (thereby taking dead aim at hegemonic white working-class masculinity and associated perks and practices), coupled with enough evidence of rising domestic violence in this class fraction to be of potential consequence in the long run. The re-making/transformation of class then, when examined *over time* and in relation to new global economic conditions and political economy, can *only* be understood as nested in both race and gender, as it is dynamics associated with both race and gender that enable class to be produced and reproduced, although in different form, at its own lived-out semi-autonomous level.

The particular role of Yemenites in this community must be considered, as this group offers a specific racial "other" around which whiteness swells.[6] I conducted the follow-up interviews prior to September 11, 2001, a moment that, at least in the popular discourse and imagination of Americans, changed the world forever (Giddens, 2003). As noted earlier, Yemenites have lived in Freeway since the mid-1940s, and white working-class identity has been forged at least tangentially in relation to this group since their arrival. However, there have been key changes with respect to the Yemenite community in this particular urban area.

To begin with, in the mid-1980s when I conducted the original research, identity work among young white men in Freeway High swirled around gender, heterosexuality, and race, but did not rest fundamentally upon the construction of an "Arab" other. Rather, the work of whiteness/class/heterosexuality and gender was done largely in relation to black Americans (who represented approximately 20 percent of the school population), where black Americans, particularly young black men, were set up as the unacceptable sexual "other," enabling young white men both to assert publicly their own heterosexuality at a time of intense surveillance and subsequent negative consequences associated with "inappropriate" sexuality, and at the same time establish and reveal their protectionist stance in relation to white girls/women. In addition, by using black men as a foil, Freeway boys articulated the limits of acceptable heterosexual behavior at the boundary of race—in other words, the behavior of black American men (and women to some extent) was seen to be over the boundary of what was acceptable whereas their own behavior was deftly established as normative, underscoring the normativity of "whiteness" in a wide variety of areas (Fine et al., 2004). The defiant heterosexual moment was, then, inscribed with and against race, particularly in relation to black Americans, a phenomenon that cannot be seen/theorized as only an on-site production, as historic, economic, and social relations between African-Americans and the white working class have fueled such co-constructions for over a century (Morrison, 1992; Ogbu, 1988, 2002; Weis, 1990).

Although there were certainly instances of overt racism involving Yemenites in the mid-1980s (as Ed stated in 1985, "Nabil, the only thing you know how to play is polo on camels"), such racism does not evidence comparable history as that between African-Americans and whites, nor do such instances reach deeply into the white adolescent psyche or the crevices of sexuality. As these white men and women "grow up," however, Yemenites take on particular significance in this community, as whiteness continues to be asserted and inscribed as *good* in a grown-up world of valued family and community living space, but such whiteness is now asserted in relation to Yemenites.

At the moment of the 2000–2001 interviews, an appreciable number of Yemenites live on the "white" side of town—living among the grown-up version of those whom I interviewed in the mid-1980s. It is fair to say that class-linked whiteness is now inscribed on a day-to-day basis in relation to Yemenites, but the key point here is that it is *whiteness* that continues to be inscribed and valued at one and the same time as Yemenites (Arabs) become thoroughly inscribed as *racially different*, in spite of the fact that Arabs are classified as white in the US census. The racial project around Yemenites thus becomes a way of categorizing a group as racially different at the *lived* level, at one and the same time as it "stretches" the existing US racial dichotomy—a dichotomy that rests largely along a black–white continuum (Omi & Winant, 1994; Seller & Weis, 1997).

As white working-class men and women continue, under the press of the global economy and associated demands for the neo-liberal subject, to contest such demands by "fixing race"—their own as well as that of others—they simultaneously expand the racial "other" in significant ways, making it possible to center on whiteness without necessarily having to engage a less immediately present (yet constructed) black other, although, as Toni Morrison and others make clear, such black "other" is always embedded in the white US imagination. This represents a significant turn of events in US racial history, paralleled, perhaps, by the racial project surrounding the internment of Japanese-Americans during World War II, where whiteness was, again, forged in relation to a group other than African-Americans. As we see here, though, at least in this particular community, the former industrial proletariat instantiates its own whiteness and at the same time marks the boundaries of this whiteness in relation to a relatively new group.

That this group is linked to current international politics is obviously important, enabling the white working-class fraction in this particular community to situate their own whiteness and goodness in relation to a negatively defined discursive (now *racial*) other in the context of a broader set of world politics. It is important to recall, however, that this racial project was apparent in this community years before anyone in Freeway knew of Osama Bin Laden. My point here is that this specific set of racial dynamics is attached to a larger project around the more general elaboration of whiteness in the new white working-class fraction rather than being tied entirely to the position of this group in the international political arena.

Affirming my earlier point regarding the nested nature of class, this set of dynamics cannot be read as linked only to race. Gender is key here, as it is arguably the case that since Yemenites exhibit highly circumscribed gender roles and relations on a day-to-day basis, this actually helps white working-class men swallow their own reconfigured and devalued position in the economy and family of the latter quarter of the twentieth century. The highly visible patriarchal family embedded in the Yemenite community perhaps enables such men to see themselves in a more positive light. They are now the "good guys"—the ones who push strollers, meet the school bus, take a turn at cooking and laundry, and tend to a myriad of family responsibilities their fathers and grandfathers would never have touched (as Jerry notes in 2001: "Not in a million years")—unlike their Arab neighbors who "pack a lot of relatives into the house," insist that their women be covered, and "drive around in Lexus's" while their women tend to all home-based duties, largely by never leaving the home. The fact that media images are sent instantaneously from the Middle East to the USA, thus reinforcing the already observed deep (and unfamiliar to even the most patriarchal male American eye) oppression of women, undoubtedly helps working-class white men retain some dignity in the face of their own re-arranged masculinity. The Muslim/Arab "other" in this community, then, plays an important role both in the stabilization of whiteness and the grudging acceptance of a new gendered order in a virulently patriarchal class fraction of the not too distant past.[7] As John said in 2000, while preparing dinner and calling his son indoors while his wife was at work: "My dad would never have done any of this stuff. . . . For him, dinner was on the table at five and the kids were kept quiet."

Young Freeway women looked toward possibilities in high school even as their male counterparts held tightly, and hopelessly, to retrograde cultural forms. It is indeed striking that the sixteen-year-old girls who I interviewed in the mid-1980s all informed me that they didn't want to be "dependent on a man"—that, as Lorna (now a teacher) stated, "men tell you what to do; where to go," and that they wanted no part of it. The reality of their own lives encouraged them to move in this direction, as many saw their mothers and/or grandmothers both beaten physically by men in their lives and simultaneously bereft of options as the steel industry collapsed around them. Young women watched their fathers drink, "sit around and do nothing," and their homes fall to pieces and/or lost altogether as money dried up. Quite simply, young white working-class women did not want this life, saw a way out as a result of economic re-arrangement, and went for it. The largely unacknowledged women's movement was critically important in this respect, in that it offered a discourse of possibility for white working-class women in the mid-1980s as well as actual school and work-related options tied to this discourse, options keyed, of course, to the needs of a rapidly changing economy in global context. Although largely rejecting ties to the feminist movement, white working-class women plunged forward—holding, at the same time, the overall class project together.

Young Freeway men wanted something different; they wanted to bring back patriarchal relations associated with the earlier years of their fathers and grandfathers. This was not to be the case, however, as women poured into colleges/universities and subsequently the labor market, while men lost their lucrative financial edge associated with the steel mill and other such industries. As "Freeway boys" faced their own rearranged position in the family, neighborhood, and work place, "Freeway girls" surged forward, building, with their men, a fragile class fractional alliance, one heavily dependent on rearranged gender/masculinity and an accompanying set of co-constructions which instantiate whiteness. Most importantly, such re-convergence around whiteness papers over, perhaps temporarily, potentially destructive fracture along the lines of gender. Thus working-class men and women continue, under neo-liberalism, to construct privileged identities as whites but the contours of such privilege have shifted within and between gendered and racial boundaries. Most importantly, they fundamentally construct class thematically and practically around and in relation to race and gender, as situated inside political economy of the final quarter of the twentieth century. If not for the particular iteration surrounding the dynamic production of class uncovered here, one which can only be understood as nested in race and gender, it is arguably the case that far more of the children of the former white industrial proletariat would simply be poor. In the final analysis, then, the discrete class fraction explored here would not have materialized.

What I do not know is what will happen from here. In the latter quarter of the twentieth century the white working class has engaged in the process of re-making itself in light of a restructured global economy and accompanying worldwide press toward neo-liberalism. Reconstituting itself on a daily basis, the white working-class fraction is effectively staging its own "class reunion"—a class reunion which, given the fundamentally altered world economy and the particular place of the former industrial proletariat inside this new economy, embodies deep restructuring along gender lines. As men and women of the new US white working class collectively assert whiteness, the class fraction solidifies, offsetting the potentially destabilizing effects of deep gender tensions and re-alignment. How long the class "project" will hold is open to question.

Questions for discussion

1. What are the major differences between the author's two distinct studies relative to the impact of external forces on the process of identity formation? To what does Weis attribute these differences?
2. Discuss neo-liberal initiatives to de-stabilize and de-moor race. Why do you

imagine the former industrial proletariat continues to insist on being a classed, raced, and gendered subject?

3. Weis employs a longitudinal ethnographic method. Why do you suppose the author chose this research method? What are the perceived advantages and/or disadvantages in using a longitudinal approach for this particular study?

4. In addition to race and gender, should we consider other nodes of difference as both wrapping class and serving to produce it? Give examples of these other nodes and explain why they too should be considered in conjunction with class, race, and gender.

5. Do you suspect most couples originate from the same or similar class backgrounds? Why or why not? Does domestic partnership/marriage change or influence one's class location if they are indeed different? If so, in what ways? Whose class location would be considered primary?

6. Why do you suppose members of the white working class of Freeway are more inclined to blame Arabs for economic erosion and deteriorating life conditions circumscribing their communities rather than blaming national and global trends? How might this be extended to the recent discussion on immigrant labor in the USA?

7. Why does neo-liberalism demand "women's independence" and thus participation in the labor force? Although the women of Freeway do not wish to depend on men, to what might we attribute the rejection of ties to feminist movements?

8. As illustrated by this chapter, the process of "Othering" functions deeply within US society. Which groups might be viewed as candidates for being labeled as "Others" (against the white working class) in the USA today? How do you explain the shift in perceptions of racial other from one group to another (for example, from African-Americans to Yemenites in the community under consideration)?

Notes

Data for this project were collected with support from the Spencer Foundation and the Baldy Center for Law and Social Policy, University at Buffalo, State University of New York. Thanks to Mustafa Sever and Michael Olneck for comments on an earlier version of this chapter. Thanks also to three anonymous reviewers who commented upon a much different version of this piece but one from which select insights are drawn for purposes of this writing.

1. In the Americanized version of *The Full Monty*—originally a British film of the same name—six unemployed steel workers turn their attention to creating a strip act at a local club as a way of making money in the face of the dole. In the BBC serial, *The Missing Postman*, a postman wanders about Europe, continuing to deliver one last letter before being laid off. In the postman's absence, his wife remakes herself as an interior decorator of some note. Camera crews waiting to greet the working-class postman upon his return instead turn their attention to his wife when they note her transformation. Both pieces probe what working-class men in first wave industrialized nations see as loss ahead of them under massive changes in the global economy, unable to face what feels "like a loss of manhood and feminization" or what Cohen and Ainley (2000, p. 83) call the loss of "musculatures of the labouring body." It is within this context that I heard and saw the Freeway youth with whom I worked in the 1980s grow up. These grown-up youth are the subject of this chapter.

2. Details related to method, including selection of subjects and specificities in regard to treatment of data, can be found in Weis (1990) and Weis (2004). See also *Working Method* (Weis & Fine, 2004).

3. The ways in which the shifting global economy affects working-class lives on the ground is fully explored in both *Working Class Without Work* (Weis, 1990) and *Class Reunion* (Weis, 2004). The practical manifestations of this shift are most evident in the fact that occupational data for 1960 to 2000 suggest that the most striking decreases in the area are found in the categories of "Construction, Extraction, and Maintenance Occupations" and "Production, Transportation, and Material Moving Occupations." These two major categories constitute virtually all the traditionally coded "blue-collar jobs," thus indicative of the loss of jobs in the area for the group under consideration. When combined over the forty-year period, data suggest a relative decline of close to 100 percent of jobs in these categories, with an absolute change of close to 17 percent. In particular, this area has been impacted by the closing of Freeway Steel, a closure that sent shock waves through the community, resulting in the loss of over 18,500 positions. Despite negotiated buyout deals, 95,000 production workers later lost health and life insurance benefits as the giant steelmaker declared bankruptcy.

4. At one and the same time as whites are instantiating and stabilizing whiteness, Guinier and Torres (2002) suggest that there is some "promise of a cross-racial and democratically committed alliance whose leaders are people of color but who struggle together against hierarchies of power at the right historical time" (p. 252). While not being overly romantic about this possibility, Guinier and Torres suggest that Hispanics/Latinos who already live at the hyphen of the black–white binary could spearhead such a multiracial movement.

5. This becomes rather complex, as the stabilization of whiteness is, in contradictory ways, related, in this case, to a simultaneous stretching of lived-out notions of the racial "other." In other words, Yemenites (Arabs) are now considered racially different even though, by official US census classification, they are white. This is happening at one and the same time as persons of Middle Eastern descent (often no matter what their nation of origin/language or heritage) in the USA are often mistakenly characterized as Arab, which makes the situation even more complex for the people of the region. My thanks to Mustafa Sever for pushing me on this point.

6. I am absolutely convinced that the overall white working-class fractional project in the USA swirls fundamentally around whiteness. In the particular community under consideration here, Yemenites play a key role in this class production. In other communities the ways in which whiteness is instantiated will differ, but whiteness will, nevertheless, be a key part of the production of class, as the white working class re-makes itself in relation to constructed bordering groups of color, whether physically or virtually. The ways in which class emerges in nested relation to race/ethnicity and gender in particular national/geographic locales, offers a significant subject for further study.

7. Again, the fact that Yemenites live in Freeway serves a day-to-day function for these particular white men. I am certain, though, that media images which surround a now well established international "enemy" help white working-class men across the USA swallow, to some extent at least, their own devalued and feminized, under the strictures of hegemonic masculinist discourse, positions in both home and work place. Obviously the politically motivated and linked representations of "others" are far more complex than indicated here; I raise this issue only in relation to the re-articulation of gender in the USA and its meaning for the white working-class fraction.

References

Anyon, J. (1981) Social class and school knowledge. *Curriculum Inquiry, 11*(1), 3–42.

Apple, M. (2001). *Educating the "right" way: Markets, standards, God and inequality.* New York: RoutledgeFalmer.

Bensman, D., & Lynch, R. (1987). *Rusted dreams: Hard times in a steel community.* New York: McGraw Hill.

Cohen, P., & Ainley, P. (2002). In the country of the blind? Youth studies and cultural studies in Britain. *Journal of Youth Studies, 3*(1), 79–93.

Cornbleth, C. (2003). *Hearing America's youth: Social identities in uncertain times.* New York: Peter Lang.

Dolby, N. (2001). *Constructing race: Youth, identity and popular culture in South Africa.* Albany, NY: State University of New York Press.

Edwards, R. (1979). *Contested terrain: The transformation of the workplace in the twentieth century.* New York: Basic Books.

Everhart, R. (1983). *Reading, writing and resistance.* Boston, MA: Routledge and Kegan Paul.

Fine, M., Weis, L., Pruitt, L., & Burns, A. (2004). *Off white: Readings in power, privilege and resistance.* New York: Routledge.

Foley, D. (1990). *Learning capitalist culture: Deep in the heart of Texas.* Philadelphia, PA: The University of Pennsylvania Press.

Giddens, A. (1991). *Modernity and self identity: Self and society in the late modern age.* Oxford: Polity Press.

—— (1998). *The third way.* Malden, MA: Polity Press.

—— (2003). *Runaway world.* New York: Routledge.

Guinier, L., & Torres, G. (2002). *The miner's canary: Enlisting race, resisting power, transforming democracy.* Cambridge: Harvard University Press.

Hall, S. (1996). Introduction: Who needs identity? In S. Hall & P. DuGuy (Eds.), *Questions of cultural identity* (pp. 1–17). London: Sage.

Hunter, A. (1987). *The politics of resentment and the construction of middle America* (unpublished paper). Madison, WI: Havens Center for Social Structure and Social Change, University of Wisconsin, Madison, p. 9.

McCall, L. (2001). *Complex inequality: Gender, class and race in the new economy.* New York: Routledge.

McCarthy, C. (2003). Race, identity and representation in education, unpublished manuscript.

McCarthy, C., Crichlow, W., Dimitriadis, G., & Dolby, N. (Eds.). (2004). *Race, identity and representation in education, Vol. III.* New York: Routledge.

McChesney, R. (1999). Introduction. In N. Chomsky (Ed.), *Profit over people: Neoliberalism and the global order* (pp. 7–16). New York: Seven Stories Press.

McRobbie, A. (Ed.). (1978). Working-class girls and the culture of femininity in women's studies group. *Women take issue.* London: Huchinson.

Morrison, T. (1992). *Playing in the dark: Whiteness and literary imagination.* Cambridge: Harvard University Press.

Ogbu, J. (1988). Class stratification, racial stratification and schooling. In L. Weis (Ed.), *Class, race and gender in American education* (pp. 163–82). Albany, NY: State University of New York Press.

—— (2002, Winter). Black American students and the achievement gap: What else you need to know. *Journal of Thought, 37*(4), 9–33.

Omi, M., & Winant, H. (1994). *Racial formation in the United States: From the 1960s to the 1990s.* New York: Routledge.

Reich, R. (1991). *The work of nations: Preparing ourselves for 21st-century capitalism.* New York: Alfred A. Knopf.

—— (2001). *The future of success.* New York: Alfred A. Knopf.

Rogers, J., & Teixeira, R. (2000). *America's forgotten majority: Why the white working class still matters.* New York: Basic Books.

Seller, M., & Weis, L. (1997). *Beyond black and white: New faces and voices in US schools.* Albany, NY: State University of New York Press.

Walkerdine, V., Lucey, H., & Melody, J. (2001). *Growing up girl: Psychosocial explorations of gender and class*. New York: New York University Press.

Weis, L. (1990). *Working class without work: High school students in a de-industrializing economy*. New York: Routledge.

—— (2004). *Class reunion: The remaking of the American white working class*. New York: Routledge.

Willis, P. (1977). *Learning to labour: How working class kids get working class jobs*. Farnborough, UK: Saxon House Press.

Chapter 20

The ideological blackening of Hmong American youth

*Stacey J. Lee**

I was in junior high school when I first heard my mother explain that *money whitens*. As a Chinese-American growing up in Mississippi during the 1940s and 1950s, my mother's social experiences were shaped by the black and white discourse on race. My mother explained that as her parents, grocery store owners, became more economically successful the whites in the town were "friendlier" to them. Most significantly, my mother recalls that there were social advantages, including attending white schools, which came with being whitened. For Chinese-Americans in the Mississippi Delta, the process of being whitened simultaneously involved being de-blackened. Although my mother recognizes that she experienced significant privileges as someone who was whitened, she has always pointed out that she and other Chinese-Americans were never viewed as being actually white. In Tuan's (1998) language, Chinese-Americans in the Mississippi Delta achieved the status of "honorary whites." As "honorary whites," Chinese-Americans were always subject to the scrutiny of whites. My mother's tenuous status as a whitened Chinese-American was driven home when her high school principal denied her the right to make the graduation speech, a right she had earned as the salutatorian of her graduating class.

My mother's story is not entirely unique to her or to Chinese-Americans in the segregated south. Various scholars have made similar observations about the significance of social class and the position of Asian-Americans in the racial hierarchy (Okihiro, 1994; Ong, 1996). Today the experiences of newer Asian-American immigrants are similarly influenced by the largely black and white discourse that continues to shape understandings of race in the United States (Lee, 2005; Lei, 2003; Ong, 1996; Reyes, 2007). Ong (1996) asserts, "non-white immigrants in the First World are simultaneously, though unevenly, subjected to two processes of normalization: an ideological whitening or blackening that reflects dominant racial oppositions and an assessment of cultural competence based on imputed human capital and consumer power in the minority subject" (p. 737). The educational and economic success of many East Asian and South Asian immigrants has perpetuated the stereotype that Asian-Americans are model minorities (i.e., near whites). On the other hand, the high rates of poverty and low rates of educational attainment among many Southeast Asian immigrants have led to their ideological blackening. In her ethnographic study of Southeast Asian youth, for example,

---

* Professor of Educational Policy Studies at the University of Wisconsin-Madison and Professor in the Program in Urban Education, CUNY Graduate Center.

Reyes (2007) observed that the youth "have fallen prey to these familiar stereotypes traditionally assigned to African-Americans, as they settle in impoverished urban areas across the United States and participate in gang culture. . . ." (p. 12).

As it was during my mother's childhood, the racist discourse on race associates whiteness with all that is valued in dominant society (e.g., economic self-sufficiency and self-reliance) and blackness with failure and laziness. Groups who are identified as being like whites earn social privilege and economic opportunities. On the other hand, being associated with blackness has potentially negative social and economic consequences. Although economic self-sufficiency is certainly tied to the process of whitening, money alone does not lead to the process of whitening. In order to be viewed as "near white" (Okihiro, 1994) or "honorary whites" (Tuan, 1998), Asian-Americans must adopt cultural characteristics associated with the dominant white middle class, and distance themselves from Asian (i.e., foreign) cultural norms. In my maternal grandparents' case, for example, this meant becoming Southern Baptists.

Similarly, the process of blackening also involves more than an evaluation of a group's economic circumstances. If the process of blackening were simply linked to poverty, working-class and poor Chinese-American residents of Chinatowns would be subject to ideological blackening. Instead, these individuals are identified as perpetual or "forever foreigners" (Tuan, 1998). Chinatowns are seen as exotic locations where the residents speak "foreign" languages and eat "foreign" foods. Segregated from other ethnic and racial groups, Chinese residents of US Chinatowns are viewed as foreign others who exist outside the category of citizens (Lowe, 1996). In contrast to Chinatown residents who remain outside of the black and white discourse of race, Vaught (2006) found that Samoan youth in the Pacific Northwest are blackened in the eyes of their teachers and their peers. In the case of the Samoan youth, issues of poverty, low academic achievement, and the fact that they lived in predominantly black neighborhoods appeared to contribute to their blackening. While poverty is certainly associated with blackness, these examples suggest that the process of racialization is complex and multifaceted.

For immigrant students, there are serious educational consequences that come with being whitened or blackened. Asian-American groups who have achieved a model minority or "near white" status are held to high academic expectations and are often favored by teachers (Lee, 1996). Although this may appear to be an advantage, members of this group who fail to achieve model minority success may be overlooked by teachers, and may suffer from shame. Like their African-American peers who face racial barriers in education, Asian-American groups who are blackened face low expectations and marginalization in schools (Lee, 2005; Vaught, 2006).

In this chapter I will examine the ideological blackening that Hmong American students undergo in the Midwest. The Hmong American students' experiences illustrate the role that schools play in the racialization of immigrant youth. The specific focus in this chapter will be on the ways high rates of poverty within the Hmong community, Hmong cultural expressions of family, Hmong American youth styles, student achievement, and issues of space intersect in the process of blackening that Hmong American youth undergo. The data in this chapter come from my ethnographic study on Hmong American high school students living in a mid-sized Midwestern city that I call Lakeview (Lee, 2005). This study explored the ways race, class, and gender informed the academic and social experiences of Hmong American high school students at a school I call University Heights High School (UHS). I conducted fieldwork (e.g., participant observation of Hmong American students inside and outside of school, interviews of students and staff) from January 1999 until June 2000. Although located in a predominately white, middle to upper-middle-class neighborhood, UHS draws students from the south side of the city where the majority of the Hmong American and African-American students live in lower-income housing.

The Hmong: Historical background

The first Hmong arrived in the United States as refugees from Laos thirty years ago. During the Vietnam War the Hmong were US allies in the "secret war" against communism in Laos. The Hmong suffered tremendous casualties during the war, and many more died in refugee camps before being resettled in the United States and around the world (Quincy, 1995). Early Hmong refugees faced significant linguistic, cultural, and economic barriers in their adjustment to life in the United States. Hmong culture in Laos was primarily oral, and children learned cultural traditions and day-to-day skills by observing their elders' daily routines. Few boys, and even fewer girls, had access to formal schooling. Scholars estimate that up to 70 percent of the Hmong refugees were non-literate when they arrived in the United States (Takaki, 1989). Early research on the educational experiences of Hmong refugees highlighted the problems that Hmong students faced, including high dropout rates from middle and high school (Goldstein, 1985; Trueba, Jacobs & Kirton, 1990).

According to the 2000 census, there are 186,310 people who identify themselves as Hmong living in the United States (US Census Bureau, 2000). The largest Hmong American communities are in California, Minnesota, and Wisconsin. As is the case in other immigrant communities, the Hmong American community is young, with a median age of 16.1. The Hmong community continues to suffer from high rates of poverty. According to the 2000 Census, 37.8 percent of Hmong lived under the poverty line, compared to 12.4 percent of the US population overall. Half of the Hmong who lived under the poverty line were individuals under the age of eighteen (Pfeifer & Lee, 2004).

Hmong American students: "At risk"

UHS enjoys an excellent reputation in the city and throughout the state of Wisconsin. Despite this reputation, however, there is a significant achievement gap at UHS that reflects race and class lines. Few Southeast Asian, African-American, or Latino students are on the honor roll or in the higher academic tracks. In conversations with teachers, guidance counselors, and administrators at UHS I found that they used similar language to talk about Hmong American and African-American students. Hmong American students, for example, were described as experiencing high rates of poverty that put them "at risk" for academic failure and for becoming members of the "new underclass," both terms historically associated with black people (Lipman, 1998). The language used to describe Hmong and other Southeast Asian students stood in stark contrast to the characterization of East Asian American students. While Hmong students were typically described in deficit terms, East Asian students were described as model minorities. As high-achieving model minorities who were in the advanced classes and participated in high status extracurricular activities, East Asian students at UHS achieved a whitened or near white status. One of the vice-principals, for example, asserted that many East Asian students at UHS were "outstripping white kids in terms of attendance and probably achievement" (Lee, 2005, p. 48).

UHS educators suggested that the neighborhoods where Hmong American students lived put them "at risk" for underachievement and deviant behavior. Although the city of Lakeview has become increasingly diverse in the last two decades, the neighborhoods are highly segregated by race and class, with most African-Americans and Southeast Asians living in low-income neighborhoods where there were few whites. Most of the East Asian students were middle class, and lived in predominately white neighborhoods, a fact that may have contributed to their "near white" status. The great majority of Hmong American students, on the other hand, qualified for free or reduced lunch and lived in low-income housing on the south side of the city, an area that teachers described as being economically disadvantaged and dangerous. Not insignificantly, the south side of Lakeview had been identified as a low-income black neighborhood long before the first Southeast Asians settled there in the mid-1970s. Educational researchers have highlighted the relationship between social space and identity (Perry, 2002; Weis, 2004). In her longitudinal ethnography of white working-class adults, for example, Weis (2004) clearly demonstrates the fact that white working-class adults believe that their distinct identities as whites depends on living in white neighborhoods. At UHS, it appears that the fact that Hmong American students lived in poor black neighborhoods played a role in how educators perceived the Hmong community, specifically the way educators racialized them.

The fact that most of the second-generation Hmong American students have adopted hip-hop styles of dress and speech that the UHS teachers associated with African-American youth was used as evidence that Hmong American youth were Americanizing in "bad ways" and "at risk" for academic failure and delinquency. UHS educators assumed that hip-hop culture was inherently dangerous and anti-school. The process of blackening intersects in particularly significant ways for Hmong American boys. Like African-American boys, Hmong American boys were viewed as being potentially dangerous and therefore in need of control (Ferguson, 2000). Many UHS educators expressed fear that Hmong American boys were "gang involved." Not insignificantly, teachers interpreted Hmong American boys' hip-hop style clothing as "evidence" of gang involvement. While there were white, middle-class boys who dressed in hip-hop clothing, they were not identified as being in gangs. Despite the teachers' assumptions regarding the prevalence of gang activity among Hmong Americans, I did not find any evidence of a gang problem among Hmong youth. When I asked Hmong American youth about gangs most laughed and said that the Hmong students at UHS were simply gang "wannabees." Significantly, the teachers who were most convinced that Hmong American youth were involved with gangs were the ones who admitted that they didn't have much contact with Hmong students.

Interestingly, some non-Hmong students at UHS characterized Hmong American students as "acting black." In the following quote, a student explains the ways Hmong American students are stereotyped by their non-Hmong peers.

> Like the stereotypes that people have are like a lot of the Hmong—the Hmong stereotype is that they're all gangsters and they follow, like, the "black path" of wearing baggy clothes and being cool and forming gangs and not coming to school, and being truant, you know, all the time.

Not insignificantly, contained within the stereotype of Hmong American youth are problematic and racist stereotypes of African-Americans.

Blaming families

Ethnic culture, race, and social class have all been found to shape the nature of family life (Fine & Weis, 1998; Heath, 1983; Lareau, 2003; Valdes, 1996; Weis, 2004). In her ethnography of working-class and middle-class families, Lareau (2003) captures the many ways social class informs "critical aspects of family life: time use, language use, and kin ties" (p. 236). Furthermore, Lareau (2003) uncovers the way class-based differences in childrearing practices play out in schools and contribute to the reproduction of inequality. Hmong American families share many of the characteristics identified with working-class and poor families, including hierarchical relationships between parents and children, and emphasis on extended family relationships. The UHS educators' middle-class ideas regarding family and about parental involvement in schools led them to view Hmong families as being dysfunctional.

While middle-class family life revolves around the nuclear family, working-class and poor families have been found to emphasize the centrality of extended family (Lareau, 2003). For the Hmong, extended family and clan are central to identity. The importance of extended family was reflected in the fact that Hmong families will often travel great distances, and youth will miss school, in order to attend family funerals and/or weddings. UHS educators appeared to view these family obligations as being barriers to Hmong students' academic achievement. In discussing Hmong American students' academic problems, one teacher sighed as she explained that "Hmong students will miss school for several days to attend funerals." Although this teacher understood the significance of funerals and weddings in Hmong culture, she suggested that these "traditional" practices placed Hmong youth "at risk" academically.

Echoing the cultural deprivation language that originally targeted African-American families, another UHS educator observed:

> African-American kids, Hmong kids, Hispanic kids . . . Some families, you know I shouldn't generalize, but some families are . . . some push those kids to go and get education and are very pro-education. Some families have a kind of culture of not being involved in schools and not valuing education. So it's kind of sometimes put on a back burner . . . the immediate needs of the family come first. Some kids might have to get a job, they might have to baby-sit sometimes when they are the only option, so they might miss school.
>
> (Lee, 2005, p. 46)

Both of these UHS educators concluded that Hmong parents simply don't place a high enough value on education. The educators' individualistic values prevented them from seeing the potential value of family-based decisions.

Within the Hmong community, the extended family serves as an important safety net and a form of control. One practice that Hmong families have adopted in the United States in order to control recalcitrant teens is sending them to live with family members in other communities. One of my research participants, for example, lived with her aunt because her parents wanted her to get away from "bad kids." Although this student was doing well in school, UHS educators who knew her viewed her living situation as being less than ideal. Her social studies teacher, for example, whispered when she said, "I'm not sure who she lives with, but I think she lives with her aunt." Although this teacher did not directly criticize the family, the fact that she lowered her voice and shared this information when discussing her concerns for the girl suggests that this family arrangement was understood to be inherently dysfunctional.

Most UHS educators identified early marriage and early childbearing as the two biggest challenges facing the Hmong community, particularly the girls. Although an increasing number of Hmong American girls are postponing marriage until they complete high school, the general perception among UHS educators is that Hmong girls are pushed into early marriage. The subject of early marriage within the Hmong culture has received a lot of attention from academics and journalists, and the practice of early marriage has typically been understood as evidence of the traditional and vastly different culture (i.e., foreign) that Hmong immigrants/refugees have brought to the United States. In the conversations about early marriage, teachers slipped back and forth between the language of blackening and language that positioned Hmong students as perpetual foreigners. UHS teachers, guidance counselors, and other staff viewed early marriage as being quintessentially foreign. They described Hmong families that advocated early marriage as being "traditional." Most UHS educators were convinced that if the Hmong community did not abandon early marriage they would be "at risk" economically. The few girls who were married and had children were simultaneously described as victims of a traditional culture and as "teen moms" who were destined to become part of the "new underclass."

Finally, the fact that Hmong parents did not exhibit the kind of parental involvement valued by schools was seen as further evidence that Hmong families did not really care about education. UHS educators regularly complained that they had "trouble getting African-American and Hmong parents involved in the PTO [Parent Teacher Organization]." These UHS educators reasoned that the problems that Hmong students faced in school were linked to their parents' "lack of involvement" in educational matters. Although Hmong parents did not participate in their children's educations in the ways identified by UHS educators as "involved," Hmong American students all reported that parents consistently stressed the importance of education. Like other low-income parents of color, most Hmong parents lack the time, resources, and/or knowledge to participate in their children's educations in ways valued by the school.

Blackening and educational opportunities

For Hmong American youth at UHS there were negative educational consequences to being ideologically blackened. The racist assumptions regarding black students were extended to include Hmong American students. As such, Hmong students were held to low expectations and given little encouragement to take upper level courses or to pursue higher education. One guidance counselor explained his perspective on Southeast Asian students, including Hmong American students, in an interview.

A lot of them are not intellectually motivated. These are Southeast Asians I'm talking about now. They are polite, they're nice, they never tell me what, where to go and that sort of thing, I'm a counselor. But they don't have a background of working hard academically, and they don't feel like it now.

(Lee, 2005, p. 45)

While there were individual teachers at UHS who worked hard to advocate for Hmong American students and other students of color, most UHS educators appeared to have given up on them. Labeled "at risk" (i.e., blackened), Hmong American students were understood to be beyond the responsibility of the school. Their academic struggles were identified as being rooted in their social class, families, neighborhoods, cultures, and identities. By blaming the students and their families, these UHS educators were able to relieve themselves of the responsibility to serve Hmong American students.

Perspectives of Hmong American students

Hmong American students' understandings of race and the racial hierarchy were shaped by their experiences at UHS. Hmong American youth were painfully conscious of the fact that whites were positioned at the top of the racial hierarchy at UHS and in the larger society. Furthermore, they were aware that non-Hmong people looked down on the Hmong culture and community. Significantly, Hmong American youth equated whiteness, middle class-ness, and American-ness. Hmong American students appeared to view whites as the only "real" Americans, as evidenced by the fact that they reserved the term "American" to describe whites, while using ethnically specific terms to describe themselves and other people of color.

Hmong American youth have internalized racial stereotypes about whites, African-Americans, and East Asians. When I asked Hmong American youth to describe "Americans," they typically described the stereotypic blue-eyed and blond-haired white person. Hmong American youth reported that "Americans" (i.e., whites) and East Asian Americans were "good" students. Based on their observations of the middle and upper-middle-class white students at UHS, and what they have learned from popular culture, Hmong American youth concluded that Americans (read: whites) are all wealthy. One Hmong American girl described her image of the typical white family in the following quote.

When I think of the mainstream I think of a White family, I guess. As both parents working . . . have really good jobs and maybe one kid or two kids, three at most. And the kids are doing house chores and everything, they like have good grades and even when the girl grows up, the woman, the mom has a good job like a doctor or something.

(Lee, 2005, p. 71)

Although Hmong American girls and boys dreamed of "being rich," and many of the girls admired the gender equity they assumed exists in white families, most Hmong American youth could not identify with whites and did not want to be like white people. Hmong American youth asserted that whites were "selfish" and could not be trusted. Specifically, Hmong American students didn't trust white people to treat Hmong people with respect. One student explained,

For me, I feel, I just feel like some White people neglect me. I mean as much as I try to be nice to them, give them respect, they don't give it back to me. Why should I even bother with them? Because I feel like I really don't need people like that . . .

(Lee, 2005, p. 68)

Hmong students' relationship with whites influenced their attitudes towards blacks. Specifically, Hmong students identified with African-American students at UHS because both groups were subordinate to whites, both groups lived in the "ghetto," and both groups did poorly in school. One Hmong American student asserted that it was "the Hmong way" to be at least one year behind in school.

Hmong American students, however, were not simply passive victims of racialization. Their participation in hip-hop culture expressed resistance to the racial and class inequality they faced at school and in the larger society. Hmong American youth were well aware of the fact that hip-hop language and clothes were associated with African-Americans, and often teased each other for talking and dressing "ghetto" (code for black). Here, "ghetto" appears to be a space of oppositional racial power. Similarly, Reyes (2007) found that low-income Southeast Asian youth in Philadelphia were deeply involved with hip-hop culture, and often teased each other for "acting black." Although Hmong American youth identified with blacks, they maintained a distinct Hmong American identity. Hmong American youth who expressed a hip-hop aesthetic were quick to assert the importance of "Hmong pride" and lyrics from Hmong hip-hop songs often drew on Hmong cultural themes and encouraged ethnic pride.

UHS educators failed to see Hmong American students' adoption of hip-hop style as a legitimate form of social critique. Like many members of the dominant culture, UHS educators viewed hip-hop culture as inherently dangerous. The fact that Hmong American youth were adopting hip-hop styles confirmed UHS educators' belief that the Hmong are like blacks, and therefore "at risk." Thus, the students' resistance helped to confirm the process of blackening.

Conclusions

My research joins the work of other scholars who have identified schools as powerful sites of racialization (e.g., Fine, 1991; Fordham, 1996; Lei, 2003; Lipman, 1998; Olsen, 1997). Significantly, the process of racialization is intimately linked to ideas about social class. Teachers and other educators at UHS interpreted Hmong American students' family cultures, neighborhoods, clothing styles, academic achievement, and social class through the lens of race. The ideological blackening experienced by Hmong American youth demonstrates that ideas about race and class are conflated in the minds of the dominant group. In the dominant imagination, whiteness and blackness are both classed positions. Ideal whiteness is implicitly associated with middle-class status, and blackness is associated with poverty. As in my mother's youth, Asian-Americans are judged by the standards of whiteness (i.e., white, middle class) and are subject to ideological blackening if they are deemed to fall short of the criteria for being whitened. In other words, Asian-Americans are blackened when they lack the human capital and cultural capital associated with middle-class whites. Far from being neutral, the process of racialization involves privileging whiteness and denigrating blackness. Hmong Americans and other groups who are ideologically blackened are subject to racial bias and unequal educational opportunities that African-Americans have historically faced.

When I told my mother that I was writing a piece about blackening, and was writing about her childhood experiences with whitening, she responded, "Money does whiten, but the other day some stranger commented on how well I speak English. What nerve! The idiot was surprised I didn't have an Asian accent." My mother, clearly irritated, had once again encountered the stereotype that Asians are essentially foreign. My mother's recent experience suggests that social class plays a central role in determining whether Asian-Americans are whitened or blackened, but middle-class status does not protect Asian-Americans from being cast as perpetual foreigners. My data suggest that while Hmong American youth are blackened, they are also subject to being identified as perpetual foreigners. At times, UHS educators interpreted Hmong cultural norms to be simultaneously foreign and deficient. It appears that Asian-Americans are simultaneously subject to being judged by the black and white discourse of race, and subject to being seen as foreign.

Questions for discussion

1. Lee argues that the school plays a powerful role in the differential racialization of Hmong and East Asian youth. What does this mean? Does/did school play the same role in your educational experiences? Give reasons for your response.
2. Hmong American students only referred to the white, middle class as "American." What does this suggest about the power and invisibility of race and class in the United States? How does this notion work to reinforce existing power structures and group inequalities?
3. Although we know that US society has been racially diverse, why does the notion of blackness and whiteness still shape the dominant discourse on race?
4. Why are Asians ideologically associated with different racial categories in the United States? How do these categories influence their daily experiences?
5. Why did the UHS educators view parenting and cultural practices of Hmong families as dysfunctional?
6. How does the Hmong youth's social critique and resistance, in the form of their hip-hop cultural expression, limit their educational opportunity?
7. Drawing from your experience, explain the relationship between space and identity. Near the town in which you grew up, is there any area which people usually consider as dangerous or poor? What is the common perception of the residents living there? Is it similar to UHS educators' perception of Hmong youth?
8. Based on Lee's findings, what kinds of educational practices and policies would be helpful for racial minorities in the US, particularly for the education of Southeast Asian youth?

References

Ferguson, A. (2000). *Bad boys: Public schools in the making of black masculinity*. Ann Arbor, MI: University of Michigan Press.

Fine, M. (1991). *Framing dropouts: Notes on the politics of an urban public high school*. Albany: State University of New York Press.

Fine, M., & Weis, L. (1998). *The unknown city*. Boston, MA: Beacon Press.

Fordham, S. (1996). *Blacked out: Dilemmas of race, identity, and success at Capital High*. Chicago: University of Chicago Press.

Goldstein, B. L. (1985). Schooling for cultural traditions: Hmong girls and boys in American high schools. PhD dissertation, Department of Educational Policy Studies, University of Wisconsin-Madison.

Heath, S. B. (1983) *Ways with words: Language, life, and work in communities and classrooms*. Cambridge, England: Cambridge University Press.

Lareau, A. (2003). *Unequal childhoods: Class, race, and family life*. Berkeley, CA: University of California Press.

Lee, S. (1996). *Unraveling the model minority stereotype: Listening to Asian-American youth*. New York: Teachers College Press.

—— (2005). *Up against whiteness: Race, school, and immigrant youth*. New York: Teachers College Press.

Lei, J. (2003). (Un)necessary toughness? Those "loud black girls" and those "quiet Asian boys." *Anthropology & Education Quarterly, 34*(2), 158–81.

Lipman, P. (1998). *Race, class, and power in school restructuring*. Albany: State University of New York Press.

Lowe, L. (1996). *Immigrant acts: On Asian American cultural politics*. Durham, NC: Duke University Press.

Okihiro, G. (1994). *Margins and mainstreams: Asians in American history and culture*. Seattle: University of Washington Press.

Olsen, L. (1997). *Made in America: Immigrant students in our public schools*. New York: New Press.

Ong, A. (1996). Cultural citizenship as subject-making: Immigrants negotiate racial and cultural boundaries in the United States. *Current Anthropology, 37*(5), 737–62.

Perry, P. (2002). *Shades of white: White kids and racial identities in high school*. Durham, NC: Duke University Press.

Pfeifer, M., & Lee, S. (2004). Hmong population, demographic, socioeconomic, and educational trends in the 2000 census. In Hmong National Development Inc. & Hmong Cultural and Resource Center (Eds.), *Hmong 2000 census publication: Data and analysis* (pp. 3–11). Washington, DC: Hmong National Development, Inc.

Quincy, K. (1995). *Hmong: History of a people*. Cheney: Eastern Washington University Press.

Reyes, A. (2007). *Language, identity, and stereotype among Southeast Asian American youth: The other Asian*. Mahwah, NJ: Lawrence Erlbaum.

Takaki, R. (1989). *Strangers from a different shore*. Boston, MA: Little, Brown and Co.

Trueba, H. T., Jacobs, L., & Kirton, E. (1990). *Cultural conflict and adaptation: The case of Hmong children in American society*. Bristol, PA: Falmer Press.

Tuan, M. (1998). *Forever foreigners or honorary whites? The Asian ethnic experience today*. New Brunswick, NJ: Rutgers University Press.

US Census Bureau (2000). Race alone or in combination for American Indian, Alaska native, and for selected categories of Asian and of Native Hawaiian and other Pacific islander. At http://factfinder.census.gov/.

Valdes, G. (1996). *Con respeto: Bridging the distances between culturally diverse families and schools—an ethnographic portrait*. New York: Teachers College Press.

Vaught, S. (2006). *The peculiar institution: Racism, public schooling, and the entrenchment of whiteness*. Unpublished PhD dissertation, University of Wisconsin–Madison.

Weis, L. (2004). *Class reunion: The remaking of the American white working class*. New York: Routledge.

Chapter 21

Schools, social class, and youth

A Bernsteinian analysis

*Alan R. Sadovnik**

In a recent article in the *New York Times Magazine*, Paul Tough (2006) examined "what it takes to make a student." He reviews the sociological literature on black underachievement and a number of schools, including the KIPP (Knowledge is Power Program) Academies and North Star Academy Charter School in Newark, New Jersey, which have been successful in producing high academic achievement for low-income African-American students. Abigail and Stephen Thernstrom (2003) profiled both schools in their book *No Excuses* as having the type of curriculum and pedagogic practices necessary for these students to achieve. The Thernstroms, KIPP, North Star build upon Lisa Delpit's critique of progressive education that invisible pedagogies disadvantage low-income African-American children because they often cannot read or misread the codes (Delpit, 1995). Rather, based in part on Delpit, KIPP and North Star believe that these students need an explicit set of pedagogic codes that are rooted in middle-class educational success. Critics of such an approach (Horn, 2006) argue that KIPP is trying to socialize low-income African-American children into a middle-class white student culture and in doing so rob them of their African-American identities.

The purpose of this chapter is to apply Basil Bernstein's code theory to schools such as KIPP Academies and North Star Academy. First, I will use North Star as an example of the type of effective pedagogic practices described in Tough's article. Second, I will present a brief summary of Bernstein's code theory. Third, I will examine how Bernstein's work, despite its primary focus on social class, necessitates a broader examination of the intersection of social class, race, ethnicity, and gender. Finally, I apply Bernstein's code theory to schools such as North Star.

North Star Academy Charter School

North Star Academy Charter School in Newark, New Jersey is one of the most successful public schools serving low-income and minority students in New Jersey, at least as measured by student test results (Gordon, 2005; Sadovnik & Gordon, 2005). Founded as a 5–8 charter school in 1997 by a former Newark teacher, Jamie Verrilli, and NYC non-profit organizer, Norman Atkins, the school expanded to grades 9–12 in 2002 and recently had its charter expanded to the K–4 grades beginning in 2006. Its co-founder, Atkins, left in 2004 to start an all boys charter school in Brooklyn and to found

* Professor of Education and Sociology at Rutgers University, Newark, New Jersey.

Uncommon Schools, a collaborative non-profit that is planning to open a number of new charter schools in Massachusetts, New York and New Jersey in the coming years, based on the North Star model and its success. North Star is a traditional school, with students wearing uniforms, with rigid disciplinary structures and with directive pedagogical practices. However, it is also a school with a partially Afro-centric curriculum, with exhibitions and alternative assessments at the middle school and high school levels, and a variety of rituals including a "morning circle" that provide a sense of belonging and community for administrators, teachers, students, and parents.

NSA is located in the city of Newark, New Jersey, which has one of the highest poverty levels in the United States and whose district schools were taken over by the NJ Department of Education in 1995 for a variety of reasons, including financial and managerial problems and low student achievement. NSA serves a predominantly minority and low-income population, with 90 percent of its students receiving free lunch. Eighty-five percent of its students are African-American and 15 percent of its students are Hispanic.

North Star was initiated by the collaboration of its founders and a parents' council in 1997, immediately after the passage of New Jersey's Charter School law in 1996. As a charter school, it is independent of the Newark Public Schools (NPS) and receives state and local public school funding of less than $10,000 per student. As a charter school, it does not receive any Abbott funding (additional funding to the 31 low-income urban Abbott districts in NJ from the state's landmark Abbott v. Burke Supreme Court decision). Thus, like all charter schools in Newark, NSA receives significantly less funding than the almost $16,000 per pupil received by the NPS.

NSA's goal is to eliminate the achievement gap that exists between urban students and students attending non-urban schools by high school and to prepare all of its students for college. Its mission is to serve Newark children by building an uncommon school where students partake in a rigorous, eleven-month, extended day, academic program that gives them the means to beat the odds in school and life.

Taken through a lottery at the end of the fourth grade, NSA students arrive below the Newark Public School average on the fourth grade NJ ASK 4 examinations in mathematics and reading/language arts, and by the eighth grade, NSA students are significantly above NPS and NJ students as a whole on the grade eight proficiency assessment (GEPA) and eleventh grade high school proficiency assessment (HSPA), examinations in mathematics, language, arts and literacy, and science. There is currently a waiting list of over five hundred students.

The data indicate that North Star has effectively closed the achievement gap between urban students and the rest of the state on statewide assessments, but NSA students are significantly below the statewide average on the SAT examinations. In almost every category, North Star's eighth graders practically doubled the Newark average and performed higher than the statewide average (New Jersey Department of Education, 2006).

What makes NSA successful, with respect to student achievement? According to its administrators, it is because it has an eleven-month program (two hundred days versus one hundred and eighty days), an extended school day, gives two hours of homework assigned each night, has special Saturday classes (eighth, tenth, eleventh) for GEPA, HSPA, and SAT preparation, before-school reading groups (targeting fifth and sixth graders), after-school honors group for seventh graders (read *To Kill a Mockingbird*), tutoring, performance tasks aimed at developing critical thinking and research skills, middle and high school portfolios and exhibitions before teachers, students, and external jurors (similar to CPESS), and community morning circle where students and teachers share goals and inspirational stories as a community.

At North Star Academy, longer days, a longer school year, committed and talented faculty, rigorous academics, and parent involvement all contribute to its high achievement. Most important, effective leadership has created a culture in the school community that reflects commitment and dedication to all children. It is understood that all teachers, administration, and parents will utilize numerous strategies and interventions for a child to succeed. Academic curriculum is rigorous and class sizes are small, which facilitates achievement. Additionally, learning is maximized and discipline alleviated through the creation of a well-structured environment. Finally, there are positive teacher–student relationships created through advisory groups, mentoring, sports, clubs, and the classroom. Although North Star is structured and disciplined, it nonetheless incorporates many progressive practices, including advisory groups, portfolios, and exhibitions. It also spends a great deal of time on test-taking strategies and preparation.

Another accomplishment of North Star Academy is that 100 percent of its three high school graduating classes are attending college. All seniors were accepted to college—an average of six acceptances each—and every general education student is attending four-year universities, such as Boston College, Mount Holyoke, Spelman, Syracuse, and Rutgers. Such results offer hope when compared to the Newark District, where only 26 percent of the graduating seniors report planning on attending four-year colleges (Annual Report 2003–4, p. 4).

North Star Academy, with its more traditional, standards based and often more authoritarian pedagogic practices, reflects the type of curriculum and pedagogy that Delpit and the Thernstroms see as more successful for this population; one that provides the necessary order and structure that low-income students may require. Its student success on state-wide tests indicates that such a curriculum and pedagogy can be highly effective. However, it is important to note that NSA's discipline is not the type of rigid authority often found in urban schools. Rather, it is part of an overall philosophy that attempts to get students to internalize authority and responsibility and, by high school, NSA students are engaged in the type of independent work more characteristic of schools with more affluent populations. NSA, although more structured and disciplinarian, also provides a caring community for its students.

What seems clear is that NSA provides students with a caring and respectful community where achievement is stressed. It has created a secular religious environment in which its pedagogic codes, through ritual, curriculum rigor, and explicit pedagogic rules, result in student internalization of an identity that includes academic success and college attendance as virtues. Whereas critics may see this as an imposition of white middle-class culture on African-American students, North Star administrators view this as the assimilation of what Delpit has termed the "codes of power," which is necessary for school and economic success. Although North Star believes that their students should retain their "local" cultural identities by becoming bicultural, they do not apologize for equipping their students with what they see as the tools for success.

Code theory: Basil Bernstein's contribution to understanding education[1]

Code theory is the term used to describe the theoretical and empirical project of British sociologist Basil Bernstein. This approach is concerned with how the macro-level (social, political, and economic structures and institutions) is dialectically related to the way in which people understand systems of meaning (codes). For over three decades, Bernstein was one of the centrally important and controversial sociologists, whose work influenced a generation of sociologists of education and linguists. From his early works on language, communication codes, and schooling to his later works on curriculum and pedagogy (teaching methods), Bernstein attempted to produce a theory of social and educational codes (meaning systems) and their effect on social reproduction. Bernstein's sociology drew on the essential theoretical orientations in the field—Durkheim, Weber, Marx, and interactionist—and provided the possibility of an important synthesis.

Bernstein's early work on code theory was highly controversial because it discussed social class differences in language that some labeled a deficit theory (Bernstein, 1973a, 1973b). Nonetheless, the work raised crucial questions about the relationships among the social division of labor, the family, and the school and explored how these relationships affected differences in learning among social classes. His later work (1977a) began the difficult project of connecting macropower and class relations to the microeducational processes of the school. Whereas class reproduction theorists such as Bowles and Gintis (1976) offered an overtly deterministic view of schools, viewing education as exclusively influenced by the economy without describing or explaining what goes on in schools, Bernstein's work attempted to connect the societal, institutional, interactional, and intrapsychic levels of sociological analysis.

The concept of code is central to Bernstein's structural sociology. From the outset of its use in his work on language (restricted and elaborated codes), the term referred to the rules that define a system of messages, especially with respect to language, curriculum, and pedagogy (Atkinson, 1985, p. 136). Bernstein's early work on language (1958, 1960, 1961) examined the relationship between communication, authority, and shared meanings (Danzig, 1995, pp. 146–47). By 1962, Bernstein began to develop code theory through the introduction of the concepts of restricted and elaborated codes (1962a, 1962b). Bernstein's sociolinguistic code theory developed into a social theory examining the relationships between social class, family, and the reproduction of meaning systems.

For Bernstein, there were social class differences in the communication codes of working-class and middle-class children, differences that reflect the class and power relations in the social division of labor, family, and schools. Based upon empirical research, Bernstein distinguished between the restricted code of the working class and the elaborated code of the middle class. Restricted codes are context dependent and particularistic, whereas elaborated codes are context independent and universalistic. For example, when asked to tell a story describing a series of pictures, working-class boys used many pronouns, and their stories could only be understood by looking at the pictures. Middle-class boys, on the other hand, generated descriptions rich in nouns, and their stories could be understood without the benefit of the pictures. Although Bernstein's critics (see Danzig, 1995) argued that his sociolinguistic theory represented an example of deficit theory (alleging that he was arguing that working-class language was deficient) Bernstein consistently rejected this interpretation (see Bernstein, 1996, pp. 147–56).

Bernstein countered that restricted codes were not deficient, but rather were functionally related to the social division of labor, where context-dependent language is necessary in the context of production. Likewise, the elaborated code of the middle classes represents functional changes necessitated by changes in the division of labor and, as a result, by the middle class's (the professional and managerial class that developed in the early part of the twentieth century) new position in reproduction rather than production. That schools require an elaborated code for success means that working-class children are disadvantaged by the dominant code of schooling, not deficient. For Bernstein, difference becomes deficit in the context of macro-power relations.

Bernstein developed code theory from its sociolinguistic roots to examine the connection between communication codes and curriculum and teaching methods (Bernstein, 1977a). In this respect, code theory became concerned with the processes of schooling and how they related to social class reproduction. Bernstein analyzed the significant differences between different forms of educational transmission and suggested that social class differences in curriculum and pedagogy are related to inequalities of educational achievement between working-class and middle-class students. Schools that serve middle-class students have different curricula and teaching methods than schools that serve working-class students, and these differences result in educational inequality. Through an examination of the inner workings of the dominant forms of educational practice, Bernstein contributed to a greater understanding of how the schools (especially in the UK and the United States) reproduce what they are ideologically committed to eradicating—social-class advantages in schooling and society. For example, Bernstein's work helps us understand the processes through which schools in the United States, despite their ideological commitment to equal opportunity and meritocracy, advantage the affluent and disadvantage the disadvantaged.

Code theory and pedagogic practice

Bernstein developed code theory from its sociolinguistic roots to examine the connection between communication codes and pedagogic discourse and practice. In this respect, code theory became concerned with the processes of schooling and how they related to social class reproduction. In order to understand the microprocesses of schooling, Bernstein analyzed the differences between two types of educational practices, one with explicit rules and the other with implicit rules. He suggested that the differences in the classification and framing rules of each pedagogic practice (visible pedagogy [VP] = strong classification and strong framing; invisible pedagogy [IP] = weak classification and weak framing) relate to the social-class position and assumptions of the families served by the schools (Bernstein, 1977b). Classification refers to relations between categories regarding the social division of labor and is related to the distribution of power. Framing refers to the location of control over the rules of communication. (For a detailed analysis of this aspect of Bernstein's work, see Atkinson, 1985; Atkinson, Davies & Delamont, 1995; Sadovnik, 1991, 1995.)

Classification, framing, and code

The concept of classification is at the heart of Bernstein's theory of curriculum. Classification refers to "the degree of boundary maintenance between contents"

(Bernstein, 1973a, p. 205; 1973b, p. 88) and is concerned with the insulation or boundaries between curricular categories (areas of knowledge and subjects). Strong classification refers to a curriculum that is highly differentiated and separated into traditional subjects; weak classification refers to a curriculum that is integrated and in which the boundaries between subjects are fragile.

Using the concept of classification, Bernstein outlined two types of curriculum codes: collection and integrated codes. The first refers to a strongly classified curriculum; the latter, to a weakly classified curriculum. Drawing upon Durkheim's analysis of the changes in the division of labor in the nineteenth century, Bernstein analyzed the way in which the shift from collection to integrated curriculum codes represents the evolution from mechanical to organic solidarity, with curricular change marking the movement from the sacred to the profane. For example, in modern societies rituals and symbols that were considered sacred in traditional societies become ordinary and routine. In schools, uniforms are replaced by individual dress and teachers addressing their students formally by their surnames (Mr. or Miss) is replaced by using their first names. Traditional curriculum whose purpose was to pass on the heritage of traditional societies is replaced with a broader curriculum representative of changes in the groups in modern society.

Whereas classification is concerned with the organization of knowledge into curriculum, framing is related to the transmission of knowledge through pedagogic practices. Framing refers to the location of control over the rules of communication and "refers to the degree of control teacher and pupil possess over the selection, organization, pacing and timing of the knowledge transmitted and received in the pedagogical relationship" (1973b, p. 88). Therefore, strong framing refers to explicit power relations between teacher and students and a classroom with discipline; weak framing refers to implicit power relations and a classroom where students have more freedom.

In keeping with a Durkheimian orientation, Bernstein's analysis of the organization (curriculum) and transmission of knowledge (pedagogy) related changes in classification and framing to the evolution of the social division of labor. He demonstrated how the move to an integrated code with weak classification and weak framing represents conflicts between the old and new middle classes in the social division of labor and provides an illuminating examination of how pedagogic discourse and practice are structurally related to shifts in social structure (1977b). That is, the new professional and managerial classes that developed in the early part of the twentieth century, and whose work occurred in the field of social reproduction, wanted their children to have a less strict and traditional education than the old middle classes, whose work occurred in the field of economic production. Although Bernstein was not a Marxist, he incorporated class and power relations into an overall structural theory.

Thus, Bernstein's work on pedagogic discourse and practice was concerned with the production, distribution, and reproduction of official knowledge and how this knowledge is related to structurally determined power relations. What is critical is that Bernstein is concerned with more than the description of the production and transmission of knowledge; he is concerned with its consequences for different groups. Whereas his work on pedagogic discourse was concerned more with the classification rules in the production and reproduction of knowledge, his work on pedagogic practice was concerned with framing rules and their role in the transmission of knowledge. Central to his analysis was the manner in which social class and power relations affect pedagogic practice.

Theory of pedagogic practice

Bernstein's analysis of pedagogic practice looked at the process and content of what occurs inside schools in terms of the "how" and the "what" of schooling. The theory of pedagogic practice examines a series of rules that define its workings and considers both how these rules affect the content to be transmitted and how they differentially affect groups from different social class backgrounds (1990, p. 63).

Bernstein examined "the social class assumptions and consequences of forms of pedagogic practice" (1990, p. 63). Finally, he applied this theory first to conservative/traditional versus progressive/child centered pedagogic practices and, second, to oppositional types within the conservative/traditional form. He differentiated between a pedagogic practice that is dependent on the economic market—that emphasizes vocational education—and another that is independent and autonomous of the market—that is legitimated by the autonomy of knowledge. Through a detailed analysis of these two competing traditional ideological forms, Bernstein concluded that both forms, despite their claims to the contrary, will not eliminate the reproduction of class inequalities. Thus, through a careful and logical consideration of the inner workings of the dominant forms of educational practice, Bernstein contributes to a greater understanding of how the schools (especially in the United States) reproduce what they are ideologically committed to eradicating—social-class advantages in schooling and society. That is, despite their commitment to equality of opportunity, schools in the United States provide different curriculum and pedagogic practices to students from different social-class backgrounds resulting in an achievement gap. However, since the dominant codes convince students that they have been given an equal opportunity, if and when they fail, they blame themselves and not the schools, thus legitimating the reproduction of inequality.

Bernstein's analysis of the social-class assumptions of pedagogic practice is the foundation for linking microeducational processes to the macrosociological levels of social structure and class and power relations. His basic thesis is that there are significant differences in the social-class assumptions of VPs and IPs and, despite these differences between what he terms "opposing modalities of control" (1990, p. 73), there may indeed be similar outcomes, especially in the reproduction of power and symbolic control.

Bernstein's analysis of the relationship between social class and pedagogic practice resulted in his distinction between visible and invisible pedagogy. Bernstein's thesis, that these pedagogic practices represented differences between the old and the new middle classes and their different placement in the division of labor, is confirmed by Jenkins' research (1990) on the social class basis of progressive education in Britain. Through an analysis of articles in the *Journal of the New Education Fellowship* between 1920 and 1950, she supported Bernstein's central thesis about the social class basis of invisible pedagogy, which Jenkins argued was precisely what the progressives were talking about. Semel (1995) further supports this thesis as applied to independent progressive schools in the United States from 1914 to 1935. For example, her work on the Dalton School and the City and Country School, both founded in the early part of the twentieth century in New York City, indicates that their students came largely from the new professional, managerial, and artistic middle classes and that the schools' pedagogic practices reflected the Deweyan progressive education of the era. Although their curricula was interdisciplinary and thematic, it nonetheless was college preparatory and contained the foundations of elite knowledge and cultural capital (Semel, 1995; Semel & Sadovnik, 1999).

Thus, as Sadovnik (1991, 1995) concludes, Bernstein's theory of pedagogic practice suggests that what is usually labeled progressive education in the United States (weak classification = integrated curriculum and weak framing = child-centered, democratic education) is more likely to be found in schools that serve upper-middle-class, affluent families; and more traditional education (strong classification = discipline-centered curriculum and strong framing = teacher directed and more authoritarian) is more likely to be found in schools serving low-income, working-class, and minority families.

Semel and Sadovnik (1999) argue that one of the significant research questions unanswered empirically by their historical study of US progressive education is whether this type of education can work for working-class and minority students. Delpit (1995) argues that progressive education is often inappropriate for working-class and especially minority students, as it requires a middle-class code, which these students do not bring to school. Although Bernstein argues that progressive education has been primarily the domain of the affluent, he does not rule out the possibility that such pedagogic practices can work for less affluent children, if a number of conditions are met, including (1) careful selection of teachers; (2) adequate preparation time for teachers; (3) time to construct lessons that allow students to recognize themselves; and (4) regular parent–school meetings (Bernstein in Sadovnik, 1995, pp. 419–20).

Social class, schooling, and youth: Applying a Bernsteinian perspective

Code theory, then, argues that youth identity is the outcome of a complex set of processes that are rooted in the relationship between the economic field of production and the symbolic fields of reproduction situated in the family and schools and, most recently, in the media. Families with different places in the division of labor use different forms of communication codes and have differing forms of social and cultural capital, which they transmit to their children. Once in school, often with children of similar social class backgrounds, children are exposed to different pedagogic codes, which often reproduce these social class differences in identity. Like other social reproduction theorists, such as Bowles and Gintis and Bourdieu, Bernstein sees schools as sites for the reproduction of social class based inequalities. Unlike these theorists, however, Bernstein places more emphasis on the ways in which the rules of pedagogic practice and discourse affect the minds and hearts of students. That is, social class differences in pedagogic codes within schools produce different pedagogic identities. These identities are functionally related to the inequalities in the economic field of production and the symbolic fields of reproduction, ultimately preparing children for their place in an unequal division of labor. Thus, Bernstein, like Durkheim, sees schooling as producing a collective conscience through the transmission of codes. Unlike Durkheim, however, these codes are social class based and produce collective conscience within different groups, but not across them. Thus, rather than schools producing the type of functional societal order envisioned by Durkheim, they produce conflict among different groups within a stratified society. In the postmodern world, however, since most, if not all, groups have access to the media through television, movies, and the internet, the boundaries that traditionally separated groups are weakened. Thus, the weaker classification of pedagogic identities results in less clearly defined social class based identities making social reproduction more complicated. Despite these differences, Bernstein understood that social class based identities remained powerful transmitters of privilege and that schools remained important institutions for their reproduction.

In his later work, Bernstein broadens his earlier exclusive focus on social class to include more of an emphasis on race, ethnicity, and gender. Although social class remains a central feature of his theory, he became more interested in how social class, race, ethnicity, and gender interacted to form identities. In part, Bernstein was reacting to profound demographic changes in the UK that by the 1990s transformed its schools into far more multi-racial and ethnic organizations. Unlike the schools of the 1960s, where schools were divided along primarily social class lines, but with mostly white students, by the 1990s schools in London and other cities, although still largely social class bounded, now had students from numerous racial and ethnic backgrounds under the same roof. Given these changes, Bernstein's later work became increasingly sensitive to the interaction of these different demographic variables. Nonetheless, the primacy of social class remained central to the end of his life.

Although a small group of researchers has continued to develop and test Bernstein's theories,[2] most sociological work in the United States ignores Bernstein, even though his work is directly applicable. The works of Annette Lareau (2002, 2003) and Jamie Lew (2006) demonstrate that, although race and ethnicity are important interdependent variables, social class remains a crucial, if not predominant, one. Lareau's ethnographic study of African-American and white middle- and working-class families indicates that there are larger differences based on social class than race. White and African-American families engage in a child rearing process she terms "concerted cultivation," whereas white and African-American working-class and poor families engage in what she terms a "natural growth" model of child rearing. Although Lareau uses a Bourdieuian theoretical perspective and argues that these practices result in different social class based habitus, her research supports a Bernsteinian perspective that these practices result in different pedagogic codes.

Lew's (2006) research on Korean-American students clearly demonstrates both the importance of social class in the construction of identity and the interdependence of race and ethnicity. Lew argues that the most significant difference between her two samples of successful Korean-American students in an elite magnet high school in New York City and unsuccessful high school dropouts returning to a GED center also in New York City was the social class background of their families. The successful students for the most part came from middle-class families; the unsuccessful students came from working-class backgrounds. Most importantly, the two groups had significantly different pedagogic identities. The successful students defined themselves as Korean-American or Asian-American and separate from white and African-American students. The unsuccessful students were far more likely to define themselves in an adversarial relationship to white students and were far more likely to identify themselves with their African-American and Latino classmates. Although Lew's work demonstrates the continuing importance of social class, it also supports Bernstein's later thesis that other categories such as race and ethnicity have become central to pedagogic identities. Further, it demonstrates that pedagogic identities and school success or failure are the outcomes of a complex interaction among family, community, and schools.

The late John Ogbu's work has been the subject of intense debate, particularly with respect to his and his colleague Signithia Fordham's "burden of acting white" theory of African-American underachievement (Fordham & Ogbu, 1986). Although Ogbu and

Bernstein's works are rarely discussed as complementary, there are significant similarities. Ogbu (2004), in an attempt to defend and clarify his theory, argues that black identities are formed in relation to the historical and structural conditions from slavery to the present, which required that African-American identities be defined in relation to white oppression. The process of identity formation included language, dress, rituals, and other forms of expression, which Bernstein would have defined as codes. Ogbu (1999), in an analysis of Ebonics, argues that African-American student ambivalence about the use of standard or White English must be understood in the context of the historical development of Black English and how the construction of African-American identity represents a complex social psychological response to domination. Although Bernstein did not write about Black English, his sociolinguistic code theory is clearly applicable to Ogbu's analysis.[3] For Bernstein, the issue would not be whether Black English is "culturally deficient." Rather, he would have argued that it developed as a functional linguistic system in response to structurally created conditions and that unequal power relations and the privileging of Standard English in the schools turned difference into disadvantage or deficit.

Although Bernstein's work has been criticized as too complex and difficult, it is undeniable that it represented one of the most sustained and powerful attempts to investigate significant issues in the sociology of education. Over thirty-five years ago, Bernstein began with a simple but overwhelming issue: how to find ways to "prevent the wastage of working-class educational potential" (1961). Taken as a whole, Bernstein's work provided a systematic analysis of the relationship between society, schools, and the individual and of how schooling systematically reproduces social inequality. It remains an important theoretical tool for understanding the complex relationships between social class, race, ethnicity, gender, and identity and how these relationships affect school success and failure for different groups.

North Star and KIPP Academy: Applying Bernstein

Paul Tough's article raises significant questions about the types of pedagogic practices employed at schools such as North Star Academy and KIPP Academy. Using Ogbu, a criticism is that these schools are socializing students to act white. From a Bernsteinian perspective, they are socializing them to follow white middle-class codes, but unlike schools that educate largely white and middle-class populations, they are making these codes explicit, where for white middle-class children, the codes are implicit, having been learned in the family.

Using Bernstein's theory of pedagogic practice, NSA is a traditional school, with strong classification and framing. It has a more strongly classified curriculum and more strongly framed pedagogic practices than schools with white middle-class populations. However, in some ways it also has more progressive features. It has a strongly classified disciplinary curriculum, which is linked to the discipline-based New Jersey Core Curriculum Standards. Its pedagogic practices, especially in grades 5–8, are strongly framed, with strict discipline and authority relations. Students wear uniforms and, in the morning circle, students who have been absent or late apologize publicly to the entire North Star community. The relations of authority and academic expectations are made explicit to all students. Once these are internalized by students, usually by the high school, the framing becomes a little weaker, but nonetheless remains strong. However, many of the pedagogic practices are student-centered and involve significant student participation. The end of year exhibitions for grades 8–12 in which they present their work to teachers and visiting judges is similar to the portfolio exhibitions at more progressive schools and are an example of a much weaker set of framing rules.

From a Bernsteinian perspective, the reaction to the Tough article was both predictable and troubling. Horn (2006) compares KIPP and its methods to the eugenics movement of the early twentieth century. A colleague of mine, a revisionist historian of education, called their methods just a new way of making black people white. Another colleague, a radical sociologist of education, labeled KIPP the latest attempt to blame low-income African-American families for the dysfunctions of their children's schools by placing the blame on a culture of poverty, rather than school dysfunction.

For Bernstein, the reality would have been far more complex than these negative portrayals of schools such as KIPP and North Star. Schools reward dominant cultural identities and these schools believe that since low-income African-American students often do not learn the codes of power at home, their schools have to have explicit pedagogic practices that teach them. Research on the history of progressive education in the United States (Semel & Sadovnik, 1999) indicates that strong classification and strong framing have dominated the schooling of low-income children, but without the high expectations and caring environment of North Star. It also points to examples of successful progressive pedagogic practices for these students, where weak classification and weak framing have had successful results. For example, Central Park East Secondary School (CPESS) in East Harlem, under the direction of Deborah Meier in the 1980s and early 1990s, used more progressive pedagogic practices successfully for low-income children of color.[4] What seems clear is that both CPESS under Meier and schools such as KIPP and North Star, with very different pedagogic practices, used a caring environment with high expectations, to create the conditions for high academic achievement by their students. Having attended the North Star graduation ceremonies held at Rutgers University-Newark, it is apparent looking at the joy and happiness of the graduates' families, most of whom have no postsecondary education, that these families do not believe that assimilation or perhaps partial assimilation is too high a price to pay for their children's acceptances to college. It is also clear from the opening march accompanied by the rhythms of African drums that North Star has not obliterated their students' African-American identities. The criticism of cultural imperialism leaves me puzzled as to whether the students in Newark's comprehensive high schools, with a 50 percent drop out rate and between 20 and 40 percent passing rates on the state's HSPA examinations, are better off having not had the codes of power "imposed" on them.

The still unanswered research question is whether or not low-income African-American children need the "tough" pedagogic practices discussed by Tough in order to succeed academically. Research on the more progressive practices currently being implemented by the small schools movement, often more characteristic of the pedagogic practices of schools with more affluent populations, may provide important answers to this question.

For Bernstein, the key to these debates is an understanding that codes are related to power and that power unequally advantages those with it and unequally disadvantages those without it. Codes originate in the economic field and are transmitted first through families and then through schools. Although his work focused on the social class basis of codes and how these codes resulted in different social class identities, currently in the

United States the intersection of social class, race, and ethnicity are at the heart of questions of efforts to reduce the achievement gaps. The ongoing question is whether low-income children of color need to become "white and middle class" to succeed in school and in doing so must lose their own racial and ethnic identities. From a Bernsteinian perspective, there are no easy answers to this question and simplistic charges of cultural deprivation, eugenics, and domination do not capture the complexities of code theory.

Questions for discussion

1. Discuss Basil Bernstein's code theory. How does Sadovnik apply this theory of codes to schools serving high achieving, low-income, African-American students?
2. Bernstein's theory was criticized when referred to as a "deficit theory." Discuss Bernstein's response to this point of contention. How is the term "deficit" dissimilar to his notion of "disadvantaged?"
3. Discuss the differences between invisible and visible pedagogy. How are these terms related to symbolic control?
4. Sadovnik compares Bernstein to various other social theorists and his code theory to various other social theories. Discuss how Bernstein's theory differs from other theories mentioned in this text. What makes his code theory so appealing to Sadovnik through its practical application within North Star?
5. The author claims: "The ongoing question is whether low-income children of color need to become 'white and middle-class' to succeed in school and in doing so must lose their own racial and ethnic identities." What must we consider when responding to this question? How would you begin to answer the question posed by Sadovnik?
6. What constitutes "elite knowledge?" How are these forms of knowledge related to the concepts of cultural capital and social reproduction? Discuss how elite knowledge might be legitimated through educational institutions, including those outside of schools.
7. Sadovnik describes a partially Afro-centric curriculum as a positive point of influence within North Star classrooms. How might a less "white-male-centered" curriculum benefit students of all racial, ethnic, and classed identities?
8. The author notes North Star's success as measured by student test results. Do you find test results to be strong and accurate ways of assessing the success of students? What other means might we use to measure success in education while also considering Bernstein's code theory (by way of Sadovnik)? Why might Sadovnik focus on test results?

Notes

1. This section up to p. 322 on Bernstein's theory is adapted and revised from Sadovnik (1995, pp. 1–35; 2007, pp. 9–11).
2. Since 2000, four international Bernstein research symposia have been held, in Lisbon (2000), Cape Town (2002), Cambridge (2004), and Newark, NJ (2006), with a fifth scheduled for

Cardiff (2008). Volumes based on the first three have been published (Moore, Arnot, Beck & Daniels, 2006; Morais, Neves, Davies & Daniels, 2001; Muller, Davies & Morais, 2004), with a fourth in preparation (Sadovnik, Muller, Power & Singh, 2006).

3. See Sadovnik (1995) for a discussion of the criticisms of Bernstein as a cultural deficit theorist and the claims by Labov that Bernstein's work argued that Black English was deficient. Bernstein consistently argued that he was not a deficit theorist. In my conversations with him prior to his death in 2000 about Ogbu's work, he indicated that although his own work was more concerned with the effects of social class, he believed that Ogbu's work captured the effects of codes based on race.

4. See Meier (1995) for a description of CPESS. Since Meier's departure, CPESS became increasingly ineffective and, in 2004, was closed and reopened as two separate schools, CPE Middle School and CPE High School.

References

Atkinson, P. (1985). *Language, structure and reproduction: An introduction to the sociology of Basil Bernstein*. London: Methuen.

Atkinson, P., Davies, B., & Delamont, S. (1995). *Discourse and reproduction: Essays in honor of Basil Bernstein*. Cresskill, NJ: Hampton Press.

Bernstein, B. (1958). Some sociological determinants of perception. An enquiry into sub-cultural differences. *British Journal of Sociology, 9*, 159–74.

—— (1960). Language and social class: A research note. *British Journal of Sociology, 11*, 271–76.

—— (1961). Social structure, language, and learning. *Educational Research, 3*, 163–76.

—— (1962a). Linguistic codes, hesitation phenomena and intelligence. *Language and Speech, 5*, 31–46.

—— (1962b). Social class, linguistic codes and grammatical elements. *Language and Speech, 5*, 221–40.

—— (1973a). *Class, codes and control: Vol. 1*. London: Routledge & Kegan Paul. (Original published in 1971.)

—— (1973b). *Class, codes and control: Vol. 2*. London: Routledge & Kegan Paul. (Original published in 1971).

—— (1977a). *Class, codes and control: Vol. 3*. London: Routledge & Kegan Paul. (Original published in 1975.)

—— (1977b). Class and pedagogies: Visible and invisile (rev. ed.). In B. Bernstein (Ed.), *Class, codes and control: Vol. 3*. (pp. 116–56). London: Routledge & Kegan Paul.

—— (1990). Social class and pedagogic practice. In B. Bernstein (Ed.), *Class, codes and control: Vol. 4. The structuring of pedagogic discourse* (pp. 63–93). London: Routledge.

—— (1995). A response. In A. R. Sadovnik (Ed.), *Knowledge and pedagogy: The sociology of Basil Bernstein* (pp. 385–424). Norwood, NJ: Ablex Publishing Corporation.

—— (1996). *Pedagogy, symbolic control and identity: Theory, research, critique*. London: Taylor & Francis.

Bowles, S., & Gintis, H. (1976). Schooling in capitalist America: Educational reform and contradictions of economic life. New York: Basic Books.

Danzig, A. (1995). Applications and distortions of Basil Bernstein's code theory. In A. R. Sadovnik (Ed.), *Knowledge and pedagogy: The sociology of Basil Bernstein* (pp. 145–70). Norwood, NJ: Ablex Publishing Corporation.

Delpit, L. (1995). *Other people's children*. New York: The New Press.

Fordham, S., & Ogbu, J. (1986). Black students' school success: Coping with the burden of "acting white." *The Urban Review, 18*(3), 176–206.

Gordon, P. (2005). *North Star Academy Charter School and urban educational reform in New Jersey*. Paper presented at the Annual Meeting of the American Educational Studies Association, Charlottesville, VA, November, 2005.

Horn, H. (2006). *KIPP as new age psychological sterilization*. EDDRA, December 8, 2006.

Jenkins, C. (1990). The professional middle class and the origins of progressivism: A case study of the new educational fellowship, 1920–50. *CORE, 14*(1). University of London, Institute of Education.

Lareau, A. (2002). Invisible inequality: Social class and childrearing in black families and white families. *American Sociological Review, 67*(5), 747–76.

—— (2003). *Unequal childhood: Class, race and family life*. University of California Press.

Lew, J. (2006). *Asian Americans in class: Charting the achievement gap among Korean American youth*. New York: Teachers College Press.

Meier, D. (1995). *The power of their ideas*. Boston: Beacon.

Moore, R., Arnot, M., Beck, J., & Daniels, H. (2006). *Knowledge, power and educational reform: Applying the sociology of Basil Bernstein*. London: Routledge.

Morais, A., Neves, I., Davies, B., & Daniels, H. (2001). *Towards a sociology of pedagogy: The contribution of Basil Bernstein to research*. New York: Peter Lang.

Muller, J., Davies, B., & Morais, I. (2004). *Reading Bernstein, researching Bernstein*. London: Routledge Falmer.

Ogbu, J. U. (1999). Beyond language: Ebonics, proper English, and identity in a Black-American speech community. *American Education Research Journal, 36*(2), 147–84.

—— (2004). Collective identity and the burden of acting white in black history, community and education. *The Urban Review, 36*(1), 1–35.

Sadovnik, A. R. (1991). Basil Bernstein's theory of pedagogic practice: A structuralist approach. *Sociology of Education, 64*(1), 48–63.

—— (Ed.) (1995). *Knowledge and pedagogy: The sociology of Basil Bernstein*. Norwood, NJ: Ablex Publishing Corporation.

—— (2007). Theory and research in the sociology of education. In A. R. Sadovnik (Ed.), *Sociology of education: A critical reader* (pp. 3–21). New York: Routledge.

Sadovnik, A. R., & Gordon, P. (2005). *North Star Academy and urban school reform*. Paper presented at the Annual Meeting of the American Educational Research Association, Montreal.

Sadovnik, A. R., Muller, J., Power, S., & Singh, P. (2006). Proceedings of the Fourth International Basil Bernstein Research Symposium. July 3–9, Rutgers University-Newark, NJ.

Semel, S. F. (1995). Basil Bernstein's theory of pedagogic practice and the history of American progressive education: Three case studies. In A. R. Sadovnik (Ed.), *Knowledge and pedagogy: The sociology of Basil Bernstein* (pp. 337–58). Norwood, NJ: Ablex Publishing Corporation.

Semel, S. F., & Sadovnik, A. R. (1995). Lessons from the past: Individualism and community in three progressive schools. *Peabody Journal of Education* (Summer 1995), pp. 56–84.

—— (1999). *"Schools of tomorrow," schools of today: What happened to progressive education*. New York: Peter Lang.

Thernstrom, A., & Thernstrom, S. (2003). *No excuses: Closing the racial gap in learning*. New York: Simon and Schuster.

Tough, P. (2006). What it takes to make a student. *New York Times Magazine*, November 26, 2006.

Chapter 22

Spatial containment in the inner city

Youth subcultures, class conflict, and geographies of exclusion

Jo-Anne Dillabough, Jacqueline Kennelly, and Eugenia Wang[*,1]

Introduction

Drawing theoretically from cultural geography (e.g., Massey, 1999) and from the sociology of youth culture, this chapter examines the relationship between social space and social exclusion as expressed by economically disadvantaged male and female youth (aged 14–16) in one inner city urban concentration in Ontario, Canada. The experiences which such urban youth themselves offer about this relationship are worthy of investigation because they help us to grasp an important dimension of the ways in which *neo-liberal* school cultures are currently impacting on the class formation of youth subcultural identities in the modern urban Canadian city.

We define *neo-liberalism* broadly as a set of free-market policies which are premised upon the economic concepts of choice, competition, and risk. Within the context of education, the aims of neo-liberalism are largely achieved through increases in standardized testing, school choice policy, and reduced public spending. In Canada and elsewhere, increasing research attention has been devoted to the relationship between urban youth, neo-liberal education, and social policy and social exclusion (CCSD, 2000). Such research is linked to cross-national evidence suggesting that young people in urban settings are experiencing heightened forms of social exclusion due, in part, to global restructuring as it is manifested in urban cities at the local level (Smyth & Hattam, 2004). Such restructuring has led to the rationalized closure of public education programs and alternative schools for youth (CCSD, 2000); to urban re-zoning policies and cuts in public housing; to falling school retention rates (Ball, Maguire & McCrae, 2000); and to the criminalization of disadvantaged youth who are "at risk" of homelessness and to changes in urban family structures, exacerbated by reductions in social provision (Lee, 2000; The Mayor's Homelessness Action Task Force, 1999).

For urban youth, the effects of these changes are most pronounced in areas of concentrated urban poverty where the incidence of youth poverty has risen dramatically over the last two decades (see The Mayor's Homelessness Action Task Force, 1999). Youth economic disadvantage of this kind may best be understood as a product of the social pressures attendant upon a "lost economy," no longer linked in any straightforward way solely to national interests, but increasingly to patterns of globalization. There is clear

* Jo-Anne Dillabough is an Associate Professor and Jacqueline Kennelly a Killam doctoral fellow in the Department of Educational Studies at the Peter Wall Institute for Advanced Studies, University of British Columbia. Eugenia Wang is a PhD candidate in Human Geography at the University of British Columbia.

research evidence that social problems relating to disadvantaged urban youth are a contemporary educational feature but the nature of the local differentiation of such problems, particularly in relation to the situated perceptions of young people themselves, has yet to be systematically researched in Canadian cities. Our central aim, then, following Reay and Lucey (2003), is best understood as a local exploration of the ways in which today's working-class young people are "tied to the geography" of urban cities and school life under the late modern dynamics of neo-liberal change.

Reconfiguring class disadvantage in urban space: Cultural geography and youth subcultural theory in new times

As youth researchers, we need some way of acknowledging how social experience is lived meaningfully through what Massey names as "emblematic class related spaces" in new times. We therefore seek to approach *late modern* class formations of new youth subcultures as functioning in some degree, "both as a response to, and a connection between, macro and micro forces of social change" (Gardner, Dillabough, & McLeod, 2005, p. 11) in urban cities. This kind of theoretical orientation allows us to engage with the semantic repertoires of classed meaning upon which young people simultaneously draw as they navigate the contours of urban change and the varied forms of alienation to which their lives are tied. In our research, we have come to understand such alienating experiences as contradictions emerging from novel forms of class and cultural conflict in which the interaction between space and identity become paramount. We therefore wish to reveal something of what young people "do with the cultural commodities they encounter" (Williams, 1977, p. 17), and the ways in which such activity constitutes a new "structure of feeling" (see Williams, 1977) emerging from contemporary urban spatial arrangements. Following Williams (1977), we might understand a young person's *structure of feeling* as a classed embodiment of larger social conflict which represents "thought as felt and feeling as thought: practical consciousness of a present kind, in a living and inter-relating community" (p. 132) organized spatially. Practically speaking, then, young people's feelings emerge as both *embodied* in elements of youth subcultural identity and as a form of *sociality* which are deeply implicated in young people's experiences of social exclusion and the navigation of social space in urban cities.

Our conceptual argument has two aspects. First, drawing upon the results of a year-long ethnography, we argue that a range of competing social processes are at work in re-contextualizing contemporary female and male youth subcultures and their perceptions of urban city life—processes which are compounded and heightened in intensity as a consequence of young people's localized positioning within "demonized schools" (Reay & Lucey, 2003).[2] In what do these processes consist? Within the changing demographic contexts of the urban city, the following elements of neo-liberal change are powerfully evident: the re-organization of urban inner city space and schools; the effect of low familial income and contractual employment upon young people's engagement with their schools; and the deeply entrenched influence of cumulative disadvantage across successive generations. What, we need to ask, is the combined impact of these processes upon young people's modes of self-representation and their conceptions of urban life as they pursue social status and recognition in the new urban city?

Second, we argue that a strong, if often covert, relationship between contemporary youth subcultures as both pre-existing social groups (i.e., historical entities) and global and local forms of "symbolic domination" (Bourdieu, 1998)[3] operates beyond, as well as within, "demonized schools." The impact of powerful modernizing forces such as educational restructuring has also resulted in a profound social distancing of disadvantaged urban youth from established "cultures of success" within an educational market marked by complexity, spatial division, and hierarchy. This tendency has been exacerbated by the heightened operation of local forms of gender, race, and intra-class conflict in schools, as well as by the wide range of more general contemporary risks, contingent largely upon neo-liberal restructuring, constantly faced by economically disadvantaged urban youth. For this reason, we are reluctant to assume that modernization in the forms articulated by scholars such as Ulrich Beck (1999)—as essentially increasing individualization—impact on all young people in quite the same way. Rather, we note that forms of historically informed domination continue to impinge strongly upon young people's subcultural identifications and notions of selfhood both in the temporal present and in the projected future (see Figure 22.1). This means that many of the cultural strategies young people utilize in their everyday lives resemble what Lois McNay (2000) has identified as deeply sedimented forms of cultural reproduction or, in Valerie Walkerdine's terms, "objectified modes" of the social order. These strategies are also shaped by the "subcultural capital" (Thornton, 1996) that young people may accumulate as spatial divisions and social relations intersect (see Stahl, 1999) to shape young people's

Figure 22.1 "This is me as a professional soccer player".

imaginative conceptions of the urban city. Thornton refers to *subcultural capital* as insider knowledge about the prescribed youth performances which position young people successfully within the competitive cultures of class conflict and spatial division. *Subcultural capital* often emerges as a form of retrieved social power in the face of marginalization and is thought to lead to social recognition among peers. As we will show, it is crucial to exercise one's *subcultural capital* in an effort to maintain social status and a sense of security in the face of increasing social divisions in urban cities.

The chapter has three parts. First, we describe our theoretical framework as it relates to youth subcultural identity, exploring the links between urban space, inner city schooling, and young people's "phenomenologies of meaning"[4] (Gardner, Dillabough & McLeod, 2005). Second, we sketch the characteristic urban contexts where young people's phenomenologies of meaning in relation to their exclusion have been established. The final section draws upon interview data from a year-long ethnography in one inner city urban concentration to illustrate the links between youth subcultural identity and urban space.

Theoretical framing

Our theoretical approach is interdisciplinary. In addition to a broad focus on youth subcultural theory, we address a persistent concern with what we identify, borrowing from Lois McNay (2000), as *sedimented cultural narratives* (i.e., emergent properties of the intersection of culture and the history of class conflict) and the field of *cultural phenomenology*. Taken together, the approaches signaled by these terms are valuable for their illumination of urban youth subcultural narratives, the characteristic forms of everyday meaning making that young people undertake, and by which they may account for their social exclusion. The researcher's role in such work is to engage in a *radical interrogation* of the meaning systems young people use to make sense of their contradictory worlds under the dynamics of change. The value of approaches of this kind is that they open up new theoretical perspectives on youth exclusion which are not bound by mutually exclusive divisions between structuralist or culturalist orientations which often position conceptions of youth identity at two polarized extremes. On the one hand, purely culturalist accounts of youth culture often find themselves tied to the significance of culture as locally derived sets of discourses (i.e., as pure pop culture) or as inherited social practices which regulate young people's commitments to this or that subcultural identity. Here, youth subjectivity is seen as ever-changing, fluid, and unstable, operating not as a form of local historical sedimentation, but as features within that which Nayak (2003) has referred to as a hybridized youthscape.

On the other hand, contemporary structuralist or high modernist positions suggest that youth identity is shaped largely by elements of late modern social change and global structures which are outcomes of what Ulrich Beck (1999) has termed "reflexive modernization." Under this view, youth identities are seen as shifting in response to advanced forms of modernization which are quite oblivious to entrenched class histories or unique local cultural communities. From this perspective, wider global forms of class stratification and de-ritualized forms of change become the focal point of interest. These two distinctive theoretical approaches are however oddly united in the negative fact that the idea of spatially organized forms of class sedimentation or deeply felt, *embodied* forms of class conflict do not figure substantially in either.

In addressing this debate, our position is that elements of youth individualization on the one side, and sedimented class positions together with spatial forms of meaning-making on the other, may in fact be seen to be simultaneously at work in identity formation and patterns of urban exclusion. At the same time, we argue that inherited mechanisms of masculine/symbolic domination (see Bourdieu, 1998) persist as a sedimented element of class conflict, continuing to shape the conditions underlying the formation of youth subcultural identity and the *maps of meaning* (see Cohen, 1999) youth draw upon in navigating urban cities. What this implies is that neither deeply entrenched inherited culturalist formations nor modernizing global forces can on their own be seen as solely responsible for the formation of youth subcultural identity. The relational negotiations achieved by youth, along with their associated phenomenologies of meaning, are rendered possible precisely through their daily exposure to complex cultural, spatial, and historical milieux, organized at local, national, and global levels. Spatial divisions in urban inner cities therefore "demarcate difference in physical locales" (Stahl, 1999, p. 20) and shape young people's conceptions of shared urban sites: "these include symbolic differentiations and collective fantasies around space, the resistance to dominant practices and resulting forms of individual and collective transgression" (Stahl, 1999, p. 20).

Our theoretical position anticipates that space represents an inherited yet shifting dimension of social life, which is underpinned by material realities reproduced over time through forms of social conflict which diverse young people embody in the temporal present. We can therefore envision how young people's conceptions of meaningful urban spaces often represent embodied forms of class conflict which provide the context for engagement with social life at the micro-level of urban space. Spatial divisions thus play some part in both extending and limiting a young person's "horizon for action" and operate as productive contexts for the formation of youth subjectivity. Following from these arguments, we can begin to conceptualize the link between youth subcultural identities, social exclusion, and "micro-geographies of exclusion" (Massey, 1995) as they operate in urban concentrations of poverty.

Contextual and epistemological dimensions of urban space

We refer to the contextual dimension as the local contours of urban space which bring together a nuanced range of local urban configurations of inner city life. By contrast, the epistemological refers to the ways in which these contexts are embedded in forms of meaning for those young people who interpret them. The latter also refers to the ways in which young people draw upon the semantic elements of urban space as they imagine who they think they are becoming, should become, or will be. Both dimensions can be seen to operate at local and national spatial levels. The spatial, as we have defined it here, comprises the multi-layered contexts of the urban landscape that youth inhabit and which play a major role in the regulation of youth identity. The spatial arena also comprehends what Lefebvre refers to as *spatial practices* (e.g., zoning, demographic change, historical elements of the urban site), *spaces of representation* (i.e., public imaginary about the space), and *representations of space* (i.e., dominant knowledge forms) (see Stahl, 1999). Below we contextualize the urban landscapes in which the young people of our local study were situated.

The urban inner city where the study took place has a long history of occupation by distinctive ethnic and class communities. From the late twentieth century, industrialization began to lose its dominant place as a source of employment for many working-class communities and the former industrial area experienced varying degrees of economic disadvantage which have persisted until the present day. Currently, the area is character-ized by low-cost tower apartments, together with housing which is self-owned, rented, and/or subsidized by the state. In the years between 1980 and 2003, a number of impor-tant urban transformations took place.

First, social support for families living in this part of the city was cut substantially, forcing many with children to engage in extended full-time employment, as well as some-times making use of their children's part-time income. Many parents of the young people in our study were sometimes working two to three contractually negotiated jobs each, or were working in factories outside of the neighborhood, usually due to the relocation or closure of businesses.

Second, the nature of the neighborhood itself was shifting as a result of recent zoning policies which allowed for transient forms of social housing, recently built low-cost non-state housing, and state supported housing. While it is important not to pathologize a neighborhood dedicated to public projects, urban re-zoning nonetheless contributed here to the loss of "traditional local integration" (see also Cohen, 1999) and to the re-shaping of the neighborhood as a site of "spatial containment" (Wright, 1997). In the late 1990s rental prices did in fact temporarily rise, leading to a partial gentrification of the area. At the time of the study, there were some signs of the emergence of an urban mix between those identifying themselves as lower middle-class and professionals (e.g., "teachers"), alongside underemployed families or families who lived in state-funded housing. Cumulatively, what is perhaps most significant about this area is that it was widely seen by many young people in the study as a site of abandonment by government and the city officials. The local school upon which our study focused—and which we have dubbed "Tower Hill"—drew both from "migrant" and "refugee" communities, as well as from local white working-class and Italian and Portuguese communities. Many of the young people involved in the study were children of working parents, single parent families, and families who might be underemployed or classified as the "working poor."

The nature of urban inner city space has to be understood at the national as well as the local level, and in this respect a number of broader cultural shifts are significant for the lives of the young people in the study. The gentrification of inner city centers shifted the location of urban economic disadvantage to neighborhoods on the fringes of the city proper. At the same time, youth economic disadvantage rose generally across urban Canada from the 1980s (see CCSD, 2000), increasing by 46 percent in little more than a decade. Rising levels of youth economic disadvantage in these years were closely associ-ated with a pronounced anti-welfare reform stance, legal and educational reforms (e.g., anti-squeegee laws, zero tolerance policies), and the spatial reorganization of urban cities in many Canadian provinces.

Schools located in the inner city are substantially affected by broader economic shifts of the kind noted above, particularly in terms of educational choice policy and the publi-cation of league tables.[5] If schools appear, particularly in the inner city core, as "demon-ized" then many middle-class parents who live in surrounding areas of the school (e.g., "regenerated" neighborhoods) increasingly "choose" to send their children to other "higher performing" settings. This creates both competition between schools across class communities and a tendency which some young people in the urban school context referred to as a "ghetto" or "warehousing" effect. This school stratification effect was compounded by larger global trends which were manifested locally in the school context. For example, in 2000, the Ontario Ministry of Education instituted a Literacy Test for all Grade 10 secondary school students. Students were obliged to take this test regardless of their schooling history or their domestic language situation, despite the fact that literacy support was absent. School success was rendered more difficult as the conditions for learning had been undermined by cuts to programs which would traditionally have supported this group of young people. At the same time, the student population was becoming increasingly transient, with many young people forced to move out of public housing complexes that were overcrowded and, in many cases, having to change schools. Students lived both with the burden of the stigmas attached to "failure" and with the deleterious effects of urban transformation. While participants did not discuss these difficulties directly in the terminology of neo-liberalism, it was eminently clear that they understood the role that "the test" and related educational and urban social reforms were playing in their lives. There were also times when students took the responsibility of blame upon themselves. The constant reminders, operating through heightened forms of individualization in educational rhetoric, that they were not truly deserving students when compared to middle-class pupils, meant that the levels of fear associated with neo-liberal regimes of testing were particularly acutely felt.[6]

Spatial landscapes of ethnographic inquiry: Phenomenology and the investigation of cultural meaning

A combination of spatial and cultural ethnographic techniques which align with a phenomenological approach were utilized in the study. A key emphasis was placed upon how cultural ethnographic approaches provide a framework for exploring particularly important aspects of youth subcultural identity in local settings such as "peer rivalry," "being in the know," and the "front." As Goffman (1959) writes: "the front is [. . .] that part of the individual's performance which regularly functions [. . .] to define the situation for those who observe the performance" (p. 22). While often neglected within ethnographies of youth culture, concepts such as the "front" or "being in the know"—as reconfigured and obviously more complex elements in the temporal present—still play an important role in the cultural processes of class stratification.

Over the course of one year, the first author engaged in both classroom observations and joint ethnographic projects in classrooms with young people at Tower Hill. We utilized a project-based approach which allowed young people to engage in a variety of activities across a period of one year.[7] In classroom contexts, we asked students to complete activity-based project work involving, for example, developing time-lines on the subject of exclusion, work, and social change. The research design also involved the completion of photo-narratives (using disposable cameras) on urban social space, capturing young people's diverse experiences of school inclusion/exclusions. To contextualize these narratives, we gathered substantial qualitative data on the urban neighborhood and its surrounding areas, including tracking zoning policies and urban transformations in the area over time.

The lead author also engaged in open-ended individual interviews with the young people. Interview questions concentrated upon students' accounts of their schooling and social experiences across aspects of urban space and schooling in times of change; their view of themselves in relation to peers, popular culture, and issues of cultural identity;

and the impact that urban life had on their school experience. In conducting interviews, we were constantly reminded of Reid's (2002) caution in relation to the interviewing process: "sociologists' queries are likely to be alien to interviewees' ways of understanding their world—and to be successful, sociologists must pose and answer their own questions without simply imposing their own problematics" (p. 344). Sociologists must therefore face the severe challenge of finding ways of interpreting youth accounts which "do not allow the discipline simply to find itself in the other it studies" (Reid, 2002, p. 344). In attending to this warning, the data represented here explicitly focus upon young people's reflections on their ties to urban arrangements and the ways in which their experiences of exclusion have been structured in part by the spatial practices of the urban school and neighborhood.

Young people's phenomenologies of meaning and their struggle to "classify"

In the data analysis which follows, we focus upon two prominent themes. The first of these—*Corridors of Power*—consists largely of a gender analysis concerned with exposing how dominant forms of sexuality emerged as powerful modalities of youth subcultural regulation, organized according to traditional dimensions of territoriality and operating through deeply classed spatial divisions in schools. We then move forward to examine data that moves beyond school experience and focuses more substantially on the structural dimensions of anxiety experienced by young people living in a demonized area of the urban inner city. Our aim here is to demonstrate how elements of urban space play some part in framing the forms of alienation and contradiction working-class young people embody as they navigate the urban inner city.

Sexualized territories and school "corridors of power": Peer rivalry, space, and the gendered front

The individual narratives which emerged from interviews may best be seen as objectified modes of discourse which are spatially bound and historically located in particular forms of masculinity and femininity. The continuing symbolic power inscribed within them means that the "subjective work" involved in accommodating the gender "ideal of the perfect girl" (Reay & Lucey, 2003) or "perfect boy" combines the exercise of gender power with a standardized and narrow definition of student success. The result is high levels of anxiety as young people pursue deeply conflicted social and personal objectives. In our study, larger discourses of the gender order and territoriality were often exploited by young people in an effort to gain "symbolic control" (see Cohen, 1999) over both their local educational and urban landscapes. We define territoriality here as an element in the "classification struggles" (Bourdieu, 1998) in which young people engage in to establish their own social status within a peer group. Cohen (1999) writes:

> The function of territoriality is [] to [] provid[e] a material basis for a system of positional rules which preserve the boundaries of the loose knit peer group network, and assigns the entire youthful population, big and little, boy and girl, to a place which cuts across these distinctions . . . Friend or Foe.

(p. 66)

Like Cohen, we try to show here that this seeking out of Friend or Foe—operating within the parameters of more traditional class, race, and gender conflict—is often one of the key mechanisms for the emergence of a *gendered front* in schools. It also forms the basis of intra-class and racial conflict between young people pushed to the margins through new modalities of spatial division. Peer rivalry thus emerged as the paramount site for the official and unofficial classification struggles that young people undertook in their efforts to reclaim meaningful symbolic territory in their lives. This highly contested symbolic territory constituted both a primary "landscape of choice" and a defining "horizon of action" (see also Ball et al., 2000) for the defense of strongly drawn youth identifications through the gendered acquisition of subcultural capital. At the same time, elements of strong group identification were often seen as a threat to a certain notion of freedom, authenticity, and autonomy which, despite all constraints, continued to hold out the future promise of becoming any kind of person at any time. As Rodrigo, a sixteen-year-old second generation Portuguese boy, remarked:

JD: So who do you hang with? How would you classify yourself? I hear about the Thugs, there's Rockers, there's Ginos.
R: Oh yeah. There is a whole bunch of people.
JD: So how do you classify yourself?
R: I'm myself.
JD: So you're not any one of those things?
R: Well yes, I could be all of them, well no not really . . .
JD: So you listen to rap music?
R: Yeah.
JD: And you say that you are kind of "gangster" like?
R: Yeah . . . and I don't like rock music and . . . the school is filled with Ginos . . .

[INTERVIEW CONTINUES]

JD: Well if you drop out of school what are you going to do?
R: I have no idea. . . .
JD: So what?
R: Probably like every other Portuguese, construction.
JD: Construction, that's what you think you'll do? . . .
R: Yeah, basically that's a Portuguese person's [destiny].
JD: So you don't mind that kind of future?
R: Well I would mind but I wouldn't mind the money but you know if I go to school and whatever, people tell me, I can get a better job [. . .] hmmm [. . .] So well most of the girls go to class, pass, do their homework, and the [. . .] guys you know they are just too cool for school [. . .] Actually even the girls do bad in this school [. . .] Most of them are Ginas . . . All Ginas like Ginos.
JD: So that doesn't bode very well for the Thugs does it if they only like the Ginos.
R: No they don't really like the Ginos . . . [] I've seen a couple of fights, mostly fist fights.

In an under-resourced inner city school, each element of school life imposes a complex set of cultural codes, its own meaning sets and positional rules. Young people are

therefore bound together, as Rodrigo tells us, as much by similarities and shared allegiances (i.e., the position of Portuguese families in the labor class) as by perceived radical
differences. This meant that while young people often saw themselves as relatively autonomous in matters of subcultural style, the interplay between economic disadvantage and
the structures linked to the demonized urban school were also deeply embedded in
gendered forms of youth subcultural classification. In drawing boundaries around such
classifications, elements of pop culture serve as key positional markers. As a First
Nations boy of sixteen remarked:

R: Like Rockers [the boys] usually stay together and listen to rock music basically. . . .
   Ginos are Portuguese kids that listen to like Techno-type music . . . and a Thug is
   just a guy who belongs to a gang that listens to rap music basically . . . they basi-
   cally stay in their own groups . . .
JD: And what about the girls? Do they all belong to these groups too?
R: Nah . . . I notice there is not much black girls in the school so they really stick
   together. . . .
JD: So what about you? []
R: I just hang around with anyone, well not anyone [. . .] I'm just saying I'm not into
   these group things.

Beyond the more spectacular iconographic markers underlying claims to subcultural
identity or the emerging contradictions in its denial, the key locus at which these identities encountered the organization of symbolic power in the "demonized school" was
often most visible through territorial gender practices in the school corridor. For
example, within the space of the corridor, both boys and girls moved around in groups
of three to four both as forms of self-protection but also to mark out a defined area of the
school as a primary site for the enactment of sexualized power and a *"revolt into style"*
(see Cohen, 1999)—what might have been seen in an earlier period of subcultural theorizing as a deeply gendered or racialized front. Young people thus drew heavily upon the
space of the corridor as a site where both gendered and racialized forms of youth subcultural style could be claimed, and where the desire for symbolic territory was at its most
visible but was also at its most dangerous. Consequently, the corridor presented itself
both as a space of intra-class alienation and symbolic control in the expression of youth
subcultural style. As Lola, a fifteen-year-old self-proclaimed Gina, remarked:

JD: [You mentioned that] some kids [gangster girls] are bullies, do you think the
    majority?
L: I think most are bullies and the others, you know.
JD: Have you had any experience with that?
S: Well I have once cause I had my skirt too long, my kilt and they're calling me
   [spoon], they would tease me well roll up your kilt or they'd push me around.
JD: Ah-hah.
L: So . . .
JD: Physically push you?
L: Yeah.
JD: Girls or boys?
L: Some kind of girls/boys, but now I'm used to it. I just roll up my kilt now.

JD: So they wanted it to be shorter.

L: Yeah.

JD: Not longer? Right. Why? Why do you think?

L: Cause they thought I was geeky and nerdy and all the—

JD: To wear it too long?

L: Yeah.

A young Portuguese boy (Randy) who referred to himself as a *Thug* (a signifier of Gangsta culture) confirmed during an interview that Lola was the target of much sexualized disciplining:

R: One of the girl's gets picked on [in the corridor].

JD: Why does she get picked on?

R: I dunno they say it's cause she fingers herself with a spoon, whatever so they call her spoony and stuff.

The corridor thus emerged as "an emblematic class related place" (Massey, 1999) where gendered regulation could be exercised as a reaction to new modalities of youth class conflict. Within this context, racialized and sexualized slurs, derived from wider derogatory discourses, were a common currency in defining the identity negotiations for which the corridor was an open and appropriate site. As one fourteen-year-old Filipino girl illustrated in remarking upon the language characteristically used to describe the visible minority teenage girls in the school corridor:

A: They'll [the girls] use this language ... they don't care ... every kind of bad word ... Slut ... I don't know. ... Motherfucker ... I don't know ...

JD: So why these names, slut, whore, what's this all about?

A: Probably that's the only way they can get their anger out.

Phenomenologies of meaning and the confining elements of urban space: "ambivalence," "anxiety," and spatial containment[8]

> Things are always going on in the bad streets. I don't feel safe in the street ... It's people talking bad about other people, lots of fighting, across the streets, close to the park.
>
> (Carrie, age 14)

Some aspects of the complex geographies of exclusion lie outside the range of schooling or the more obvious forms of subcultural peer rivalry associated with the school. Here, we turn away from the corridors of power in urban schools to the local contexts of urban neighborhoods. Once more following Reay and Lucey (2003), we explore young people's conception of space "as deeply ambivalent understandings of their social context." As Rodrigo remarked:

R: My apartment is not safe 'cos there's ways to get in the building, like through the steps, [. . .] and everything is always unlocked and in my area of [Tower Hill] there's a lot of dumb people ... [coming in and out of the building].

JD: How do you feel about that?

R: Not really [too bad], 'cos my brother's usually home 'cos he's still young right, but when he gets older and you see all these kids together [. . .] so I think they do drugs [. . .] and there's always a problem.

The social confinement of youth to particular places can be seen to contribute to what one young person referred to as "warehousing kids" and what Bourdieu saw as being "chained to a place" or as positional suffering (Bourdieu, 1998; see also Reay & Lucey, 2003). This chaining effect was often expressed by young people as both ambivalence and as social constraint. It was either through interpellation (e.g., "lots of dumb people") or through contradiction that *a structure of feeling* about place—especially in response to questions about home—emerged. This attitude toward neighborhood—as both confining and as "home"—can be seen in the following interview with Clara, a fourteen-year-old girl who had recently arrived "as refugee" from West Africa:

C: [Referring to photo narratives] What I would like about this place is it's very quiet and lovely.

JD: Is it very quiet?

C: Yeah, it's very quiet.

JD: And no problems on the street or anything?

C: No.

JD: So you live there with your family [sister]?

C: Yeah. [] She doesn't have a job right now. My building [] someone got killed there. Yeah, in the elevator.

JD: Oh, what happened?

C: [] I'm not really sure but I heard this guy got killed inside the elevator. I went there, I seen, yeah, and the guy got killed inside the elevator cause he . . . I think he was dealing with drugs or something.

In the photograph to which Clara is referring in this interview stands one of the tower apartments common to this inner-urban neighborhood; above it, Clara has written "Home Sweet Home." The story which is hidden but immanent in this account is of the progressively worsening cuts in social support and public housing subsidies for economically disadvantaged young people from the early 1990s onward. Clara's construction of space here was, in fact, intimately related to the temporal configurations of social change and neo-liberal transformations of her urban neighborhood. In understanding her spatial location in the urban city, she bears the "weight of the world" (Bourdieu, 1998) as it manifests itself through working-class neighborhoods in post-welfare economic regimes. Her words convey how, as Massey (1994) puts it, "space is constituted through social relations and material social practices" (p. 337). In this new spatial context, young people living on the hard edge of the economy must sometimes read their own lives as *outside* those who fall into the same class category—as other, as "deviant," as "noise," and as interference into the progress of their potential for a middle-class existence. Paradoxically, they must also read their lives as an adaptation to the apparent invader of their space or as a collective effort to make "noise" and classify as a response to "semantic disorder" and contradiction (see Hebdige, 1979). Any deviation from the expected narrative codes or sedimented cultural narratives regarding this space, regardless of the degree of desire a young person may hold, is likely to have very disorienting outcomes. As Cecilia remarks:

JD: So this is just where people hang and sometimes there are fights. Is this where you got into some of your fights, too, in that neighborhood?

C: Yup.

JD: Yeah. Would you rather live some place else or are you happy there []?

C: I'm kind of happy but my mom just had a baby so I don't think it's the proper neighborhood for the baby to grow up in. Right?

JD: Yeah? What are you gonna do?

C: My mom's trying to move out of there.

In her photo narratives, Cecilia documents the "shortcut" that she uses to get to school when she is running late ("This is usually every day," she notes). Her photo narrative consists of an image of a long empty hallway that appears to be underground. In a second photograph, she has captured the local bus shelter, which she notes is one of two that she uses. Captioning this photograph is the following comment:

> I live in the downtown area which isn't the worst or greatest area. The reason being is because lots of homeless and criminals live in this area and many bad things occur. But it isn't the worst because there are many other places that make my place the best.

This personal struggle between recognizing her "place" as being one marked by multiple dangers, yet also striving to reconfigure it as one that "isn't the worst," indicates the degree of ambivalence emerging from the pressures contingent upon middle-class aspirations and the recognition that one is broadly "working class." Althusser, often forgotten in contemporary sociological theory, reminds us that this tension must not be read as a *personal feeling*—expressed here as ambivalence—but instead represents a classed form of interpellation necessary in coping with the realities of working-class life.

Young people in the study also mentioned strategies they drew upon to keep themselves safe, such as saying "Hi" to an imaginary person in a doorway if they saw someone "suspicious" nearby. Many also spoke of the regular drug use that they had witnessed on the streets and in the school. Some commented on the fact that these activities were taking place with impunity, as they perceived no police presence to curb them. Such accounts provide insight into a "structure of feeling" founded upon circulating social fears of abandonment and exclusion (see Williams, 1977) which are grounded in the spatial divisions and material conditions underwriting the lives of young people at Tower Hill.

These *structures of feeling* and *forms of interpellation* are not located inside the marked bodies of economically disadvantaged individuals who are sometimes seen to own such feelings as free liberal subjects in the new "global city." Nor do young people possess the degree of autonomy they imagine even if such imagined freedom emerges as a response to heightened individualization operating in the early twenty-first century. Rather, their feelings can be better read as attempts to make sense of their lives—to find what Hebdige (1979) refers to as a *magical solution*—in light of deeply contradictory social messages and experiences. On the one hand, young people living at the turn of the twenty-first century are expected to absorb the dominant belief that their situations are theirs to make the best of ("we are not what we are but what we make of ourselves"; see Giddens, 1998, p. 34), and that they are limited only by their own "skills" and "willingness" to persevere. On the other hand, they daily confront circumstances which are wholly beyond their control, largely the products of the neo-liberal restructuring of urban cities and schools targeted as "demonized." This ambivalence often extended beyond students' urban location to their families' working situation where young people consistently affirmed that their situation was tolerable, was "okay," even after sharing family experiences which appeared objectively as deeply challenging. "Things," in the characteristic words of one particularly disadvantaged young woman of fifteen, were "working out okay."

There are myriad ways in which the "structures of feeling" our excerpts have demonstrated may be theorized. For example, Reay and Lucey (2000) describe ambivalence as a form of working-class resilience or refusal, a manner of seeing things as bearable, "even okay," in order not to be overwhelmed. In bearing the weight of their worlds, they argue that young people are engaging in the process of "reclassification." "Reclassification" is the action young people undertake to survive and make sense of the class conflicts between home, unfamiliarity, and risk. Another more spatially oriented interpretation we might offer is that when a place (such as public housing) does not belong to the individual but rather the individual must belong to it, ambivalent readings should not be unexpected (see Wright, 1997). Indeed, feelings of placelessness as a form of positional suffering may dominate the consciousness of those who are not choosing a place called "home" or a "demonized" school. Clearly, most middle-class youth have more advantaged spatial resources. They are often driven home in cars, live in property owned by their families, or walk home through leafy neighborhoods and have little cause to worry about the "dangers" of urban inner city life. Such early degrees of spatial mobility reinforce social advantages accorded to those who live in privileged areas of the city. Against the knowledge of such mobility, the experience of economic disadvantage and "failing schools" confirms economically disadvantaged young people's distinctiveness to others and to themselves as marginal non-citizens. Young people are, to borrow from Bourdieu, obliged to navigate the path of a particular distinction but this navigation always requires a *double consciousness*. There is a feeling of anxiety both in deviating from "home" and in the recognition of being chained to a place. In this way, place and youth subcultural identity are closely intertwined within the inner city. As Bourdieu reminds us, the urban city and "demonized" school—often celebrated as sites of opportunity—are re-emerging as a kind of spatially organized, permeable container for "potential outcasts," who experience them as both contradictions and novel class conflicts "associated with the type of education that is an end in itself . . . all one can do is to try and prolong the period of time in the state of uncertainty that itself keeps him/her from mastering that period of time" (cited in Reid, 2002, p. 351).

Conclusions

Since the publication of Paul Willis' (1977) seminal work on *Learning to Labour*, sociologists of education have debated over whether schools are still profoundly implicated in the social reproduction of economic disadvantage. Willis, however, was not primarily concerned with questions of urban space nor are contemporary sociologists (e.g., Beck) who target individualization as the dominant element of youth identity in late modernity. In contrast to Beck's individualization thesis, evidence from this study, from Tower Hill and its students, from the school corridor to urban space, suggests that economically disadvantaged youth are still tied in part to deeply "sedimented" forms of social relations.

Yet there are also signs of change in how diverse groups of economically disadvantaged youth think about their futures in relation to urban space and contemporary school life. First, unlike working-class youth in earlier studies such as those portrayed in early British Cultural Studies research, male and female youth at Tower Hill showed strong desires to break their own class ranks and to escape their feelings of entrapment in particular urban spaces. Paradoxically, however, these desires were often trapped in a political economy of urban constraints and "structures of feeling" that young people held toward the inner city spaces and schools in which they were confined. The outcome was deep ambivalence toward the spaces they inhabit, as well as toward its ability to provide security under the dynamics of neo-liberal retrenchment. Yet, the class conflict associated with the abandonment of such spaces or a lack of social recognition linked to moving on seemed an impossible future for many of the young people.

We should not be surprised, then, that we still witness forms of noise generated by youth through particular subcultural identifications, especially those associated with style, rivalry, and space. Forms of style and rivalry have emerged as local and global adaptations, playing some part in new social divisions, particularly heightened intra-class conflict. We have argued that these intra-class conflicts are linked to elements of social location (e.g., race) and "geographical arrangements of power" in urban schools and cities. We also suggest that young people who are tied to particular geographical spaces might be seen as engaging in "classification struggles" over the social meanings of youth subcultural identity. These classification struggles are an outcome of both inheriting and challenging classed, gendered, cultural/racialized, and spatial positions which are historically significant. This local inheritance does not function as it might have done in the past—to simply determine and reinforce class positions—but rather shapes the ways in which young people construct cultural meanings of everyday life and education through youth subcultural communities, creating perhaps more (rather than less) anxiety about their ability to perfect themselves for an imagined future in new times.

Second, we argue that any links made between neo-liberal school cultures and the spatial elements of social exclusion should reconsider the symbolic power of ritual and territoriality. This return to a focus on territory is significant, as late modern accounts of youth identity imply that young people are less and less tied to ritualistic cultural practices. The data we have considered here suggest, however, that rituals still carry substantial symbolic meaning in youth subcultural identity formation and are powerful forms of regulation in the struggles young people undertake to gain social status in their respective youth communities. They also represent examples of how feelings might be structured by space and expressed by young people who must navigate their lives in highly individualistic urban spaces. Young people are therefore still bound at least in part by classed codes of cultural inheritance (i.e., the front), serving as vehicles of social meaning, and as such, in Bourdieu's terms, as the embodiment of both domination and anxiety. Despite heightened individualization, young people do not perform domination or objectify gender symbols as free, unfettered agents of the state but, rather, as constrained social subjects, who must resolve the contradictions which accompany social containment. At the same time, they are also actors who struggle daily to move beyond such embodiment. But one must be clear that the range of youth subcultural expressions available are substantially narrowed by symbolic economies of social exclusion operating on a far broader scale. Undoubtedly then, theories of de-traditionalization have exaggerated the degree to which cultural norms have been reconfigured and favor changes experienced by middle-class youth, and have grossly inflated the so-called freedoms now thought to be generally available to economically disadvantaged youth (see also McLeod, 2002). Like many other contemporary youth theorists (see Nayak, 2003), we therefore wish to maintain the position that structural forces and forms of historical and contemporary culture shape the everyday meanings young people construct about their social position in the state, and about the local spaces to which they find themselves tied. At the same time, the phenomenology of meaning making among young people is culturally and symbolically located in the local formation of youth culture itself. It also impacts upon the material conditions underwriting young people's social circumstances and, very likely, their future destinies. We do not therefore assume that young people are a product of their own making or that they are determined, as positivist sociological accounts might have us believe, by their "class." We need instead to view young people as responding and reacting to contested local histories as they confront contemporary social change. Such a position will best allow us to understand young people's complex phenomenologies of meaning as emerging from a reconfigured history of marginalization "set in motion" in the present.

Questions for discussion

1. What do the authors mean by "geography of exclusion?" To what extent do geographic boundaries contribute to and exacerbate class conflict? If so, in what ways?
2. Discuss how the authors illustrate the complex relationship between gender and class for urban youth. Why is it important for social scientists to complicate social constructions, rather than isolate and simplify their structures?
3. Why do young people living in the urban city develop feelings of ambivalence toward their neighborhoods? In what kinds of paradoxical situations might they situate themselves as a result of feeling this ambivalence?
4. How do particular schools become "demonized?" Which social, economic, or cultural forces are thought to contribute to the demonization of these schools and their student populations?
5. One of the respondent's (Cecelia's) photographs is used as a narrative to understand the perception of neighborhood and school. How does this approach demonstrate that class is deeply "felt?"
6. Why do you suppose urban youth are the focal point of this chapter? What distinguishes youth narratives from adult narratives in this shifting social climate? Why should we listen closely to the voices of urban youth?
7. This chapter draws upon the ethnographic method. In what ways is ethnographic research advantageous or disadvantageous to the study of class? What do we learn and not learn by employing this research method?
8. Geographically speaking, reflect upon your knowledge of (or experience within)

rural spaces in contrast to the urban locations studied in this chapter. Would an ethnographic study of youth in rural settings present similar findings? Might there be such a thing as rural "containment?" Do rural areas summon "subcultural" narratives similar to those of the urban contexts studied?

Notes

1. Jacqueline Kennelly and Eugenia Wang were research assistants on this project. This paper was originally published in a longer format in the *Journal of Curriculum Theorizing* (Summer, 2005). A second version of this paper, shortened and adapted for publication in *Education and the Spatial Turn: Policy, Theory, Geography* (Gulson, K., & Symes, C. (Eds.)), is in press. This chapter is a substantially revised version of the original journal publication. JCT does not hold copyright over their publications. This notwithstanding, we wish to thank JCT for allowing the original paper to be published as a revised paper, as well as a reprinted version. The author order has been altered here to reflect the order in which revisions to this version of the JCT paper were undertaken.
2. Following Reay and Lucey (2003), we define *demonized schools* as those sites which carry with them, as their institutional burden, a long history of "under-performance" relative to middle-class schools, often maintaining low enrollments and which are under-resourced. Such sites are often threatened with closure or changes in administration as a result of their social/academic status.
3. Pierre Bourdieu (1998) refers to "symbolic domination" "as a masculine 'logic' which structures social life in a highly variegated fashion yet asserts normatively that there are 'real' differences between the sexes. These differences are legitimized and evolve dialectically through deep-rooted, structural, and symbolic mechanisms in the social order. What makes the logic of symbolic domination so deeply problematic is that it imposes itself as neutral, as normal and therefore, self-regulating and perpetuating. It emerges as a symbolic construction—a 'sexually characterized habitus'" (see Dillabough, 2005, p. 129).
4. We refer to *phenomenologies of meaning* as the interpretive meaning sets young people draw upon as they encounter the temporal present drawing upon the intersection of everyday lived culture and the burdens of their collective and individual pasts.
5. League tables refer to school rankings by municipality on achievement scores emerging from provincial testing and graduating averages.
6. Teachers reported that funds designed to enhance literacy among various communities of youth had dissipated through program cuts. In this context, teachers themselves were being asked to do literacy training (many of whom had not been trained in ESL practices).
7. We completed these activities either alongside the classroom teacher, or in team-teaching situations.
8. Wright (1997) identifies "spatial containment" as a structured and cultural property of cities whereby economically disadvantaged communities are often contained in urban spaces which are ultimately pathologized.

References

Ball, S., McGuire, M., & McCrae, S. (2000). *Choice, pathways, and transitions Post-16: New youth, new economies in the global city.* London, UK: RoutledgeFalmer.

Beck, U. (1999). *The risk society.* London, UK: Sage.

Bourdieu, P. (1998, Edition du Seuil). *Masculine domination.* Stanford, CA: Stanford University Press.

Canadian Council on Social Development (CCSD, 2000). *Thinking ahead: Trends affecting public education in the future.* Accessed from: www.ccsd.ca/pubs/gordon/part2.htm.

Cohen, P. (1999). *Rethinking the youth question: Education, labour, and cultural studies.* Durham, NC: Duke University Press.

Dillabough, J. (2005). Gender, "symbolic domination" and female work: The case of teacher education. *Discourse, 26*(2), 129–48.

Gardner, P., Dillabough, J., & McLeod, J. (2005). *Disenfranchised youth, class conflict, and educational exclusion: An international comparison.* Social Sciences and Humanities Research Council Grant (Part B).

Giddens, A. (1998). *The third way.* Cambridge, UK: Polity Press.

Goffman, E. (1959). *The presentation of the self in everyday life.* New York: Barnhardt.

Hebdige, D. (1979). *Subculture: The meaning of style.* New York: Methuen and Co., Ltd.

Lee, K. (2000). *Urban poverty in Canada: A statistical profile.* Ottawa, ON: Canadian Council on Social Development.

Massey, D. (1994). *Space, place and gender.* Cambridge, UK: Polity Press.

—— (1995). *Spatial divisions of labour.* London, UK: Macmillan.

—— (1999). Imagining globalization: Power-geometries of time-space. In Brah, Hickman, & Mac an Ghaill (Eds.), *Global futures: Migration, environment, and globalization.* Basingstoke and London, UK: Macmillan.

McLeod, J. (2002). Working out intimacy: Young people and friendship in an age of reflexivity. *Discourse, 23*(2), 211–36.

McNay, L. (2000). *Gender and agency: Reconfiguring the subject in feminist social theory.* Cambridge, UK: Polity.

Nayak, A. (2003). *Race, place, and globalisation: Youth cultures in a changing world.* New York: Berg.

Reay, D., & Lucey, H. (2000). "I don't really like it here but I don't want to be anywhere else": Children and inner city council estates. *Antipode, 32*(4), 410–28.

—— (2003). The limits of "choice": Children and inner city schooling. *Sociology, 37*(1), 121–42.

Reid, D. (2002). Towards a social history of suffering: Dignity, misery and disrespect. *Social History, 27,* 343–58.

Smyth, J., & Hattam, R. (2004). *"Droping out," drifting off, being excluded: Becoming somebody without school.* New York: Peter Lang Publishing.

Stahl, G. (1999). Still "winning space?": Updating subcultural theory. *Invisible Culture,* 1–32.

The Mayor's Homelessness Action Task Force (1999, January). *Taking responsibility for homelessness: An action plan for Toronto.* Toronto: City of Toronto.

Thornton, S. (1996). *Club cultures: Music, media, and subcultural capital.* Middleton, CT: Wesleyan University Press.

Williams, R. (1977). *Marxism and literature.* Oxford, UK: Oxford University Press.

Willis, P. (1977). *Learning to labour: How working-class kids get working-class jobs.* Farnborough, UK: Saxon House.

Wright, T. (1997). *Out of place.* Albany, NY: SUNY.

Chapter 23

Class and the middle

Schooling, subjectivity, and social formation

Julie McLeod and Lyn Yates [*]

"There is no single set of constitutive criteria to appeal to in characterising complex social practices."

(Seyla Benhabib, 1995, p. 27)

Addressing "the way class works" entails a debate about the usefulness of different theories and conceptual lenses as tools for depicting the world. It is to take a position on which issues deserve to be prioritized and which are silenced in that story. It is also to consider a range of different arenas of life—individual experience and subjectivity, work and social relations, schooling, social formation. And it brings with it concerns about politics and action: where and how might things be changed. These are all central issues for the study of schooling.

In this chapter we explore the usefulness and problems of working with "class" today, particularly in relation to understanding the formation of individual subjectivity and larger social patterns in the context of schooling. We argue that class is a vital yet also always a problematic lens, and that there is not a single way to work with the concept or category of class. Our interest in this chapter, and in the longitudinal project on which we draw, is not one of providing an ethnographic picture of the lives of a particular pre-defined group of people ("working-class white women" for example). Rather, here we consider schooling as a period when *both lives and social patterns are in formation*, and in which questions about class and its salience relate to what is in the process of being formed in the future (both for individuals and as social formations) as well as to what is being lived in the present. Distribution, subjectivity, and political values are all part of this story.

Historically, the language of class has provided an influential explanation of social and distributive inequalities. The relationship of class to person formation has also been a dimension of conventional class analysis, such as in Bourdieu's account of habitus or Althusser's concept of interpellation. However, recent feminist and social theories have given a particular prominence to questions of subjectivity and social relations. Two related lines of feminist enquiry have been especially important for our discussion here. One strong line of feminist analysis has argued that subjectivity exceeds the social discourses and categories that define or are said "to construct identity." Subjectivity is

[*] Julie McLeod is an Associate Professor in the Faculty of Education and Lyn Yates is Foundation Professor of Curriculum at the University of Melbourne, Australia.

more than an aggregation of discourses or subject positions (Hollway, 1994; Nielsen & Rudberg, 1995) and more than the intersection of different identity and social categories (Brown, 2005); it is historically and contextually embedded and involves desires, projections, and fantasies that are not neatly accounted for by sociological categories. Second, a wide range of feminist scholarship has argued for taking seriously the realm of emotions and interpersonal dynamics in relation to understanding social processes (Ahmed, 2004). Understanding the relationship between class and subjectivity thus involves more than only documenting the educational, social, and economic differences and inequalities in the pathways and outcomes of individuals and classes of people. It also involves, we argue, understanding the subjective, emotional, and embodied resonance of class-based differences (Reay, 2004; Skeggs, 1997, 2004; Walkerdine, Lucey & Melody, 2001), including the articulation of values and cultural orientations, and the impact of the politics and practices of both "distribution" and "recognition" on subjectivity (Fraser, 1997).

Class as an analytic category

To name what we attend to as "class," or to talk about what we "find" as "class," or to designate someone as "working class" or "middle class," is to inscribe it (and them) in a particular way. It encompasses attention to social distinction, hierarchy, power embodied in individual identities and in the patterns of social relationships between individuals, as well as patterns of work, including the form of paid and unpaid work, the structure of what types of jobs people from different backgrounds enter, and the dispositions, capital, power, and lack of capital and power that pertain to different kinds of jobs. Today, none of these are simply replicating their historical forms: the challenge is to consider what class means now and as "new times" are in formation.

Moreover, as an analytic concept, the idea of class as a foundational category for analysis of political and social life has now been challenged from a number of quarters—from the globalizing spread of neo-liberal politics and the power of the market construction of autonomous individuals, from critiques of master narratives and the rise of anti-foundationalist accounts of the social, from the impact of new social movements and identity politics and associated new political configurations, and calls for intersectional analyses (Brown, 2005; Crenshaw, 1994). Class, like other sociological categories such as gender or race and ethnicity, is frequently invoked yet also greeted with some ambivalence and theoretical and political suspicion. To only analyze class (or gender, or race . . .) is now understood as a political and analytical act of exclusion.

The notion of intersectional analysis has been one response to such dilemmas. Instead of isolating or examining discrete categories, intersectional analysis turns to class, for example, as one element among intersecting factors. It acknowledges the complexity of affiliations and categories that frame individual lives, and works against reducing or elevating one as more or less important than the other. As such, it can be seen as a corrective to some of the gender essentialism of feminism, or the gender blindness of class analysis, or the neglect of race and ethnicity on the part of both class and gender-based analysis.

However, an intersectional approach has its own limitations. Intersectional portrayals of particular groups can elide specificity and context. Subjectivity tends to be represented as a kind of replica or aggregate of external, even if intersecting, categories, as an "end point," rather than as an embodied "process of becoming" that is dynamic, cumulative, and recursive (McLeod & Yates, 2006). And the categories themselves (class, gender, race) tend to be deployed as if they are static rather than enmeshed in historical and locational change. Further, subjectivity is not constituted by categories of identity in an additive or linear way. As Brown (2005) argues, subjectivity is "historically complex, contingent, and occurs through formations that do not honor analytically distinct identity categories" (p. 123).

In the longitudinal schooling project we discuss in this chapter, we did want to keep a focus on those different conceptions in play. But the way we attempted to do this (see McLeod & Yates, 2006) was not by telling a single intersectional story of particular individuals or groups in our study. Rather we wanted to take up, in turn, different lenses on our study, so we could focus more directly at different points on gender, or race and national identification, or class, and so we could give adequate attention both to the empirical and the category or concepts or bigger picture beyond the story. In this chapter we try to show some aspects of this approach as a way of talking about the way class works. It is an approach that says "the way class works" is not just a story about how particular lives are being lived, but about how social formation and future lives are being developed.

A longitudinal qualitative study

Our longitudinal study, located in Australia and begun just over a decade ago, followed secondary students at four schools over seven years, and into their first year after leaving school (McLeod & Yates, 2006). It was designed to explore the interaction between biographies and schooling, and to take a fresh look at the production of subjectivities and inequalities over time through schooling in a period and national setting where gender rather than class had become the marked category of interest. In relation to class, we wanted to revisit schooling's part in both the politics of distribution—"who gets what"—and in the politics of recognition—values, identity, difference (Fraser, 1997). The study included young people attending an elite school and a school in a disadvantaged area, as well as two schools in the middle (that is, high schools that were neither "disadvantaged" nor "elite" in their intakes and outcomes). We were interested in following comparatively over time what happened to students from different backgrounds (class, gender, ethnicity) attending the same school, and to students from similar backgrounds attending different schools. We were particularly interested in schooling's part in the construction of gendered identity and the different forms this takes—in values that are formed about what is constituted as the norm, as right ways of thinking about who, what, and how is constituted as "other." We saw "distribution" and "recognition" not as antitheses but intimately linked in understanding what schooling does to produce fairness and unfairness, advantage and disadvantage, and lesser and greater forms of social equality.

What relevance has "the middle" to class?

One response to a request to focus on "class" might be to draw from the experiences of students at the two class extremes, and to tell a somewhat familiar story about those who represented the most elite and the most disadvantaged backgrounds and school settings in our study. A large body of sociological literature on schooling and class reproduction has explored this kind of perspective in ways that continue to resonate (Teese, 2000; Teese & Polesel, 2003). In the elite group, those whose parents were doctors and judges and lawyers, the young people not only in fact ended up at eighteen beginning to enter the most elite post-school courses, but also, in their own subjectivity, began, among all the students we interviewed, to most voice a neo-liberal discourse that saw society as composed of individuals with similar rights and opportunities whose outcomes were the result of their own efforts:

> Like people, any one of the lowest of people can get up and find themselves a job [. . .] some people try every now and then, but not try hard enough, and I think they're the people who shouldn't get our help because they're not trying either [. . .] I sometimes think, oh, it's just because people are really slack and because they don't have top qualifications and they're not even going to try. But I mean all my friends at school, we'll just walk into a place and say, "oh, excuse me, do you have any work?" and you know about three out of five times they'll get a job, and that's how I got my job.
>
> (girl at private school, aged 16)

At the other end of the class continuum, we could tell a story of those whose parents had learnt to expect nothing of school, who, on average, ended up in schools with the worst patterns of outcomes, and whose mantra about the future was a repeated "take it as it comes."

We could also, using those same two schools and groups on the extremes, tell a somewhat more gender-differentiated version of this familiar account of social reproduction. Among both the elite and the most disadvantaged young people we studied, girls were in the process of forging future lives somewhat differently to their male peers, with a new sense of possibility and self-reliance. With the elite girls this took the form of wanting to have everything—to be a future model and lawyer and travel the world as well as have a life that was not so pressured as their parents' lives.[1] The girls from poorer backgrounds, compared with boys of the same background, also conveyed some stronger sense of future possibility, though in a terrain that was very different from the girls from private school. For example, when their male counterparts were failing to finish school or find employment, these girls were persisting into basic qualifications via nursing assistant courses or McDonald's training courses. Many of these young women had seen their mothers return to study and get more qualifications during the educational and economic changes of the 1990s, and had a lived sense of expanding work and educational opportunities (though they might still express their lives in terms of "take it as it comes" rather than ambition or career planning). With the elite boys, there was a continued story of expected success, but also signs of some bewilderment about where the world was going and what their future life would be like. With the country working-class boys, there was a sense that they were pinning their hopes on a job and social structure that no longer existed—they hoped for apprenticeships and factory work, but could not accept the new role of extended schooling in enabling even the first steps of that employment to happen. These brief observations show the value of attending to class in interaction with other differences.

However, we now want to consider our study of class from a different starting point: what was going on in the schools and for the individuals who were "in the middle"—not the classic working class or disadvantaged, and not the private school middle class? If, as we have been arguing, class refers to both subjectivity (the individual student's own formation, self-understanding, values and trajectory) and to the production of social patterns (the ways groups of people are set up relative to each other), then class is not only located at the extremes. As identity and as analytic category, class is relational.

In this chapter we want to focus on some aspects of "the middle" in relation to class, but need to be clearer about what we are attempting to look at. We are not here working primarily with self-described categories of class—in Australia as well as the USA and even in contemporary England, people do not readily self-describe in class-differentiated terms, and there is a tendency for everyone to see themselves as middle class. Nor do we want here to focus on a social stratum that has been of major interest in recent sociological studies of schooling and the issue of "middle-class" advantage (Ball, 2003; Brantlinger, 2003; Power, Edwards, Whitty & Wigfall, 2003). "Middle class" in those studies refers to the professional and "new middle class" who are relatively affluent and well educated, and whose children in general do well from school. What we want to focus on here, however, is an account of those who are not "middle class" in that advantaged sense, nor "working class" in the sense of being heavily socially disadvantaged and marginal—in fact the bulk of the population in a country like Australia. We have used the term "in the middle" in a similar sense to the way in which it is used in a study of the values of "middle Australia" by Michael Pusey (2003). Pusey's study drew its national sample for focus group interviews by excluding those at the top and bottom deciles of the socio-economic status categories used by the Australian Bureau of Statistics. Pusey found that this large "middle" in Australia had been particularly affected by intensified working conditions arising from neo-liberal, market-driven policies. In these new conditions, both women and men are expected to fully participate in paid work as autonomous individuals, yet have to manage their family life in the context of withdrawal of traditional forms of public welfare in the form of free or subsidized education, health, and social security arrangements.

A traditional approach to studying class (and gender) in the context of schooling is to take a group who are pre-defined as losers or winners in the schooling system, and to study them to show what class looks like: what material and identity resources a certain group brings to their encounter with schooling, and what results from that interaction. Yet schooling is not only about success and failure in this distributional sense. Schooling is about both individual lives and inter-generational social forms *in formation*—that is, how social patterns are forming and how subjectivities are "becoming" in relation to schooling. The work of schools is thus part of the broader creation of a social and cultural zeitgeist about who matters and what matters and what counts as fair and unfair treatment of individuals and groups. This school-mediated process becomes taken up in an individual's sense of themselves, their values, their capacity, their significance, and their potency in the world. Collectively, these formations impact upon, in turn, citizenship, labor regulation, discrimination, and interpersonal experiences. In this respect, what happens *to everyone* should be part of the story of class: class is not just a possible way of describing the cultural particulars of one group—it does not simply mean working class. It is also about social processes and relationships between groups.

Class, values, and particular schools

> Do you think the school you're at makes much difference to where you end up in life or what kind of person you become?
>
> Well it does. I think so. Because different schools attract different sorts of people, and they also I think help mold you into sort of beliefs and that sort of thing.
>
> (17-year-old male high school student, 1999)

Much of the writing about class and schooling emphasizes a general story of how the institution of schooling confronts and reshapes young people of different kinds of class background. But there is a question too about particular schools and their effects.

The two "middle schools" in our study both drew students from a range of family backgrounds—from poor and unemployed to small business people, and parents working in professional occupations. In other words, these were high schools not so typed as "disadvantaged" that no "middle-class" children entered them; they were schools with some positive reputation, and where some students have gone on both in the past and in the current study to tertiary studies; but they are not selective schools or confined to a narrowly middle-class population. One of the schools ("Suburban High") is located in a largely middle-class suburb of Melbourne, and has a reputation for being slightly "alternative" with a very strong visual and communication arts curriculum. The other school ("Regional High") is located in a large provincial city, enjoys a high reputation in the local community for its academic standards and discipline, with many families moving houses to live in its catchment zone.

We want to begin with the end point of the study. Australian high schools are six years in length, with students usually beginning at age twelve in Year 7, and completing Year 12 at age seventeen or eighteen; students can legally leave school at age fifteen (usually Year 10); and overall nationally about 75 percent of young people complete Year 12. All our students began secondary school in 1994. Seven years later, of the eight students followed at Suburban High: one had left school in Year 10 to take up an apprenticeship, but has dropped out before completing this; one had hoped to get into a university course in an information technology area, but got a disappointing end of school examination result, and is doing a technical college one-year course in a similar area; two were still at school because they had not taken a full program of studies the previous year; one student had gone on an overseas exchange in Year 11, and had not, as he had originally planned, returned to finish his schooling, but was in casual employment; three began university courses, and of these, one had dropped out within two months of commencement, one was considering dropping out when interviewed mid-way through her first year, and the other was continuing and had found a subject area she enjoyed (Women's Studies).

These somewhat diverse students gave an overall impression of not being highly driven to get on the career track, or to have a work-related ambition to "get on in the world"; they were unlikely to express a strong commitment to a particular job or field of study. Many conveyed a kind of "aimlessness," a sense of uncertainty about their immediate and distant futures. For some students this uncertainty caused concern, for others it was understood as part of growing up, of "finding yourself." A high value was placed on self-awareness and introspection and school promoted a therapeutic ethos—in terms of both care of the self, and valuing of interpersonal relations.

By contrast, at Regional High, in the year after completing Year 12, all except one of the students were firmly on a vocational track. Here the dominant ethos was one of enterprise and hard work, and a commitment to securing individual achievement and developing personal goals. Three of the six students were at university (all doing directly vocational courses); one was at technical college in her chosen field (hotel management); one was accepted at university but chose to enter the police force directly rather than via a university qualification; and one student had left school previously as soon as he was legally old enough (15) to do so. All the other students had clear plans about what they were doing and where they were going, and indeed most had further plans about what they were going to do next, and were taking steps to make that happen: for example, going to the gym regularly to pass the police fitness test; applying for an air-force scholarship as a means of completing nursing on full pay; finding out options for continuing beyond the current degree to do a graduate degree in medicine. Our account of these two schools, the cohorts of students, their trajectories at the end of school, as well as their different values and cultural orientations cultivated by the different schools, shed light, we argue, on the way class works today.

First, let us consider the patterns of distribution and advantage most associated with the everyday use of the concept of class. Many sociologists have explored the diverse ways in which schooling contributes to social inequality by giving success to those groups who already possess cultural and material advantage, yet appears to be rewarding *individual* intelligence and effort. The work of Pierre Bourdieu has been a very influential account of this process (Bourdieu, 1984, 1998; Bourdieu & Passeron, 1977; and see also Ball, 2003; McDonald, 1999; Teese, 2000). In schooling, unstated, implicit, yet powerful "distinctions" operate whereby those who come from backgrounds not already familiar with and/or successful in the education system are made conscious of their otherness, and this sense of otherness intensifies the closer one gets to the levels and markers of academic success. More widely, "habitus"—the acquired dispositions related to particular family social locations—ensures that groups and social classes learn to value the things that lead to the reproduction of their situation. For example, in his classic study of working-class lads, Willis (1977) found that bright working-class boys valued behavior marked by disdain for academic schooling. Recently Ball (2003) and Power et al. (2003) in the UK, and Brantlinger (2003) in the USA, have added a further layer to such accounts of class and schooling by examining some of the ways in which the school curriculum and ethos is deliberately steered by professional middle-class parents.

These concepts of class capture part of the story of the students we followed at the two schools in the middle. Overall, the students came from family backgrounds that were neither as in tune with the academic curriculum nor as alien to it as the students at private and the disadvantaged schools in our study, and the overall outcomes of these students reflected that background. Within each school cohort too, some effect of family habitus could be seen in the different results and trajectories of students we followed. At Suburban High, for example, the girl who ended up doing Women's Studies at university had parents who were teachers; while the boy who was going on to technical college rather than university had parents who worked in unskilled jobs.

Of course, as Bourdieu and others show, subjectivity is formed from family habitus as well as school, and in the cases of the two schools at the extreme we discussed above, the schools heightened the family-formed subjectivity, either by reinforcing those values in the case of the elite school, or emphasizing the distance from "academic" knowledge, for the disadvantaged group. Nevertheless, through studying the cohort of students in each school over six years, we are able to see better what each school adds to or allows to be re-framed or emphasized from that family habitus. In the two schools in the middle we studied, although a few students in each case had parents who had made deliberate choices for them to be there, others were there simply because they were in that school's zone. Those we followed in each school were not a uniform group (demographically or in the ways they saw themselves and their world) at the beginning of our study, and we were able to see as we proceeded how they began to express some common political and social values by school that were different from those expressed in the other school.

The comparison over six years of the two schools and groups of students "in the middle" allows us to notice not only how students with different backgrounds and habitus see, and are seen by, their schools, but also to notice what is "in formation" both as individual subjectivity and as social patterns. These processes of "becoming" happen over six years in the context of particular schools, and on top of the family and biographical differences that students bring to school. Issues about distribution, recognition, and "class" in new times are thus inter-related.

Regional High is a school that overtly values winning and academic success and has the reputation of being an academic and sporting school; and it is attuned also to the types of distinctions that mark out social hierarchies and the claims to be among the elite. Relativities of positioning in the economic and status social hierarchy are emphasized and taken as an explicit agenda for both the school and individual. When we ask students at this school what they think of the school, or how the school compares with other schools, they talk at great length (compared with students from the other three schools in our study) about the comparisons involved. They constantly refer to material facilities, behavior, reputation *with the public*, and, above all, participation in a sporting activity associated with elite schools as the things that mark this as a "good" school. Making a comparison to another high school in the same city, one student says:

> Yeah, they have a higher [academic achievement result], but they don't have like a too good a reputation. Because all fights and stuff break out over there, and it's a dirty school. That's what a lot of people say and that. So I think we have a better reputation than a lot of other schools.
>
> (Year 7 girl, 1994)

At Regional High an interest in distinction, and in the way public (state) schools might measure up to elites, was prominent. The students already could speak at length about these issues when we first interviewed them in grade six, prior to coming to the school. As they progressed through school, the interest in comparisons and social distinctions remained high. The students both explicitly and implicitly reflected (and constituted) a particular school ethos in their ongoing concerns about success, the artifacts of success, and class relativities. They constantly talked about the importance of *public* appearances, reputation, and achievements, as a symbol of how good their own school was (and their own identity as part of this); and constantly drew comparisons with private schools (which they were like) and other high schools (which were inferior, "dirty," and violent, and lacked their own markers of status).

In terms of what the school produced as outcomes, and in terms of how students talked, Regional High generated a sense of a world in which individual effort and hard work bring rewards, and constant effort and vigilance is needed to keep up with those at the top of the social hierarchy, who are always an explicit point of comparison. The outcomes for individuals are positive in terms of the types of things parents and policy-makers worry about: attachment to career routes, taking action, being strategic, hard-working, and pro-active. Students who make it through to Year 12 acquire a strong sense of their own responsibility and efficacy to take action to shape their own future. But in doing this, students learn to mis-recognize existing class and school patterns and their own disadvantage (relative to the private school in our study). Listening to their experiences makes clear the amount of disciplinary work by the school that goes into being seen "as good as" the private schools—and of course "as good as" itself carries the message that you are not one of them. These students are also being nurtured into individualist ways of thinking that puts the responsibility for one's fate on the individual, one that carries with it relatively little empathy for those who struggle or who may be victims of, for example, bullying or racism:

> [in response to a question about causes of unemployment] Some of them I don't think want to go out and work. A lot of people that have been out of work for a while, and that sort of thing just leads to alcohol and drug use in the, ah, how would you put it, lesser rich populations of [this city].
> [He is then asked: "What do you think are the causes of unemployment?"] Probably the way they think about themselves, or the way they dress, or, um, yeah, the way they think because of where they live. They don't have much self-esteem. . . .
>
> (16-year-old male, Regional High)

> I think everyone should be able to get a job, because then they get responsible and they have to, everyone has to learn how to be responsible, how to be reliable, how to do things, because that's just the way society is, that's the way life is, that's the way everything goes. And the world runs like that. So for people that aren't employed and don't want to be or are finding it hard to get a job, I would try to encourage them as much as I could because you've got to, it's important and it's good for you, you'll benefit from it.
>
> (16-year-old female, Regional High)

> [talking about Indigenous Australians] I think they get too many rights over us and it's always we have to apologize for what our ancestors did to their ancestors.
>
> (16-year-old female, Regional High)

Regional High was thus a school whose central motifs were concerned with distinction, hard work, and winning. Students learned to think about some aspects of how social superiority and advantage worked, but were less attuned to simultaneous changes in social formation. The lack of overt ethnic diversity in the school, the lack of embedding of its culture in new forms of cosmopolitanism, meant that when students moved to the larger city at eighteen, a number of them were struggling with those cultural contexts.

Ah, it's very different [at university] from what I've encountered in the past. There's a fairly strong, ah, ethnic flavor to the students there, which is [. . .] not really something that you're used to.

(18-year-old male in post-school year after Regional High)

In contrast, Suburban High was a school with some pride in a tradition of being a little "alternative" and inclusive and of looking after its students. In interviews over the seven years of our study, young people at this school conveyed a strong sense of a school that paid a lot of personal attention to students, tried to help them and give them second chances, and where there was genuinely less racism than at other schools. Students spoke very warmly of teachers—both in general and in relation to particular teachers, and reported one of the strengths of the teaching as being its ongoing commitment to "giving you another chance." Individual students reflected that they felt nurtured and valued. When they made comparisons with other schools, students did not focus on social hierarchy so much as on the style and the culture of this school, especially its informality and ethnic diversity and inclusiveness. As individuals, students felt less pressure, and one consequence seemed to be that in the immediate post-school phase many had not advanced along the educational pathways to the extent that they might have at another school. Many reported that they did feel not highly pushed in terms of academic work, and were more consumed with working themselves out. One boy, for example, spoke of wanting to continue his studies, but just could not get himself organized to do this; another was vaguely dissatisfied with the university course she began, and found traveling there by public transport too much trouble—and had dropped out within two months of beginning the degree.

Suburban High, at least as reported by students, was highly sensitive to cultural and ethnic diversity, and nurtured the valuing of good relationships; it cultivated a sense of commitment to social collectivity and inclusiveness. For example, students' political values were largely sympathetic to those who found themselves unemployed:

Well, there's not enough jobs, and then people get discouraged because they can't get a job, so they give up . . .

(16-year-old female, Suburban High)

In interviews after leaving school, a number of students mentioned, without prompting, issues of racism they had spoken out against. They also did not perceive unemployment as a personal reflection on the unemployed, but as something that happens for reasons outside their control.

Both Regional and Suburban High are shaping students in particular ways, constituting immediate longer-term educational and work pathways, and individual orientations to the social world. In terms of values and orientations, Suburban High was doing well on "the politics of recognition"; but distinctly less well on the distributive side. Regional High was strong on pathways and on establishing an individualized sense of the self and of the social. The young people here were developing a sense of social status in which some people were superior and others dirty, and also an ideological sense that portrays unemployment as simply the result of one's own individual lack of effort.

Subjectivities of becoming and class/social arrangements in formation

The very brief account we have given of one part of our findings about young people and their cohort experience over time at two schools "in the middle" might seem to be an unsatisfactory way of getting at "class." We have drawn from it because we think even this rather summary account allows a glimpse of some of the different ways we need to think and talk about "the way class works"; and that for different purposes, different kinds of theoretical interests, and different foregrounding of data, are appropriate.

Questions about specificity of context and the purpose of a particular analysis or research account are not peripheral to a consideration of the meaning of class; they are part of what gives it significance and salience. An argument against a single, or definitive model of class pertains not only to the point made by Benhabib, with which we opened this chapter, of the conceptual impossibility and undesirability of settling on one single theory or model as an adequate account of a complex phenomenon. It also refers to the contexts in which research on class takes place, and the purposes and audience for any such research. To take a simple but significant example: writing in a policy context about the impact of class background on schooling outcomes in a climate of accountability and school effectiveness calls for a different way of representing class than does a discussion of class in relation to feminist political theories on social justice where the intention might be to highlight the limitations of certain definitions of class.

We have deliberately in this chapter focused on one way of reading class in our longitudinal study, by emphasizing a story about school cultures that we have built up by listening to different students over time, and by hearing common patterns and themes in the values articulated within each school. Our account emphasizes that the particular practices, history, and culture of a school come together in distinct ways and that this has ramifications for how individuals see and act on themselves and their possibilities, and for how they think about others, as well as what "outcomes" they directly experience from school. We have not in this discussion emphasized differences, of gender, of ethnicity, or of individual biography, among the students at particular schools. For example, at Suburban High, the dominant school ethos and cultural codes had a differential impact on two boys who came from ethnic minority backgrounds. We have also not looked specifically at gender differences and class. However, as with class, our argument is that to properly consider either race or racism or ethnicity and difference, we cannot simply put this together into a single chapter-length account, but need to focus directly on the conceptual questions (about modernity and colonialism and identities of national belonging) and the story that we saw in our project in relation to these (McLeod & Yates, 2003). We have examined class not as a single category or identity, but as a relational concept and embodied experience that is central to how social relations and practices work and take shape. Schooling (and particular schools) contributes to this formation, not only in the immediate distributive sense of "who gets what," but also by setting up for individuals ways of thinking about the self, the social, politics, and possibilities.

Explanations of class influenced by the concepts of habitus and cultural capital can easily slide into a reproductive model in which habitus of family and school are conflated, and in which the different modes and cultures of particular schools are glossed over (McLeod & Yates, 2006). This is where some comparison of Suburban High and

Regional High is of interest. Accepting broadly arguments about class-based cultural advantages and disadvantages of different students in Australia, we have in these two schools, with some broadly similar (though certainly not identical) intake, two different ways of relating to the "cultural arbitrary," two different representations of what is valued. At one school, relativities of positioning in the economic and social status hierarchy are emphasized and taken as an explicit agenda for both school and individual; at the other, it is a submerged discourse, not part of the school's strong agenda. We have argued that these different modes create significant differences both in terms of the fate of the individual students, and in terms of the broader values they produce.

For young people at Regional High, the ongoing battle of this school to be "as good as private schools" created an obsession with markers of social differentiation. In that (limited) sense, "class" became an emphasized category in what they noticed about the world, what they noticed about themselves in the world, and what they assumed they might achieve in the future. Class in this sense was part of their self-conscious identity. It was a form of class consciousness likely to reproduce class difference—to see others as "dirty" or "lazy"—alongside a little class mobility, but it was not class in the sense of class solidarity. At Suburban High, the world was seen above all as ethnically and culturally diverse. In terms of identity categories, race and ethnicity rather than class (or gender) were more noticed in social relations and patterns. This is not to say that "class" was irrelevant in the lives and opportunities available to these students. Rather, it is to suggest that their positioning of themselves in relation to others, and articulation of self–other relations more generally, was not principally expressed through a class-based language and imaginary. Attention to cultural diversity was congruent with an introspective individualism, in which becoming "your own person"—a non-conforming individual—was a marker of distinction. This engagement/mobilization of discourses of difference, diversity, and being an individual does not easily fit with conventional forms of class analysis. The Bourdieuian analysis of practices of cultural distinction perhaps captures part of it, but the desires for being an individual, and knowing yourself, were not.

The two schools responded to the overall problem of cultural capital and social advantage and disadvantage of the students in two different ways. Regional High accepted the norms as they stood, and drove students to learn the dominant modes and compete on that ground (with some, but limited, success—they had much higher drop-out rates than private schools). Suburban High adopted an approach that had students focusing on who they were themselves, rather than what the playing field consisted of. This too has been identified as a key feature of contemporary times—incitements to self-reflexivity and the (therapeutic) regulation of the autonomous self (Beck & Beck-Gernsheim, 2002; Rose, 1999). Such forms of subjectivity—flexibility, reflexive, self-managing—are also highly desirable features of the new worker, and in this respect the cultivation of such dispositions articulates with a very traditional agenda of "class" analysis—that is, the kind of resources called on and exploited in the labor market and in the contemporary neo-liberal economy (Chappell et al., 2003; Du Gay, 1996; Gee, 1999; Gee, Hull, & Lankshear, 1996).

Final reflections

Understanding "the way class works" involves examining how class produces identifications (self-conscious as well as unconscious) and desires as well as its political effects in the production of inequalities. The argument that class is about social patterns and distributional issues of who gets what and who ends up on what pathway remains important and necessary. But class, as we have been arguing here, is also about subjectivity—how one understands and positions self and other, rationally and emotionally, and one's sense of potency and possibility. For example, the mode of relating to others as inferior or superior was different in the two schools discussed here, as were the dominant rhetorics for understanding "who one is." At Regional High, being hardworking, goal-oriented, and competitive was highly valued, and there was a strong concern with asserting the superiority of the school and knowing the local markers of distinction. At Suburban High, the codes of distinction were based more on the aesthetics of choice and individualism, and in the overall orientations to cultural inclusiveness, class differentiation was underemphasized.

Schools distribute success and failure; they also teach people things beyond formal curriculum knowledge; and they impact on individuals and groups in both the short term and the long term. With students from two "middle" high schools in our study, we can observe some "school effects" not just on immediate post-school outcomes for young people in them, but on their social values and orientations, some different ways of seeing what matters, and of thinking about relations between individuals, group characteristics, and the social whole. In each case, issues of "distribution" and "recognition" are intertwined; in each case, the directions set in motion have some consequences both for the individuals themselves, and for the broader development of Australia's polity, economy, and relations between its citizens.

But is it helpful to name any of this as about "class?" Both as theory and as category in broad social use, "class" is typically associated with particular places ("old" Europe) and histories (elites based on birth) and times (nineteenth-century industrial society). Nevertheless, and accepting that after feminism and critical race theory there is no way to retrieve a single master theory or model of what class or class/race/gender look like, we do want to go on struggling with this issue. When considering the schooling of middle Australia, for many purposes, to omit class is to ignore an obvious presence. Whether or not class is a self-conscious identity category, in Australia and in the USA, and indeed in all the OECD countries, a very strong relationship of schooling to "socio-economic status"[2] persists, whatever the problems in trying to operationalize that concept adequately, and whether we are considering this alongside or within other categorizations, such as race or gender (Connell et al., 1982; OECD, 2006; Teese, 2000; Teese & Polesel, 2003; Thomson, 2002). This is not to claim that class has universal effects, or is universally the most significant form of inequality or discrimination in education—race currently has a strong claim to that dubious prize in many countries, and religion is strongly on the horizon, while gender had a brief day in the sun in the 1970s and 1980s. Rather, it is to argue that keeping analytical distinctions and historical and theoretical insights in play is an important part of thinking about how processes of subjectivity and social formation work. Researching gender or race without asking questions about class is to diminish those enquiries. And, as we have attempted to illustrate in this chapter, in asking questions about class, for some purposes at least, there is value in thinking about "the way class works" as relational and discursive (or ideological), as conceptual, and as also about formation over time, not just as an empirical study of the ways of life of particular groups of people.

Questions for discussion

1. Discuss McLeod and Yates' use of the term subjectivity in relation to schooling and social class. Based on your experience, how do schools work to shape students' values and sense of self-worth?
2. Drawing from McLeod and Yates, how can one understand social reproduction from a gendered perspective? What are the interrelations between gender and social class?
3. In discussing their research approach, McLeod and Yates state that "it is an approach that says 'the way class works' is not just a story about how particular lives are being lived, but about how social formation and future lives are being developed." What are the authors asking us to think about in regard to class reproduction? What are they asking us to think about in regard to micro and macro social structures?
4. What is a "marked category of interest?" What, in your opinion, is the current "marked category of interest" in your location and why? If you chose a category other than class, in what ways is it related to class?
5. Why might students at the most elite school visited by the authors express their firm belief in the equality of rights and opportunities? Discuss the ways in which these students are influenced by these ideological beliefs.
6. The authors noted that most people in the UK, US, and Australia tend to self-identify as middle class. How is the institution of schooling related to the pervasive adoption of middle-class-ness? How does the myth of meritocracy factor into the equation?
7. Discuss the differences in student outcomes between Regional High and Suburban High. How do the differences in the schools' ethos impact students' outcomes? How does social class work to shape the schools' ethos?
8. McLeod and Yates imply that the meaning of class has evolved. What do you think class means now "as 'new times' are in formation?" What theoretical and experiential perspectives inform your definition? How does your definition differ from more traditional definitions of class? What components are most salient or crucial in your definition? Do you think McLeod and Yates would support your definition, and why?

Notes

1. Some interesting similarities and a more extensive psycho-social interpretation of middle-class white girls today have been explored in studies by Walkerdine, 2003 and Walkerdine, Lucey & Melody, 2001.
2. SES is not the same as "class" of course, and has not been able to be adequately put together as a single hierarchy once there was an attempt to adequately include women's work, but it is one proxy for setting up certain investigations of the latter that has salience in relation to school.

References

Ahmed, S. (2004). Collective feelings or the impressions left by others. *Theory, Culture and Society, 21*(2), 25–42.

Ball, S. (2003). *Class strategies and the education market: The middle classes and social advantage.* London: RoutledgeFarmer.

Beck, U., & Beck-Gernsheim, E. (2002). *Individualization: Institutional individualism and its social and political consequences* (P. Camiller, Trans.). London: Sage Publications.

Benhabib, S. (1995). Feminism and postmodernism. In S. Benhabib, J. Butler, D. Cornell & N. Fraser (Eds.), *Feminist contentions: A philosophical exchange.* New York: Routledge.

Bourdieu, P. (1984). *Distinction: A social critique of the judgement of tastes.* Cambridge, MA: Harvard University Press.

—— (1998). *The state nobility: Elite schools in the field of power.* Oxford: Polity Press.

Bourdieu, P., & Passeron, J-P. (1977). *Reproduction in education, society and culture* (R. Nice, Trans.). London: Sage.

Brantlinger, E. (2003). *Dividing classes: How the middle class negotiates and rationalizes school advantage.* New York: RoutledgeFalmer.

Brown, W. (2005). The impossibility of women's studies. In W. Brown (Ed.), *Edgework: Critical essays on knowledge and politics.* Princeton: Princeton University Press.

Chappell, C., Rhodes, C., Solomon, N., Tennant, M., & Yates, L. (2003). *Reconstructing the life-long learner: Pedagogy and identity in individual, organisational and social change.* New York: Routledge.

Connell, R. W., Ashenden, D., Kessler, S., & Dowsett, G. W. (1982). *Making the difference: Schools, families and social division.* St. Leonards: Allen & Unwin.

Crenshaw, K. W. (1994). Mapping the margins: Intersectionality, identity politics, and violence against women of color. In M. A. Fineman & R. Mykitiuk (Eds.), *The public nature of private violence* (pp. 93–118). New York: Routledge.

Du Gay, P. (1996). *Consumption and identity at work.* London: Sage.

Fraser, N. (1997). *Justice interruptus: Critical reflections on the "Postsocialist" condition.* New York: Routledge.

Gee, J. P. (1999). New people in new worlds: Networks, the new capitalism and schools. In B. Cope and M Kalantizis (Eds.), *Multiliteracies: Literacy learning and the design of social futures.* London: Routledge.

Gee, J. P., Hull, G., & Lankshear, C. (1996). *The new work order: Behind the language of the new capitalism.* St Leonards: Allen & Unwin.

Hollway, W. (1994). Beyond sex differences: A project for feminist psychology. *Feminism & Psychology, 4*(4), 538–46.

MacDonald, K. (1999). *Struggles for subjectivity: Identity, action and youth experience.* Cambridge: Cambridge University Press.

McLeod, J., & Yates, L. (2003). Who is "us?" Students negotiating discourses of racism and national identification in Australia. *Race, Ethnicity and Education, 6*(1), 29–49.

—— (2006). *Making modern lives: Subjectivity, schooling and social change.* Albany, NY: State University of New York Press.

Nielsen, H. B., & Rudberg, M. (1995). Gender recipes among young girls. *Young: Journal of Nordic Youth Studies, 3*(2), 71–88.

OECD (Organization for Economic Co-operation and Development) (2006). *Education at a glance: OECD indicators 2006.* Paris: OECD.

Power, S., Edwards, T., Whitty, G., & Wigfall, V. (2003). *Education and the middle class.* Buckingham: Open University Press.

Pusey, M. (2003). *The experience of Middle Australia: The dark side of economic reform.* Cambridge: Cambridge University Press.

Reay, D. (2004). Gendering Bourdieu's concept of capitals? Emotional capital, women and social class. In L. Adkins & B. Skeggs (Eds.), *Feminism after Bourdieu.* Maiden, MA: Blackwell Publishing.

Rose, N. (1999). *Powers of freedom: Reframing political thought*. Cambridge, UK: Cambridge University Press.

Skeggs, B. (1997). *Formations of class and gender: Becoming respectable*. London: Sage.

—— (2004). *Class, self and culture*. London: Routledge.

Teese, R. (2000). *Academic success and social power: Examinations and inequality*. Melbourne: Melbourne University Press.

Teese, R., & Polesel, J. (2003). *Undemocratic schooling: Equity and quality in mass secondary education in Australia*. Melbourne: Melbourne University Press.

Thomson, P. (2002). *Schooling the Rustbelt kids: Making the difference in changing times*. Sydney: Allen & Unwin.

Walkerdine, V. (2003). Reclassifying upward mobility: Femininity and the neo-liberal subject. *Gender and Education, 15*(3), 237–48.

Walkerdine, V., Lucey, H., & Melody, J. (2001). *Growing up girl: Psycho-social explorations of class and gender*. London: Palgrave.

Willis, P. (1977). *Learning to labour*. Farnborough: Saxon House.

Chapter 24

Rereading class, rereading cultural studies

*Jennifer Logue and Cameron McCarthy** [*]

Say Cockney fire shooter. We bus' gun
    Cockney say tea leaf. We just say sticks man
    You know dem have a wedge while we have corn
    Say Cockney "Be my first son" we just say Gwaan!
    (quoted in Paul Gilroy, *There Ain't No Black in the Union Jack*, p. 196)

"The problematic of a word or concept consists of the theoretical or ideological framework within which that word or concept can be used to establish, determine and discuss a particular range of issues and a particular kind of problem."
    (Althusser & Balibar, 1968; quoted in Hebdige, *Subculture*, p. 142)

Could a cockney translation of cultural Marxism, its overall perceptual, conceptual, and linguistic apparatus, provide insight into the basis on which to imagine and build networks of affiliation across race, class, gender, and national divides? What does a conversation between aspects of contemporary popular culture and scholarly discourses of cultural Marxism reveal? And why is it important to ask?

Illuminating the way discourses of resistance function to reinforce aspects of the very power structures they aim and claim to subvert, we subject the analytic apparatus of cultural Marxism to scrutiny. Reading it contrapuntally (Logue, 2005) through the lenses of cinematic and literary representation, we begin to see how the units of analysis in the discourse of cultural/historical materialist revolution are incapable of encapsulating the dynamics of power at work in past and present social and global relations. Here, we juxtapose analysis of the nostalgic and unified nationalist structure of feeling with which the neo-Marxist discourse in post-war Britain is silently aligned to the problematization of tradition we see in cinematic and literary representation. This provides an opportunity to (re)examine the conceptual tensions and categorical contradictions existent within this discourse of resistance, the terms of which seem to undermine the possibility of adequately diagnosing the dynamics of power and resistance it portends.

The tendency to at once universalize and pathologize particularity in a manner disavowed allows terms such as "tradition," "culture," "class," "power," "privilege," et cetera, to be deployed as though they weren't riddled with complexity, contradiction,

[*] Jennifer Logue is a doctoral student in Educational Policy Studies, specializing in Philosophy of Education and Gender and Women's Studies, and Cameron McCarthy teaches Mass Communications Theory, Cultural Studies, and the Sociology of Knowledge in the Department of Educational Policy Studies and the Institute of Communications Research at the University of Illinois's Urbana campus.

and antagonistic genealogical formation, an age-old strategy in the struggle for domination. Of course, the persistent assignment of particularism and atavism to the vast wastes of the Third World begins with Karl Marx himself as well as Max Weber and Emile Durkheim in their particular staged model of historical evolution of human societies. This practice continues in contemporary thinking in the attribution of the same scarlet letter to the new social movements and the rejection of identity politics in the writings of Marxist scholars such as Todd Gitlin (Gitlin, 1995). This essay bucks this trend, restoring a corrective valence to the whole enterprise of the analysis of culture. We read all of this against the troubling of tradition and the past in recent films on the working-class subject such as *Billy Eliot* (2000) and *The Full Monty* (1997) as well as George Orwell's discourse on tradition, power, and privilege in his essay, "Shooting An Elephant" (1946/1981). In reading back and forth between Birmingham and Burma, a new light is shed on recombinant particularism (*There Ain't No Black in the Union Jack*) that the analytic framework of cultural Marxism seems to have foreclosed.

Examining the status of tradition and the past within cultural Marxism as a way of clearing a path to the future, looking particularly at the work of historical recuperation within Marxist cultural humanism and its tendencies towards the universalization of the particular, a sharp light of attention is focused on British Cultural Studies, its anxiety of influence, and its graven desire for plenitude of the socially and materially constructed demarcations of the modern world. One is reminded here of the definition of culture and cultural studies advanced by John Fiske in his essay, "British Cultural Studies and Television." "Cultural studies," argues Fiske, "is concerned with the generation and circulation of meanings in industrial societies (*the study of non-industrial societies may require a different theoretical base . . .*)" (Fiske, 1987, p. 254). Cultural Studies' search for the vanishing point, the origins of consciousness, and general mythologization, and valorization of the industrial working-class subject is nestled within a peculiar narrative and play of national endowment, affiliation, and ethnic and localist distinctiveness in its founding arguments and concerns.

This valorization of the traditions of the industrial working class has had several consequences (beyond the mistaking of spitballs for revolution) not always adequately accessed or diagnosed to date. One is the disavowal of particularism being no different in structure and tone than what could be found in the patterned variables and structural functionalism overall in the work of mainstream social scientists such as Talcott Parsons. Of course, an integral feature of the reverence for working-class traditions is the methodological overlay of field-bound ethnographic rules and the visual culture documentary impulses that flow from Bronislaw Malinowski, E. E. Evans-Pritchard, Radcliffe Brown, and Margaret Mead and monumentalist classical anthropology into the critical sciences in education and elsewhere. These ethnographic impulses parallel the rise of visual culture as a whole in silent and sound film, television, and radio broadcasting and the like.

Interrogating the foundational assumptions and technical terms deployed in the discourses of cultural Marxism, we foreground the epistemological, ethical, and political implications of not investigating what it is these conceptual tools enable us to open up and what it is they foreclose. Does the concept of "class," for example, as deployed within cultural studies research, properly capture the contradictions experienced by category members in their everyday, lived existence and their class trajectories as they intersect with the new social subjects of the modern world—the diasporic "Pakis" and "West

Indians" of British urban ethnographic lore (carriers of class histories of a different order)? How are the class affiliation and performative practices of Willis' "ear'oles" to be understood within this paradigm particularly when these putative class members no longer seek to align themselves with the traditions which theorists of the working class describe? Is the working-class concept equipped to theorize the collective formation of agents with shared interests as members of interpretive communities comprised of individuals that may or may not share the same relation to the means of production? Should it be? And what happens to sex/gender/sexuality when class becomes the primary category of analysis? What follows is a critical conversation between foundational texts of cultural Marxism and forms of popular culture to illuminate some of these complexities captured on the big screen and in the ill-fated peregrinations of the working-class/lower-middle-class subject in modern literature. Reading these discourses, texts, and conceptual tools contrapuntally through the lenses of cinematic and literary representation magnifies the need to reconfigure language, perception, and desire so that the conversation and transnational hybridity that is culture can take place and be grappled with collectively.

Demystifying the demystifiers

A central task of this essay, then, is to demystify the demystifiers on the problem of tradition and particularism, which the classical sociologists had assured us would diminish with the advance of capitalism. The tendency to shunt particularism off to the periphery is therefore consistent with this core form of thinking. The ethnographic impulse that underlies cultural Marxism fuses action and interpretation, experience and text, worlding the world from the metropolitan center into its visible hierarchies of class and culture. Standing at the center of this panopticon, the whole social field spreads out before the Marxist observer like a vast unscrolling map. This cartographer of the modern world measures and weighs its social distinctions with the finality of a puritan and with the fervor of what Rey Chow calls "the protestant ethnic" (Chow, 2002). In the cultural Marxist's elective epiphany, the third world subject would virtually perish (*There Ain't No Black in the Union Jack*). But in this disavowal, particularism returned like a plague of innocence. Read on its own terms as a quest for scientificity, cultural Marxism divines class from the entrails of the social present and past, and ethnicity disappears. Read against the grain as a reluctant form of autobiography, the root book of cultural Marxism reveals its protagonist dressed in his solipsistic bright suit of ethnic privilege. And here, by this strategy, ethnic particularism appears. It is this deep-bodied ethnocentrism, paradoxically attached to the generalizations and trans-historical statements about the industrial working class and human societies associated with the theorizing of critical social scientists, which Horace Miner satirizes in his classic essay, "Body Ritual among the Nacirema" (Nacirema spelled backwards, of course, is "American"). Here, Miner talks about the mouth rites of the Nacirema, in the process exposing the classic norms underlying the cultural description that constituted the *leitmotif* of culturalist scholars writing about others:

> The daily body ritual performed by everyone includes a mouth rite. Despite the fact that these people are so punctilious about the care of the mouth, this rite involves a practice which strikes the uninitiated stranger as revolting. It was reported to me that

the ritual consists of inserting a small bundle of hog hairs into the mouth, along with certain magical powders, and then moving the bundle in a highly formalized series of gestures.

(Miner, 1956, p. 503)

The everyday practice of brushing the teeth is elevated to the realm of magic. The magician, the social observer, and his besotted humanism are defamiliarized here. And, the anthropological gaze of the West upon the third world subject is turned back on power for an evanescent moment full of illumination.

When we look, too, at the writings and founding motives of cultural studies, we find a similar hidden subject within the text that attaches itself to the working class and hides its own anxieties and its professional updraft. When we look at the work of Richard Hoggart or Raymond Williams or E. P. Thompson, or later, Paul Willis and Dick Hebdige, we find an ethnographic Marxism alloyed to a visceral nationalism, an ethnic particularism and wish fulfillment that it denies. How else can we read the intellectual history of Williams' *Culture and Society, 1780–1950* (1966) but as a formidable and unrelenting recuperation of the Leavisian moral sensibility and purpose of British cultural form—the dream of the whole way of life as the encoding and decoding of national ethos in the British industrial novel and literary works? How else are we to read the brilliant E. P. Thompson, who at the end of *The Making of the English Working Class* (1980) makes the disclaimer that he was not competent to speak for any other working class than the English . . . not even the Scots or the Welsh? How else are we to read Paul Willis and his lads of Hammertown Boys, who reduce the postcolonial other to the metonymic "Pakis" and "Jamaicans?" In this rude awakening from methodological slumber, British Marxist historians would disconnect from the work of international socialism, the CP, and found its own distinctive theories of the origin of the British working class in the revival of working-class radical traditions (Dworkin, 1997; Hall, 1980). This working-class construct, for the subcultural theorists of resistance at Birmingham, was defined around a militancy of style, distinctive accoutrements of dress, argot, and the like. This characteristically muscular construct, as Angela McRobbie (1997) would note, folded the working class into a singular, homogenous structure, powerful against its class adversaries, its semiotic chora set against the "ear'oles," and contemptuous and disdainful of the periphery.

In its radical ethnocentrism, cultural Marxism closed off the White working class from its racially minoritized other, orientalizing the latter—whether they were from Asia or the Caribbean—as metonymic attachments: the Pakis or the Jamaicans. A deadly consequence of this self-centered impulse is that the working-class subject and the nature of power were not presented in a sufficiently complex or nuanced way. Indeed, it would be left to the filmic culture and the literary culture to present more complicated views of class power and class subjects. Films such as *Educating Rita* (1983), *The Full Monty* (1997), *Billy Eliot* (2000), *Sammy and Rosy Get Laid* (1987), and *My Beautiful Laundrette* (1985) exemplify some of this complexity. While in the literary world, Wilson Harris's *Carnival* (1985), Samuel Selvon's *The Lonely Londoners* (1956), Kazuo Ishiguro's *The Remains of the Day* (1989), George Lamming's *The Emigrants* (1954/1994) and *Water with Berries* (1971), and V. S. Naipaul's *The Mimic Men* (1967) and *Half A Life* (2001) seem to do a better job at grappling with dynamics of power than the scholarly discourses we have been discussing. But before we turn to the filmic and literary culture for insight, let us try to spell out a little more thoroughly the nature of the conceptual tensions that stem from this radical ethnocentrism.

Conceptual calamity and lexical apse: Who fills in the gaps?

The lack of unity and fluidity found within different lived realities within nations and around the globe are not/cannot be contained in the concepts we have with which to articulate them. These concepts include "*the* working class," which has been the animating and organizing category deployed in much contemporary "neo-Marxist" analysis. Crucial aspects of what it means to be a socio/discursively constructed subject differentially positioned in a nebulous network of power relations are overlooked when definitions of culture, class, and power involve a nationalist monologue at the expense of intercultural dialogue and exchange. Language, here, is of primary importance, for not only does it serve to articulate and delimit a set of criteria for establishing whether or not one belongs to a given tradition, or rather, where they belong in relation to it, but language often seems to reinforce the very social structures it is invoked to subvert.

Historicizing the concept of class, for example, reveals not only that common contemporary usage of the term too often fails to adequately absorb and embrace crucial distinctions and complex variations found within "it," but also that "class" is then disembedded from its proclaimed tradition, thereby eliding paradoxical implications of forms of resistance achieved by revolutionary discourses past and present. How, for example, is the Marxian distinction between *Klasse en sich* (*class in itself*) and *Klasse fuer sich* (*class for itself*) placed within the work of cultural Marxism? Marx theorized *class in itself* to signify those who share a common location with regard to their relations to the means of production and *class for itself* to pertain to members of a group who consciously recognize their shared predicament and common interests, actualizing their needs and desires through networks of communication and resistance by organizing around their shared conflict with the opposing class. The two contending classes here, for contemporary Marxism, included the proletariat, destined to become *class for itself* and the bourgeoisie, incapable of formulating class consciousness beyond the pursuit of individual self-interest. What was less spelled out, however, were the dynamics, shifts, and conflicts found within *class in itself*. For when one tries to figure out how factors of race, gender, and sexuality figure into the operationalization of the definition of the proletariat/ "working class" *in itself*, one may be inclined to suggest that there were numerous formations and reformations of *class for itself* within the "working class" and that these variations on the theme were of less urgency for Marx (and later neo-Marxists) to articulate. Continuing in this vein, early postwar cultural studies theorists failed to track the dynamic patterns of migration, dislocation, and rearticulation that had begun to feed into the class experience of working-class subjects in England and that brought new elements, new potential conscripts, to membership within the industrial working class. They had failed to adequately assess the changing map of spatial relations and the interior realities of British urban life itself as part of a broad-scale set of effects brought on by late-capital—effects that were now stalking modern industrial societies. It seems that, here, the seeds of an under-theorized dynamic involving the mis(sed)-diagnosis of the impact of networks of global communication, movement and migration of economic and cultural capital, and the amplification of representations and images had been consolidated. What was nurtured instead was an ethnic and nationalist myopia planted firmly in the soil of an agrarian England transcoded onto the urban setting. The nurturing work of much of the historical recuperation of British radical traditions such as that of E. P. Thompson or Raymond Williams always, then, had a backward glance. Time and space essentially stood still. And, for instance, Willis would find in the Hammertown Boys School in *Learning to Labor* (1981) that the progeny of the working class grew from seedlings that were planted by their fathers on the shop floor. This backward glance rendered problematic the entire analytical apparatus of the cultural studies discourse on class and change. In affirming the class essence of the industrial proletariat, this nostalgia has a particular methodological effect concerning class analysis as deployed within cultural studies: a tendency to gloss over contradiction, variation, and multiplicity.

Is this affirmation of traditional essence and the latent but virile proposition of the indivisibility of the working class, in a sense, what Hebdige accomplishes by writing of reggae and punk as seemingly equivalent subcultures in *Subculture: The Meaning of Style* (Hebdige, 1979). Rather than emphasizing these formations and modes of resistance as mutually constitutive, reggae figures in as an expression that culminates in the response of the punks. Neither is reggae considered counter-cultural or as more than an articulation of style, despite the fact that Hebdige cites its having created its own language, religion, and vision of the future. Are we to understand the White and Black factions described herein as manifestations of *class for itself* contained within the "*working class?*" How are the lived realities and cultural achievements of the diaspora/Black Britain subsumed by this move? Does it contribute to the idea that tradition and culture can be claimed as the moorings of an ethnically invisible yet distinctive group that remains forever threatened by that which it codes as deviant?

What happens if we take seriously Michel Foucault's assertion that the concept of class struggle evolved out of (was extracted/de-historicized from) the discourse of race war/race struggle (*Society Must be Defended* [2002])? Foucault's genealogy of the discourse of history reveals that racism is imbricated in revolutionary thought coming from the moment when the discourse of race struggle was being transformed into revolutionary discourse, where the state functions no longer as an instrument that one race uses against another: the state becomes the protector of the integrity, the superiority, and the purity of the race. Foucault reminds us that the concept of class struggle is found first in the discourse of the French historians—in the works of Augustin Thierry, Francois Pierre Guizot, John Wade, and others. Thierry is defined as the father of the "class struggle," which is used to replace the notion of "race struggle." The effort to recode race struggle into class struggle is read as a manifestation of the shift in focus on race as existing whenever one writes the history of two groups that do not have the same language, to the term race becoming pinned to a biological meaning. This shift in race as linguistic difference to race as biological is what will become actual racism. This racism, according to Foucault, takes over and reconverts the form and function of the discourse of history, which was hitherto a discourse on race struggle/race war. Racism is born, then, of the shift in historical discourse. Once reporting on the theme of historical war with its battles, invasions, victories, and defeats protagonists record history with a new post-evolutionist theme. Racism, then, at its inception, becomes manifest in the idea that foreigners have infiltrated society, which is to be safeguarded from deviants, who serve to foreground class conflict by being coded as factors that complicate it.

Foreclosing examination of its own origins, disembedding the discourse of class conflict from the discourse of race struggle impairs analysis of the complex organization of hierarchical social relations and resistance to them. Not only does the term class commonly function as though it were a static, impermeable category with an invisible ethnically particular tradition, but it fails to connote the actual strategies through which social subjects forge collective oppositional identities from the grounded pragmatics of cultural hybridities. Rather than attending to the centrality of sexual orientation, gender, and ethnic affiliation in cultural formations and transformations, in creating networks of communication and association, these categories are too often treated as complications contained within the already-established organized relations to the means of production. And while the insights and methodological breakthroughs of cultural Marxism are important, like the emphasis on the popular imaginary, style, and other forms of often overlooked resistance, might not the struggles and forms of active resistance to what cultural Marxism lauds as the "working class" be better described as strategies developed by those differentially positioned in a complex web of power relations? It seems as though some of these overlooked dynamics of power and resistance are better captured in the very popular culture that cultural Marxism sought to interpret. Yet, while cultural Marxism begins to analyze popular culture, does it really converse with it?

Leaping out of the lexicon: Cinematic and literary representation

BILLY ELIOT'S DAD: Ballet?

BILLY ELIOT: What's wrong with ballet?

BILLY ELIOT'S DAD: What's wrong with BALLET?

BILLY ELIOT: It is perfectly normal . . .

BILLY ELIOT'S DAD: Perfectly NORMAL? . . . For girls, not for lads, Billy . . . Lads do football, or boxing or wrestling. . . . Not Frigging Ballet!

BILLY ELIOT: What lads do? . . . Wrestling? . . . I don't see what's wrong with . . .

BILLY ELIOT'S DAD: Yes you do!!!

BILLY ELIOT: No, I don't!!!

BILLY ELIOT'S DAD: Yes you bloody do!!! . . . Who you think I am?

BILLY ELIOT: What are you trying to say dad . . .

(From *Billy Eliot*)

Contemporary filmic representations offer complex and nuanced accounts of the transforming circumstances of working class lived and commodified existence, revealing fault lines of contradiction and multiplicity. Indeed, the vaunted traditions and the folkways of the past, so celebrated in the cultural studies' ethnographic portrayal of the proletariat from Hoggart to Willis and Hebdige, now hang like proverbial dead weights upon the new working-class subject. As Billy (Jamie Bell) of the film *Billy Elliot* (2000) demonstrates, the shop floor and the coalmines belong to a distant past and now exist as straitjackets constraining the desires of youth. Billy, instead, chooses a future in the Royal Ballet, in dance, rather than in the Victorian role of male provider of the coalmines and the deunionizing labor of North Durham, England. And in the end, when his latecomer dad comes to his performance, he gets to see his son leap, soar, literally and metaphorically out of the terms of existence that fashioned his life.

And while Billy's doing ballet demonstrates the falling and collapsing—the ephemerality—of tradition, as well as the ability and desire to leap out of it with passion and grace into creative self-transformation, what does our youthful subject have in common with that weary and worn-out working-class subject featured in the spotlight of much media in the mainstream as well as with the scholarly and political discourses of the radical left? It portrays the young White (presumably straight?) "working class" male as triumphant; the battle scars, struggles, and defeats of the racially and reproductively marginalized others (always present even in their absence) are subsumed in the spotlight of his victory over those forces that constrain and oppress *him*. We can see here how the construct of the working class constricts those who find themselves in it and casts out those who provide the other side of the boundary line, for it is not just the capitalists that constrain him and over whom he seeks to triumph, there are so many more lines drawn in the sand.

Providing for him an unnamed but central aspect of his co-authored identity, Debbie Wilkinson (Nicola Blackwell), the daughter of his dance teacher, his potential friend (or rather, girlfriend), could have had a voice and purpose of life beyond becoming his worshipping subject seeking to possess him for herself at all costs. This one visible female counterpart is vanquished in the representation. Rather than being portrayed as a potential ally with agency, she is pitted against him, so they remain alienated from each other as well as the structures that define and code them. Moreover, the way whiteness functions (for anyone possessing it) as property (providing a special but spectacularly hidden ethnic particularity), cultural capital, and symbolic power, which translate into material profit, remains unexplored. But the depiction of the "traditional" masculinist working-class subject united against an identifiable enemy with similarly positioned others is indeed challenged here, opening the door for analysis of the underground economies of national identity, sexual orientation, and ethnic affiliation.

In a somewhat different way, but with similar intensity of the uprooting of the past and tradition, Gurinder Chadha's *Bend It Like Beckham* (2002) is yet another refreshing depiction of the flat-lining of tradition, but this time the star of the show is a young Asian girl, Jesminder. Jess is the youngest daughter in a rather orthodox Sikh family living in Britain, who struggles to participate in family tradition while at the same time pursuing her dream to "bend it like Beckham." A wonderful football (soccer) player who feels she may be destined to kick the ball around only in parks when no one is looking, Jess manages to get picked up by the Hounslow Harriers women's team, where she is soon to become a star, until her parents find out and ban her from playing. Her mother scolds her, "Who'd want a girl who plays football all day but can't make chapattis?" Willing to gender-bend on some level (but oblivious to the ways in which his daughter's sexual orientation has been questioned by her best friend's mother), her father eventually comes around, preferring his daughter's happiness to the confines of "tradition." We are presented with wonderful depictions of his daughter's ability to participate with agency in seemingly separate traditions laid out side by side. Complications of sex/gender/sexuality collide in Deepa Mehta's *Fire* (1998), where same-sex desire overrides the dictates of tradition for two Indian housewives whose "trial by fire" signals the purity of their new found love that dares to, but cannot, speak its name. "There is no word to describe what we are to each other in our language," utters Sita (Nandita Das), the more rebellious of the two.

Again we see the notions of the past and the "tradition" of the "working class" challenged when the six unemployed steel workers of *The Full Monty* (1997) form a male striptease act, literally defrocking and leaving nothing but their Poulantzian number plates on their backs. Shelving their overalls and dungarees for the regular beat as male strippers, the Full Monties of Sheffield literally search for, and then abandon, their iron-mongering past in the decayed industrial rubble of the once-thriving manufacturing city of Sheffield. Going a few years back in filmic representation, we must not forget the telling sentiment: "We're not English, We're Londoners," as Sammy explains in *Sammy and Rosie Get Laid* (1987). After numerous depictions of what might have made Hoggart turn in his grave, Sammy is depicted doing seven different things simultaneously while trying to unwind: eating fast food, watching the news, listening to the radio, flipping through a porno magazine, sipping beer, and indulging in a line or two of cocaine while conversing with his father. We have here a depiction of the shifting and fragmented nature of co-authored identities' dis-identification with the ethnic particularity of the "Nation" and its culture, even as they seemingly indulge in what it has to offer. An alternative representation of desire and romantic/domestic partnerships is pursued here as well as the building of alliance across class lines (as conceived or portrayed in its strictly material sense). The confines of compulsory heterosexuality and notions of ethnic purity and distinction are subverted as alliances and love affairs transpire between members who are differentially placed within the categories of race, class, and sexuality. Depictions of interracial and homoerotic desires are indeed a sight for sore eyes in *Sammy and Rosie Get Laid* and in the depictions of love and desire outside the confines of heteronormativity in *My Beautiful Laundrette*. We can't forget that the space is owned by "Pakis," who are the employers and lovers of White working class, Jonny.

And with an eye to the under-theorized pathologies of imperial domination, we also get a glimpse in these films of the perils of privilege lived out by its perpetrators. Sammy's father's (Ravi's) involvement in British imperialism leads him to commit suicide after he finds that relocating to Britain fails to drive the brutal memories from his mind of how perhaps his own involvement in maintaining his notion of tradition contributed to its demise. Notably, the wealth and riches he received from his affiliation with the colonizers provided neither luxury nor peace of mind, alienating him from his family who cried, but did they mourn his death? The very privilege promised by tradition seems to have driven him to take his own life, not celebrate it. But where is the guilt or the consciousness of the White colonialist? Though not depicted here, the film helps to demonstrate that thinking of class merely in terms of one's relationship to the mode of production does not allow for the building of allies outside shared relationships to the means of material production. The film thus offers an excellent example of what networks of affiliation and interpretative communities could look like.

Oppositely privileged individuals—both of whom are alienated from their assigned class/social function—are portrayed in film, demonstrating once again the way in which crucial aspects of lived social relations form and reform with those who may or may not share the same relationship to the means of production. As Paulo Freire would be inclined to point out, both "oppressor" and "oppressed" are alienated, dehumanized in relations that prize hierarchy and cultural/traditional superiority. In *Educating Rita* (1983), we see this alienation in the lives of White working-class Rita and her fleeting mentor/professor, Frank. Aspiring to cross over the confines of their class distinctions, both are disillusioned by the promises of becoming that are offered in dominant ideologies. We get a sense of the ways in which identity is not a finished product with which one is bestowed at birth, but rather a project always in process, an ongoing ever-changing conversation and exchange with Others. Filmic representations such as these depict the world of change driven by consumer durables. The logic of mobile privatization, which made Hoggart so uncomfortable, has followed a relentless line to the disembedding of the lads. All that is left is resentment, as Michelle Fine and Lois Weis so effectively underscore in *The Unknown City* (1998).

Depictions of tradition in the literary imagination

> "Then he said, 'On my travels I visited an Indian tribe known as the Hopi. I could not understand them, but in their company they had an old European man, Spanish, I think, though he spoke English to us. He said he had been captured by the tribe and now lived as one of them. I offered him passage home but he laughed in my face. I asked if their language had some similarity to Spanish and he laughed again and said, fantastically, that their language has no grammar in the way we recognize it. Most bizarre of all, they have no tenses for past, present, and future. They do not sense time in that way. For them, time is one. The old man said it was impossible to learn their language without learning their world. I asked him how long it had taken him and he said that question had no meaning.
> "After this we continued in silence."
>
> (Winterson, 1989)

Like cinematic representations, the literary imagination troubles notions of tradition, power, and privilege, revealing those dynamics of power and privilege that seem to be foreclosed in scholarly discourses of working-class resistance. Orwell, for example, presents the working-class ear'ole or lower-middle-class actor "divided to the vein," conflicted to the bone (as Derek Walcott says of his identity struggle in "Far Cry from Africa" [Walcott, 1986, p. 17]). As Uma Kothari (2005a, 2005b) has told us, many of the colonial bureaucrats who went out to the colonies were often of working-class or "ear'oled" backgrounds, sponsored up to the public school, Eton or Harrow or whatever, and deployed to the imperial periphery with all their hang ups. Read against this phalanx of national assertion, George Orwell's "Shooting an Elephant" (1946/1981) presents a picture of the lower-middle-class subject operating overseas, confronting the periphery inhabitant on his native soil, in a different light . . . more internally divided, more complexly linked to England and Empire, more uncertain about self and role in the elaboration of Britishness. The ethnographic lens now puts the Western actor under the microscope. And, Orwell portrays the everyday negotiation of class and power in the imperial outpost of Burma through the mediation of modernizing energies and subaltern subversions ("the weapons of the weak"), the anticipation of the waning of Empire and the dubiousness of civilizing missions abroad. The story draws on Orwell's experience as a colonial officer and it concerns the angst of an environmentally conscious, uncertain British police officer who, egged on by a crowd of natives to shoot a rogue elephant, compromises his own agency and his hegemonic subjectivity. The narrator/police officer does not want to shoot the elephant, but he feels compelled to by the Burmese agro-proletarians and peasants, before whom he does not wish to appear indecisive or cowardly. The situation and events that Orwell describes underscore the hostility between the administrators of the British Empire and their "native" subjects. But, at another level, it is a deep examination of power. And, it foregrounds what the anthropologist James Scott calls the "weapons of the weak" (Scott, 1985). Here, the native is not the butt of Paki jokes for the lads or the source of Black cultural economy of symbols for the punks.

Orwell problematizes power and the agency of so called dominant subjects, carefully depicting the colonial situation as one in which the "subjection of the ruled also involves the subjugation of the ruler," showing us how "subjects of colonies controlled rulers as much as they were controlled by them" (Nandy, 1983, p. 39). Plagued by divided consciousness, unable to act in accordance with his own volition, the protagonist is tormented by guilt, hatred, and fear, and forced to suffer the felt contradictions of his precarious position "in the utter silence that is imposed on every Englishman in the East" (Orwell, 1946/1981, pp. 148–49). Having decided long ago that "imperialism is an evil thing," this colonial official claims to be on the side of the Burmese population but feels "stuck between the hatred of the empire" and "rage against" the villagers who try to make his job so utterly impossible. One part of the official, we are told, views British rule as "an unbreakable tyranny" clamping him down while the other part of him feels that the "greatest joy in the world would be to drive a bayonet into a Buddhist priest's guts" (Orwell, 1946/1981, p. 149). These feelings, we are told, are the "normal by-products of imperialism" (Orwell, 1946/1981, p. 149). And, while it is certain that the torment and suffering of those on the other side of the foul smelling "lock-ups" could never be equivocated, the dominant subject in Orwell's narration is clearly not enjoying the promise his "privilege" provides.

Challenging simplistic notions of the ways in which power operates and who creates and belongs to the "British" tradition, on the most telling event of the day in question we learn that the colonial official is far from being decisive, all-powerful, fully authoritarian, or in control. Rather, he feels like an "absurd puppet," a "hollow posing dummy" unable to do that which he most desires. Having been ordered to find a work elephant that was wreaking havoc about the town in which he was posted, the subject in question follows his orders, armed and ready to serve and protect. He sets off to pursue the rogue elephant but is met with resistance from the villagers who claim neither to have seen the elephant nor even to have heard of its havoc, though clearly standing right there in its midst. This non-cooperation on the part of the "helpless" unarmed Burmese population was yet another "normal" element of daily life one counts on as a colonial official, he adds. After almost giving up on his search, thinking the whole thing to be "a pack of lies" (p. 150), the narrator finally stumbles upon the large beast's most recent victim. The official spots the elephant up ahead in the distance and halts momentarily in his steps and reports, "As soon as I saw the elephant I knew with perfect certainty that I ought not to shoot him" (p. 151); moreover, he adds, "I did not in the least want to shoot him" (p. 152). He decides that the best thing to do is to keep an eye out for a while to ensure the elephant does not turn savage again, and go home for the day. But then he sees the crowd:

> I looked at the sea of yellow faces above the garish clothes—faces all happy and excited over this bit of fun, all certain that the elephant was going to be shot. They were watching me as they would watch a conjurer about to perform a trick. They did not like me, but with the magical rifle in my hands I was momentarily worth watching. And suddenly I realized that I should have to shoot the elephant after all. The people expected it of me and I had got to do it; I could feel their two thousand wills pressing me forward, irresistibly. And it was at this moment, as I stood there with the rifle in my hands, that I first grasped the hollowness, the futility of the White

man's dominion in the East. Here was I, the White man with his gun, standing in front of the unarmed native crowd—seemingly the leading actor of the piece; but in reality I was only an absurd puppet pushed to and fro by the will of those yellow faces behind. I perceived in this moment that when the White man turns tyrant *it is his own freedom that he destroys*. He becomes a sort of *hollow, posing dummy*, the *conventionalized figure* of a sahib. For it is the condition of his rule that *he shall spend his life in trying to impress* the "natives," and so in every crisis he has got to do what the "natives" expect of him. *He wears a mask, and his face grows to fit it.* I had got to shoot the elephant.

(Orwell, 1946/1981, p. 152)

The choice is no simple matter for the official in question, who repeatedly insists, "I did not want to shoot the elephant" (p. 153). Yet, knowing with perfect certainty what he *ought* to do, he looks again at the crowd and he reflects that there "was only one alternative" (p. 154). He loads the cartridges into the rifle and fires. A slow and agonizing death tortures the struggling gasping elephant while the official is tormented by the sight and the need to keep shooting, continuing to fail to put the beautiful gasping living being out of the misery he'd inflicted upon it.

The privileged subject, here cast, is condemned to conform to a tightly scripted code of conduct with which he does not identify. Three metaphors from the story, the gun, the gaze, and the mask (Logue, 2004), serve as useful devices with which to depict what Césaire termed the "boomerang effects of domination" (*Discourse on Colonialism* [1972]). The gun symbolizes the moment of usurpation as one in which his imposed superiority coerces him to be what he has forced the other to see him as. Paradoxically, the instrument through which he performs his fantasy of superiority becomes the vehicle through which he suffers his own agentic demise. Unable to affirm his freedom, the dominant subject finds himself sentenced to an unending struggle for status and justification, symbolized through the inescapable look of the Other. This gaze represents the instability and precariousness of his usurpation, his becoming a victim of his own unconscious. In the desperate attempt to shield against this hideous onslaught of unruly emotion and external threat, he projects them onto the other who now constitutes that which he most needs to defend himself against. The mask signifies the onset of his own dehumanization, for in wearing it, he can only reach for the gun. A self-destructive vicious circle is begun. The "posture of absolute domination" (Theweleit, 1989), adopted by Orwell's "hollow, posing dummy" (p. 152), and the processes through which he brings about his own destruction, help to illuminate the way in which culture is a conversation and not the final property of an ethnically superior tradition. How are these tensions grappled with in neo-Marxist cultural analysis?

What do the imminent deaths of the elephant, Sammy's father (*Sammy and Rosie Get Laid*), and hopes that "traditional" parents (*Billy Eliot*) have for their children signify? Could it be that with the death of the subject lies the death of tradition, an imperial tradition on the wane? And isn't it the case that Billy Elliot's grandma, who has Alzheimer's, stands in her dream-like silence as the scrambled riddle of past attachments, past associations, and feeling? Do our perceptual and linguistic apparatuses allow for the articulation of the complexities of lived social relations and networks of affiliation?

Conclusion: Transforming contexts, transforming traditions, transforming identities

It seems cultural studies analysis in its treatment of class has been overtaken by events. It seems the perceptual/conceptual/linguistic apparatus of socio-cultural analysis on the whole is now unable to diagnose the global predicament we are in, seemingly reinforcing the very structures we seek to subvert. Our entire perceptual, conceptual, and linguistic apparatus is in need of overhaul as we come to recognize the rise of networked societies in which traditions, affiliations, "cultures"—subcultural or not—are now disembedded from the moorings of the final property of any group. There has been a flattening out of cultures and traditions integrated into global expansion of markets and flexible models of production of capital pursuing new sites of value in ever-increasing alienated contexts. We have reached a stage in this new millennium where the old "conflict" versus "consensus" metaphors—"your traditions versus mine"—do not seem to apply. Instead of models based on conflict and resistance, increasingly social groups are being defined by overwhelming patterns of transnational hybridities, new forms of association and affiliation that seem to flash on the surface of life rather than to plunge deeper down into some kind of neo-Marxist substructure. This new model of power could now be called "integration." It does not have a negative pole. It is what Foucault describes as a "productive" not "repressive" model of power. It articulates difference into ever-more extensive systems of association, flat-lining the edges of culture into a pastiche of market-able identities, tastes, neuroses, and needs, processed through the universalization of the enterprise ethic. It lays traditions down side by side, layering them in ever new ephemeral patterns and intensities; whole elements and associations given in one place can be now instantaneously found in another. Paul Willis's nationally and geographically inscribed "lads" are now being replaced by Jenny Kelly's (2004) Afro-Canadian youth, who are patching together their identities from the surfeit of signs and symbols crossing the border in the electronic relays of US television, popular music, and cyber culture. Post-apartheid South African youth now assign more value to markers of taste—Levis and Gap jeans, Nikes or Adidas, rap or rave—than ancestry and place in their elaboration of the new criteria of ethnic affiliation (Dolby, 2001). All these developments are turning the old materialism versus idealism debate on its head. It is the frenetic application of forms of existence, forms of life, the dynamic circulation of and strategic deployment of style, and the application of social aesthetics that now govern political rationalities and corporate mobilization in our times. The new representational technologies are the new centers of public instruction providing the forum for the work of the imagination of the great masses of the people to order their pasts and present and plot their futures. They are creating instant traditions and nostalgias of the present in which our pasts are dis-embedded and separated out as abstract value into new semiotics systems and techniques of persuasion, new forms of ecumenical clothing that quote Ché, Mao, Fidel, and Marx, and "revolution" in the banality of commodified life.

Who now owns the terms that define the authentic traditions of radicalism that inform our works? Who now has final purchase on the terms "resistance," "revolution," "democracy," "participation," and "empowerment?" The massive work of textual production is blooming in a crucible of opposites—socially extended projects producing the cultural citizen in the new international division of labor, in which the state may not be a first or the final referent. Naomi Klein (2001) reminds us ultimately of this radical disembedding. Spadina Avenue, the garment district of Toronto of the 1930s, is now in post-industrial limbo and a center of a masquerading consumerist heaven. Its transformation to its new millennial identity—of warehouse flowering apartments, Sugar Mountain, retro candy, edible jewelry, and dispensing of London Fog coats—owes its genesis to the cruel juxtaposition with Jakarta and the flight of its garment industry to Indonesia. And while there is not much need for overcoats on the equator, "increasingly," according to Klein, "Canadians get through their cold winters not with clothing manufactured by the tenacious seamstresses on Spadina Avenue but by young Asian women working in hot climates . . . In 1997, Canada imported $11.7 million of its anoraks and ski jackets from Indonesia . . ." (Klein, 2001, p. xvi).

The outlines of this new global context have precipitated a crisis of language in neo-Marxist scholarly efforts to grasp the central dynamics of contemporary societies, bearing on the question of "tradition" and the centering term "culture." The latter developments have led to a depreciation of the value and insightfulness of neo-Marxist analysis in our time. Old metaphors associated with class, economy, state ("production," "reproduction," "resistance," "the labor/capital contradiction") are all worn down by the transformations of the past decades in which the saturation of economic and political practices in aesthetic mediations has proceeded full scale (Klein, 2001). The scale and referent for all of these organizing terms of analysis had been set and bounded at the nation, defined in the localist anthropological/ethnographic terms of "traditions," "ritual," "culture," which are understood on the localizing plain of community, ethnic group, society, et cetera. The new circumstances associated with post-fordist capital— that is, the new international division of labor, movement and migration, the amplification of images, and the work of the imagination of the great masses of the people, the great masses of our times driven forward by computerization, the internet, popular culture, et cetera—have cut open particular traditions, spilling the entrails of so much fluttering fish around the world. New working units for understanding modern life are needed. Maybe not the nation, not the state, not society, but the "Globus," the "Global City," ultimately the "Globe," may be the new unit of analysis, the new referent, connecting nodes and networks of affiliation where traditions are attenuated, even as the public sphere and the life world have become more susceptible to re-feudalization, sectarianism, and fundamentalism.

Questions for discussion

1. What is the purpose of reading cultural Marxism through the lenses of cinematic and literary representations of the working class?
2. Discuss Marx's terms "class in itself" and "class for itself." What are the ways in which the terms are useful for looking at class productions/reproductions? How can these terms help us to illuminate the complexities of class as interconnected with race?
3. In the words of the authors: What happens to "sex/gender/sexuality when class becomes the primary category of analysis?"
4. Compare British cultural studies (as relayed through this chapter) to US cultural studies (as relayed through your knowledge and experience) relative to the

study of social class by mimicking the kind of analysis presented by Logue and McCarthy.

5. Logue and McCarthy argue (along with a multitude of other scholars) that language/particular words possess inherent limitations when caught up within a system of dominant discourse, in this case one that universalizes particularities. Explain how these limitations function within the contemporary world relative to social class. How does the language of class (i.e., working class, middle class, and so forth) work to reinforce popular conceptions of these groups and borders between them?

6. Has the concept of "working class" changed over time within the USA? If so, how is "working class" both deployed and analyzed today as compared to its historical descriptions as a categorization?

7. If "class commonly functions as though it were a static, impermeable category with an invisible ethnically particular tradition . . . fail[ing] to connote the actual strategies through which social subjects forge collective oppositional identities from the grounded pragmatics of cultural hybridities," would the obliteration of terms such as class, working class, and middle class extinguish that which is linguistically problematic? Would doing so only result in another linguistic turn towards a "new" word/s that continue to hold and circulate power? Explain your answers.

8. How does fiction confront fact within this text? Do works of fiction provide alternative ways of addressing social complexities? Do you think fiction proceeds or precedes lived reality?

Note

Jennifer Logue is a graduate student in Educational Policy Studies and Gender and Women's Studies at the University of Illinois, Urbana-Champaign.

Cameron McCarthy is Communications Scholar and University Scholar at the University of Illinois. He teaches Mass Communications Theory, Cultural Studies, and the Sociology of Knowledge in the departments of Advertising and Consumer Studies, Educational Policy Studies, and the Institute of Communications Research at the University of Illinois' Urbana campus. With Lois Weis and Greg Dimitriadis he recently published *Ideology, Curriculum, and the New Sociology of Education: Revisiting the Work of Michael Apple* (Routledge, 2006). Correspondence to: Cameron McCarthy. Institute of Communications Research, College of Communications, University of Illinois at Urbana-Champaign, 228 Gregory Hall, 810 South Wright Street, Urbana, IL 61801. Email: cmccart1@uiuc.edu.

References

Althusser, L., & Balibar, E. (1968). *Reading capital.* London: New Left Books.

Césaire, A. (1972). *Discourse on colonialism* (J. Pinkham, Trans.). New York: Monthly Review Press.

Chow, R. (2002). *The Protestant ethnic and the spirit of capitalism.* New York: Columbia University.

Dolby, N. (2001). *Constructing race: Youth, identity, and popular culture in South Africa.* Albany, NY: State University of New York Press.

Dworkin, D. (1997). *Cultural Marxism in postwar Britain*. Durham, North Carolina: Duke University Press.

Fine, M., & Weis, L. (1998). *The unknown city*. Boston: Beacon Press.

Fiske, J. (1987). British cultural studies and television. In R. Allen (Ed.), *Channels of discourse*. Chapel Hill, NC: The University of North Carolina Press.

Foucault, M. (2002). *Society must be defended: Lectures at the College de France, 1975–76*. New York: Picador.

Gilroy, P. (1991). *There ain't no black in the Union Jack*. Chicago: University of Chicago Press.

Gitlin, T. (1995). The rise of identity politics: An examination and critique. In M. Berube & C. Nelson (Eds.), *Higher education under fire* (pp. 305–25). New York: Routledge.

Hall, S. (1980). Cultural studies: Two paradigms. *Media, Culture and Society, 2*, 57–72.

Harris, W. (1985). *Carnival*. London: Faber and Faber.

Hebdige, D. (1979). *Subculture: The meaning of style*. London: Methuen.

Ishiguro, K. (1989). *The remains of the day*. New York: Vintage.

Kelly, J. (2004). *Borrowed identities*. New York: Peter Lang.

Klein, N. (2001). *No logo (required)*. London: Harper and Collins.

Kothari, U. (2005a). Authority and expertise: The professionalisation of international development and the ordering of dissent. *Antipode, 37*(2), 425–46.

—— (2005b). *Recruitment criteria: Character, sport and class*. Unpublished essay, Institute for Policy Development and Management, University of Manchester, England.

Lamming, G. (1954/1994). *The emigrants*. Ann Arbor: University of Michigan Press.

—— (1971). *Water with berries*. London: Longman.

Logue, J. (2004). *Agentic ambiguity and the politics of privilege: Recognition versus re-evaluation of privilege in social justice education*. Unpublished MA thesis, OISE/University of Toronto.

—— (2005). Deconstructing privilege: A contrapuntal approach. In K. R. Howe (Ed.), *Philosophy of education* (pp. 371–79). Urbana, IL: Philosophy of Education Society.

McRobbie, A. (1997). More! New sexualities in girls and women's magazines. In A. McRobbie (Ed.), *Back to reality?—Social experience and cultural studies* (pp. 190–209). New York: Manchester University Press.

Miner, H. (1956). Body ritual among the Nacirema. *American Anthropologist, 58*, 503–7.

Naipaul, V. S. (1967). *The mimic men*. London: André Deutsch.

Nandy, A. (1983). *The intimate enemy: Loss and recovery of self under colonialism*. New York: Oxford University Press.

Orwell, G. (1946/1981). Shooting an elephant. In G. Orwell (Ed.), *A collection of essays* (pp. 148–56). New York: Harcourt Inc.

Scott, J. (1985). *Weapons of the weak: Everyday forms of peasant resistance*. New Haven, CT: Yale University Press.

Selvon, S. (1956). *The lonely Londoners*. London: Longman.

Theweleit, K. (1989). *Male fantasies. Volume 2: Male bodies: Psychoanalyzing the white terror*. Cambridge, UK: Polity Press.

Thompson, E. P. (1980). *The making of the English working class*. Harmondsworth: Penguin Books.

Walcott, D. (1986). Far cry from Africa. In D. Walcott (Ed.), *Collected poems, 1948–84*. New York: Noonday Press.

Williams, R. (1966). *Culture and society, 1780–1950*. New York: Harper and Row.

Willis, P. (1981). *Learning to labor*. New York: Columbia University Press.

Winterson, J. (1989). *Sexing the cherry*. New York: Grove Press.

Index